# THE ARCHAEOLOGY OF POLITICS AND POWER

*Where, When and Why the First States Formed*

Charles Maisels

Oxbow Books
Oxford and Oakville

Published by
Oxbow Books, Oxford

© Charles Maisels 2010

ISBN 978-1-84217-352-7

A CIP record for this book is available from the British Library

This book is available direct from

Oxbow Books, Oxford, UK
(Phone: 01865-241249, Fax: 01865-794449)

and

The David Brown Book Company
PO Box 511, Oakville, CT 06779, USA
(Phone: 860-945-9329; Fax: 860-945-9468)

or from our website

www.oxbowbooks.com

Library of Congress Cataloging-in-Publication Data

Maisels, Charles Keith.
  The archaeology of politics and power : where, when, and why the first states formed /
Charles Maisels.
     p. cm.
  Includes bibliographical references.
  ISBN 978-1-84217-352-7
  1.  Social archaeology. 2.  Political anthropology. 3.  State, The--History. 4.  Power (Social
sciences)--History. 5.  Violence--Political aspects--History. 6.  Civilization, Ancient. 7.  Politics
and culture--History. 8.  Political culture--History. 9.  Social structure--History.  I. Title.
  CC72.4.M35 2010
  930.1--dc22
                                                                2010000522

*Front-cover image shows a mannequin dressed in replicas of objects from Tomb 1, The Royal
Tombs of Sipan; courtesy of Christopher B. Donnan, Fowler Museum of Cultural History,
University of California, Los Angeles.*

*Back-cover images from the British Museum.*

Printed and bound in Great Britain by
Hobbs the Printers Ltd., Totton, Hampshire.

Dedicated to the lives and achievements of Robert Stevenson (1772–1850), Thomas Hamilton (1784–1858), Alexander 'Greek' Thomson (1817–1875) and John James Burnet (1857–1938); four great Scots builders who had no need of a 'Scottish Government'; and to the memory of two great scholars who died in the same year: Andrew Sherratt (1946–2006) and Bruce Graham Trigger (1937–2006), both sorely missed.

'If humans follow their desires, how will they ever come to a limit?' (A line from the nature poet Xie Lingyun, early 5th century AD, in Mark Elvin's translation (2002: 14)).

*Noxiae mentes caeco semper in facinus furore rapiuntur.*

# TABLE OF CONTENTS

# LIST OF FIGURES

## Chapter 4

## Chapter 5

# Chapter 6

# Chapter 7

## Chapter 9

# ACKNOWLEDGEMENTS

First I would like to thank Jonathan Haas, who read the whole work, gave great encouragement and made a host of excellent suggestions. Then to Jennifer Maisels, whose hard work produced such a fine Index. Thanks also to Paul Butterlin, Mark Elvin, McGuire Gibson, Kevin Hammond, Vicky Hammond, David Harris, Frank Hole, Li Liu, Michael E. Moseley, Gregory Possehl, Mitchell S. Rothman, David Waugh, Harvey Weiss, David Wengrow and Toby A.H. Wilkinson.

For illustrations I am obliged, first and foremost, to the British Museum for their high-quality images and excellent service. I am indebted to Li Liu for gracious permission to use a number of her fine illustrations. Also to Altimira Press, The Brown Reference Group Ltd., Harper-Collins, London and SAR Press, Santa Fe.

This work could not have been written without the resources of the University of London libraries, especially the library and friends at the Institute of Archaeology (UCL).

## Why are NGOs necessary?

International charities such as Oxfam, Médecins sans Frontières and Save the Children, are called NGOs, which, of course, stands for Non-Governmental Organizations. There are hundreds of international NGOs and they are engaged all over the world in a great variety of essential tasks from emergency relief to economic development and through every kind of health activity, preventative and curative, to educational and cultural work, the protection and promotion of the welfare of women and children, the environment, and so on. In other words, Non-Governmental Organizations do all the kinds of work that states ought to do, but don't! How can this be? The justification for the existence of states, their controls and their taxes, is that they serve the needs of the public for security, order, development and welfare. In rhetoric (spin), a state exists to promote the quality of life of its population. Most do not; they serve the interests of those in power, and that is why there is always a struggle for control of the state. Power, after all, enables those wielding it to obtain goods and services that those providing the goods and services would not voluntarily provide. In the purchase of goods and services the parties to the exchange must agree that to do so is in their mutual interest. Power, by contrast, is coercive and one-sided. When the rhetoric is stripped away, the basis of power is violence, implicit or explicit, and I argue below that violence is intrinsic to human nature. Male human instinct is for self-assertion and thus aggression; that is what testosterone is for. Self-interest causes violence and only self-interest can restrain it. Society either makes violence 'worthwhile' (for instance in the role of professional soldier, or in the sport of boxing), or it restrains violence by rigorous penalties that makes resorting to violence too 'costly'. For example, it either sanctions wife-beating as a male prerogative or it proscribes it as domestic violence against the individual, where individuals possess equal value and are entitled to equal protection. "Natural selection is a mechanistic process and thus morally neutral: discovering a genetic influence on murder does not condone it. In fact, it may only be a proper understanding of underlying biological causes that will grant us the *choice* not to follow the subtle coercion of genes" (Byrne 2006: 96; original emphasis).

Every part of every continent except Antarctica is contained within some state or other; why do so many of them consistently fail the populations they are supposed to serve? The UN report into the spending by governments of the 5.6 billion GBP raised globally for rebuilding after the Indian Ocean Tsunami of December 2004, found that:

"Hotels and big business have been allowed to build in beach resorts while many families have been uprooted and forced to live in shacks.

In India, the government has denied food, water and shelter to people of low caste, it was claimed.

The Sri Lankan government has paid compensation only to men – sometimes ex-husbands – while mothers struggling to raise families have been left penniless, the UN said.

…Aid workers who visited more than 50,000 people in 95 towns and villages affected by the disaster were said to be shocked by the way basic rights to food, health, housing, work and compensation were being neglected. Women and children endured sickness, starvation and sexual abuse at refugee camps, it was claimed.

In Thailand, the authorities forced villagers out of their traditional homes in favour of commercial interests and the 'local land mafia', the report said.

UN official Miloon Kothari said: 'Even in the face of an overwhelming tragedy, governments have failed to uphold the human rights of their most vulnerable citizens'.

Ramesh Singh of Action Aid International, added: 'Emergency help should reach all those who need it, not a selected few. They should be ashamed of their record'" (Metro 2/2/06).

Getting to the origins of things and tracing their development is often a good way to find out why things are the way they are today. As the eminent archaeologist and theorist Frank Hole (2000: 191) succinctly put it: "it is not too much to say that the foundations of what we consider to be the basic attributes of our civilization were established during the Neolithic".

So this book is about why and how states formed in the places where they first came into existence according to the archaeological record. Those places are Egypt, the Levant, Mesopotamia, northern China and the Andes of South America. In counterpoint, the Harappan civilization of the Indus plains is discussed here as a large, complex and urban society that was not state dominated. I do not discuss Mexico/Central America in this work as it would make a lengthy book even longer.

Specifically, I want to address the questions:

1) why do states exist at all; what is the reason for their existence, or non-existence in the case of Indus Civilization (in Northwest India during the third millennium BC)
2) why different types of state arose where and when they did
3) what such an analysis can tell us about the fundamentals of human nature, for some claim that there is no such thing as 'human nature' (e.g. Ingold 2006).

The thesis to be tested and perhaps demonstrated in this book is that states formed to privilege the elites in control of them, and not to 'manage complexity by integrating proliferating sub-systems' as anthropological jargon has it. According to the rationale that has become standard in anthropology/archaeology over the past forty years, as societies grew larger in population and extent their functioning came to depend on command and control mechanisms that we recognise as the state. But in whose interests? *Cui bono?* The brazen non-response of the military rulers of Burma to the suffering of the population caused by cyclone Nargis in 2008, their strategy of retaining total control by keeping the country closed despite the scale of the disaster and the desperate need for assistance, plus the reluctance of other states to sweep away that contemptible regime, all makes my case. However, some might argue that this, as in the case of Zimbabwe, is an 'extreme example' and that in origin at least states were not like that, but rather 'served the people'.

The archaeological evidence suggests otherwise, but the evidence is detailed and lengthy. This is because the emergence of the state can only be understood as the outcome of a long process starting in the Neolithic farming villages of each region. There is little point talking generalities about increases of population and social complexity that is not grounded in survey, excavation and comparison. So for each region it has been necessary to describe early settlement, the origins and development of farming, hierarchy formation, the functions of towns and of cities, and the domestic, ideological and political order at each stage. Those evidence-based trajectories are of value even if the main theses of the work are rejected. *Felix rerum cognoscere causas* (It is fruitful to know the causes of things). However, for those whose interest is simply in the mechanics of state formation and not in the archaeology, then the first two and the last two chapters will provide a summary view; always bearing in mind Rothman's (2004: 109) warning that "If we want truly to understand the origins of complexity, our data must be able to live up to our theory".

# CHAPTER 1

# The Science of History

**History is philosophy from examples**, wrote the Greek historian Dionysius of Halicarnassus, in the first century BC.

By 'philosophy' Dionysius meant politics, sociology, economics and psychology, and by 'History' he meant the corpus of historical writing or historiography. So in addition to the uses of History set out below, one of those is as the record of a global psychology laboratory. If it is true that the mainspring of History is human agency (cf: H.T. Wright 2007), then it follows that its substrate is human psychology, underlying which is the evolutionary inheritance we call instinct. This is scarcely surprising as neuroscience now shows that the conscious functioning of the brain is the least part of its activity.

> "Young children, whose intentions and sympathies are not merely 'constructed' by us, show that our own language and cognitions are more products of a natural organismic process than our politicians, judges, theologians and philosophers, and many of our scientists, pretend to believe" (Trevarthen 2006: 240).

Building on Dionysius, I will begin by offering my own definition of history: *History is about understanding how we came to be where we are now, through the study of processes, people and events in the past.*

Understanding History is both cognitively satisfying (situating ourselves) and instrumentally useful ('learning from history'); both good to know and useful to know. Its study helps us understand how societies are constituted and how they change as a consequence of human actions (culture, technology, warfare and politics) in the context of underlying forces (geographic, ecological and economic). *Science consists in demonstrating mechanism*; social science similarly consists in laying out chains of cause and effect (which is what mechanisms or systems are). History does not stop or 'leave you alone' because you are ignorant of its processes. Ignorance just means that you are swept along like a stick in a river. If we substitute the phrase 'flow of events' for the term 'history', everyone knows this is true. It's what we've done that makes us who we are, as individuals and as societies.

## A: Politics and Ideology

The state is a dominant organization backed by force: physical, economic and ideological. But all states are different, even now, even in 'united' Europe. They were even more diverse when they first emerged. Mesopotamia gave rise to the earliest cities and to the city-state, derived from large business-like households. Those households were organized around the temples as a community resource and the temples became the nuclei of cities in Sumer. Egypt produced a large territorial state from chiefdoms dominating villages. In China, which generated no city-states, the territorial state ('village state') was produced by clans dominated by aristocrats, with other members pushed down to the condition of subjects. "Individual choice disappears when a person has a duty to be a member of a group, or, to say it the other way around, when a group has the right to claim him as a member" (Goodenough 1970: 59).

The state arose in the Andes on a similar basis, that of the descent group. In north-west India, around the Indus, an extensive, populous and complex society existed for half a millennium without state domination. Contrasting the social structures of the two large early territorial states, Baines and Lacovara (2002: 27) observe that "Egyptian societal organization was 'political' rather than kin-centred. ... Egypt did not have extended lineage structures; where cults of lineage ancestors are an essential moral focus that coexists with central values, as in China, there is an intricate nesting of social groups and ideologies".

Politics are the traffic between economic power, physical force and ideology. Politics affect all human activity; at home, in the workplace, in the educational institution, at social gatherings and, of course, in the state. Wherever there are humans there is politics. Politics is an arena of contest between the three socially crucial resources already mentioned – Ideology, Economy and Physical Force (i.e. violence and the threat of violence) – that, starting in 1984, I have represented as a triangle, the sides of which consist of specific social relations (Figure 1.1).

The system of contest-exchanges by no means applies only to public or state-level activities, but operates at domestic, village, clan; every level, from the hippiest most egalitarian commune to the line managements of big (or small) business. We personally and daily encounter the politics of the bedroom, of the household, of the boardroom,

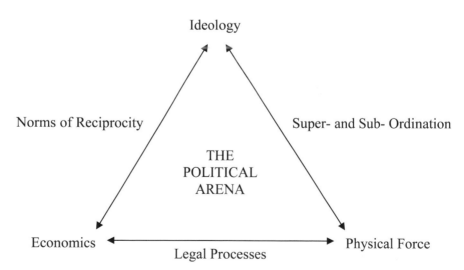

*Figure 1.1: How Ideology, Physical Force and Economy create the political terrain (from Maisels 1984, 283).*

the common-room and so forth; the social nexus is a political one.[1] Indeed human brain-size, and language itself, evolved in response to the complexities of living in large social groups (Dunbar 1993: 681), having to deal continuously with enemies and allies, mates and rivals, both within one's own group and in those surrounding. Originally dyadic grooming and then language served to form a network of 'strategic friendships' where "These primary networks function as coalitions whose primary purpose is to buffer their members against harassment by other members of the group. The larger the group, the more harassment and stress an individual faces the more important those coalitions are" (Dunbar 1993: 683). Such dealings constitute politics, and for just such situationally dynamic reasons Primates, (*Prosimian and Anthropoid*) have also evolved politics (Byrne 1995; Dunbar 1988, 1993). Coalitions are, of course, combinations of self-interest; a shared fear or goal is what the participants have in common. The problem with combinations is that defection is easy so soon as one or several members find that their interests are best served elsewhere. This is where ideology can serve a key purpose in convincing members that they share more than just a narrow and expedient self-interest, but rather that some higher, broader or deeper purpose is being served, thus making the attachment stronger by making the appeal emotional. As societies are essentially coalitions, or more accurately coalitions of coalitions, ideologies are a key means of holding them together. The other is the existence of the state, specifically of its apparatuses, one of which, for the reason just given, is bound to specialize in ideology. The functions of ideology are fourfold: to legitimate, mystify, motivate and control.

This is a book about what caused the rise of the state. I define the **state** as control over people and territory exercised from a centre through specialized apparatuses of power that are: (1) military; (2) administrative (mostly tax-raising); (3) legal and (4) ideological. I define **power** simply, following Schortman, Urban and Ausec (1996: 62), as "the ability to direct and benefit from the actions of others".

As for **political power**, Garth Bawden (2004: 118) has a very neat formulation: "At its most basic level, political power denotes the ability of an agent to advance partisan interests in the face of opposition. As such it is a universal accompaniment of human society, exercised in all aspects of human discourse". Power, however, is not to be understood simply as manifest or latent force, but also, importantly, as the ability to set the social agenda such that meaningful opposition does not arise. Hence the importance attached in this work to ideology, which, when successful, convinces others with objectively different interests, that in fact there is a community of interest.

As for the political power of the state, John Locke (1689) is at his most pithy: "Political power, then, I take to be a right of making laws with penalties of death, and consequently all less penalties, for the regulating and preserving of property, and of employing the force of the community..." (An Essay Concerning the True Original Extent and End of Civil Government).

---

[1]  I understand Aristotle's *zoon politikon* in this sense and not in the usual senses referring to city life and/or civilized existence. In this sense all the world's problems can be regarded as political and the way of resolving deep political problems, which are fundamentally psychological ones, can only come through education in Emotional Intelligence. However, to produce the globally effective 'New Enlightenment' that is required, it will, like the original, be a century-long process.

The mechanism for the generation of power is the ability to command sufficient amounts of ideological, economic or physical-force resources in a given situation, to advance one's own interests or to block or deflect those of others advancing their interests at one's expense. A state usually commands more of those three key resources and so normally wields the greatest power. Of course states differ in power relative to one another, according to their ability to mobilize and manage different quantities of those resources (Hui 2005). But a state needs ideological justification to be considered legitimate and thus stable; cathedrals are required as well as castles. Natural disasters, failure in war on in economic adequacy will strip away its ideological cover – religion, ethnicity, nationalism, tradition – and the state, or at least the regime, will fall, depending on the seriousness or cumulative nature of the failures. Russia in 1917 and again in 1991, are major examples in the last century. Now I can define the state simply as: *a coercive centre of ideological, physical and economic force.*

Ideology has those defining characteristics: (1) it is the public representation and justification of private or sectional interests, which (2) can be material or immaterial, real or imagined, while (3) the fact that the ideology represents and furthers the interests of a particular group is disguised by the claim of 'universal benefit', and/or the claim that 'high principles' are involved which are in the interests of the whole of the nation, society, or humanity; from which it follows that (4) ideological justification selects only those facts that can be spun as favourable to its claims with counter-facts ignored, denied, denigrated or suppressed.[2] Thus (5) ideology can combine with the emotions to such an extent that it is no longer thought but felt; ideology is then experienced as an emotion.

One either spins or adopts an ideology to represent one's own interests, or one is entrained in the ideology of others. It is the all-embracing, potentially all-consuming nature of ideology that makes it so dangerous. Its psychological sources are threefold: (a) in the stories we tell ourselves about our motivations, (b) in the excuses we make for ourselves about our actions, and (c) in the phenomenology of everyday life, that is, in the way that the natural and social environment appears to us. For example, on the pattern of human experience, natural processes appear to be agent driven, the consequence of 'will', hence the universal belief in spirits and deities as transempirical entities accounting for empirical processes that are not understood (Boyer 2001: 160–161), when in fact it is our own cognitive processes, specifically our use of ontological categories ('templates'), that we don't understand (*ibid.*: 90, 109).

(Self-) interest of groups, individuals or institutions, is what distinguishes ideology from failed science. This is equivalent to the difference between a lie and a mistake. A lie is a deliberate falsehood, whereas a mistake is simply an error in attempting to tell the truth. Pre-Newtonian science thought that planetary orbits were circular rather than elliptical. This was a mistake, not a lie. But lying to oneself helps convince others that one's self-interested claims are for the general good, as Frank (1988: 131) explains: "If liars believe they are doing the right thing, observers will not be able to detect symptoms of guilt because there will not be any. With this notion in mind, Robert Trivers suggests that the first step in effective deception will be to deceive oneself, to hide 'the truth from

---

[2] "Within science the term *fact* refers to aspects of the actual occurrence of an event. More importantly, scientists generally attribute factual status to 'recognisable' singular events that occur at given times. While a *fact* exists in an event or part thereof that occurs once and is gone forever, *data* are the representations of facts by some relatively permanent convention of documentation" (Binford 1987: 392).

the conscious mind the better to hide it from others.' He describes an evolutionary arms race in which the capacity for self-deception competes for primacy against the ability to detect deception.

"Extensive research shows that self-deception is indeed both widespread and highly effective. People tend to interpret their own actions in the most favourable light, erecting complex belief systems riddled with self-serving biases" and lots of excuses; even excuses for making excuses. So when ideology fails, as it must, more ideology is slapped on top to cover it up, in a potentially infinite regress until reality hits really hard.

Claims to special privilege, especially the 'right' to rule, are most stable when other social groups can be convinced that partisan interests are not really partisan, but are in fact universal; beneficial to society as a whole because of some special role that the interest group has (e.g. in ritual) or some special skill that it possesses (e.g. in warfare). A dominant (i.e. rulers') ideology forms in this manner by "condensing the conceptions that represent reality for its adherents and affirming those to the public at large through codified visual symbolism and participatory ceremonies" (Bawden 2004: 119); also by verbal narrative and pronouncement. A ruler's ideology is most stable when it can shape worldview:

> "Ideology is driven toward 'deriving' its social myth from a world-view, a *Weltanschauung*. We might call this 'method' of world-mythologizing the method of 'isomorphic projection'. In other words, the same structural traits which characterize the social myth are projected on the world as a whole as a total myth. Then, after this projection has been accomplished, the ideologist claims to 'derive' his social myth as a special case of world myth" (Feuer 1975: 99).

Ultimately everything is about power and its prerogatives; consider the power pyramid where you work. Two further tropes are commonly used by ideologists: (1) if you can invoke 'the general good' for a proposition, then you can sell it as 'principle', and an antisocial act or political position can be justified by appeal to 'principle' or 'conscience', despite its adverse impact on the public good, rhetoric and reality being different things; and (2) the hiding of a politico-ideological agenda behind alleged 'practicalities'. So instead of coming out and admitting that one is opposed to certain things on ideological grounds – which would admit interest – one says that certain laws or initiatives should not be implemented because they are 'counterproductive', 'excessive', 'impossible to administer' or just 'unfair', a suitably vague term.

Art is part of the currency of power. To be effective, power must be felt by a population as both latent and present, implicit and explicit. This combination is manifest in art, ritual and ceremonial. All three are forms of display that stop short of the actual use of force, but all three can readily be combined with displays of the naked instruments of power, as at Nuremberg Rallies or parades through Red Square. The balletic qualities of such rallies are part of their impact. In terms of pictorial propaganda, two aspects impress viewers in addition to what is actually represented: the technical skill with which it is accomplished, and the act of framing, that is, of selection and the concentrated focus that the act brings to the content (cf: Verhoeven 2002b: 6). All three aspects are designed to convey the message that something 'extra-special', even 'transcendental', is being seen.

Ideology does not respect facts. Arguments and evidence are weighed against interests, or rather perception of interests, for interests are immaterial as well as material, real and

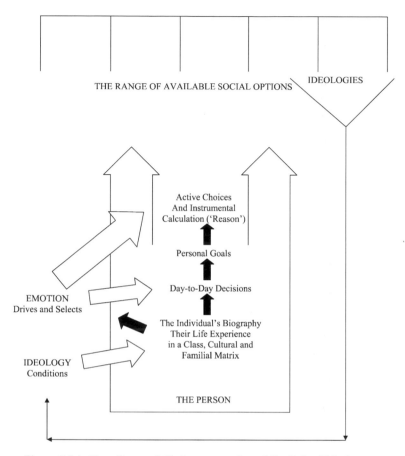

THE RANGE OF AVAILABLE SOCIAL OPTIONS        IDEOLOGIES

Active Choices
And Instrumental
Calculation ('Reason')

Personal Goals

Day-to-Day Decisions

EMOTION
Drives and Selects

The Individual's Biography
Their Life Experience
in a Class, Cultural and
Familial Matrix

IDEOLOGY
Conditions

THE PERSON

*Figure 1.2A: How Personal Choices are made and the Role of Ideology.*

imagined, and they can be misconstrued. An individual's perceived interests are a product of: 1) age, ethnicity, social class and gender 2) the individual's familial and biographic trajectory 3) the ideology that has been absorbed or developed in the course of that trajectory. Figure 1.2A shows how Ideology and Emotion informs personal choices and goals in the social opportunity space.

Biology, Biography and Ideology shape the Emotions and the Emotions select goals and the means to achieve them, for "emotions are powerfully innate and … they shape reasons" (Trevarthen 2006: 233). Indeed, emotions set our goals and reason is the means we employ to attain them. Sometimes, however, reason is scarcely in play even with crucial life-changing decisions; consider the choice of marriage partners in societies where marriage is not arranged! Reason is instrumental, emotion is fundamental.

> "In the beginning was the emotion; then came the idea and last the deed. The emotional need for an ideology is the primary theme in the history of intellectuals; it is their longing for a generational myth of a mission, and of the validation of their claim to rule. It follows consequently that so long as there are new generations of young intellectuals,

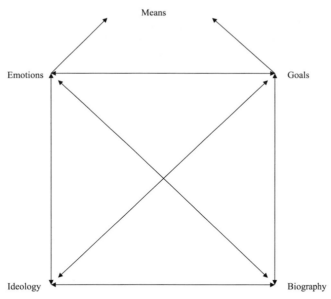

*Figure 1.2B The choosing of Means (M).*

ideology as a mode of thought will be recurrent. Every so-called generation in politics, literature or art will have its corresponding ideology" (Feuer 1975: 79).

This selection process can be represented by a skeleton diagram (Figure 1.2B). Finally, I define symbolism as the visible representing the invisible, conceptual or non-present; an artefact, activity or sign 'standing in for and pointing to' an idea.[3] Thus a 'T' on a roadsign warning of a junction ahead; a flag representing nationhood; cutting a tape to declare a structure open; a cross, a star or a crescent representing religion, and writing representing spoken language. The roadsign (panneau) indicating that traffic-lights (signals = devices that prompt action) are ahead, uses symbols (conventional representations) of traffic lights as well as words (which are signs). Mathematical symbols by contrast, e.g. powers, square roots, fractions, brackets, or the signs for addition, subtraction, multiplication and division, represent operations, something that you do or find (cf: Appendix B). Maps contain symbols yet are not themselves symbols, but models, for they aim to represent physical relationships using empirical data. A model is a graphic, mathematical or physical representation of a system, process or object.

## B: Chiefdoms

Is a chiefdom equivalent to a state? Not in my definition, nor that of Jonathan Haas (1987). A chiefdom, which arises within traditional modes of authority, still has a large consensual element in its functioning,[4] although this diminishes markedly as a

---

[3] Note Trevarthen's (2006: 237) remark that "symbols are taught to the young as reliable decontextualized referents to important ideas".

[4] "Chiefdoms imply a secular or semi-secular authority in which the chief is a pivotal individual whose standing,

chiefdom moves from simple (few thousand people) to complex (tens of thousands of people). A state can simply command a whole society, a chiefdom cannot at least not for long. Webb (1987: 166) speaks of "the kinship bonds, ceremonial obligations and traditional restraints that tie the hands of chieftains". Further, it is not the case that all states are preceded by chiefdoms (see Maisels 1987). Whatever its basis,[5] the state emerges after a rupture with previous modes of authority when the military, ideological and economic sources of power are united under the control of a monarch or 'supreme leader'. That is why in the Old World, accounting and writing systems accompany state formation: they function as tracking and control devices (Postgate, Wang and Wilkinson, 1995). Chiefdoms are rank societies. A key transition is the turning of rank (held by noble families) into posts at court, thence (often much later) into leading roles in a permanent state apparatus paid for out of taxes. The very first full census we know of was held by Den, a king of the mid First Dynasty (3050–2890 BC) of the unified Egyptian state (cf: Millett 1990). It was, like the Domesday Book of AD 1086, a census of people, lands, animals and installations (notably in England, mills), taken for the express purpose of levying sustainable taxation. So a chiefdom if and when it becomes a state, does so by installing a hierarchical control structure (diversified line management) supplanting the 'general purpose' decision-making of the chief with a few members of his family or entourage.

A method of conceptualising the components of a state-ordered society can be seen in Figure 1.3. The contrary facing arrows indicate that the sub-systems are not smoothly integrated. Also, Soft and Hard infrastructural systems are functions of developed states and empires.

It has become established in the literature that a two level settlement hierarchy is indicative (not proof) of a simple chiefdom, a three-level settlement hierarchy of a complex chiefdom, while a state will manifest itself by a four-level settlement hierarchy of city, towns, villages and hamlets; or cities, towns, large villages, small villages and hamlets (Wright and Johnson 1975). With his usual perspicacity Flannery (1998: 16) states that "'administrative hierarchy' and 'settlement hierarchy' are not synonymous". Settlement hierarchy or its absence can result from non-political but instead from topographic and economic features, such as the presence of deserts, routeways, good or bad farmland, coastlines and mountains.

As a complement or alternative, I suggest that administrative control structures manifest cross-cultural and cross-organizational regularities in state-ordered societies ranging from the third millennium Sumerian temple to the third millennium capitalist corporation.

---

based on economics, kinship, or religion, is paramount within a local or regional system" (Kembel and Rick 2004: 75). In the development of chiefly authority from the simple to the complex and perhaps onwards to the state, Weber (1947: 347) wrote that "With the development of a purely personal administrative staff, especially a military force under control of the chief, traditional authority tends to develop into 'patrimonialism'", where the chief sees his office as his personal possession. "Where absolute authority is maximized, it may be called 'Sultanism'. The 'members' are now treated as 'subjects'". Dealings of equality now only take place between rulers, manifested in the exchange of valuables and wives.

[5]   Webb (1987: 167) refers to a proto-state as a 'regional polity' in order to neutrally designate this stage, and I agree with Butterlin (2009a) that pre-state communities of the Near East undergoing urbanisation are best designated 'communautés proto-urbaines'. "Ce terme ne préjuge en rien de la nature des mutations à l'oeuvre at encore moins de leur échelle".

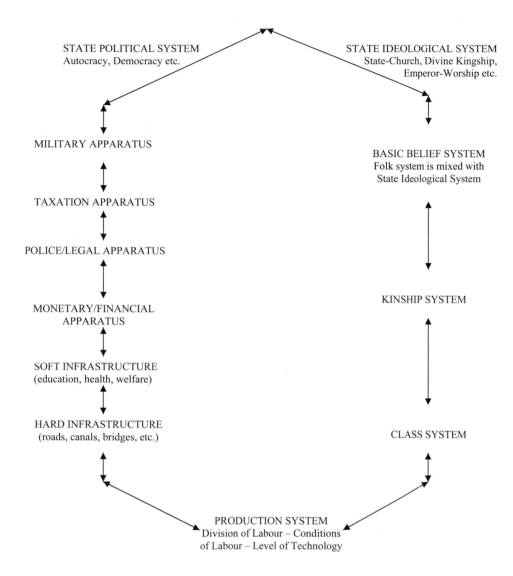

STATE POLITICAL SYSTEM
Autocracy, Democracy etc.

STATE IDEOLOGICAL SYSTEM
State-Church, Divine Kingship,
Emperor-Worship etc.

MILITARY APPARATUS

BASIC BELIEF SYSTEM
Folk system is mixed with
State Ideological System

TAXATION APPARATUS

POLICE/LEGAL APPARATUS

MONETARY/FINANCIAL
APPARATUS

KINSHIP SYSTEM

SOFT INFRASTRUCTURE
(education, health, welfare)

HARD INFRASTRUCTURE
(roads, canals, bridges, etc.)

CLASS SYSTEM

PRODUCTION SYSTEM
Division of Labour – Conditions
of Labour – Level of Technology

*Figure 1.3: The Sub-Systems of a State-Ordered Society.*

Administration is about control, and control is done on behalf of the beneficial owners. So, in terms of the capitalist corporation, the owners are the shareholders and they elect a Board of Directors to administer the business. This is Level 1. They in turn appoint the Chief Executives (Level 2) who in turn appoint Managers (Level 3), who appoint Technical Experts (Engineers etc., Level 4), while beneath them, but also appointed, are Foremen and Overseers (Level 5) who are directly engaged with Labour, on the job, skilled, semi-skilled and unskilled.

This should be compared directly to the hierarchy of control in the Sumerian temple (Gelb 1979: 14; Maisels 1987: 355–6; Maisels 1999: 166).

I:      *abba-abba-me* 'elders' ; the Board of Directors
II:     *sanga* or *sabra*, the CEO
III:    Officials, i.e.: Top Managers who are specialists: archivist, field surveyor, grain store supervisor, chief overseer of workers.
IV:    Middle Managers: scribe-of-the-plough-animals; accountant (sar-ra-ab-du).
V:     Overseers of plough animals and chiefs of plough teams.

Beneath them the gurush, or 'hands'. The beneficial owners were, originally, the citizens of the city-state, but later the greatest benefit was to the elite and the monarchy. Another comparison can be made to Anglo-American university structure:

I:      Senatus Academicus/ Board of Regents etc.
II.    Presidents/Vice-Chancellors
III:    Heads of Department
IV:    Professors
V:     Lecturers/Readers/ Associate Professors.

The beneficiaries here are 'the community at large' and 'the world of learning' generally, specifically, the students.

Interestingly, all three (sub-system) hierarchies are relatively meritocratic in contrast to state power as such, which is overtly political, usually patrimonial and originally attached to the court. Indeed, there is normally something like an 'outer' and 'inner' court, the former conducting administration and developing state ideology, the latter where the real political and military power lies (Hsu 1998: 183). The 'chief officers of state', the ones with real executive power, are most often members of the aristocracy, even in the traditional Chinese 'nine-ranks system' which was nominally meritocratic. "In the first reigns of the Han dynasty, political power was monopolized by a small group consisting of imperial kinsmen and meritorious generals and their descendants. The absorption of literate men into government service was viewed as expedient for the discharge of archival and clerical tasks. ...Thus, literati had grown into a system or, more precisely, a sub-system within the imperial system, which originally was essentially political. More important, during its growth this subsystem acquired an ideology [Confucianism] that justified its existence, a structure of regeneration that co-existed with the political power structure" (Cho-Yun Hsu 1998: 183).

Originally there were only three ranks in the Catholic Church: Bishops, Priests (Presbyters) and Deacons. This has evolved into scores of present grades of the hierarchy, but the 'rungs' are now:

1.   Patriarchs, of which the Pope is the first, Chief Patriarch, as Bishop of Rome
2.   Cardinals
3.   Archbishops, Primates and Metropolitans
4.   Bishops and Eparchs
5.   Canons
6.   Priests (Pastors, Presbyters)

The presence of the Roman Curia, the Pope's 'cabinet office', which is the central government of the Catholic Church, alerts us to the presence of bureaucracies within bureaucracies (there are also Diocesan and other curia) as well as to parallel rankings, most notably those of military as well as of civil control, all of which nominally come together in the power of the head of state, or, in this case, church.

## C: Types of State

There are various ways of categorizing states: by what can loosely be called *composition*, by *politics* and by *structure*.

A:  Under *composition* I recognize qualitatively different types of state: 1) territorial states of various sizes, which when large and agrarian, I have previously described as Village-States because they are territorial states characterised by a capital city, a few towns and a mass of villages; 2) city-states, a less common type of state, comprising a city and its immediate hinterland (actually its *Umland*). They tend to form in groups in a restricted period and habitat, such as fourth/third millennium Mesopotamia, seventh century Greece or twelfth-century Italy (the *città*); 3) empire states, consisting of an existing territorial or more rarely in origin a city state that has conquered other, usually adjoining, polities with a shared culture that it attempts to make a permanent part of the conquering state. Such were, amongst others, the Inca and Chinese empire states. The Inca lasted a bare two centuries (before becoming part of a 'conventional' empire of metropole and colonies) while the Chinese empire-state, despite so many vicissitudes, continues to this day. In modern times Prussia under Bismarck formed the German empire-state by force of arms. On 18 January 1871, William I – King of Prussia and the Kaiserreich – was declared 'His Imperial and Royal Majesty, William the First, by the Grace of God, German Emperor and King of Prussia etc..' (other titles) in the Hall of Mirrors at Versailles upon the defeat of France. By contrast, the Austro-Hungarian Empire that Bismarck defeated in 1866 in the process of forging the German national state,[6] was just a 'conventional' empire that disintegrated into its different nationalities upon defeat in the First World War. Germany itself became the Weimar Republic and did not disintegrate, but its imperial impetus was reactivated by Hitler.

B:  In terms of *structure*, territorial states can be unitary, federal or coalition states, the difference between the federal and the coalition, being that a coalition state has no dominant centre, though it will probably have a pre-eminent one (*primus inter pares*). In Chapter 7, I suggest that the Moche State was a Coalition State and also the early Nasca state in southern Peru to have been a Sacerdotal State, a state run by priests, such as the Vatican (formerly Papal) State.

C:  In terms of *politics*, states can be either monarchies or republics, and more or less autocratic or oligarchic, despotic or not, depending upon who participates in power and at what level. But of overriding importance is whether the state is one of **consent** or **terror**. Historically, city-states best conform to states of consent, as

---

[6]  On defeat of Austria in this 'Seven Weeks' War', Prussia annexed Hannover, Schleswig-Holstein, Hesse-Kassel, Frankfurt, Nassau and parts of Hesse-Darmstadt.

citizens constitute the political class (defined below) while territorial states, as in China during the regime of Qinshihuangdi (and many of his successors), were (are) too often states of terror in which the rulers treat the populace as chattel and the country as one big prison camp. In between are states of **acquiescence** in which the populace rather passively accepts the regime so long as their own personal condition is not adversely impacted.

Territorial states can be large or small, but city-states are always relatively small (hence Hansen's [2000b] term 'micro-state') though densely populated. Size however, is not the main differentiating characteristic; the nature of the political economy is, and this is clearly seen in city-states. There, the tight clustering (nucleation) of houses, workshops, public buildings etc., occurs within city walls that serve for self-definition as well as defence. The city has its own presiding deity resident in the main temple(s) that, with supporting cult in Sumer as in Greece, unites it to its countryside (Steinkeller 2007: 206; de Polignac 1995 {1984}: 154). As Nicholas Postgate (1992: 75) tersely puts it: "If the city's religious identity is expressed in the temple, its fortification walls represent its political identity". Together with the political institutions, they define the collectivity. The *urbs* of the *polis*, that is, the cities of the city-states, are religious as well as economic centres (*astu* is the physical city as central place, *chora* its food-producing land), but they foster a sense of citizenship as well as some form of democracy for those deemed citizens. "Athens was a group of *metrioi*. Every *metrios* had a share in the community, and no one else had any share at all" (Morris 1997: 97).[7] So the polis can be regarded as a 'citizen-state'. Even Aristotle, not a native of Athens but of Stagira on the peninsula of Chalcidice, never became a citizen of Athens and remained a *metic*, a resident alien.

A city-state can be initially defined as a densely co-resident political, economic and cultural community occupying a compact area and possessing its own government, thus forming a self-conscious civic polity, a *Stadtgemeinde*. Crucially in the polis, "State authority rested to a remarkable extent on the willingness of the individual citizens to fulfil their obligations, and did not constitute a power external to the citizens themselves. ...*The polis was a community of citizens*, not a mass of subjects under a differentiated elite" (Morris 1991: 44, 48, original emphasis). In sum, it is the city-state that nearest approximates the 'social-contract' view of state existence found in Locke and Rousseau (Melleuish 2002: 331). "Here were individuals distinct from the State, and yet in their communion forming the State. ...The city formed a moral being, with a set character of its own" (Barker 1960: 2, 5).

By contrast the cities in territorial states (Hansen's 'macro-states') are politico-ideological centres, something fairly easily identified archaeologically by the amount of open ceremonial space within them. Dependent on peasant tribute, their centres are dominated by the residences of the elite – usually sectioned off by walls – and by their ideological apparatuses such as temples, pyramids and plazas. Everyone in such a city is there at the behest of the elite. There are no independent merchants or craftsmen. Andean cities are particularly clear examples of village-state centres. As succinctly put by Alan Kolata (1997: 246–7):

---

[7]  "The grant of Athenian citizenship to outsiders was always therefore in principle a privilege, conferred sometimes on individuals, more rarely on groups" (Austin and Vidal-Naquet 1977: 95).

"Andean cities were centres for elite cultural definition and self-expression; a large resident population of commoners was inimical to their purpose and function. Apart from commoners incorporated into the cities in a retainer capacity, the masses rarely participated in urban culture, except on ritual occasions. Not surprisingly several – perhaps most – Andean capitals were focal points for pilgrimages".

The vast majority of the population in large territorial states live in villages, so, as mentioned above, I (1987, 1990) have termed those *village states* in contrast to city-states which are urban in attitude and ways of life. By contrast, referring to territorial states as *village-states* draws attention to the type of settlement characteristic of the society and to the type of economy in which the overwhelming majority of the population is engaged. It is what Geographers call 'primary activities': agriculture, fishing, mining, forestry exploitation. The term 'village-state' was coined to indicate a certain type of territorial state: basically a large agrarian state with a primate capital and very few, if any, other cities, the other largish settlements comprising only garrison towns and/or trading centres/ports. Early China or early modern Russia would be major examples of Village-States (Blum 1961: 504–8). Indeed, Underhill *et al.* (2008: 25) in their study of regional settlement patterns in south-eastern Shandong, China, have identified a process of increasing ruralization in the transitions from Zhou to Han periods "since the percentage of the population in rural communities increased at the expense of the cities."

The Village-State is, then, an extensive agrarian regime with the bulk of the population living as peasants in villages dominated by a capital/administrative centre/garrison. In city-states the division of labour is organic in Durkheimian terms, namely complementary rather than mechanical, which is the redundant multiplication of relatively few occupations.[8] The organic economy is more than the sum of its parts.

---

[8]  While agreeing with Bruce Trigger and I that formative China did not produce city-states, Liu and Chen (2003: 147) have criticised my (1990: 12–13) characterisation of the village-state as, they say, "a political/cultic centre surrounded by a large number of small villages which produced the same items by identical methods". While I greatly value their work and draw upon it extensively, their summary is a gross oversimplification of what I said: "Chinese cities, in common with those characteristic of what I have [previously] called the village-state mode of production, were essentially political and cultic, not economic centres. Or rather, the wealth consumed in such cities was not produced in them in association with an immediate hinterland, as in Mesopotamia or Greece. Instead they drew revenues – tribute, taxes, corvee, etc – from a very wide area populated by basically autarkic villages producing largely the same items by largely identical methods. Accordingly, village states covered territories of orders of magnitude greater than city-states, and cities in them were never clustered, as they were in Mesopotamia and Greece". This last phrase of course means that as village-state cities were regional or procurement centres or royal capitals, they were necessarily distant from each other. My ideal-type model was constructed to contrast cities in territorial states, such as Egypt (the earliest) with city-states, such as those of Mesopotamia (the earliest); see my 1999: 354–5. This does not mean that no subsistence production was undertaken by the population of village-state cities; rather that, in contrast to city-states, economic activity was not their formative rationale. So I totally accept Liu and Chen's contention (p. 146) that "urban centres at Erlitou and Zhengzhou not only produced prestige goods such as bronzes, but also manufactured utilitarian products such as pottery and bone artefacts for the non-elite population". The key distinction is between city-*forming* activities (the raison d'etre of the city) and city-serving or settlement-*sustaining* activities, which are internal servicing functions. In this case food and artefact production would count as city-serving, because the city-forming function was political and not to provide central place functions to a hinterland. In other words the city rationale was the concentration and disposition of military and ideological power, not a centre generating economic power, as say Venice did historically or as Singapore does today. Liu (2004: 232) concedes this when she says: "These centres in the Erlitou rural areas constituted focal points in regional economic systems by producing and extracting

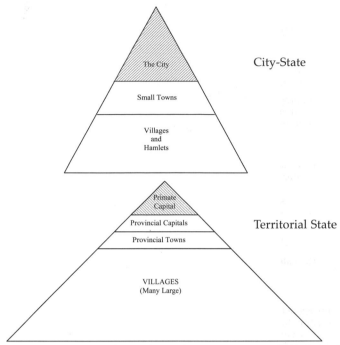

*Figure 1.4: Relative proportions of the urbanized population in city and territorial states.*

It is highly interdependent, cohesive, transformative and usually monetized. Village states are, as has been said, territorial states, characterized by the presence of villages as the very extensive base of the settlement pyramid; that is, they are by far the most numerous type of settlement. This does not mean that regional and sub-regional urban centres (towns and cities) do not develop, constituting the upper levels of the (minimally) four level settlement hierarchy that is an attribute of territorial states. Nor does it mean that no craft, exchange or service activities develop at those levels. It does mean that village states are overwhelmingly agrarian, and therefore that the settlement pyramid, like the demographic pyramid in the Third World today, has a very wide base and a low apex, as illustrated in Figure 1.4.

Settlement distribution is only one of the dimensions that make city and territorial states qualitatively distinct. Others are listed in the summary table (Figure 1.5).

The royal/imperial courts as the ruling engines of village states have need of recording methods and develop a group of literate specialists for this purpose. Accordingly large

---

both subsistence goods (e.g., food, stone tools, and construction materials) and elite goods (white pottery) for the urban centre. Given the fact that no high-level prestige goods (jades and ritual bronzes) have been found in the Erlitou hinterland, the economic relationship between urban and rural settlements appears to have been asymmetrical, suggesting a tributary system (cf: Wright 1977: 381–2)." Lastly, I said that the villages were "basically autarkic" not 'small'. No doubt they ranged in size, depending on terrain, transport links and locally exploitable resources. As early as the Longshan and Liangzhu some were very large, with a population of many thousands, as in China and India today.

*Figure 1.5: Distinguishing Characteristics of City as against Territorial States.*

| | CITY-STATE | SMALL TERRITORIAL | LARGE TERRITORIAL |
|---|---|---|---|
| Urban form | Nucleated (synoecism)[1] | Aggregated (clustered) | Aggregated (clustered; core-and-satellite) |
| Urban economy | Basically autarkic Citizens farm and trade | Relies on tribute/taxes Peasants are squeezed | Relies on tribute/taxes Peasants are squeezed |
| Settlement pattern | High proportion of total population lives and works in or from the city | High proportion of total population lives in villages | Overwhelming majority of total population lives in villages |
| Culture | (1) civic: institutions of civil society. (2) deity (Athene, Nanna etc) represents civic identity and cult. (3) culture is common to other city-states of the region: Mesopotamia, Greece, Italy etc.) (4) relatively widespread literacy | (1) court/aristocratic culture versus peasant/ folk culture. (2) state ideology: divine kingship, son of heaven, pontifex maximus etc. (3) some elite literacy | (1) court/aristocratic culture versus peasant/folk culture. (2) royal/imperial ideology: divine kingship, son of heaven, pontifex maximus etc. (3) some elite literacy; corps of literate functionaries |
| Politics | Participatory | Confined to dynastic/ court struggles | Confined to dynastic/court /military struggles |
| Military | Citizen army: 'phalanxes' of hoplites | Royal core plus infantry levies. | Standing army plus mass levies. |

[1] Synoecism is a concept derived from Aristotle that refers to the formation of a town by the fusion of several villages. It can also apply to the fusion of several towns into a city, as happened in Staffordshire, England in 1910 when Stoke-on-Trent was formed from the fusion of six contiguous towns. Historically Venice and Dortmund are well-known instances of synoikismos in this sense of fusion. And of course Thucidides (2.15) says that Theseus formed Athens in this way. Myths notwithstanding, settlement seems to have continued at Athens after the Mycenaean collapse. Both processes are, however, distinct from the process of organic city growth (e.g. of London) whereby the city expands into its surrounding agricultural land and, continuing to expand, absorbs distinct but smaller settlements into the growing mass of built-up area. Previously (1990: 13) I have used synoecism in another fashion, namely to refer to urbanism as a way of life, arising from: (a) nucleation (compact morphology); (b) the ownership of diverse means of production by townsfolk; (c) the civic consciousness and pattern of daily interaction that arises from (a) with (b).

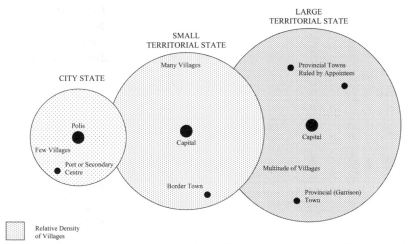

*Figure 1.6: Settlement Attributes of City States, Small and Large Territorial States.*

agrarian (i.e. village) states are sometimes referred to as 'agro-literate'. Another way of visualising the contrasts is as in Figure 1.6 (above).

## D: Hierarchy, Heterarchy and Complexity

The key distinction is between social complexity and social hierarchy, for the consolidated form of the latter is the state. The trick is, as Wengrow (2006: 175) observes, to "project hierarchy as a necessity, rather than an arbitrary feature of human existence". Most importantly, while the state cannot arise in the absence of social complexity, social complexity does not inevitably produce the state, although it usually does. In some instances a *heterarchy* may emerge to integrate a society through a series of overlapping and interacting competencies in different activities in adjacent geographical areas. In contrast to vertical integration by *hierarchy* (top down), a heterarchy is a mode of horizontal integration between different but complementary places and organisations. Hierarchies can exist within a heterarchy, each in its own sphere, but no hierarchy within a stable heterarchy is so dominant as to be able to subject the whole society. The outstanding instance is Indus civilization, where there is no dominant centre or class of rulers. This does not mean that there are no differences of wealth or standing. There surely were a whole set of gradations in wealth and standing, but not the usual dichotomy between a 'mass' of producers and a dominant elite who ran society in their own interests as consumers of the social surplus. In multi-faceted city-state society there is also a high degree of heterarchy (Stone and Zemansky 1995) and indeed social mobility (Stone 2007b: 228).

What then is meant by social complexity? The basis is the Neolithic Revolution when settled farming communities emerged in the place of the mobile hunting and gathering mode of life that had characterized *Homo sapiens* since its inception. However, as will be shown below, the Neolithic Revolution was revolutionary in its long-term outcomes, not in its actual speed of transformation of subsistence or culture. The occurrence of diverse specialization, the cause and consequence of technological advance beyond mere subsistence production, only occurred during the Chalcolithic or 'Copper Age'. The Chalcolithic is a period confined to the Old World and it comes between the Neolithic and the Bronze Age. Whereas the Bronze Age was the period of the first states and cities, the Chalcolithic was the period of towns and explosive specialization, such as characterized the Ubaid period in Mesopotamia (Hole 2006: 1) at which time "the industrial nature of pottery production … is evident enough from the huge quantities of potsherds found on the larger sites… (A.M.T. Moore 2002: 74–5).

I do not believe that the state came into being because it alone could perform important social functions in societies of increasing size and complexity (Maisels 1990: 203–214). This 'functionalist' or 'adaptationist' view was clearly expressed by one of the founding fathers of anthropological archaeology, Elman Service. "The earliest government" he writes (1975: 8) "legitimized itself in its role of maintaining the whole society. Political power organized the economy, not vice versa. Personal wealth was not required to gain political power. And these first governments seem clearly to have reinforced their structure by doing their economic and religious jobs well – by providing benefits – rather than by using physical force". And Jean-Daniel Forest (2005: 203) who has done valuable excavation in Iraq, wrote of the process of state formation, that "It is the society which, through its members and especially the most eminent ones, adopts the most appropriate solutions for mastering problems encountered, in particular the necessity of integrating increasing numbers of people". A similar view has recently been articulated in a major work by NormanYoffee (2005: 33,17):

> "In the evolution of the earliest states, new groups were created to transform, create and marshal the symbolic and ceremonial resources that allowed the recombination of the differentiated groups into a new social collectivity.
> "…The emergence of a political centre depended on its ability to express the legitimacy of interaction among the differentiated elements. It did this by acting through a generalized structure of authority, making certain decisions in disputes between members of different groups, including kin groups, maintaining the central symbols of society, and undertaking the defence and expansion of society. *It is this governmental centre that I denominate as the 'state', as well as the territory controlled by the governmental centre*" (original emphasis).

In this view, then, the state arose in order to integrate increasingly diverse social categories in societies of advancing complexity. As already mentioned, I do not believe that the state arose for this reason, which is one of pure functionalism and managerialism. As expressed by Yoffee and Forest, among others, the state arose as a system-serving entity (to overcome social problems), whereas I contend that the process of its emergence was self-serving on behalf of the elites. So the circumstances of, and real motivations for, state formation, are what we need to know. What is not in doubt is that the "movement of human beings from small hunter-gatherer groups to large and complex states can be viewed as one of the two or three defining characteristics of world history during the last 100,000 years. Considered in the 100,000 year span of human history it has been revolutionary" (Melleuish 2002: 322).

## E: Subsistence, Households and Survival

States can only arise on the basis of widespread settled farming, not on the basis of shifting cultivation or horticulture (or herding). This fact, which is effectively a truism, has a key consequence: insecurity. Farmers are at the mercy of Nature, of their neighbours and of strangers. So security from want and from attack, and conversely of support in times of scarcity and when under attack, are crucial. Accordingly, the nuclear family living and working on its own (as in some 'frontier' myths) is an impossibility. It has to be embedded in a larger structure affording protection against the vagaries of nature, environmental and human. Those larger structures can be of two types, depending on the environmental situation encountered as farming develops: *proximity* and *incorporation*.

1.  By **proximity** I mean that small, possibly nuclear household units function as minimal lineage units in a descent structure that groups together in a locality those with shared descent lines. They are para-resident, that is, the family units occupy individual houses in one or several hamlets or villages (most famously the Chinese 'single-surname village', e.g. Gao, below). At village and area level lineages group into clans in order to contest with other clans. Since lineages or clans are at base agonistic entities competing for resources, one clan or lineage becomes dominant and subjects the others, offering them protection, or else. But crude 'protection' under the

threat of violence cannot be sustained. A state can only emerge where other forms of protection are incorporated so that a rounded security package is offered: (a) ideological – protection from the wrath of the gods; (b) economic – redistribution, stores against famine, infrastructure development; (c) defence – against attack from without and against criminals within.

2.  By **incorporation** I mean co-residence in a single but essentially large household. It is a large permanent structure with controlled and ritualised space, containing several generations, siblings, plus their families of procreation. It may also include dependents from ruined households, and they may be related to the proprietors or not. Slaves may also be incorporated. The household, central to an ancestral estate, will always be under the control of the senior generation who are still active, and this usually means control by the senior male, thereby the patriarch. Even his children are subject to him and females even more than males. Marriages are arranged and used for strategic purposes. Where such extended and stratified households are the building blocks of society, as in ancient Mesopotamia, Archaic Greece and Rome, then a democracy of patriarchs emerges with the city-state.

3.  The wealthy and the political elite in societies structured by clanship can also form large households. It is at once a manifestation of their power and their instrument of power. However the roots of power in such societies lie not in the household but in the kinship structure (e.g. the Andean *ayllu*, below), specifically in its ideological justification with reference to ancestors. A large powerful household is the best machine for transmitting privilege in any society, including ours. Consider this analysis of Moche, the first and formative state in the Andes: "There exists at Moche a clear variability in the size, level of internal segmentation, construction quality and occupation continuity of houses. These elements also have a tendency to co-vary. The larger dwellings housed extended families or polynuclear family households organized in corporate groups, pooling a variety of resources, and adapted to a wider set of production and distribution strategies. The smaller households would have relied upon a narrower economic base and the contributions of a smaller number of participants. These smaller dwellings demonstrate, through their size, construction quality and short occupation, less permanence than the wealthier houses. This suggests less durable cross-generational kinship relations as well. The larger, wealthier households demonstrate a more effective permanence strategy from one generation to the next, clearer evidence for household ritual, and a higher level of integration in terms of membership. This translates into a more advantageous reproduction strategy reflected in the transmission of privileged socio-economic status to one's offspring, resulting in the formation of extended, multigenerational households" (Gijseghem 2001: 270).

4.  As the sources of power in any society are only three: ideological, economic and physical force; then, being a privileged member of the large household puts one in a good position to deploy some combination of those three sources to further one's ambitions. Blanton (1994, 1995) has conducted a cross-cultural study of peasant households, whose attributes, such as post-marital residence, he has treated statistically. He contrasts the egalitarian household (usually smaller and less ritualized) that he calls incorporative (my 'inclusive') and

which has a greater degree of freedom for its members, with the centralized, where a high degree of subordination of its members is instituted. Mechanisms to ensure acceptance of this subordinate range of household positions are of course required and Blanton (1995: 114–5) "suggests that, whether as a result of ritual or ritualized everyday behaviours, sanctification of a cultural code comes about from the establishment of an affective response to domestic symbols. ... This sanctification, not ideology alone, is proposed here as the basis for the primitive government of the centralized household systems, through its ability, as expressed by Kelly and Rappaport (1975: 33) to 'certify messages that might otherwise strike receivers as dubious'". Partly this is formalized household ritual as in the worship of household gods and/or ancestors; partly it resides in the allocation of space, where, literally, everyone knows their place, for instance women's rooms and women's work. The 'masters' might eat their meals privately, while the rest eat later and communally; and so forth.

5.   This is certainly an important mode of justification for inequality. Another, probably the most basic, is membership itself. The benefits of membership might be unevenly distributed, but at least the member does have a locus and his/her basic needs, material and psychological, are likely to be met in some form. Those outside or on the margins of society, where society is structured by households (as it always is in some form), are the persons in the most unenviable position, and who therefore are attracted by millenarian ideology looking toward the 'total overturning' of the established order.

In a lineage-based society the step beyond the chiefdom[9] is the segmentary lineage state. To the extent that it is segmentary it is structured as if every segment was a chiefdom in its own right, with its own internal hierarchy. To be called a state a segmentary state must have a king exercising hegemony over the segments. However to be a true state the king must gain control over the segments and reduce their relative autonomy, changing the system of stratification from one that is segment based and focused to one that is court based and focused. Only then can a monarch deploy the apparatuses of power, characteristic of a developed state, that make his will felt throughout the kingdom. So a segmentary state is a transitional or stalled form.

## G: Four Propositions

P1:  The state did not come into existence to serve the population in management, coordination or integration functions, but to serve the interests of the rulers, providing them with a much higher quality of life than their subjects.

P2:  All states are nevertheless different in origin and construction because the societies from which they emerge are different. The Neolithic is the key formative period

---

[9]   A chief depends upon prestige, kinship and generosity for his position. Anglo-Saxon chiefs' prestige depended on their success as warriors and on their generosity to companions and kinsmen (cf: Bazelmans 1999, Wallace-Hadrill 1971). They had no apparatuses of power; whatever had to be done they had to do themselves. In the tradition of Anglo-Saxon chiefs (cf: Beowulf), the last Anglo-Saxon king, Harold Godwinson, died at Hastings on foot, in the front ranks, fighting shoulder to shoulder with his men.

in pristine state formation, as the processes leading to state formation are path dependent. The subsequent trajectory is also path dependent.

P3:   After the state has emerged some socially useful functions are undertaken by it. However, this is usually the minimum necessary to keep society going and thus the rulers in place. Those in power traditionally extract from society much more than is returned in constructive services.[10]

P4:   Where the interests of the ruling class clash with those of the rest of the population, the interests of society will be sacrificed, as the elite will insist on their privileges at any cost, including the ruin of society as a whole.

## H: The architecture

Paradoxically, I will begin in the chapter after next, by describing a society of great size and complexity that enjoyed a high quality of life in terms of health, broadly spread wealth, urban order, the absence of war – and which achieved those in the absence of the state. Indeed, it could be argued that this was only possible in the absence of the state, as the population's surpluses were not drained away to build monstrous monuments, and to maintain palaces with all their retainers, hangers on, military apparatus and so forth. This stateless society was the Indus Civilization, and is the only complex stateless society known. As Gregory Possehl so well expressed it in the title of an article (1990), this represents a 'Revolution in the urban revolution'. Later (2002: 5) he explicitly stated that "The Indus Civilization is an example of archaic socio-cultural complexity, but without the state"; as have I (Maisels 1991, 1999).

Propositions 2, 3 and 4 will be substantiated in the subsequent chapters by an archaeological account of the earliest state occurrences in the Old and New Worlds, namely those of Egypt, Levant/Mesopotamia, China and in the Andes of South America. For reasons of space, early state formations in Mesoamerica are not discussed.

Lastly, I wish to make clear the distinctions between pristine, primary and secondary states. A pristine state is one that is the first to arise in its region and which has developed on an indigenous basis from less complex arrangements. A primary state, by contrast, is simply the dominant state in its region and period, such as the Roman Republic and Empire was in the Mediterranean.

Secondary states form in response to the emergence of primary and pristine states. Their elites will have become familiar with the culture and at least some of the technologies employed by pristine and primary states and deploy that knowledge to build their own.

---

[10]   "The formation and maintenance of elites, and then of elites within elites, lie at the heart of civilizations: inequality is fundamental…Moreover in the absence of advanced technology or gross exploitation of outsiders, the production of elite high culture adversely affects the material culture and living standards of the rest… Rather, elite high culture appears to stand in contrast to a poverty or an absence of distinctive materialised ideology for others" (Baines and Yoffee 1998: 234, 238, 240).

CHAPTER 2

# On Human Nature: Rhetoric, Relativism and the Realities of Violence

What are the reasons for the dichotomy between the Andes with East Asia and the rest of Asia? The Americas presented huge open frontiers to colonists, as also did 'China' to farming communities well into the first millennium BC. Under such conditions the lineage comprising several households, served as the unit of mutual aid. This was necessary both for subsistence and for security reasons. Farming is a risky activity, exposed both to environmental and human violence. Even hunter-gatherer society was a violent one. As Gat (1999: 567) points out in her excellent survey, "…the pattern of 'primitive warfare' manifests itself independently everywhere". It has the general characteristic of 'asymmetric fighting', which is "fighting against weakness and fighting only at highly favourable odds". Thus ambush of individuals or the massacre of women, children and the old while men are away has always been favoured. Thomas Harriot, scientist, pioneer colonist and the first person to learn and write accounts of a North American language (Algonkian), wrote in 1587 that the Indian's favourite method of fighting was "by sudden surprising one another, most commonly about the dawning of the day or moon light" (cited Milton 2000: 382); which is why native settlements were palisaded. In South America "Late Andean prehistory was profoundly shaped by warfare. ... In short, when Europeans arrived in the sixteenth century, they found indigenous Andean cultures steeped in military experience, strategies, and expertise" (Arkush and Stanish 2005: 3).

Prehistoric Britain and Europe was no different (Pearson and Thorpe 2005). Even in the Arctic and Sub-arctic warfare was an ever-present danger, as indicated by all the lines of evidence: (1) settlement data (defensive sites and structures, nucleation, relocation, burning, refuge villages); (2) skeletal evidence, including decapitation, scalping, perforations at joint surfaces of postcranial skeletal elements indicative of trophy taking; (3) violent injury from weapons, and (4) weapons themselves, such as the bow and arrow, more suitable for attacking humans than animal prey (Lambert 2002: 212–3).

Lambert (*op. cit.*) provides the following instance: In the fourteenth century the Inuit settlement of Saunaktuk on the Mackenzie Delta in the Northern Territories was attacked by Athabaskans while the Inuit men were away whaling. "Old men, women and children were tortured, murdered and mutilated. Inuit accounts do not describe cannibalism, but body parts and bones do seem to have been treated in ways consistent with this interpretation (Melbye and Fairgrieve 1994)". A minimum of 35 people died, indicated by their disarticulated, defleshed and broken remains (Lambert 2002: 212). That is why both Inuit and New Guinea highlanders made armour, respectively of bone and of tree-bark fibre and woven cane (illustrated LeBlanc 2003b: 23).

Male hunters are professional predators, so I am surprised that anyone is surprised by this behaviour, but ideology always conflates 'is' with 'ought' statements.[11] In addition to direct physiological evidence, there is locational and economic evidence from Southeast Alaska in the late prehistoric period. "Food remains and village location indicate a change at this time from subsistence strategies emphasizing foods like herring and halibut obtained by small task groups, to those such as salmon that concentrate at single locales and can be exploited by whole villages. ...These shifts are hypothesized to have minimized the risk of attack during performance of subsistence tasks", such as befell the village of Saunaktuk while the men were off whale hunting.[12]

Lambert (2002: 216) states that "the origins of war are more obscure, but archaeological and ethnographic evidence from the Northwest Coast suggests that absolute food shortage was not paramount among them. On the other hand, status clearly was, at least during the historic period". So once the usual 'pressure' excuses have been disposed of, I contend we are left with predation itself: the fundamental cause of warfare is the desire to get something for nothing, something(s) that formerly belonged to others: food, land, women or sheer gratification (in which category I include status). This is the sense in which 'taking heads' or scalps or genitals is done: to augment your own life force by stealing that of others. Not long ago the fascination of anthropologists with the Yanomamö (Chagnon 1968) was that they were very violent and in this regard supposedly exceptional for pre-class society (Ferguson 1995). They should have been forewarned by Jules Henry's 'Jungle People', a study of the Kaingáng Tribe of the Highlands of Brazil (1941, 1964), for whom "it is in the story of feuds and murder that the Kaingáng reveal the dominating drives of their life … for murder and rage are as much a part of their lives as the tapirs they kill and the houses they build" (Henry 1964: 125, 132). In any event, a study of any part of the world from prehistory to date will all too clearly show that males have always indulged in violence to get what they wanted, from raiding, warfare and genocide to Saturday-night bar-fights, killings and rapes (Wrangham and Peterson 1996: 115), and it is dangerous dissembling to pretend otherwise.

Having reviewed all regions of North America, Lambert (2002: 229) concludes that "how war was conducted appears to have varied in accordance with local traditions, technology, economy, and political system. Various parameters of the physical environment, such as topography, resource distribution and rainfall likely also

---

[11] Is to Ought statements require a linking proposition which is either ideological or utilitarian or more likely, a combination of the two. Thus the Is statement 'Not everyone has access to healthcare' followed by the Ought statement: 'Everyone should have access to healthcare', requires a linking Proposition such as: 'Everyone is entitled to healthcare' (by dint of shared humanity) and /or 'Universal healthcare improves national efficiency' etc. The Proposition necessarily involves an explicit appeal to a 'general category', such as 'humanity' or 'efficiency'.

[12] There is no point proliferating examples; Lambert 2002 has a most useful Bibliography, as do the works she cites. Wrangham and Peterson (1996) provide an indispensable comparative ethology of primate violence, including the species *Homo*.

influenced when, where, and how war was conducted. Most of the archaeological and osteological evidence suggests that relatively small-scale engagements predominated, involving a limited number of aggressors and resulting in relatively few victims per encounter. Quantitive analysis of victim frequencies reveals, however, that even this low-level warfare could result in very high death tolls overall, particularly for certain sex and age classes (*e.g.*, Bridges *et al.*, 2000; Jurmain, 2001; Lambert 1994, 1997; Milner *et al.*, 1991). In addition mass graves and/or large numbers of unburied bodies showing signs of trauma are known from several regions and document outbreaks of highly lethal, genocidal violence. Large-scale massacre is best known at sites on the northern Great Plains (Crow Creek, Fay Toilten, Larson), but apparent massacres have also been identified at sites in the northern Southwest (Wetherill's Cave 7, Battle Cave, Castle Rock, Sand Canyon Pueblo) and southern Southwest (Casas Grandes), the Canadian Arctic (Saunatuk), and possibly in the Southeast (Pinson Cave). As Milner notes (1999), it is likely that other such outbreaks occurred, but were not preserved because no one survived to bury the dead". War-crimes did not await the arrival of the state. As Haas (2001) trenchantly observes: "the archaeological record demonstrates that warfare is not just an ugly stepchild of complex centralized societies".

On the contrary, and contrary to received wisdom, Keeley (1996) provides comparative evidence that males in nonstate societies are far more likely to face armed combat than is the average male citizen of a modern state. Whether it is called feuding, vendetta or warfare makes no difference to the violent reality, and neither does calling it 'ritual'[13] or religious, as if the all too real combat, death and mutilation was some kind of sacralized pantomime. Some scholars even see ancient Chinese warfare in this light, despite the fact that during the Qunqiu period ('Spring and Autumn' 770–484 BC) warfare reduced the number of states in China from 162 to only 14 (Kolb 1990–1). This even prior to the Warring States period (484–221 BC) when China was unified by warfare in the longest and most massive series of military mobilizations and battles anywhere in the world until the First World War. Such groundless orientalizing assumptions are thoroughly disposed of by Shaughnessy (1996). Despite their well-known military rituals and care to pacify and even incorporate the gods of the defeated, no-one claims that Roman warfare was 'ritualistic'. Arkush and Stanish (2005: 10–11) rightly remark that "warfare of all kinds and scales can be ritualized, including warfare that involves the killing of enemies, the taking of property and people, and the appropriation of land". The Geneva Conventions are part of our ritualization of warfare, as is the British practice of commissioning recognized artists to produce work representing military activities in times of war (official 'war artists' as distinct from journalistic illustrators). As Ghezzi (2008: 69) observes in regard to late Early Horizon warfare in the Andes: "the reluctance to accept that the graphic depiction of dismembered body parts being trodden on by weapon-bearing figures at Cerro Sechín was grounded in the reality of war, reflects the tendency to see the ritual and secular aspects of warfare as mutually

---

[13] Ritual is repeated, conventionalized symbolic behaviour, externally (publicly) and internally (psychologically) actualizing aspects of a belief system (ideology). cf: Firth (1951: 222) for whom ritual is "a kind of patterned behaviour oriented towards the control of human affairs, primarily symbolic in character with a non-empirical referent, and as a rule socially sanctioned".

exclusive. Such an 'either-or' approach to warfare ignores that, as a cultural institution, warfare is multi-dimensional and cannot be so reduced".

It is a cruel paradox that those wishing to minimize violence in human affairs, as we all should strive to do, think that they further this end by an anti-historical and anti-biological form of pacifistic wish-fantasy (Hastorf 2005: 17). Those opposing what they see as the 'naturalistic fallacy' (in this form 'the way of nature is how people behave') adopt the 'reverse-naturalistic' or 'moralistic fallacy'[14] wherein our preferred values can just deny facts and by doing so abolish them. They forget the fundamental distinction between Is and Ought statements: namely, that in order to get to where you want to be ('the way it should be') you first must be clear about where you are ('the way it is'). This is just basic map work. If Is and Ought are conflated, a path to the goal – how we get from present conditions to those desired – that is, from here to there, cannot be charted. Implicit in Ought statements are Is statements, but the reverse is not true. We must be clear about the Is before we can advance the Ought because an instrumental link must be provided showing how it is to be done. The diminishing number of scholars who deny evolutionary entailment, do so not because of lack of evidence, but because they wish to believe that 'nurture' not 'nature' is decisive in human behaviour and that if only social institutions could be rectified, then human behaviour would be too. However, while social arrangements can modulate, modify, shape and even direct some behaviours, what they cannot do is produce a tabula rasa by abolishing evolved structures (Barkow, Cosmides and Tooby 1993).

Instead, Keeley (1996: 39) argues, "the archaeological evidence indicates that homicide has been practiced since the appearance of modern humankind and that warfare is documented in the archaeological record of the past 10,000 years in every well-studied region". However, in terms of area studies, only in the last ten years, has "a major philosophical obstacle been overcome: the lack of recognition of war as an important social process in prehistoric North America" (Lambert 2002: 230; cf: Walker 2001: 588). In Central and South America, Flannery (1994: 105) finds that "evidence for armed conflict, raiding, and terrorism is everywhere in Nuclear America at the rank society or 'chiefdom' level of evolution. From Cerro Sechín on the north coast of Peru, with its graphic carvings of trophy heads, enemies quartered and disemboweled, to the fortification walls and defensible locations of Late Formative sites in Mexico's Valley of Oaxaca, or the carved scenes of decapitation in Chiapas, it is clear that rank societies were violent societies".

Another locus, in northern Chile, has implications for the latter part of this work. The coastal Palaeolithic/Mesolithic Chinchorro people of the Arica region were fishers, shellfish-gatherers, seaweed collectors and hunters of marine mammals; not only pre-state but pre-farming in this most northerly part of Chile. Chinchorro population numbers were only at hunter-gatherer levels, but were localised in permanent settlements without permanent architecture (Rivera 1991). Movement seems to have been seasonal from a base-camp. The Chinchorro were producers of the world's earliest mummies, preserved by the aridity of the Atacama Desert (Arriaza 1995). The

---

[14]   For instance, the Seville Statement on Violence (1987) prepared on behalf of UNESCO. See Wrangham and Peterson (1996: 176–7).

excellent state of preservation that resulted and the international, multidisciplinary study of the remains that has been undertaken over two decades, demonstrates that a remarkable proportion of the population died violent deaths at the hands of other members of that population. Further, evidence such as the longitudinal splitting of leg longbones strongly suggests cannibalism, something frequently inferred, but hotly contested, in North America also.

In the Old World Palaeolithic too, the site of Gebel Sahaba in the south of Egypt (Qadan industry) around 12,000 BP, has a cemetery containing 59 individuals, of whom "twenty-four showed signs of a violent death attested either by many chert points embedded in the bones (and even inside the skull) or by the presence of severe cut marks on the bones. The existence of multiple burials (including a group of up to eight bodies in one grave) confirms the picture of violence" (Hendrickx and Vermeersh 2000: 30), especially as about half of this population are women and children. Given the small scale of Palaeolithic populations, this represents a major loss of life and indeed reproduction potential.

During the Late Intermediate Period, northern Chile, along with the highlands of south-western Bolivia and north-western Chile, experienced endemic conflicts (Nielson 2005: 18). This is "supported by several lines of evidence, including rapid population aggregation, shifts to defensible locations for settlement, fortified sites, new weapons or changes in the frequency or design of existing ones, cuirasses, helmets, 'trophy heads' and rock-art representations of fighting. Those indicators have not been recorded everywhere, but seem to be present to some extent in areas with significant human occupation all the way to the Argentine province of Cajamarca". Indeed the indicators listed by Nielson are among the multiple lines of evidence that Haas (2001: 332) and Arkush and Stanish (2005: 15) argue produce convincing evidence of warfare. But it is not warfare *per se* that is most interesting in regard to violence and social complexity in the Andes. Rather, it is that overt violence is bound into the fundamental ideology of social and natural exchanges, with nature and its terrestrial representatives the dominant parties. "In the representational art of prehistoric Andean society, the pervasive iconography of violence, predation, and sacrifice, juxtaposed or conflated with symbols of agricultural fertility and cosmic regeneration, attest to the crucial role that sacralized violence and ideologies of reproductive-consumption played in Andean prehistory" (Swenson 2003: 261). "As such," Feuer (1975: 17) remarks, "an ideology is never content with the narrative of the myth; the drama must be shown to be deducible from the laws of existence itself."

The Rousseauesque fantasy of the 'peaceful savage' is accompanied by the equally fanciful notion of 'peaceful Nature' in opposition to 'Nature red in tooth and claw'. In this view plants and animals do not compete but, at a deep level at least, cooperate. Combined, they produce the myth of prehistoric/pre-contact people at home in, and at one with, a pacific Nature, as intuitive environmentalists (Kay 1989). Some people need to believe that somewhere, out there or, more probably, back there, 'originally', this state of affairs actually existed. This is just Garden-of-Edenism got up with some social science figleaves (Pinker 2002). Garden-of-Edenism is, however, a dangerous fantasy because it is manifestly counter-historical and as such enables ideologues to spin all kinds of tales (Feuer 1975: 7). Peace and plenty is not a default position, but has to be striven for, in the full knowledge of human propensities. However, "the psychological motive to believe in peace appears to have a strong influence on the way we look upon ourselves. By remaining largely ignorant of the way warfare weaves its web through human endeavours, people can believe in the myth of peace" (Gilbert 2004: viii), and an essentially pacific human nature.

Likewise with regards to criminality and violence, in societies 'at peace'; that is, not at war. No one imagines that if police forces, courts and prisons are abolished all social behaviour will be benign. Nonetheless, only a few years ago, Stephen Lekson (2002: 618) felt obliged to apologise for his analysis of the causes and periodization of violence amongst the Pueblos of the US Southwest, since indigenous peoples are supposed to be 'naturally' peaceful. I cannot put the case against Rousseauism or Arcadianism any better than has Walker (2001: 590): "The search for an earlier, less-violent way to organize our social affairs has been fruitless. All the evidence suggests that peaceful periods have always been punctuated by episodes of warfare and violence. As far as we know, there are no forms of social organization, modes of production, or environmental settings that remain free from interpersonal violence for long". And if that is the case the root cause must reside in our emotions and instincts, that is, in human nature itself: self-preservation, self-gratification, the sex drive and the drive for power that privileges individuals and groups in society. Accordingly, only those forms of society are legitimate that recognize and strongly counter those 'natural' propensities.[15]

> "Many rationalists accept that, while reason facilitates and helps to control human behaviour, it does not motivate it. Reason has evolved to serve drives that are rooted in human nature. Human nature, in turn is grounded in a common biology that expresses itself in similar organic needs, forms of intelligence and psychology, that generate similar impulses and drives"(Trigger 2003b: 5–6).

As for an earlier ecological accommodation, deforestation, soil and habitat destruction were already extensive in the Neolithic (Rollefson, Simmons and Kafafi 1992; Rollefson and Kohler-Rollefson, 1989, 1993), even in the British Isles, which came late to the Neolithic and where Holocene soils have not been short of moisture. Most of the British Isles were deforested well before the arrival of the Romans, which is why there are no forests in Britain, only woodlands (Rackham 1986: 72). Islands around Britain, even major ones like the Isle of Man, fared even worse. Now British people think

---

[15]   On the evolutionary basis of ethics and its cultural manifestations, see Ayala 2006 and the other contributions to Jeeves ed., Human Nature. Emotions shape ideologies and philosophical tenets, as Feuer (1975: 58–9) makes plain: "No combination of philosophical tenets with its corresponding set of expressed and repressed emotions is ever in a state of stable equilibrium. ...The next philosophical tenets will express those emotions which were most repressed by the previous philosophical scheme. ...The component of repressed emotion, associated with every philosophical tenet, is obviously the crucial one in the history of ideology. One might call it the source of 'Jamesian waves' in the history of ideology. It is founded on one psychological postulate: that the goals and longings of human emotions do not constitute a consistent system; men are driven by both love and aggression; they alternate between competitive drives and cooperative aspirations; they seek both autonomy and self-donation; they hold fast to material interests even as they long for transcendental ideals. No ideological doctrine can satisfy these incompatible vectors, unless some powerful emotions have been super-added to repress partially one of them. But the repressed element always presses for an overhauling of the ideology".

of bare hills as 'natural' and therefore 'beautiful' and so oppose reforestation.[16] Even the trees that grow at the highest altitude in the world, *Polylepis,* are not safe from human destruction. *Polylepis* (queñoa) form low forests close to the snowline in the equatorial Andes and farther south in the Lake Titicaca basin, or rather used to: they have been largely destroyed for firewood and replaced by *paramo* steppe (Whitmore 1981: 269), which is a tundra-like biome. People have always been, what they are now, ecological disaster (Deckers and Riehl 2004). We have wiped out countless species over the past ten thousand years, especially, and shortly after, the Americas and the Pacific islands were colonized. As Ridley (1996: 219) observes: "In all, as the Polynesians colonized the Pacific, they extinguished twenty per cent of all the bird species on Earth". He rightly concludes (*ibid*.: 225) that fable and wish-fantasy will not enable us to save the planet; only stark realism will achieve that, for "the conclusion that seems warranted is that there is no instinctive environmental ethic in our species – no innate tendency to develop and teach restrained practice. Environmental ethics are therefore to be taught *in spite of human nature*, not in concert with it" (my emphasis). All ethics, not just environmental ones, need to be taught in spite of human nature. Human nature hasn't changed: as accelerating forest destruction again proves, we are greedy, narrow-minded, short-sighted and given to incessant excuse-mongering, often elaborated into ideologies or expressed through them. What has changed is our sheer numbers and the level of technology we can use for destruction. Until recently it was thought that the technology of our destruction would be nuclear. It is now apparent that it is the technologies of sheer consumption that will consume us. "Human motivations are always a complex mix of the practical, the emotional and the frankly irrational. Whatever the specific reasons, leaders (and others) on all but the simplest societal levels tend to want more" (Webb 1987: 167). Hence the mottos on the Dedication page.

Our intra-species and extra-species behaviour (hierarchy, violence, victimization, predation) is continuous with that of our closest relations, the chimpanzees (who routinely hunt monkeys and victimize or kill other chimps) and with other primates such as lemurs (even though the latter are female dominated) and monkeys such as baboons, who eat vervet monkeys and birds (McGrew 2004). Capuchins (tool-using New World monkeys) have large canines for fighting and more are killed by other Capuchins than by predators. Macaques (Old World monkeys), the most widespread and adaptable non-human primate, even have an aristocracy. Yet another parallel chimpanzee characteristic is male violence against females: "Male attacks on females, so consistent and regular an aspect of chimpanzee life, might best be described by the term *battering* – as it is used to describe domestic violence among humans, most often when a man attacks and beats up a woman with whom he has an ongoing relationship" (Wrangham and Peterson 1996: 145–6). The battering of infants and rape is another chimpanzee and human characteristic. After all, we had a common ancestor only 5 million years ago and, sharing 98.4 per cent of our genes with chimps, we could be regarded as the third chimpanzee species (Common Chimpanzees, Bonobos or pigmy chimps and us). This is our family tree (Figure 2.1).

---

[16] In fact most British people are afraid of forests, for they are outwith their personal experience (Rackham 1986: 93; Maisels 1978; Ridley 1996: 105).

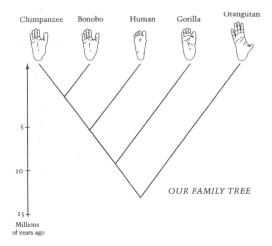

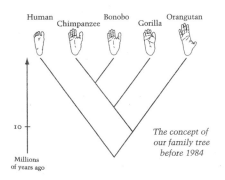

*Figure 2.1: Our Family Tree (from Wrangham and Peterson 1996, Appendix).*

We flatter ourselves, and conflate emic with etic categories when we talk about victimization, mutilation, torture and murder as 'ritual sacrifice', as if sacralizing it (whatever that may mean) makes it okay. Or perhaps the victims are somehow less human than us and do not suffer as much? Would you say this about the millions of recent victims of such abominations in Rwanda, Congo, Sudan or Sierra Leone? Or Khmer Rouge Cambodia or in Nazi concentration camps? After all, the perpetrators had a 'sacred' mission too! As Quilter (2002: 172) observes of the Moche and more generally: "There is also the question of the emotional power of participating in or watching fellow human beings being transformed into chunks of rotting flesh, flayed skins, and dismembered carcasses. Perhaps it is a relic of the era when archaeology attempted to be objectively scientific that consideration of emotions seems to have no place in our studies of the past. Ancient sacrifices in which one group of people did nasty things to another are described as if victims and victimizers were members of the congregation at an Anglican evening prayer service. But in stripping the emotion out of these acts we lose a perspective in understanding them (see Carrasco 1999)". As Robert Redfield (1968: 156–7), that man of good sense, said over half a century ago: "It is easy enough to be objective towards objects; but the human individual refuses to be only an object. ... Ethnographic research calls for as much objectivity as can be combined with the necessity to come to know the values of the people one is studying. ... But I do not think that it asks of me that I divest myself of the human qualities, including valuing. I could not do my work without them." Barry Kemp (2006: 2) expressed similar sentiments when introducing the second edition of his key work on ancient Egypt, and added that "There is no clear and absolute answer as to where the line should be drawn between too much empathy and too little".

Or for that matter in understanding the lure of the Roman amphitheatre and contemporary bull-'fights', cock-fights, bull and bear 'baiting', to say nothing of hunting for 'sport'. As a consequence first of the conquest of Italia and then of the whole Mediterranean basin, Rome itself had long been filled with an idle (a third and then one half of the year given over to official holidays!) ignorant and bloodthirsty mob, which had to be fed rations and constantly diverted by (very expensive) gladiatorial and other games, theatres and circuses (*ludi*). Indeed Samuel Dill in his classic work ([1898]1958: 54) acutely observes that "the amphitheatre gave a sort of consecration to the old savage instinct for cruelty, as the [Roman] theatre gratified the pruriency of low desires. ...Men can find a justification for any established institution, and those cruel displays were defended, even by good and eminent men, as the virile amusements of a warlike race, accustoming it to make light of death". So addicted were the population to those 'amusements' that they were still staged and fully attended as the Empire came crashing down around them.

Doubly unfortunate is the fact that for humans (as for chimpanzees), violence is both instrumental and itself gratifying, that is, pleasurable. It provides an adrenalin high, as in this account of chimpanzees in Tanzania's Gombe National Park in 1970 described by Wrangham and Peterson (1996: 17):

> "At one point [the Kasekela group] sat still on a ridge, staring down into the Kahama Valley for more than three-quarters of an hour, until they spotted Goliath, apparently hiding only 25 metres away. The raiders rushed madly down the slope to their target. While Goliath screamed and the patrol hooted and displayed, he was held and beaten and kicked and lifted and dropped and jumped on. At first he tried to protect his head, but he soon gave up and lay stretched out and still. His aggressors showed their excitement in a continuous barrage of hooting and drumming and charging and branch-waving and screaming. They kept up the attack for eighteen minutes, then turned for home, still energized, running and screaming and banging on tree-root buttresses. Bleeding freely from his head, gashed on his back, Goliath tried to sit up but fell back shivering. He was never seen again."

Chimpanzee hunts of chimpanzees and other primates are instrumental in forging male solidarity because killing is a gratifying manifestation of power.[17] "And in every place, the chimpanzees' visceral reaction to a hunt and a kill is intense excitement. The forest comes alive with the barks and hoots and cries of the apes, and aroused chimpanzees race in from several directions. The monkey may be eaten alive, shrieking as it is torn apart. Dominant males try to seize the prey, leading to fights and charges and screams of rage. For one or two hours or more, the thrilled apes tear apart and devour the monkey. This is bloodlust in its rawest form" (Wrangham and Peterson 1996: 216), akin to the carnage in Rwanda in 1994.

Mankind spent a long time as professional predator. "Indeed, animal motifs played a significant role during all periods of Egyptian military history, and so far it has not

---

[17] And not just male power, as this report from the Metro newspaper on December 15, 2005, shows: "A girl of 14 led a gang of sadistic misfits who killed for fun during a Clockwork Orange-style spree of violence. She was one of four grinning thugs who were 'seeking violence for its own sake' when they kicked bar manager David Morley to death in a happy-slap attack. The gang assaulted eight people in just one hour. The teenager, who wanted to film attacks to distribute them on the Net, pointed her mobile at Mr Morley and said: 'We are doing a documentary on happy-slapping. Pose for the camera'. She then ran up and 'kicked his head like a football'. The 37 year-old victim was chatting to his friend, Alastair Whiteside, on London's South Bank on October 30 last year when he was attacked. He was kicked and punched by the 'smiling and laughing youths' and left for dead". Which he was. "His 44 injuries would be more commonly seen in someone who had been in a car crash or had fallen from a great height, a pathologist said".

been possible to distinguish between the image of the hunter and that of the warrior" (McDermott 2004: 11). Just as the pleasure we get from sex is evolution's inducement and reward for propagation, so it would be surprising if evolution did not have similar psycho-emotional reward mechanisms for violence. And so it proves, for the brain produces Dopamine, the feel-good neuro-transmitter, when engaging in violence, just as it does when engaging in sex.

> "Men enjoy hunting and killing, and these activities are continued as sports even when they are no longer necessary. If a behaviour is important to the survival of a species (as hunting was for man throughout most of human history), then it must be both easily learned and pleasurable. ...Evolution builds a relation between biology, psychology, and behaviour and, therefore, the evolutionary success of hunting exerted a profound effect on human psychology. Perhaps this is most easily shown by the extent of the efforts devoted to maintain killing as a sport" (Washburn and Lancaster 1968: 299).

It all comes down to the level of the individual psyche. So it doesn't do to sociologize, relativize and 'contextualize' everything; those are the opiates of the chattering class. Some things just are biological, physical, neurological, somatic, instinctive, that is, evolved:

> "Social scientists must cease analysing human behaviour without reference to humans as biological entities. Evolution, both biological and cultural, is a process that adapts humans with specific but as yet poorly understood biological, social and psychological predispositions and needs to the natural and social environment in which they live" (Trigger 2003: 686).

Humans are born with an innate capacity for language – "the human brain is born listening for human talk" (Trevarthen 2006: 225) – and for pattern recognition, which makes writing, counting and representation ('art') possible. *What* is written, counted or represented is a social construct; the capacity to do so is not (Pinker 1994). A refrigerator is a machine to preserve food, and a motor vehicle, bottom line, is a means of transport; even Hitler's 'people's car'. As Picasso said when asked about the symbolic meaning of the chicken in his famous Guernica picture: 'it's just a chicken!' Sometimes things just are what they appear to be, mundane as that is. As Joseph Ball and Jennifer Tascheck (2007) trenchantly and refreshingly put it: "Sometimes a 'stove' *is* just a stove: a context based reconsideration of three-prong 'incense burners' from the Western Belize Valley" (their emphasis). Not symbol, not ritual, just cooking.

"On the one hand then, we have the Andean peasantry revelling in sacrifice, and on the other, we have the anthropologists busy trying to clean up after them with exchange theory" (Gose 1986: 298). Given the determination of some cosmic lawyers to provide excuses for everything, I reproduce without further comment the following short report (from The Metro, a London newspaper, Thurs. July 14, 2005: 20):

> "Kenya: At least 50 people, up to half of them children, were killed in a raid on a remote village by Ethiopian bandits yesterday. They died after a 500 strong raiding party armed with rifles, hand grenades, machetes and spears, surrounded a school in Tubi. Survivors said the gang struck out indiscriminately; one mother said they killed her two children and beheaded her husband while she watched. More than 20 children, many in their school uniforms, were among the dead. Police say they

> pursued the bandits, killing 16 of them, but most escaped back across the border. They also recovered about 5,000 sheep, 200 cattle, ten camels and four donkeys from the raiders."

No doubt the cosmic lawyers will argue that they needed food.


## The state as parasite and predator

In this work I argue for a different kind of exchange theory, namely negative reciprocity, wherein the elite take from the producers much more than they ever return; taking even their lives. Maurice Bloch (1992) calls this 'the consumption of vitality'. As the ethnographer Gose (1986: 306) further observes in regard to the worldview of the Andean peasantry: "Politics consists of the transcendental assimilation of the ruled by the rulers, and is correspondingly violent". This is true even of peaceful enterprises: in Europe we only have to consider the sacrifice of at least one hundred thousand lives made by 'Peter the Great' in building his new capital of St. Petersburg.

One of the key claims by which a state justifies its existence is by the imposition of 'law and order', such that fighting is reserved to itself in a monopoly of force, violence in general is repressed, and the strong are not allowed to oppress the weak such as widows and orphans. The earliest written law codes, those of Mesopotamia in the late third and early second millennia BC (most famously Hammurabi's) make just such claims to legitimacy. Some four centuries earlier Ur-Nammu, the founding ruler of the Third Dynasty of Ur (and builder of the best preserved ziggurat) issued a law code that survives from copies produced in the scribal schools of Nippur and Ur. Part of the over hundred lines of preamble reads: (ll.31–35)

> "After [the principal gods] An and Enlil had turned over the Kingship of Ur to Nanna [city-god of Ur] … at that time did Ur-Nammu, son of (the goddess) Ninsun, for his beloved mother who bore him … in accordance with his (i.e. the god Nanna's) principles of equity and truth… (ll 104–113). Then did Ur-Nammu, the mighty warrior, king of Ur, king of Sumer and Akkad, by the might of Nanna, lord of the city (of Ur), and in accordance with the true word of Utu [the sun god, son of Nanna], establish equity in the land (and) he banished malediction, violence and strife" (Finkelstein 1975: 31–32).

As part of which it was necessary for Ur-Nammu to dispose of corrupt, grasping officials. No change there.

In other words, once the state has arisen it must justify its existence by showing some social benefit in exchange for its high running costs. Costs are however lower and benefits higher in city-states, as the populace has at its disposal various means of action against the ruling elites, ranging from democratic assemblies and military formations of the armed citizenry to riot, assassination and revolution. Autonomy and prosperity are the reasons why the citizens of city-states fought so strongly to retain their city-states against territorial ones. Instances range from Sumer, through ancient Greece and the cities of Renaissance Italy to the resistance of the Low Countries against Spanish domination in the 16th Century. Siena too, despite over two centuries of internal faction fighting that produced revolution and counter-revolution, banishments and tyrannies, yet fought valiantly against the Spaniards, only being overcome in 1555 after a heroic siege.

The fundamental condition for the emergence of city-states is either priority of emergence, or if not chronologically prior, then emergence into a political arena of weak and fragmented powers. So, if urban formation is prior, then a city-state is likely to form, but if state formation is prior to urbanization, then territorial state formation is much more likely. Conversely, if urbanism can survive the collapse of a territorial state, as in post Roman Italy (La Rocca 1992: 161) but not in Britain (Dixon 1992: 156–7), then city-state polities can emerge. Urbanization was later elsewhere in Europe, and without doubt it was the weakness of territorial powers in mediaeval Europe and their fragmentation, that allowed the formation of city-states in Italy, Germany, the Netherlands and Switzerland (Clarke 1926, Hui 2005).

## Environmental Conditions

Under the 'open' conditions of expanding frontiers and with life and property at stake, warfare would have been rife and the power of a single, simple lineage quite inadequate once several other lineages had banded together using the ideology of shared descent. The more ramified (extended) the lineage structure one could count upon, the more power and security one had. This would, of course, instigate an arms race whereby those without clan protection would be forced to join one or be wiped out. In a short period clans would dominate the entire social landscape.

Archaeologically, we see clan organization at the earliest stages of the Neolithic in the Andes, and in China at the Neolithic villages of Jiangzhai, Beishouling, Shijia and Banpo (Gao and Lee 1993; Maisels 1999). Janusek (1999: 110), in discussing specialization amongst *ayllus*, (often translated as 'clan'), characterizes the Andes at contact as populated by "loosely coalescing segmentary polities, in which economic organization and social power were distributed among constituent, mutually nested *ayllus*. ... An encompassing macro-*ayllu*, much like an ethnic group, shared a common ancestor and social identity, but gathered largely during political confrontations and major rituals". He graphically represents the nesting of Macro, Major and Minor *ayllus* as can be seen in Figure 2.2.

*Alasaya* means 'upper half', *majasaya* 'lower half'. Each square represents a major ayllu grouping of micro-*ayllus*. This corresponds to traditional Andean

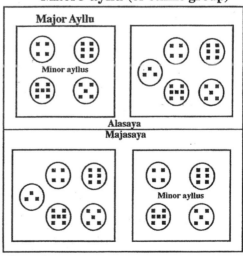

**Macro-ayllu (or ethnic group)**

Major Ayllu

Minor ayllus

Alasaya
Majasaya

Minor ayllus

▪▪▪ = Micro-ayllus, estancias, or communities

*Figure 2.2: Schematic Structural Model of the Andean 'ayllu' (from Janusek 1999: 110; cf: Albarracin-Jordan 1996: 186).*

dualities, spatially to *hanan* and *hurin*, respectively upper and lower (Shady Sollis 2008: 36).

Janusek later (2002: 37) observes "the nested and unequal relations among *ayllus* were often described as intimate family relations, with political leaders as metaphorical 'elder-brothers'. ... Thus, *ayllu* conjured an intricate and flexible sense of place and identity, but it also condensed complex relations in a hierarchical sociopolitical landscape, bestowing on them intimate family terms. *Ayllu* defined social identity but it also was political ideology".

Recent work by Makowski (2002) in the Tablada de Lurin in the Lima area of Central Peru, focussing on the end of the Formative period (*c*.200 BC–AD 200), confirms that the structuring institution was the *ayllu*[18] This is indicated by the clustering and re-use of burial chambers in the enormous cemetery. Male and female, old and young were buried together in a cluster, and, most significantly, wealthy and poor existed within each cluster. It was not the case that some areas were reserved for the wealthy and powerful while others, the majority, were just poor, undifferentiated commoners. Instead, each *ayllu* had its more wealthy and powerful members. This period in the Lurin Valley, Makowski (2002: 115–6) characterizes as being occupied by a cohesive ethnic group with the political structure of a complex chiefdom; that is, as encompassing a few tens of thousands of population, whereas a simple chiefdom would typically comprise a population of only a few thousand.

For nomadic pastoralists and cattle-keepers of historical periods and the present, clanship serves as protection for their flocks and pasturelands against other clans, and against states. Indeed, groups of clans (tribes) were sometimes in a position to conquer states, as the Amorites did in early second millennium Babylonia, organized as they were in a structure specifically designed for mobility and combat. The conflictual basis of the clan is still highly apparent in contemporary China (Chapter 6). Kinship, after all, is "the product of strategies (conscious or unconscious) oriented towards the satisfaction of material and symbolic interests and organized by reference to a determinate set of economic and social conditions" (Bourdieu 1977: 36). The ferocious adherence to clan and tribe in contemporary Afghanistan, Somalia and Sudan is clearly a consequence of endemic warfare in those areas (Krapf-Askari 1972: 20), as indeed in the Highlands of Scotland pre-1745, in Japan before the Meiji Restoration, and over much of sub-Saharan Africa today. Since politics is the continuation of war by less-destructive means, even when actual fighting dies down, competition ensures that clan and tribe identities are

---

[18] The *ayllu* descent group model derives from Inca society at contact. Not all Andeanists are convinced that pre-Inca society was structured by the ayllu, or even that it existed prior to the social re-organizations imposed by Inca imperialism, or by earlier state-building episodes. While Moseley (1993: 94) and Kolata (1991: 113) are amongst those who think that the ayllu existed from the early Neolithic, some six thousand years ago, William Isbell (1997b: 136) has argued that the ayllu is a late innovation of pre-Hispanic Andean society. As will become clear below, the existence of the ayllu is a strong working hypothesis accompanied by much circumstantial archaeological evidence (Bandy 2008: 225–7). However, archaeological correlates are not yet conclusively in its favour, although most Andeanists assume its existence at least as far back as Moche times. For a succinct discussion with some new evidence, see Valdez, Bettcher and Valdez (2002). My own position is close to that of Bermann (1997 and below) which sees the ayllu rooted in the Neolithic transition, but assuming different configurations according to the political and economic situation. Its existence makes the most sense in the light of monument building processes and also the vertical archipelago.

strongly maintained during periods of relative peace, especially when fighting for positions in, or control over, the state.

Each area of state emergence has to be examined in its own right using archaeological evidence and the earliest written evidence. In the Andes, for example, states were late to emerge after a long drawn-out Neolithic transition, during which cities form in the pre-ceramic period and where metals are of only ritual importance.

The following table (from Maisels 1999: 30) shows parallel phases in evolution from Palaeolithic ('Old Stone Age') to Bronze Age across the Old World, indicating sites and cultures in each trajectory. As categories such as Chalcolithic and Bronze Age do not apply to Latin America, Andean cultures are not included in this composite table (Figure 2.3).

In terms of chronological priority, Mesopotamia is earliest, forming as city-states (most notably Uruk) during the fourth millennium. In chronological terms Egypt was only a few centuries behind, but the state form on the Nile was that of the territorial state, the world's first. So city-state and territorial state have similar antiquity. Urban society emerged in north-west India from the mid-third millennium (the Mature Indus period) and terminated with that millennium. States formed in parts of what became China in the first half of the second millennium. Although its period of state-formation is the latest of the major civilizations of the Old World, China shows the strongest elements of continuity from Neolithic to the present.

Certain key facets of Chinese culture history have their origin in the Neolithic: animism (veneration of natural phenomena), hierarchical family structure sanctified by ancestor worship (Keightley 2008: 426; Liu 1999: 602), central importance of family (stem-family), lineage and clan, hierarchic ranking of lineages. A consequence was the early emergence of 'lords' with control of people and territory, sanctioned by genealogical rank plus ritual, and defended by force. This form of class domination produced the territorial state in the particular form of Village-State (Maisels 1987 and above). From this matrix there emerged a congeries of states in competition, alliance and conflict during the Bronze Age, and which reached its height during the first millennium BC. The Warring States Period (484–221 BC) marked the final break-up of the formerly hegemonic Zhou regime. The Warring States Period ended with the victory of the state of Qin (pronounced 'chin') and its ruler became the first Emperor as Qin Shi Huang Di. The victory of Qin, turning China into an empire state, is why we call the central kingdom (Zhongguo) 'China'.

## SITES OR CULTURES REPRESENTATIVE OF THE NAMED PERIODS IN:-

| PERIOD AND CHARACTERISTICS | EGYPT UPPER (South) | EGYPT LOWER (North) | EGYPT FAYUM (North West) | NEAR EAST LEVANT | NEAR EAST MESOPOTAMIA | INDUS | CHINA |
|---|---|---|---|---|---|---|---|
| **LATE-PALAEOLITHIC** (Microliths/Compound Tools) | Wadi Kubbaniya, Makhadma | | | KEBARAN | ZARZIAN | Sanghao Cave, Rabat, Baghor I & III | Xibaijianfang, Xiaonanhai, Xiaogushan, Xiachuan, Xueguan#, Daxianzhuang* |
| **EPI - PALAEOLITHIC** (Pounding/Grinding Tools) | | | FAYUM B (Qarunian) | NATUFIAN | Zawi Chemi/ Karim Shahir | Chopani Mando, Baghor II | Shayuan, Huduiliang, Xijiaoshan, Layihai, Zengpiyan |
| **NEOLITHIC** (Villages, Agriculture) | BADARIAN | MERIMDE/ EL OMARI | FAYUM A | PPNA, PPNB, PPNC, YARMOUKIAN, JERICHO IX, WADI RABA | PRE-PROTO-HASSUNA, PROTO-HASSUNA, HASSUNA, SAMARRA, HALAF | Mehrgarh I (aceramic), Mehrgarh IIA (ceramic) | YANGSHAO (Zhongyuan), DAWENKOU (Shandong/East Coast), HEMUDU (Zhejiang) |
| **CHALCOLITHIC** (Craft Specialization, Towns) | AMRATIAN (Naqada I), GERZEAN (Naq.II) | BUTO-MAADI, Minshat -, Abu Omar | MOERIAN | GHASSULIAN | UBAID | Mehrgarh IIB - III | LONGSHAN (East Coast/Zhongyuan), HONGSHAN (Dongbei), QUJIALING-SHIJIAHE (mid-Yangzi), LIANGZHU (Tai Hu Bandao) |
| **EARLY STATE** Centralization of Force, Cult and Tribute/Tax | PROTODYNASTIC: unification process -- Dynasty 0 | | | | URUK, JEMDET NASR | KOT DIJI, SOTHI & AMRI-NAL synthesis = EARLY HARAPPAN | ERLITOU (= XIA?), LOWER XIAJIADIAN (Dongbei), Sanxingdui |
| **BRONZE AGE STATES** (Writing, Calculation, Cities, Monumental Building) | EARLY DYNASTIC (Dynasties 1 + 2) | | | | CITY - STATES (Early Dynastic I-III) | MATURE OR URBAN HARAPPAN OECUMENE | SHANG, WESTERN ZHOU (to 770 B.C.), EASTERN ZHOU |
| **BRONZE AGE EMPIRES** (Bureaucracy) | OLD KINGDOM (Dynasties 3-8) | | | | SHORT - LIVED EMPIRES (Sargonic, Ur III, Hammurabic) (BABYLON 1763 B.C.- 539 B.C.) | LATE HARAPPAN (Devolution) Castes Develop | QIN UNIFICATION (221B.C.), HAN EMPIRE |

1) Cultures are shown in upper case, sites in lower case.
2) This is a classificatory, not a chronological chart. Alignment does <u>not</u> imply synchrony.
3) The Levant column stops with the Chalcolithic.

\# An area in Shanxi Province comprising 16 sites.
\* The most northerly of a number of East China sites that include (N-S): Xiacaowan, Lianhua Cave, Sanshan Island.

*Figure 2.3: An Evolutionary Classification of Sites and Cultures from the Nile to the Yellow River.*

# CHAPTER 3

# Indus-Sarasvati Civilization ('Harappan' Civilization)

It might seem odd to provide the counterexample to state-dominated society first, before the other substantive chapters that exemplify state formation, especially as neither the book's premises nor its conclusions depend upon Indus-Saravati civilization not being state controlled. The reason is to try to explain why it is that analysts today equate complex societies with the presence of the state, and to show that it is not necessary so.

Ideology wishes to force all forms of social life into boxes. This is even true of social science, which has taken over the ideological proposition that all large-scale complex societies are necessarily state ordered and that the state is responsible for, or at least thoroughly implicated in, the emergence of social complexity. Here I intend to show: (a) that large-scale complex society is indeed possible in the absence of the state; (b) that the social division of labour, an economic and not a political relationship, can be primary; and (c) that true complexity emerged during the Chalcolithic (between the Neolithic and Bronze Age), after which most Bronze Age societies were state ordered. It is, however, the 'anomalies' that tell us so much about the dynamics of social evolution (Maisels 1991).

In social as in natural evolution not all earlier entities have modern representatives. Heavily reliant upon ethnographic or historic models for the reconstruction of social patterns (Verhoeven 2005: 255), archaeological explanation has floundered where they are absent (or even where they are present; Verhoeven 2005, passim). I find this to be particularly true in discussions of Indus Civilization, but it also obtains in regard to prehistoric Mesopotamia, which is otherwise much better known. Mesopotamian city-states are an example of what Blanton, Feinman, Kowalewski and Peregrine (1996: 2) call a 'corporate polity', where "the distribution of power is structured, determined, legitimated and controlled within the limits set by the prevailing cognitive code"; that is, power is shared. This in contrast to the 'exclusionary power strategy', in which "political actors aim at the development of a political system built around their monopoly control of sources of power", as applies in the territorial state (or in the city-state when tyrants emerge; cf: Morris 1991: 48: "Tyranny was the antithesis of the polis").

Blanton *et al.* (1996: 14) conclude their programmatic discussion with the suggestion that "it will be of particular importance to advance our understanding of corporate systems, since the discipline has tended to devote most of its attention to exclusionary strategies and their outcomes. Thus we think that Sahlins (1983: 522) misleads us by pointing to the need for a new sociology of ruler-centred societies founded upon what he terms 'heroic history'. There is an abundance of theory of this type already. What is needed instead is an expanded theory capable of addressing the nature and development of the corporate political economy and its processual relationships with the exclusionary political economy".

In this chapter I aim to contribute to this 'expanded theory', by discussing in detail a post-Neolithic complex society, namely Indus Civilization of the Mature or urban period, which extends from the middle to the end of the third millennium. Its analysis has long perplexed scholars and continues to do so (Possehl 1998: 290). I contend that this is because no similar forms of social organization exist in the modern world or in the recorded past to serve as models. Instead, the Bronze Age Harappan (and Late Neolithic Halaf of northern Mesopotamia) have been forced into sociological pigeonholes that cannot accommodate them: 'chiefdom' and 'state' respectively. I will not repeat what I previously wrote (1987, 1990) regarding evolutionary trajectories in general and the place of chiefdoms in particular, which have no place in formative Mesopotamia (Butterlin 2009a). Rather, I have already argued (1999: 136–46) that the simpler of the two mentioned, Halaf, manifests a novel pattern of social organization (the 'distributed network') whose 'interactive autonomy' shows how localism can be overcome and security provided without recourse to hierarchical structures. This removes the rationale of 'social integration' for the coming of the state so beloved of several generations of anthropologists. Halaf villagers achieved pastoral-arable and intervillage integration without any 'higher authority' (Akkermans and Duistermaat 1997, 2004; Akkermans *et al.* 2006, and see discussion below).

Another, but related organizing principle applies to the later, more extensive, populous, complex and urban Indus ('Harappan') Civilization. It is also 'stateless' and structured instead by the complex division of labour itself. In doubting whether Harappan Civilization, although large, urban and complex, was class hierarchical and state organized, I (1991, 1999) have been anticipated by Jim Shaffer (1982a, 1982b and 1987) who believes, as I do, that here "in South Asia, a unique experiment in the development of urban, literate culture, was underway"(1982a: 49) and the reason for this, that "the contingencies of the Indus Valley Cultural Tradition's food producing economy may have generated concepts of land tenure, wealth and socio-economic organization very different from prevailing situations elsewhere" (Shaffer and Lichtenstein 1989: 120). This view of Indus Civilization as a 'non-state' is also shared by Gregory Possehl (1998: 288–9), who observes "there is no evidence for kingship ... there were few if any bureaucrats and public administrators. Crafts and trades were highly developed". Accordingly, "The sense that the defining quality of the Mature Harappan was a distinct new ideology, leads one to suggest that those beliefs may have been used as the force that bound these decentralized units together, giving them a powerful common ground".

I further argue that the devolutionary process from urban civilization in the early second millennium led to the emergence of caste-ordered society (*jati*, which are the operative occupational sub-castes) as a hierarchical substitute for state ordering, and I produce a (revised) model for this.

# THE INDUS CIVILIZATION

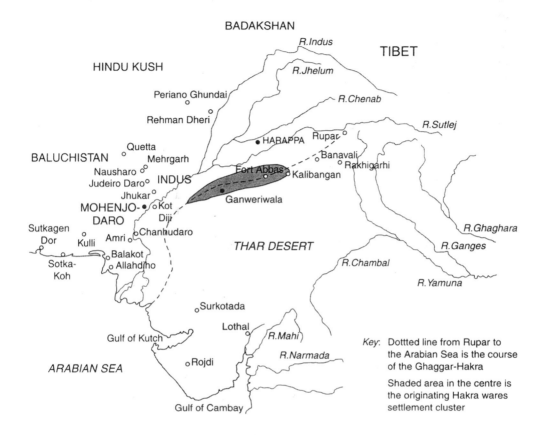

*Figure 3.1: Map of the Greater Indus Drainage.*

## A: Background and Chronology

Extending over more than 1,000,000 km², Indus Civilization (sometimes called 'Harappan Civilization', now more correctly Indus-Sarasvati) came into its 'Mature' or urban phase around 2500 BC and by the time of Hammurabi of Babylon (1792–1750 BC) had definitely come to an end as a complex civilization. Indeed the last substantive contacts with Mesopotamia, to whom the Indus area was known as Meluhha, seems to have been in the early part of the preceding Isin-Larsa period (2017–1763 BC). A terminal point for Harappan civilization would therefore be 1900 BC (Possehl 1998: 261). See Figure 3.1.

There are in total 1,019 settlements of the Mature Harappan (Urban Indus) Period, according to Gregory L. Possehl (2002: 47), who keeps the best gazetteer of Indus sites (see also his 2007 for Gujarat). For this period there are nine settlements with

| Phase/Stage | Number of Settlements | Settlements with Size | Average Size (hectares) |
|---|---|---|---|
| Mature Harappan | 1,019 | 537 | 7.25 |
| Early Harappan | 477 | 281 | 4.51 |
| Kechi Beg and Hakra Wares | 256 | 184 | 5.22 |
| Togau | 84 | 48 | 3.51 |
| Burj Basket-marked | 33 | 19 | 2.58 |
| Kili Ghul Mohammad | 20 | 9 | 2.65 |

*Figure 3.2: Settlement Data from Pre-Harappan to Mature Harappan.*

areas between 50 and 100 hectares (*ibid.*: 63). Figure 3.2 (from Possehl 2002: 47) lists the number and size of settlements from the Kili Gul Mohammed phase, which he calls 'the beginnings of village farming communities and pastoral camps' (7000–5000 BC), through to the Mature (Urban) Harappan phase (2500–1900 BC), with average site sizes.

The best Neolithic exposures we have are located in the Bolan river valley in Baluchistan. The Bolan valley opens onto the Kachi plain, which is an extension of the Indus plains. The Bolan is not only an important watercourse but an important route from the Indus plains to Afghanistan and onward to the Iranian plateau. The Bolan valley has three sites worked by a French team since 1977. Those are Mehrgarh and Nausharo, the latter 5 km to the southwest, and Pirak to the east, (see Figure 3.3).

Fortunately those three sites span the whole epoch of Indus Civilization, from the aceramic Neolithic at Mehrgarh (sub-periods 1A and 1B), commencing around 7000 BC (J-F Jarrige 2000: 259). At Nausharo, Periods I to IV extend from 3000 BC to the very end of the urban period at around 1900 BC (C. Jarrige 2000: 237), while "by 1800/1700 the Pirak culture marks the beginning of a new period in the whole Kachi/Bolan area and in other parts of Baluchistan" (J.-F. Jarrige 1997: 16). In fact we are doubly fortunate with the discovery of Mehrgarh, since "the historical roots of the Hakra Wares are found at Mehrgarh and Sheri Khan Tarakai in Bannu" (Possehl 2002: 35). The Hakra Wares Phase (3800–3200 BC) immediately precedes the Early Harappan (3200–2600 BC) which has four broadly contemporaneous regional aspects: Amri-Nal, Kot Diji, Sothi-Siswal and Damb Sadat. The Early to Mature Harappan Transition took place between 2600 BC and 2500 BC (Possehl 2002: 29). This particular century does seem to represent a cusp: Possehl (1990: 274) refers to "a paroxysm of change". Figure 3.4 (from Possehl 2002: 41) shows all Early Indus sites. Especially notable are the two major clusters in the headwaters and confluence of the Hakra drainage (west of the Yamuna river):

## B: Mehrgarh

Mergarh has three main periods and a series of radiocarbon dates, placing the end of Period IB around 6000 BC and with Period III, the Chalcolithic, extending from 5000 to

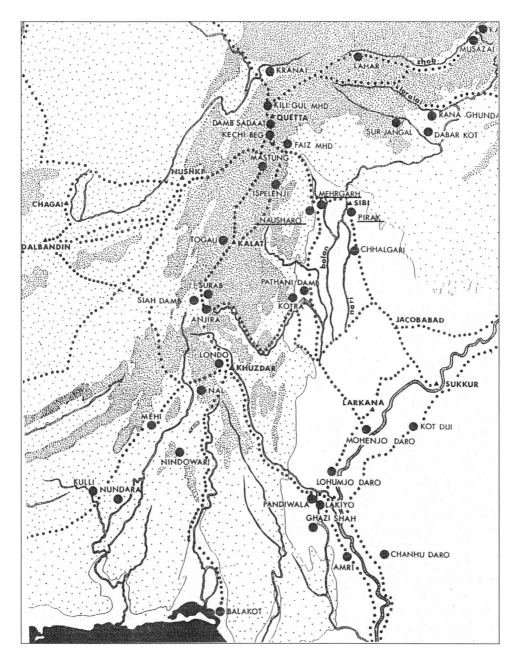

*Figure 3.3: Map of the Kachi Bolan region (from J.-F. Jarrige 1997: 12).*

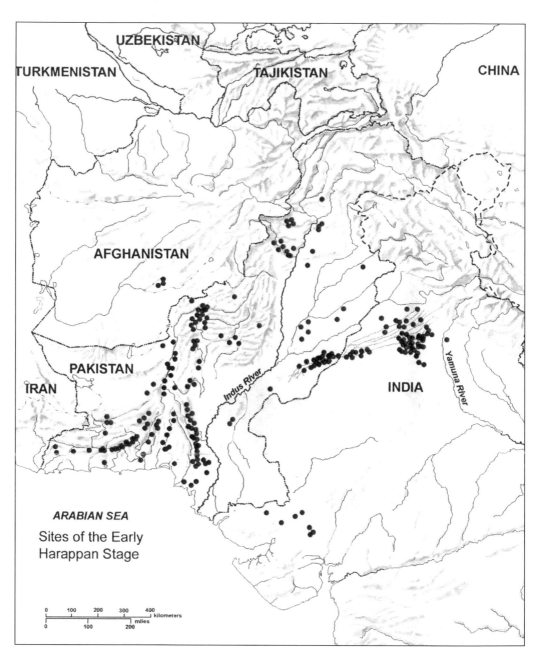

*Figure 3.4: Map of All Early Indus Sites (from Possehl 2002:41).*

4000 BC (J.F. Jarrige 2000: 282). Its remains extend over about 300 ha., representing a succession of compact, nucleated village-sized settlements, with rectangular structures built of mud-brick in the 'classic' fashion.

"Wheat and barley were the important crops throughout the Neolithic. The archaeobotanical remains documented the contemporary exploitation of wild and domesticated species of two-row barley, of domesticated six-row barley, rounded seeds of spherococcoid barley, einkorn, emmer and free-threshing wheat. The presence of fruit stones of Zizyphus [jujube] and Phoenix [date palm] has also been documented. In later periods, grape pips became very common..." (Constantini and Lentini 2000: 136). The dominant crop during Period I was naked six-row barley, and barley continues as the dominant crop, as in Mesopotamia, throughout the Mature Harappan period. In addition to einkorn and emmer, free-threshing durum wheat is also present. Indeed, Meadow (1993: 301) has even suggested that durum wheat "could have originated as easily in the Pakistan area as in north-western Iran", because emmer and goat-face grass occur in Baluchistan, and so could have crossed locally. This conjecture remains to be demonstrated.

The general view at present is that the presence of emmer and einkorn indicate that domesticated crops were introduced by population movement from the west. However, since pollen analysis suggests to Constantini and Lentini (2000: 155) that "part of the Kachi plain was covered by annual herbaceous vegetation (mainly Graminae and Leguminosae) forming large open zones" some now suggest (e.g. Possehl 2002) that much or all of the domestication process took place in situ. This is certainly the case for the sphaerococcal (club) form of wheat and barley, both of which occur at Mehrgarh and Naushero (Constantini 1990: 326). Like zebu cattle, they are locally adapted. Possehl (2002: 28) ventures that sheep and goats were also locally domesticated. He admits that "the earliest inhabitants of the site came [to Mehrgarh] with a broad suite of fully domesticated food grains, including both wheat and barley" (*ibid*.: 29), but contends that, as a consequence, Mehrgarh is not the site at which to see the domestication process in action. Rather, he maintains, it is more like an early PPNB site in the Levant, with the earliest phase analogous to the PPNA undiscovered in Baluchistan as yet. Changing tack, he also urges us to consider the whole of the Near East, Iran and the Afghan-Baluch region [the mountains of Baluchistan, the Northwest Frontier and Afghanistan] as the 'nuclear zone' for domestication, so that "rather than ending in the Zagros mountains of Iraq/Iran, it spread all the way across the Iranian Plateau to the Indus Valley. The early Holocene peoples across this vast region, from the Mediterranean to the Indus, were engaged in the development of food-producing practices at that time" (*ibid*.: 28). But this is trying to have it all ways. Either domestication of sheep and goat took place in northwest India or it did not. My guess is that it did not.

Possehl is absolutely correct, however, that we still suffer from the absence of a range of well-excavated, well-analysed Neolithic sites in the north-west of the subcontinent. Nonetheless, there has been some interesting recent work in Kashmir (Mani 2004–5) and Omran Garazhian's (2009) highly significant cluster of Pre-Pottery Neolithic sites at Darestan in Kerman province, south-east Iran, show a part of a possible transfer route. Bricks are similar to those at Mehrgarh (F. Jarrige 1984) as are the remains of wheat and barley (Constantini 1984). So far the strong probability is still that an early

*Figure 3.5: Chlorite bowl from Khafaje (British Museum) shows a fertility figure seated between two zebu bulls and grasping streams watering vegetation and a palm tree.*

Neolithic population arrived in the Bolan with some domesticates, notably barley, emmer and pulses (Mani 2004–5: 11–12) and probably sheep and goats too, and added others from local resources, notably cattle, as shown on Indus seals. Indeed, it seems to me that cattle and their secondary products were thereafter always a key resource and accordingly that their sanctification had its origins even in pre-Harappan cattle-keeping, reinforced by Late Harappan pastoralism.

Figure 3.5 above shows a chlorite bowl from Khafaje (British Museum) with a fertility figure seated between two zebu bulls and grasping streams watering vegetation and a palm tree. Zebu cattle (*Bos primigenius indicus*) are not native to Mesopotamia or Iran but to India. Khafaje, ancient Tutub, *c*.80 km north-east of Baghdad, lies on a major trade route through the mountains onto the Iranian plateau.

Like the early Neolithic sites in the Near East, the Bolan sites were chosen for their hydromorphic conditions. Constantini and Lentini (2000: 155) conclude that "the results of pollen analysis show that from *c*.8000 BP to *c*.6000 BP the region was probably dominated by a semi-lacustrine or humid environment with a riparian vegetation, characterised by Populus, (poplar) Salix (willow), Fraxinus (Ash), Ulmus (Elm) and Vitis (grape), associated in a typical hydrophytic complex, arranged in dense gallery forests [along the banks of rivers]. It is notable that a comparable vegetation, with Populus, Tamarix, Fraxinus, Ulmus, Vitis and many aquatic plants, was still present in Iranian Sistan during the Bronze Age, as documented by the analysis of a large collection of woods, charcoals and macroremains found at Shahr-i-Sokta".

## C: Nausharo

Period 1A-1B corresponds to Mehrgarh periods VI and VII, about 2900–2700 BC (Samzun 1992: 245). Period 1D (not present at Mehrgarh) has three levels and dates to the transition century, 2600–2500 BC. Period II is Early Indus (2500–2400 BC), while Period III has the Mature Indus assemblage (2400–2100 BC).

Nausharo's earliest level contains a well-preserved mud-brick building with nine rooms of various sizes and possibly also a courtyard and staircase. Interestingly in the light of what has been said about trans-Elamite influences/connections, its general layout shows close affinities with the buildings of Shahr-I Sokhta, Period III–IV and Mundigak, Period IV, I (*ibid.*). The rooms contained fireplaces and tanoor ovens with charcoal. Soil samples indicate the presence of cow dung (*ibid.*).

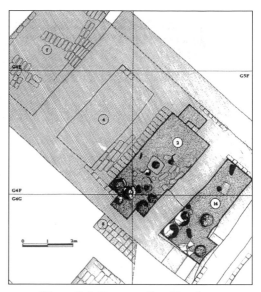

*Figure 3.6. Structure II at Nausharo.*

The latest level of Period 1D is the burnt layer, such as is found all over the Indus oecumene at the onset of the Mature (urban) Harappan. It contains Structure II which Samzun (*ibid.*: 252) does not think is a dwelling, but a 'monumental complex'. It has thick walls and three rectangular loci (Loci 4, 2, 14, average dimensions 3.70 x 1.20 m) and a room (Locus 3) largely destroyed by gullying (*ibid.*: 246). Structure II is illustrated from Samzun (1992: 247) as Figure 3.6.

"From locus 2 there is a door giving access to Locus 14. In the middle of Locus 2, a square-shaped fireplace bordered by bricks was revealed with a container at its centre. This kind of structure is exceptional at Nausharo for the pre-Harappan levels, for fire-structures are usually oval or circular in shape; this square one is the only example known so far. Still, it is reminiscent of the fireplaces from Mundigak Periods III and IV, and those from Shahr-I Sokta Period IV..." (*ibid.*). As can be seen from the Figure, Loci 2 and 14 contain many objects, mostly pottery painted and unpainted, but also including grinding stones and a stone bowl or mortar, a couple of necklaces and fragments of human figurines. The unburned Locus 3 contained two large unpainted jars, a painted goblet, three human figurines and two metal objects.

However the outstanding finds are the four decorated jars with everted rims, distributed in each of the three rooms of Structure II. The motifs are painted in black directly onto the reddish-buff ware or on a red slip (jars nos. 1, 2 and 4), as illustrated from Samzun (1992: 249) in Figure 3.7.

The plant with large leaves is pipal, a leitmotif of Harappan imagery[19] and the bulls are tied to them and to other types of shrub. Samzun (*ibid.*: 248) thinks that the frieze

---

[19] Saxena (2004–5: 30) states that the pipal leaf motif first appears at Rehman Dheri I around 3600 BC.

Characteristics of the Pre-Harappan Remains, Pottery and Artefacts at Nausharo

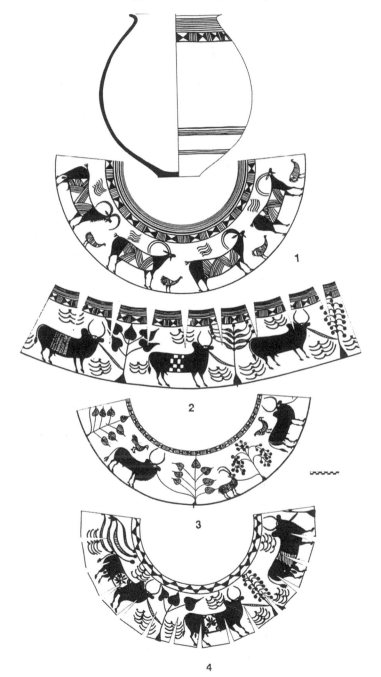

*Figure 3.7: Decorated Pottery Found in Structure II at Nausharo.*

Characteristics of the Pre-Harappan Remains, Pottery and Artefacts at Nausharo

*Figure 3.8: Male and Female Figurines from Nausharo.*

of jar 1 shows "wild goats associated with birds" (and that the smaller animal in the middle of the jar 3 frieze is a goat), but the animals on jar 1 could be cervids.

Overall the pottery is stunning as seen in the variety of items, including globular jars and goblet, bearing fish-scale designs, pipal leaf and other plant motifs, illustrated by Samzun (1992: 250).

The human figurines, for example the group of six male and one female terracotta figurines, one male carrying a baby, found in a room of Period ID (c.2600 BC) at Nausharo and discussed by Catherine Jarrige (1997: 38), are remarkable for their directness and potency. In complete contrast Rao (1973: 142) illustrates thirteen much more schematic figurines from Harappa and Mohenjo-daro apparently demonstrating yogic poses. The drawings of those seven examples from Nausharo can be seen in Figure 3.8 (from Samzun 1992: 251).

Samzun (*ibid.*: 252) concludes that "The dynamic cultural phase between 2600–2500 BC represents a formative transition reflecting strong links between Baluchistan and the Indus valley and clearly indicates close connections with Southern Afghanistan (Mundigak) and Eastern Iran (Shar-I Sokhta) as well as Central Asia (Altyn Depe)." Links to the west and north in several periods are also stressed by C. Jarrige (1997) and J.F. Jarrige (1997).

After the transition Nausharo became a small town with remains spreading over six hectares, constructed on the "typical layout of the Harappan city, [with] a 'citadel' and a 'lower town', oriented to the cardinal directions" (C. Jarrige 2000: 241). All the other Harappan attributes are present, including bathing platforms, water outlets in fired brick, domestic drains, collective sewers and cylindrical clay containers.

## D: Indus-Sarasvati Civilization

Indus civilization in its developed form is the shortest lived of the seminal Bronze Age civilizations of the Old World, lasting 'only' about half a millennium; equivalent in British history to the span from the first of the Tudors (AD 1485) to the present-day. As a civilization it is doubly remarkable, both because it was the only complex

| Period | Site counts | Settled area (hectares | Average size (ha.) |
|---|---|---|---|
| Early Iron Age (Painted Grey Ware) c.1000?- 500 BC | 14 | 36 | 2.6 |
| Posturban (or 'Late') Harappan (Cemetery H) c.1900–1700 BC | 50 | 255 | 5.1 |
| Mature Harappan c.2500– 1900 BC | 174 | 974 | 5.6 |
| Early Harappan (Kot Dijian) c.3200–2600 BC | 40 | 256 | 6.4 |
| Hakra Wares c.3800–3200 BC | 99 | 643 | 6.5 |

*Figure 3.9: Site counts, total settled area and average site size for Cholistan, from the formative Hakra Wares period to the Early Iron Age (Mughal 1997:40).*

society either of antiquity or the modern world that operated without marked social stratification and the state; and, in what may be a related phenomenon, an agrarian society in which the villages were not oppressed by the towns. Doubtless the absence of royal or state capitals is significant in this; which is certainly not to say that towns and cities were absent, rather that they were not ruling centres.

But the name Indus Civilization (which is used synonymously with Harappan) is a misnomer. It is so-called from the excavations initiated in the 1920s by Sir John Marshall upon the sites of the cities of Harappa and Mohenjo-daro located on the Indus river system. The civilization is now referred to by Indian scholars as Indus-Sarasvati civilization (Gupta 1996; Misra 1996). Following M. Rafique Mughal's seminal survey work in Cholistan (locally called Rohi), we now know that the greatest densities of early villages are clustered in the 300 mile long Hakra depression (Mughal 1994: 53). This river, which finally dried-up around 1000 AD, follows a course east of, but parallel to, the Indus. This once major but long dry river Indians call the Sarasvati, while geographers refer to it as the Ghaggar-Hakra drainage system.

Sarasvati settlement clusters are early (*c*.3800–3200 BC) and dense, with Hakra sites and wares clearly preceding the early, Pre-urban Harappan (3200–2600 BC). This periodization of sites, with the average site size and settled area in Cholistan can be seen in Figure 3.9 (from Mughal 1997: 40).

Remarkably, the collapse in site numbers by about seventy-five per cent from the Mature (urban) Harappan to Posturban Harappan, only sees a small decline in average site size (nine per cent), clearly showing that regional abandonment was the dominant factor.

Further, work in the last two decades has shown that Mohenjo-daro and Harappa do not lie at the centre of maximum density of village settlement, but rather at peripheries. At the southern end of the Hakra Wares cluster lies a city comparable in size to Harappa and Mohenjo-daro. It is called Ganweriwala, is probably older than either Harappa or Mohenjo-daro and was certainly moribund before they were. Excavation would surely tell us a huge amount about the rise and fall of Indus-Sarasvati Civilization. It shames the Pakistani authorities, the international archaeological community and UNESCO that they did not begin work at Ganweriwala within a year or two of its discovery, decades ago. I have already argued (1999: 253) that the decline of the Harappan heartlands along the Ghaggar-Hakra/Sarasvati interior drainage in Cholistan removed critical mass from Indus Civilization and led to its decline and fall. See Figure 3.10 (Mughal 1994: 54).

Dotted lines show the dry course of the Hakra River, formerly fed by the Sutlej (top right). The map also shows the location of Harappa, which stands in relative isolation and functions as a gateway city for northern exchanges with pastoralists and for the import of minerals such as carnelian and lapis lazuli from Afghanistan. As excavations by Kenoyer and Meadow (1997: 72) indicate, craft production was important at Harappa from its origins around 3300 BC. They also identify a local aspect of the Hakra Phase which they name the Ravi Phase (*ibid*.: 59). On the basis of new radiocarbon determinations from Harappa, Kenoyer and Meadow (2000: 55) construct a Provisional Chronology for Harappa as can be seen in Figure 3.11.

Period 2 they call the 'initial urban phase' (Meadow and Kenoyer 2003). On the basis of very limited excavations in the Cemetery H area, Periods 4 and 5 (1900–1300 BC) are

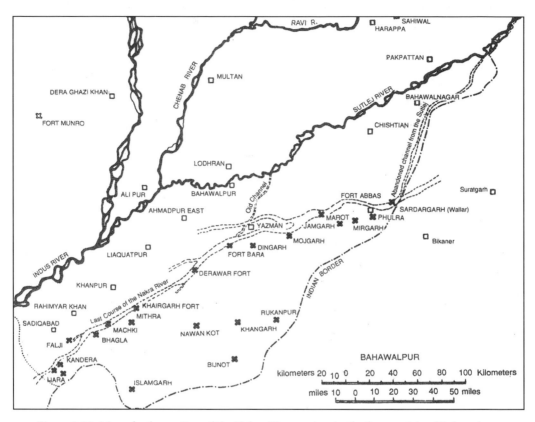

*Figure 3.10: Map of a dry section of the Hakra River system in the former state of Bahawalpur.*

| Period 1A and 1B | Early Harappan/Ravi | *c.*3300–2800 BC |
|---|---|---|
| Period 2 | Early Harappan/Kot Diji Phase | *c.*2800–2600 BC |
| Period 3A | Harappan Phase A | *c.*2600–2450 BC |
| Period 3B | Harappan Phase B | *c.*2450–2200 BC |
| Period 3C | Harappan Phase C | *c.*2200–1900 BC |
| Period 4 | Post-urban Harappan | *c.*1900–1700 BC |
| Period 5 | Late Harappan Phase (Cemetery H) | ?- <1700 BC |

*Figure 3.11: Provisional Chronology for Harappa*

claimed to show that "in contrast to earlier interpretations of decline and abandonment, the city was in fact thriving and at the centre of important cultural and economic transformations"(*ibid.*). By contrast, some scholars think that Period 5 is not Harappan in any meaningful sense and so should not be called Late Harappan at all (cf: Mughal 1997; Possehl 2007). At the craft and trading site of Gola Dhoro in Gujarat, "occupation of the site continued in the post-urban period up to 1700 BC. In the last phase there are indications that the trade activities and the production of various craft items, use of the fortification wall, writing and making steatite seals all came to an abrupt end" (Bhan *et al.* 2005: 5).

Historically, Sarasvati is a major Hindu goddess representing abundance and nourishment, and this now dry river-system was the formative core of Harappan civilization (Maisels 1999: 246–49). Its progressive loss to settlement by geologically induced drying caused Harappan civilization to lose critical mass, tore the heart out of it, and set in train a devolutionary process which resulted in the system of occupational caste called *jati*. Beginning early in the second millennium, Harappan civilization thus went from being a complex stateless society to being a much less complex, stateless and city-less society. The uniquely acephalous condition of Harappan civilization explains the uniqueness of the subsequent Hindu caste system, which is not otherwise explicable except as the product of indigenous 'Dark Age' economic adaptation. At the head of this system of adjusted economic specialization, Aryan invaders placed themselves in the latter part of the second millennium (as Brahmins, priests, and Kshatriyas, the warrior-aristocracy) while providing ideological justification in terms of the four Varna categories. But this was just spin for their domination of a pre-existing division of labour, namely one which had accommodated itself to devolution from an extensive, urban centred division of labour to local, village-based systems of production and exchange.

This view of post-urban Indus-Sarasvati society as diverse yet interdependent, economically stratified but stateless and stable, receives support from the mathematical modelling of Henrich and Boyd (2008: 722) on the division of labour, economic specialization and the evolution of social stratification. They emphasize that their model applies to the emergence of occupational specialization in general and they deploy their model in a Supplement "to interpret an ethnographic case involving the stable coexistence of highly interdependent specialized occupational castes in the Swat Valley, Pakistan (Barth 1985)". In that supplement, 'A', they conclude that "The qualitative lessons of our model can be applied to a range of empirical settings. While the model can certainly be interpreted as laying a foundation for the emergence of elite controlling groups of priests, warriors, or resource managers, it also applies to situations in which social groups (perhaps ethnic groups) have evolved to occupy niches in a regional economy, which may or may not be ruled by a single political establishment such as is associated with a hereditary nobility" (2008: 715).

There are economic parallels in China. Accounting for the breakdown of the Later (Eastern) Han regime (AD 25–220), Cho-yun Hsu (1988: 189) observes that "the Han exchange network was built upon the need for regional interdependence. ... It was delicately balanced and could easily be upset by disturbances such as war or natural calamity, which could break down the national network into several regional networks. Further breakdown could then occur, disintegrating a previously integrated system into

| Domain | Time | Site count | Average site size (hectares) | Settled area (hectares) |
|---|---|---|---|---|
| **Sindhi Domain** | | | | |
| | Mature Harappan | 86 | 8.0 | 688 |
| | Jhukar | 6 | 5.6 | 34 |
| **Cholistan Domain** | | | | |
| | Mature Harappan | 174 | 5.6 | 974 |
| | Cemetery H | 41 | 5.1 | 209 |
| **Kulli Domain** | | | | |
| | Kulli and Quetta | 129 | 5.8 | 748 |
| | Posturban | 0 | 0 | 0 |
| **Sorath Domain** | | | | |
| | Sorath Harappan | 310 | 5.4 | 1,674 |
| | Late Sorath Harappan | 198 | 4.3 | 815 |
| **Eastern Domain** | | | | |
| | Mature Harappan | 218 | 13.5 | 2,943 |
| | Posturban | 853 | 3.5 | 2,985 |

*Figure 3.12: Estimated Settlement Data for the Mature and Post-Urban Harappan, by region.*

a group of communities sustained by local self-sufficiency". And local self-sufficiency is the very basis of the *jati* system, with its occupational caste members spread across the villages of a region.

The devolutionary process of Indus Civilization to a post-urban, Eneolithic condition was, of course, relatively slow, occupying a couple of centuries (Mughal 1982: 83, 1990: 143). Early signs appear, most significantly, in Mohenjo-daro, possibly as early as *c*.2200 BC, when the Warehouse and the great Bath were abandoned (Possehl 1997: 458). That both the ritual centre and what may have been the central civic storehouse/strategic reserve could no longer be sustained indicates a growing crisis. Possehl (2002) thinks that a too-well integrated ideology and society resulted in social entropy that meant it was unable to overcome new challenges. However, he does not say what those new and ultimately fatal challenges actually were.

The actual process of de-urbanization is perfectly clear from Possehl's (2002: 241) summary table (Figure 3.12) comparing the Mature Harappan and Post-urban situation in every region.

All regions show a decline in site numbers and sizes, except for the Eastern Domain, where the average site size fell to around a quarter of what it had been in the Mature Harappan period. Nonetheless, this was the only area where the total settled area remained the same in the Posturban as in the urban period, due to a rise in the number of sites in this domain, indicating a major population shift from west to east.

The consequences for social organization of the devolutionary process can be modelled (Figure 3.13 (revised from Maisels 1991: 264, with ethnographic evidence)).

This is the socio-economic structure encountered by the Aryans entering India later in the second millennium. By imposing the Varna system of four major castes, they make themselves the largest landowners, the principal priests and the dominant warriors.

Caste formation, unique to India, is best explained by what else is unique to India, namely a complex but stateless society in decline early in the second millennium BC. Support for the initial stages of this model comes from Massimo Vidale's study (1989:

manufacturing villages/city sectors decline with the ending of urban society → craftsmen and then other occupational groups 'locally reinforce their socio-economic bonds' → lineage name supplanted by Occupational name (e.g. Smith, Tanner, Weaver, Barber, Potter) → specialised lineages link through endogamy to similar occupations in neighbouring villages, suppressing competition → a common ritual and economic position emerges in a static, stateless society → (sub-) CASTES (*jati*) have formed extending across a region → they are ranked according to economic and ritual status, with subordination beneath the large landowners who wield political power locally.

*Figure 3.13: The Devolutionary Emergence of Caste (*jati*).*

180) of craft industries in Mature Harappan urban contexts, that also helps explain the observed near uniformity of craft output:

> "In the manufacturing cycles so far analyzed, one often recognises a strongly repetitive character, required undoubtedly to fulfil the needs of an intensive production standard. These cycles are sometimes interconnected by specific forms of recycling or 'lateral cycling' (Schiffer 1976), pointing to the existence of well-defined socio-economic bonds among the different groups of craftsmen working or living in the cities. In some cases, the technological similarities are so strong that one suspects the presence of some sort of inter-site economic and social patterning of the labour-force employed in craft production. These forms of social organization could have allowed a very accurate training of apprentices".

Further support for the occupational and endogamous basis of caste comes from an unlikely source, namely fourth millennium Mesopotamia. Henry T. Wright (2001: 138–9) argues that "if skilled crafts have emerged as social categories guarding craft secrets, there will be a motivation for endogamous marriage. Since there may be relatively few families skilled in a given craft in any one community, young people seeking partners may have to look to distant communities. The increasingly broad homogenization of Uruk material styles may simply be a result of the changing organization of the crafts..." Of course the relative homogeneity of craft products in Harappan society has often been noted. But why did this craft endogamy not result in caste formation in Mesopotamia? Because states always existed there from the fourth millennium onward!

What began with urban craftsmen in Mature Harappan urban contexts spread, in a kind of reactive imitation, to other occupations as society became more 'ruralized' in the period of urban decline.

Formerly, when Indus-Sarasvati cities existed to focus and integrate the division of labour on a society-wide basis, the division of labour was itself structuring and productive of organic solidarity, represented by a shared belief system that Possehl (2002: 244) regards as its ultimate undoing. He states (*op. cit.* 250) that "The Indus ideology is expressed in some form at all of the [known] 1,052 Mature Harappan sites"; and he characterizes this ideology as "proxied by urbanization, nihilism, technology and technological innovation, and water in terms of symbolic and physical cleanliness", the last sometimes referred to as wasserluxus.

Lamberg-Karlovsky (1999: 94) argues that, given the manifest statelessness of Indus Civilization, its social structure can best be explained by the existence of caste organization (*jati* and *varna*: the former occupational sub-castes, the latter the four over-arching political categories already mentioned, dressed up as religious ones). He cites Quigley's (1993: 145) acute observations that "caste depends on the relative failure of centralization and the parallel persistence of kinship in shaping social institutions. The second is the expression of common culture through ritual rather than through the written word". Lamberg-Karlovsky (*op. cit.* 94) also correctly notes the interpenetration of kinship and caste, and the central role of (sub-)caste (*jati*) endogamy in maintaining the system. Nonetheless, he neither provides nor even suggests a mechanism for the emergence of caste as early as the mid-third millennium, the period of urbanization, merely observing (*ibid.*: 87) that caste organization, being society-wide, can account for the "astounding degree of cultural homogeneity and standardization over a vast geographical area". But on this basis, perhaps caste formation should be placed even earlier, possibly in the mid fourth millennium during the Hakra Wares Phase? Sensing a lack of groundedness, Lamberg-Karlovsky concludes (*ibid.*: 108) that "the case for a caste system within the Indus [urban phase] remains both speculative and circumstantial. It will remain so until research designs specifically address the issue," a sentiment I heartily endorse. Nonetheless, until better evidence comes forward I remain convinced that it was the decline of Indus Civilization into a non-urban period that produced the caste system.

## The Sarasvati River is the key to origins and decline

At the northern end of the Sarasvati village concentration lies the major site of Kalibangan, while at the southern end lies Ganweriwala: at 81.5 hectares almost identical in size to Mohenjo-daro (83 hectares) with only Harappa significantly larger at over 150 hectares, according to Meadow and Kenoyer (2003), with separate walled areas ranging from 10 to 25 ha. each.[20] Both of the excavated cities seem to be specialized as gateway cities (Ratnagar 1982: 261), though Mohenjo-daro also appears to have important cultic functions, and it is mostly constructed of fired brick. Harappa, by contrast, uses much less. Nonetheless, given the association of Ganweriwala with the originating village heartlands, when excavations belatedly take place there it may be more accurate to refer to Harappan civilization as Ganweriwalan or Sarasvatian civilization. As mentioned several times above, Indian archaeologists already refer to the civilization as Indus-Sarasvati Civilization.

There are few cities in such a large area of the Indus drainage and considering that only one of them exceeds 100 hectares in extent, this tells us a great deal about the nature of the civilization. The most important points are that:

1) The cities contain no palaces or temples (Kenoyer 2000: 99), only cultic facilities for fire and water on high platforms in the so-called 'citadel' areas, that were sources of ritual purification for the whole settlement

---

[20] Ethnologically based densities ranging between 100 and 250 persons per hectare, are used to estimate the population of settlements, depending on type of settlement and region. See Postgate 1994.

Figure: 3.14: Terracotta goddess figurines from Mohenjo-daro (British Museum).

Figure 3.15: Lapis, gold and carnelian necklaces from the Royal Tombs of Ur in the Early Dynastic III period (British Museum).

2) The cities only contain a small fraction of the total population, most of whom lived in villages
3) Within the cities there are few disparities of wealth or power and this is reflected in the architecture of households. Instead, differences in size are functional, reflecting family size
4) Skeletal studies show no health disparities such as would indicate depressed or oppressed classes
5) The use of copper implements is very widespread and indeed standardized in form, indicating a general availability (Bhan *et al.* 2005), something untypical of other Bronze Age Civilizations. In China for instance, bronze objects, especially tripods, are associated with only the most powerful lineages. In the third millennium, Meluhha, as the Indus was known in Mesopotamia, supplied copper, silver, gold, lapis lazuli and carnelian, either directly to Mesopotamia or through Dilmun, modern Bahrein (T.F. Potts 1994: 148–9; 159–165). See Figure 3.15.

In sum, Indus civilization is by far the most egalitarian of any of the pristine Old or New World Civilizations, and that by a long way and by any measure. It is true that we do not have all the survey and excavation evidence that we would like (do we ever?), for instance, to discuss settlement hierarchies, but such evidence as exists points toward an extensive, complex, urban and stateless society, and so far no evidence to the contrary exists, only the assumption amongst some that such a state of affairs is 'impossible'.

## An Absence of Models, Ethnographic or Historic

### Modelling a Stateless Society

The root of the problem is that Indus civilization fits none of the established sociological or ethnographic models. Walter A. Fairservis (1961, 1967, 1971, 1986) therefore hypothesized that Indus civilization remained at the socio-cultural level of the chiefdom, failing to attain what he called the 'second level of civilization', namely that characterized by what he termed 'higher abstract thought'. However that may be – and by it Fairservis probably alludes to developed writing systems – in anthropological theory it is the state that is seen as the next advance in complexity. Fairservis' attempt to fit the Indus case to the existing categories of acephalous band, tribe, chiefdom, state, just shows how limited those categories really are (cf: Maisels 1987). The fact is that there is a distinct lack of evidence for the presence of a state at any stage of Indus civilization even the fully urban. However, as this is still a contentious matter amongst scholars of Indus civilization, some extended argument is required. It is additionally valuable for demonstrating the range and quality of evidence that archaeology can provide to illuminate social organization.

Jonathan Mark Kenoyer (1991: 371), who, with Richard Meadow is currently excavating at Harappa, "propose(s) that the Indus state was composed of several competing classes of elites who maintained different levels of control over the vast regions of the Indus and Ghaggar-Hakra Valley. Instead of one social group with absolute control, the rulers or dominant members in the various cities would have included merchants, ritual specialists, and individuals who controlled resources such as land, livestock,

and raw materials. These groups may have had different means of control, but they shared a common ideology and economic system as represented by seals, ornaments, ceramics, and other artefacts. This ideology would have been shared by occupational specialists and service communities, who appear to have been organised in loosely stratified groups". "It is probable", he continues, "that the cities were more rigidly stratified and segregated than the rural settlements, which would have included larger numbers of farmers, pastoralists, fishers, miners, hunters and gatherers, etc. The largest cities may have been relatively independent, with direct political control only over local settlements and lands. Political and economic integration of the cities may have been achieved through the trade and exchange of important socio-ritual status items".

*Figure 3.16A: Painted Jar from Harappa showing peacocks, pipal and other motifs.*

*Figure 3.16B: Other painted forms from Harappa.*

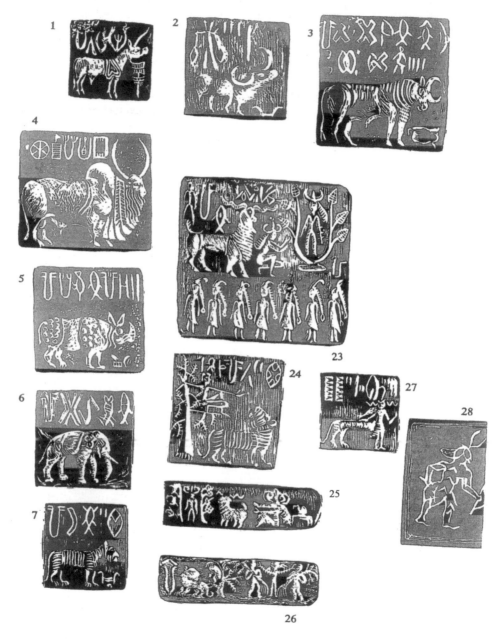

*Figure 3.17: Selected seals of steatite carved intaglio (from Fairservis 1971: 274–280).*

I have no problem with that characterization, which Kenoyer subsequently repeated in almost identical form (2000: 98–9), but I don't see how, having said what he has, he can refer to that situation as 'the Indus state'. The condition described above is such an example of organic solidarity – social integration based on complementarity in the division of labour – that Durkheim, had he known of it, would have regarded as it as archetypal. The diversity that Kenoyer recognizes is indeed remarkable, but nowhere has he indicated the presence of a ruling centre or apparatus – indeed he even points to their absence (2000: 98) – or even what stratum might constitute a ruling class. On the contrary what he describes are competing and collaborating, but essentially diffused loci of power. Kenoyer is, therefore forced into contortions in order to establish statehood: "The use of cubical stone weights can be seen as an economic indicator of wealth and a symbol of ideology regarding the economic systems of the Indus state. In the absence of evidence for military coercion, the economic system was most probably supported by a common ritual ideology that legitimized the enforcement of such rigid standards" (2000: 102).

Further, there is no 'iconography of power' such as is manifest in the other regions where the existence of the state is not in doubt. From the earliest state-formation period in Egypt, for example, we have images of the king in action, both military and ritual, in a variety of media. Seeing those, we have no need of writing to make clear to us that a ruler is represented as shown in Figures 5.15 and 5.16.

In complete contrast, the power(s) represented on Indus seals, which, Kenoyer (2000: 101) says "may identify hereditary merchant communities, sodalities, clans, or even different classes of administrative officials", is the power of Nature and the cult venerating it, involving the likes of sacred bulls and their feeding, adoration or sacrifice (Fairservis 1971: 274–5). Also central is the cult of sacred trees, especially a tree still revered in India, the Nim or Neem, *Azadirachta indica* (*Anteaea indica*). It yields Margosa (Nim or Neem oil) from seeds, used, amongst other things, to treat skin diseases. An extract prepared from the bark, Cortex Margosae, is used in preparations that reduce dental caries and inflammation of the mouth (Moore 1981: 242). All trees deserve sacred status, this one particularly so. The tree-deities illustrated in Figure 3.17 are the prototypes of yakshis (*yakṣīs*), female tree spirits, whose male counterparts are *yakshas*. They live in the forks formed by the limbs of large trees, or in hollows within their trunks, becoming an integral part of the tree.

The images in Figure 3.17 show:-1–7 naturalistic representations of bull, buffalo, rhinoceros, elephant and tiger; 23: Tree deity being worshipped with animal (ram?) brought for sacrifice before pigtailed (probably female) celebrants; 24: tree-deity (or shaman) with bangle-less outstretched arms and tiger; 25: another tree-deity/sacrifice scene, incorporating the 'outstretched arms figure'; 26: another view of the braceleted 'outstretched arms figure' between two figures uprooting trees, with Asiatic lion on the left; 27: composite man/tiger figure; 28: hunter with ram headdress. The justly famous 'Pasupati' seal from Mohenjo-daro shows the yogic figure with arms full of bangles, while the (so far unique) 'dancing girl' copper figurine from Mohenjo-daro has her left arm covered in bangles from shoulder to hand, while her right arm has two at the elbow and two at the wrist.

Central to the problem seems to be the all-too-common assumption that complex society equals state-ordered society, with, I suspect the implicit value-judgement that

*Figure 3.18: Photograph of four seals (British Museum).*

somehow state-level society is superior. I regard Indus-Sarasvati civilization as a 'civilization', using the term in a specific, non-normative, non-judgemental sense, broader than the conventional usage that a 'civilization' is a state-ordered society. To me, 'civilization' is the materialization of Culture, where materialization includes everything a society has made, done or built and Culture is defined as the inter-generational cumulation and transmission of beliefs, institutions and techniques, with the expectations and outlook that arise therefrom. The result is a certain mentality derived from the concepts and information available to a population sharing a culture. Hence the collectivism of 'collective representations'. Culture and, in this sense, 'civilization' commonly survives changes of political regime. The French, currently in their 'Fifth Republic', are well aware and indeed proud of, the continuity of their Civilization (e.g. from Charlemagne to Charles de Gaulle)[21] as also are Russians, Chinese and indeed Indians, amongst many others. Central to culture is language, central to civilization is History.

The integrative mechanisms of Indus-Sarasvati society seems to reside in the division of labour itself and the interdependency of regions, with family, lineage or clan ownership of the means of production.

The occupational or familial units shared a worldview of common values structured around distributed religious powers. This makes 'everyone his own officiant', reflecting the fact that pantheism is a set of fluid and overlapping beliefs without a fixed or official cosmogony, where all-important natural and social forces are personified. It thus has no hegemonic centre or organized 'church', as indeed is the case with Hinduism today.

## Another Mode of Production

In 'The Emergence of Civilization' (1990) I set out an apparatus for modelling a society's Mode of Production (MOP), defined as: 'what is produced, by what means, by and for whom' (or 'who produces what, by what means, for whom'). There I set out MOP models of foraging societies (1990: 264), of chiefdoms (*ibid.*: 265) and for the Asiatic Mode of Production (*ibid.*: 267) redescribed as the Village-State MOP. I also produced an operational model (*ibid.*: 272) for the mode of production of third millennium Mesopotamia. With application to all MOP's, I defined the Relations of Production as

---

[21]   Indeed, France can claim to be the province of the Roman Empire with the most direct continuity (Dill 1958).

the Forms of Productive Cooperation (how work is organized) on the one side, and the Forms of Ownership and Control on the other. Together they animate the Forces of Production. The forces of production comprise the Instruments of Production (tools, machines, motive power) the actual Labour Process (the energy and skill expended in the work done) and the Objects of Production, this last being what is worked upon: land, raw materials etc. (Maisels 1990: 263–4). *Accordingly, members of a social class are those with a shared position in the Relations of Production.*

Here I produce a composite model of the Mode of Production characterising Harappan Civilization. I say composite because this model includes the cultural dimensions that inform the core order of household and village community. The social structure is of course the pattern of roles, which I previously (1990: 223) defined as "repeated, because culturally stabilized, interpersonal relationship(s), ultimately dyadic (1:1). They are specific practices that status allows. Accordingly, roles are patterns of expected behaviour, directed to certain social ends. It is, then, the grid of social positions, which are role-bearing locations that I consider to be the social structure".

In Figure 3.19, the pattern of roles (and thus the social structure) deriving from the Mode of Production are shown interacting with the cultural realm. Here: (1) central

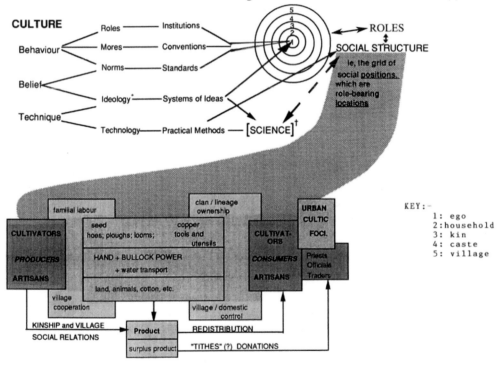

*Figure 3.19: Composite Model of Harappan Mode of Production.*

rectangle is the Means of Production; (2)
the adjoining rectangles represent forms
of cooperation (left) and (right) ownership
and control; (3) the boxes to their left
and right show the producers and the
transfer of some of their output through
kinship and village social relations to other
cultivators and artisans, but with most of
their output being self-subsistence; (4) while
their surplus product goes through tithes,
donatives and trading profits to support
the cities. In the Post-Harappan centuries
there are of course no urban centres, and
the caste 'ring' appears in the Core Order,
with the surplus product appropriated
hierarchically by the dominant castes
(Mayer 1956; Berreman 1979).

Harappan civilization was characterized
by a wide dispersal of resources. It is,
after all, the concentration of resources –
economic, ideological and military – that
characterizes the state. As to the absence of
'ruling engines', Kenoyer (1991: 363) holds
that "many of the complex and sometimes
massive structures at Mohenjo-daro and
Harappa could have been elite residences,
centralized administrative structures
or even temples, but later disturbances
obscured their primary function" (*ibid.*).
When later?! During the devolutionary

*Figure 3.20: Reconstruction of the so-called
'priest-king' figurine.*

period? During abandonment? During nineteenth-century railway building? And
why should their 'primary function' be so obscure if universal state forms are indeed
present? What Kenoyer would have to do to prove his case would be to demonstrate
that a certain elite stratum with control of one of the major sources of power had
managed to integrate this with the other two, thereby mastering society by deploying
apparatuses of control.

Significantly, Kenoyer (1991: 364) helps to destroy what some have assumed (e.g. by
Mortimer Wheeler 1968) to be evidence of a state-religion: a damaged stone statuette of
a seated, bearded male in a trefoil-decorated robe, with one leg bent under, the other
bent in front, taken to be a 'priest-king'. Kenoyer (*op. cit.*) declares that "at present, we
cannot clearly associate the stone sculptures, seals, or any other set of symbols with a
'state religion' as opposed to a less structured cult". Indeed we cannot; but we can go
in a different direction, though not to Sumer, where the 'priest-king' was the EN, the
high priest of the temple who assumed the role of city leader, at least by the Jemdet
Nasr (Uruk III) period (Jacobsen 1980: 77; Maisels 1999: 171–73).

Ardeleanu-Jansen (1991) recognises the so-called 'priest-king' (with some similar examples) as belonging to the category of 'seated man' figures seen on a vase from Bactria. However, those seated men are drawn in profile, are active, and certainly not in repose.

Elsewhere (1999: 231–2) I argued that the 'priest-king' figurine is late, atypical and possibly foreign-influenced. It was actually found by Marshall in the DK-B Area of Mohenjo-daro, where all the architecture is of the latest and poorest phase of occupation. It may have had some cultic function, but most likely for recent incomers from the north (the Bactria-Margiana Archaeological Complex).[22] If actually Harappan it is more likely to represent some religious officiant, guru or a buddha-type individual. This is evident from both posture and demeanour, as reconstructed in Ardeleanu-Jansen (1989: 204). See Figure 3.20.

As to the elite monopolization of prestigious raw materials, Harappan Civilization is the only one of the major Bronze Age societies in which copper/bronze artefacts were widely distributed throughout the population, and were actually used primarily for production and decoration rather than for warfare and ritual. The locus classicus of the latter, showing total elite monopolization, is of course China. However, in regard to craft specialization, technological and stylistic uniformity and the supply of raw materials around the Indus, Kenoyer (1989: 186) himself has stated that, "based on an ethnographic model of similar craft communities in South Asia today, this uniformity can be explained, not as the result of centralized authority but on the basis of networks for supply and distribution that were defined by kin-ties or socio-economic alliances between the distant groups. These kin relations or alliances involve the sharing of resources, technology and stylistic expressions. Hereditary, kin related learning processes and alliances have resulted in standardization and uniformity in technology, raw material and stylistic features of the finished objects". In other words, those of Rothman (2004: 101): "The presence of specialized production does not in itself indicate the need for administrative regulation. Perhaps scale as a causal factor also should apply to specialization in economic activity as well as to population size and geographical extent". Indeed so.

So far there is precious little evidence of Harappan soldiery in any form, let alone the professional warriors and mass levées that are so characteristic of the other major civilizations. Weapons certainly existed, as did walls around settlements, but were often too flimsy and easily penetrated to resist serious attack. Rather, as at Mohenjo-daro and Kalibangan (Kesarwani 1984: 66; Maisels 1999: 224–5), "walls around settlements are often multifunctional, offering flood protection, defining the limits of settlement [and making the inside/outside contrasts clear] and regulating the comings and goings of people and animals (both wild and domesticated), as well as providing defence" (Possehl 1997: 435). Also perhaps providing tolls to fund the local administration in this most decentralized of societies. Lothal is a major (port) settlement where 'ramparts' functioned as flood defences (often breached, repaired and raised) against the rivers Bhogavo and Sabarmati (Sharma 1991: 67). The relationship of the enclosing peripheral wall to the river bed and nullah (a normally dry watercourse filled only during the

---

[22]  For earlier Trans-Elamite influences upon and derivation of Harappan imagery, see Winkelmann 2000.

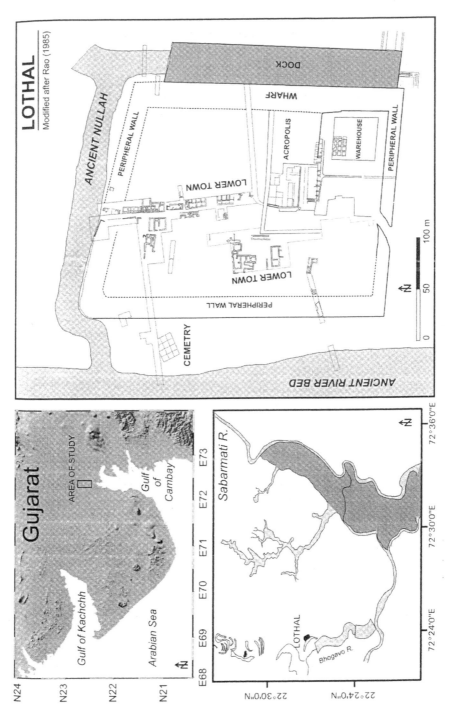

*Figure 3.21: Site, Situation and Location of Lothal in Gujarat.*

monsoon) is clear in this plan (from Khadkikar, Rajshekhar and Kumaran 2004: 897) whose work is a model of rigour and clarity. See Figure 3.21.

All Harappan settlements had walls of some sort, geometrically set out, and those with a clear site-plan had a separate 'acropolis' area with its own circumvallation (as in Lothal), setting it apart from the middle or lower town (Rao 1985). In multi-period sites the walls usually originate in the pre-Harappan period, as famously at Kot Diji, Lothal, Kalibangan, Rehman Dheri and Harappa itself (Meadow and Kenoyer 2003). Walls were usually rebuilt to a higher standard in the Harappan period, but so too was the whole urban fabric. What the walls seem to be telling us is that the cities were corporate entities that had to look to themselves for protection from attack by floods, bandits or any other threat. No imperial army or corps of engineers was coming over the horizon to their rescue. Indeed, without a peace centrally imposed and patrolled, (self-) protective measures were all the more necessary, and in regard to human threats weapons were also necessary.[23] How then are the commonalities of settlement structure to be explained? Quite simply by a shared belief system which held certain attributes to be necessary in the built environment, most prominently in the 'acropolis'/ lower-town contrast, clear boundaries, circumvallation, and concern for drainage both of surface water and sanitation. Fairservis (1971: 273) puts it most eloquently:

"There is a formality about the Harappan sites – village, city, or town – which argues for a 'formal' and authoritative mother tradition rather than an authoritative and coercive administration. In other words, the old tradition of 'this is the way we have always done things' typical of village life was still a paramount factor in the daily activity. From what we know about Harappan village sites, there is characteristically an 'acropolis' as well as a habitation area, if only on a much smaller scale than on the urban sites. The 'acropolis' in the village would seem to be simply a public building set above the habitation areas. This structure, too small to be inhabited, must have been used to perpetuate something shared across the Harappan world. It is difficult to conceive of this as having been anything else but a religion". Note too that the Acropolis of Athens was a civic/cultic structure and not a castle or garrison.

---

[23] Edward Cork (2005) has argued that scholars who saw an absence of warfare in the Indus Civilisation (ultimately deriving from Marshall 1931) did so because of a perceived 'inadequacy of metalwork' to produce the required weapons, and his article produces some evidence to suggest that Harappan weapons were not very different from some of those recovered from Near Eastern or Egyptian sites (*ibid.*: 416). Cork sees 'the absence of warfare' as "having major implications for the interpretation of the internal organisation of this civilisation. Primarily this has meant the explanation of social coercion and control in terms of ideology rather than physical force" (*ibid.*: 411). Having stated at the outset that "this paper does not, however, argue for the presence of standing armies and organised war in the Indus Valley" (p. 411), Cork paradoxically concludes that "it does not necessarily follow, however, that the Harappan elite did not use weapons, or use warfare as a method of social control, or for political and/or territorial gain, or that the nature and function of elite power did not involve these weapons" (p. 421). It is hard to prove a negative and anything is possible, but none of this has been established in his paper, and while he states (*ibid.*: 420) that "it is not within the scope of the present paper to properly address all these issues" that is, the interlocking issues of Harappan social, political, ideological and economic organisation; the mere presence of weapons that could actually be useful in combat tells us nothing about the constitution of Harappan society. I only claim that the state was absent – a coercive centre of economic, ideological and military force – not that strife was absent. Given what we know of human nature, postulating a society without conflict would be very naïve indeed.

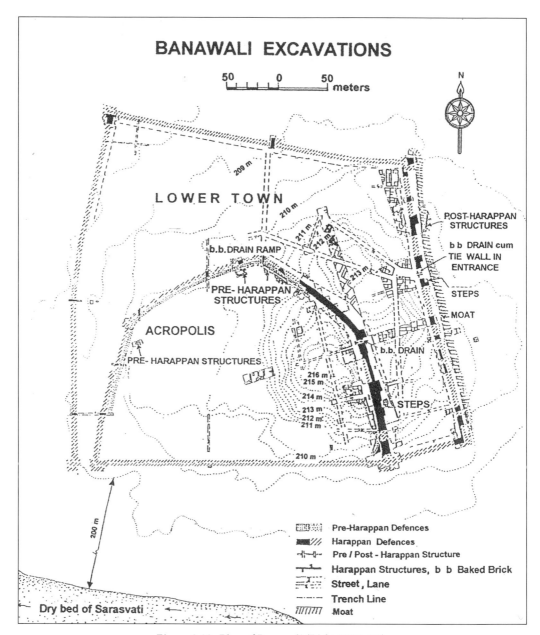

*Figure 3.22: Plan of Banawali (Bisht 1999: 33).*

*Figure 3.23: Artist's impression of the interior of a Harappan house in the Mature period (from Fairservis 1971: 294).*

Very noticeable, but not receiving the attention its significance requires, is the Harappan concern for geometry. This can be seen most clearly, perhaps, in two quite dissimilar but recently excavated settlements, namely Banawali and Dholavira, respectively village and town/city. At Banawali, instead of the usual separation of acropolis from the town proper, we find, in Bisht's words "a glaringly unusual formation – an apsidal citadel (with)in a trapezoidal town" (1999: 15). He finds and tabulates (*ibid*.: 25) many more complex geometric ratios in the built environment of Dholavira, in form quite unlike either Harappa or Mohenjo-daro. See Figure 3.22.

So much for state-imposed 'uniformity' of urban layout. Banawali is a village in Haryana, which lies on the right bank of the lost Sarasvati River. Its total area is only about 9 ha (this and subsequent information from Bisht 1999). It too has pre-Harappan origins (corresponding to Kalibangan I/Sothi). The initial period, 1A, was that of an open village with no circumvallation. Houses, made of sun-dried bricks in mud mortar were oriented to the cardinal directions. Interestingly, those bricks laid in a single course of headers, had a length/width/thickness ratio of 3:2:1. This was an ideological, not a functional property, as this shape of brick does not make for strong bonding.

Period 1B commenced with the construction of a thin, poorly made boundary wall, only 1.40 m wide, with no tapering. It soon started to tilt and split vertically. The outer face was also damaged by water action. Attempts at bolstering having failed, a massive brick wall was built onto the existing one from the outside. The width of this 1B wall was now 3.60 m. Accordingly 1B is called the initial defence phase. Houses of this phase remained low with thin walls. But square bricks with a new 3:3:1 ratio appears, perhaps for strengthening purposes.

The next phase, 1C is the Proto-Harappan Period. While the previous range of ceramics continues, "it is characterized by drastic changes in planning, architecture and antiquities. It is singularly significant, not only in that it witnessed the debut of certain typical items such as the bricks marked by a novel ratio of 4:2:1, triangular cakes and 8–shaped nodules of terracotta, chert blades and a few proto-Indus pottery forms and designs which would become later on regular and standard cultural companions of the following Mature Harappan Period, but also in that the entire settlement was enlarged into a bipartite township. The interior of the settlement was planned and constructed de novo. All the pre-existing residential structures were razed to the ground and fresh ones were raised with the newly introduced bricks and with thicker walls of better workmanship" (Bisht 1999: 16). However, the orientation of the houses was scarcely changed although a new street system was introduced. The town wall was doubled in width and what Bisht (*ibid.*) calls "the precedent fortress, thus reinforced and rebuilt, was converted into a citadel, and on three sides viz., the east, north, and west, the lower town was laid out within a larger framework of fortification, designed like a trapezoid, within which the citadel, planned in the form of a horseshoe with its apex towards the north, occupied a large south-central area".

Period II at Banawali is the Harappan Period. Once again all existing houses were demolished and rebuilt within a new street system, which was rigorously adhered to for the next five centuries. The town wall seems to have acquired a v-shaped moat at this period, 5.70–6.50 m wide and 3.60 m deep, with a road running between it and the wall, which is now tapered. The main gate so far excavated is East Gate, where five major streets meet on a broad piazza, which was provided with a well. This gate-complex "was provided with a frontal moat, flanking bastions, a broad passageway, a postern stairway and a storm-water drain" (*ibid.*: 20). The sort of entrances so far excavated and the lack of ruts in the streets suggest that vehicular access was highly restricted. If this is so it must have been an impediment to trade, or even the local supply of foodstuffs to the town, though there is evidence of cart tracks in the street leading from a northern gate. The area of the citadel covers 2.7–2.8 hectares, about one third of the area of the whole town. Half or even more of the citadel's area comprised open space, which Bisht (*op. cit.* 19) considers was given over to a range of public activities. So far there is no evidence of differentiation in the quality and types of houses available. The only differences seem to have been in the quality of the bathing facilities in the citadel compared to the lower town. In the citadel some houses contained fired brick bathing platforms. In the latter bathing areas comprised platforms made of terracotta nodules and potsherds. "For sanitation, pottery jars connected to house drains of baked bricks, were placed in the streets or lanes" (*ibid.*: 20).

## The mystery of Dholavira

Owing to the lack of ethnological models already referred to, and also the absence of continuous, decipherable texts that might illuminate aspects of their society, much about Indus-Sarasvati civilization is puzzling. As Possehl (2002: 6) so aptly puts it: "The Indus Civilization comes across as a kind of counterintuitive civilization, possibly 'strange'..." I describe the town of Dholavira in detail below, because it exemplifies some new dimensions of that 'counterintuitive' puzzle.

Dholavira is a large multi-period site lasting perhaps a millennium and a half, located on the island of Khadir (only 196 km²) in the Rann of Kutch, Gujarat. Dholavira is situated on what was formerly a saline lagoon giving access to the sea. Kutch itself lies on the uncertain margins of the summer monsoon, making droughts and famines common. "There are no perennial rivers, lakes or springs. The groundwater is, by and large, brackish and saline and unfit for human consumption and even for cultivation" (Bisht 1999: 26). Overall, the environment is harsh and hostile, making one wonder why any settlement, let alone a town, was placed there. We shall suggest some answers below.

Khadir Island today receives only 262 mm of rain, largely absent in winter, so summer evapotranspiration is exceedingly high. The settlement is wedged between two streams, the Mansar to the north and the Manhar in the south, presently storm-water channels (nullah = wadi = arroyo, not quebrada, which technically is a dry canyon). The site is sloping, 13 metres from north-east to south-west, and occupation debris extends over about 100 ha, but the walled Harappan city encloses only 48.67 ha assuming closure of the rectangle. If the dams on the Manhar in the lower right quadrant are indeed Harappan, then we can assume no stream vagrancy (and therefore erosion of the city area). However such stability of stream channels would be most unusual over a period of four and a half millennia. This could be explained if the streambed was cut down into bedrock, like the reservoirs, in which case the channels may form part of the original boundary of the Harappan city in the southeast. By stabilizing the channels, the inhabitants would have facilitated damming. The layout, including the nullas and their dams (northwest and southeast), is seen on Figure 3.24.

So far there is evidence for two dams on the Mansar and three for the Manhar. The stone block dams appear principally to function to divert ponded overflow into no less than 16 reservoirs (in Stage III, the Mature Harappan period) spread along the northern, western and southern sides of the main settlement and to the east of the citadel. Filling the reservoirs was made possible by a gradient of 13 m from north-east to south-west, such that Bisht (*ibid.*: 27) says that "one can visualize the existence of a descending cascade of reservoirs..." It is apparent that life would be impossible at Dholavira without a lot of stored water. Bisht (*ibid.*) estimates that the total area of the reservoirs was 10 ha, which he reckons (*ibid.*: 21) to be ten per cent of the total area of 100 ha covered by the city and its cemetery. However, measured from the plan the whole circumvallated area assuming a closed rectangle covers only 32.5 ha, a sizeable settlement, but a town rather than a city. Ten per cent of 32.5 ha is of course 3.25 hectares or 32500 m², still a large area, although it is cubic capacity that is decisive. It is hard to see from the plan where 10 ha of reservoirs might be located.

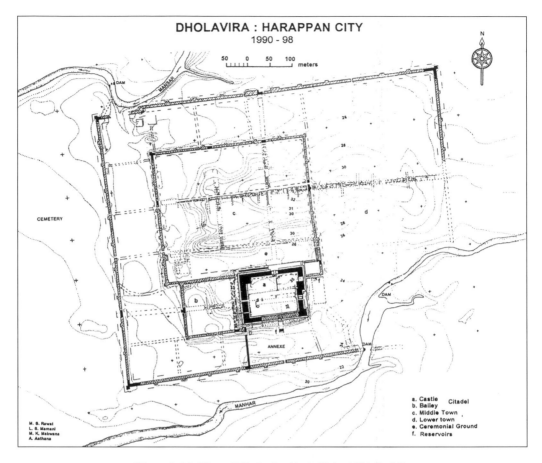

*Figure 3.24: Plan of Dholavira (from Bisht 1998–9: 34).*

## Dholavira: Harappan Town

One definite reservoir, described as one of the two "excellent examples of reservoirs" (Bisht 1998–9: 28), lies to the immediate east of the 'castle' and south of the small stadium. Approached by 31 steps, it is 70 m long, 24 m wide and 7.50 m deep, giving a volume of 12,600,000 litres or 2,769,230 gallons. The other of the two lies between the 'castle' and the annex. Its dimensions are 90 m x 11 m x 3 m (crudely averaged), giving a volume of 3,135,000 litres or 689,011 gallons. Crudely averaging the two (since the others remain unexcavated) and multiplying by the stated 16 (although 14 would be safer) for Stage III (III and IV represent the Mature Harappan period), gives a total storage volume of 125,880,000 litres or 27,665,934 gallons. Removing the area of the southeast corner (2.21 ha) from the surface area of the walled settlement (32.5 ha), plus the 3.25 ha of reservoirs and the 1.31 ha area of the main stadium leaves a total city area of 25.73 ha. If we assume an averaged population density of 125 persons per hectare for the remaining area, the town has a population of 3216. At 150 per hectare the population numbers 3859. A population of around 3,500 seems to be the right order of magnitude.

With a population of 4000 there is available in storage 31470 litres or 6916 gallons per person per year assuming all the reservoirs are filled each year. This ignores the possible widespread use of wells (seen, for example in the 'castle'), which would both supplement the stored supply and make the population less dependent upon it. On a daily basis the stored supply would provide 86.2 litres or 18.9 gallons per person. However, even in a good year not all of that water would have been accessible, so perhaps 25 per cent would have been too muddy, brackish or foul, or would just have evaporated. This rather optimistic assumption leaves 64.65 litres or 14.175 gallons per person per day. This is adequate for a person's drinking, processing, cooking and washing needs, with perhaps some to spare (young children would need less than adults). One reservoir or tank could even have been given over to bathing. I make those calculations because of claims for a much larger population at Dholavira. But the volumes calculated do not leave enough for irrigation on any scale larger than a kitchen garden using wastewater. No wonder that the 'bailey' or 'castle' was largely given over to a reservoir (*kaccha*) filled by runoff from the 'castle' walls through a complex system of drains (fresh water only; no waste). Indeed some of the town's drains were large enough to enable a person to walk upright through them (Patel 1997: 102). If Dholavira had a significantly larger population it must have relied on wells, and those should be archaeologically visible. It is worth testing at various points and depths to see whether the groundwater is saline.

The 'castle' itself contained a complex arrangement of a well linked to two water tanks, located in the south-western quarter. The well was masonry-lined and had a diameter of 4.125 m. Presently, the wellhead can be reached 24 m deep. Water was drawn by leather bag, connected by rope to a wooden pulley on a horizontal wooden pole, supported by either masonry or wooden posts at the side of the well mouth. (Bisht 1998–9: 29). The raised water was poured into an adjoining stone-lined tank, which was accessed from the north side by steps reaching halfway down into the tank, sealed with gley (*ibid.*). Next to the large tank is a smaller one, apparently filled by a high inlet drain. It is furnished with a plughole for drainage and what appears to be a seat accessed by an easy flight of steps, suggesting that it functioned as a bath.

A key function of the town's walls must have been to protect the precious water supplies. So far 14 gates, elaborate and simple have been found. The castle has five, the bailey two, the stadia four, the middle town one, the annex two, but none so far in the lower town (*ibid.*). A clue to one use of the main stadium is provided by the North Gate of the 'castle', which is the most impressive of all the gates. See Figure 3.25.

In addition to its mass, with heavy inner and outer wooden doors supported by masonry columns cased in wooden panels, it seems to have been the main processional port, as its passage opened onto a terrace 12 m deep, 33 m long and 5.6 m high. To the east it opened onto a 9 m wide ceremonial pathway and ceremonial ground through another gate. The North Gate overlooks the large stadium, the middle town, lower town, and beyond. Within this pre-eminent gate with its "grandiose proportions and

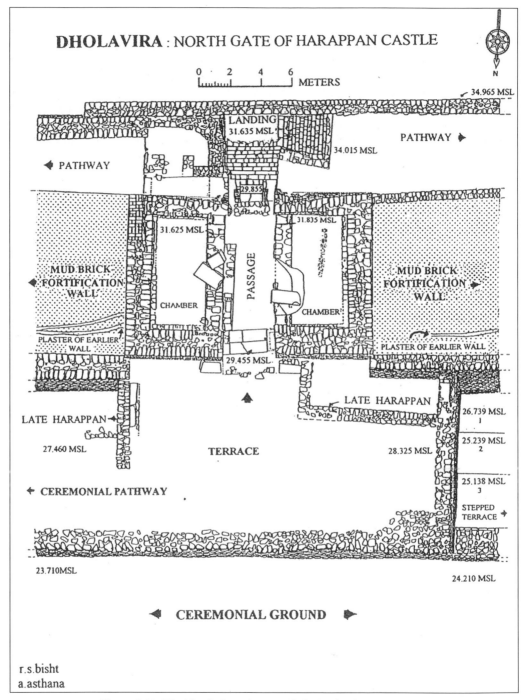

*Figure 3.25: The North Gate Area at Dholavira (Bisht 1998–9: 29).*

majestic appearance highlighted by its lofty and projected terrace" (Bisht 1991: 79), he found an inscription of "10 large-sized signs of the Indus script" (1998–9: 29) lying on the floor of the western chamber of those flanking the entry passage. Bisht postulates (1991: 80) that the passage and chambers were linked by a bridging floor to form a single chamber, 7.20 m by 12.80 m. Here, he conjectures, "the supremo might have had his seat with a large inscription hanging over his head. This may be a probable reason for that inscription of 10 letters lying on the floor of one (the western) of these chambers". He describes each 'letter' (1991: 81) as about 37 cm high and from 25 to 27 cm in width. They are carefully composed of cut pieces of a crystalline material, that may be either a solid mineral or a paste composition. A single character was made up from several pieces and it seems that the characters were let into a wooden board. Of course those signs would only constitute a script if they represented speech, such that whatever could be said in natural language could be said in writing.

Early Mature Period (III) deposits (in some places 10 m deep) include seals, sealings, weights, various types of beads, bangles and other ornaments of gold, silver, copper, lead, semi-precious stones, shell and clay. There are a variety of clay objects, including cakes, balls, marbles, model frames and stoppers. There is also a range of shell items, including ladles, spoons, inlay pieces, bangles and rings, "all essential attributes of Indus civilization", as Bisht (1991: 77) remarks. He also observes, however, that "terracotta figurines, human or animal, so profuse in the adjoining Sindh and farther north and north-east of the Indus cultural area are either absent or bafflingly rare". Perhaps, then, Dholavira was a trading port with a large resident foreign population. If not a port then perhaps there were important mineral deposits nearby. Of course the two functions are not mutually exclusive. Waterborne traffic would have been the best way to move goods either internally or for export.

At any rate, it is to be expected that only a valuable resource would keep a relatively large population in such an area. It is hard to imagine that the settlement occupied a strategically important location militarily. There was some groundwater and some, but not extensive, fertile soil, and also some grazings which, "while restricted in the dry season, are rich when the monsoon rains come. In a good year, people historically have brought their animals from Sindh and Rajasthan to feed on the lush vegetation. And when the rains are good, the population of wild animals, including black buck, gazelle, nilgai and wild ass or hémione, can increase dramatically, only to die away during a series of bad years" (Patel 1997: 102). On the basis of faunal analysis, Patel suggests that the people of Dholavira pursued a pastoral economy, exploiting a mix of hunted and domesticated animals. The latter encompassed water buffalo and cattle, sheep and goats, with the ovicaprids in roughly equal proportions. Suines may have been wild, domestic or both. Patel (*ibid.*: 108) also suggests that differential access to meats is seen as between the Bailey where wild animals and caprines are better represented, and the Middle Town in which bovines overwhelmingly dominate all assemblages. This could represent a socio-economic difference, with the Bailey consuming the choicer food (*ibid.*). Or it could just be differential recovery.

Stored water was insufficient to irrigate fields that could provide food for the populace. Further, the monsoon, active from June to August, can fail for 3–5 consecutive years, destroying not just wildlife but most vegetation too. If the *nullas* didn't fill with overland flow then the dams would not work to fill the reservoirs. No wonder that the excavator (Bisht 1991: 70) states that "the location of such a large city as Dholavira indeed poses an enigma and as such a challenge to archaeologists for a satisfactory solution". Just about everything regarding Dholavira is puzzling. Amongst many attributes requiring explanation is the function of the citadel, and also the presence of a large and a small stadium; the larger measuring no less than 283 m E-W and 47.50 m N-S, provided with terraced stands, one of which was 12 m wide with four tiers (Bisht 1998–9: 32). As far as we know (but who was looking?) no other Harappan settlements have stadia, or processional routes, or such massive gatehouses, or the quantity and complexity of water storage arrangements, although the presence of the latter at Dholavira is explained environmentally. It is the sole characteristic that presently has a good explanation. Perhaps its early foundation provides a clue (below). The high consumption of animal products is explained ecologically as the area is unsuitable for farming, but the raison d'etre of Dholavira is probably not that of a pastoral distribution centre.

## An Analogue of the 'Uruk Expansion'

Sonamane (2000: 141), reviewing the distribution and character of the 500 known sites in Gujarat, observes that they fall into two categories: those belonging to local (regional) Chalcolithic traditions which interacted with but did not contribute directly to the formation of Harappan civilization; and those settlements that were a product of Harappan civilization. Significantly the former were in the vast majority, continuing to rely on agriculture with herding, while the latter number only 25 sites, 15 of which are in Kutch itself. He contends that those sites were (then) coastal, either actually on the sea or else on the margins of the Ranns, hypothesized as then forming an arm of the Arabian Sea before the drying of the Sarasvati. Lothal, Nageswar, Padri, Kuntasi and Bagasra in Saurashtra; Nagwada and Zekhada in north Gujarat; Dholavira, Shikarpur, Surkotada and Pabumath in Kutch; all of those are located on the coast or along the Rann margins which strongly suggests that "their locations clearly demonstrate that they were settled for trade and access to raw materials required by the Harappan urban centres" (*ibid.*); and, in the case of Dholavira, settled during the formative Harappan phases (Bisht 1999: 22), Kuntasi only during the Mature Harappan (Dhavalikar 1993: 559).

Most importantly Sonawane (*op. cit.*) concludes that "the southward expansion of the Mature/Urban Harappan into Gujarat was marked by an accelerating process of acquiring natural resources by colonizing selective ecological regions, a process driven by the requirement of trade rather than a political domination [Sonawane 1992: 169], similar to the establishment of the initial European colonies in India during the 17th century". So again the trading/manufacturing/port settlements form two groups, one containing (Punjabi or Sindhi) Harappans, notably Kuntasi (Dhavalikar 1993:566), and now Gola Dhoro with seals and sealings (Bhan *et al.* 2005); the other, comprising sites such as Nageswar, Kuntasi, Padri, Rangpur and Zhekada, plus Rojdi A and B, containing a mix of local culture and Harappan inventories, indicating that they were acculturation sites of local people participating in the Greater Harappan market. For

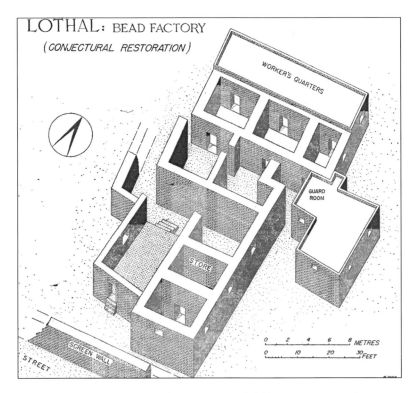

*Figure 3.26: The Bead Factory at Lothal (from Rao 1973: 71).*

almost all of the trading/manufacturing/port sites "are associated with the manufacture of specialized items of semi-precious stone, steatite, faience, chank shell, ivory and copper for the purpose of trade. Regional centres like Lothal and Dholavira definitely acted as trading and administrative stations demonstrating the dependence of the central Indus urban centres on the outlying resource regions of Gujarat" (Bisht 1999: 22). Indeed the size of Lothal's dock measuring 37 x 22 metres with a depth of 4.3 metres, argues strongly for international trade taking place there, and coastwise trade also. Today the town of Khambhat, at the head of the Gulf of Khambhat on the other side of the Sabarmati River from Lothal, has several thousand people engaged in the manufacture of beads from the materials listed above. See Figure: 3.26.

In the far north on the Oxus River in Afghanistan, Shortugai was a settlement of true Harappans (around 2200 BC) as indicated by the pottery which is not imported but locally made (Echallier 1981: 118). The painted ceramic shows keynote motifs of intersecting circles, peacocks and pipal leaves (Francfort 1984: 172). Harappan presence is also demonstrated by an Indus seal depicting a rhinoceros, elements of the characteristic toy carts, a terracotta figurine of a zebu, etc. (*ibid.*). Both copper and lapis were worked on site during Shortugai I (*ibid.*). Shortugai, where raw lapis has been found (Lyonnet 1981) existed principally to funnel lapis lazuli south to the ports, thence up the Gulf to Mesopotamia.

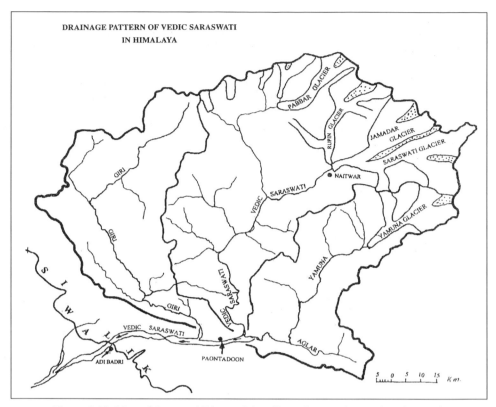

*Figure 3.27: Map of Sarasvati River origins (from Gupta, after Puri and Verma).*

In addition to Dholavira, at least two other settlements in Kutch, notably Surkotada and Pabumath were quite strongly fortified. It is remarkable that those three settlements, north to south, Dholavira, Pabumath and Surkotada, are grouped together in the Rann and are each other's nearest neighbour. Perhaps, in the absence of an overarching state, each was fighting the other for resources and trade. Or possibly each separately or collectively had to face Gulf piracy and raiding. Given their situation it is unlikely that there was much by way of local population to control in the hinterlands, although relations with pastoralists might have been a problem. But we are much clearer about the environmental problems causing the collapse of the whole Harappan oecumene.

## Tectonics, climate, decline and de-urbanization

Highly germane to this process are Mughal's (1997: 248) survey findings of qualitatively distinct settlement patterns in the north (Punjab) in contrast to the south (Sindh) of the Harappan core lands. In the Punjab "the entire plain was densely settled at least from the beginning of the fourth millennium BC", which is the Hakra wares period, whereas in Sindh "the locational pattern of Harappan sites is similar to that of Cholistan and the Bari Doab, where sites of all periods are essentially concentrated along the flood plains of the rivers. In upper Sindh also, most Harappan sites are located along the abandoned river channels locally known as Reni, Nara, Wahind and Hakra".

Those are in fact all local names for parts of the Sarasvati channel. Indeed there are others: Sotar, Ghaggar and Sarsuti (Gupta 2000–1: 31). One of the key points to have emerged from recent geological work summarized by Gupta (2000–1), is that the Sarasvati River origins are not Himalayan (Garhwal), but are actually glacial, as shown on Figure: 3.27.

The Palaeo-Sarasvati had its origins 5 km south of Naitwar, at the confluence of the Rupin and Tons Rivers, which are glacier fed. The rapid retreat of glaciers during the Holocene was, by shrinking the Sarasvati Glacier's original area of 206 km², enough to continuously reduce the ice mass from which meltwater could come. This was compounded by the loss of two perennial tributaries, the Sutlej (Shatudri) and the Yamuna (Drishadvati), diverted by a series of tectonic movements to the Indus and Ganges systems respectively. This goes far towards explaining how and why Harappan society could continue while the Sarasvati River, in effect a large inland delta and the area of densest settlement, was drying. In the rise of Harappan civilization developments were uneven, enabling urban society to compensate its losses for a while.

Possehl (1997: 463) rejects the cessation of Mesopotamian trade as an explanation for the civilization's decline, as I do. Likewise, he ties collapse to the drying of the Sarasvati system and specifically to the situation in Sindh, the core region of Harappan civilization which he says might have been the Mature Harappan breadbasket. And he also sees decline as a slow process, already visible around 2200 BC with the abandonment of the Great Bath and Granary at Mohenjo-daro.[24] Marshall (1931), the excavator, provides this isometric plan of the Great Bath at Mohenjo-daro, just one of the cluster of public buildings there (Figure 3.28).

As already mentioned, Possehl (2002: 244) proposes that "a failed Indus ideology is … the socio-cultural flaw" which brought down Indus Civilization, but if this is so it must be seen in the context of deteriorating economic and social circumstances predicated on environmental ones. As an explanation of decline and fall, I prefer 'undermining due to environmental change', and I cannot put it any more succinctly than has D.K. Chakrabarti (1995: 274): "Once the civilization in its heartland weakened due to the slow but inexorable drying up of the Sarasvati-Hakra channel and had to transform itself into a number of densely distributed but much smaller agricultural communities, the process could not but affect the entire Harappan distribution area, and Harappan urbanism, as we know it in its mature form, was easily lost". In other words it ceased to be a complex and integrated society, becoming instead a series of regional and local societies slowly devolving. Regional cultures – Bagor, Hakra and Kot Diji – or rather aspects of them had fused to form the classic Harappan culture in the first part of the third millennium (Shaffer and Lichtenstein 1989: 123). With its decline regional traditions reasserted themselves, even, as at Pirak, sometimes

---

[24] At Harappa, Meadow and Kenoyer (2003) found no direct evidence that the Granary had indeed that function, nor did they find evidence of threshing at the circular working platforms, or more specifically, at the eighteenth such platform which their HARP project discovered.

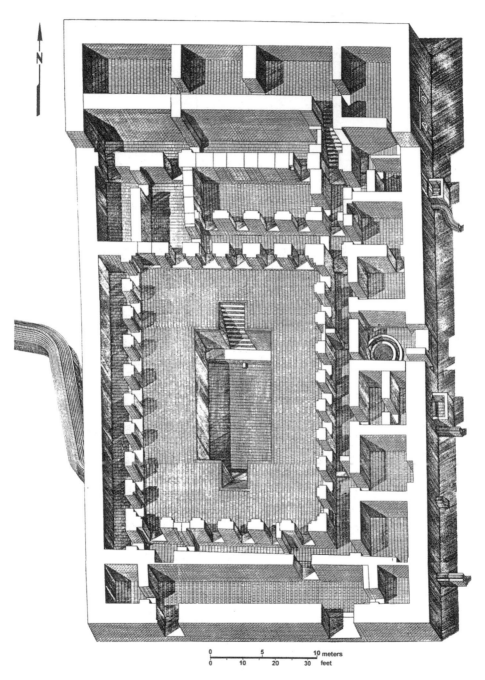

*Figure 3.28: Isometric Reconstruction of the Great Bath at Mohenho-daro.*

fusing different traditions to form new entities. "It is obvious that in the so-called Harappan empire extending from Shortugai in Afghanistan to Gujarat and from the Makran border to the Ganga-Jamuna Doab near Delhi, local cultural traditions were probably not eliminated everywhere. If, in what can be considered the cradle of Indus Civilization in which Naushaso was included at the beginning of Period II, the Indus civilization was quite homogeneous, we know that in the Indian Punjab, Rajastan, Haryana or Gujarat, local contemporary or earlier traditions were maintained" (J.-F. Jarrige 1997: 31).

The westernmost groups of settlements effectively ceased to exist, suggesting that the monsoon, a series of notoriously unreliable precipitation pulses, entered a period of secular decline during which it was weaker and failed to reach as far west and inland as hitherto (Staubwasser and Weiss 2006). An advance of the boundary of the Arabian sub-tropical high would block the advance of the south-easterly monsoon. This blow to intensive summer farming (*kharif*) would, of course, only compound the problems of a drying river system with its cropping based on extensive winter floodplain farming along the Indus. After the spate between June and September, the hot wet season, wheat and barley are sown without ploughing, as *rabi* crops for harvesting during March-April, before temperatures peak in May (Maisels 1999: 254–5). October to February is the warm dry season, but October-November is the cyclone season. And we must not forget that north-east India is prone to devastating earthquakes, as the Indo-Australian tectonic plate drives northward into the Eurasian plate. As both are continental plates (equivalent density) neither is subducted, so the consequent collision creates the world's largest mountain mass. The earthquake in January 2001 at Bhuj in Gujarat was 7.9 on the Richter Scale. India's biggest earthquake since 1956, tremors were felt as far away as Bangladesh. At least 30,000 died, 55,000 were injured and about half a million made homeless. Repair of buildings and infrastructure was estimated at £2.2 billion, half of which was requested as a loan from the World Bank. Such devastation occurring in the Bronze Age would surely be a motive for regional abandonment, quite apart from long-term disruption to basin drainage patterns.

## Summary

Social complexity has both horizontal and vertical dimensions. What seems to be the problem is the inability to imagine extensive horizontal complexity (the division of labour) that is not determined (promoted or organized) by the vertical, hierarchical component. If the division of labour and the complementarity that it brings is able to develop in depth and extent before a command centre (kingship) can develop by merging the different sources of power, and if this corporatist-egalitarianism (Blanton 1998: 151) is able to develop an appropriate cosmology for itself, then there is little social space left in which kingship and the state can arise. Indeed, perhaps this is what the 'burned layers' found at Kot Diji, Gumla, Amri and Naushaso represent, namely a 'social levelling' during the crucial and rapid transitional phase between the Early and Mature Harappan periods, c.2600–2500 BC, the aforementioned 'paroxysmic change'. Perhaps also, as part of this process, and as Possehl (1998: 272) suggests, "the peoples of the Mature Harappan clearly preferred to find new places to live, cutting their historical ties with the older Early Harappan settlements", in an act of destruction and renewal that put all core communities on an equal footing, removing and merging previous ethnicities (Shaffer and Lichtensten 1989: 123).

If internal means of developing an authoritarian centre are thus closed off, only external imposition remains. The Indus valley was early enough and distant enough from both Mesopotamia and China for imposition to be unrealistic. So it went its own way until its internal, geological, circumstances changed. Is this a case of geographical determinism? It certainly is! Determinism? What is meant by determinism? 'Something that causes something to happen causes something else to happen' (Douglas Adams: The Hitchhiker's Guide to the Galaxy, 1979); in this case a combination of tectonic forces with Holocene warming and drying caused the dissolution of a complex, urban but stateless civilization.

# CHAPTER 4

## The Levant and Mesopotamia

If Indus-Sarasvati is the least known large pristine civilization, then the Near East, extending from Egypt to Iran, and from Turkey to the Gulf, is the best known. There are three main reasons for this: the Near East is the locus of 'biblical archaeology' which for a century and a half has sought to identify Biblical places and events; the region has long been suspected of having the oldest cities and states in Eurasia; antecedent to this it was inferred, and subsequently proven, to be the region in which permanent settlement, farming, plant and animal domestication first occurred.

By the law of unintended consequences 'biblical archaeology' has shown much of the biblical historical narrative to be unhistorical. For example, "Without archaeology we would never know that the Omrides established the first real territorial state in the Levant, a state which covered both the highlands and the lowlands, with their various populations, a state which engaged in extensive trade with Phoenicia, Cyprus, and the south" (Finkelstein 1999; 2005: 211). The Levant of course is the eastern coastline of the Mediterranean, containing the modern states of Lebanon, Israel, Jordan and Syria and in ancient times the famous coastal cities of Phoenicia that spread alphabetic writing east and west. Prior to this, Byblos, the two-harboured port some 60 km north of Beirut, was originally a Neolithic settlement that became an important city-state and key trading centre in the Bronze Age Mediterranean. Those are only a few indications of why the Near East is important archaeologically and historically. We want to know how all of this happened, where and when, and what the connections are.

The origins of permanent settlement and farming in Eurasia do indeed commence in the Levant, but the formation of cities and states took place farther east, in present-day Iraq, around the rivers Tigris and Euphrates. The earliest states are city-states, most famously the Uruk (Sumerian **Unug**) of Gilgamesh, the first hero-king in the earliest literature.

So to understand the long transition from hunter-gatherer bands to literate civilization as represented first in Mesopotamia, we have to start at the end of the last Ice Age, look at how the Neolithic happened and then the transition to towns in the Chalcolithic ('copper age') and on to the cities of the Bronze Age with their literacy, numeracy, astronomy and class-stratification.

CLIMOSEQUENCE

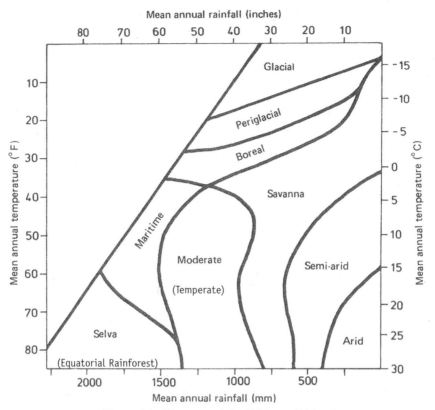

Figure 4.1: Climogram (after Whittow 1984: 99).

## Human Ecology and Geography

Climate and terrain are the keys to civilization, for it depends upon agriculture.[25] There are also scale effects to be considered, bearing in mind that the existence of even a complex chiefdom requires a population of tens of thousands, something not possible with a hunting and gathering way of life. The relationship between precipitation and temperature in biome formation is illustrated in Figure 4.1.

The trigger for human behavioural change is of course environmental change, as we are currently reminded (cf: Wood 1998). The ending of the last Ice Age and the onset of the present warm period, the Holocene, is what ended the Palaeolithic ('old stone

---

[25] Climate is the outcome of at least four independent variables, each with multiple subsystems. The major variables are: (1) insolation or sunshine levels, which are a function of latitude (distance from the Equator) (2) interiority, which is a major determinant of cloudiness, with the cellular nature of the atmosphere the other determinant. Interiority is often called continentality, a measure of distance from oceans, hence the reciprocal term, oceanicity. (3) Winds (direction, strength, temperature and moisture content) and (4) topography (height and shape of surface landforms). For example, the Himalayas have an enormous effect on the climate of South and East Asia.

age') hunting and gathering way of life and ushered in the Neolithic way of life based on farming and permanent settlement, with villages that spread rapidly over the landscape. As the late and much missed Andrew Sherratt (1997: 283; my emphasis) indicated, "environmental change is not simply a background to evolution: it is a principal reason for major episodes of biological change. ... Dessication precipitated *modern behaviour* [in already *anatomically* modern humans, *c.*50,000–45,000 years ago] which (after some dampness and then a little more dessication) precipitated farming – a socio-subsistence system that thereafter spread like an epidemic. Agriculture was an accident waiting to happen (and it is scarcely surprising that it happened so soon in the Levant)", a mid-latitude, easily traversed corridor with a wide variety of flora, fauna and terrain (cf: Colledge, Connolly and Shennan 2004).

The ending of the last Ice Age some 10,000 years ago not only caused temperatures to rise across Eurasia, but moisture levels too. Global circulation patterns altered with the shrinking of ice sheets back toward the Arctic, releasing water for precipitation, raising temperature and permitting a higher level of water 'pickup' by onshore winds. The consequent higher levels of rainfall at interior locations, particularly in the hinterlands of the Eastern Mediterranean, raised total biomass in the areas affected, and thus the components available for human consumption, especially nut and fruit-bearing trees and the cereal grasses. Hunter-gatherer diets in the Holocene could thus be expanded in quantity and diversity; foods could be stored, groups could come together for longer and, in principle, populations could grow (at first very slowly; cf. Maisels 1990: 123–130).

The region that earliest benefited from an expanding resource-base, were the hunter-gatherers of the Levant. Thus the Geometric Kebarans, as the Upper Palaeolithic culture of the Levant is called, became the semi-sedentary hunter-gatherers known as the Natufian Culture, who additionally, as a complement to and back-up for their other subsistence activities, stored wild grains at their proto-village sites. Using sickles of flint-blades hafted in bone, they reaped wild barley and wheat, which they did not sow or cultivate. "It seems that the Natufians adopted the use of sickles for harvesting because of their need to maximise yields and minimize time, the reason being the limited availability of fields of wild stands" (Bar-Yosef 1998: 164–5).

Hillman (1996: 190) shows how, after 13000 BC (uncorrected radiocarbon), a wave of terebinth-almond-hawthorn woodland spread eastwards from the northern Levant, followed a millennium or so later by oak-dominated woodland. Advancing with the pioneer terebinth-almond woodland were annual grasses which formed huge expanses and which were later to undergo domestication, including "both the wild einkorns (*Triticum monococcum* subsp. *boeoticum* and *T. urartu*), wild barley (*Hordeum spontaneum*) and perhaps wild annual rye (*Secale cereale* subsp. *vavilovii*)" (*ibid.*: 188).

The consequence was "massive and abrupt increase in carrying capacity [which] started at the western end of the northern Fertile Crescent around 13,000 BC and progressed slowly eastwards, thereafter to spread southeast down the Zagros and reach the Zeribar area around 9,000 BC" (*ibid.*: 192). However this increase in biomass was not uninterrupted. Between 12,800 and 11,500 years ago a partial return to colder, drier conditions occurred, known as the Younger Dryas. According to Munro's (2004) careful study of Natufian hunting and consumption practices in Western Galilee, the

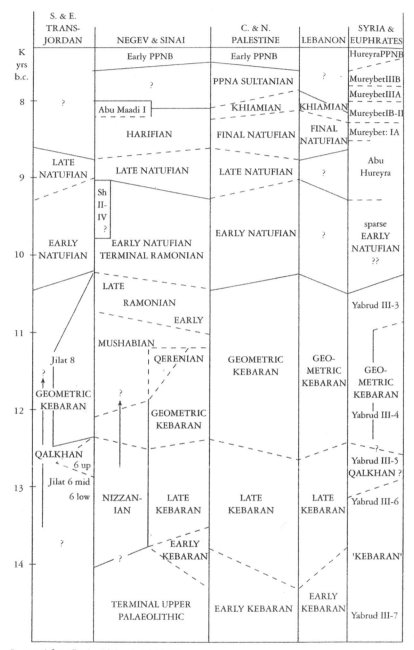

Source: After Goring-Morris 1989:11

*Figure 4.2: Chronological Scheme of Cultural Developments in the Southern Levant, Palaeolithic to Early Neolithic.*

THE LEVANT AND MESOPOTAMIA

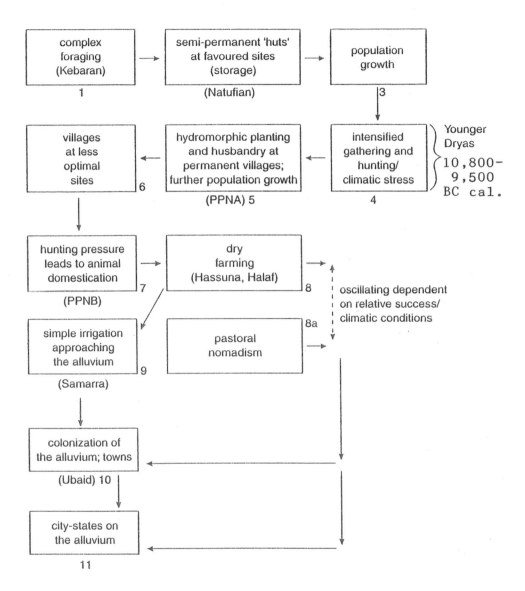

*Figure 4.3: Flowchart of social evolution from hunter-gathering to city-states in the Near East. Younger Dryas Stadial 10,800 – 9.500 cal. BC cal. Source: Maisels 1990: 70.*

onset of the Younger Dryas, producing lower overall foraging returns (productivity), caused the (Late) Natufians to reduce their population levels and to increase their mobility, in contrast to the Early Natufian period. With use of wild resources already intense and with the resource ceiling lowered climatically, the Late Natufians had no alternative, further intensification being impossible. As their overall social complexity did not decrease, intensive exploitation of available plant and animal resources took place, 'pre-adapting' Natufians to cereal management, such that "when conditions did improve *c.*10,000 years ago, cereal agriculture was adopted immediately" (Munro 2004: 21).

The sequence of Epipalaeolithic cultures (and their successors) in the southern and eastern Levant during the Terminal Pleistocene and Early Holocene is indicated by this Table (from Maisels 1999: 88). See Figure 4.2.

In the Levant it all begins with the Natufian, the hunter-gatherers who first began to reduce their mobility sufficiently to adopt semi-permanent residence, storage of foodstuffs and some elements of fixed architecture. Thereafter, in the Pre-Pottery Neolithic (PPN) of the Levant, permanent villages emerged, at first exploiting wild flora and fauna, then domesticating grains and pulses, sheep and goat, cattle and pig. The transition was, nonetheless, a slow one lasting at least a thousand years (Kuijt 2004: 305), and evolutionary rather than revolutionary. Or rather, the outcomes were revolutionary but the process was one of piecemeal emergence.

Figure 4.3 illustrates this process. It demonstrates the 'course of unintended consequences' resulting in permanent settlement and agriculture, with all the further unintended consequences that flowed therefrom.

No one anticipated the advent of agriculture; still less did they 'invent' it. Even plant and animal domestication was not invented, but the outcome of incremental human control and manipulation. Rather, change was induced by doing what the actors thought would consolidate the existing situation by doing a bit more of what they already did. At the outset this was bit more gathering with the surplus stored; then it was just reducing mobility a bit farther to fully utilize those stocks; later it was the extension of agriculture across the whole landscape by budding-off new villages from those that had become too large because of population growth; later still, extending ditches into canals meant that new, arid zones could be populated. At all stages people went unwittingly down a path that incrementally transformed the entire scale and complexity of society. That is, they qualitatively changed their society and culture when the real intention was to secure what they already had.

In a recent ethno-archaeological analysis of 43 ethnic groups, Marion Benz (2004: 27) found that "when hunter-gatherers are forced to stay in one place and food shortages subsequently occur, their social system breaks down". From this unsurprising consequence was developed a four step model that starts "when hunter-gatherers become dependent on locally restricted resources". This is what Benz (*ibid.*) calls 'the territorial commitment' brought on either by periods of food stress or population growth. The territorial commitment is accompanied by a reduction in the food and other reciprocities (sharings) that characterize hunter-gatherer groups, and this is Step 2. The abrogation of generalized reciprocity is essential to the practice of longer term storage, particularly of seeds, Step 3. Step 4 would then be the sowing of seeds and the harvesting of crops, where formerly there had only been the harvesting of wild plants but this is only worthwhile where the actual cultivators 'reap' the benefits.

The relationships between climatic variation and cultural development at the end of the Upper Pleistocene and the Early Holocene periods, are neatly illustrated by Paul Sanlaville (1996: 25) in Figure 4.4.

## The Natufian (*c.*12,500– *c.*10,000 BC)

It has been called the "gazelle culture" (Cope 1991: 341), as gazelles account for 60–90 per cent of ungulate remains at most sites (Lieberman 1991: 52), but with small game, notably tortoises and birds also significant (Munro 2004: 10). In fact, despite hunting pressure resulting in younger animals being taken, gazelle predation remained a mainstay of Levantine populations for millennia, its importance lasting right through the Pre-Pottery Neolithic Period (PPN, A, B or C) during which the shift from hunting and gathering to farming was made.[26] PPNA is the transition period to farming that involved 'pre-domestication cultivation', particularly of cereal grasses and legumes, that is, wild resources were being harvested/culled, but not sown or raised. We await with great interest the faunal and floral finds from the important new PPNA site of Körtik Tepe in the province of Diyarbakir, Eastern Anatolia, dating from the tenth millennium in at least six phases. The village consists of stone-built circular houses 2.5 m to 3.0 m in diameter, with evidence of fishing, weaving, storage and possessing remarkably well-decorated stone vessels found in tombs under house-floors (Vecihi Özkaya & Aytaç Coşkun 2009). The excavators (*ibid.*) state that "The differences in the quantity and quality of grave goods – such as stone vessels, thousands of stone beads, stone axes, and other tools – show variants of belief and social status among the earliest permanent community", making this a potentially very revealing site.

Bar Yosef (1995: 197–200) has identified four major characteristics of this initial Neolithic period in the Levant: (1) "pluvial conditions of the PPNA period ensured the existence of numerous small lakes and ponds"; (2) "common attributes among PPNA sites are found in their lithic industries. Khiam points and aerodynamic arrowheads were documented from southern Sinai (Abu Madi I) to Jebel Sinjar in northern Iraq (Qermez Dere)" the occurrence of those points marking the PPNA interaction sphere; (3) "extensive use of mudbricks that began in the PPNA which undoubtedly reflects a change in the hierarchy of values within Neolithic society", and (4) "The PPNA period's main change was in increased village populations (to 250–400 people) which lived all the year round in the same location." Work since 1995, has, however, tended to reduce estimates of the size of PPNA village populations. Further, an argument can be made that there were no true villages before the PPNA and note that Körtik Tepe (above) is stonebuilt.

Despite the crucial role of the Natufian in preparing the transition from hunter-gathering to agriculture, Natufian sites have with few exceptions been sampled rather than extensively excavated, even despite the fact that such sites are relatively small.

---

[26] Or to hunting, herding, cultivating and foraging during the Early Late Neolithic (8,000–7,500 BP) in the limestone steppe and Azraq Oasis of Eastern Jordan (Martin 2000: 100).

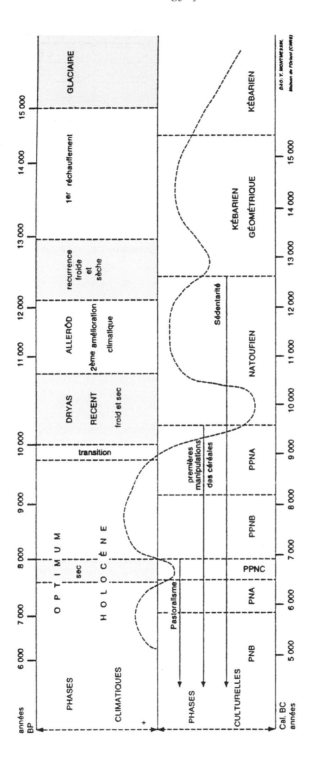

*Figure 4.4: The relationships between climatic variation and cultural development (Dates on the top line are BP (radiocarbon), those on the bottom line Calibrated dates BC, that is, calendrical. For a long overview starting in the Pleistocene, see Richerson, Boyd and Bettinger (2001)).*

| Chronological Period | Start Cal BC | End Cal BC |
|---|---|---|
| Pre-Pottery Neolithic A | *c.*9800 | c.8800 |
| Early Pre-Pottery Neolithic B | *c.*8800 | c.8400 |
| Middle Pre-Pottery Neolithic B | *c.*8400 | c.7500 |
| Late Pre-Pottery Neolithic B | *c.*7500 | c.7000 |
| Final Pre-Pottery Neolithic B/ | c.7000 | c.6500 |
| Pre-Pottery Neolithic C | | |

*Figure 4.5: Aceramic Neolithic Chronological Periods and Approximate Date Ranges (from Colledge et al. 2004: 40, after Kuijt 2000: 3013).*

Two of the largest are Nahal Oren and 'Ain Mallaha, each of which covers around 2000 m² and contain clusters of stone-built circular or semi-circular dwellings, ranging from 2 m to 6 m in diameter. They are shown on this Map of the Levant and south-east Anatolia as locations 3 and 15 (Figure 4.6).

## Early Neolithic

Their successors were the Pre-Pottery Neolithic (PPN) cultures of the Levant – *c.*9,800 to *c.*6,500 Cal. BC – who were the very first to occupy fixed village sites. The transition to the Neolithic was prompted by macro-scale environmental changes, but it was necessarily effected through social, psychological and political developments. In fact for the first couple of millennia, that is until around 7,500 BC, the Epipalaeolithic way of life of hunting and gathering continued largely unchanged and most habitation sites were not substantial villages with permanent architecture, but transient stopping places with merely temporary shelters (Akkermans 2004: 285). Even the permanent settlement sites were small, only 0.5–1 ha (*ibid.*). The number of inhabitants was probably only a few dozen, which is the number of members in a hunting and gathering band. However, because the mounds (incipient tells) formed by permanent residence were so relatively few, they formed key features in the landscape, and so "the mounds became centres of social engagement, where people regularly or seasonally gathered for the benefit of ceremonies and initiation rites, the re-confirmation of social bonds and allegiances, and the exchange of commodities and marriage partners" (Akkermans 2004: 290); and, of course, ideas (Akkermans *et al.* 2006: 123–4).

Comparison of the socio-political consequences in the Old and New Worlds is particularly instructive. For instance, the societies of China and the Andes have striking structural resemblances. Both areas are structured around clanship as the fundamental social order and the basis of hierarchy and the state. The Americas were peopled from East Asia during the Late Palaeolithic (*c.*16,000–11,000 years ago) so it cannot be the case that immigrants to the Americas (the 'Native Americans') brought this social order with them. All they could bring was what was common to all Palaeolithic hunter-gatherers across the whole of Eurasia, namely animism, shamanism and hunting magic (Seaman and Day 1994).

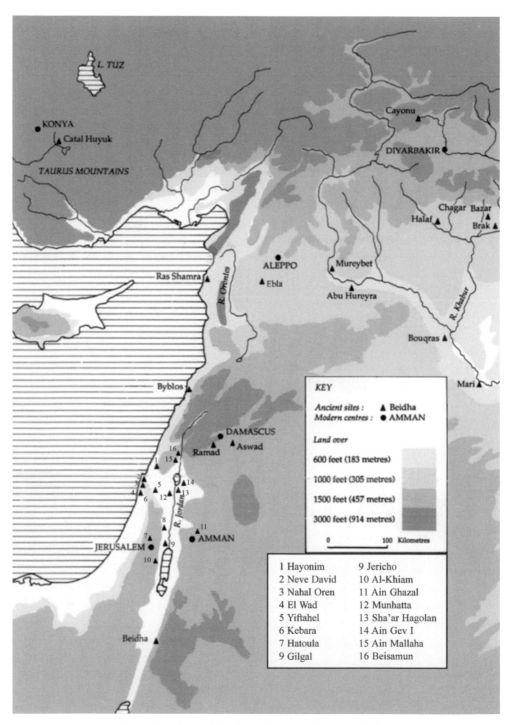

*Figure 4.6: Map of the Levant and south-east Anatolia.*

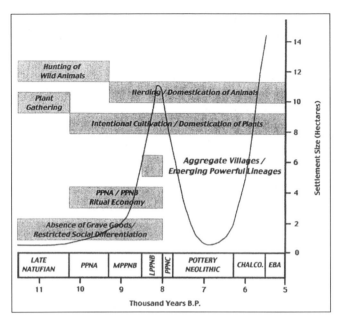

*Figure 4.7: The relationship of settlement size to social organization and economy (from Kuijt 2000d: 86).*

A marked divergence took place during the Neolithic between East and West Asia. While East Asia became organized by lineage and clan, West-Asian social structure was predicated on the household.[27] In the Near East the organizing principles consisted of the nested elements: nuclear family/household, village community, and inter-village community, perhaps connected by affinity (Kuijt 2000b, 2000c, and pers. comm.; Banning 2001 and pers. comm., Gilead 2001 and pers. comm.). Theoretically and in practice the head of a household could be politically and economically active at all levels prior to the advent of the state, and often even after it, as in Mesopotamia and the Levant.

In regard to the Levant, Syria and south-east Anatolia, Marc Verhoeven (2002b: 5) observes that "...instead of the suggested structuring principles in the PPNB [Pre-Pottery Neolithic B] of communality, dominant symbolism, vitality and people-animal linkage, Pottery Neolithic rituals were marked by what has been called domesticity. In the apparent absence of clear social hierarchy and leadership in both the PPNB and the PN – apart from probable village meetings – communal ritual in the PPNB and pottery decoration in the PN are regarded as having been (symbolic) systems which helped to regulate society". More, it enabled populations undergoing domestication to come to terms with the transition from hunting and gathering to settled agriculture. It did this through three levels of ritual: individual (magic), household (household continuity) and public, meaning 'in public', but not necessarily involving the whole population of a village or area. (Verhoeven 2003: 253).

---

[27] Notwithstanding the early (*c.*8500–6000 Cal BC) phenomenon of 'lineage houses' in the Central Anatolian Neolithic (cf: Düring 2005).

Ian Kuijt (2000d: 86) relates settlement size to social organization and economy in Figure 4.7 and Byrd (1994: 644) noted the social significance of changes in architecture at the well-known site of Beidha in Jordan during the Pre-Pottery Neolithic (PPNA and PPNB). Early communality represented by circular buildings, sharing common walls and adjacent spaces, gave way to initially freestanding rectilinear buildings where decreased visual contact and heightened privacy increased social distance and respect for private property. "A decrease of visual contact into buildings and open areas over time and more restricted circulation flow and access patterns are significant archaeological correlates".

Figure 4.8 is a reconstruction of a Late PPNB house at Basta, Jordan. House entrances became narrower and approached by stone steps, and their openings oriented away from 'public' areas. This marked the household 'individualizing' itself. To compensate for such losses in community cohesion, more formal political and ceremonial institutions were required. Those were housed in large, centrally situated non-domestic buildings characterised by a distinctive architectural style, and further distinguished by their location within the site, the range and layout of features, the *in situ* artefacts and the absence of trash dumping (Byrd 1994: 647). They contained neither domestic artefacts nor storage facilities, which were held by individual households. All of the non-domestic buildings, seven in all (one from Subphase A2, four from Phase B, and two from Phase C) were situated near the centre of the village and opened directly onto the main courtyard. They were sequentially occupied, with only one in use at a time (*ibid*.: 656) and persisted throughout the settlement's existence. "The large non-domestic buildings of the early Neolithic were no doubt where community decision-making and group rituals took

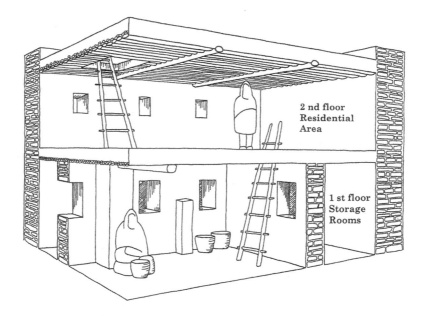

*Figure 4.8: Reconstruction of a Late PPNB house at Basta, Jordan (from Kuijt 2000d: 92).*

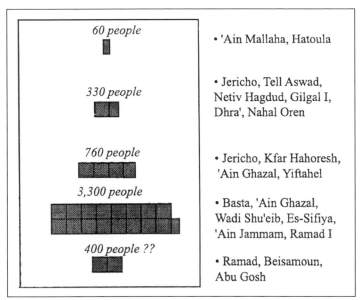

*Figure 4.9: Estimates of Community Sizes from the Late Natufian to the Pottery Neolithic (Kuijt 2000d: 90).*

place" (*ibid.*: 660), as an essential compensation for increasing individualism.

In sum, "decreased sharing of production and consumption activities within the community, more restricted access between domestic buildings and greater distinction between public and private space facilitated competition, insecurity and ambiguity with respect to information and material goods" (*ibid.*).

Ian Kuijt (2000d: 90) provides estimates of community sizes from the Late Natufian to the Pottery Neolithic periods derived from the following named sites (Figure 4.9). It is apparent that population numbers, densities and settlement crowding in the south-central Levant peaked in the Late PPNB at sites such as 'Ain Ghazal, Basta 'Ain al-Jammam, wadi Shu'eib and Es-Sifiya, situated along the ecotones of the Jordanian highlands. Their failure and abandonment around 8000 BP has been ascribed to various factors, particularly environmental degradation (cf: Rollefson 1996), but Kuijt (2000d: 98) sees the failure of social organization as equally important, if not more so:

"From this perspective, then, the abandonment of LPPNB aggregate village communities along the Jordanian highlands can be seen as a failed experiment in balancing antiquated systems of shared social power with the need for developing new means of organizing and directing increasingly large urban communities with competing House leaders". However, I think that part of the problem was that the agglomerated villages were insufficiently 'urban'. Manifesting no division of labour except by age and sex, the villages were just assemblages of similar roles and thus statuses. Indeed, in a thoroughgoing analysis of Pre-Pottery Neolithic figurines, Kuijt and Chesson (2005: 176) argue that "in masking differences, MPPNB people stressed a collective community identity, and emphasised egalitarian values and limited social differentiation within the community, just as we see in mortuary practices and in the built environment".

As their table 1 (*ibid.*: 158) lists some Middle to Late PPNB/C settlements exceeding a population of 750, the lack of a developed division of labour produces only mechanical solidarity which, in the stresses of aggregated living, is easily dissolved as neither subsistence nor ideology depends upon it. Conversely, an organic division of labour, where tasks are inter-dependent, produces a mutual dependency from which a powerful ideological system can arise to make communities of thousands of people cohere. As a consequence the LPPNB/C was followed by the Pottery Neolithic, when people lived in small hamlets where social interactions were manageable. The advent of pottery use in the Levant at this time is not coincidental, but a function of social re-constitution (Rosen 2002: 13) and initially may even be more symbolic than functional (Gopher and Goren 1995: 224–5).

## The Neolithic Revolution in South-west Asia, had four principal components:

a.  the sowing of plants and the rearing of animals, replacing mere culling and harvesting of wild resources
b.  permanent settlement in villages with durable architecture in order to benefit from (1)
c.  the emergence of a new social order based on household and village community
d.  an ideological and cultural revolution accommodating and representing the previous three factors.

Cauvin's (1994) *Naissance des divinities, naissance de l'agriculture* argues that the Near Eastern Neolithic was triggered by a religious revolution. One doesn't have to accept religious priority (and I do not) to acknowledge that the Neolithic was indeed revolutionary, though not sudden, and necessarily involved a revolution in religious belief and practice (cf: Cauvin 2001; Schmidt 2000a, 2000b, 2001; Verhoeven 2002). So while Levantine societies experimented with the likes of 'head reverence' during the Pre-Pottery Neolithic (Verhoeven 2002: 251) as represented by the so-called 'skull cults' (illustrated in Cauvin 2000: plates II–VI), with, for example two stone masks and six skulls with asphalt coating on the posterior side at Nahal Hemar (Bar-Yosef 1995: 203) and possibly even trophy heads at Çayönü (Verhoeven 2002: 338–9), they were also experimenting with temples as a community focus. 'They', may mean the whole community, but it is much more likely to refer to the community leaders, or at least the leading households, which had most to lose and to gain. Temple structures are particularly well represented at the large PPNB/C village of 'Ain Ghazal in Jordan, and at Cayönü, Göbekli Tepe[28] and Nevali Çori in Turkey (Hauptmann 1993; Rollefson 1998;

---

[28] Excellent photograph of an ithyphallic stone pillar from Göbekli, with carved aurochs, fox and perhaps crane, in Peters *et al.* (1999: 34). Colour plates of Göbekli, 'Ain Ghazal and Çatalhöyük in Lewis-Williams and Pearce 2005.

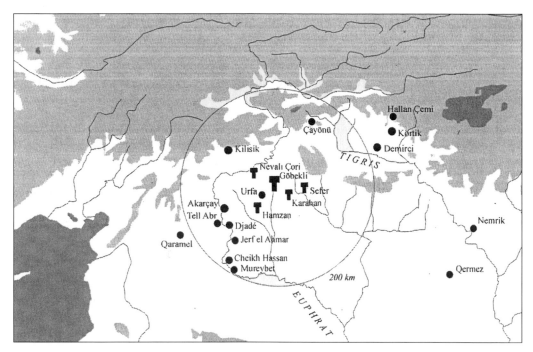

*Figure 4.10: Map of important PPN sites in Upper Mesopotamia (from Schmidt 2005: 14).*

Schmidt 2001; Maisels 1999: 108–118). Significantly, EPPNB Nevali Çori provides the earliest examples of domestic eikorn wheat (*Triticum monococcum*) so far found, while the earliest domestic emmer wheat (*Triticum dicoccum*) occurs at Cayönü, according to Peters *et al.* (1999: 40). See Figure 4.10.

Necessarily, then, a key part of the Neolithic Revolution in West and South Asia was a cultural revolution, which Jacques Cauvin has referred to as 'a revolution of symbols' (1994, 2000a, 2001) and the 'birth of the gods'. The symbols he has chosen to make his argument are primarily figurines from the southern Levant, though with much reference to the iconography of Çatal Höyük. Unfortunately "As with Schmandt-Besserat, Cauvin's approach to figurine interpretation leans heavily upon materials from later periods and from a broad geographic area, decontextualizing materials and weakening his interpretive framework" (Kuijt and Chesson 2005: 171). Worse, the figurines are reduced to only two categories: female figurines representing a goddess, and bulls representing male power. Changes in frequency over time suggest to Cauvin that the 'male principle' overtakes and supplants the female. This echo of *Das Mütterrecht* is however vitiated by the ambiguous attributes of the figurines themselves, some of which are just geometrical (Kuijt and Chesson 2005: 177). In any event, the figurines are too few and too poorly understood to support such a construction (*ibid.:.* 178).

In Cauvin's view this symbolic revolution was the instigator of the Neolithic revolution and not a consequence of it. The conventional view, which I share, is that increasing human populations and with it the heightened complexity (and difficulty) of living together, was accompanied by increasing ritual and symbolism, as spectacularly seen at the site of Göbekli Tepe in South-eastern Turkey (Schmidt 1998, 2000, 2002, 2005) and at Jerf el Ahmar on the middle Euphrates in Syria (Stordeur and Jammous 1995; Jammous and Stordeur 1999, Stordeur 2000). The need for such psycho-social outlets was felt even at Kfar Hahoresh, a M-LPPNB site in the Nazareth Hills of Israel, which functioned as "a regional funerary and ritual centre, a site exclusively devoted to burial", in the words of Galili *et al.* (2005: 15). Kfar Hahoresh has good evidence for large-scale feasting, perhaps involving up to 2,500 people consuming wild aurochs, with their bones used in caching rites (Goring-Morris and Horwitz 2007: 902).

Ritual activity goes back to the Epipalaeolithic at least, but the 'explosion' of ritual life that took place in the PPNB clearly indicates that it followed the establishment of farming villages, and did not give rise to them, as Cauvin claims. The fact that human interments were sometimes accompanied by parts of domesticated animals need not imply that there was a symbolic motive for domestication; rather that the novelty and importance of domesticated animals made them 'worthy' of being interred with humans. Each heightened the significance of the other.

History shows that under stress human populations turn to ritual and heightened symbolism. Grosman (2003: 576) argues that the pressure dissolving the larger Late Natufian settlements caused by the Younger Dryas environmental drying episode between 10,800 and 9,500 cal. BC (Willcox 2004: 51) intensified ritual practices as society in the hilly Mediterranean zone was forced to become more mobile. In other words, this was a method of retaining social cohesion and group identity in a time of instability.

## Revolution in the Religion

What was so revolutionary in South-west Asia was that the powers and processes involved in hunting magic, animism and shamanism were eventually supplanted by anthropomorphic deities (and ultimately a single, creator deity) which are transcendent human agents (Boyer 2001: 164; cf: *The Pantheon of the Sumerian City-State*, Appendix A in Maisels 1990). Hunting magic, animism and shamanism did not disappear with the onset of farming, but their former pre-eminence was supplanted by named deities with specific functions and their ministrants. Lewis-Williams and Pearce (2005: 85) see this process as the "escape from the highly varied intricacies of the labyrinthine subterranean passages and chambers that Upper Palaeolithic people negotiated", replacing the animal spirit/cave/cavern/shaman process with "new, 'above ground' arrangements for representing and for accessing the tiers of the cosmos, arrangements that sometimes necessitated major construction..."

Akkermans and Schwartz (2003: 45–6) refer to the transformation that accompanied 'the Neolithic world of agriculturalists and herdsmen' as "the rise of a new spiritual order ... a new set of social and economic values centring around the house, the dead buried in and around the house, and the production and storage of staples". This in contrast to the Göbekli situation which should "most likely be viewed as as the culmination of final Palaeolithic developments rather than as the initiation and emergence of new ideas", in the words of Goring-Morris and Belfer Cohen (2002), cited with agreement by Schmidt (2005: 18). But we should, with Gebel (2005: 28) go a bit further than this: "Sedentary foragers should not be mistaken as representing Epipalaeolithic ritual life … but instead they should be understood as having developed a site-bound incipient Early Neolithic ritual life using an Epipalaeolithic heritage".

Perhaps the best-known example of a large village in the southern Levant is Jericho. It covered 2.5 hectares, part of which had 34 consecutive PPNA phases, representing archaeological material nine metres deep. Jericho's inhabitants relied on the farming of wheat and barley for their calories, and on hunting, mostly gazelle, for their protein. Only during the seventh millennium were domesticated sheep and goat added to the arable farming regime, but with deleterious consequences for the immediate environment. The original adaptation lasted until about 6,500 BC, the end of PPNC, by which time it was bankrupt, due to the narrowness of the farming base in terms of the domesticates and the technique employed, aggravated by, as well as aggravating, aridification.

The archaeobotanist, Mark Nesbitt (2004: 38) states that "there is no archaeobotanical evidence – the only reliable form of evidence for plant domestication – in the Levantine PPNA, and therefore no evidence that agriculture started there first". Indeed, "it is not until the mid-PPNB that a well-established and homogenous package of crops is present throughout the region" (Nesbitt 2004: 39) and I contend that the new values and deities were not fully 'in charge' until the Chalcolithic (*c.*4500–3600 BC). Even after that, extending up to the present day, magic and shamanism of some kind (witchcraft, sorcery, astrology) remain important in folk religion and popular belief (Boyer 2001: 316), as does an implicit notion of 'the great chain of being', revived in our time under the banner of environmentalism. In the ancient Near East the excavation of temples and the recovery of texts has skewed our views of religion. Too many authors write as if the religion we recover was anything other than elite or state religion that impinged more or less frequently on the lives of the population at large, though certainly more frequently with regard to the patron deity of the city. The daily lived religious experience would have been domestic, focussing (a domestic religious term from ancient Rome) on household gods, ancestor veneration and local deities. Indeed this situation may only have changed with the advent of the monotheisms and then only after long struggles and not completely, despite the fact that monotheisms are key aspects of the political life of political societies. By contrast Hinduism celebrates its domestic shrines as complementary to the temple and, paradoxically, many devotional Catholic households have what are, in effect, domestic shrines.

As Gary Beckman (2005: 376) observes:

> "And as for the Hittites, the religious beliefs and practices of the common people of Mesopotamia, Syria and Palestine are far more poorly understood at present than those of the state and the literate elite. To judge from the case of Hatti, the ordinary men and women of these regions too probably paid scant attention to the great deities of their land, and directed their worship primarily to their own ancestors and to secondary deities and forces whose rank within the cosmos was analogous to their own place within human society".

Indeed, Van der Toorn (1996: 77) sees at least three different dimensions of private religion in ancient Mesopotamia, corresponding to three different functions: "The anonymous house god (and house goddess) symbolize the house and the household as a specific residential unit. The cult of the family god outside the house links the household to the larger social group of clan, town and neighbourhood. The cult of dead kin, finally, which had its focus within the house, identifies the family as part of a diachronic reality, linking the living with their ancestors".

In magic, a charismatic individual tries to tap and direct supernatural forces on behalf of other individuals, in the home or in some informal setting. Or as Isaac Gilead puts it (2001): "Magic is an activity performed to manipulate supernatural entities in order to influence the well-being of group members", that is, group members as individuals. In religion, by contrast, authorized individuals acting in the name of the community conduct ritual activities in a formal setting (temples, churches, 'high places') on behalf of the community or congregation as a whole. *Religion is belief in, deference to, and reverence of, unknown, immanent or transcendental powers.* Transcendental powers are 'transempirical', that is, are not directly observed but assumed. Religion is instrumental, seeking a good harvest, a good life, a good afterlife; also a search for meaning in causality since everyone wants their life to have meaning and value. Accordingly, Lewis-Williams and Pearce (2005: 25) see religion, as I do,[29] as comprising three interlocking dimensions: religious experience (which has a physiological basis),[30] belief (socially and linguistically based) and practice (ritual, symbolically based).[31]

## Parting of the Ways

Inevitably "the most significant issue concerning the Neolithization process is the fact that it encompassed a combination of Palaeolithic phenomena together with events and procedures that had never been previously experienced or addressed. In this sense the origins of the Neolithic represent both 'ends' and 'beginnings'" (Belfer-Cohen and Goring-Morris 2005: 22).

As early as the Pre-Pottery Neolithic A in the Taurus foothills of eastern Anatolia, collective temple-like structures appear at Hallan Çemi Tepesi in the tenth millennium BC (9986–9284 BC and 9346–9225 BC – Stordeur 2004: 51).

Hallan Çemi is a village of settled hunter-gatherers still practising hunting (sheep and deer, goat and pig) and gathering (almond, pistachio and pulses) – all high protein, high fat and energy items. Indeed it is the oldest fully settled village so

---

[29]   However, I do not accept their proposal of altered states of consciousness (ASC) as the explanation for Palaeolithic art, but support Hodgson's (2006) Neurovisual/Evolutionary explanation. For a broader, evolutionary view of religion, see Boyer (2001).

[30]   When emotions are strong, mixed, confused and undirected and also contain unfocussed mental sensations of perplexity, wonder or awe, the resulting effect is said to be 'spiritual'.

[31]   Religion is belief in, deference to and reverence of, unknown, immanent or transcendental powers. Those powers are conceived of as wilful agents called gods or spirits. Religion is characterized both by faith in a god or gods and belief in the stories describing the relationships between god(s) and humans. The former without the latter is just deism, not religious belief. Accordingly, most of the modern British population is not religious, but deistic. Religion is actualised by prayer and ritual, where ritual is repeated, conventionalised behaviour, manifesting by symbolic actions, aspects of a belief system. Prayer is an act designed to induce a presumed deity to change some external (social/natural) condition, and/or it seeks to change an individual's interior (mental/emotional) condition.

far known from eastern Anatolia, and one of the very earliest villages in the world. Pig domestication is said to be 'incipient' (Rosenberg *et al.*, 1995: 5), but Peters *et al.* (1999: 41) doubt this and suggest that pig domestication in south-eastern Turkey occurs well into the Middle PPNB.

A half hectare, four level site (1 uppermost) in the upper Tigris drainage, the excavators (Rosenberg and Davis 1992, Rosenberg and Redding 2000) estimate the population of Hallan Çemi to be around that of a hunter-gatherer band, namely about 25. At least in the three levels that have been excavated the layout comprises structures and features arranged around a central activity area, over 15 m in diameter (2000: 44). The entrances to the stone-built 'c' or u-shaped houses, of which two are known in Level 1, face away from this communal area, providing a measure of privacy (*ibid.*: 48). More than this, it possibly indicates that individual households are 'turning their backs' on the generalised sharing of hunter-gather life and forming individual 'private' household units. If the notched stone batons were indeed tallies registering goods or services exchanged or due, then notions of private property, or at least 'measured reciprocity' had arisen well before the onset of farming, but after permanent settlement.

In this regime where storage is essential to residential permanence (and an inducement to it), each family must gather and store enough to see itself through the annual round. There are no storage pits in any level, but circular platforms occur constructed of stone, packed mud or a plaster-like material. Their preserved height is about 40 cm and they range from 1 m to 2 m in diameter. The platforms are assumed to be the bases of silos (*ibid.*: 47). However, the sharing of meat, at least on special occasions, does seem to continue important aspects of hunter-gatherer commensality (see the Benz Model below). This is both traditional and doubly functional. Flesh does not store well without special processing techniques, so inviting others to consume a substantial carcass prevents waste. And reciprocation means that everyone eats from every substantial kill. Secondly, with advancing individualization, some means of heightening community spirit is necessary. The central area of Hallan Çemi contains inordinately dense concentrations of animal bones and fire cracked stones (*ibid.*: 44), so one of the means of heightening social solidarity seems to have been community feasting using resources specially garnered for that purpose. Community solidarity would have been further strengthened, and alliances made, when hosting neighbouring communities. Perhaps this is what the decorated stone bowls and fancy animal head sculpted pestles were for: to impress visitors.

Also in level 1, however, are two remarkable stone semi-subterranean structures, with a diameter between 5 and 6 m. The pit level is lined with sandstone slabs, which rise up out of the pit. Above ground the wall consists of coursed slabs. The buildings were roofed, with regularly spaced gaps in the walls presumed to hold roof supports. A stone feature in the centre probably served as the foundation for a central support. Floors of both large structures were covered by a thin sand and plaster mixture, many times resurfaced. Hearths were also of plaster. Against the walls were semicircular stone benches/platforms. Mundane plant and animal remains were scarce within those two large structures as were objects that could be regarded as ground stone processing equipment. However, copper ore was associated with those large structures, one of which was the (sole) obsidian knapping site. In this structure a complete aurochs skull was found that appeared to hang on the north wall, facing the entrance. The other large structure contained several partially preserved sheep skulls and deer antlers. The special size and attributes of the large semi-subterranean structures mark them out as something beyond the ordinary household.[32] Rather they seem to be houses where the whole community gathers; one perhaps just a meeting house, the other for solemn-ritual purposes. As the evidence of large, community buildings is best for the latest level, level 1, and if that is not just a consequence of limited excavation, it could mean that the community sensed that, if it was to function as a co-resident community undergoing increasing individualization, some powerful integrating institutions were essential. These appear to have been found in a formal congregation for religious purposes in addition to an informal meeting space.

Speaking of this period and the sites of Syria and south-east Anatolia in general, Stordeur (2004: 49) remarks that their "communal buildings become more specialized and they appear to be more and more dedicated to symbolic ritual activities. This becomes more and more spectacular from the earlier to the later periods, but also from south to north. The 'megalithic' expression is found only in Anatolia".

By the Pottery Neolithic of the Near East, I contend that transcendent sky gods, distant and distinct from human society had won out over family gods, but, as argued above, had displaced not replaced them. At Sha'ar Hagolan, a large Yarmukian (early Pottery Neolithic) village currently under excavation on the north side of the Yarmuk River in Israel, a statue around 35 cm high, about three times larger than the typical Sha'ar Hagolan figurines (of which over 200 have been recovered so far), was discovered during the 1997 season in the courtyard of a large monumental building (Garfinkel, Korn and Miller 2002: 190). It was found as part of a small cache that includes a head, a leg and additional small fragments of an anthropomorphic figure. While figurines are usually found individually in domestic contexts, at Nevali Çori and Göbekli Tepe statues were associated with a central cult building (Hauptman 1993: Schmidt 1998) and the excavators of Sha'ar Hagolan assume this to be true at their site also (Garfinkel, Korn and Miller 2002: 190).

## Göbekli Tepe

This site of the 10th and 9th Millennia BC (Schmidt 2006: 38) has been taken by some, not least the excavator, as confirming Cauvin's argument that religious motivations, here the requirements of religious assembly, demanded the development of farming. Spectacular iconography is still being revealed at this site (Figure 4.11).

---

[32] A household is a co-residential unit of production and reproduction, which "perpetuates itself through the transmission of its name, its goods, and its titles down a real or imaginary line, considered legitimate as long as this continuity can express itself in the language of kinship or of affinity and most often both" (Levi-Strauss 1982: 174). Accordingly, the households which prosper will be those where (a) strategic management of household resources is good; (b) a considerable amount of labour is available internally, with more that can be called upon externally (c) health of its members is good (d) relations with kin and affines are good. Those factors will translate into political influence or power, which in turn will help the household to expand its resources and prosper (cf: Figure 9.1, point 4).

The resources upon which Göbekli Tepe depended were wild. In the PPNA this includes: Persian gazelle (43 per cent of faunal remains), wild cattle (20 per cent), Asiatic wild ass (*Equus hemionus*, 10 per cent), wild boar (8 per cent), plus wild sheep (*Ovis*, 11 per cent) (Peters *et al.* 1999: 35).

Schmidt (2002a: 24) argues that the round or oval enclosures (and there are many) with a pair of pillars at the centre bearing reliefs of wild animals belonging to the PPNA/EarlyPPNB, "was accomplished not by a village farming community, but by

*Figure 4.11: Göbekli Tepe Pillar 43, Enclosure D (from Schmidt 2006: 39).*

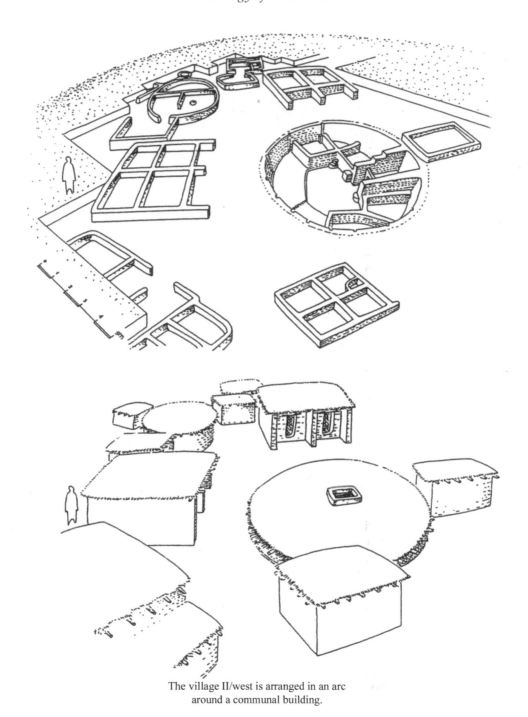

The village II/west is arranged in an arc
around a communal building.

*Figure 4.12: Jerf el-Ahmar, a Murebetian site with a PPNA-PPNB transition period (from Stordeur 2000: 3).*

a hunter-gatherer society. It seems obvious that only organized meetings of several groups of hunter-gatherers from territories around Göbekli Tepe would be able to provide the capabilities for such a purpose, meetings that were rooted in a ritual background". The site's position on top of a limestone ridge most likely 'heightened' its propitious character as well as its visibility in the landscape.

Schmidt goes on to claim that such gatherings, by placing serious stress on the local food supply, provide "the starting point for incipient cultivation" (2002a: 25). This is, as it were, an active 'materialization' of the Cauvin proposition. Schmidt further suggests (2002b: 12, 2005: 14) that people from a distance of up to 200 km, including those from Çayönü , Jerf el-Ahmar, Nevali Çori, Tell 'Abr, Nemrik and Tell Qaramel, amongst others, foregathered at the Göbekli site, where, however, there are no traces of daily life, only ceremonial activities (in the Sondergebäude). Accordingly he (2005: 15) regards Göbekli as an *amphictyony*, that is, where a central shrine serves a large area of those living 'round about'. This in contrast to Çayönü and Nevali Çori, which he calls "real settlements" (2001: 10). Nonetheless a radius, or even a diameter of 200 km centred on Göbekli does seem to encompass a very large area and a long way to travel. "Being aware of this, we may question the 12,000 km² religious 'catchment' area around Göbekli proposed by Schmidt..." (Belfer-Cohen and Goring-Morris 2005: 23). I also agree with them that, beyond 'communication' and cult activity, "the repeated annual aggregation of groups engaged in ritual activities at certain locales can best be explained as a mechanism for the retention of a viable genetic pool, and the need to maintain a specific population size" (*ibid.*).

One of the settlements Schmidt suggested as belonging to 'the' amphictyony (there are likely to be many) is the (now drowned) site of Jerf el-Ahmar on the Syrian Euphrates (Figure 4.12). This plan and impression of the village (Level II/west knoll) is from Stordeur (2000: 3).

So in respect of Göbekli, 'living together' assumes a special meaning: those who built it were not living together at the site, but by building and sharing it, relieving the stresses of their individual settlements by communication with each other and with the forces they saw as shaping their lives. "This exchange, of course, also entailed shared spiritual values; and it promoted – and ultimately demanded – the use of a symbolic system. Many pillars at Göbekli Tepe are marked with a series of abstract signs and animal representations" (Schmidt 2005: 16). Equally important, other sites in the amphictyony contained object groups and iconographic motifs that indicate close connections between them (*ibid.*: 15). Nonetheless, building activity at Göbekli seems to have ended in the MPPNB for reasons unknown (Schmidt 2005: 18). Perhaps this was owing to the 'internalisation' of the ritual centres within the settlements themselves (*ibid.*), in response to the strains discussed above and below. Nonetheless, as Frank Hole (2005: 31) points out: "Ritual architecture does not necessarily imply religion, for example we construct 'ritual' or 'communal' architecture in which to play football or baseball. ...One may regard the structures as religious in nature, but equally they could just reflect the ebb and flow of life itself and provide the arenas for dancing [cf: Garfinkel 2003] and telling tales of hunts and times past"; more of a secular than a sacred theatre. *Ritual, after all, is repeated, conventionalised behaviour, manifesting by symbolic actions aspects of a belief system.* In the cases of football or baseball or cricket, the belief system includes notions such as 'the importance of sport', of 'our' team representing our town or country winning, of technical skill and athleticism etc. The Olympic Games is of course the highest expression of such a belief system and set of rituals with its material manifestations. Kafafi (2005: 33) also suggests that not all 'non-domestic' buildings were religious or ritual structures and that at 'Ain Ghazal, the lack of cultic or ritual objects within those structures admits the possibility of a different explanation, and indeed a secular one:

"Our own personal observation suggests that, in the southern Levant, (Jordan and Palestine) villages used to and still are building special houses in which they gather in the evenings, known as *diwan* or *madhafa*. In this room a fire-place is built in the centre of the floor and people use to sit around it and chat about all kind of subjects". In this interesting piece of direct ethnographic analogy, Kafafi further observes (*ibid.*) that prayers may sometimes be made in such meeting places, and so, on those occasions, they fulfil what he calls socio-ritual functions. Additionally, as Frank Hole (2000: 30) suggests, construction itself could be the ritual and/or construction would involve rituals.

Returning to the Cauvin/Schmidt thesis: there is just no evidence that the need to procure a food supply for an occasional event set in train the process of agricultural and pastoral development. This was a long, slow and scattered process in which Göbekli cannot be seen to have been either central or catalytic. Further Kfar Hahoresh clearly shows that periodic large-scale gatherings can be fed by wild resources as late as the Middle to Late Pre-Pottery Neolithic (Goring-Morris 2000; Goring-Morris and Horwitz 2007: 902) so the necessity of developing farming in order to feed the multitudes is just absent, even assuming it was practicable.

## Fission and Fusion

Early village societies are well known to fission when they reach a certain size, the splitting induced by social tensions ('scalar stress'; G.A. Johnson 1982). This can and does occur until the terrain is full of relatively small villages, at which point either distant out-migration must occur or settlements expand their populations. For such expansion to occur, means of ideological cohesion and conformity need to be developed, and this is the function of heightened cultic practices in the Neolithic. The process of fissioning produced by scalar stress and the development of materialized (artefactual) means of promoting community cohesion has been well demonstrated archaeologically for villages on the Taraco Peninsula of the southern basin of Lake Titicaca in Bolivia (Bandy 2004). Fissioning during the Early Formative Period (1500–800 BC) was succeeded in the Middle Formative (800–250 BC) by the emergence of the Yaya-Mama ('male-female' or 'father-mother' in Quechua) religious tradition that served as an integrative ideology with its material focus in the public ceremonialism of sunken courts and their associated facilities, ceramic burners (*incensarios*) and trumpets (*ibid.*: 330). "The Yaya-Mama Religious Tradition can therefore be thought of as a kind of social technology that allowed the establishment of a system of large stable villages in the Middle Formative Period" (Bandy 2008: 233).

Back in the Levant, Gary Rollefson (2005: 9) discussing conditions at the end of LPPNB, a period of environmental stress, observes that: "whatever integration had been facilitated by MPPNB community-wide participation in such events as skull caching [Kuijt 2000: 151–9], perhaps this became too weak in the face of new population levels that now were 3–5 times as large as during the MPPNB. If ancestral linkage was an important element of MPPNB social identity, the enlarged settlements such as 'Ain Ghazal and Wadi Shu'eib and the newly founded megasites including Basta and 'Ain Jammam faced new challenges. A focus on clan/lineage identity represented by the skull cult became divisive and centrifugal in terms of community because of the enormous pressure on the availability of necessities..." Accordingly a community building and ideology was required that all could share, represented by "the sudden appearance of new ritual buildings like those at 'Ain Ghazal'."

By the Chalcolithic in the Levant, the large temple compound of En-Gedi shows this in developed form (Ussiskin 1980); that is: *a temple is a god's house, where the god lives, in contrast to a shrine, through which the gods can be accessed.* Gods' houses, explicitly addressed as such and using the normal words for house, **é** (Sumerian) and *bīt* (Akkadian), occupied central and dominant positions in the cities of Mesopotamia.

However, as in ancient Rome, family gods did not necessarily disappear. They merely became subordinate. In Rome, for example they functioned domestically (as *lares et penates* and Vesta/Hestia, the latter goddesses of the hearth and storeroom) in a subsidiary capacity to the public or city-gods (and latterly the deified Emperor). Public gods had, however, clearly won the Neolithic contest in the Levant and Mesopotamia where they formed a divine society, individual members serving as patrons of city and state (cf: Westenholz 1998 for a clear exposition).

In East Asia and the Andes the transition to Neolithic farming and settlement was, for geographical reasons, longer and slower. Accordingly, the social order did

*Figure 4.13: The principal gods of the Sumero-Akkadian pantheon on a greenstone cylinder seal of the Akkadian period (British Museum). Central is Inanna/Ishtar goddess of sex, war and reproduction, carrying a cluster of dates. To her left Enki/Ea, god of fresh and subterranean water, and to his left Isimu, his two-faced vizier or chief-minister. To Inanna's right, full-face and holding a bow stands Enlil/Ellil, fiercest of the main gods with a lion at his side, while the sun god Utu/Shamash, with rays rising from his shoulder, is cutting through the mountains with a serrated sword as he rises at dawn. The cuneiform inscription identifies the seal's owner as Adda, described as dubsar, scribe.*

not initially change into one based upon household and village community, which is how nearly all specialist scholars characterize the Neolithic social structure of Southwest Asia (cf: the contributors to Kuijt ed. 2000). Rather, as already mentioned, in East Asia and the Andes social structure was predicated upon the segmentary collectivism of lineage and clan, and so the religious ideology became that of ancestor worship plus shamanism. Ancestor worship is the key to strong lineage formation (Maisels 1999: 360–1). Consanguinity demands descent from common ancestors, so worshipping originators is sacralizing the line (Li Liu 1999: 603); it is as genitor that ancestors are being reverenced by their descendants (cf: Abraham as founding father or originating patriarch); and also because they are dead, have 'passed over' and so are in touch with the spirit powers. Hence the Chinese injunction to 'Serve the dead as one would the living'.

The Pre-Pottery Neolithic of the Levant was succeeded by the Pottery Neolithic. The Levant lost the priority it had possessed since the Epi-Palaeolithic and the running was taken up to the east, in Mesopotamia. There major rivers produce deep alluvial soils and permit large-scale irrigation to exploit them. On the basis of intensive agriculture and rigorous organisation, the large agricultural surpluses that could be produced allowed a cluster of cities to form there, the world's first such cluster. In Steven Pinker's (1994: 253) striking sentence: "Farming is a method for mass-producing human beings by turning land into bodies".

## The Heartland of City-States

The triangular wedge between the Tigris and Euphrates north of ancient Agade (the area of present-day Baghdad) is called the Jezira, literally 'the island'. There shortly after the adoption of pottery around 7,000 BC we find Mesopotamia's first extensive Pottery Neolithic culture, termed Hassuna, after the eponymous site by the Tigris. Recognisably Hassuna culture commences around 6,800 BC(Calibrated).[33]

Domestic arrangements took the classic Neolithic form of a homestead with rectilinear walls made from packed mud or mud brick and roofed with beams and a type of thatch (Tekin 2005). Farming too had assumed its classical form of grains and pulses, sheep and goats, cattle and pig. So successful was this adaptation, that within half a millennium a derivative culture called Samarran, had pushed down

---

[33] This example of current chronology using Baysian analysis of date distributions to calibrate selected dates in the Levant and Mesopotamia, is by E.B. Banning, University of Toronto, who continues to refine the technique:

| Arpachiyah Classic Halaf | 5961/5882 cal BC – 5830/5682 cal BC |
|---|---|
| Girikiciyan Halaf | 5921/5852 cal BC – 5201/5092 cal BC |
| Sabi Abyad 2–1 | 5931/5912 cal BC – 5581/5402 cal BC |
| Sabi Abyad 3 | 5951/5932 cal BC – 5931/5912 cal BC |
| Sabi Abyad 4-5 | 5981/5952 cal BC – 5951/5932 cal BC |
| Tell es-Sawwan level III | 6111/5972 cal BC – 5911/5832 cal BC |
| Yarim Tepe II 3 | 5821/5752 cal BC – 5761/5612 cal BC |
| Tell es-Sawwan level I | 5341/5242 cal BC – 5281/5182 cal BC |
| Yarim Tepe II 6 | 5491/5432 cal BC – 5411/5312 cal BC |
| Yarim Tepe II 7 | 5581/5522 cal BC – 5491/5432 cal BC |
| Yarim Tepe II 8 | 5721/5582 cal BC – 5581/5522 cal BC |

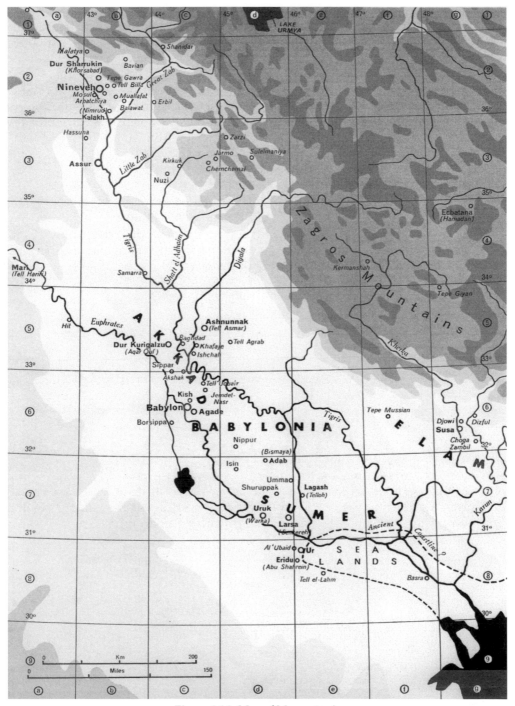

Figure 4.14: Map of Mesopotamia

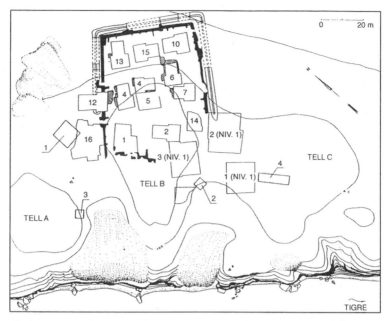

*Figure 4.15: The location on the Tigris of the Samarran site of Tell es-Sawwan (after Breniquet 1992: 6).*

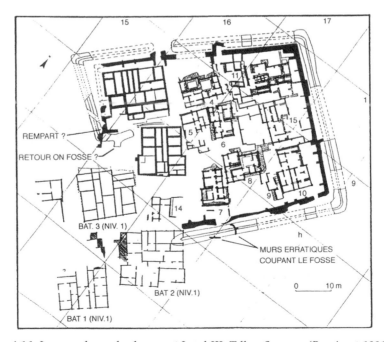

*Figure 4.16: Large and complex houses at Level III, Tell es-Sawwan (Breniquet 1991: 78).*

the Tigris beyond the zone of sufficient rainfall (the 300 mm isohyet) and in so doing pioneered three seminal developments: irrigation techniques, the extended and stratified household (**oikos**), and nucleated settlements. All agriculture is inherently risky and pioneering new areas and techniques is more risky still. The key response to this risk was making household units large and diversified enough to cope (Maisels 1984, 1987, 1990). The households also clustered together around a central reserve, the temple, for mutual support and coordination. The social dynamics of this expansion can be suggestively illustrated from Michael Sheridan's ethnographic work (2002: 87) on irrigation agriculturalists in pre-colonial North Pare, Tanzania:

> "Given the low population density, slow rate of population growth, and productive banana groves of precolonial North Pare," for which substitute fertile alluvial soil in Mesopotamia, "irrigation seems to have been a means to attract both local and long-distance immigrants and assemble them into communities. By building up a group of dependent neighbours, the founder of an irrigation system achieved a degree of social mobility for himself and his descendants. This status also had pragmatic material benefits because the new settlers increased the pool of labour for work groups and strengthened the localized network of reciprocal social obligations. From the perspective of new settlers (who may have been immigrants from as far away as Usambara or Nguu or newlyweds from a more densely settled part of North Pare), joining such a community reduced both social and ecological risks."

This accords very well with the phenomenon discovered by Adams (1981: 69–70) in his classic archaeological survey of the central floodplain of the Euphrates. At the onset of the Uruk period at the start of the fourth millennium, he found a rapid, massive process of population growth, with "something closer to a tenfold increase than to a doubling ... within a period not exceeding two centuries. Favourable natural conditions, to be sure, must have encouraged vigorous natural growth. But in addition it is virtually certain that we are witnessing either an extensive pattern of immigration into the region, the rapid conversion of large numbers of formerly semi-sedentary folk into settled agriculturalists, or, more likely, both together".

Figure 4.15 (after Breniquet 1992: 6) shows the location on the Tigris of the famous Samarran site of Tell es-Sawwan, dating from around 6000 BC (calibrated). It is quite obviously and remarkably a township enclosed by a wall. Internal structures are distinct units, namely large and complex houses, clearly seen here at Level III (Figure 4.16 (Breniquet 1991: 78)).

Not only is Sawwan the type-site for Samarran pottery, but hundreds of stone anthropomorphic statuettes from the two bottom levels have been found there (Ippolitoni Strika 2000, with several new photographs). They occur almost exclusively in burials within "huge tripartite buildings of the earliest two levels" (*ibid.*: 654).

Within another half millennium the successor culture to the Samarran, called Ubaid, emerged. Ubaid is named from the type-site of Al-Ubaid, 5 km west-north-west of Ur on the southern reaches of the Mesopotamian alluvium. The descent/evolutionary relationships between Mesopotamian cultures from the Neolithic to the Bronze Age is shown in Figure 4.17 below (from Maisels 1999: 135). Cultural continuity between the Prehistoric and Protohistoric is not in doubt (Ippolitoni Strika 2000: 656); straightforward linearity is, however.

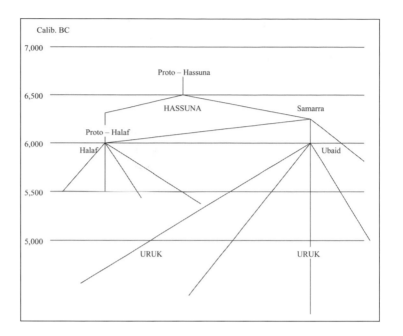

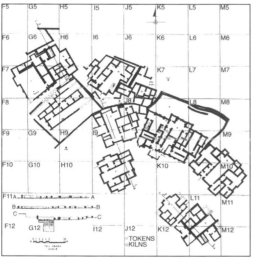

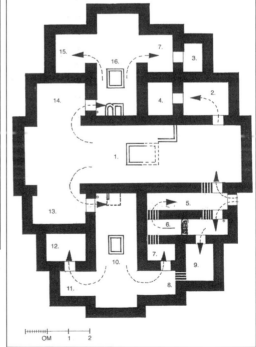

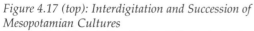

*Figure 4.17 (top): Interdigitation and Succession of Mesopotamian Cultures*

*Figure 4.18 (above): Level II at Tell Abada (Jasim 1985(2) fig. 13).*

*Figure 4.19 (right): The Ubaidian site of Kheit Qasim III showing circulation.*

Ubaidian settlements in Mesopotamia manifest the clustered or nucleated township layout, and indeed its individual structures are even more imposing than those seen at Tell es-Sawwan. The example in Figure 4.18, is from Level II at Tell Abada (Jasim 1985(2) fig. 13).

So just what does it represent? This becomes clearer when we look at this houseform from the earlier Ubaidian site of Kheit Qasim III (Figure 4.19) for it is striking in its clarity and symmetry (after Forest 1884: 119 and Forest-Foucault, 1980: 222). What we have here, I contend, is three dwelling-units, all of which are T-form, but two of which are subsidiary, being at ninety degrees to the main axis, the central and dominant T, which I take to be the main hall and hearth (in the centre) belonging to the *paterfamilias*. It is those types of structure (and they vary) that are referred to as 'tripartite'.

All three share a common entrance, but the existence of separate hearths and storage bins in each, I have argued (1984, 1987, 1990) to represent a household consisting of father and married sons (or the joint household of brothers of whom the oldest is senior), forming semi-independent domestic units in a shared household with, therefore, common resources. Such a household would be called **é** in Sumerian, *bitum* in Akkadian or *oikos* in Greek (Weissleder 1978) and *oikiai* are what I have characterised as *augmented and stratified* households (Maisels 1984, 1990, 1993, 1999). They arose as corporate units during the Samarran period as a means of marshalling and managing labour and other resources needed to pioneer irrigation and exploit the rain-deficient alluvium. The successful advance down the alluvium to the head of the Gulf was made possible by this corporate unit. Clusters of such households, with the gods' households at the centre, served as the nuclei of city-formation on the southern alluvium, the earliest in the world. The temple households originated as community focus, storehouse and clearinghouse, which is why we find them at the centres of settlements of all sizes and periods. As Pollock (1999: 87) observes: "In the long succession of Ubaid temples from Eridu, artefact repertoires quite similar to those of houses were recovered, including equipment for food procurement and processing as well as textile production..."

However, advancing urbanization, stratification and output is manifest in both the development of control techniques and the simplification and standardization of output, seen, for example in the plain unornamented utility of Ubaid pottery compared with the superb artistry of decorated Samarra and Halaf wares. With regard to the transition from Naqada II to Naqada III (the state-building period in Egypt), Wengrow (2006: 156) observes of the ceramics in the Naqada III cemetery of El Kab, just north of Hierakonpolis, that: "Gone entirely is the figural painting of the predynastic period, and pottery assemblages as a whole exhibit a much greater degree of homogeneity and repetition of form", something paralleled throughout Egypt.[34] See for example Figure 4.20 below.

---

[34] So an argument can be made, as by Wengrow (2006: 151–4), and it is one I support, that this indicates if not the material impoverishment of the lower classes upon the advent of the state, at least their social, cultural and probably inter-personal impoverishment The state and the elite reserved to themselves meaningful initiative and cognitive development, and, no doubt, leisure too. And this certainly slowed, if it did not fully stifle, intellectual development, as Kemp (1989: 89) observed: "the success of court art

*Figure 4.20: A Halaf Bowl from Arpachiya, Early Sixth Millennium (British Museum).*

"The presence of seals in a late Ubaid Eridu temple indicates the role of temple personnel in authorizing transactions. Elsewhere, the architecturally elaborate Late Ubaid (level XIII) buildings – generally thought to be temples – from Tepe Gawra, located at the edge of the foothills in northern Iraq, were furnished with numerous spindle whorls, grinding stones, clay mullers, and chipped stone tools, as well as finely crafted pottery seals [Tobler 1950; Rothman 1993]. This evidence suggests that temples were differentiated from houses by their architectural elaboration [and decoration] and the presence of some finely crafted luxury or ritual goods, although their inventories of domestic items resembled those of houses" (Pollock 1999: 87).

As already mentioned, those houses, at least the larger ones, were *hierarchically organised augmented and stratified households*, structured for production. Butterlin (2009b) rightly sees them as the basis for social stratification and ultimately for the advent of the city-state in Mesopotamia. Many clustered 'tripartite' (i.e.: *oikos*) households, many

---

and the tendency towards mass stereotyped production of artefacts sapped local creativity." As described elsewhere in this work, in its place the state installed distracting spectacle, replacing participation by mere viewing. This process is marked today by the global hegemony of state-supported or commercially driven spectator sports, propagated through all media, as against the relatively miniscule number of participants in sporting activities. The pinnacle of state-sponsored spectator ('elite') sport, global and comprehensive, is of course the Olympic Games.

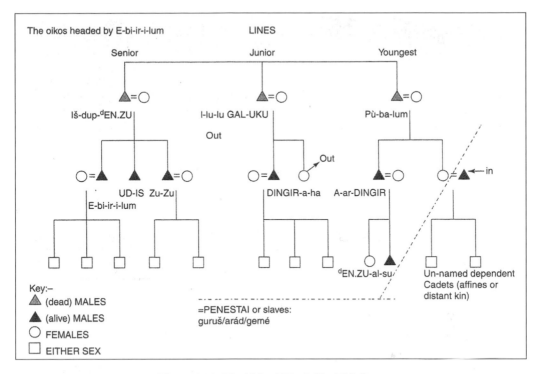

*Figure 4.21: The 'Oikos' Headed by Ebiirilum.*

proto-urban clusters; those facts alone explain the appearance of many city-states on the alluvium and the absence of 'chiefdoms' (Maisels 1984, 1987).

Using I.J. Gelb's work (1979) on boundary markers called *kudurrus* as my foundation, I have modelled (1993: 174) the internal structure of the oikos (Figure 4.21).

Here we have three siblings, their children and grandchildren, occupying the three distinct halls of the *oikos*. Also attached are dependents: distant or ruined relatives, plus servants and field workers whom we know lived apart in a separate multi-purpose building, as seen at Kheit Qasim III (illustrated in Figure 4.19).

Figure 4.22 below is an attempt to model[35] the contributions to production and the beneficiaries of output in the private (family) oikos. This should be compared with the public (temple) *oikos*, modelled in Fig. 4.27.

Support for and illumination of this archaeological and textual reconstruction of the private or family *oikos* can be found in Michael Sheridan's (2002: 85) ethnographic work already referred to:

---

[35] The basic model derives from Wilk (1990). Some of the data for the public or institutional oikos comes from Gelb's (1979) study of ten texts from the temple households of Lagash in the Ur III period. Input/output flows are derived from Jones' (1976) discussion of Sumerian administrative documents. The ecology of the private household is informed by Foster's (1982) work on household archives of various sizes in Gasur during the Sargonic period.

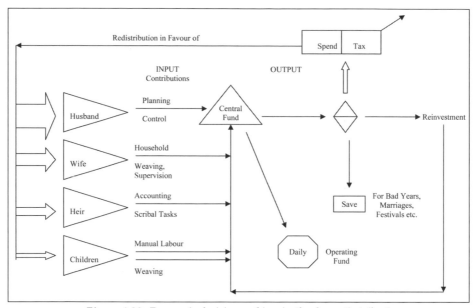

*Figure 4.22: Economic decision making in the domestic 'oikos'.*

"The patriarch's public role was as manager of all the people in the compound, and his interests largely lay in bridewealth arrangements, livestock investments, dispute settlement, tribute collection, and political affairs. His dependents' roles as farmers and herders were established well enough that he did not actually have to assign tasks on a daily basis (except for *vazoro* debtors); rather, he ratified critical decisions, such as borrowing cattle, applying for irrigation water, of selling crops in the marketplace. Domestic relations had a high degree of coercion. As one elderly woman described these precolonial intrahousehold processes: 'Marriage was like being purchased as a slave'."

## Uruk and Kish, writing and history

Ubaidian social organization spread throughout and beyond Mesopotamia during the 5th millennium, and is the substratum of the score of cities that subsequently emerged on the Sumerian (southern) alluvium during the last half of the fourth millennium – Uruk, Ur, Eridu, Nippur, Lagash etc. – strung out like pearls on the lower courses of the Euphrates (see Figure 4.23). According to one version of the Sumerian Deluge Myth, the five sacred cities are Uruk, Badtibira, Larak, Sippar and Šuruppak (Kramer 1983: 116).

We find similar *oikos* structures in the subsequent and proto-historical Uruk period too, as at Tell Qalinj Agha (Figure 4.24) and in the early historic periods at Shuruppak, the city where the original flood legend was set with its hero Ziusudra or Ut-napishtim, much later known as Noah. Early-Dynastic period (first half of the third millennium) examples are found in the towns of Khafajah and Asmar, and in the city of Ur itself, whence, over two millennia later, came that most famous patriarch, Abraham.

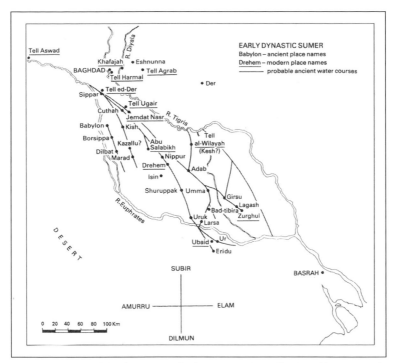

*Figure 4.23: Watercourses and Settlement on the Mesopotamian Alluvium (from Maisels 1990: 152).*

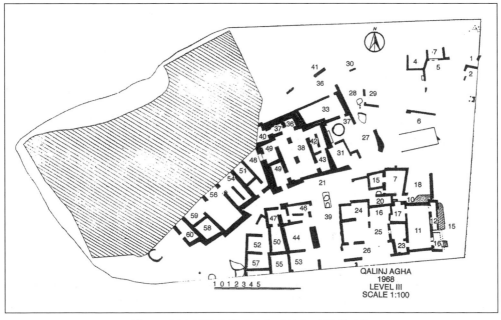

*Figure 4.24: Tell Qalinj Agha (Al-Soof 1969: 39).*

Palaces and kingship only emerge in Mesopotamia during the Early Dynastic period in the early centuries of the third millennium. Specifically they emerge from the Semitic populations of the 'Kish Culture' in the northern part of the alluvium that, including Mari on the Euphrates (Gelb 1992), extended at least to Ebla in Western Syria, where a magnificent palace has been found at Tell Mardikh, about 55 km (35 miles) south of Aleppo (Pettinato 1991). It is at Early Dynastic Kish, which is in the northern part of the alluvium near Babylon, that the earliest palaces have been found. It was also at Kish that the earliest royal inscription was found, that of En-mebaragesi. The King List (see Maisels 1990: Appendix) states that Kish held the kingship (hegemony) 'after the Flood'.

By contrast, leadership on the southern alluvium where the earliest cities (such as Ur, Eridu and Uruk) are located, was exercised by temples, which originally were not just cultic foci but, as already mentioned, community resources. There, capital and labour-intensive agriculture and, importantly, marsh management (Pournelle 2007), was developed on a large scale as part of diverse and vertically integrated production. Ubaid contains a

*Figure 4.25: Gypsum statuette deposited in a temple to pray for the donor – a votive offering of Early Dynastic III Period (British Museum).*

large temple complex dating from Early Dynastic III, *c*.2,500 BC, while at Eridu, some 24 km south-south-west of Ur – said by Sumerian literature to be one of the most ancient cities and home to the god Enki, Lord of the Deep – excavations exposed no less than eighteen successive levels of temple rebuilding, with the earliest dating to Early Ubaid (Safar, Mustafa and Lloyd 1981).

The city of Uruk is structured around not one but two cultic precincts, the Eanna precinct in the east and the Anu ziggurat precinct to the west, also known as the Kullab. Eanna, the 'House of Heaven', is dedicated to supreme god (of the sky/heaven) An, and to Inanna, a syncretic goddess of sex and fecundity, war and peace. With Enki, she is also god of the *me*'s, which are the norms[36], structures and attributes of

---

[36] Norms are types of behaviour people expect others to exhibit. Norms and institutions are mutually supportive. The 'state of matrimony' is an institution, but *the expectation* (by family and society at large) of getting married and procreating, is a norm. Indeed, one could say that matrimony is an originating institution since kinship is fundamental to society and as Fortes (1953: 201) says: "Kinship is used to define and sanction a personal field of social relations for each individual". The logic, as I previously (1999: 361) said, is that: "Everything starts

civilization in the Sumerian worldview. This is reflected in the Balag hymn to the goddess, concerned with the blessing of King Urninurta by the chief gods, An(u) and (his enforcer) Enlil, god of the storm; collated and translated by A.W. Sjoberg (1977).

> "Inanna, (she is) foremost, with all *me*'s, surpassing among the divine Ladies,
> She makes perfect the rules of kingship; to 'restore' it
> (And) to provide justice for the black-headed people and to let them have a stable governance,
> She has set her mind and truly yearned for;"

In the version of the Sumerian Deluge ('Noah') Myth edited and translated by S.N. Kramer (1983: 117), Enki, one of the senior gods and friend to mankind says of them (ll. 41–46): -

> 41. Let them build the *me*-endowed cities, I would refresh myself in their shade,
> 42. Let them lay the bricks of the *me*-endowed cities in holy places,
> 43. Let them erect the *me*-endowed *ki-eš* in holy places,
> 44. I have directed there the fire-quenching holy (?) water
> 45. I have perfected the divine rites (and) noble *me*,
> 46. I have watered the earth,[37] I would establish well-being there.

The Limestone Temple, the Stone Building and the Stone Cone Temple in Uruk date from around 3600 BC. At the very origins of writing in the Jemdet Nasr period (3200–3000 BC), at the site of Jemdet Nasr near Baghdad, we find a group of 240 tablets concerned with the running of the temple's economic affairs, administering land, animals, people and crops. The scientifically managed irrigated fields in the south had rates of return to seed not bettered until the twentieth century AD. By contrast, northern alluvium fields were smaller and less intensively managed (Liverani 1996), while the northern population had less to do with manufacturing and much more to do with the pastoral nomads who operated around the edges of the alluvium and in the piedmont areas.

The most important temples, usually at the heart of the city as in Uruk, had several shrines and a ziggurat.[38] Surrounded by a perimeter wall enclosing shrines, storehouses, workshops, bakeries, breweries and courtyards, an integrated precinct was formed. Indeed the very names for the cities of Uruk (Unug), Ur and Zabalam (amongst others) are written with the sign for 'shrine': EŠ₃.

Texts tell us that originally priesthood and temple stewardship are pre-eminent. The temple gave rise to the leadership position of EN, the high-priestship, known as a title as early as the Jemdet Nasr period, by which time it had already assumed the

---

from *spouseship* (recognised marriage) producing legitimate = licensed *offspring* = filiation, thus *descent* (serial filiation) and *siblingship*; thence *co-lineal descent* producing *collateral relatives* and thus kinship".

[37] The third of the four most important deities in the Sumerian pantheon – An, Enlil, Enki and Nintu – Enki was 'Lord of the sweet waters', that is, fresh, especially rainwater and riverwater. He is Lord of the Apsu ('abyss') thought to be the great underground reservoir of freshwater, hence his appellative *nagbu*, 'source, groundwater'. See Figure 4.13, where water and fish flow from his shoulders.

[38] Forest (2005: 193) considers the 'White Temple' close to the Anu-ziggurat in Gawra, and the 'Painted Temple' at Uquair to be "actually a council room built on a high terrace, where eminent people (most probably lineage leaders) gathered in order to manage public affairs.

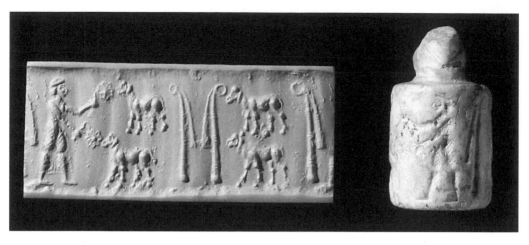

*Figure 4.26: A Jemdet Nasr period cylinder seal from Uruk showing the EN ritually feeding sheep in front of a shrine to Inanna (British Museum).*

significance of 'priest-king', given, Jacobsen (1980: 77) postulates, the general warlike conditions. Figure 4.26 shows the EN in his cultic role.

The office of king, *lugal* ('big' or 'great man') is substantially later, his power coming from the size of his household, armed following and no doubt success in battle (cf: Langdon 1924, Excavations at Kish I: Plate XXXVI.1, for a war scene found in the audience hall of Palace A at Kish). Nonetheless the Epic of Gilgamesh (the world's oldest work of literature) informs us that this violent mytho-historical king of Uruk, infamous for hubris, still had to get approval from (one of) two councils for his resistance to, and attack upon, Akka of Kish. One council comprised the 'seniors', whom I have interpreted (1984, 1987) as *paterfamiliae* (*oikosdespótes*), namely the heads of *oikos* households;[39] and another, irregular council, or better, assembly, consisting of all the men of the city able to bear arms.[40] There is a historical parallel for this from someone with equal quantities of hubris. This of course was Julius Caesar, who, in the year of his consulship and facing strong opposition in the Senate to a land-settlement bill he proposed on behalf of Pompey's veterans, appealed instead to the people in the Forum. By a mixture of demagoguery and intimidation the bill was passed and the Senate silenced.

In regard to conciliar institutions, there is a very suggestive example from ancient Egypt, as observed by Eyre (1999: 43):

---

[39] "In Ottoman Egypt or Palestine, village headmen were not appointees so much as the recognised local leaders, and in practice the heads of the most important local families" (Eyre 1999: 43).

[40] Without a standing army or police force, the citizen army that fought on foot in phalanx formation – as hoplites in the city-states of classical Greece – was the ultimate arbiter. For Snodgrass (1991: 19) "hoplite armies shaped rather than merely echoed the history of the polis. ... The hoplite, in the first place, served primarily, and increasingly only, the state; secondly, he and his fellows comprised a substantial proportion (typically, about one third) of the adult male population; thirdly, he was, at his own expense, equipped and protected so well that for centuries he could only be resisted on the battlefield by other hoplites; fourthly, his pre-eminence sooner or later received the ultimate accolade, that nobles themselves came to fight as hoplites in the phalanx" (Snodgrass 1991: 19). The phalanx formation was the ultimate expression of community solidarity.

*Figure 4.27: Eannatum of Lagash leads a phalanx against the city of Umma (Louvre, Stele of the Vultures).*

"At Deir el-Medina the local foremen and scribe(s) held a dominant position in the village, but we do not find them acting as authoritative headman. Rather they acted more or less in concert as a group, leading the local council (*qnbt*). The membership of this body fluctuated considerably from case to case, but in matters of communal importance the entire male adult population of the village were present" (Eyre 1999: 43).

Note text above and below the phalanx on Figure 4.27.

## City-state political economy

Thus even when kingship came to be dominant from the middle of the third millennium, and for at least a millennium beyond this, representative bodies acting for civil society at state level still ensured the continuation of the community character of city-states (Steinkeller 2007: 209–10). And, as argued earlier, those structural differences are what distinguish city-states, even large, dominant ones like Uruk and Lagash, Athens and Venice, from territorial states of any size. Nonetheless, the degree of equality and democracy in city states should not be exaggerated: only citizens and male citizens at that, enjoyed full rights. Mediaeval Italian city-states were rarely democratic; they were

*Figure 4.28: Square stone plaque of the ED III period (British Museum) fastened to the wall by a stone or wooden peg through the square hole, used for securing temple stores with a sealed cord. The upper register shows a naked priest pouring libations before a bearded god who holds a vessel, while the lower register shows worshippers carrying offerings to the temple, symbolised by the façade, while the priest again pours libations of what is most likely beer, a key item of Mesopotamian diet.*

guild-corporatist and usually ruled by a Patriciate of nobles and *haute bourgeois*, and when their rule was overturned, then tyrants assumed power. In stark contrast to the rural-urban integration of Mesopotamian and Greek *poleis*, Italian cities failed to incorporate the surrounding peasantry into the state as citizens and exploited them oppressively. This was also the fate of conquered towns, as shamefully, Pisa by Florence. Accordingly, when the armies of Charles VIII of France entered Italy in 1494 it was a signal for revolt, and "the streets rang with shouts of 'France and Liberty' (Clarke 1926: 165). "For this reason," Clarke continues, "the city-state in Italy never became an organic unit; the canker which destroyed it was its refusal to admit conquered subjects to citizenship".

In regard to the condition of what Gelb (1979: 24) has called the serfs or helots to indicate their semi-free status in third millennium Mesopotamia, Van Driel (2000: 497) remarks that he "is inclined to share Englund's well-publicized pessimism: much work, as little to eat as possible, and the occasional beating".

This may be true of conditions on some of the large estates, but seems not to be true of urban or rural conditions generally, according to Elizabeth Stone (2005: 163): "The consistency of these patterns [of household size and form] over both space and time suggests significant stability in Mesopotamian social relations, a view which contrasts with the impression of volatility which is how the changes in genre in written documents have often been interpreted. Moreover, the similarity in house sizes to those occupied by modern urban residents, the proximity of houses of the rich and poor, and the wealth of objects recovered from both large and small houses in cities in northern Babylonia, southern Babylonia and the Diyala River region, suggest an overall degree of prosperity. This evidence indicates that we can no longer sustain earlier views of Mesopotamian cities where exploitation by political and religious elites was seen to result in the impoverishment of the bulk of the population".

As far as we know, Mesopotamian city-states were internally stable in contrast to Rome's early plebeian revolts and those of the later Italian city-states, which were, to put it mildly, turbulent.[41] As Nicholas Postgate (1992: 26) said of Mesopotamian city-states: "both excavation and surface survey substantiate the picture of a fairly uniform class of major population centres distributed widely across the southern plain, with

---

[41] Though this impression may be due to our limited sources.

strong local identities expressed in their allegiance to a city god and their pride in the temple". Of the Greek city-states Barker (1960: 9) observes that "Religion was an aspect of the political life of a political society: it was not another life, and it entailed no other society" (Barker 1960: 9).

Following Maeda one can go farther in defining the relationships between the city, its god and its ruler. "The city-god had an absolute status", Maeda (2005: 26) concludes on the basis of a major study of the royal inscriptions of Lugalzagesi and Sargon, rivals in the mid 24th century. "We need to acknowledge that there was an insurmountable barrier between the superior city-gods and the inferior personal gods of rulers" throughout the third millennium. "While the status of personal gods changed, the status of city-gods never changed. The city god was master or lord of the city *and city ruler, and the ruler was a servant of the city-god* (my emphasis). Even though a king gained the status of overlord, he addressed deities as 'his master/mistress (lugal/nin-a-ni)' in each city. He still recognized his relationship to the city-god as that of master and obedient servant. This never changed in the time from the Early Dynastic Period to the Third Dynasty of Ur Period" (*ibid.*).

Just the same obtained in ancient Greece, where "communal state cults stood at the very heart of the polis" (Snodgrass 1991: 17) and, he argues, building a temple for the god's sanctuary indicates the civic self-consciousness of the polis at the point of its formation. Trigger (2003: 639, 656) neatly contrasts identities and authority between city-states and territorial states: "In city-states, temples and palaces tended to express community identity as well as royal and divine authority, while in territorial states palaces, temples, walled administrative compounds, forts and rulers' tombs signalled royal authority. ... Distinctive art styles symbolized the political unity of particular territorial states, the broader cultural affiliations of member polities of city-state systems, and the separate identities of individual city-states."

## Households beget the state in Mesopotamia

So what does all this tell us about the emergence of the Mesopotamian state, apart from the fact that there was not a single unitary state but a couple of dozen city-states clustered together on the southern alluvium (which includes Khuzistan in SW Iran) from the fourth to the second millennia? It makes abundantly clear the crucial role of the local ecology and economy.

Samarran origins and organization determine the subsequent political trajectory into Sumerian urban civilization. The process of colonizing the rain-deficient alluvium – which early in the Ubaidian period had reached all the way down to the permanent marshland at the head of the Gulf – was impossible for separate nuclear, or even extended families. Instead, a series of augmented family units incorporating subordinates under tight managerial control emerged to co-ordinate the wide range of economic activities – irrigation farming, marsh exploitation, herding, processing, weaving, manufacturing – that produced the self sufficiency requisite to pushing forward the boundaries of settlement.

Temples played a key role in city formation, serving as their nucleus and functioning as a kind of reserve bank, particularly for lean years and in the case of disasters. Given

| Hassuna | 6800–6300 | |
|---|---|---|
| Samarra | 6300–6000 | |
| 6200–5350 | Halaf | (6200–6000 Pre-Halaf; 6000–5900 Transitional; 5900–5350 Halaf ('classic')) |
| 6000–4200 | Ubaid | |
| 4200–3200 | Uruk | |
| 3200–3000 | Jemdet Nasr (southern Iraq only) | |
| 3000–2750 | Early Dynastic I | |
| 2750–2600 | Early Dynastic II | |
| 2600–2350 | Early Dynastic III | |
| 2350–2230 | Dynasty of Akkade (Sargonic Dynasty) | terminated by: |
| 2230–2113 | Gutian Interregnum (Gudea's dynasty continues at Lagash) | The Guti were invaders from the Zagros |
| 2113 | Conquest by Ur-nammu; Ur III Period commences | |
| 2029 | UrIII period ends with conquest by Amorites and Elamites | |
| 2025 | Isin /Larsa period begins with Naplanum at Larsa; 2017 Išbi-Erra at Isin | |
| 1794 | Isin conquered by Larsa | OLD BABYLONIAN PERIOD *c.*2000–1600 BC |
| 1763 | Rim-Sin of Larsa conquered by Hammurabi of Babylon (First Dynasty of Babylon) | |
| 1761 | Hammurabi conquers Assyria | OLD ASSYRIAN PERIOD: 1950–1761 BC |
| 1759 | Mari conquered by Babylon. | |
| 1749–1712 | Samu-iluna son of Hammurabi | |
| 1712 | Iluma-Ilum launches Sealand Dynasty in the south | |
| 1711–1684 | Abi-esuh, son of Samsi-iluna, king of Babylon | |
| 1595 | Conquest by Mursilis. Kassite period begins. | |

*Figure 4.29: Outline Chronology of Prehistoric and Early Historic Mesopotamia; dates BC calendrical.*

their coordinating role (Stone 2007b: 224–5) temples also functioned as trading foci to secure for the alluvium a supply of such necessities as construction timber and metals, neither of which was available on the alluvium, whose basic resources were fertile soil, water, the diverse marsh resources that water provided (Pournelle 2007) and palm trees, not suitable for most building applications, but providing in dates one of the dietary staples. The temple was in many respects like a private household, with a priestly/management hierarchy and body of dependent workers, who were probably more like employees ('hands') than in the condition of quasi-serfdom. For "apart from the slaves, who never formed a large sector of the population, people could vote with their feet" (Stone 2007b: 228). Figure 4.30 indicates the political economy of the temple estate.

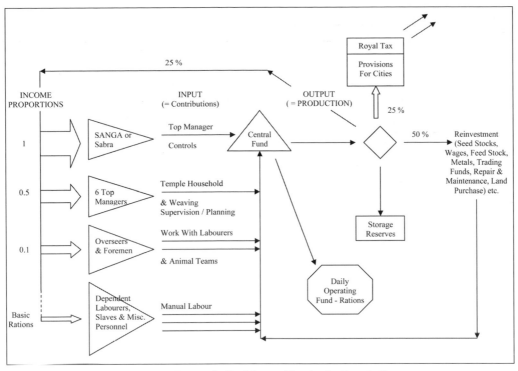

*Figure 4.30: Economic Decision-making in the Temple Estate.*

A city formed around a public household – the temple as nucleus – by autarkic (i.e. self-sustaining) private households, would then, with its dispersed powers, be democratic in the sense that (and for similar reasons that) classical Athens was democratic, namely, fundamental decisions were taken by assemblies of adult male citizens.

Mesopotamian towns and cities are densely nucleated around temples and, later, palaces; they are made of brick, have walls, gates and public open spaces, and are continuously rebuilt on the same site so raising a mound (*tell*) on which the living settlement sits. Civic deities, private property and a kind of democracy gave those urbanites a sense of belonging. Attempts at unification into an encompassing territorial state, most famously by Sargon in the 24th century BC, were fiercely resisted not just by the elite but also by the citizenry. There was little ecological or economic rationale for the existence of an overarching structure that would reduce city-states to mere provinces. To provide justification for what was really sheer ambition, Sargon launched a major ideological offensive employing all cultural media, especially the visual. "Sargon devoted a large part of his propaganda to legitimising his authority [the other, complementary, part was devoted to stressing his might and personal greatness] on the one hand by stressing the continuity between Early Dynastic and Akkadian [i.e. his] sovereignty and, on the other, by celebrating the religious legitimacy of Akkadian kingship" (Nigro 1998: 85).

*Figure 4.31 (above): White calcite (marble) cylinder seal of ED II period (c.2700 BC) showing 'mastery of the animals' type combat scene featuring a 'bull-man' struggling with lions, while a 'hero', centre, subdues gazelles (British Museum).*

*Figure 4.32 (left): An ED III spouted silver jug from the 'Queen's Grave' in the Royal Cemetery of Ur (British Museum).*

Clearly such a state, with the costly standing army of which Sargon boasted, would not serve the interests of the citizenry, but rather the ego and ambitions of a king who would call himself 'king of the universe' (Frayne 1993).

The next attempt at a territorial state subsuming the individual city-states was undertaken by the Neo-Sumerian Third Dynasty of Ur (Ur III). However, its bureaucratic costs of centralization were huge and its economic sclerosis such that it too was short-lived, to be followed by a much more market-oriented series of regimes in the second millennium. Writing and its associated complex numeracy appeared in Mesopotamia in the latter part of the fourth millennium in order to keep track of economic transactions within and between households, public and private (Rothman 2007: 253). Temples, palaces and the larger private households acted as 'firms' or economic enterprises for whom the bottom line was, of course, to maximize income by undertaking the most efficient production and exchange possible. Temple and palace estates were the 'economic corporations' of Mesopotamian society making huge capital investments in, for example, complex plough teams and in storage and transport. They provided the disposable surpluses available to the elites and the state (Van Driel 1999–

2000: 91) and they provided a large part of the population with a proportion of their subsistence requirements. Those institutions, however, by no means encompassed the whole of an economy that had space, physically and structurally, for non-institutional farmers. However this 'independent' sector reached a low in the highly centralized Ur III period during which Steinkeller (2007: 209) reckons that "At least two-thirds of Umma [province's] rural population were members of the royal [central state] sector. Best described as military colonists, they cultivated about two-thirds of the arable land." It is unknown how representative this is of the whole Ur III territory.

Amongst many other firsts, scientific agriculture was invented and extensively applied in Mesopotamia, where all parameters and input/output ratios were known, at least in the larger estates. Similarly for animal raising. This was accompanied and accomplished by the 'scientific management' outlined above.

All factors of production could be and were calculated in the universal equivalents of money and labour-time. In addition to concepts of equivalence and ratios, which are arithmetical, mathematics proper was also developed. As Robert McCormack Adams put it (2000: 189) the Early Dynastic was "a time of decisive advances in administrative sophistication and density, in the ability through writing to disseminate information and store, systematize, and deploy memory for political as well as religious and economic purposes, in the utilization of tin-bronze, in the elaboration of more sophisticated irrigation technology, in the at least protoindustrial production of textiles for long-distance trading purposes, and much more."

The Early Dynastic period (3000–2350 BC) was the heyday of the city-state in Mesopotamia, extending from Ebla in Syria to the shores of the Persian Gulf. Independent political entities, what they shared was a civilization, as did Greek and later Italian city states; so too the cities of the Hanseatic League, which arose out of the 'Hansa of German Merchants' (*Hansa mercatorum Alemannie*) in 1358.

## The Ubaid Continuation and the 'Uruk Expansion'

Samarran culture clearly gave rise to the Ubaidian which, having colonized the whole alluvium with all the social and technological developments that were involved, in turn engendered the Uruk period and the Heartland of Cities. Yet, while this thumbnail is not incorrect, it is much too simplistic. Things did not proceed in quite so linear a fashion.

In the Late Neolithic Halaf, Hans Nissen (2001: 169–70) recognised the existence of a network, "which I assume operated on the basis of equal partners ('symmetric', as others would call it), [and which] would have been the basis and the context for swift exchanges of both information and goods". He argues that it characterizes the Ubaid too. In fact he argues against the previous implications of an Ubaid 'takeover' of 'the north' from the southern alluvium and instead maintains that the 'Ubaidization' of Greater Mesopotamia is essentially a technological phenomenon, wherein local cultures, formerly included in the Halaf network, adopt the tournette or slow wheel as an adjunct of cultural integration:

> "What the potters shared across Greater Mesopotamia was a series of new techniques that, when used to elaborate older local designs, produced seemingly similar,

homogenized local styles that looked more similar than they actually were. ... I argue that this near uniformity in Ubaid-period artefact style should be seen as the result of a new technique in pottery manufacturing introduced by the end of the Halaf phase, rather than as the result of southern Mesopotamian migrations"(*ibid*.: 169). Indeed we have no need to invoke migrations at all, if we accept, as I do, the account of Stein and Özbal (2007: 342) that "the spread of the Ubaid into neighbouring regions reflects the gradual, peaceful spread of an ideological system that was translated into a variety of different local cultural schemes, forming what are, in effect, new, hybrid social identities in these outlying areas".

Two concepts are key: (1) Overlapping and interacting networks of various types and scales: "intermarriage, short-range and long-distance trade, ceremonial and ritual events, the role of mobile groups in maintaining links and carrying ideas, riverine and maritime connections by boat etc. The means of transmission need not be the same throughout all regions and all time periods, and there may be multiple means operating at any one place and time" (Carter and Philip 2006: 2), thereby sets of networks rather than a singular network. (2) Changes in material culture are graded through space (Carter and Philip 2006: 1) and such changes can signify different things in different parts of their range. Graham Philip (2002: 223) earlier criticised general contact models on the grounds that they "do not take adequate account of the highly contingent nature of relationships between different regions and communities".

Nissen's insight has been reinforced by contributors to the Ubaid Conference held at Durham University (UK) in April 2006, a product of which has just been cited (Carter and Philip). As most clearly articulated by Stuart Campbell, Peter Akkermans and Jean-Daniel Forest, and post-Conference by Frank Hole, the danger of seeing whole cultures (and cultural transitions) in pottery styles lies in reifying them into bounded entities, on the pattern of modern nation states. In contrast to this traditional 'top-down' approach, the conference consensus was rather to see development from the bottom-up, that is, to think about what people were actually doing and responding to. This approach posits Neolithic and post-Neolithic cultures as comprising a range of settlement sizes and adaptations that certainly have much in common in a particular time and space and which can be represented as 'interaction spheres'. However interaction is by no means bounded within interaction spheres, but rather techniques, social practices and beliefs can be adopted and adapted from other 'spheres' within and beyond what may be regarded as 'natural regions' (Hole 2006: 3). Within the Samarra and Halaf 'cultural ranges' or provinces, there exists "a growing amount of evidence for stylistic and technological diversity at both the site level and the regional level. While similarities indicate inter-relationships between communities, the differences point to autonomy and independence of local groups" (Akkermans *et al.* 2006: 153). That is the point: autonomy and independence without isolation (cf: Philip 2002).

In regard to the Ubaid, the early dates (around 5200 BC at Tell al-'Abr and Tell Kosak Shamali on the Syrian Upper Euphrates) now available from the north, that is, from beyond the alluvium proper, suggests that Ubaidisation as it took place across the whole northern arc did not rely upon a reflux of Ubaidians from the southern alluvium (Nissen 2001: 169). Indeed Jean-Daniel Forest (2006: 7) is of the opinion that while Halaf settlements were quite fluid and the population relatively mobile, Ubaid settlements and populations were not. On the alluvium there were relatively few good sites for agriculture, as opposed to many in the Halaf rain-fed range.

As Ubaid culture advanced in complexity it did so in communication with other settlements, notably of those characterised as Halaf, itself not a uniform culture. They contributed to and adopted Ubaidian characteristics in whole or in part, as suited their particular political economy. Indeed Jean-Daniel Forest (2006: 7) observes that "the newly-formed Northern Ubaid represents a series of particularisms (that is, features not to be found in the Ubaid proper) which bear witness to its Halafian origins, and prove we are dealing with a culture of its own".[42] Stein and Özbal (2007: 335) go farther, and argue in regard to Tepe Gawra, which they see as archetypal in northern Iraq and south-east Turkey: "People quickly took on markers of Ubaid identity in the public domain, especially in contexts relating to community affiliation and hierarchical social status. However, at the same time, the inhabitants of Gawra retained a distinctively Halaf personal identity, which they expressed primarily in the private or domestic domain".

This kind of push-pull synchrony is of course more difficult to conceptualize than established linear thinking. But it does seem to account much better for the evidence now coming from sites in Syria, Turkey, Western Iran and even the Southern Caucasus, with emulation/selective adoption obviously playing a defining role. The concept of *co-evolutionary interaction* gets beyond, though it incorporates, prior conceptions of exchange mechanisms, now seen to be much too thinly drawn. J-F. Forest (*op. cit.*) sees, for example, the mechanism of Halaf/Ubaid fusion as brought about by the intermarriage of the populations along the initial contact zone that included Samarra, Mandali and Sa'adiyeh. As Halaf is the 'painted pottery culture' *par excellence,* this interpretation is in conformity with the general observation that most 'Ubaid' sites have a high proportion of painted pottery in their early levels, which subsequently declines. However, "no trait other than pottery extends across the entire Ubaid domain" (Hole 2006: 2); not architecture, seals and sealings, or even subsistence activities. Nevertheless, "the fifth millennium saw the first really convincing evidence of the building of temples, a sign of emerging social complexity. By mid-fifth millennium there were well-established different secular and religious roles for individuals and settlements" (Hole 2006: 1). Significantly though, distant 'Ubaid-adopting' settlements such as Degirimentepe in Turkey, lack "the clear functional differentiation between the sacred and the residential of the southern Ubaid. (Özbal 2000: 12). Instead, nearly all the central court areas of the tripartite structures, although clearly domestic, yield ritual evidence as well..." (Stein and Özbal 2007: 336-7).

By the Late Ubaid/Early Uruk periods, the equilibrium of the broader 'exchange system' was increasingly upset by the growth of population and settlement in the

---

[42] Indeed the 'proto-Hassuna' also appears as a cluster of localized Neolithic cultures. "But at the same time, within part of that core area, namely in North Iraq, the change from an Hassunan way of life to an Halafian way of life was undertaken by different communities at different times, and essentially as a switch rather than through a gradual transition" (Watkins and Campbell 1987: 436). Sudden transitions amounting to 'switching' are precisely characteristic of self-organizing network formation. Significantly, at the other end, the process of Ubaid 'takeover' was gradual and certainly not one of 'switching'.

southern alluvium induced by its productive advantages (Algaze 2004: 16; 2007) and accompanying organizational changes.

"It thus was primarily southern Mesopotamia where quantitative changes [facilitated by climatic ones] were transformed into qualitative (and recognizable) ones. ... An increase in size, density and agglomeration of population seems to have catalysed conflicts and social problems" (Nissen 2001: 171), as settlements grew in size and number.

The necessity of keeping the exchange networks going in the face of increasingly marked socio-economic disparities along with the increased demands placed upon the system, led to the phenomenon referred to as the 'Uruk Expansion'. Central to this concept is the placing of 'Uruk' colonies in the most important resource area for imports to the alluvium, namely the 'far north', which were the mineral and timber-rich areas (Nissen 2001: 172). This, according to Nissen (*op.cit.*), was essentially a 'stabilizing' process (his term, p.173), although as Algaze (2001: 71) and Stein (2001: 302) have recognised, one undertaken not by Uruk-Warka alone but competitively by emergent urban centres in the south. Perhaps however, given the distances involved and the possible economies of scale, it was done cooperatively, in everyone's best interests. The work done on sourcing the large quantities of bitumen found at Hacinebi (Stein 2001: 289) showed that no single southern city controlled the trade or the colonies and indeed that the colonies were of different types (cf. p. 129 below). Indeed Rothman (2002: 58) "argue(s) that the Uruk expansion represents an increase in economic exchange, which benefited leaders in the North and South, as well as groups of entrepreneurs and craftsmen in both areas. That is to say, this process was not one of dominance or colonialism."

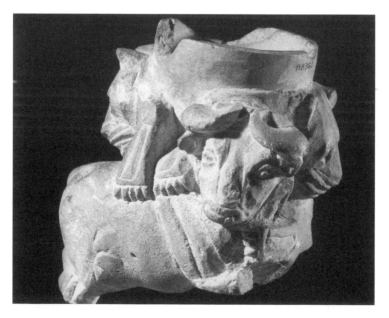

*Figure 4.33: A stone cult vessel of the Late Uruk Period showing two lionesses attacking a bull (British Museum).*

Timothy Potts (1994: 181–2) discussing the sources for and utilisation of minerals in Sumer at this time, observes that "Already in the late prehistoric period a range of more distant materials was also exploited, especially at Uruk IV-III where, in addition to the usual light stones, there is granite, basalt, obsidian, bituminous limestone, slate/schist, variously coloured marbles, green calcite ('aragonite') and 'serpentine'. It is tempting to associate this variety of materials with the widespread network of Late Uruk colonies in Syria and Iran." So-called 'serpentine' "which was commonly used for Late Uruk cylinder seals virtually disappears in Uruk III after the collapse of the Euphrates settlements" (*ibid.*). However, Henry Wright (2001) shows that many useful minerals were available much closer to home. Figure 4.33 shows a stone cult vessel of the Late Uruk period (British Museum) with two lionesses attacking a bull.

Perhaps surprisingly, there are a number of good historical analogies for some aspects of the 'Uruk' expansion. One comes from the age of the English Merchant Venturers, as related by Carus-Wilson (1967: xvii): "It was a very usual practice in the Middle Ages for merchants from one city, or a group of cities, doing business in some foreign mart, to form a 'fellowship' or 'hanse' to further their common interests. Thus associated, they could jointly negotiate concessions which would ensure them favourable conditions for trade, such as freedom from vexatious restrictions, permission to set up an authority of their own to order their affairs and settle disputes among themselves, and power to exclude from the trade any of their fellow townsmen who were not of their fellowship."

## Hacinebi

Located in what was open oak forest, Hacinebi is a 3.3 ha Late Chalcolithic settlement overlooking the Euphrates, about 30 km north of Carchemish and the border with modern Syria (Bigelow 2000: 84). There are three phases: Pre-contact phase A (*c.* 4,100–3,800 BC), Late Pre-contact phase B1 (*c.*3,800–3,700 BC) and the Contact phase, B2, *c.*3,700 to 3,300 BC, when a relatively small colony of Mesopotamians lived separate lives as part of a sophisticated local settlement during this Middle Uruk period. This suggests to Schwartz *et al.* (2000: 82) that "control over trading colonies in Anatolia was not held by Mesopotamian city-states," and that "certain areas of Mesopotamia were trading different goods with the Anatolians." Perhaps this provides an insight to the reality underlying Jacobsen's (1957) putative 'Kengir League' of cities on the alluvium, an idea supported by the 'city sealings' (Matthews 1993, Maisels 1999), that indicate cooperation between cities in the matter of goods transfers.

In the period terminating the Uruk, namely the Jemdet Nasr, the existence of an association of Sumerian cities is indicated by archaeological finds in the city of Jemdet Nasr. In a huge building measuring 92 m by 48 m, which was either a palace or a storehouse (or both), an archive of 240 clay tablets bearing very early writing (Eanna III) was found. Thirteen tablets bore a seal impression that conjoins the major cities of Ur, Larsa, Nippur, Uruk, Kish, Zabalam and Urum, amongst others (Matthews 1992: 199–200; Matthews 1993 and pers. comm.). Such collective sealings are also known from Ur. Moorey (1976: 105) suggests that Jemdet Nasr, with its central position, functioned as a kind of clearing house. Perhaps a large part of the necessity for such a clearing process

| Date B.C. | | Sumer | Iran | Syria | Upper Euphrates | Tigris | Southern Mesopotamia |
|---|---|---|---|---|---|---|---|
| 3000 | LC 5 / Late | IVA Eanna IVB V; Nippur XV–XVII | Godin V; Early 17 Susa Acropole | Habuba Kabira Jebel Aruda; Sheikh Hassan 4; Brak TW 12 | Hassek Höyük; Arslantepe VIA | Mohammad Arab Late Uruk; Nineveh (Gut) Spâturuk Ninevite 4; L: 31–20 | Late Uruk |
| 3400 | LC 4 | Eanna VI; Abu Salabikh *Uruk Mound*; Eanna VII; hiatus?; Nippur XVIII | Late 18 Susa; Early 18 Sharafabad | Qraya; Sheikh Hassan 5–7; Brak TW 13; Leilan IV | Arslantepe VII; Hacınebi B2 | Norduruk B; L: 37–31 | Late Middle Uruk |
| 3600 | LC 3 | Eanna IX–VIII; Nippur XX–XIX; Eanna XI–X | Susa 19–22 | Sheikh Hassan 8–10/13; Brak TW 14–17; Leilan V | Hacınebi B1 | Tepe Gawra VIII; Norduruk A; L: 45–37; Tepe Gawra IX–X | Early Middle Uruk |
| 3800 | Late | | Susa Acropolis 23–27; hiatus?; Geoy Tepe M | Hammam et Turkman VB; Brak TW 18–19 | Hacınebi A | Tepe Gawra XI/XA; L: 59–45 | |
| 4000 | LC 2 / Early | Eanna XII | | | | | Early Uruk |
| 4200 | LC 1 | Eanna XVI–XIV | | Hammam et Turkman VA; Hammam et Turkman IVD | Arslantepe VIII | Tepe Gawra XIA/B; Gawra A; hiatus?; Tepe Gawra XII; L: 60 | |
| | Term. Ubaid | | | Leilan late VIb | | XIIA–XIII | Ubaid transitional Ubaid 4? |

*Figure 4.34: Chronology for the Late Chalcolithic/Uruk Period (Table 1.1 from Rothman 2001: 7). LC stands for 'Late Chalcolithic' (1–5) chosen to provide a more neutral and more widely applicable framework than the 'southern' one traditionally used (far right column).*

was the complexities of trade 'off the alluvium', with various cities sending and receiving different types and quantities of goods both directly and via third and fourth parties. Such a network would be complementary to one that, perhaps, circulated goods for cultic and other purposes, such as alliances cemented by marriage. By this time however, southern cities were re-orienting their trade to the east (cf: T.F. Potts 1994).

From later literary material, Jacobsen (as already mentioned) inferred the existence of a political league or confederacy with a central assembly at Nippur to which the rulers of the various cities went to decide matters of common interest, and later to adopt or confirm a hegemon. However, collaborative relations between certain cities based simply upon mutually advantageous 'out of alluvium' trading interests on the one hand and perhaps shared cultic interests on the other, require no higher order political structures, only cooperation facilitated by good record-keeping.

*Figure 4.35: An alabaster 'eye idol' with small 'child' eye figure below, from Tell Brak, north-eastern Syria, about 3500–3300 BC (British Museum).*

## Uruk Colonies

The so-called 'colonies' were, as already observed, of markedly different types, and spanned a period of over 600 years in the fourth millennium, from about 3700 BC until around 3100 BC (Rothman 2001: 6; Stein 2001: 301) Those types are, minimally: 1) indigenous urban settlements prior to the 'expansion': Arslantepe, Hacinebi, Tell Brak, Gawra; 2) small forts/trading outposts such as Hassek Höyük; 3) large fortified settlements of southerners: Habuba Kabira South, Jebel Aruda and Sheikh Hassan. Note the longevity of Tepe Gawra on the Tigris, of Arslantepe on the Upper Euphrates and Tell Brak in Syria, site of the famous Eye Temples excavated by Max Mallowan in 1947, and by others subsequently. Those are settlements that precede and outlive the Uruk expansion. Butterlin (2009a) refers to Gawra as one of the centres of a veritable proto-urban archipelago that stretch out along the foothills of the Zagros Mountains in the east, to the foot of the Taurus in the west.

One type of 'colony' was the small fort/trading outpost like Hassek Höyük, Tiladir Tepe and Şadi Tepe (cf: early modern European trading 'factories' in the Orient; Keay 1991). Godin VI in the Kangavar Valley of highland Iran, on the most important east-west route through the Zagros Mountains, seems to be most like Arslantepe, where

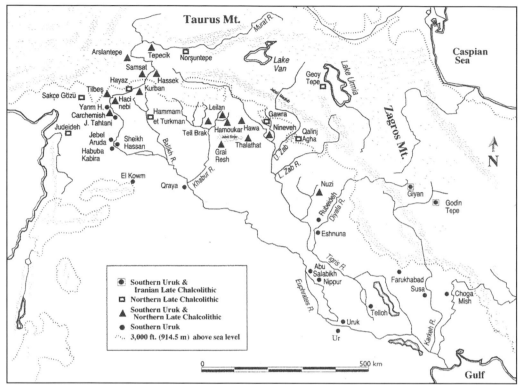

*Figure 4.36: Sites of the Late Chalcolithic/Uruk period are shown on the map (from Rothman 2001: 6).*

indigenous complexity was augmented by contact with lowland consumers, but without the resident 'Urukian' population (Gopnik and Rothman eds., 2009). The famous walled oval compound of 560 m², placed on what would have been the highest part of the mound, is best explained as the 'headquarters' of a locally emergent elite at this time (Rothman pers. comm.). Sites of the Late Chalcolithic/Uruk period are shown on the map from Rothman (2001: 6 (Figure 4.36)).

Another type, characteristic of the Late Uruk period, were the large fortified settlements like Habuba Kabira, Sheikh Hassan and Jebel Aruda, which contained mainly southern immigrants and employed southern town-planning. It seems that their presence evoked enmity or envy, for as Kohlmeyer (1996: 91) states, though at first unfortified, Habuba Kabira was later surrounded by a city wall enclosing about 10 hectares: "Parts of this three metre thick wall were uncovered to the north and to the west", as shown in Figure 4.37(1) (from Kohlmeyer 1996: 90). "Eight towers or bastions protected the northern front, twenty-nine are still preserved on the western front, as well as two gates. They have large broad rooms as gate chambers. An outside wall served as the first obstacle. At the south gate a third, niche wall was added which surrounded the southern part of the city and obviously belonged to the most recent period." Walls, gates and nucleated town layout are clearly visible from her

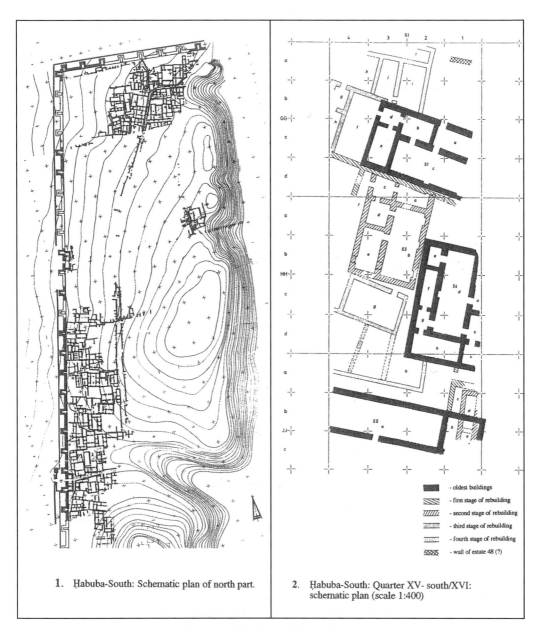

1.  Ḥabuba-South: Schematic plan of north part.

2.  Ḥabuba-South: Quarter XV- south/XVI: schematic plan (scale 1:400)

- oldest buildings
- first stage of rebuilding
- second stage of rebuilding
- third stage of rebuilding
- fourth stage of rebuilding
- wall of estate 48 (?)

*Figure 4.37(1) (left): Habuba Kabira*
*Figure 4.37(2) (right): Some details of the domestic architecture at Habuba Kabira*

*Figure 4.38: The classic tripartite flanked-hall household and its variations (from Kohlmeyer 1996: 101).*

plan showing the northern part of the town. Across the river the much smaller site of Sheikh Hassan has similar fortifications. Figure 4.37(2) shows some details of the domestic architecture.

We are also indebted to Kohlmeyer (1996: 92) for laying out in such rigorous detail (including the metrics) all the variations upon the classic Mittelsaalhaus, i.e. the fully-flanked main-room house type, with and without transverse extension on the short wall (back). Figure 4.38 (from Kohlmeyer 1996: 101) illustrates the classic tripartite flanked-hall household and shows just some of the range of variation upon it, including smaller and presumably poorer households whose house lacked the central hall (*Mittelsaal*). Also, see the discussion of functionality in Butterlin (2009b).

Although the Habuba Kabira excavations were rescue archaeology in the Tabqa Dam area, no other site, north or south, provides us with such an extensive view of the range of domestic architecture of the Uruk period. We are further indebted to Kohlmeyer for the nomenclature she has developed for classifying and analysing those house types. Henceforward all serious students of Uruk (also Ubaid and Samarran) architecture will be obliged to use it (cf: Maisels 1984: 1987: 349–352; 1990: 160–168).

Yet another type of settlement involved a group of southerners living and working within long established and flourishing indigenous urban centres at distances of over 1000 km from Warka (Uruk) or from Susa in south-west Iran. Such were Arslantepe and Hacinebi Tepe in Turkey or, rather less distant, Tell Brak in Syria. The southerners were present at Arslantepe and Hacinebi Tepe because the local elites – already linked by ideological elements and economic exchanges with each other (Schwartz *et al.*: 2000: 82) – wanted the networks to flourish in order to develop their own power (Stein 2001: 279). This may also be the case at Brak (Oates 2002: 121), which, by 3,900 BC was a site exceeding 50 ha.

Uruk networks thus appear to be successors to the Ubaidian, Halafian and earlier ones, which were, as has been already argued, "open systems ... based on equal partnership" (Maisels 1999: 143, Nissen 2001: 173). However, only part of the Uruk system was based on equal partnership, as at Arslantepe and Hacinebi. The other two categories, namely the 'forts' and the *coloniae* on virgin soil, such as Habuba Kabira and Jebel Aruda, probably dominated and exploited the surrounding countryside.

*Figure 4.39: Late Uruk stone vase, probably cultic, 1.2 m high, showing cattle and sheep (British Museum).*

Perhaps too, many or parts of the so-called colonies comprised displaced persons, refugees from emergent servitude or land-hungry peasants (Schwartz 2001: 260). As yet the archaeology is insufficient to support any particular model. What is fairly certain is that southerners founded some wholly new settlements, were merely present as minorities at other pre-existing settlements and that a single 'trade and dominion' explanation is much too simple. Henry Wright (2001: 127) has said explicitly what several of us think, namely that "At any time, the Uruk world probably contained scores, if not hundreds of discrete polities, of different scales [and longevity] and organized in different ways"; for Gil Stein (2001: 302) "The locational data are completely consistent with the idea of multiple competing urbanized polities in a pattern analogous to the Early Dynastic social landscape".

Habuba Kabira and 8 km to its north, Jebel Aruda, were founded in the Late Uruk as completely new settlements on virgin soil. Though a large settlement, Habuba Kabira appears to have been a short-lived single period site lasting two centuries at the most. Given that their material culture was completely southern, this must indicate a movement of people south to north in significant numbers (Schwartz 2001: 255). By contrast, the relatively small enclaves in existing indigenous centres like Arslantepe are more likely to have been established by enterprising individuals (if not actually traders), refugees or exiles. In regard to Jebel Aruda, the excavator, G. van Driel (2002: 191) "consider(s) the most reasonable explanation for the situation of the settlement was its function as a subsidiary service centre to a major sanctuary on the summit of Jebel Aruda. The settlement is thus primarily a sign of the depth of the Late Uruk implantation in the area and is unlikely to have fulfilled any specific role in regional administration or long distance trade networks". This is a salutary warning against drawing 'obvious' (=facile) conclusions about the functions of a settlement.

Schwartz (2001: 259), following Wilkinson, observes that both clusters of Uruk settlements in the Syrian Euphrates were most likely far enough north to be within the zone of rainfed ('dry' i.e. unirrigated) farming. Accordingly those Uruk settlements would have been able to support themselves in foodstuffs, and would not have had to rely upon imports either from north or south for subsistence. Indeed, Schwartz (2001: 260) argues that the availability of good farmland itself explains the existence of the Habuba enclave. The matter of self-sufficiency is undoubted at Hacinebi farther north in the piedmont zone of the Syro-Anatolian borderlands (Bigelow 2000: 89). It was well watered with a flourishing agriculture and had exchange relations with similar centres in the Syro-Anatolian piedmont. As already noted, Hacinebi in Phase B2 contained a small Uruk enclave with full southern characteristics and population. It maintained itself over a period of three to four hundred years, that is, from about 3700 BC to perhaps as late as 3300 BC (Stein 2001: 299). It acquired, refined and despatched copper south, and was "economically autonomous in the sense that it produced its own crops, pastoral products, and crafts" (*ibid.*). As suggested above, its population was most likely also autonomous in that they were not under the control of the homeland but were in direct communication with it. The inhabitants of Hacinebi and the southerners lived parallel and peaceful lives (Stein 2001: 295). "This autonomy can be seen in the encapsulated nature of craft production, subsistence, and exchange-related administrative activities"(*ibid.*). It is also apparent in food preferences and other lifestyle attributes, reinforcing the impression that actual Mesopotamians lived in Hacinebi (Stein 2001: 293).

At any event Gil Stein's excavations at Hacinebi, taken with the evidence from Sheik Hassan and Tell Brak means that "we can no longer view the Uruk Expansion as a short-lived phenomenon. Instead the Uruk Expansion must be seen as an interregional trading relationship that lasted from the Middle Uruk almost to the end of the Late Uruk period – a time span possibly as long as 500 years" (Stein 2002: 152).

Whatever the reasons for the 'Uruk expansion' and its collapse or transformation, clearly in the Late Chalcolithic we are dealing with qualitatively different types of network from those that existed in the Neolithic and Early Chalcolithic. The Halaf network was established between autonomous, essentially egalitarian villages and served as a conduit for *circulation* rather than exchange. By this I mean that it served to transmit information about farming/herding and other subsistence matters such as zones of abundance or scarcity, possible marriage partners, events elsewhere in the sub-regions ('news') and information about others on the periphery of the network. Here the actual exchange of goods, whether that be obsidian, fine pottery or sub-regional specialities, was a means to an end, namely communication, rather than the network's prime rationale. The conductors of that circulation would primarily have been the mobile, pastoral section of the Halaf population, who used the famous seals and tokens to register their exchanges and credit with their home village (and perhaps others), as convincingly argued by Akkermans and Duistermaat (1997, 2004 and pers. comm. Akkermans 2005), making the mobile/settled exchanges the nearest thing to Halaf 'trade'.

By contrast, the Uruk and later networks existed primarily to service urban centres, or more specifically their elites, supplying both luxury items and what in their political economy was regarded as essential goods, for instance building and decorating materials (such as lapis lazuli) for temples. The culture established by the world's first cities and states continued into the period of territorial states, dominating the second millennium and beyond. So powerful was this first impulse however, that we still inhabit its cultural legacy.

> "The most remarkable innovation in Mesopotamian civilization is urbanism. The idea of the city as a heterogeneous, complex, messy, constantly changing but ultimately viable concept for human society was a Mesopotamian invention" (Leick 2001: xvii).

*Figure 4.40: Statue of Kurlil, official in the city of Uruk, c.2500 BC, in attitude of prayer to Damkina (Ninhursag) at Tell al'Ubaid (British Museum).*

# CHAPTER 5

# Egypt

Egypt was the world's first territorial state and on formation it was a large one, encompassing most of the territory it would ever have: from the First Cataract at Aswan to the Mediterranean, a distance of 1,360 km. Entirely dependent on river flooding for agriculture, the plain averages only 10 km wide, but can reach 50 km. The area of the Nile Valley with the Delta is a mere 37,540 km², which is more than Belgium but less than the Netherlands (see Figure 5.1).

There are two remarkable features of Egypt's emergence, and they are not pyramids and mummies. The first is that "the Nile valley did not possess a long tradition of sedentary village life prior to the period of state formation" (Wengrow 2006: 77); and the other is the speed of pristine state formation in under two millennia of Neolithisation (5th to end of the 4th), with kingship emerging as early as the end of the Naqada I period, around 3600 BC (T.A.H.Wilkinson 2002: 237). Such rapidity is unparalleled elsewhere and this compressed development supports three propositions, one economic, the other two political: (1) that the key domesticates of the Neolithic were introduced ready-made from the Levant, and (2) that if unequal exchange and domination can take place it will certainly do so, and that (3) hierarchy will consolidate itself in the form of a state given the right conditions.

This is apparent even during the earliest Neolithic in Egypt, the Badarian of the fifth millennium.

> "The Badari district lies on the east bank of the Nile about 30 km south of Assyut. Badarian settlements and graves extend over a distance of 33 km southward in the Mostagedda and Matmar region. ... The survey by Brunton and Caton-Thompson [between 1922 and 1931] revealed 41 cemeteries and 40 habitation sites in the low desert overlooking the floodplain under the cliffs of the high desert limestone plateau. One site, Hemamieh, has a two metre sequence from the earliest confirmed Predynastic in Middle/Upper Egypt to the late Predynastic"(Hassan 1988: 153).

Excavation by Sami Gabra at the Badarian site of Deir Tasa revealed a settlement of around 5000 m², but the cultural deposits were very uneven in depth, ranging from only a few centimetres to a few tens of centimetres, suggesting that at no time was the whole area occupied simultaneously. Rather, repeat usage of certain preferred locations over the generations is indicated. The habitations were lightly made huts or windbreaks, associated with hearths. Large, well-shaped granary pits up to 3 m deep and 2.7 m in diameter were present, probably for holding barley and emmer, as found in the graves at Matmar and Mostagedda. Large sunken ceramic pots were

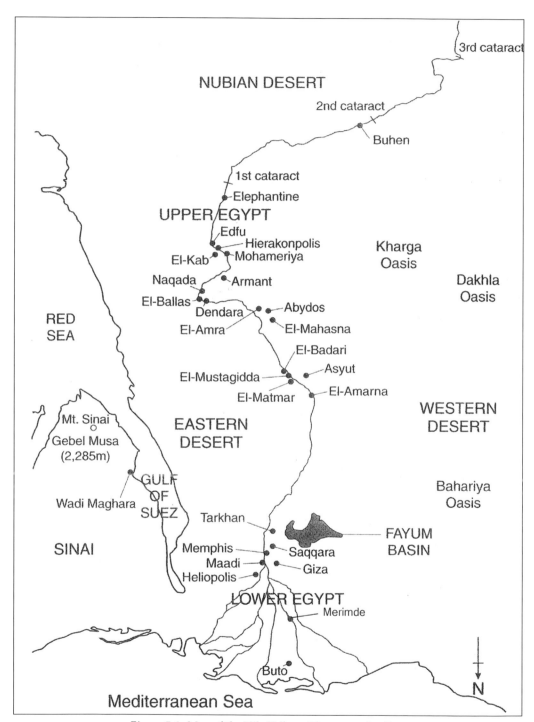

*Figure 5.1: Map of the Nile Valley with some early sites.*

also used to store grain. Pottery is the distinctive black-topped red ware, the most distinctive being 'rippled' ware, made by pulling either a catfish spine or a comb across the unfired clay, then, with wet hands smoothing off the marks and firing the pot. Hendrickx *et al.* (2002: 289) have suggested that "the earliest Meidum bowls, the small carinated jars, the small storage jar, and possibly early Maidum bowls, all served for the processing and storage of milk during the Early Dynastic period"; and that, at least in Upper Egypt, milk was available from the Badarian period onwards (*ibid.*: 289). Given its very short life as fresh milk, they argue that from the beginning, milk was likely to have been consumed in the fermented acidified form. Vessels with relatively closed shapes to restrict oxygen exposure are optimal for the lactic acid bacteria which thrive best in a micro-aerobic environment (*ibid.*: 290)[43]. Much use, utilitarian and decorative, was made of ivory and bone, but the Badarians also used copper, probably from Sinai, for small tools and personal ornaments. A very well-made hollow base projectile point is an artefact shared with the Fayum and Lower Egypt.

*Figure 5.2: Figure of a woman carved in hippo ivory with inlaid eyes of lapis lazuli, from Badari (British Museum).*

As soon as even minor surpluses became available, ranking emerged, as Wendy Anderson (1992) has established from a study of 262 burials in the seven cemeteries at El Badari in Upper Egypt. Having first looked to see whether differential grave goods were a function of age and/or sex criteria, she found statistically that there was no association. She did however find that "all may be interpreted as a manifestation of the unequal distribution of material wealth amongst the grave occupants and thus an indication of differential access to resources" (*ibid.*: 61). This is with regard to settled communities. It does not seem to be true of the proto-Badari or Badari-related cattle pastoralists of Gebel Ramlah in the South Western Desert, despite the fact that the human burials were accompanied by valuable imported objects such as turquoise (from Sinai), shells and mica (Red Sea coast) and ivory (from Equatorial regions), suggestive of a prosperous community with abundant jewellery (Kobusiewicz *et al.* 2004: 577).

---

[43] Similarly beer fermentation requires restricted, or better total absence of oxygen in the mash vats (*ibid.*: 292). Egyptian beer was made from bread, dates and water (see also Valdez 2006).

*Figure 5.3: Tulip beakers with flared rim and incised exterior and interior decoration, from Gebel Ramlah, Badarian period.*

Group size and mobility obviously play a role; however, real wealth differences, if such there were, would exist in the number of cattle owned by individuals or more likely by family groups, as amongst contemporary Nilotic cattle keepers. Thus any distinctions in wealth would occur between, rather than within, family groups. The graves with multiple burials in the Gebel Ramlah graveyard are suggestive of family plots (Kobusiewicz *et al.* 2004: 572) and indeed of equality (*ibid.*: 571), for "there is an overall lack of skeletal pathology. The dentitions of all adults also exhibit good oral health; only minor attrition (wear) and enamel hypoplasia (an indicator of childhood stress) are evident".

However, in regard to *settled* Badarians, Hoffman (1982: 146) came to a similar conclusion as Wendy Anderson. From his work leading the Hierakonpolis Project, he concluded that "what is surprising is the earliness of the processes of social economic differentiation. Already by Early Predynastic times, there were large 'special' tombs which were richly furnished. Whatever we call the individuals who once occupied these tombs, it is clear that a good deal of time, care and economic surplus was being lavished on them (or at least their tombs)".

One from several centuries later is Tomb 23, recently discovered by Barbara Adams (2002) in Locality 6 at Hierakonpolis. Dating to Naqada IIAB (3600–3500 BC) at *c.*5 m x 3.10 m and 1.20 m deep, it is larger than any other tomb of its period. Not only is it anomalously large, but it "is set in the earliest funerary complex yet discovered. … The entire enclosure will be at least 9 m wide and probably 18 or 20 m long, forming a rectangle around Tomb 23" (*ibid.*: 25). Special objects are associated with Tomb 23: "The first, large greywacke cosmetic palette with a bird-head decoration found in the cemetery, fine bifacial flint arrowheads, calcite and limestone scorpion amulets, part of a modelled pottery cow bed and very fine black topped red, intact pottery vessels" (*ibid.*). And to cap it all, at the end of the 2000 season, parts of a limestone, life-size human sculpture that seemingly is seated on a throne were recovered (Adams 2002: 27).

Accordingly, in regard to Egyptian conditions, I contend that the state did not arise in order to serve the needs of society, but was the inevitable outcome of a trajectory of privilege institutionalization: from ranking (Badarian) through elite stratification (Amratian/Naqada I) to proto-state formation (Gerzean/Naqada II), thereby serving a minority at the expense of the majority. By Naqada II times, for example, not only was there fine pinkware pottery with scenic (later, IIc) and geometrical designs painted on them (earlier IIb), but additionally the elite had very fine, very labour intensive stoneware vessels made for themselves, using the hardest rocks, such as basalt, gneiss and diorite. "Inherited status was clearly a feature of Predynastic society in the mid-Naqada II period, even in a place like Matmar, comparatively remote from the centres of developing political and economic power" (Wilkinson 2002: 240).

In Naqada II labour-intensive objects in gold, silver and lapis lazuli proliferated, as did copper objects in the form of adzes and axes, bracelets and rings. In evolutionary

| Upper Egypt and Post Unification | Date | Lower Egypt |
|---|---|---|
| Badarian | 5000–3900 BC | FayumA<br>Merimda<br>El Omari |
| Amratian (or Naqada I) | 3900–3600 BC | Maadi/Buto I-IIA |
| Gerzean (or Naqada II) | 3600–3300 BC | Buto IIB |
| Naqada IIIA | 3300–3150 BC | Buto III |
| Dynasty 0 (Naqada IIIB (Scorpion, Ka, Narmer)) | 3150–3050 BC | Buto IV |
| 1st Dynasty (Aha – Qa'a) | 3050–2890 BC | Buto V |
| 2nd Dynasty (Hetepsekhemwy- Khasekhemwy) | 2890–2686 BC | |
| Old Kingdom (3rd-8th Dynasties) | 2686–2160 BC | |
| First Intermediate Period | 2160–2055 BC | |
| Middle Kingdom | 2055–1650 BC | |

*Figure 5.4: Outline Chronology of Egypt from Neolithic to the Middle Kingdom, using an Upper (Southern) Egyptian framework, with northern correspondences.*

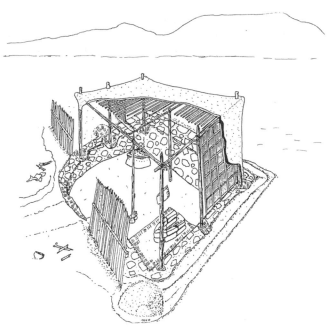

*Figure 5.5: Reconstruction of an Early Predynastic (Amratian) House at Locality 29, Hierakonpolis (from Hoffman 1982: 138). Poles are of Tamarix or Acacia and the matting from Halfa grass (Desmostachya).*

terms, by creating the state (not fully-formed until Naqada III) a small minority is able to permanently transform its own conditions of life and reproductive success.

## The Neolithic

Domesticated goat was present on the Red Sea coast of Egypt around 5,800 cal. BC (Close 2002). However the suite of standard domesticates, emmer wheat and barley, sheep and goat arrived in the Fayum Depression around 5,200 cal. BC (Shirai 2005: 12). This was made possible by the commencement of a period in which rainfall isohyets deflected at least 20 km southwards. An overland transfer of domesticates across Sinai was now viable (Smith 1996: 33).

As already indicated, the prehistoric cultures of Egypt are the Badarian, Amratian and Gerzean in the Nile Valley (Upper and Middle Egypt). Named from the type-site of El-Gerza, only 5 km (3 miles) north of the Meidum pyramid and near the Fayum, the Gerzean extended all the way south into Nubia. The mechanisms of this spread are discussed below. The Buto-Maadi culture of the Delta extended to Sedmet, about 100 km south of Cairo (Lower Egypt). Importantly, Buto-Maadi people had connections with the Levant, which went well beyond trade, with Palestinian groups settled at both Buto and Maadi.

Although in the Fayum there is no evidence for dependence upon agriculture until historic times, there certainly is at **Merimda (Beni Salama)**, (possibly) a 20 hectare site on the south-western edge of the Delta, around 60 km north-west of Cairo. The locality of Merimda was occupied for much of the fifth millennium, with the bones of cattle, pig and goat dating to the earliest levels, around 5000 BC, which is of course at least as early as the earliest Badarian farther south. The remains of donkey were also found. As in the Fayum, to which the pottery and lithics are similar, the settlement early in the millennium consisted of insubstantial, pole-framed oval huts and windbreaks, with the hut entrances facing away from the prevailing westerly or north-westerly wind. Hearths were of various types: simple round or oval fire-pits; hearths hollowed out in the centre to receive a cooking pot; or fire trays above which a cooking pot rested on firedogs or andirons of conical mud (see Figure 5.5).

Towards the end of the millennium, perhaps around 4300 BC, houses at Merimda were of semi-subterranean type. The living floor was a plastered mud oval 1.5–3.2 metres in diameter. Walls were made of layers of Nile mud or of rough blocks of mud containing straw as binder. The structure was roofed with reeds or rushes supported on posts. The houses were ranged in ragged rows, with workspaces, on either side of winding alleys. Storage was in pottery jars and in bins sunk into the ground. The cordiform, flat-topped *pithoi*, about 1 m deep and 60 cm in diameter had a capacity of about 60 kilograms of grain, while the bins, which were hemispherical in shape and mud-lined, held fruit and emmer wheat. Also embedded in the floor or placed against a wall, was a pottery jar for water.

Subsistence was provided by wheat and barley, with sheep/goat, cattle and pig. Hawass *et al.* (1987: 74) state that this subsistence regime, common to the Predynastic of Upper Egypt at Naqada and Hierankopolis, relied little on game, with the exception of aquatic resources and birds. However, the excavations of Hawass *et al.* (1987: 35), though limited, produced fragmentary (tooth) remains of hippopotamus, and Hassan (1988: 148) observes that "the exploitation of hippo must not be under-emphasised as a food resource", until of course, like the otter and other animals, they were totally wiped out in Egypt.

If we assume that late in Merimda's existence the full area of the locale, 180,000 m² was occupied simultaneously, then the population could have been 1,000 to 2,000 persons, though this does seem improbable. A much better suggestion comes from David Wengrow (2006: 83). Noting the generally 'light and ephemeral' nature of the housing and that "the largest concentrations of human activity are defined by lateral spreading of cultural material along a horizontal axis, rather than the vertical tell-urbanisation of Mesopotamian towns", he asks whether "in attaching growing numbers of people to particular places, and in reproducing those attachments over generations, the urbanisation of the dead may have been more important than the urbanisation of the living, the density of social memory more vital than the massing of permanent dwellings." Thus the layout of early Egyptian settlements and the materials used in their construction might indicate a more fluid habitation, with a significant proportion of the inhabitants absent or 'on the move' at any one time, but drawn back by "the density of social memory", kinship and, of course, certain property rights.

A cluster of mid-fifth millennium sites lying on the east bank of the Nile in the Helwan area (just south of Cairo) is named **El Omari**. They cover about 750 m x 500 m in an open area just south of the entrance to the Wadi Hof (Debono and Mortensen

1990: 13). Wadi Hof and Wadi Garawi to the south allow access to the Red Sea and Sinai. Permanent architecture is lacking, the only clay structures being small walls like windbreaks around hearths (*ibid*.: 22) and this again is similar to the Fayum and the early phases of Merimda. Only post holes remain, so light wattle-and-daub type houses are the most likely. The site is dotted with storage pits, which, when empty, were filled up with rubbish. Debono and Mortensen (*ibid*.: 79) state that "all objects of the earliest phases are those of a simple economy based mainly on fishing and perhaps also hunting". El Omari is ceramic, pottery being mainly red or black with little decoration. Local clay was used in the early phase to produce predominantly open and half-closed shapes, "which were used for the storage of objects and various food items, as well as for eating. Cooking may have been possible with the vessels having knob handles" (*ibid*.).

From the beginning of the settlement some cereals were grown, to make bread as well as porridge. Pieces of carbonised bread have been found, but the grains were crushed rather than ground. Carbonised grains were found in pits from all phases (*ibid*.: 80). Cereal grains were always found mixed, however, with emmer predominating. The diet of the Omaris was mainly based on fish, domesticated pork, cereals and vegetables (*ibid*.) The small number of sickles found suggest that cereals were just pulled out of soft, moist ground, and this indicates that the area growing cereals was not large, and in turn that cereals were not very important in the diet. The principal food source seems to have been fish. Other possible foods were hippopotamus and tortoise.

El Omari represents a local development by the indigenous Palaeolithic population in some degree of contact with Levantine populations. It would seem that El Omari was occupied for about 200 years, from *c*.4,600 to 4,400 BC (*ibid*.: 81) and that in terms of development, in which it was effectively autonomous, it was much closer to the Fayum Neolithic than the relatively advanced culture of Maadi near the apex of the Delta.

## Maadi

Maadi is a linear settlement located on a terrace, between the mouths of the Wadi Digla and the Wadi el Tih, overlooking the floodplain. It is oriented east-west, and extends over 1.5 km, but is only 150–200 m wide, resulting in a site of *c*.18 ha. House types are insubstantial light huts, wind-breaks and/or fences, with hearths and storage pits of various sizes and shapes (Hartung 2003: 8). Subsistence was a mix of agriculture, the breeding of goat, sheep, pig and cattle, combined with fishing (Hartung 2004: 338). Caneva *et al.* (1987: 106; 1989: 288–9) report a wide range of cereals from about 380 m², an area said to be undisturbed. Finds include einkorn (*Triticum monoccocum*), emmer (*Triticum dicoccum*), hexaploid or bread wheat (*Triticum aestivum*), spelt (*Triticum spelta*) and cultivated barley (*Hordeum vulgare*), as well as peas and lentils. Also recovered were large quantities of animal bone, with more than 15,000 identified so far, and also horn, hair and skin. Those remains come overwhelmingly from domesticated sheep and goats, cattle, pigs, donkeys and canines. The bones of wild animals are rare (Caneva *et al.* 1987: 107), but fish, turtle and bird remains were not. Remains of donkey found at Maadi are the earliest for domesticated donkey found anywhere in

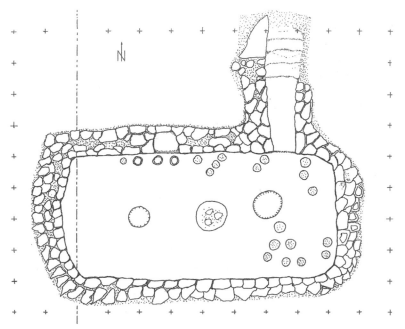

*Figure 5.6: A subterranean stone-built structure at Maadi-West, described as a 'magazine' (Badawi 2003: 3).*

Africa (Caneva *et al.* 1989: 289). At Maadi-West Badawi (2003: 7) found circular pits with depths ranging between 0.50 and 0.90 m used as repositories. Those lined with clay were most probably used to store grain, others to hold vessels, whose types are known from the rest of the Maadi site.

Despite earlier assumptions, it is highly likely that the six anomalously stonebuilt subterranean structures (four in the eastern and two in the western part of the site) recently discovered at Maadi by the German Institute of Archaeology, Cairo, belong to persons originating from the Chalcolithic Beersheba (or Beersheva) Culture of southern Palestine (Hartung 2003: 9).

In an apparent paradox, Hartung (2004: 338) suggests that "in the recent trenches there was no indication that trade played such an important role as is often stated. Imported objects or raw material from Upper Egypt as well as Palestine occurred very rarely." Derivation and even continued connection does not of itself necessitate or imply trade – the systematic exchange of goods – which must be demonstrated by other means. The odd find does not indicate trade.

Watrin (2000: 1753) suggests that **Buto**, deep in the Delta, whose remains cover about 1 km², is several centuries older than Maadi and that Buto I is contemporary with the Ghassulian Chalcolithic culture of the southern Levant (see Maisels 1999: 119–122 for the Ghassulian).[44] Buto IA would then be contemporary with the Late Badarian or Naqada

---

[44] Grigson (2001: 6) provides a concise summary: "The Beersheva and Ghassoulian cultures seem to be roughly contemporary and are indeed considered to be facets of the same broad cultural Late Chalcolithic phase. Churns

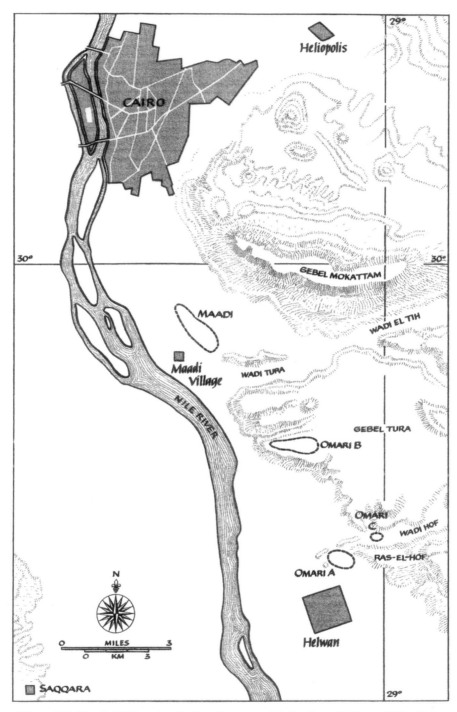

*Figure 5.7: Maadi, El Omari and other sites around Cairo (from Hoffman 1979: 193).*

IA. However, the subterranean structures found at Maadi between 1999 and 2002 affect this picture. Hartung (2004: 353) concludes that "the rural settlement of Maadi seems to have existed for approximately 300–350 years, and corresponded to parts of the Late Chalcolithic and EB Ia in terms of southern Levantine chronology" (see Figure 5.7).

The style, mineral temper and turned fabric of pottery found at Buto – painted v-shaped bowls of different sizes, bowls with thumb-indented rims, a fragment of a churn, *pithoi*, and holemouth jars, some with plain ledge handles and loop handles – are clearly Palestinian products and indicate a residential Palestinian population at Buto (Watrin 2000: 1752). According to Watrin (*ibid.*: 1755) this Palestinian population disappears in the second half of Buto IA. Somewhat later, dating to E(early)B(ronze)1, the great quantities of Levantine lithic tools found at Maadi indicate the presence of resident Palestinian craftsmen, most probably in connection with the copper industry. Three

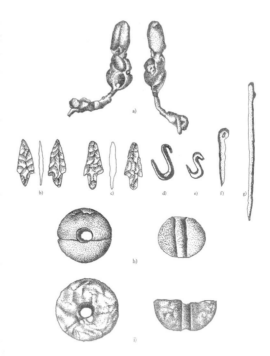

*Figure 5.8: Copper statuettes, fishhooks and pins, plus other finds from Maadi-West (from Badawi 2003: 8).*

cast copper ingots as well as a few pieces of copper ore were found, in addition to small pins, chisels, fishhooks and pieces of wire (Rizkana and Seeher 1984: 238). However, Rizkana and Seeher (1989: 13–18) report finding no evidence that igneous metallurgy took place there. This is not surprising, as Maadi is distant both from sources of ore and also fuel. Even for house construction tamarisk had to be used, and the posts employed were very thin, ranging between 0.07 and 0.15 m at Maadi-West (Badawi 2003: 7). Copper products were most likely made for local consumption from refined copper, hence the ingots (see Figure 5.8).

Badawi (2003: 10) claims that Maadi manifests the earliest known stone architecture in what he calls a "huge magazine for storing provisions of food and liquids", in addition to "many traces of the earliest Egyptian metallurgy and evidence of a strong Palestinian presence".

Maadi dies out as a settlement during Naqada IIb, to be succeeded by Tell el-Farkha Ia, Tell el-Eswed A str. III-I and Buto IIa, where there is a hiatus between periods I and II (Watrin 2000: 1760). By Naqada IIc the Delta and Palestine are linked into long-range

are common to both [cf: the 'secondary products revolution'], but cornets are more frequent in Ghassoulian sites. … Sites of the Beersheva culture range from Shiqmim in the west, through Beersheva itself, to various points in the wadi system further to the east. This culture is characterised by subterranean structures, stone foundations to walls, and artefacts related to copper and ivory industries, as well as rather crude lithics. All these sites are situated in areas where the present rainfall is 200 mm a year or less."

trading circuits that extend to Anatolia and Iran, evidenced by the presence of obsidian in the Delta and of lapis lazuli in the tombs of Middle and Upper Egypt (Matmar 2645, Mahasna H107, Naqada 822, El-Amra A139 and El-Badari 3730). By around 3,300 BC, Levantine products, notably wine, oil, timber and resin, had important roles in elite Egyptian patterns of consumption and display (Wengrow 2006: 137). Further, in regard to the southern piedmont of the Levant, which offered good opportunities for cereal farming, Wengrow (2006: 138) remarks that "dietary habits based on the consumption of leavened bread and beer [which use overlapping technologies] were transferred to this region from the Nile alluvium, along with associated ceramic forms (made in local fabrics) and simple techniques of administration using cylinder seals and pot-marks".

After the conquest of the Delta by Upper Egyptian kings of Dynasty 0, the Egyptian state had a strong presence in southern Palestine at two of Van den Brink and Braun's (2003) four settlement types, namely Tiers 1 & 2. Tier 1, may have been wholly populated by Egyptians or had large Egyptian majorities as indicated by the predominance of Egyptian ceramic imports and their local imitations (Van den Brink and Braun 2003: 78). Such settlements included Tell es-Sakan, perhaps Tel Ma'ahaz I and 'En Besor III. Tier 2 included Tel Lod and Small Tel Malhata (Van den Brink and Braun 2003: 80) which are indigenous Late EB1 sites with possibly resident ethnic Egyptian populations, but where Egyptian ceramic imports and local copies are a significant part of the repertoire (Braun 2004: 512; Van den Brink and Braun 2003: 79). Tier 3 settlements are defined as those with little Egyptian influence or contact ("a modicum of Egyptian material" in Tier 3A (Van den Brink and Braun 2003: 80)), notably Megiddo and 'Ein Assawir cemetery; Tier 4 having none (*ibid.*: 78).

Speaking of 'En Besor III as an actual state outpost, "generally acknowledged to be a small garrison or enclave of ethnic Egyptians" (Van den Brink and Braun 2003: 78) with a number of *serekhs*[45] and *bullae* found there, Watrin (2000: 1773) observes that "these installations are contemporary and located at the crossroads of great commercial routes. 'En Besor controls the most important springs of the Negev and the routes linking Egypt to Palestine through the north of Sinai. Tel 'Erani and Tel Halif control the way to Shephela. Lod, situated in the south of Yarkon, controls the routes to the north and represents the deepest penetration of the 'Egyptian advance' into Palestine". Nonetheless, Van den Brink and Braun (2003: 85) suggest that at least during the second half of EB I (approx. the last quarter of the fourth millennium) "any suggestion of military domination seems unwarranted". Also to be considered is the existence/substitution of a sea route from the Delta to the southern Levant, as indicated by Late EBI Tel Lod, given the quantities of directly imported and Egyptianizing pottery found there, plus of course the pottery incised *serekhs* of [Horus] Ka and [Horus] Nar[mer].

There are also prehistoric sites in the Fayum depression. However, during the 'Fayum Neolithic' people there relied mostly upon hunting and especially fishing, and as there

---

[45]   A serekh is a rectangle containing two smaller rectangles the larger of which represents the vertical panelling called 'palace façade', (*per-aa*: 'great house', palace) while the other rectangle contains a king's Horus name. Accordingly a falcon (Egyptian *bik*) which is the symbol for Horus, perches on top of the enclosing rectangle (full discussion in O'Brien, 1996). *Bullae* are found in Mesopotamia and Egypt. Egyptian examples are roughly shaped balls of clay covered with sealings and with a hole through the centre to attach them to goods for identification and tracking purposes.

| Absolute Chronology (BCE) | Chronology of the Naqada Culture | Southern Palestine Chronology | Egyptian Sites and Relative Chronology of the lower Egyptian Cultures | Palestinian Sites |
|---|---|---|---|---|
| 3900-3700 | Late Badari Naqada Ia Early Naqada Ib | Late Chalcolithic | Hammamiya Buto Ia Early Buto Ib | Gilat Nahal Mishmar Wadi Ghazzeh Site O |
| 3700-3650 | Late Naqada Ib | Transition Chalc./EB I | Late Buto Ib Ma'adi settlement-Digla I | *Hiatus?* Tell Halif Silo Site IV? |
| 3650-3500 | Naqada Ic-IIa | Early EB I (EB Ia1) | Ma'adi settlement Digla II-Heliopolis Matmar tomb 3131 Mahasna tombs H 30-41 | Afridar-Marina Tell Halif Silo Site III Nizzanim V-Lakhish Wadi Fidan 4-Yiftahel II |
| 3500-3400 | Naqada IIb | Early EB I (EB Ia2) | Buto IIa Tell Eswed A-str. III-I Hammamiya tomb 1728 El-Adaïma tomb 404 | 'En Besor Site H Taur Ikhbeineh V/IV Erani D |
| 3400-3300 | Naqada IIc | Middle EB I (EB Ib1) | Buto IIb Tell Eswed A-str. VI-IV Tell Ibrahim Awad 7 Hierakonpolis tomb 100 Naqada tomb 1298 | Taur Ikhbeineh III Erani C1 Hartuv III Taur Ikhbeineh II |
| 3300-3200 | Naqada IId Naqada IIIa (Early Dynasty 0) | | Buto III-Minshat I-II Abydos tombs U 127-134 Scorpion I tomb (U j) | Azor tombs 1-4-40 Hartuv II. 'En Besor IV Erani C2 |
| 3200-3100 | Naqada IIIb-c1 (Late Dynasty 0) | Late EB I (EB Ib2) Serekh phase | Buto IV-Minshat III Abydos B Narmer tomb (B17-18) | Erani V/VI-Lod-Palmahim II-Horvat Illin Tahtit IV-Arad IV Tell Halif II-'En Besor III |

*Figure 5.9: Chronological Chart of the Relationships between Egyptian Periods and Sites and those of Southern Palestine (from Watrin 2000: 1774).*

are no significant permanent settlements in the Fayum until the Middle Kingdom (Wenke et al., 1988: 46), the Fayum population is more Mesolithic than Neolithic.

## The state formation process

Barry Kemp (1989) in his seminal reconstruction of early state formation in Egypt sees a stage there of the emergence of a proto city-state during the fourth millennium, after a late Neolithic period that only became established in the fifth millennium (which is late for the Near East). However this is not the type of organic growth of cities seen in Mesopotamia, but one of centralization based on conquest, or at least of the hegemony of a dominant settlement over a number of villages strung out along the narrow floodplain of the Nile. Those local entities are absorbed into one of the three regional entities by about 3,500 BC: Naqada, Hierakonpolis and This, the latter becoming hegemonic under the Thinite kings (i.e. the kings of the region in Upper Egypt called This). The site has not been found but is thought to be near modern Girga. The town of Abydos, whose foundation dates from about 3,150 BC (Naqada III), "was probably closely bound up

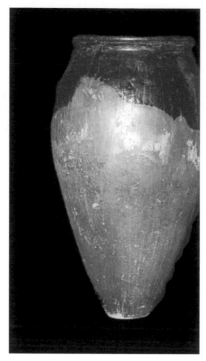

*Figure 5.10: Blacktopped redware jar of Naqada II, c.3200 BC, from a tomb at Abydos (British Museum).*

with the process of state formation" (Wilkinson 1999: 355); that is, with the ambitions of the Thinite kings. As Dreyer (1993: 10) succinctly puts it: "Abydos, 500 km (300 miles) south of Cairo, is virtually the centre of where the Naqada culture – the main basis of pharaonic Egypt – flourished in the fourth millennium BC. Its last stage, Naqada IIIb, runs smoothly into 'Dynasty 0', the final period of the unification."

Seidlmeyer (1996: 108) is eloquent on the impact of state formation on the nature of Egyptian urbanization:

> "The fusion of Predynastic chiefdoms to form a first national state in Egypt did not affect only the geographical size of the political unit(s); rather, it entailed profound changes in socio-economic structure, evident, among other indications, in the settlement pattern. Most conspicuous, archaeologically, are the remains documenting the establishment of the royal residence in the Memphite area, where the social elite and all expressions of high culture came to be concentrated; the rest of the country, including the former centres sank to a level of provincialism. Social and economic relations of unprecedented asymmetry between centre and country provided the basis for the achievements of civilization; on the condition, however, that a stable integration of the social system as a whole was still maintained. ... One may wonder, indeed, whether Old Kingdom Egypt is more remarkable for her early success in meeting this requirement, or for her ultimate failure".

Part of that ultimate failure was failure to innovate. Baines and Malek (1980: 14) observe that "it is a striking feature of native Egyptian culture at all periods that it is not technically innovative. Possibly the very prodigality of the land was and its water has not encouraged invention." It has certainly encouraged high population levels from antiquity onwards: but as to innovation we have seen that ancient and too many modern states innovate very little upon their legacy at formation. The power holders are too concerned to keep a tight grip on power to innovate (except in control techniques) while the productive mass of the population is too concerned with survival. This makes both rulers and ruled generally risk averse. Only in exceptional circumstances, such as during the Renaissance or in the course of the Industrial Revolution is innovation sustained, as social innovation must accompany technological innovation in a feedback loop. Such a process is currently underway in China, however unevenly.

It is conceivable that had there been tighter nucleation earlier,[46] on the Samarran-Ubaidian pattern (which was undergoing a Chalcolithic revolution while Egypt was still in the throes of the Neolithic revolution) then critical mass might have been achieved, allowing city-states to form along the Nile in the way they did on the Lower Euphrates. Instead geography (the absence of deep hinterlands), ecology and chronology favoured territorial state formation in Egypt. The linearity of settlement along the river and ease of access by land and water, made conquest logistically easy. The river is Egypt's main highway and has always been used for trading and raiding. The outcome at the end of the fourth millennium was the conquest of the northern culture of the Delta and Lower Egypt (Buto-Maadi Culture) by the hierarchical and militaristic culture of the south (Upper Egypt), once its three chiefdoms had been reduced to one from the mid-fourth millennium. Occupation at Maadi came to an end in the Naqada IIc/d phase.

The formation of the Egyptian state thus has nothing whatsoever to do with notions of 'hydraulic management' as promoted most famously by Wittfogel (1957). In this functionalist explanation, the demands of a complex irrigation system calls forth a management coordination structure that, essential to the functioning of a society dependent upon irrigation, becomes the state. Then as now, Nile irrigation was in fact annual inundation of a strip comprising the fields of individual farmers. What they had to do annually was to level their fields for maximum areal coverage and pound back some of the retreating floodwater for maximum soil penetration. Then, upon recession of the flood, seed was broadcast into the fresh, moist silt. Barbara Adams (1995: 80) is clear: "The theory that control of irrigation for a basin system of agriculture led to leadership and ultimately despotism is not tenable as the main reason for the rise of Egyptian kingship..." However once kingship has arisen, control of the economic base becomes essential for the continuance of domination. So Adams continues: "there is no doubt that local administrative control under a single ruler of agriculture and produce was an essential component in the patronage system. The feudal system of government headed by the Pharaoh and laboured under for millennia by serfs in Egypt may have had its origins in Hierakonpolis [Nekhen]" as the first centre of the unified state. It is certainly true that Hierakonpolis was a major population centre during Amratian and

---

[46] Nucleation refers to the built environment; concentration refers to population distribution. A nucleated settlement will have a relatively high population density, but a primate city, which concentrates population relative to the region or country, need not itself be highly nucleated. Indeed it may well be one of the 'core and satellites' type discussed in chapters 6 and 7. However, pressures on land-use over time will tend toward nucleation, as in Mexico City or many of the large cities of Latin America.

Gerzean times due to the presence of the Great Wadi (Hoffman 1982: 122), initially a virtual oasis. Social hierarchy has deep roots in the Hierakonpolis area, so it is not surprising that the final stage of state formation occurred there (Hoffman 1982: 140).[47] After all, "Hierakonpolis has produced the largest Early Predynastic graves ever found and allows us to trace the rise of an apparently indigenous elite up to the unification of Egypt under the first kings of the First Dynasty about 3100 BC" (Hoffman 1982: 144–5). The Scorpion Macehead and the Narmer Palette, famous assertions of kingship, were found in this area.

## The basis of hierarchy and the emergence of the state

Barry Kemp (1989: 34–5) has located the roots of prehistoric Egyptian hierarchy in the territoriality of the egalitarian farming village, which allows "a powerful urge to dominate [to] come to the fore". Such urges are of course not confined to the banks of the Nile, but obtain everywhere. Explaining the central importance of feasting in egalitarian Neolithic communities in China, Li Liu (2004: 244) observes that "factional competition may have been the common social relationship in Neolithic communities, which suggests a context within which some individual households or social sectors sought to obtain power when circumstances allowed" (cf: Figure 9.1, item 4).

In Kemp's model, therefore, the start condition is small egalitarian communities in competition with one another; originally perhaps mainly for prestige and precedence, but no doubt also for control of the best fishing locations, village boundaries relative to flood waters and so forth. Village territories included a range of resources from riverbank to desert-edge. Fishing was and is a key resource on the Nile (cf: El Omari above) while the valley edge contains a range of valuable minerals. Between the river and the cliffs lies the farmland whose fertility would be renewed every year if the floodwaters reached it in sufficient depth for a sufficiently lengthy period. Accordingly, since not even floodplains are truly flat, some land was more worth having than others; the nearer to the river the better.

The next step is the emergence at the valley edge of a "large low-density farming town", essentially a large village, the function of which is to facilitate exchanges across the area, and which also supplies to the whole area services that villages could not provide for themselves, namely those of specialists.

By the third stage some of those 'farming towns' have become larger, fortified and dominant over the immediate farming landscape. They extract taxes to support an urban elite, whose tombs are located on the valley-edge, beyond the floods and the farmland.

Kemp (*op.cit.*: 32) then asks us to imagine "a board game of the 'Monopoly' kind. At the start we have a number of players of roughly equal potential. They compete (to some extent unconsciously) by exchanges of different commodities, and later

---

[47] Of all the formative civilizations of the Old World, irrigation in the true sense of complex, capital and labour intensive canal building and their associated control works, only existed on the alluvium of southern Mesopotamia. And, as just discussed, ancient Mesopotamia was characterized not by an integrationist territorial state, but by dozens of competing city-states strung along river courses. As we have seen in the previous chapter, managerialism did have much to do with the rise of the Mesopotamian city-state, *but not directly*, rather at the level of household enterprises within civil society.

more openly by conflict. The game proceeds by means of a combination of chances (e.g. environmental or locational factors) and personal decisions [plus demography]. The game unfolds slowly at first, in an egalitarian atmosphere and with the element of competition only latent, the advantage swinging first to one player and then to another. But although hypothetically each player's loss could later be balanced by his gains, the essence of gaming, both as a personal experience and in theoretical consideration, is that the initial equality amongst the players does not last indefinitely. An advantage that at the time may escape notice upsets the equilibrium enough to distort the whole subsequent progress of the game. It has a 'knock-on' effect out of all proportion to its original importance. Thus the game inexorably follows a trajectory towards a critical point where one player has accumulated sufficient assets to outweigh threats posed by other players and so becomes unstoppable. It becomes only a matter of time before he wins the whole game by monopolizing the assets of all, although the inevitability of his win belongs only to a later stage in the game." This would then be the Thinite victory, described above.

But what if ecological conditions induce inequalities from the outset? Thomas Park (1992) has argued, on the basis of Chaos Theory and his own fieldwork amongst flood-recession agriculturalists on the Senegal River, which has a regime similar to that of the Nile, that where the height and duration of floods are critical, and where, as also on the Nile, the extent of flooding is unpredictable ('chaotic'), then to achieve the flexibility demanded the human population will become hierarchical.

This is still far from the advent of ruling or managerial classes. Rather, the 'original' or best-established families or minimal lineages will assume preferential access to village lands, such that in good years they have rights to the best, which are those parts of the flood basin between the levees and the lowest depressions. "Those were the prime areas for cultivation of the single annual crop of barley, emmer wheat, beans chickpeas and other vegetables" (Park 1992: 106).

In bad years there is insufficient land of satisfactory quality (wetness + structure) for 'non-priority users'. Those families or groups are thus forced to pursue some other means of livelihood: fishing (always the main protein source), hunting, mining, trading, pastoralism or working for those with sufficient land. Those so 'excluded' would, for a time, retain some rights of return when conditions improved. However, most are likely to be disadvantaged by their absence from agriculture, and would only gain access to 'surplus' land, that of poorer quality, or else have to pay 'rent' for the better. To this would be added social disabilities, such as exclusion from important cultic and leadership positions.

Thus social evolution is like natural evolution, for both require only a source of variation, an independent force of selection, plus a means of preferential propagation of advantageous traits. Here the human population faces unpredictably variable river-flow plus differential land quality. It selectively employs aspects of environmental conditions to serve material and psychological ends through a social framework The institutions and organizations thus established serve to transmit practices that enable permanent farming villages to thrive. It so happens, however, that this involves some families, lineages and clans being more equal than others, an inequality amounting to ranking that can be extended and reinforced by trade.

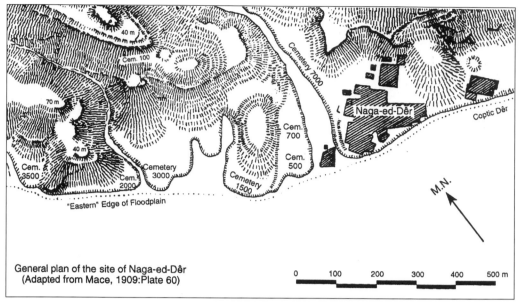

Figure 5.11: General plan of site of Naga-ed-Der and its location (from Savage 1997: 233).

Analysis substantiating this model has recently been conducted by Stephen H. Savage (2001) on graves at Naga-ed-Der, just downstream and on the opposite (eastern) bank from Abydos. For a general plan of the site of Naga-ed-Der and its location (see Figure 5.11).

The wadi edge cemetery site N7000 (centre top) was used from about 3800 BC to around 3090 BC, in four phases. Based on combined AMS radiocarbon (2 sigma p), the phases are: 1: 3800–3630; 2: 3640–3500; 3: 3510–3340; 4: 3360–3090, Calendar years BC (Savage 2001: 126).

Using correspondence analysis and k-means analysis, Savage (*op. cit.*) identified six clusters, which he suggests might be descent groups, probably representing clan-type organizations in Predynastic society. He finds that they are highly unequal in wealth, power and respect, the graves of the weak clans being robbed by the strong as a demonstration of their power. From the grave goods, he observes that:

> "Cluster 1 appears to have controlled the ivory, suggesting that their power was based on trade with the south, where the ivory probably originated. Cluster 3, at the time of its ascendancy and greatest power in Phase 3, appears to have controlled the products associated with Mesopotamian trade. At some time between Phases 1 and 3 the trade with the south appears to have collapsed and was later replaced with trade to the north. The group that controlled trade to the south, Cluster 1, declined sharply from Phase 2 to Phase 3, at precisely the point where Cluster 3 experiences its ascendancy" (*ibid.*: 126).

Cluster 4 graves are located on a lower terrace of the cemetery suggesting lower status compared with burials on the upper terrace. Indeed Cluster 4 burials contained so few grave goods that none of its graves could be used in the seriation study (*ibid.*).

From which Savage concludes that "descent (based on kinship), power and competition appear as powerful organising principles in the Predynastic at Naga-ed-Der"(*ibid.*: 125). Intensifying competition is indicated by increased plundering of graves, the elaboration of grave architecture and mortuary ritual, plus the increased inclusion of grave goods over time (*ibid.*: 126).

A way of integrating all of this, namely Kemp's game-theory with his three-step model, Park's stochastic-hierarchic model and Savage's descent group competition, is by means of my processual one, which, however, requires six levels and fifteen steps to The Emergence of the Egyptian Territorial State (Figure 5.12).

*Figure 5.12: Emergence of the Egyptian Territorial State.*

1.  Farming Villages form as internally stratified settlements with leading lineages that:
    a)  Compete for prestige
    b)  Which comes from success in farming and family augmentation (reproductive success)
    c)  Which proves the ritual potency of its representative
    d)  Which proves his overall 'leadership qualities'

2.  Agricultural Towns
    e)  Form from successful farming villages
    f)  Compete for the leadership of villages in their hinterlands
    g)  Fight to control hinterlands and fortify themselves

3.  Fortified Towns
    h)  Dominate the landscape
    i)  Fight for predominance in a given region
    j)  Rulers (chiefs) emerge

4.  Regional capitals
    k)  Naqada, Hierakonpolis, This and Abadiya emerge around 3,500 BC dominating their own regions
    l)  Hierakonpolis absorbs the Naqada polity sometime towards the end of Naqada II. Sites in this region go into decline at this time (Savage 2001: 129) the late fourth millennium; Hierakonpolis grows larger as an urban centre. From Naqada II comes a large painted mural from the tomb (tomb 100) of an Upper Egyptian ruler at Hierakonpolis.[48] It shows large boats, armed men hunting, fighting and killing, and even contains a Mesopotamian style 'master of the animals' (presumably lions) 'hero' image, indicating that armed men and powerful logistics were the basis of this ruler's power. Nile boats, capable of travelling distances in open water, may even date from as early as the seventh millennium (Usai and Salvatori 2007).
    m)  At about the same time, namely late Naqada II, This probably extends its dominance in the Nile valley and into the Delta as far as Minshat Abu Omar, enabling it to control the overland trade with Canaan, notably in wine. Maadi itself ceases to be occupied in the Naqada IIc/d phase. The 12 chambered royal tomb U-j at Abydos, the grandest burial from Predynastic Egypt and obviously the sepulchre of a king – Serrano (2003: 99) following Dreyer says Scorpion I – dates to Naqada IIIA1 (*c.*3300 BC) and has more than 200 wine jars imported from Palestine. It has calibrated radiocarbon dates ranging between 3490 and 3100 BC as outer limits (Gorsdorf, Dreyer and Hartung 1998: 171). As the oldest measurement is 3490–3470 cal. BC on a roofbeam from *A. nilotica* (*ibid.*), this must be old wood and so does not indicate when the tomb was constructed but when the tree was growing. One of the 150 ivory or bone labels is inscribed with numerical and pictographic prototypes of Egyptian writing (Kahl 2001), which are the earliest examples we have from a secure source.[49] The Delta town of Bubastis is (probably)

---

[48] This highly important source demands a full-scale study.

[49] See Vernus (1993) for the distinction between a symbolic system and a writing system. The elements of a writing system are symbolic, but not all symbols form part of a writing system, by which is meant one that can record sustained and flexible discourse paralleling speech. This may be the case with the symbols on Indus seals.

recorded as rendering taxes. Cylindrical wavy-handled jars (W-class pots), of which there are over a hundred, have cursive inscriptions in ink. In the Delta only Buto remains independent, continuing seaborne trade with Canaan. (Figure 5.13).

5.   Unification in the South
    (n)   This unites with Hierakonpolis either by conquest or by marriage (or both), initiating Dynasty O [zero]. It is possible that the event depicted on the wedding macehead depicts a union between Narmer of This and Neith-hotep of Hierakonpolis (Savage 2001: 133). And if the bride was of Naqadan origins (Wilkinson 1999: 70) then the unity of the three original super-chiefdoms was the better assured. Narmer was of course the last ruler of Dynasty 0, and the predecessor of king Aha/Menes (Dreyer 2000: 6).

6.   Unification of the 'Two Lands'
    (o)   This, already in control of the rest of Egypt, completes what is to become the Egyptian state by conquest of the Buto/Sais region after what was most likely a protracted struggle. However Ciałowicz (2000: 576) maintains that "there are no findings testifying to the existence of elites in the delta before the arrival of the Nagadians", or at least no elites whose power would be in any way comparable to that of the elites in the south (Upper Egypt). Suddenly in Nagada III there is a marked expansion of settlement in the Delta, in which large, hitherto unknown, mudbrick buildings appear, with grain silos, ovens and brewing complexes. Stone tool repertoires also undergo a marked change and rectangular sickle elements appear in unprecedented numbers. "In the southern Levant their adoption is associated with early evidence for the use of draft animals… (Wengrow 2006: 162)" and both longhorn and shorthorn cattle have been identified at Tell el-Farka (Chlodniki and Ciałowicz 2002: 113). Together this amounts to an organisational and economic revolution, its suddenness strongly suggesting imposition from Upper Egypt no matter what symbolist revisionism contends.

The Gebel el Arak knife handle and the Tjehenu Palette possibly depict battles against Buto (Savage 2001: 131, 134). Final conquest launches the First Dynasty, in possession of all of Egypt and in control of trade routes, overland and by sea.

It now seems highly likely that (at least a major battle in) the final conquest of the Buto/Sais region is depicted on the famous Narmer Palette (in the Egyptian Museum, Cairo, shown below). Its reverse side is dominated over four fifths of its height by the figure of the king, significantly wearing the white crown of Upper Egypt, with a mace smiting and despatching long-haired enemies. The obverse, centre panel, shows the two lands united by the intertwining of the necks (controlled by ropes!) of fantastic animals, while in the bottom register the king, represented as a bull, has broken into a walled city and is trampling on one of its defenders, an image repeated several times on the 'Towns Palette' of around 3100 BC. In the top and widest panel the king processes in triumph, led by standards representing districts, while laid out before him in rows are bound and decapitated bodies.

The imagery on the Narmer Palette (Figure 5.15) is repeated on the ivory tag (Figure 5.16) recently discovered by the German Archaeological Institute (DAI) in the spoil from Cemetery B at Umm el-Qaab, Abydos, along with imagery of bound prisoners on an ivory cylinder of Narmer from Hierakonpolis. They apparently refer to the same event, namely smiting the 'Libyans' (shown bearded on all three images). Indeed the upper register of the tag from Abydos can be read as "Smiting the Libyan marshland people by Horus Narmer, celebration (of the victory) at the palace", the first such event known in Egyptian history (Dreyer 2000: 6–7). The key here is reference to 'marshland people', not 'Libyans', which is a later reading. In those days the Delta could have been described as marshland (Wilson and Gilbert

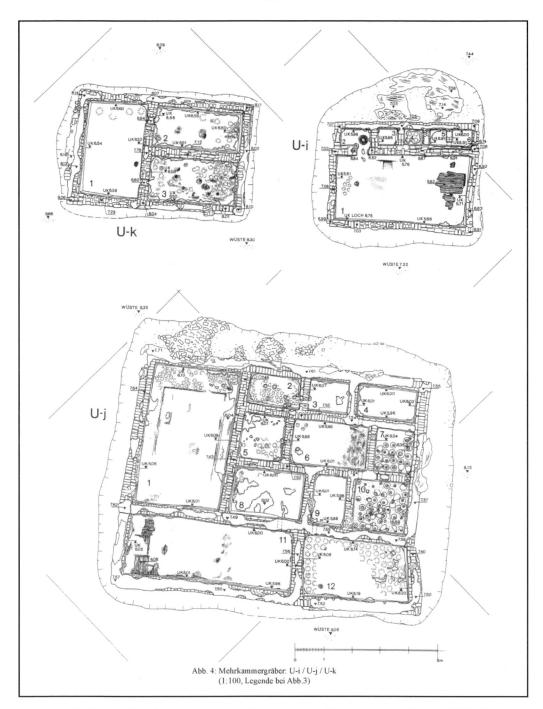

Abb. 4: Mehrkammergräber: U-i / U-j / U-k
(1:100, Legende bei Abb.3)

*Figure 5.13: Tombs U-i, U-j and U-k at Umm el-Qaab (from Dreyer 1993 = MDAIK 49: 33; Nachuntersuchungen im frühzeitlichen Königsfriedhof. 5./6. Vorbericht).*

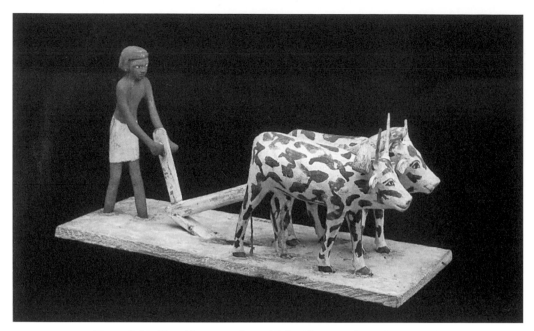

*Figure 5.14: Ploughing team, later third millennium (British Museum).*

*Figure 5.15: The Narmer Palette (after B.J. Kemp 1989).*

*Figure 5.16: Ivory label (c.2980 BC) for King Den's sandals, showing the usual smiting, the scene filled with royal iconography, such as the Serekh (centre: Horus hawk on palace or temple façade); standard with the Seth animal (right) and the Ka symbol (far left), a pair of protective arms representing the king's life-force (British Museum). A good study of smiting scenes and defeated foes is in Gilbert 2004: 88–97.*

2002: 12–13) and indeed the land of the papyrus. Accordingly, Jimenez-Serrano (2003: 119–20) accepts Gardiner's (1961: 404) reading of the scene on the Narmer Palette as: "The falcon-god Horus (i.e. Narmer) leads captive the inhabitants of the papyrus country."

Narmer was "the first pharaoh of whom irrefutable traces can be found not only all over Egypt but also far outside it" (Adams and Cialowicz 1997: 61), from the Eastern Desert (rock surfaces) to the southern Levant (pottery).

A further indication that the 'unification of the lands' was a matter of conquest and not merely of acculturation, is that the last king of the Second Dynasty (c.2890–c.2686) and the last ruler at Abydos, Khasekhemwy, had to fight a fierce civil war against 'rebels' described as 'marsh dwellers' to achieve the re-unification of Egypt. This war was particularly bloody if the number of claimed dead, in excess of forty-seven thousand, is to be believed. History shows that wars of secession always incur heavy casualties. If the unified Egyptian state was so beneficent, why the bloody rebellion or rather civil war? After its suppression Khasekhem, as he was originally called ('the power that appeared') changed his name to Khasekhemy ('the two powers have appeared') using Seth, symbol of Lower Egypt, on his *serekh* in addition to the Horus falcon. His predecessor Sekhemib ('Hope of All Hearts') had changed his Horus name in favour of a Seth name, Seth-Peribsen. So the civil war probably started under Sekhemib/Peribsen.

The last king of the Second Dynasty, Khasekhemy built for himself the last tomb to be constructed in the royal cemetery at Abydos. At 68 m long by 39.4 m at its widest point, it comprises one long gallery divided into 58 rooms with a central burial chamber measuring 8.6 x 3 m and 1.8 m high. It is the earliest known large-scale stone construction in Egypt.

## Royal Ritual

Khasekhemwy's successor, Djoser, first king of the Third Dynasty (2686–2613) was secure enough to build his famous six-stepped pyramid – or rather Imhotep built it for him – the centre-piece of a vast complex contained within a rectangular enclosure of limestone blocks in the architectural form of the 'palace façade'.[50] The whole mortuary complex could only be entered through a ceremonial colonnaded hall. It gave access to a courtyard for the Sed festival (royal jubilee, below). This *heb-sed* court was faced by a series of barrel-vaulted dummy shrines representing parts of the king's domain. At the southern end of this court was a pavilion holding two thrones representing the Two Lands, upon which the king would have sat, in turn presumably donning the White crown of Upper Egypt, then the Red crown of Lower Egypt. Beyond lay the much larger South Court at the rear of which is the important South Tomb approached by a steeply sloping shaft leading to a series of small, finely decorated chambers. It probably contained Djoser's viscera removed as part of the embalming process. The South Tomb's importance is further indicated by three relief panels, carved to show the king performing the *heb-sed* ritual. Wearing nothing but the White Crown, a loincloth and beard that may not be real, he is pictured running between boundary markers that he probably had to strike with the small flail carried in his right hand.

During the *heb-sed* renewal rites the king dressed in special robes and wore an unusual headdress, (both shown on Djoser's limestone statue found in the *serdab* (illus. Baines and Malek 1980: 145)) and sat under a special canopy on a double-stepped, double-throned dais, symbolising his mastery of both Upper and Lower Egypt. The latter was represented by the cobra goddess Wadjit of Buto, the former by the vulture goddess Nekhbet of el-Kab. The initial part of the proceedings were presided over by Sekhmet-Hathor, the leonine form of the cow-goddess Hathor, probably the divinity with the widest range of attributes (syncretism suggesting great antiquity), who suckled the god-king. From his thrones he viewed a line of temporary shrines in timber and matting that represented the gods of the various provinces under his dominion and doubtless paying homage. At the step-pyramid a double row of those formerly temporary shrines was rendered in stone, for eternity. Despite this, later rulers favoured the 'traditional' wood and wattle temporary structures for their 'jubilees'. Of course, only courtiers, the royal family and members of the elite would be present at the *heb-sed*.

Ritual and art, the sharing of preciosities (to reinforce status) and wealth, are necessary for retaining the allegiance of the elite; while cult, ceremonial, symbolism and respecting traditional, and thus expected, living standards are required for the elite to keep control of the populace.

By the north-east corner of the step pyramid are situated the House of the North, noteworthy for its stone columns carved to represent the papyrus plant, and the House of

---

[50]  For a detailed analysis of this important piece of iconography, see Jimenez-Serrano (2003).

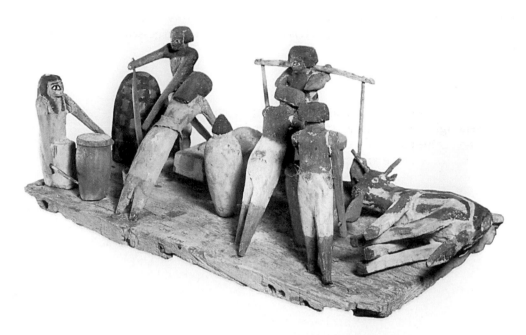

*Figure 5.17: Bread-making, beer-making and butchery (British Museum).*

the South. To their north and west runs another huge enclosed area as yet, surprisingly, unexcavated. So Djoser's pyramid was not just his tomb with his personal stairway to heaven, but the centrepiece of a massive ceremonial precinct making a key political statement about the pivotal role of kingship in society and state and, specifically, of his ability to mobilise resources for his own purposes.

In sum, "the formation of a state is the last stage and not the first link from which everything begins" (Adams and Ciałowicz 1997: 34). It requires "a marked consolidation of the bureaucratic and priestly elite and the development of central administration controlling the entire country" *(ibid.*: 61). Finds in tomb U-j at Umm el-Qaab show that hieroglyphic writing was already quite well established by the Naqada III period (Dreyer 1993: 12). Cylinder seals had arrived in Egypt during Naqada II, and an impression survives listing the first five kings of Dynasty I, from Narmer to Den in their historical order (Spencer 1993: 64). In the second half of the First Dynasty marked changes took place in the ways in which the staples beer and bread were produced and in the provision of wine for 'an elite way of living'. Hendrickx *et al.* (2002: 299) conclude from this that "the changes in food technology are to be considered the consequence of the strongly increased levels of social differentiation during the Early Dynastic period and the organisation of the centralised state implying the presence of a growing number of professionals in the administration, religion and crafts, who had to be provided with food"; and not just any, but superior food and in greater variety.

Figure 5.18 shows the organization of those 'professionals in administration' in the Early Dynastic Period.

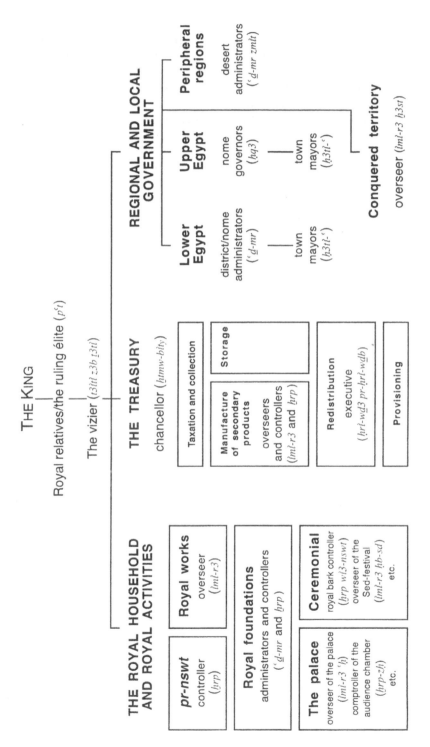

*Figure 5.18: Wilkinson's Model of Early Dynastic state administration in Egypt.*

## Urbanism in Egypt

City-states are the product of localised organic growth. The 'local' refers to a specific and limited productive topography; 'organic' refers to growth through success in exploiting those resources. By contrast, territorial states are the consequence of conquest, even if, like Rome, they began as city-states. The urban form is intrinsic to the existence of the city-state. By contrast, the conquest of territory and then rule from a centre (which may not even be a city) is what defines the territorial state. A city-state may have some villages and perhaps a town or two in its hinterland, but an agrarian territorial state, as all *large* territorial states were in antiquity, will have its territory populated by many villages, hence the term 'village-state' to contrast with city-state. Most of the population of a city-state live and work in the city. In village states, the overwhelming majority of the population live and work in villages, as was the case in Egypt.

The analogy for the formation of territorial states is with business enterprises that wish to grow quickly, or rather whose bosses wish to grow the business quickly. Rather than expanding the business by working at organic growth, the tactic is to use a temporary advantage of some sort (e.g., high share price, high profits, difficulties in a rival's new product launch, etc.) to take the rival over and merge it into one's own business. If there were three original players and one takes over another, the third is then at huge disadvantage and very likely to be swallowed-up in a short time, if the initial merger can be made to work. This is what seems to have happened in Egypt, explaining unification (from regional groupings) in not much more than a century.

One consequence of the process outlined above is that cities' principal role in ancient Egypt was to function as royal capitals, religious/ceremonial centres or administrative/control settlements, notably for the gathering of taxes. Given the number of their inhabitants, towns and cities necessarily acquired secondary functions as market centres. But this was not their primary purpose. Which is, of course, very similar to the situation in Bronze Age China, that other great territorial state. Otherwise the population continued (necessarily) dispersed in their villages strung along the banks of the Nile and over the Delta. There, the kings planted their private estates. Further, throughout the whole country, the developed system was one of "villages and estates providing for the royal cult, [which] was not just the economic background of individual temples, but, since it was run as a unified network by the administration of the palace, it functioned as the backbone of the economy of the state at large" (Seidlmeyer 1996: 124). But it was not the whole economy. Indeed the economy that provided for the population at large was that of the relatively independent peasant operating within "the local family-based enterprise rather than a bureaucratic organisation of dependent workers. The great estate is to be envisaged as a lordship, not a bureaucracy, and the rural population as individuals, working to their own economic advantage within the socio-economic constraints of their village or estate, not a regimented mass" (Eyre 1999: 52).

Toby A.H. Wilkinson (1999: 145) models the administrative structure of the Early Dynastic state in Figure 5.18.

This alerts us to an issue of general importance when discussing urbanism; namely that we must *clearly distinguish settlements that are involved in the rise of the state, as against those*

*Figure 5.20: Top centre: King Den seated in his festival pavilion, flail in hand, and wearing the double crown of Upper and Lower Egypt; top right, the king running; behind the pavilion his serekh (British Museum).*

easy to cut, was used and faced with fine white Tura limestone from the Mukattam hills. At 110 by 125 metres the Step-Pyramid is not square and neither is it isolated as a monument. Still an imposing pile on the Saqqara skyline, it forms part of a grand funeral complex contained within a walled enclosure, at the south end of which is

> "a great mastaba which is a duplicate set of chambers reproducing those immediately connected with the burial chamber of the pyramid. The walls of some of the rooms under the mastaba and pyramid are decorated with blue glazed composition tiles, arranged to represent primitive hangings of matting, and fine low reliefs showing Djoser performing various religious ceremonies. On the north side of the Step Pyramid is a mortuary temple and a small chamber containing a statue of the dead king. The former was intended for the practice of the funerary cult of the king and the latter as a substitute for the body for the reception of offerings" (James 1979: 176–7)

Matting patterns were also standard decoration on the exterior mud-brick walls of mastabas. The great plaza formed by the enclosure was the setting for the most important ceremony undertaken by the king in his lifetime. As already mentioned, this was the Sed festival (*heb-sed*, 'royal jubilee') of renewal, "a great jubilee celebration of the king's earthly rule over a period which was ideally thirty years, although second and third celebrations could subsequently take place at shorter intervals" (Kemp 1989: 59).

A First Dynasty oil-jar label from Abydos (*c.*2900 BC) shows King Den during the Sed/jubilee renewal festival wearing the White Crown of Upper Egypt and running between two markers symbolising the borders of Egypt (Figure 5.20 above).

Earlier still, such a ceremonial courtyard was in use from Gerzean (Naqada IIb-

d) times until early in the First Dynasty. This is site Hk29A at Hierakonpolis and is described by Hoffman (1987) as a 'temple-workshop complex', perhaps the *pr-wr* (Friedman 1996: 33–4) reverencing the elephant (Jimenez-Serrano 2003: 122). It lies in the desert and consists of a large parabolic courtyard over 32 metres long by about 13 metres wide, surrounded by a mud-covered reed fence and later by a mud-brick wall (Holmes 1992a: 37). Adjoining the northern (long) side are at least five rectangular buildings, some of which were specialized production centres for flint tools and carnelian beads. On the facing (south) side are a line of four enormous post holes, with a maximum diameter of 1.5 metres. Their ceremonial role is suggested by the occurrence of another, serving as a flag or totem pole, located at the 'top' or apex end of the enclosure, while the entry gate is at the other end, on the north fence/wall (*ibid.*).

The Fourth Dynasty (2613–2494 BC) was the first period in which true mummification – involving the removal of the body's soft internal organs – commenced. It was still a fairly unsuccessful process of preservation, but was an advance on the use merely of linen bandages and resin-moulding of features that had been the practice during the earlier dynasties (Spencer 1982: 35).

The Fourth Dynasty also marked the peak of pyramid building, notably of the Great Pyramid of Cheops at Giza, by Memphis. Cheops, whose Egyptian name is Khufu, an abbreviation of Khnum-khuefui ('Khnum is protecting me') was the second king of the dynasty. It was the first king of the Fourth Dynasty, Sneferu, who was responsible for having built the first 'true', plane-sided pyramid at Meidum, some 53 km south of Saqqara. This was achieved by 'filling in' an eight-step pyramid.[52] *Mastabas* continued to be built for the elite in large numbers. Indeed around the pyramid at Medum and Sneferu's northern pyramid at Dahshur, there were what Malek (1995: 101) calls extensive fields of *mastabas* built according to an overall plan and separated by streets intersecting at right angles. Unique to the Fourth Dynasty, they were built not only in brick but also in stone, their superstructures faced with fine limestone from the royal Tura quarries. Such prestigious stone was available during, but not after, the Fourth Dynasty, for this arrangement was part of the 'new dispensation' of royal/elite accommodation at the time. Quarrying stone was, after all, a royal prerogative, as was gold mining.

As Roth (1993: 33) sums it up:

> "The advent of the Fourth Dynasty of Pharaonic Egypt marked a radical break with the first three dynasties. The break is most visible in the new shape of the era's most substantial archaeological remains, the royal pyramids and their surrounding mortuary complexes. In the Third Dynasty, royal tombs took the form of stepped pyramids, surrounded by dummy buildings and enclosed in a rectangle of high, niched walls, with its long axis north-south. During the reign of Snefru, royal tombs became true pyramids of vastly increased size [and cost!], built at the western end of a complex of new components and proportions, which extended in an east-west line from the border of cultivation [onto the desert margin]".

---

[52] Pyramid types and their construction methods are brilliantly illustrated on pp.138–9 of Baines and Malek 1980.

## Pyramid costs

With regard to the economy, two principal myths have held sway. The older one, influenced by the Bible, is that pyramids were built by slave labour, much of it foreign. However, in the second part of the 20th century AD, another myth replaced it in the wake of Keynesian economic policy. This was that, rather than slave labour, native Egyptian peasants were (almost exclusively) employed in the 'off 'season for agricultural labour during the annual inundation. This supposedly provided peasants with much-needed seasonal employment that benefited both individual families and the economy as a whole, since seasonal underemployment is a characteristic of agrarian regimes. Both are myths.

While "coercive state mechanisms, such as police, were conspicuous by their absence; people were tied to the land and control over every individual was exercised by local communities that were closed to outsiders" (Malek 1995: 101). The work of *mastaba* building was onerous enough but the load on the peasantry increased by orders of magnitude when pyramids were built. As agricultural techniques did not improve, the state drove the intensification and extensification of agriculture to increase output. Higher levels of production and state extraction were needed in order to provide for the full-time pyramid builders and to gain supplies for the unskilled but heavy labour employed seasonally. Intensification involved the replacement of privately-owned land by royal estates coordinated through *nome* (provincial) administrative centres, while extensification was undertaken by increasing the area cultivated. At the same time a more rigorous census and tax regime was imposed. All of this made the subsistence economy more unstable. Consequently,

> "Egypt during much of the Old Kingdom was a centrally planned and administered state, headed by a king who was the theoretical owner of all its resources and whose powers were absolute. He was able to commandeer people, to impose compulsory labour, to extract taxes, and to lay claim to any of the resources of the land at will, although in practical terms this was tempered by a number of restrictions. During the 3rd and 4th Dynasties, many of the top officials of state were members of the royal family, in direct continuation of the system of government of the Early Dynastic Period" (Malek 1995: 102–3).

It is true that the state developed storehouses and moved food supplies around to deficit areas in time of shortage, although this system tended to break down during periods of famine. It also suppressed local conflicts and imposed its own law and order. It is clear from all of this that the state emerged to secure and extend elite privileges and that any benefits provided to society at large, such as security, were merely a part of its self-serving operation.

So to return to human nature with Hoffman (1982: 148): "The distinction between public piety and private venality, always inherent in human society, was exacerbated by the development of the state which reinforced the development of a complex division of labour, and the importance of ascribed over achieved status".

It should always be borne in mind that ascribed status does not fit the best people to key roles in the division of labour, but rather puts in charge those who happen to be born of elite parents.

State formation in Egypt was clearly a product of violence (Spalinger 2005: 245). The original iconography is particularly graphic, not just in terms of the 'smiting king' imagery where enemies are literally trampled underfoot, but also in the more subtle form of imagery of the *rekhyt*-bird (a kind of lapwing or plover) that, in being depicted as hung by their necks from the standards of the Buto-Maadi culture area, symbolize that the territory had been totally conquered by late Predynastic King Scorpion. "Both ideologically and economically, the acts of conquering *and ruling* were inseparable from the idea of absorbing new wealth into the estates of the king and the major religious cults" (Shaw 2000: 329, emphasis added). In this Egyptian kingship was no different from kingship in Mediaeval Europe, it just lasted longer.

*Figure 5.21: Granite statue of Ankwa, shipbuilder to the king, with an adze at his shoulder. Third dynasty, c.2650 BC (British Museum).*

# CHAPTER 6

# *China*

The China we know today, that is China as an *empire state*, came into existence in 221 BC with the victory of the state of Qin over the others comprising the central Chinese culture area, of which Qin was originally on the margins. Ultimate victor in the massive conflicts of the 'Warring States' era (475–221 BC), its ultimate architect, the notoriously brutal and driven King Zheng of Qin, became Qinshihuangdi, 'First August Emperor' (more literally 'August Celestial Deity'). The 'universal empire' having been established, thereafter China remained an empire state except in periods of 'disunity'. However those were merely 'intermediate periods'; then as now both the population and rulers of China envisage the country as a unified empire ruled from a single centre, thus an *empire state*.

States existed in some of the territory that was to become China for at least a millennium and a half prior to the formation of the empire state. On the central plains (Zhongyuan) of the Yellow River (Huanghe) a succession of three states or regional hegemonies are traditionally recognised. Referred to as the Sandai, they are Xia, Shang and Western Zhou. Traditional dates are: Xia (21st–16th century BC), Shang (16th-11th century BC) and Zhou periods (11th century–221 BC). As mentioned above, 221 BC is the date of the first unification of China, which resulted from the state of Qin's success in war, undertaken with extreme ruthlessness and cunning.

Liu and Chen (2003: 84) conjecture that the Xia dynasty, if it existed, began as a Late Neolithic Longshan 'chiefdom'[53] that only crystallised into a state around 1800 BC, during Erlitou Phase II. Indeed, Liu (2004: 238) positively declares that "The earliest state-level society that can be unmistakeably recognized from the archaeological record is Phase II of the Erlitou culture (*c*.1800 BC)". One indication of this is that the Erlitou site, which reached 456 hectares, was where both residential and mortuary segregation existed for the first time (*ibid*.: 244), dividing rulers from ruled in both life and death. Another has to be the large palatial structures in a 10.8 ha walled-off compound near the centre of the site but off to the southeast. To its north lies the 'sacrifice zone' and to its south, near the site's perimeter, is the bronze foundry. However, the lack of stable cemetery sites at Erlitou, suggests to Liu and Xu (2007: 894) that "the Erlitou population was characterised by many small and unrelated kin groups, who were bound together by an urban setting", and at least for some, service to the elite in the palatial complex, which "formed the core of the urban expansion" (*ibid*.: 893).

---

[53] See Demattè's (1999: 119) argument that "the use of the chiefdom concept for the Chinese evidence is not particularly useful or explanatory". However, see Y. Kuen Lee's argument (2004) that it is.

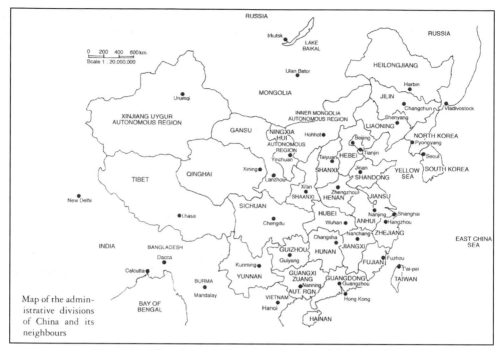

Map of the administrative divisions of China and its neighbours

Figure 6.1: Map of present-day administrative divisions of China.

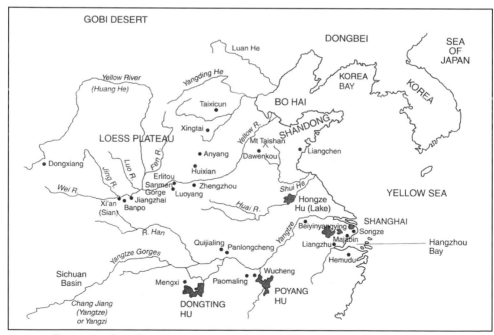

Figure 6.2: Some key sites, such as Erlitou, in relation to the major river systems.

This is the phase (1800–1700 BC) during which white pottery vessels, which were the model for the earliest bronze ones (*jue, gui/jia* and *he*) were most prevalent (Liu 2003: 20). Liu (2004: 240) puts Erlitou's core area at 5689 km² and its population at 54,000–82,000 persons, a range suggesting a complex chiefdom rather than a state, and below I propose a model for its transition to true statehood. The central provinces are shown on the map of present-day administrative divisions of China (Figure 6.1).

**Erlitou** and the other sites of what became the 'capital district' of the northern interior along the middle reaches of the Yellow River, are centrally located with respect to the loessic (originally wind-deposited) soils that are deep, fertile, well-drained and easily worked with simple tools. The key tributaries defining the middle reaches of the Yellow River are the Wei (joining from the west), the Fen (joining from the North) and especially the Luo/Yi from the south-west. Figure 6.2 shows some key sites, such as Erlitou, in relation to the major river systems.

From the Palaeolithic to the Iron Age the territory of what is now China comprised different culture-provinces reflecting ecological differences between north and south, interior and coast. Determining features are the mountain masses to the west, the deserts and steppe of the north-west and north, the so-called central plains (Zhongyuan, actually in the north), the great rivers originating in the western mountain mass but running east into the China Sea, and the lush, sub-tropical south. Those ecological differences are clear in this map from Liu (2004: 26) Figure 6.3. Note that present-day China extends south of the Tropic of Cancer (23.5°N).

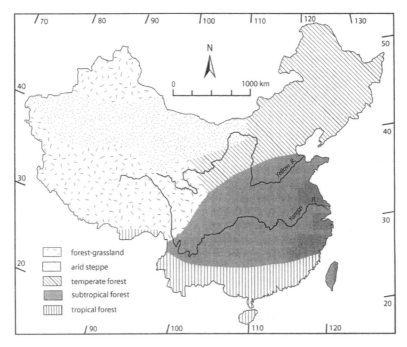

*Figure 6.3: Map of ecological differences in modern China (from Liu 2004: 26).*

China now extends from the Himalayas to the Pacific and from Mongolia to Vietnam. While the 'North-east' (Dongbei, former Manchuria) has a cold, dry, continental climate, the southernmost area (which includes Hong Kong and Guangzhou) is within the Tropics. As the earliest clearly marked state-forms are located in the northern interior on what is conventionally known as the 'central plains' or Zhongyuan, much of the discussion focuses upon this province, for it came to dominate the whole region. This, however, is just a simplification device. It should not be thought that northern plains cultures were 'the centre' and the others merely peripheral. On the contrary, so dynamic was the whole situation, and so relatively populous was 'the south', in particular the cultures along the Yangzi, that much of the time the 'central' plains were merely absorbing influences from all around.

The north is climatically and ecologically different from all the other regions, including areas farther north across the Yellow River and farther again across the Luan River, north-east of Beijing. The north was the millet culture area (and later wheat), while the south was a rice culture area, the dividing line lying broadly along the course of the Huai River, which is about halfway between the Huanghe (Yellow River) and the Yangzi (Changjiang). The process of the domestication of the two grains is quite different as also their cultural consequences, even in recent historical (i.e. late traditional) times. Northern wheat/millet dry farmers were predominantly the owner-operators of their farms, while southern wet-field rice farmers tended to be tenants of landlords.

## Palaeoclimate and the Holocene

The issues and models discussed in this section are very much in flux (Liu, Hunt and Jones 2009). As those issues are important the following sketch is provided as background to ongoing research. Given the size and regional diversity of China its archaeology was bound to be complex. Hitherto (as below) emphasis has been overwhelmingly on the origins of rice cultivation, for cultural reasons. This, however, has tended to downplay the importance of millet farming in early agriculture. Those wishing to get straight to the 'state formation processes' can go directly to the section entitled 'Early Stratification in the North: Dawenkou and Longshan'.

Lu (1999) has outlined a process for the advent of farming in China. Her tentative model begins at the Last Glacial Maximum (LGM) in China, *c.*18,000–15,000 BP (where BP is calibrated calendrical 'before present'). Sea levels exceeded -100 m below present during the LGM, and were still -40 m at 10,000 BP, the Holocene boundary (Lu 1999: 9). As in south-west Asia, warming occurred after 13,000 BP with fluctuations that included an analogue of the Younger Dryas between 11,300 and 10,000 BP, a period of deteriorating climate with inferred stress on populations. Fluctuations continued until 10,000 BP, at which time the post-glacial or Holocene proper began. At its start, temperature in the middle and lower Yangzi valley was about 1°C lower than at present, but similar to the present after 8,000 BP (Higham and Lu 1998). At 7,000 BP modern sea levels, which had been -100 m at LGM, were reached with marine transgressions inevitably following. Accordingly, this is the boundary between the Early and Middle Holocene.

"Pollen studies for the Yangzi River valley suggest little change from current conditions since the Pengtoushan Culture, about 6500–5000 BC" (Underhill 1997: 112).

As elsewhere in Asia, the Last Glacial Maximum was cooler and drier than the same latitude in the Holocene. North of the Yangzi conditions became more steppe-like, which is a grass-dominated environment. Then came the Holocene warming, interrupted by the Younger Dryas Stadial (12,800–11,500 cal yr BP). With the diminution of more desirable gathered foods, notably forest products and tubers, much more reliance had to be placed on grass-seeds, notably that of green foxtail millet (*Setaria viridis*) and broomcorn millet, *ji*, (*Panicum miliaceum*) in the north and common wild rice, a perennial, south of the Yangzi (*Oryza rufipogon*).

Though originally less desirable as food, grains were eminently storable and relatively reliable. Dependence on grain was heavy by the time that the 'Eastern Dryas' had passed, but rising temperatures and rainfall allowed populations to increase. Population density had previously increased on a localized basis, as groups crowded into parts of the Yellow River, Huai and Yangzi Valleys that continued to offer favourable conditions during and after the LGM. Nonetheless, Palaeolithic populations remained very low and widely scattered. At the Holocene, as populations grew on a wider scale, wild stands had to be supplemented by grown and eventually domesticated grains, in a process similar to that shown for the Near East. *Setaria viridis* (green foxtail) was domesticated as *Setaria italica* (*su*), *Oryza rufipogon* (common wild rice) as *Oryza sativa*. Broomcorn millet (*Panicum miliaceum*) the domesticated variety, still widely distributed in the Yellow River Valley, has the same name as the presumed wild progenitor, although some suspect that this wild grass may just be a retrogressive sub-species of the domesticated broomcorn millet (Lu 2006: 139).

Plausible as this model is for millet, it is less so for rice.[54] Although the most common wild rice species (*O. rufipogon*) can now be found as far north as 28°, this cannot have been true during the LGM, for wild rice requires a mean annual temperature of 16°C, and a minimum rainfall of 1000 mm. It is, therefore, hard to see how rice could have been collected as a major staple in the Yangzi Valley (around 30°N.) during or immediately after the LGM, as Lu (1999: 74) herself concedes. Further, if faunal and floral resources of southern China (< 28°N) were not greatly affected by the LGM, and specifically if wild rice, along with other floral and faunal resources, continued to be abundant there, on present information it is hard to see how or why rice came to be domesticated there at that time. Lu herself (2006) provides some answers.

Lu's repeated experiments (reported 2006) on growing wild rice (*Oryza rufipogon*) found that, due to its botanical characteristics – very low germination rate, infertile and shattered grains – the productivity of harvesting wild rice was very low indeed. Accordingly she concludes (2006: 145) that "incipient cultivation was probably a supplementary or even a leisure activity, without much expectation for return. The incipient cultivators were mainly hunters and gatherers and were only 'part time' or

---

[54] For a wide-ranging discussion *Antiquity's* Special Section on Rice Domestication (Malone 1998 ed.) is essential, particularly for the series of radiocarbon and AMS dates in Crawford and Chen Shen.

| ZONES | ESTIMATES (BP: uncalibrated radiocarbon) | REPRESENTATIVE CULTURAL REMAINS |
|---|---|---|
| Zone B | 2000–5000 | Pottery with geometric impressions. Domination of ground stone tools, bone tools having disappeared. |
| Zone C | c.7000 | Early pottery made by coiling method |
| Zone D | c.8000 | Early pottery made by the section modelling technique |
| Zone E | 9000–10000 | Primitive ceramics |
| Zone F | 10000–11000 | Ground stone tools. Chipped stone tools and bone artefacts are dominant, which continues until Zone C. |
| Zone G | 11000–12000 | Chipped stone tools and bone artefacts. |

*Figure 6.4: Chronologies and cultural stages at Diaotonghuan Cave in northern Jiangxi (Zhao Zhijun 1998).*

'occasional' farmers, until the production of cultivation increased to a certain level and/or until the natural floral and faunal resources were depleted by their foraging activities".

## Diatonghuan Cave

Diaotonghuan Cave, northern Jiangxi, in the Middle Yangzi region, is the subject of ongoing research, where a full-scale excavation was undertaken, directed by Richard MacNeish and Yan Wenming. The cave is situated in the small, swampy Dayuan Basin, measuring approximately 4 km east-west and 1 km north-south. It is surrounded by limestone hills on all sides and the cave is located about 60 m high in one of those hills. An area of 5 x 8 m at the centre of the cave was excavated to five metres, producing 16 clear-cut stratigraphic zones, A to P, latest to earliest.

One of the indices studied was the presence of rice phytoliths in various strata of the cave. Finds included stone implements, potsherds, bone and shell artefacts and a great abundance of animal bones (Zhao Zhijun 1998: 887). The first pottery occurs in Zone E, amongst the earliest in China. A conservative date for this zone is 9000–10,000 BP (*ibid*.: 888). Zhao provides a table of chronologies and cultural stages at Diaotonghuan Cave (Figure 6.4).

Zhao (1998: 892) found that an abundance of rice phytoliths suddenly appeared in the Zone G deposits, indicating that rice either wild or domestic became a component of local subsistence after about 12,000 BP. He suggests that "the recovery of few *Oryza* phytoliths from the lower deposits might indicate that *Oryza* did not grow in the area for most of the time during the colder Pleistocene or was a rare component of the vegetation. The sudden appearance of significant amounts of *Oryza* phytoliths in Zone G may reflect a warmer and more moist regime, beginning at the end of the Pleistocene which resulted in an extension of wild rice distribution into the middle Yangtse[55] region". What is certain is that the permissive conditions of the early Holocene encouraged the sedentary trend, and with ample subsistence resources, a rising population. The warmer, wetter Holocene climate, with mid Holocene temperatures in the Yangzi Valley possibly 3–4°C higher than today and with precipitation above 800 mm (Tang *et al.* 1993), permitted an easy path to farming to feed this rising population as excessive local pressure was put on parts of the resource base (Lu 2006: 147).

None of which is in conflict with earlier use of wild rice. Higham and Lu (1998:869) posit a scenario in the Younger Dryas (12,800 – 11,500 cal yr BP) during which "floral, and probably to a less entent, faunal changes must have had a impact on the prehistoric foragers of the region." The reduction of fruit and nuts, and the dominance of herbs might have encouraged foragers in the Yangzi valley to consume wild grasses, such as rice. According to archaeological discoveries, husks of wild rice (*Oryza rufipogon*) have been found in the Yuchan Cave in the middle Yangzi valley (Yuan 1996), and phytoliths of wild rice have been identified in Xianrendong in the lower Yangzi valley (Zhao *et al.* 1995). These discoveries suggest that wild rice was collected during the terminal Pleistocene". Potsherds also occur in Yuchan and Xianrendong caves, dated earlier than 10,000 BP. Higham and Lu (*ibid.*: 870) suggest that a prime use for pottery could have been the cooking of wild rice, which would have stimulated pottery production (for other ideas see R. Pearson 2005). At Yuchan and Xianrendong, until 7000 BP, the commonest forms are the cooking *fu*, with its round bottom and deep belly. Until that date in the middle and lower Yangzi valley, pottery is all hand, not wheel, made (*ibid.*).

Lu (2006: 151) defines the Xianrendong/Diaotonghuan group as incipient cultivators, and her hypothesis (*ibid.*: 150) based on current data, and in her own words, "is that incipient cereal cultivation in North China and the Yangzi Basin occurred approximately 11,000 to 10,000 years ago when the palaeoclimate improved after the Last Glacial Maximum and the Younger Dryas. It occurred in temperate areas where people lived with seasonally fluctuated resources, not in subtropical areas (i.e. South China) with very abundant year-round resources.

> "In addition, the incipient cultivators seem to have been small groups of semi-nomadic or seasonal collectors [Binford 1980; Murdock 1967] who scattered over the vast areas of North China and the Yangzi Basin. They first collected and then cultivated the progenitors of cultivated cereals (i.e. green foxtail millet in North China and wild rice in the Yangzi basin). These people lived in open, probably seasonal camps in North China and caves in the Yangzi Basin. Their subsistence strategies are broad spectrum, as they lived on various wild plants and animals".

This agrees with Pearson's (2005: 826) conceptions for the early use of pottery. For him, "the evidence suggests that small semi-sedentary or sedentary communities made very small quantities of pottery vessels for food preparation, since pottery is found in the living debris and is plain or minimally decorated. Vessel shapes seem to indicate

---

[55] This is his own pre-*pinyin* spelling.

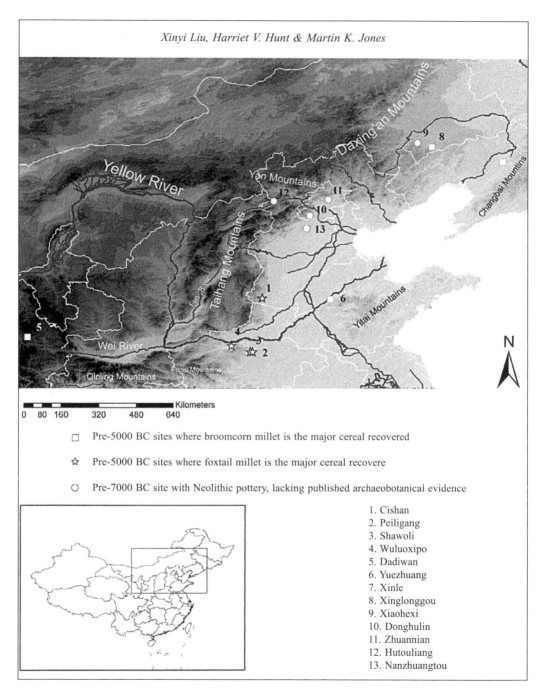

182    The Archaeology of Politics and Power

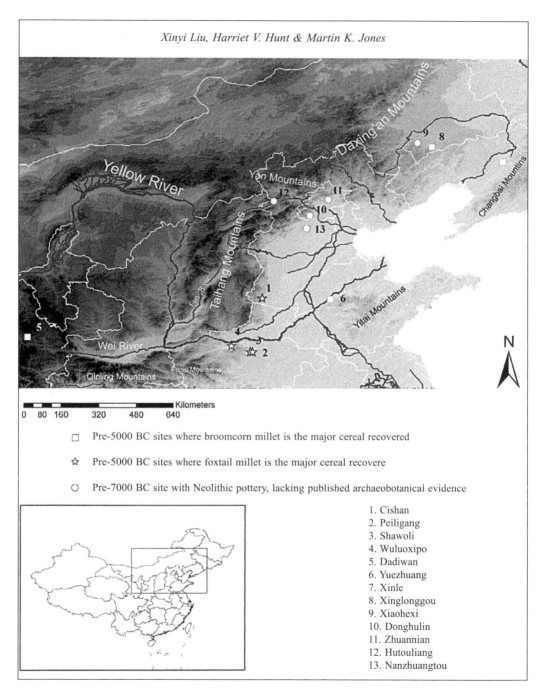

*Figure 6.5: Map of sites where millets are the major cereals recovered. From Liu, X., Hunt, H.V. and Jones, M.K. (2009: 85).*

food preparation rather than food consumption, although further research is needed to confirm this".

Liu, Hunt and Jones (2009: 93) suggest that there are more parallels between the origins of farming in south-west Asia and north-east Asia than are usually assumed, and I conjecture, as I previously have for the Near East (Maisels 1990: 71,130), that it was Holocene reduced mobility based on more plentiful food resources that led to sedentism (Lu 2006: 147). By permitting the population to expand (Bocquet-Appel and Naji 2006: 358) intensified demands were made on wild flora and fauna, not least through the 'packing effect' of proliferating villages.[56] Cultivation then arose from the desire for diversity in, and most important, the need for security of foodstuffs, coupled with the desire to have surplus food available for competitive display and feasting purposes.

## Earliest rice cultivation at Pengtoushan and Bashidang?

So far the earliest evidence for rice *utilization* comes from Pengtoushan and Bashidang, two sites on the Liyang alluvial plain south of the Yangzi. Compare this with Figure 6.5, from Liu, Hunt and Jones (2009: 85), which shows sites where millets are the major grains recovered – they are around or north of the Yellow River.

Pengtoushan and Bashidang have similar pottery, and date between 8900 and 8000 BP. In fact, although 15 pits, two houses and 18 burials have so far been excavated at Pengtoushan, no rice grains were found, and the evidence of its occurrence comes from the use of rice straw and husks as temper for the predominantly black pottery (Lu 1999: 89), much of which is cord marked. Common forms are bag-shaped jars and basins with round bases (Underhill 1997: 142). With the very earliest dates rejected, calibrated (years BC) dates for Pengtoushan fall into the 8th and 7th millennia (Crawford and Chen Shen 1998: 861).[57]

At Bashidang, which is 20 km northeast of Pengtoushang, 200 post-holes within an area of 100 sq.m suggests a village raised on piles, in turn suggesting location in a swamp, eminently suitable rice-growing terrain. There 15,000 grains of rice were found, husked and whole grain, and claimed to be an early form of domesticated rice (Zhang and Pei 1997; Pei 1998). Pei's (1998: 882) scattergram comparing the Bashidan grains with those of *hsien* (indica), *keng* (japonica) and wild *O. rufipogon* indicates that Bashidang rice is close to none of those, although it shares some characteristics with each. Pei (*ibid.*: 883) maintains therefore that "the early cultivated rice from

---

[56] Lu (1999: 115–6) found the use of the sickle to be the most efficient way to harvest common wild rice (*Oryza rufipogon*) with pulling-up and taking indoors to dry the next most efficient. She asks: "what would have been the harvesting methods used by prehistoric gatherers? According to my harvesting experiment conducted in Sanshui County, Guangdong Province in 1995, beating rice with a wooden rod into a basket is not efficient, as the panicles still contain considerable moisture and the grains won't come off until they are fully ripe. What is more, some of those grains fell into the swamp and could not be collected. But when the whole plant was pulled and left inside a house for one or two days, the panicles dried up and all the ripe seeds shattered". This scenario is, of course, eminently testable archaeologically.

[57] Underhill (1997: 142) has a broadly drawn Pengtoushan culture as spanning the period around 7000–5500 BC, with succeeding cultures of the Middle Yangzi valley, grouped as Zaoshi, *c.*5500–4500 BC. Zaoshi complex is followed by Daxi.

Bashidang represents the small-grain ancient rice at a precise history of its evolution. We suggest that it is called 'Bashidang ancient cultivated rice." Pei usefully also points out that the cultivation of rice went together with the cultivation of other wetland plants, notably water caltrop and lotus root, neither of which require soil preparation. Protective (drainage?) ditches and walled 'fortresses' are also reported from Bashidang, along with over 100 burials. Evidence from radiocarbon suggests that Bashidang is somewhat later than Pengtoushan. So too the Jiahu assemblage on the upper reaches of the Huai valley in Henan Province (33° 36'N, 113° 40'E) where we have radiocarbon from charcoal, ash, fruit stones and human bone, all of which indicate a calibrated span of 7000–5800 BC (Pei 1998: 899), that is within the Peiligang culture range (*c*.7000–5000 BC).

At Jiahu the remains of over 400 houses have been excavated, along with 300 graves in this 5.5 ha site, bounded by a lake and two rivers. "Residential patterns at Jiahu are characterized by three features: First, the settlement was divided into several residential groups; second, within a residential group small houses were arranged around one or two large houses in the centre, and the large houses may have been the locations for the kin group to conduct certain types of indoor tasks together; and third, the settlement was surrounded by a moat to protect the domestic community from the wild" (Li Liu 2004: 77).

Finds include pits, stone tools, animal bones, horns and teeth. Also kilns and several thousand pieces of pottery, mostly of poor quality because they are made from sheets or slices of clay, unevenly fired between 600 and 1000°C (Zhang and Wang 1998: 897). Most notable are round-bellied, necked jars with two pierced lugs. The assemblage includes twenty-six 7–note (single octave) bone flutes, turtle shells (*Cuora flavonmarginata*) used as rattles and bones with signs carved into them. This makes Jiahu a most interesting site, before even considering the finds of carbonised rice grains, husks and impressions of rice grains in pottery, in addition to a large quantity of rice phytoliths (*ibid*.). Early pottery at the site was sand-tempered, later ceramics were tempered by rice-husks, clamshell fragments, bone fragments, mica and talc (Li *et al*. 2003: 33). In regard to the flutes and other possible musical instruments, Li *et al*. propose "that the specially rich burials, the flutes, the incised tortoise shells and the pebbles, whether used to make musical rattles or counters to represent auspicious numbers, constitute evidence of ritual activity and divination" (2003: 42) most likely conducted by shamans. Indeed, this is ritual activity of a very high order, yet mortuary data strongly suggests that Jiahu society was egalitarian (*ibid*.: 128).

From their comparisons of the shapes of carbonised rice grains excavated at Jiahu and at Longqiozhang, and also comparing those found at Bashidang with Chengtoushan (the site of one of the oldest walled settlements in China), Zhang and Wang (1998: 900) advance the proposition that primitive cultivated rice originated simultaneously around 9000 BP in the upper Huai River region (where Jiahu is located) and in the middle Yangzi River region. However, the Huai River valley marks an ecotone transitional between the sub-tropical south and the temperate north. As a consequence of the higher selection pressures, human and natural, seen at such sites as Jiahu which is 33° 36'N, 113° 40'E, a major cool-tolerant cultivated variety, namely japonica (*keng*) had evolved there by 5,500 BP. This variety also emerged under selection pressure in the Yangzi

Valley, but there the principal variety was indica (*hsien*), which requires warmer, wetter conditions. Zhang and Wang (*ibid*.: 991) therefore conclude that, beginning the process around 7,800 BP, environmental conditions in the Huai Valley forced the speedier evolution of domesticated rice there as compared with the Yangzi valley, with 'typical' japonica farmed in the Huai by 5500 BP.

Test excavations at the nearby site of Lijiangang are also reported to have produced examples of domesticated rice (Underhill 1997: 142). Zhang and Pei (1997) claim that this rice was an ancient cultivated variety in transition to the contemporary forms *O. sativa indica* and *O. sativa japonica*. This would be an important finding were it established by thorough, and international, study. There are certainly enough rice grains to go around the specialist centres. Lu (*op.cit*.: 116) suggests that "the archaeological discoveries in Xianrendong and Yuchan in the Yangzi basin indicate that common wild rice might have been harvested in the terminal Pleistocene: and rice cultivation began by no later than 8000 BP at Bashidang and Pengtoushan." Further, the earliest pottery in the middle and lower Yangzi valley comes from Yuchan and Xianrendong, where, until 7000 BP, the commonest forms are the cooking *fu*, with its round bottom and deep belly. Until 7000 BP in the middle and lower Yangzi valley, pottery is all hand, not wheel, made (*ibid*.).

Another pile-dwelling site is that of Hemudu located in the peninsula south of Hangzhou Bay. This post 5000 BC site (perhaps 5000–4500 BC) was until recently considered to be earliest with cultivated rice. It also has the earliest painted pottery in southern China, the earliest oar for a boat, lacquer ware and also perhaps silk

| South China (southeast mainland, Taiwan) | Lower Yangzi River Valley | Middle Yangzi River Valley |
|---|---|---|
| Late Neolithic cultures, ca. 2500–1000 B.C.; both *indica* and *japonica* rice; first documented rice on Taiwan | Late Neolithic; rice, unknown varieties | Longshan Period, ca, 2500–1900 B.C.; several sites with rice, *japonica* identified at some |
| Shixia Culture in Guangdong, ca. 3000–2400 B.C.; *indica* and *japonica* rice | Liangzhu Culture, ca. 3300–2200 B.C.; *indica* and *japonica* rice | Qujialing Culture, ca. 3000–2500 B.C.; rice at several sites, only *japonica* identified |
| | Songze (ca. 3700–3300 B.C.) and Majiabang (ca. 4500–3700 B.C.) cultures; *indica* and *japonica* rice | Daxi Culture, ca. 4500–3000 B.C.; both varieties of rice |
| Dapenkeng Culture, ca. 5000–2500 B.C.; no evidence but possible cultivation of root crops and other crops such as rice | Hemudu Culture, ca. 5000–4500 B.C.; both *indica* (more common) and *japonica* rice, wild rice, soybean | Zaoshi Culture, ca. 5500–4500 B.C.; rice at several sites, *japonica* identified at some |
| | | Pengtoushan Culture, ca. 7000–5500 B.C.; unknown varieties of rice |

*Figure 6.6: Cultures in Southern China with macrobotanical evidence for cultivation of wet rice [paddy rice] and other crops (Underhill 1997: 141).*

production. It certainly has evidence for rice cultivation and domestication of, at least, the pig. The problem is, however, that Hemudu has anomalously excellent preservation, so its 'firsts' could just be an accident of preservation, with earlier to come elsewhere. One such may be Shangshan, an open site located on the lower Yangzi plain between Hemudu and Xianrendong/Diaotonghuan (Lu 2006: 138). The settlement seems to have been built on piles. The culture was ceramic, pots being slab-built, with many of them tempered with rice husks. Vessels include round-bottom cooking cauldrons, *fu*, and big basins flaring up from a small and flat bottom, with a loop handle near it (Lu *ibid.*). Vessels are mostly plain, but some are cord marked, stamped or incised. Flaked stone balls, examples of which have previously been dated from the mid to late Palaeolithic, have been found at Shangshan, as have flaked pebble tools, lithic abraders and perforated stone implements (*ibid.*). Grinding slabs and handstones also occur.

Hemudu fits into the southern rice-growing cultures as indicated by this Table (Figure 6.6, above) from Underhill's (1997: 141) thorough review of issues in the Chinese Neolithic.

## Food Preparation

Tracey L.-D. Lu (1999) advances a model that accounts well for the very early onset of pottery in China. In marked contrast to Southwest Asia, there is in China no Pre-Pottery Neolithic, followed after a couple of millennia by a Pottery Neolithic. Her elegant explanation (1999: 140) is that:

> "Grass seeds in China seem to have been only dehusked and cooked whole, instead of being milled into flour. The consequence of this simple processing is twofold: on the one hand, the labour and time required for seed processing were significantly reduced, thus making grass exploitation a much less formidable task; on the other hand, the type of cooking required the emergence of cooking equipment, thus stimulating the manufacturing of pottery. Once pottery was invented, seed cooking would have become a much easier task, and the cooked seeds were a tasteful, nutritive and easily digested food. Consequently, grass exploitation could have become much more attractive to foragers, causing continuous and intensive exploitation. When grass resources were not sufficient to meet the increased demand (caused by the decline of other resources, or the increase of population, or both), it would only be natural that methods of maintaining and increasing its availability were tried, one of them being cultivation, which eventually led to domestication."

Of course additional food sources could also have benefited from cooking in pottery, such is the flexibility that it offers.

This early adoption of pottery helps explain a number of important cultural characteristics, including the reverence for certain forms, notably the *ding*, originally a *fu* clay cooking pot with a round body, deep belly and round base, mentioned several times in previous sections. It stood on a tripod to go over a fire, which was later incorporated into the base as legs. So far the earliest *ding* known was found in Jiahu, the Peiligang culture site in the Huai Valley, the major river between Yangzi and the Yellow River. Jiahu, a large site with an area of 55,000 sq.m has already been discussed

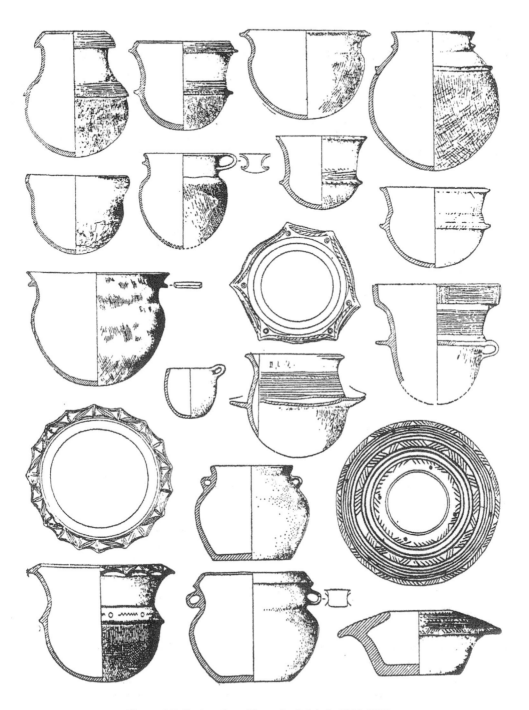

*Figure 6.7: Pottery from Hemudu (Maisels 1999: 289).*

as a possible locus of early domesticated rice. Of course the separate pot and stand precedes this, while "the over-cooked rice remains found in one *fu* in the Hemudu assemblage indicate that this vessel was used for rice cooking" (Lu 1999: 11).

In the Longshan site of Liangchengzhen in south-eastern Shandong, a Late Neolithic site putatively estimated at 246 ha, the largest in the region and studied by Crawford *et al.* (2005: 13), both millets and rice (and possibly wheat) were recovered, and "ceramic tripod vessels suitable for steaming grains or preparing gruels are common" (*ibid.*: 315). Liangchenzhen is assumed to be a regional production centre for elite items such as jades and egg-shell pottery goblets, and of utilitarian stone tools, over three quarters of which are made from sandstone, greenstone and quartzite (Li Liu 2004: 108). Indeed Underhill *et al.* (2008: 12) hypothesise that "Yaowangcheng and Liangchengzhen were centres of politically autonomous, but culturally connected regional polities during the Early and Middle Longshan periods." They also postulate (*ibid.*: 14) that both were "ritual centres for the region, where important ceremonies for the prosperity of the region took place", which likely involved feasting.

As Lu (1999: 11) observes: "in Bronze Age China, the *ding* was a symbol of the state and ruling power. The mysterious and sacred perception of this vessel in Chinese tradition suggests its antiquity and importance in prehistory". Indeed, the reverence accorded cooking vessels, especially when they assumed their bronze form with the sacred, ancestral associations, is not known to me in any other culture. Inscriptions on those revered vessels are one of our few contemporary Bronze Age sources (Keightley 1978; Shaughnessy 1991).

Much about Chinese food/cooking now becomes clear. In contrast to the 'flour' cultures of western and southern Asia, where 'daily bread' is the staple, bread and the bread-oven are not required in China. Instead fire or 'stove-top' cuisine develops based on boiling and roasting, with all their cultural/nutritional implications. When flour-based products are developed (probably earlier for the northern hard grains, notably foxtail millet) they take the form of noodles/pasta, which are boiled and not baked. Flour-based 'puddings' are steamed, as fish and vegetables often are. Even stir-frying does not seem to have been used until post-Zhou times, perhaps not common until iron utensils were. For the cooking of the Zhou period, Chang (1977: 31) observes, "their most important methods appear to have been boiling, steaming, roasting, simmer-stewing, pickling and drying". Different regions have different ingredients and recipes, but cooking methods belong to a common repertoire.

## Agriculture in Northern China

The earliest known agricultural village cultures of northern China are the **Laoguantai** in Shaanxi, **Peiligang** in Henan, **Cishan** in south Hebei and **Houli** in north Shandong, dating between 7000 BC and 5000 BC. Yan Wenming's (1999: 132) 'Early Neolithic' sites, such as Xianrendong (Spirit Cave) at Wannian, Qingtan Cave at Yingde, Dalongtan at Liuzhou, and Zengpiyan near Guilin, which are dated between 8500 BC and 6500 BC, are in fact Mesolithic. Essentially hunter-gatherer sites, it is just possible that pig domestication was beginning at those rock-shelter locations, but that remains to be seen. Even so, the Neolithic is defined by permanent villages with permanent architecture, gaining subsistence from some domesticates, supplemented by some hunting, gathering and often fishing. On those criteria, none of the pre-6500 BC sites are Neolithic. Shell mound sites of this period, maximally of 20,000 m², are found on both banks of the Pearl River in the far south, as well as along the coasts of Guangdong and Guangxi, and they are manifestly Mesolithic.

**Peiligang** in central Henan is represented by more than 70 sites (Underhill 1997:

| Northeast China | Western Yellow River Valley | Central Yellow River Valley | | Eastern Yellow River Valley |
|---|---|---|---|---|
| | | West | East | |
| Late Neolithic; none, cultivation inferred | Qijia, 2100– 1900 B.C.; foxtail millet, hemp | Longshan, 2800– 1900 B.C.; millet—foxtail, broomcorn | Longshan, 2800– 1900 B.C.; foxtail millet | Longshan, 2600– 1900 B.C.; foxtail millet |
| | Machang, 2300– 2100 B.C.; foxtail millet | | | |
| | Banshan, 2800– 2300 B.C.; broomcorn | Longshan | Longshan | Longshan |
| | Majiayao, 3400– 2800 B.C., millet—foxtail, broomcorn; hemp seeds | Late Yangshao, 3500– 2800 B.C.; millet—foxtail, broomcorn? | Late Yangshao, 3500– 3800 B.C.; millet— foxtail, broomcorn?; sorghum? | Dawenkou, 4300– 2600 B.C.; millet— foxtail, broomcorn |
| Hongshan, 4500– 3200 B.C.; foxtail millet | Yangshao, 5000– 3400 B.C.; unknown | Early Yangshao, 5100– 3500 B.C.; millet—foxtail, broomcorn; hemp? mustard seed? | Early Yangshao, 5100– 3500 B.C.; foxtail millet | Beixin, 5500– 4300 B.C.; foxtail millet |
| Lower Xinle, 5500– 4800 B.C.; broomcorn millet | Early Neolithic; unknown | Laoguantai, 6000– 5000 B.C.; broomcorn millet, rape seed | Peiligang, 6300– 5100 B.C.; millet— foxtail, broomcorn | Houli, 6200– 5500 B.C.; none, cultivation inferred |
| Earlier Cultures 6200– 5300 B.C.; none, cultivation inferred | | | | |

*Figure 6.8: Presence of cultivated millet and other possible dry-land crops among cultures of northern China (Underhill 1997: 118).*

121), mostly distributed across the Huang-Huai Plains. Site sizes range from less than 1 ha to over 6 ha and they contain stone tools with serrated edges interpreted as sickles. If sickles, they are the earliest in China. Laoguantai and Peiligang sites also contain formal pit burials with grave goods and the earliest ground-stone axes. They fit into the northern, millet-growing cultural sequence as shown in Figure 6.8.

However, Shelach (2000) argues that there are comparable dates for the earliest Neolithic from other parts of (what is now) China, including the North-east (Dongbei), locus of many sites of the ceramic Xinglongwa and Zhaobaogou cultures. Figure 6.9 (from Shelach 2000 & 2006 with modifications), compares the sequences in North-east China and the Yellow River basin.

Shelach (2000: 402) describes **Xinglongwa** and **Zhaobaogou** communities as sedentary or semi-sedentary and as containing over one hundred persons. Although Chinese archaeologists have been less than rigorous in recovering faunal and floral remains with flotation all too rare, Shelach suggests (*ibid*.: 381) that this area across the Yan Mountains north-east from Beijing[58] was where soy beans, so crucial to Chinese agriculture, were first domesticated, "because this is where wild and domesticated varieties of soybeans are most numerous, and because some of the domesticated varieties in the area have primitive characteristics".

Xinglongwa and Zhaobaogou houseforms however do not have primitive characteristics, being rectangular, in contrast to all the houses of pre-Yangshao cultures of the Yellow River basin, which are circular. In Yangshao sites rectangular forms occur, but are still outnumbered by circular shapes. Furthermore, Xinglongwa and Zhaobaogou settlements are laid out in lines or rows on rising ground or on the first terrace above the river valley, quite unlike those of the Yellow River basin or in the Chifeng area today, where most villages are sited on the edge of the floodplain. Indeed Liu, Hunt and Jones (2009: 92) argue that "The transition to millet farming may have originated beyond the [Yellow] valley itself, in locations along the foothills of two

| NORTH-EAST CHINA | CENTRAL YELLOW RIVER | EASTERN YELLOW RIVER |
|---|---|---|
| Lower Xiajiadian (*c.*2200–1600) | Erlitou (*c.*1800–1520) | Longshan (*c.*2600–1900) |
| Xiaoheyan (*c.*3000–2200) | Longshan (*c.*3000–1800) | Dawenkou (*c.*4000–2700) |
| Hongshan (*c.*4500–3000) | Yangshao (*c.*5000–3000) | Beixin (*c.*5500–4300) |
| Zhaobaogou (*c.*5250–4500) | Peiligang/Laoguantai (*c.*6300–5000) | Houli (*c.*6450–5500) Cishan (is north of Huanghe). |
| Xinglongwa (c.6200–5400) | | |

*Figure 6.9: Comparison of the Chronology of North-east China and of the Yellow River Basin (estimated BC dates). From Shelach 2000 & 2006 with modifications.*

---

[58] A rectangle formed by the Luan River in the west, the Xilamulun/West Liao River to the north, the lower Liao River in the east and Bohai Bay to the south.

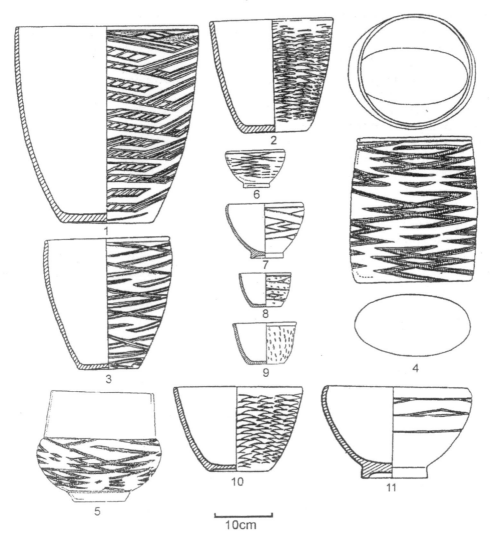

*Figure 6.10: Ceramic vessels of the Zhaobaogou culture of Northeast China (From Shelach 2000: 392).*

mountain chains in north-east China. In a smaller-scale niche surrounding each site, the run-off within hilly terrain was captured in small plots well before it reached the valley bottom".

Bifacial and ground stone tools are common at Xinlongwa sites, bone tools with inset microliths forming a cutting edge less so (*ibid*.: 384). Shelach (2000: 385) observes that "although no systematic study has addressed the function of these tools, their shapes seem to indicate a mixed economy of hunting, gathering and cultivation. The large 'hoes' and 'axes' may have been used to clear vegetation and to till the soil and the bone tools inset with microliths seem to have functioned as sickles. More direct evidence for cultivation is found at Zhaobaogou sites. In the Zhaobaogou [type-]site, among the 257 tools excavated, 163 are core tools and 94 are flake tools. ... In contrast to the Xinglongwa period, most Zhaobaogou core-tools are polished, although unpolished tools are also found. Common core tools are labelled as hoes, axes, mortars, and pestles. ... One unusual tool has been called a 'plough' (*si*) by the excavators".

However that may be, large grinding-stones are known from Xinglongwa sites and are very common at Zhaobaogou sites. As they are commonly associated with ceramic installations, acorns or other nuts/nutlets that require leaching could have been the main item ground, rather than grain. Certainly the grinding stones are different from those of the Peiligang and Cishan cultures (*ibid.*: 406). Xinglongwa pottery is mostly in coarse, sand-tempered clay, relatively soft and uneven in colour, suggesting both low firing temperatures and poor control over the kilns. All vessels are handmade, mostly by coiling, and the repertoire limited (*ibid.*: 389). The main types have been labelled as *guan*, a cylindrical jar, and *bo*, a bowl, both with flat bases. Decoration is usually by impression and incision especially of a Z motif. Zhaobaogou pottery is similar, but adds a finer, darker fabric. They remain simple in design and execution, but add other types of vessel, such as *zun* beakers. Ring footed vessels and oval bases also appear. The biggest differences are in decoration, which now includes stamping and applications; while motifs, in addition to the Z motif, include diamonds, nets, continuous and so-called 'thunder' patterns. See Figure 6.10 for examples.

Most notable are a few *zun* beakers made of fine clay and decorated with a continuous/merging pattern of intertwining animals. This example (Figure 6.11) is from the Zhaobaogou culture site of Xiaoshan ('little mountain') and shows the heads of deer, boar and a bird intertwined and combined with wings, antlers and paws of other animals.

Continuous/merging designs became a standard decorative technique during the Chinese Bronze Age, and is analogous to Andean decorative principles (see next chapter). Small, squat clay figurines which appear to be pregnant have also been found at Zhaobaogou sites.

*Figure 6.11: Decoration of a* zun *ceramic vessel (beaker) from the Zhaobaogou culture site at Xiaoshan (from Shelach 2000: 393, after Zhongguo1987: 495).*

# Yangshao

The most widespread and dense Neolithic of the northern interior is called Yangshao, originally described as 'painted pottery culture'; the earthenware pots with their swirling designs are probably mortuary ware. Banpo, probably the best preserved Yangshao site, near Xi'an, Shaanxi Province, is famous for painted designs of fish and human faces on red pottery. This rope-impressed amphora, 31.7 cm high, is an example of everyday ware. (Figure 6.12).

Concentrated on the middle stretches of the Yellow River and its tributaries, though by no means confined to them, around a thousand sites are known. An intensified East Asian monsoon and high temperatures made for a climatic optimum during the Yangshao Period (*c.*5000–3000 BC) and most sites can be described as hydromorphic (Maisels 1990: 70, Fig. 3.5).

The earliest painted pottery however, comes from the **Baijia** site belonging to the Early Neolithic (*c.*7000–5000 BC) Laoguantai culture of Shaanxi (Underhill 1997: 120). We now know that Yangshao

*Figure 6.12: Rope-impressed amphora, 31.7cm high, an example of everyday ware from Banpo.*

has three major phases (Early, Middle, Late) extending from about 5,000–3,000 BC: Banpo type, Miaodigou type and Xiwangcun type. Already lineage organization is apparent in the archaeological record, but stratified lineages are not present until the final, Late phase of Yangshao. It was succeeded by the Longshan. "The Longshan period was the first period in Chinese history to show major turmoil and upheaval that enforced cultural fusion" between what had been distinct culture areas (Shao Wangping 2000: 200).

**Jiangzhai** is a 5 ha settlement originating in the Banpo phase of the Yangshao, the earliest, with four later prehistoric levels (Li Liu 2004: 79). The centre of the site comprises a plaza of about 3 ha around which the residential area was disposed, with all the doors facing the central plaza. The residential area was surrounded by ditches outside of which burials were distributed (*ibid.*). The houses were clustered into five groups or sectors, and each group comprised small and medium houses and one large house, assumed to be of non-residential communal character as no cooking vessels were found inside them (*ibid.*).

Total population ranged between 75 and 125 persons based on settlement data and 85 to 100 persons based on burial data, giving a population density 44 to 63 persons per hectare and a mean of 53.5 (*ibid.*), a very useful reference level, since the whole of the Banpo phase settlement was excavated. "Pottery kilns and remains of workshops were found in eastern, western, southern and south-western parts of the site, both in the residential area and outside the ditches. ... The kilns were small in size, and probably could accommodate only four to eight small vessels in each firing. ... Only stone axes, made of cobbles, may have been produced in large quantities at Jiangzhai" (Li Liu 2004: 81–2).

Communal lineage cemeteries – *shizu gonggong mudi* – were standard for the Chinese Neolithic (Li Boqian 1999: 253), though we must be careful when speaking of 'China' in those early periods (below). Other Yangshao sites with communal lineage cemeteries in addition to Shijia, are Yuanjunmiao, Hengzhen and Jiangzhai. Indeed, in a comparison of general settlement patterns between two broadly contemporary villages, **Jiangzhai** in Shaanxi and **Zhaobagou,** the latter located in the Chifeng area of northeast China (between Beijing and Shenyang), Shelach's summary table shows communal arrangements at the former, while "it is quite clear that households in Zhaobaogou were much more independent in comparison with their Jiangzhai counterparts. The aggregation of activities, including storage, inside houses at Zhaobaogou suggests a restricted form of sharing – mainly within the household, as opposed to the 'open sharing' and communal orientation of households at Jiangzhai. The same is evident by examining the overall layout of the sites" (Shelach 2006: 340).

So Early Yangshao culture (*c.*5000–4000 BC) is relatively egalitarian, the poorly exposed Middle Yangshao Culture (*c.*4000–3500 BC) is transitional, with the recent discovery of several very large sites with large buildings, such as the 40 ha **Xipo** settlement in Lingbao, western Henan. By contrast, Late Yangshao culture (*c.*3500–3000 BC) with the emergence of large walled towns with palace-like public architecture (Li Liu 2004: 87) was definitely stratified. Such are **Dadiwan** in Qin'an, Gansu and **Anban** in Fufeng, Shaanxi.

An indication of merely relative egalitarianism even early in the Yangshao period, is that human sacrifice became established as a common practice at the **Banpo** site in Xi'an, Shaanxi, and in the mid-period settlement at **Miaodigou** in Shanxian, Henan (Li Liu 2004: 46). Craft and gender specialization increased markedly, as did the practice of household feasting in order to gain allies to build prestige and political power (*ibid.*: 42–6). Competitive feasting demonstrates the recognition amongst its practitioners of the necessity of bringing together 'the three elements' (Fig. 1.1) that, combined, make for secure political power: economic, in having the wherewithal to throw a feast that would need to include expensive meat (e.g. of water buffalo) in large quantities; ideology as the occasion for the feast, celebrating the ancestors, some kind of victory, good fortune or the life-cycles or fecundity of the lineage; and force, manifest as human sacrifice or the slaughter of important animals (such as turtles) in some numbers. This show of power would be even more potent were the turtle shells to be used for divination at the feast. Of house T26 at **Kangjia**, an extensively excavated *c.*19 ha site of the Longshan period (*c.*2709/2716 Cal. BC ±120; Flad 2008: 409) in Lintong, Shaanxi, Li Liu (2004: 69) concludes:

"Putting several lines of evidence together, pit H71, situated extremely close to the door of a house [T26], was probably intentionally made for a ritual event which involved

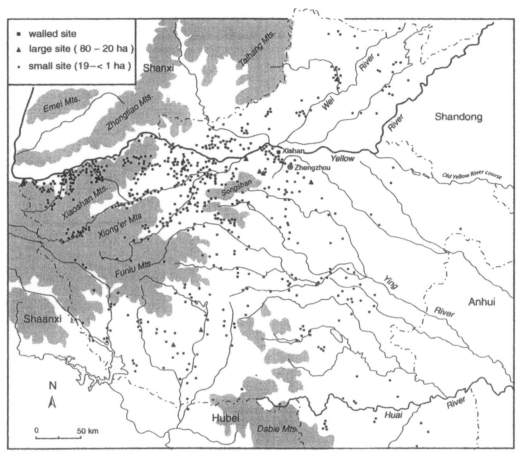

*Figure 6.13: Distribution of Yangshao sites in Henan, differentiating small, large and walled sites (from Li Liu 2004: 165).*

feasting. During this event a partially dismembered human body was buried, ritual performance using oracle bone and turtle shells was conducted, and large quantities of animal meat, shellfish and wild fruits were consumed at the same time", probably with lots of alcoholic drink.

**Dadiwan** was probably the centre for a large region, as by the Late Yangshao it approached 100 ha (Li Liu 2004: 86). Located on second and third terraces south of the Qingshui River, the settlement dates from the Early Yangshao when it approximated 10 ha, later extending up the hill slope. As with earlier Yangshao practice, settlement consisted of residential sectors, each comprising large and small buildings (*ibid.*). One of the large structures is house F405 found in sector IV. It's foundation extended over 270 m² with a large central hearth 2.34 m in diameter and 0.6 m high. The hearth, along with the floor, walls and posts were covered in lime plaster (*ibid.*). Apron structures were found on both sides of the building and three doors pierced the front and side walls. This may have been a communal building but important persons may also have lived there, indicated by the find of a white marble object, interpreted as a sceptre, a symbol of rank and high office.

In the centre of Dadiwan, about 240 m north of F405, disposed on a north-south axis lies F901, described as "a palace-like large foundation" (Li Liu 2004: 86). A multi-room structure covering 290 m² (420 m² with affiliated structures) it comprises a central large room with small rooms on both sides and at the back. At the centre of the major room is a fireplace 2.6 m in diameter, and in this room were found a set of ceramic objects not encountered in ordinary dwellings. These included a four-legged *ding* cauldron, a four-handled *guan* pot, a funnel-shaped lid, a rectangular basin and two *chao* scoops, one large and one of lesser capacity, with loop handles on top, perhaps functioning as measures. In the back-room three large pottery urns were found, which may have been for grain storage. In front of the building there are two rows of postholes and one row of stone pillar-bases, indicating that a large and imposing porch-like structure stood here. The building's three doors open onto this pavilion-like porch. With a large open plaza in front of it, F901 was ideally placed to orchestrate communal activities. So despite have been described as a 'palace-like structure' Li Liu (2004: 87) concludes that "This structure may have functioned as a central place for activities of regional communities, including perhaps feasting, redistribution, and ritual performances, rather than as an elite residence". A better description then might be 'proto-palace'.

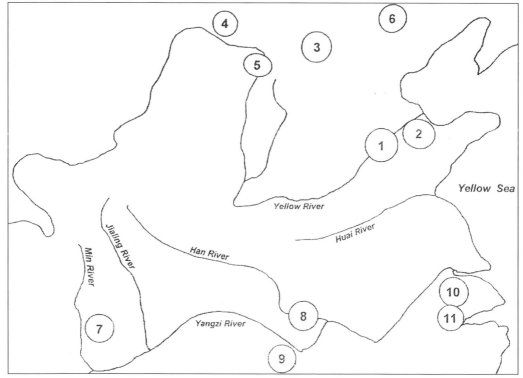

*Figure 6.14: Map of areas in China with Longshan walled cities (Dematte 1999: 124).*

If so the same must be true of **Anban**, a 70 ha site 200 km east of Dadiwan, as indicated by its layout, its building F3 similar to F901 at Dadiwan and some of the small finds, such as a large pottery scoop almost identical to one at Dadiwan.[59] So Dadiwan, Anban and Gaosituou, over 100 km south of Dadiwan on the west bank of the Xihanshui River in Lixian, Gansu, seem to be regional centres that are stepping stones to ruling centres.

**Xishan** near Zhengzhou in Henan is the largest, *c.*25 ha, earliest and best reported *walled* site of the Yangshao Period, which it spans. Located on a terrace of the Yellow River, only the northern and western parts are preserved (Li Liu 2004: 93). The walls are of *hangtu*, stamped earth, with none remaining above-ground, and measure 265 m long, 3–5 m wide and 1.75–2.5 m high. The walls are surrounded by a moat, 4 to 11 m wide and 3 to 4.5 m deep (*ibid.*). Two gates are located in the north and west, with the 10 m wide north gate shielded by a section of wall 7 m long and 1.5 m wide (*ibid.*). 6,385 m² were excavated, exposing about 200 houses, 2,000 ash pits, 150 burials and many artefacts, plus faunal and floral remains. One of the buildings, F84, built near the western gate, covered 112 m² and had a large plaza of a few hundred square metres extending to its north. It is not clear whether this was a communal public or an elite building (*ibid.*: 94). Incomplete skeletons of children inside pottery jars were found beneath the foundations of the town walls and houses. Over twenty of the pits contained whole animal skeletons suggesting ritual feasting using animal sacrifices. Some ash pits contained human skeletons "in postures of struggle mixed with animal bones, indicating violence or warfare" (*ibid.*). Indeed, the town walls constructed at the beginning of the Late Yangshao Period (3300–2800 BC) ceased to function before the end of that period, and this, in association with non-local elements related to the Dawenkou and Qujialing cultures, suggests that inter-group conflict was the reason (Li Liu 2004: 167).

## Regional Trajectories

Shao Wangping (2000: 195) lists six "macro-regions within which development toward complex civilization occurred separately during pre-historic times:

(1) The upper reaches of the Yellow River basin; (2) The middle and lower reaches of the Yellow River basin; (3) the Yangzi River basin; (4) far southern China; (5) the northern steppes; and (6) China's north-east". All of those regions are shown by Demattè (1999: 124) to contain Longshan period walled cities (see Figure 6.14).

## Early Stratification in the North: Dawenkou and Longshan

Longshan sites, which date between about 3000 and 2000 BC, cluster in Shandong along the former course of the Yellow River when it entered the Yellow Sea to the south of the Jiaodong Peninsula. (At present the river enters to the north of the peninsula).

---

[59] However some of the eight small baked–clay figurines (2.7–6.8 cm high) recovered from a pit, manifest 'non-Chinese' characteristics, such as long straight or hooked noses, one of which has a full beard. They wear pointed or flat-topped head-gear (Li Liu 2004: 88).

Figure 6.15 shows sites of Longshan and related or parallel cultures (from Maisels 1999 after Yen Wen-Ming 1981).

After the evidence of significant social stratification in the Late Yangshao, it comes as no surprise that even the Early Longshan period shows marked stratification. Longshan is contemporary with other stratified cultures such as Miaodigou II in Henan and Shaanxi, Middle and Late Dawenkou in Shandong, Qujialing in Hubei and Early Liangzhu in Zhejiang and southern Jiangsu [south of the Lower Yangzi]. **Dawenkou** is discussed next, prior to a fuller description of Longshan culture.

Because Dawenkou has Early (3900–3400 BC), Middle (3400–2900 BC) and Late Periods (2900–2400 BC), Fung (2000: 68) suggests that Dawenkou shows "the first consistent manifestations of social inequality in the Chinese archaeological record". However, Underhill (1999: 98), while extending the chronological span of Dawenkou in Shandong Province (see Map below) from *c.*4300–2400 BC, groups all of the burials at the Dawenkou cemetery into either Early or Late on the basis of cluster analysis. She further (*ibid.*: 117) identifies only very limited Early Period vertical stratification, for instance only one grave, (E78), from the Early Period has any jade. The presumed status indicators are: a large grave, log tombs, large quantities of pottery vessels especially tall-stemmed cups (probably for drinking alcohol); and objects of jade, elephant ivory, turquoise and alligator hide (*ibid.*: 120). On this basis there is very limited evidence

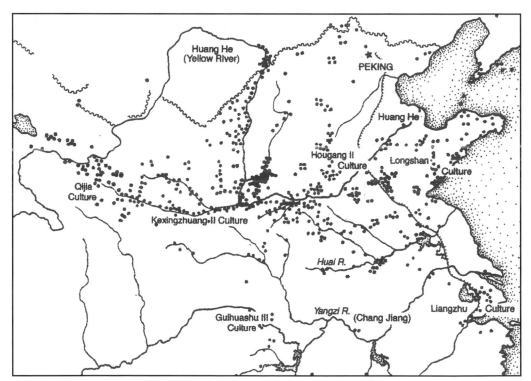

*Figure 6.15: Map showing sites of Longshan and related or parallel cultures (from Maisels 1999 after Yen Wen-Ming 1981).*

| B.C. | UP. YELLOW R. | MID. YELLOW R. | LOW. YELLOW R. | MID. YANGZI R. | LOW. YANGZI R. | LIAO R. |
|---|---|---|---|---|---|---|
| 1000 | Regional cultures | Shang | | | Regional cultures | Upper Xiajiadian |
| 1500 | | Erlitou | Yueshi | Regional culture & Erlitou | Maqiao | Low Xiajiadian |
| 2000 | Qijia | Late Longshan | Longshan | Shijiahe | Liangzhu | Xiaoheyan |
| 2500 | Majiayao | Early Longshan | Dawenkou | Qujialing | | |
| 3000 | | | | | Songze | |
| 4000 | Yangshao | Yangshao | | Daxi | Majiabang | Hongshan |
| | | | Beixin | | Hemudu | |
| 5000 | | | | | | Zhaobaogou |
| 6000 | Dadiwan | Peiligang | Houli | Chengbeixi | | Xinglongwa |
| 6500 | | | | | | |

*Figure 6.16: The succession of cultures from the Neolithic to the Shang state in some major river valleys (from Li Liu 2003: 3).*

of status differentiation in the Early period, but definite indications during the Late period, when there are even signs that use of the cemetery was becoming restricted to higher ranking families (*ibid.*: 121). The average grave size and number of artefacts per burial increases from 1.73 m² and 12.8 artefacts in the Early phase to 4.41 m² and 44.3 artefacts by the Late phase (Allard 2002: 10). The largest of those, M10, occupied by an adult female, has almost 200 grave goods, eight graves have none, while many have only one or two objects.

However, many graves contain the remains of a number of animal species, with pig remains prominent: 96 skulls, six lower jaws and numerous other bones (*ibid.*: 9). Noting that during the Late Phase large and stylistically elaborated *dou* (pedestalled serving stands) and goblets constitute a larger proportion of the ceramic assemblages of large and wealthy graves than of poorer graves, Allard (*ibid.*: 13) concludes that the *dou* and the goblets indicate the importance of social events in which those vessels were used to serve food and consume what were most likely alcoholic drinks. In the early stages of social stratification, being able to put on a good show, play host to large numbers (if not of the whole community, at least to one's faction) and appear to be engaged in some kind of redistribution, is a strategy found in many regions undergoing elite formation. This provides a plausible explanation for the appearance and significance of pig skulls and mandibles. If kin and supporters supplied pigs as part of the mortuary rituals/feasts, then their presence "may be interpreted as evidence of the degree of honour or status awarded to the deceased by survivors", as eloquently put by Li Liu (2004: 125). The use of pigs in this fashion will come as no surprise to those familiar with the classic ethnography, *Pigs for the Ancestors* (Rappaport 1968).

Similarly at **Wangyin**, some 65 km south-west of Dawenkou in Ningyang County, a large site comprising about 800 graves along with the remains of houses and pits. It has three phases, but most of the Phase I burials yielded no artefacts, while those that did contained a mere two or three grave goods (Allard 2002: 7). By contrast,

*Figure 6.17 (left): Burial M10 at Dawenkou showing a large labour-expensive burial pit (from Allard 2002: 11). Figure 6.18 (right): Burial goods recovered from M10 (from Allard 2002: 12).*

"the last two phases are marked by an increase in both the average number and the range of grave goods per burial. Wealthy graves belonging to the final phase contain ceramic vessels, along with various stone ornaments (rings, bracelets and pendants), turquoise earrings and tortoise carapaces" (*ibid.*). As at Dawenkou, ceramic vessels, all hand-made, dominate the range of grave goods provided. *Ding* tripods, cups, bowls, basins, jars and *gu* goblets were made across the life of Wangyin, but items manifesting greater craftsmanship appeared, used for display and serving (Allard 2002: 8). "One important late phase addition is the *dou* pedestalled serving stand, a dish on a splayed ring foot that could have been used to display – and serve – food" (*ibid.*: 9). The trend of the vessels towards greater elaboration across the three phases is seen in the ceramic sequence in Figure 6.19 from a to c at Wangyin (after Allard 2002: 8).

Dawenkou's successor culture, from about 2300 BC, was the **classic Longshan of Shandong**. Characteristic of the Late phase of Dawenkou are black, thin-walled vessels, which are the precursors of the well-known black eggshell pottery of Longshan (Allard 2002: 12). During the late phase of Dawenkou stone and jade ritual axes also appear.

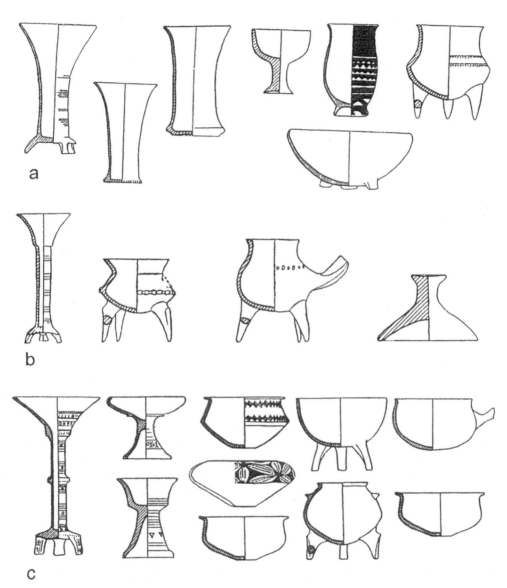

Figure 6.19: Ceramic sequence from a to c at Wangyin (after Allard 2002:8); a) vessels from early phase burials, b) vessels recovered from M139, a middle phase burial, c) vessels recovered from late phase burials. (Vessels are not drawn to the same scale).

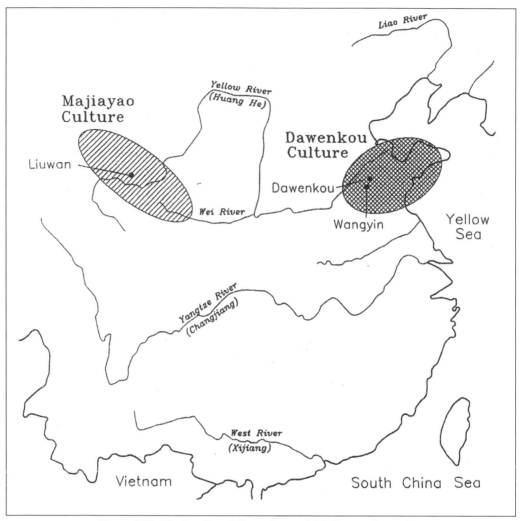

*Figure 6.20: The location of Dawenkou and Majiayao culture sites.*

## Longshan

Ubaid towns are the foundations for the development of cities and states in Mesopotamia. In China the foundations for class[60] cleavage and the state lie in the Longshan Period.

A major distinction in material culture of the Longshan (so-called from the type site of Zhengzuyai in western Shandong and meaning 'Dragon Mountain') compared with the earlier Yangshao, is that some house structures are literally 'raised-up' on stamped-earth platforms – *hangtu* – a technique identical to that used in building the town walls

---

[60] Members of a social class are those with a shared position in the Relations of Production. Thus peasants, priests, knights and large land-owning aristocrats – the state class – are the classes of mediaeval Europe.

mentioned above. That technique of ramming the loessic soil to hardness using boards was applied to construct massive city-walls with long deep ditches at the sites of Taosi and Chengzi, as examples, and it became a standard technique subsequently. So too did the cosmographic significance of walls, regulating and 'harmonising' space:

> "All these walls [of Qin times] were aimed at channelling and controlling the unseen spiritual forces of the world, as well as the movement of humans. They were intended to harmonize earthly space with the order of the cosmos..." (Yates 2001: 362).

The largest Longshan site, **Taosi**, located in the Linfen Basin of south Shanxi and dating to 2600–2000 BC, is said to have an area of 300 ha. The Linfen Basin is surrounded by mountains, some containing copper and lead. Eighteen walled towns have been found, some of them equidistant from one another, and manifesting a three-level settlement hierarchy (Liu 1996a: 1). Longshan is contemporary with an equally advanced culture south of the Lower Yangzi, called Liangzhu, which will be discussed in more detail below.

Taosi began with a rammed-earth wall enclosing 56 ha in the southern part of which a 5 ha palatial area and a 1.6 ha elite area were built (Li Liu 2004: 110). In the middle phase a much larger enclosure of 280 ha was built with walls, at 9 m wide, twice the thickness of the earlier ones. Taosi's rammed-earth enclosure is said to be the largest of the Neolithic period and it is one of the earliest sites in the middle Yellow River Valley that has metallurgy, signalled by a cast copper bell found there (Li Liu 2004: 111). In the south-eastern part of the larger site a 10 ha elite enclosure was built, containing a small elite graveyard (*ibid.*). In its late phase those walls were destroyed and with them the palatial area of the early phase, which now became a craft production area. Li Liu (*ibid.*) sees craft production as one of the reasons for the growth of regional centres in the Neolithic, and suggests that "the early use of metal at this site was not integrated with the existing prestige-goods system for expressing social hierarchy, a phenomenon also seen at other late Neolithic sites". The elite were not yet secure.

In this former palatial area more than forty skeletons were found buried in a ditch, some of the skeletons dismembered or having a weapon embedded (*ibid.*). Also the elite burials in the small enclosure were broken into and disturbed. Li Liu (*ibid.*) notes the existence of the 230 ha site that emerged at **Fengcheng-Nanshi** in the south of the Taer Mountains and says that the destruction at Taosi is consistent with military rivalry and conflict. However, it is also consistent – perhaps more so in the light of the selective destruction – with an internal revolt against increasing stratification and exploitation.

Three hectares of the Taosi site is a graveyard used across the entire Taosi period containing thousands of graves, around one thousand of which have been excavated. They can of course be categorised according to number and quality of gravegoods – especially ritually important ones such as pottery drums, alligator drums or *cong* jade tubes and *yue* jade axes – and according to size, furnishings and whether there is an *ercengtai* or (second level) offering ledge around the coffin/burial chamber. Obviously larger graves are more lavishly equipped, but there exists first and second class large graves, first, second and third class medium graves and first and last class small graves,

| Class | Subclass | Quantity | Frequency | Cultural Traits |
|---|---|---|---|---|
| Large | | 9 | 1.3% | Grave 3m long, 2–2.75m wide; all males. |
| | A | 5 | | Wooden coffin; spread cinnabar; 100–200 grave goods, including plate with dragon design, alligator drum, pottery drum, giant chime stone, large V-shaped stone knife, painted wooden board, container, plate, and stemmed cup; painted pottery; jade or stone ritual objects such as *yue* 鉞 axe, *yuan* 瑗 and *bi* 璧 disks, and *cong* tube; sets of stone axes, adzes and arrowheads; whole pigs. |
| | B | 4 | | Similar to subclass A, but without alligator drum, pottery drum, giant chime stone. |
| Medium | | 80 | 11.4% | Grave 2.2–2.5m long, 0.8–1.5m wide. |
| | A | | | Near large tombs; wooden coffin; spread cinnabar; whole set of pottery vessels including 1–2 painted ones; a few painted wooden vessels; jade or stone ritual objects; a few to a few dozen pig mandibles. |
| | B | | | Wooden coffin; spread cinnabar; jade or stone ritual objects; ½–1 pig mandible; no pottery or wooden vessel. |
| | C | | | Wooden coffin; a few grave goods including stone ritual objects and bone pin; 1–2 pig mandibles. |
| Small | | 610 | 87% | Grave 2m long, 0.4–0.6m wide; |
| | A | | | bone pin; some have 1 small pottery vessel; some have ½ pig mandible. |
| | B | | | No grave goods. |

*Figure 6.21: Classification Table of Burials at the Taosi Site (N=699), from Li Liu (1996a: 21).*

the last having nothing at all. They are all detailed in this Classification Table of Burials at the Taosi Site (N=699), from Li Liu (1996a: 21) (Figure 6.21).

Large graves occupied the centre of neat rows, with medium and small graves placed on either side. Accordingly, "the elite burials form the centre of the burial cluster in a cemetery which includes both elites and commoners, most of whom were kin, indicating that basic kin groups (families or extended families) were internally stratified" (Li Liu 1996a: 22–3). This is a clear early example of the emergence of the *conical clan*, in which a dominant lineage, localised as a major household, gains hegemony and ultimately control over the other lineages in its clan. Other lineages' subordination is justified by perceived genealogical distance from the axial or dominant lineage. The destruction seen during the late phase of Taosi may well indicate that this process did not go unchallenged by the lower orders or 'inferior' lineages, and that at this point, in this place, they had just had enough of pretensions and exactions regardless of the ideological justifications deployed.

The occupants of the 'raised-up' houses, even where, as at Donghaiyou they were only 6 x 6 metres, were socially 'raised-up' also. Here are unmistakably clear signs of social stratification, and it is occurring within lineages as well as between them. That conical stratification is not anomalous at Taosi, but is in fact typical of Longshan settlements, is indicated by the sites of Yinjiacheng, Zhufeng and Chengzi.

**Chengzi** is situated on a river terrace to the west of Chengzi village in Zucheng County, Shandong. It extends over 2 ha, of which 1300 m² have been excavated, exposing two houses, 16 pits and 87 burials (Li Liu 1996b: 230). The cemetery indicates that Chengzi was a stratified society (Li Liu 2000: 151). The 87 burials at Chengzi excavated between 1976 and 1977 lay in rectangular pit graves and group into four distinct classes based on the characteristics of their size and furnishings, "ranging from large grave pits associated with abundant grave goods, to small pits with no grave goods" (*ibid.*).

(1) large graves, with second-level (*ercengtai*) ledge, wooden chamber, and many grave goods, including invariably the thin cup on high stem (goblet), eggshell pottery and pig mandible;
(2) smaller pits, with second-level (*ercengtai*) ledge, some wooden chambers, more than 5 grave goods, sometimes including the goblet and pig mandible;
(3) small rectangular pits, with no second-level ledge or caskets, and no more than 3 grave goods;
(4) very narrow pits, barely large enough to place the body inside, with no furnishings and no grave goods.

There are altogether only five first-class graves, all male, eleven second-class graves, of those sexed, all male, seventeen third-class graves evenly split, and fifty-four fourth-class graves of mixed sexes. Significantly, the burials were clustered in four well-defined areas of the cemetery, but only three (still?) have class 1 graves. It may be that the houses shown as horseshoe shapes on the plan below, and which are later (Li Liu 1996a: 25), probably after the cemetery went out of use, have destroyed the class 1 graves in the eastern section. Nonetheless, "most lower-ranking individuals were concentrated in the eastern section, while most higher-ranking ones were concentrated in the western section. Moreover, the western section of the cemetery seems to be further divided into three sub-groups of burials arranged in parallel rows. Each of the three sub-groups contains different classes of burials" (Li Liu 2000: 151) *corresponding to internal ranking within each lineage.* There are 14 pits located in the western part of the site and associated with the elite graves, only two in the eastern section (though two are on the borderline between west and east). They contain well-known ritual items such as whole pots, stone and bone implements and pig mandibles. This indicates ongoing ancestor worship, as the pits are either contemporary with or later than the burials, in which latter case they would be commemorative sacrifices (Li Liu 2000: 153). "Therefore a deceased individual's qualifications for assuming the role of ancestor depended on his political and economic importance within his family and lineage during his lifetime" (*ibid.*). Here then ancestor worship had already shifted from being community-oriented to being family or lineage oriented (*ibid.*).

Li Liu's conclusion (2000: 151) is that "The distribution of burial ranks seems to be conical: the higher the rank becomes (or the larger and more elaborate the graves and their furnishings are), the fewer the number of burials found". Here we encounter the *conical clan* (discussed and illustrated below) in which one lineage promotes itself to the apex of a cone formed, as it were, by the branching away of related lineages from the supposedly core lineage. All lineages in reality have same time-depth, but by gathering to itself the most important sources of power – ritual, economic and physical – a lineage makes itself both central and superior, having relations of equality only with promoted lineages in other conical clans.

Chengzi site seems to have been a cemetery site, but **Yinjiacheng** in Sishui, Shandong, was a residential site with a cemetery. Much of the site has been lost in recent times, although enough survives to demonstrate five classes of grave. Indeed M15, at 5.8 m long, 4.36 m wide and 1.55 m deep, is amongst the largest Longshan examples so far found (Liu 1996a: 33).

However the largest Longshan examples known occur at **Zhufeng**, a 10 ha site on a terrace of the Mi River at Xizhufeng village in Linqu county, Shandong. There three very large burials appear to belong to different generations of a dominant lineage as they are grouped in the south-west part of the site, which was partitioned into sections for the various kin groups (Liu 1996a: 38) and belong to different phases. The three 'master' graves are M1, M202 and M203. M1 is 4.4 m long, 2.5 m wide and 1.8 m deep, and was constructed with an inner coffin, an inner chamber, an outer chamber, a side container and a foot container, all made of wood. The occupant was an adult female

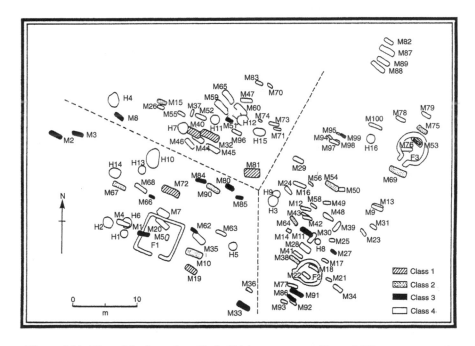

*Figure 6.22: Plan of the Longshan Chalcolithic cemetery at Chengzi (Chang 1986: 251).*

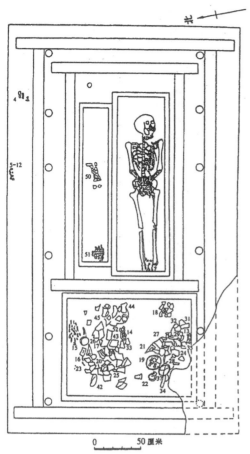

*Figure 6.23: Plan of M1 at Zhufeng (from Liu (1996a: 35).*

who had a turquoise ear pendant near the head, a small jade tube on the chest and a deer tusk in her hand. The side container held two egg-shell pottery goblets, with another six in the foot container, which held another 29 pottery vessels (*ibid.*: 36). Figure 6.23 is a plan of M1 from Liu (1996a: 35).

M202 and M203, dating to the late Shandong Longshan period were found less than 30 m to the west of M1. It was 6.68 m long and 2–2.1 m deep, but its full width has been lost. The coffin itself remains intact, and the unsexed skeleton is 1.75 m tall. Near it were jade and turquoise ornaments and jade ritual objects,[61] including a knife, two *yue* axes and, significantly, a headdress bearing a motif similar to those on jade ornaments of the Liangzhu culture, discussed below. Amongst other pottery items that included cooking vessels, pouring vessels, storage vessels and liquid containers, were egg-shell goblets and a few dozen alligator scutes (scales), which most probably came from alligator drums. The presence of alligator drums would denote very high status indeed. Some of the artefacts, such as jade objects, certainly drums and chime stones, were ritual paraphenalia, suggesting that one path to power (or to consolidate it once socially successful) was through ritual or shamanism (Li Liu 2008: 122–3).

M203, located only 3 m north of M 202, is 6.3–6.44 m long, 4.1–4.55 m wide and 1.48 -1.72 m deep. It too had a wooden coffin within which were jade and turquoise ornaments, an inner chamber with pottery and goblets, an outer chamber and an *ercengtai* ledge (Liu 1996a: 36).

At **Chengzi,** sacrifice pits were confined to the worship of elite ancestors, those of poor or broken lineages being non-ancestors. By contrast the distribution of 150 sacrificial pits distributed around the edges of 168 burials of the Yangshao site at **Longgangsi** (earlier), indicates that all forebears were commemorated in a relatively egalitarian society (Li Liu 1996a: 40). The pits, which contained ash, small pieces of

---

[61] For an extended discussion of the ritual significances of jade, see Childs-Johnson, ed., 1988. Jadeite is of course the other 'true' jade mineral.

charcoal, pottery sherds, burnt clay, crop seeds, stone tools and unbroken pottery vessels, indicate use for ritual purposes relating to the deceased in ancestral cult ceremonies (Li Liu 2004: 131). By Shang times, associated with eleven royal tombs at **Xibeigang** (below) were nearly 2000 sacrificial pits, clearly the most important ritual for Shang rulers. Until Shang times there seems to have been no ancestor temples (*zongmiao*). Accordingly, all major rites were conducted in graveyards around tombs, but without above-ground buildings at least until the historical Spring and Autumn Period (see Li Boqian 1999 for an important discussion. Chen Lie 1996: 272 states that the ancestor cult is "ultimately the core of Chinese religious belief").

## Liangzhu

The evolutionary sequence for the emergence of Liangzhu Culture in the Lake Tai peninsula (where Shanghai is situated) is, in broad terms: Majiabang during the fifth millennium BC, Songze during the fourth millennium BC, and Liangzhu culture in the third millennium BC, contemporary with the Longshan to which the Liangzhu was once assimilated. Especially difficult was the acceptance that southern Neolithic and Chalcolithic cultures could be so rich in jades, taken to be a measure of sophistication, and that there could be a culture distant from Longshan at least as advanced as it was (Sun Zhixin 1993: 19).

However, it is now clear that there were many regional cultures as advanced as Longshan and that they produced fine jades, leading some to call this Late

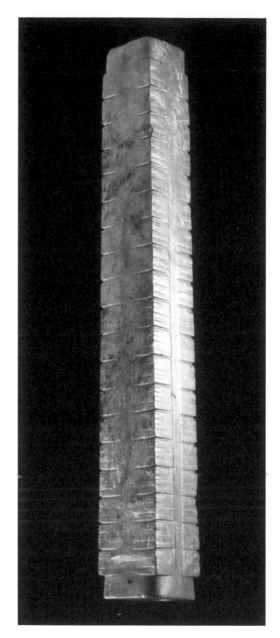

*Figure 6.24: Liangzhu jade cong; square cross-section pierced by a circular hole (British Museum).*

Neolithic/Chalcolithic period the 'Age of Jade' (Chang 1989; but see Rawson 1995: 28). In addition to the Longshan and Dawenkou of Shandong, those contemporary jade producers include the Qijialing and Shijiahe in Hubei, the Xuejiagang culture

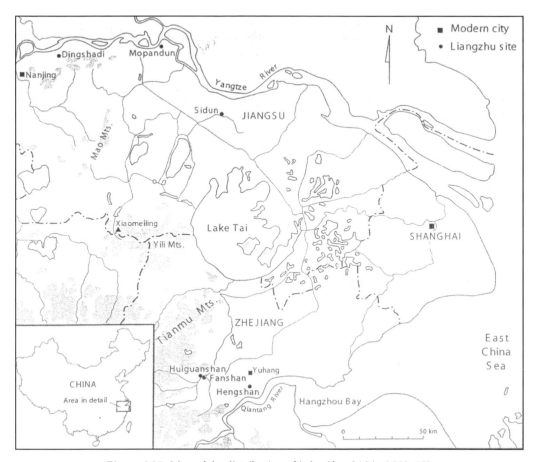

*Figure 6.25: Map of the distribution of jades (fom Li Liu 2003: 10).*

in Anhui and the Shixia culture of Guangdong (Sun Zhixin: 1993: 23). Shixia, dated between 4850 and 4500 BP, has a material culture intimately related to Liangzhu culture; bracelets, jade *cong*, pendants and slit rings link the two (Higham and Lu 1998: 874). Shixia, along with Xincun, Chuangbanling and Niling provide evidence of early rice cultivation in Lingan. Lingan sites are linked to the Yangzi valley by the rivers Ganjiang and Xiangjiang (north-flowing) and the River Biejiang (south-flowing). Nonetheless, by far the greatest quantity of jades and the best in quality come from Liangzhu sites in the lower Yangzi Basin (See Figure 6.25).

Liangzhu sites are also remarkable for clear evidence of social stratification, the profligate consumption of labour and lives in human sacrifice (as at Fuquanshan) and the iconography of power which was adopted by later regimes. From the abundance of unfinished jade objects in elite graves, Li Liu (1993: 12,15) makes two important and related suggestions concerning the Liangzhu jades: (1) that the elite made at least the ritual jade objects with their own hands; meaning that either such skill was a path to power, or that once in a position of power it was possible to consolidate it by acquiring pieces of jade and transforming them into finished articles; (2) that the position of the elite with its special ability to communicate with the ancestors through jade artefacts was destroyed by environmental forces. Those were either natural (marine transgression and flooding at the end of the third millennium) and/or human-induced environmental deterioration, against which their ideological power could, of course, not prevail. Accordingly the successor culture, the Maqiao, had little use for prestige-goods production.

Most of the jades are either *bi* or *cong*, respectively rings and tubes, the latter most probably developing from a bracelet around 3000 BC. Historically the circular *bi* were used to refer to heaven, the (sub)-square highly decorated *cong* refer to earth. Bronze rings, *huan*, and tubes, *guan*, were also made. In traditional cosmography heaven is round and earth is square and flat (Teng Shu-P'ing 2000). Zhou texts state that ritual buildings should be round on a square platform or in a square courtyard. Imperial coinage (*cash,* after 221 BC) was round with a square hole at the centre for its obvious cosmological connotations. Conversely, the large Liangzhu *bi* may in fact represent a store of wealth rather than, or outweighing, their ritual value. Some, such as those of the middle Liangzhu period from tomb 3 at Sidun, Jiangsu, weighed 1.5 kg each (Chang 1989: 27). Like western oil paintings, ritual value and exchange value could be mutually reinforcing:

> "The ancients considered jades to be 'numinous objects'. They valued the material for its durability and incorruptibility; to them, it symbolized eternity and endurance. Jade and silk – both richly imbued with the aura of refined excellence – were deemed particularly suitable as offerings to spirits and ancestors, and were therefore referred to as the 'two refined substances' (*erjing*) Indeed the character used for writing the word *li* 'ritual' is a pictograph that illustrates 'offering jade to the spirits'" (Teng Shu-P'ing 2000: 190). When bronze took over as the most important ritual substance around 1700 BC (Erlitou Phase III) it was referred to as 'beautiful metal' (*meijin*). "The association of bronze with a set of ritual practices centred on ancestral offerings first occurred at Erlitou" (Allan 2008: 420).

Made of jade and representing the sun and the sky, *bi's* had then a double charge, and woe betide any commoner who did not offer to the ruler a *bi* that had come into his or her possession (*ibid.*: 191). Li Liu (2008: 121) designates the *cong* tube, the *bi* disk and the *yazhang* tablet, a sceptre-shaped ritual item, as three of the trans-regionally occurring jade forms.

*Cong* bear the earliest *taotie* designs, formed from the fusion of human and animal characteristics that some see as indicating shamanistic transformations into a spirit animal/guide (shaman: the character *wū* 巫). Zhang Chi (1997: 66) reproduces examples of *taoties* from carved jade objects excavated at Yaoshan and Fanshan, which are but two of the elite cemeteries in a cluster of 40 sites contained in only 12 km² around Mojiaoshan in Zhejiang.

Figure 6.26 shows *taotie* designs on carved jade objects. Bottom left is a 'double taotie', where the arms, drums (hands are open and flat) and feet of the upper *taotie* form the face of a lower one.

I read *taoties* as representing the transformative properties of power, especially death. For example, a particularly grim *taotie* spans a Shang (state) executioner's axe. An

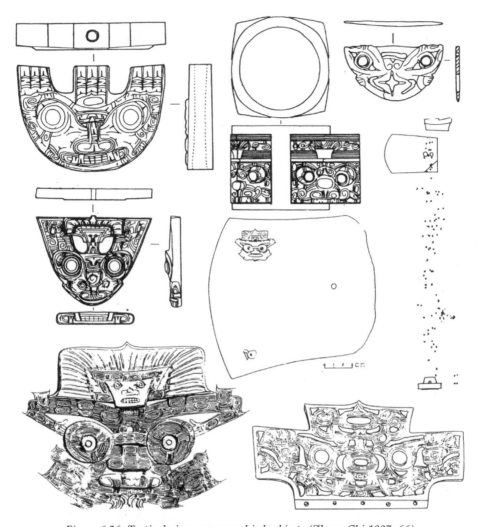

*Figure 6.26: Taotie designs on carved jade objects (Zhang Chi 1997: 66).*

aperture at the centre of a bronze axe of the late Shang forms a gaping, fanged mouth ready to devour its victims (illustrated in Rawson 1980: 47), who describes the demonic face as that of a man rather than that of a *taotie*. But the principle of terrible power is the same: two such axes were found in the outer trench at Sufutun in Shandong, (below), where the beheaded victims were laid out on the access ramp next to the main burial pit (Rawson 1980: 46; axe illustrated in Blunden and Elvin 1983: 48–9). The situation at Sanxingdui in second millennium Sichuan (below) is likely to be different. For one thing there is as yet no clear evidence of human sacrifice there.[62] However, speaking

---

[62] Nonetheless, excavations have only sampled the huge site and fieldwork reports have been notable by their absence. For example, as Jay Xu (2006: 156) states, "none of the fieldwork undertaken since 1994 has been reported".

of the many masked individuals and birds found in the Sanxingdui pits, Yang Liu's (2000: 41) anthropologically very well informed account relates that:

"Aggressive supernatural spirits of an almost demonic nature are represented on those masks. They remind us of the *taotie* animal face – the most popular motif on ritual objects of Bronze Age China that was also employed as decoration on bronze vessels in Sanxingdui. As to the *taotie*, many explanations have been offered but one early tradition referred to it as the image of a harmful spirit." In sum, a *taotie* manifests menace.

The major jades at Liangzhu come of course from elite tombs, which were centred upon wooden coffins or chambers. Excavation in 1986 at Fanshan in Zhejiang Province (the same year as the remarkable finds at Sanxingdui, below), recovered over 1,000 *bi/cong* sets (2,200 pieces) from eleven burials in a mound only 4 m high, but 90 m E/W and 30 m N/S. The following year another 635 sets were found in twelve burials cut into a rectangular ceremonial platform atop Yaoshan Hill, 5 km northeast of Fanshan. To the west of Fanshan eleven tombs in two parallel rows yielded over 3,000 jades (Sun Zhixin 1993: 20). Even the elite were stratified, and so one tomb, M20, the most lavishly furnished, alone produced over 500 jades, while the poorest had 'only' 50 (*ibid*.). The extraordinary find, however, came from M12. It was a *cong* measuring 8.8 cm high by 17.6 cm wide. Nicknamed 'the king of *cong*', it weighed a massive 6.5 kilograms. Its four sides carry sixteen elaborate double images (*ibid*.) which make up *taoties*. On *cong* and other media, what is represented is wealth and power, especially the power of life or death.

When wealth, power and ideology come together, then the internal political conditions exist for a state to form on the basis of pre-existing stratification. However Liangzhu culture appears not to have developed, or at least been unable to consolidate, its own state. Rather, the early state forms we know of arise in the Zhongyuan although that may be an artefact of traditional historiography and patchy archaeological survey and publication. However all the conditions existed for the emergence of the state in the Liangzhu culture area. Probably all that was lacking was sufficient centralization before the breakdown of the society and its replacement by Maqiao communities. In other words *charismatic catalysis* – which is point 13 on Figure 9.1 – was not achieved.

A roughly contemporary and hitherto totally unexpected civilization was recently discovered at the site of **Sanxingdui** in present day Sichuan. As presently understood, it was sacrificing remarkable objects instead of humans. Indeed the pit sacrifices carried out Sanxingdui seem to be collective rituals rather than ones conducted for the benefit of deceased royalty. It had the benefit of no contact with the Late Shang capital of Anyang and some contact with middle Yangzi civilization.[63] A bronze kneeling figure found at Sanxingdui was holding a *yazhang* tablet, which is a sceptre-shaped jade ritual item that was particularly widespread in East and South-east Asia (Li Liu 2003: 6). Jade objects with similar forms and motifs from various regions and periods are shown on Figure 6.27 (from Li Liu 2003: 7). The jades are *bi* and *cong*, *yazhang* tablets, as well as divine bird and turtle objects.

---

[63] Bagley (1999: 208–9) sees bells as indicative of the "overarching cultural unity" of the middle and lower Yangzi region, and perhaps an absence of human sacrifice is too.

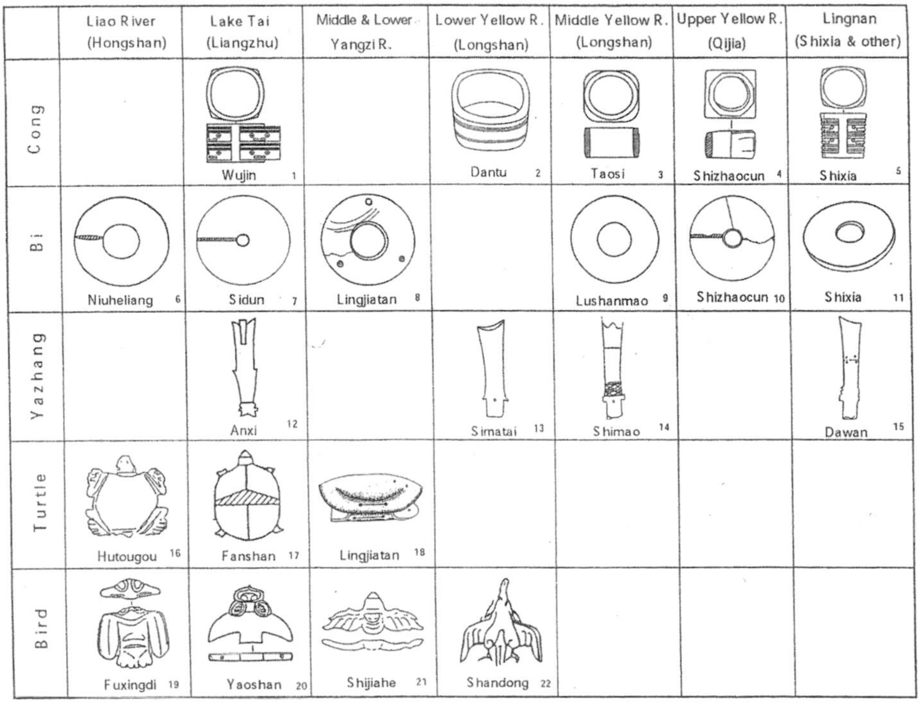

| | Liao River (Hongshan) | Lake Tai (Liangzhu) | Middle & Lower Yangzi R. | Lower Yellow R. (Longshan) | Middle Yellow R. (Longshan) | Upper Yellow R. (Qijia) | Lingnan (Shixia & other) |
|---|---|---|---|---|---|---|---|
| Cong | | Wujin 1 | | Dantu 2 | Taosi 3 | Shizhaocun 4 | Shixia 5 |
| Bi | Niuheliang 6 | Sidun 7 | Lingjiatan 8 | | Lushanmao 9 | Shizhaocun 10 | Shixia 11 |
| Yazhang | | Anxi 12 | | Simatai 13 | Shimao 14 | | Dawan 15 |
| Turtle | Hutougou 16 | Fanshan 17 | Lingjiatan 18 | | | | |
| Bird | Fuxingdi 19 | Yaoshan 20 | Shijiahe 21 | Shandong 22 | | | |

*Figure 6.27: Jade objects with similar forms and motifs from various regions and periods (from Li Liu 2003: 7).*

## The Earliest State: Erlitou?

The site of Erlitou is a multi-period one – Yangshao, Longshan, Erlitou and Erligang – extending about 2.4 km east-west and 1.9 km north-south on the south bank of the Luo River only about 12 km before its junction with the river Yi. After the junction it is called the Yi-luo River, a tributary of the Yellow river, which can be seen inset on the map below. Erlitou is located 20 km east of the modern city of Luoyang in the Yiluo River basin. By far the largest contemporary site, it is thought by many to be the centre of the earliest state in China, traditionally referred to as **Xia**, first of the Sandai, or Three Dynasties, mentioned in the opening paragraphs. Erlitou culture sites are distributed over Henan and also adjacent parts of Shaanxi, Shanxi, Hebei and Hubei (Bagley 1999: 164),[64] as seen in Figure 6.28 with key natural resources.

The culture seems to be centred in western and central Henan, especially the latter, as the Xinzhai phase of Erlitou culture developed from the Haojiatai phase of the Longshan (Li Liu 1996b: 274). Over 120 Erlitou sites have been identified, with the Xinzhai site a centre of 70 ha in the Gughengzhai settlement cluster, manifesting the

---

[64] In the following section my debt to Bagley's (1999) recent synthesis in *The Cambridge History of Ancient China* is clear. I am also much indebted to Li Liu and Xingcan Chen's 'State Formation in Early China' (2003), which marks a huge advance in our understanding of that topic.

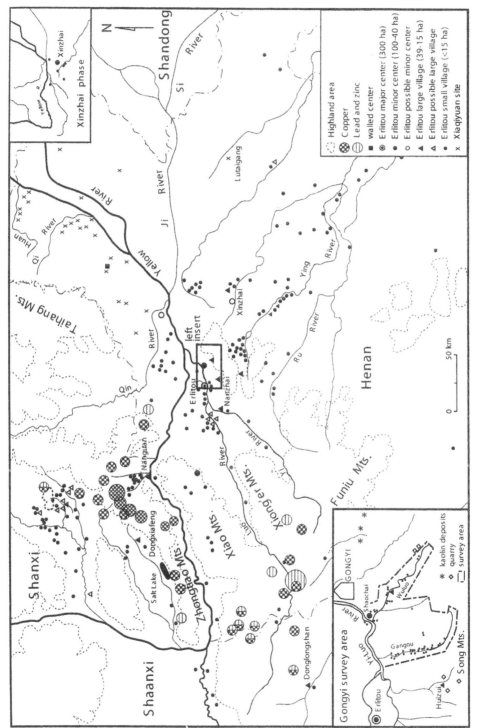

*Figure 6.28: Erlitou in its setting (from Liu and Chen, 2003: 12).*

transition from late Longshan to Erlitou (*ibid*.: 276). Other Longshan sites in the region are Luokou (20 ha) situated in the middle reaches of the Wuluo valley, and Fuxi (13 ha) in the mid Gangou valley (Lee 2004: 187). Liu (2004: 229) sees Xinzhai and its environs as pivotal, since the "core region of the Xinzhai phase is situated in the area where the Wangchenggang, Wadian and Guchengzhai sub-clusters, each with three levels of site hierarchy and two with walled centres, reveal the most complex settlement system in Central Henan". Guchengzhai and Taosi both contain large palace-like residential buildings (Liu 2004: 244).

Li Liu *et al.* (2004) have undertaken probably the first rigorous and extensive study of multi-period settlement patterns in prehistoric North China, and on this basis Liu reaches conclusions that have broad theoretical relevance: "The earliest states such as the Erlitou culture, however, were not derived from the most complex chiefdoms in the Taosi and Sanliqiao settlement clusters, which manifest three levels of settlement hierarchy and the largest regional centres. [Rather] it seems that the least complex chiefdom systems in the central and northern Henan regions, mostly with two levels of settlement hierarchy and medium-sized regional centres, were directly related to the emergence of the early states. In this regard, the hypothesis that the state developed from more complex variants of chiefdom seems to receive little support from the Chinese data used here" (Liu 1996b: 279). Accordingly, "no linear progression from the more hierarchical form of regional systems to early states can be established" (Liu 2004: 242).

This is explicable on the basis that warfare is the catalyst of state formation. Endemic violence has already been argued to be the catalyst of clan formation in an 'open environment'. In the open social and environmental circumstances of the Central Plains, where the condition is that of war of each against all, then the most militarily effective leaders will be able to establish structures that give them permanent pre-eminence. A successful military elite will also acquire land and other resources with which to reward followers and to fund sumptuary items and superior military equipment for further expansion. However, while a source of power for the early complex chiefdoms lay through ancestral cult rituals which elevated the rank of the lineage practising it, it was the less stratified, more solidary "group oriented social system, involved in intensive military conflict by relying on local resources to maintain internal solidarity against outsiders, that gave rise to the early states in north China" (Liu 2004: 248), that is, in Henan not Shandong. In Henan and Shaanxi regions, the tradition from the Yangshao into the Longshan periods was of collective efforts, for instance in building defensive walls, and of ancestors being venerated *communally* in Yangshao mortuary rituals (Liu 2004: 248). Even in the following Longshan period there is no evidence for rich burials in those areas (*ibid*.). In contrast to the elevation of individual ancestors to semi-divine status, collective religion rather reflected common subsistence concerns, with deities embodying natural forces, such as the fertility symbols and celestial bodies depicted on Hongshanmiao burial urns. At Lutaigang in Henan there is a ritual building with rammed-earth walls, the outer one being square and containing within its area a circular inner wall divided into four sectors. Akin to the form of *cong* tubes, it is surmised that the square outside and the circle inside symbolize earth and heaven (*ibid*.: 249), for as mentioned previously, in traditional cosmography earth is square and flat and heaven is round.

At some point however a lineage and its faction (or a clan) had to make a dash for elite status against the prevailing egalitarianism of the Henan Longshan communities. This mould-breaking transition seems to be what the **Xinzhai** sites represent, although they are poorly known (Liu 2004: 235).

The site of Erlitou itself has five levels, in places exceeding three metres together, but although discovered in 1959 there is as yet no proper site map. Phases 2, 3 & 4 extend from *c*.1800–1500 BC. So far there is no trace of a city wall, only a partial ditch, but individual elite compounds are walled in *hangtu* technique, which is very labour intensive. Stratum 2, the second earliest, has rich deposits and *hangtu* house foundation platforms. Stratum 3 has remains of large buildings, as well as tombs with *ercengtai*, lacquered coffins and a sacrificial pit beneath them (*yaokeng*, lit. 'waist pit'). As is well known, lacquering is a very labour intensive craft, given the number of layers to be applied and the materials employed. The fourth stratum, which contains a large number of storage pits, corresponds culturally to the Lower Erligang Phase of Zhengzhou, while the last stratum (Erlitou V) is equivalent to the Upper Erligang period at Zhengzhou, the Shang capital, named from a modern city only 85 km to the east.

Most striking at Erlitou is the bronze work, including plaques, bells and knives, but dominated by cast vessels for elite ritual purposes. They include three *jia* (tripod vessel for heating millet 'wine') a *ding* (open tripod or four-footed vessel for cooking sacrificial food), one *he* (like a flattened teapot, for mixing wine with water), fragments of a *gu* (for tasting wine) and no less than twenty *jue* (for heating wine). Those are designs based on white pottery originals (except for the *ding* cauldron), which occur here in bronze for the very first time. They become 'classics' and are carried forward for the next millennium. So too is the *ge* found here in both bronze and jade versions. It is probably the most mass-produced metal artefact in antiquity. The *ge*, which became the standard weapon of Bronze Age armies, is a kind of halberd, armed at right angles to the staff with a blade the Chinese call a 'dagger-axe'. This *ge* character, when it appears within a square box symbolising walls, is the character *guo*, meaning a state or country. Thus China, the Central Kingdom, is Zhong Guo (see Figure 6.57).

At its peak (Phase III) Erlitou's 456 hectares were divided into a number of functional zones (Liu and Chen 2003: 58). In the central palace zone, two huge structures have been excavated in an area that contains around two dozen rammed-earth foundations. 'Palace' no.1 is about a hectare in extent, while no.2, located 150 m north-east of 'Palace 1', covers 4200 m², although its rammed-earth foundation exceeds a hectare (*ibid.*). Most of the palace area consists of empty compound, containing a relatively small building set on an auspicious site within the compound. This leads some to suggest that the 'palaces' are actually temples or ceremonial structures; but they could have had all of those functions.

In the absence of local supplies of jade, turquoise is a significant material at Erlitou, something it shares with the important and broadly contemporary Lower Xiajiadian culture (*c*.2200–1500 BC; cf: Guo Dashun 1995, Flad 2002, Shelach 1994, 2000) and whose most famous site is Dadianzi to the north of Bohai Bay in Inner Mongolia. The Northeast is the region in which the earliest oracle bones were found (Flad 2008: 409). However, Lower Xiajiadian's most intriguing connections are probably with the Andronovo and other nomadic peoples of the steppe lands of Central Asia (Fitzgerald-Huber 1999:

152). Notwithstanding the quality of the bronze work at Erlitou, at Zhengzhou "a single bronze vessel from one of the Zhengzhou hoards outweighs by a factor of ten all the metal yet found at Erlitou" (Bagley 1999: 167). However, this might be a result of major elite tombs having been lost through a change in the course of the River Luo from the south to the north of the Erlitou site since the Tang dynasty (Liu and Chen 2003: 151, n. 2).

Liu and Chen (2003: 64) sum up the Erlitou period as providing "evidence of political centralization at the primary centre [that] includes the following facts: a rapid increase of urban population, the construction of a palatial complex, the institutionalization of a mortuary hierarchy, the development of various craft productions, and the emergence of state-controlled craft specialization in the manufacture of ritual bronzes". And in regard to the nature of Erlitou urbanism, they observe that "when Erlitou developed into an urban centre with a large population, which may have reached 18,000–30,000 in Phase III … its urban population was largely engaged in architectural construction and craft production. Its subsistence economy would have required the support of agricultural production in the hinterland of the Yiluo region" (*ibid.*), a region that manifested a four tier settlement hierarchy (Liu 2004: 240–1). It included the major settlements of Shaochai (60 ha), a control location at the confluence of Wuluo and Yi-Luo rivers, Luokou (18 ha), Huizui (14 ha) and Nanzhai on the river Yi, a major communication route (Lee 2004: 190).

## The Early State: Shang

Just as the archaeological Erlitou corresponds to Xia if anything does, traditionally recognized as the first state in China, so Erligang archaeology corresponds to early ('pre-Yinxu', i.e. pre-*c*.1250 BC) phases of its successor, the Shang. Approximate dates for the Erligang Period, divided into Upper and Lower, are 1600–1250 BC. The Erligang apparently derives from the Xiaqiyuan culture, east of the Qin River and north of the Yellow River.

"Some have argued that early Shang culture may have been derived most directly from the Zhanghe variant of the Xiaqiyuan culture and that the population of the Zhanghe variant, for unknown reasons, may have moved southward to eastern Henan during the late Erlitou period. … This proposition of a proto-Shang population migration is supported by the discovery of the Lutaigang site in Qixian, eastern Henan, at which ceramic assemblages show an intrusion of the Zhanghe variant into the local Yueshi and Erlitou cultures"(Liu and Chen 2003: 85). Yueshi culture spans *c*.2000–1600 BC. However, I suggest a different formative process below.

During the transition between Lower (1600–1450 BC) and Upper Erligang (1450–1250 BC) periods, power and thus the elite moved from Erlitou post Phase IV (*c*.1564–1521 BC) to Zhengzhou; certainly bronze production moved. Amidst much uncertainty, according to Liu and Xu (2007: 892) "what is certain is that production of elite goods, particularly of bronzes completely stopped after Phase IV". Only 6 km from Erlitou, lies a relatively small fortified centre called **Yanshi Shangcheng** ('Yanshi Shang city') which contained large-scale storage facilities some 100 m distant from its palatial complex. Ceramics from the earliest occupation at Yanshi include both Erlitou types and a transitional form between Xiaqiyuan and Erligang types (*ibid*.: 89). The three phases at Yanshi are comparable to Erlitou Phase IV, Lower Erligang and Upper Erligang respectively (*ibid*.). But the "Yanshi I assemblage is dominated by typical early Shang type vessels (also known as the Lower Erligang style) common in Zhengzhou" (Y.K. Lee 2004: 184).

In Phase I at Yanshi, a 4 ha rammed-earth enclosure was built around a group of palatial structures. Around this a 75 ha enclosure was built using rammed earth walls six to seven metres wide. They are referred to by Chinese archaeologists as the 'palace town' and the 'Yanshi small city' see (Figure 6.29). In the south-west of the large (i.e. 'small city') enclosure another 4 ha rammed-earth enclosure was built around house foundations, which may have been a storage and living area for craftspersons. In Phase II the town expanded to become a large walled city of about 120 ha, surrounded by a moat and possessing five gates (Liu and Chen 2003: 91). Another 'storage area' was added adjoining the eastern wall of the (original) small city wall, while palaces and other

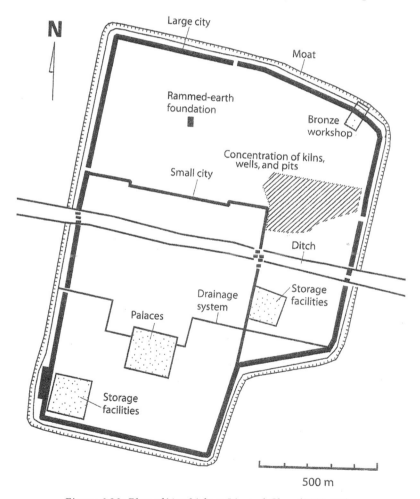

*Figure 6.29: Plan of Yanshi from Liu and Chen (2003: 90).*

facilities were expanded several times. Finally, in Phase III the palaces were expanded yet again, new ones were constructed and the storage facilities renovated. Shortly thereafter the city began to decline into an ordinary settlement, and was abandoned completely in the late phase of the Upper Erligang period (*ibid*).

Bronze production took place just outside the north-east corner of the original town enclosure walls, though despite two decades of excavation it is not known what bronze items were manufactured there. As conflict seems to have been endemic, and "the primary function of Yanshi in its early phase seems to have been more military than economic" (Liu and Chen 2003: 91), weapons are a likely product, especially as there is no evidence of bronze ritual vessels being produced at Yanshi.

Conventionally Yanshi is seen as the Shang springboard to the conquest of Xia. Alternatively, as argued by Zou Heng (1999: 202) on the basis of mostly literary evidence, Yanshi is a 'detached palace' or 'secondary capital' built by the founder of the Shang Dynasty, King Tang. Yanshi's early date in the initial Shang period is an archaeological requirement, but its location and duration make little sense in either regard. So I conjecture the heretical possibility that there was *no* 'conquest' of the Xia by the Shang and that what we see in the shift of power from Erlitou to Zhengzhou via Yanshi is but the transition from the Formative to the Early Dynastic Period, analogous to the sequence from Dynasty 0 to the Early Dynastic Period in Egypt. This suggests that the role of Yanshi was as the base of a charismatic leader effecting this transformation (see Chapter 9 for this process) – perhaps King Tang – otherwise the location of a small (originally 75 ha) settlement only 6 km from the *c.*300 ha 'Xia' site of Erlitou is inexplicable. See Figure 6.30 for the location

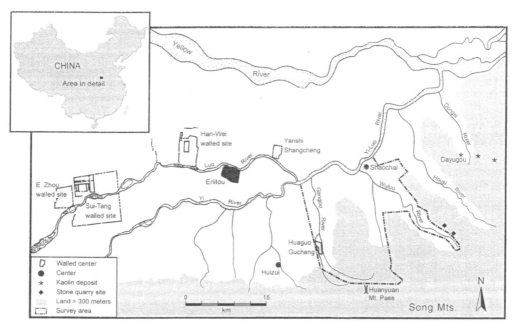

*Figure 6.30: The location of Yanshi in relation to Erlitou in the Yi-Luo Valley (Y.K. Lee 2004: 177).*

|  | | 1500 BC | 1400 | 1300 |
|---|---|---|---|---|
| **REGIME** | 'XIA' | Erlitou → Erligang | SHANG | |
| | | Transition Phase | | |
| | | | | |
| **STAGE** | Proto-state* | Charismatic Base | Early (Dynastic) State | |
| | | | | |
| | | | | |
| **LOCUS** | Erlitou | Yanshi | Erligang/Zhengzhou | |

\* during which a number of elite lineages struggled for supreme power.

"The rapid expansion of state power in the Central Plains is confirmed by the replacement of Erlitou material by Erligang assemblages, and by the intrusions of Erligang material culture into broader regions" (Liu and Chen 2003: 127).

*Figure: 6.31: The role of Yanshi in State Crystallization.*

of Yanshi in relation to Erlitou in the Yi-Luo Valley and Figure 6.31 for Yanshi's role in state crystallization.

In the light of historical knowledge, it may well be the case that clan formation and mobilization under a new leader, in the place of the many small and unrelated kin-groups that characterised the Erlitou population (Liu and Xu 2007: 894) are what made the transition and the Shang dynasty possible.[65] The transition would then later be glossed as a 'conquest' analogous to, and continuous with, the Zhou conquest of Shang ('when King Wu received the Mandate') to make the Sandai a cornerstone of continuity in Chinese cultural history (Wagner 1993: 11). It is worth noting that Wagner (1993: 16) "personally remains unconvinced that Xia ever existed" as a state.

This reconstruction as charismatic state-formation, sits well with how Blunden and Elvin (1983: 56) have characterised Shang social structure: "Shang society was probably based on two or three hundred clans, concentrated in particular localities, each with its particular emblem and serving as the focus for its members affiliations, loyalties and observances. The possession of bronze weapons, notably the 'dagger-axe' or Chinese halberd, bronze arrow-and spear-heads and bronze helmets, gave those who were privileged to have them a nearly decisive superiority in the use of force. We may surmise that this ensured both the dominance of a warrior nobility of clan leaders over their commoners, and of the Shang people as a whole over the less advanced tribes who lived around and among them. The Shang kings engaged in continual military expeditions. Plunder and tribute were part of the royal economy. Captives taken in war were either slaughtered as sacrificial victims or enslaved. ... The new power of coercion was the foundation of new political and administrative structures" not merely for the Shang state, but for much of the rest of Chinese history.

**Zhengzhou,** the ancient Bo and the first Shang capital, is situated in central Henan on the Huang-Huai floodplains with the Yellow River to the north, Songshan Mountains

---

[65] On the basis of his recent high-precision radiocarbon dates and wiggle-matching, Lee (2004: 184) declares that "The downfall of Erlitou as the regional centre of the Yi-Luo Valley, at the end of Erlitou Phase IV, can be firmly dated no later than 1520 BC".

to the south-west and the great 'central' floodplains to the south-east. Parts of the site were occupied by settlements during the Erlitou period, and likely prior to that, but most of the archaeological deposits belong to Lower Erligang Phases I and II and Upper Erligang Phases I and II (Liu and Chen 2003: 93).

Zhengzhou, as royal capital, was the centre for the manufacture of ritual bronzes. Indeed, "like Erlitou, the sites involved with bronze metallurgy in the periphery showed no sign of casting [ritual] vessels during the Erligang period" (Liu 2003: 25). See Figure 6.31.

The elite core of ancient Zhengzhou has *hangtu* walls, with sides measuring 1,690 m (north), 1700 m (east), 1,700 m (south) and 1,870 m (west), 6960 m in total, with the north-east corner at an angle in order to avoid a natural ridge (Bagley 1999: 166). Begun early in the Lower Erligang period, overall thickness at the base is around 22 m, and the greatest surviving height is nine metres. This is called the city wall, but it clearly is not. It is the enclosure around the 'inner city' containing palaces and ancestor temples, indicated by *hangtu* foundations ranging from 2000 m² to 100 m². Remains of the 'outer city' are spread over an area of about 25 km². A ritual complex has recently been found some 20 km to the north-west. Pottery and bone workshops, bronze foundries and graveyards, all are located beyond the inner city wall, as seen on the Plan of ancient Zhengzhou from Liu and Chen (2003) in Figure 6.32.

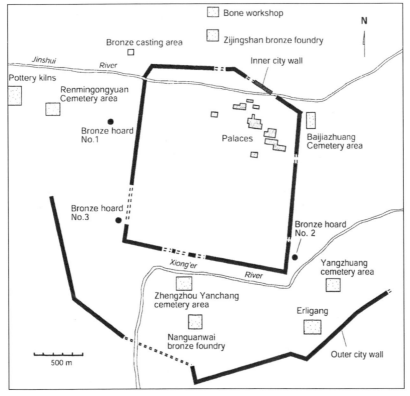

*Figure 6.32: Plan of ancient Zhengzhou ( from Liu and Chen 2003: 94).*

The pottery workshop at Minngonglu, a 12 ha ceramic production area, was large, with fourteen kilns, but must have been one of many, as those workshops specialized in only a few vessel types, namely fine-paste basins and steamers. The bone workshop used more human than animal bone (Bagley 1999: 166–7). In the vicinity of what was probably a temple near the northern wall, around 100 human skull tops, many with saw marks, have been discovered in a ditch (Liu and Chen 2003: 95).

Outside the inner-city wall, 500 m from the south-east corner, is, remarkably, the type-site of Erligang itself. Within the inner-city walls, concentrated in the north-east quarter originally the locus of pre-Erligang residential features, lie over twenty *hangtu* platforms, as already mentioned, ranging in size from 100 m² to 2000 m². This 'palace zone' covers 750 m northwest–southeast by 500 m north–south. The buildings on them were very large, one measuring 65 m by 13.5 m, another 31 m by 38 m (Bagley, *ibid*.). Nearby was the principal ritual area marked by large upstanding rocks and sacrificial pits containing the remains of humans and animals (Liu and Chen 2003: 94). Commoners' houses seem to have been small (4–6 m²) semi-subterranean structures (*ibid*.: 97). From the stone and shell sickles and bronze fishhooks found in workshop and residential areas, it appears that at Zhengzhou as at Erlitou, craftspersons had either to procure or to supplement their own food. That being the case, one wonders just what, if anything, the elite gave in exchange for the services of craftspersons.

The development of Zhengzhou peaked in the Upper Erligang Phase I period. When it collapsed, a large (144 ha) settlement developed at Xiaoshuangqiao, 20 km to the north-west (*ibid*.: 99).

Here then we have the formative pattern of the Chinese city: not a nucleated settlement on the South and West Asian pattern, but something qualitatively different, namely the **core and satellite** pattern, also found in the Andes, notably at Chan Chan and Inca Cuzco (Moseley 1975b: 225). Elite residences are grouped together and circumvallated to signal their apartness (and for their own safety?). Distributed nearby and also at some distance, are the servitor 'districts' effectively villages with their workshops. Population concentrations, around the soldiers' and servitors' locale, gives rise to the 'town' settlement, such as it is.

A similar pattern exists at **Panlongcheng** in Huangpi, Hubei, 450 km to the south where remains cover about 1 km on the banks of the She Shui. This is a tributary flowing into the Yangzi just north of Wuhan, today the major city on the Yangzi's middle reaches: river port, industrial centre and capital of Hubei Province. Similarly in the Erlitou and Erligang formative periods, Panlongcheng seems to have been a major communications centre in the Yangzi's middle reaches, supplying copper and other materials. Again, only a small part of this settlement area was walled, a mere 260 m east-west and 290 m north-south. This wall, which was built in the Upper Erligang (though settlement is earlier), is trapezoidal, and with a base width of 26 m, the wall is nearly as thick as at Zhengzhou. Within the compound's north-east corner is a large *hangtu* terrace. It carries the foundations for three large buildings, see for example Figure 6.33.

Not only do they follow the same construction technique as at Zhengzhou (cf: Xiaotun elite residence below) but also the compass orientation is identical at 20° east of north (Bagley 1999: 168). The same orientation is given to the 'city' wall and the grave,

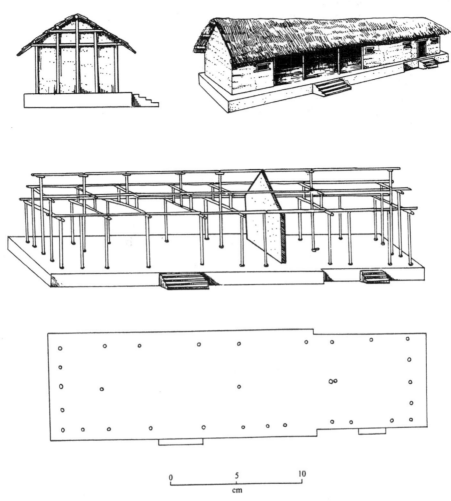

*Figure 6.33: Hall F1 at Panlongcheng.*

which is a typical elite tomb, with *ercengtai* (second-level ledge) and *yaokeng* (sacrifice shaft beneath the coffin). Here three human victims were laid on the *ercengtai* and on, or inside, the larger coffin (Bagley 1999: 170). It also held bronzes, jades, pottery and carved wooden objects. Crucibles and other casting debris at Panlongcheng indicate that the bronzes were locally made, most likely indicating the co-option of the local elite. Erligang bronzes have been found right across north and central China, and are indistinguishable from Zhengzhou bronzes no matter where they are found (Bagley 1999: 170), suggesting some form of explosive radiation from that centre.

The Panlongcheng walled town was abandoned around the end of the Erligang period, to be supplanted by Wucheng (Liu and Chen 2003: 126). Wucheng developed into a major regional centre, but one which, although influenced by the Central

*Figure 6.34: Bronze* zun *(ritual wine vessel) supported by two rams; from southern China, 13th to 12th Centuries BC (British Museum).*

Plains, nonetheless was independent of it during the late Shang period, indicated by its regional characteristics.

   **Wucheng** is situated on the Ganjiang, a river that flows north to join the Poyang Hu (Lake Poyang) at the major city of Nanchang in northern Jiangxi Province. Lake Poyang is the southernmost of the great Yangzi lakes. According to Bagley (1999: 174) Wucheng culture (Dayangzhou) represents "a notably vigorous response to contact with expanding Erligang civilization." It is thirteenth-century, one of the cultures of the 'transition period' characterised by regional diversification. The home of a distinct civilization for which large bronze bells, *nao and bo*[66], about 40 cm high, are

---

[66] *Nao* are mounted on a hollow stem, mouth upward and struck on their exterior; while the *bo* are hung from a top loop and probably struck with a clapper.

the defining artefact (*ibid.*: 173), the wealth of the civilization of which Wucheng city and the **Xin'gan tomb** (some 20 km away on the other side of the river) are examples, seems to derive from the copper trade. A large copper mine is located at Ruichang in northern Jiangxi, and it seems to have been exploited as early as the Erligang period (*ibid.*: 174–5). Certainly the Xin'gan tomb "is the second richest Early Bronze Age burial known, surpassed only by the contemporary or slightly later tomb of Fu Hao (*c.*1200 BC)" (*ibid.*: 172). The Xin'gan tomb contained 356 pieces of high quality pottery, 50 bronze vessels, four bells, over 400 bronze tools and weapons, around 150 jades, plus several hundred jade beads. Wucheng had a distinctive metallurgical technique, some of it, such as 'casting on' or casting in stone moulds, well in advance of northern methods (Wagner 1993: 20).

> "Of the 195 [bronze] vessels in Fu Hao's tomb, 105 belong to the types *jia, jue* [for heating millet 'wine' and pouring libations; both have pointed legs] and *gu* [a chalice-like, long-stemmed vessel with flaring foot and mouth, for tasting 'wine']. These types are invariable features of northern burials, but they are missing entirely from the Xin'gan assemblage, where 37 of the 50 vessels were *ding* [large open tripods or rectangular four legged vessels] and *li* [a closed cooking vessel]. The absence of the types most essential to northern funerary ritual, the predominance of *ding* and *li*, and the presence of four large bells can only mean that the occupant of the Xin'gan tomb was a not a northerner" (Bagley 1999: 174).

This demonstrates a more general point, namely that it is not necessarily contact with contemporary cultures that causes others to develop complex technology and social organization. In the case of Dayangzhou (Wucheng/Xin'gan), it was rather derivation from an earlier and common predecessor and parallel development that made it the equal of the Shang. Similar considerations apply to the stunning bronzes of Sanxingdui (see for example Figure 6.34).

## The Shang state triumphant: the capital district of Anyang

The dynasty's major centre from around 1200 BC was at **Anyang,** almost due north of Zhengzhou across the Yellow River, where the foothills meet the plains. Like other major settlements of its period, it was founded in the bend of a river, the Huan, as shown in Figure 6.35 (from Li Chi 1977: 70). Anyang is, however, not a single or integrated site but the capital district of Late Shang (Yinxu, *c.*1220–1046 BC). It extends over about 25 km² in which 17 distinct districts are so far known. Anyang lies at the centre of the Shang core territory, which is an approximately elliptical area with a long axis of around 200 km. Surrounding this core territory, but mostly to the east and south of it was the 'outer domain' comprising the Daihang Mountains, the Huanghe Corridor and the Yellow River flood zone. Only the 'inner domain' was directly administered by Shang officials, the 'outer domain' most likely (on the Zhou pattern) by detached members of the ruling lineage or its affines. Around this patchy outer domain a buffer zone would have consisted of other, independent or semi-dependent polities variously allied to, dependent upon, or opposed to the Shang, according to shifting political, economic and military interests. In any event, the size of Shang and Zhou states has generally been much overestimated: "although their cultural influence was certainly

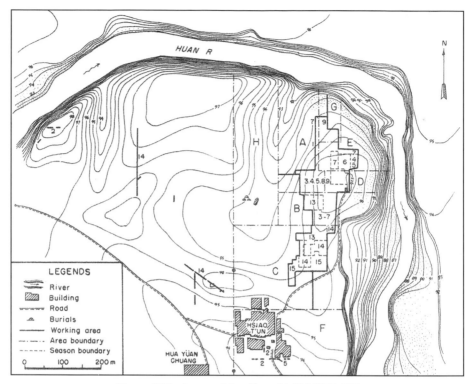

*Figure 6.35: Anyang Map (from Li Chi 1977: 70).*

widespread, it would appear that neither Shang nor the Western Zhou kings were ever able to project their political authority beyond a relatively circumscribed area, primarily along the middle and lower stretches of the Yellow River" (Shaughnessy 1989: 22).

The main areas of excavation so far have been north-east of the village of Xiaotun. But remains are by no means confined to this area. Although excavations are ongoing and have been for most of the 20th Century AD, the site and its hinterland have not been systematically explored, let alone excavated. It appears however that by end of the reign of Wu Ding (c.1200–1181 BC), supposedly the 21st Shang king and first of nine Late Shang kings, the site extended over about 15 km², reaching about 25 km² by the end of the dynasty.

Given its huge extent and non-nucleated structure, it is not surprising that so far there is no trace of a city wall. Anyang therefore, with its royal residential core near Xiaotun, surrounded by cemeteries, many workshops and 'villages' of craftsmen and servitors, is yet another core and satellite 'city', on a very large scale. Figure 6.37 shows an elite residence at Xiaotun (from Shih Chang-ju, Annals of Academia Sinica (1954)).

Toward the south of the site, at Miaopu Beidi, along with workshops, housing and cemeteries for workers, there is a bronze foundry that by the end of the dynasty covered 10,000 m² (Bagley 1999: 183). The sheer scale of the foundry indicates how important bronze was for weapons and ritual vessels. For instance, in one of the approach ramps of tomb M1004 that had been thoroughly looted, there still remained in the fill of the

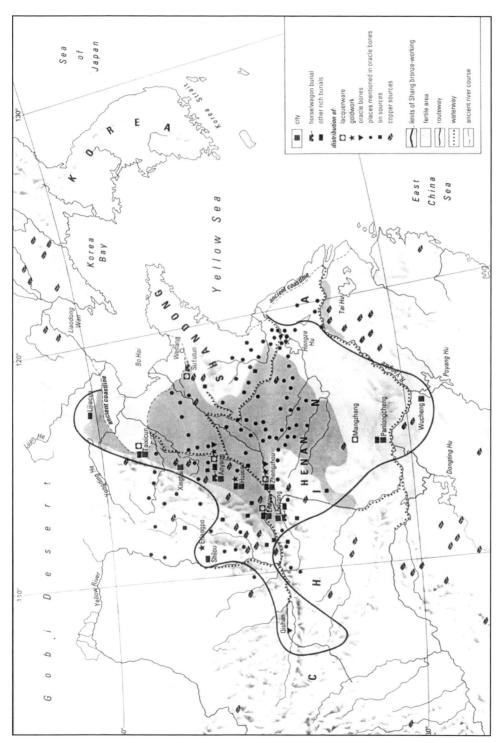

*Figure 6.36: Shang domains and sphere of influence (from Scarre 1988: 146).*

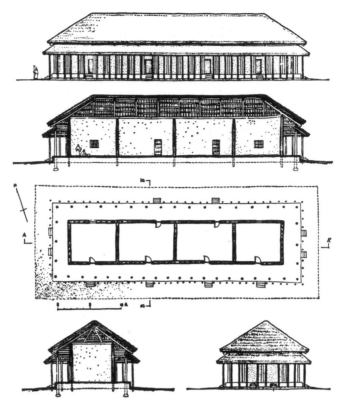

*Figure 6.37: An elite residence at Xiaotun (from Shih Chang-ju, Annals of Academia Sinica (1954)).*

south ramp (the only one that usually descended all the way to the bottom of the shaft itself) four successive layers of grave goods. From the bottom up they were: chariot fittings and the remains of leather armour and shields; in the next layer more than 100 bronze helmets and about 360 bronze *ge* blades; in the next layer, 36 bronze spearheads, and in the top layer a stone chime, one jade and two large bronze *fanding* (Bagley 1999: 185)

Anyang is also the earliest source we have for anything resembling texts in China. They are the famous 'oracle bone inscriptions' which pose questions about the timing and propitiousness of events, centred upon the king's activities. Answers come as cracks on scapulae (shoulder blades) and plastrons (turtle shells) by the king's diviners or the king himself as chief diviner and indeed shaman, as indicated by the following divinations from Keightley (1999a: 7):

> On *dingmao* (day 4) divined: 'If the king joins with Zhi [Guo] (an important Shang general) to attack the Shaofang, he will receive [assistance].' Cracked in the temple of Ancestor Yi (the twelfth king). Fifth moon.
> Divined: 'If the king dances for rain, there will be approval'.
> Divined: 'The king shall not dance (for rain, for if he does, there will not be approval)'.

The approval and assistance sought was, first and foremost from ancestors. It was they who received most cultic attention and sacrifice. There were also the natural powers conceived of as such: Mountain, Wind and (Yellow) River. Ultimately, and most distant was Di, who could not be approached directly and so received much less cultic attention than ancestors, who alone could intercede with him.

> "That Di was virtually the only Power who could directly order (ling) rain or thunder, as well as the only Power who had the winds under his control, sets him apart from [and above] all other Powers, natural, pre-dynastic or ancestral" (Keightley 1999a: 11).

It is almost certain that more mundane matters were written on perishable materials. None of those have survived however. But plastron survival is excellent. Pits variously functioned as dwelling, as grain silo or for other storage. In one of them, H127, 17,000 plastron fragments were found in 1936, while at the southern edge of Xiaotun, 5000 inscribed bones were found in 1973. Nonetheless, as Campbell (2008: 420) points out, "inscribed bones represent less than 10 per cent of those collected".

At nearby Huayuanzhuang over 500 inscribed plastrons, about 300 of which were complete, were found as recently as 1991 (Bagley 1999: 184). As well as oracle bones, Xiaotun was also the locus of palaces and temples and their associated sacrificial burials. Fifty large *hangtu* platforms have been excavated so far, some 3 m thick, depending on terrain. Many are 20 m x 50 m, but there is one building that is 14.5 m x 85 m. Construction demanded sacrifices, and dogs, horses, oxen, sheep, chariots and hundreds of humans became victims (Anyang Excavation Team, 1977).

Across the Huan River lies the site of **Xibeigang**, which is about a kilometre north of the villages of Houjiazhuang and Wuguancun. There lies one of the cemeteries of the elite, covering an area of about 450 m east-west and 250 m north–south. It contains thirteen important tombs, of which 11 were excavated between 1934 and 1935, another in 1950 and another in 1984. All 13 are oriented a few degrees east of north. The tombs are divided by a modern road into eight to the west and five to the east, along with more than 1,400 pits for sacrificial victims.

Like the palaces, apparently none of the tombs pre-dates Wu Ding's reign. The shafts ranged in depth between 10 and 13 metres, at the bottom of which a wooden chamber was constructed. Beneath this was a small pit (*yaokeng*) in the centre of the shaft floor. It contained an armed man sacrificed to guard the tomb's owner. This is the usual quota. However M1001 is different (see Figure 6.38).

One of the earliest and certainly the grandest tomb here, M1001 may have be belonged to Wu Ding himself, although thoroughly (but not totally) looted in antiquity. Including ramps, it measures 66 m north–south and 44 m east–west. The southern ramp is longest, and measures 30.7 m, entering the shaft 2.3 m above the floor. The other three ramps enter 5.5 m above the floor of the shaft, which is 10.5 m deep and cross-shaped in section. Dimensions of M1001's shaft floor, including the arms of the cross, are 15.9 by 19.15 metres.

In the floor, in addition to the usual single human sacrificial victim at the centre, an additional eight victims were buried in eight pits located at the north and south corners of the shaft floor. Each pit also contained a dog and a *ge* blade, bronze in

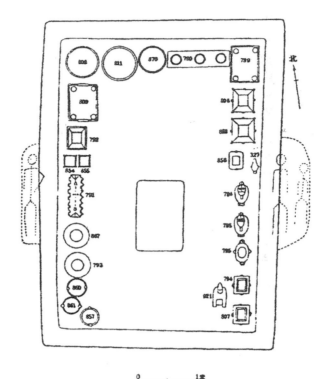

*Figure 6.38: Xibeigang tomb M1001.*

the corner pits and a 43 cm long jade in the centre pit. "No other Xibeigang tomb seems to have had more than one sacrificial pit, a *yaokeng* at the centre of the shaft, but the man in the *yaokeng* was always armed with a jade *ge* blade. If the men are interpreted as guardians, then perhaps jade *ge* found by themselves in the *yaokeng* of lesser tombs, without human victims, should be understood as symbolic guardians. No evidence connects any other jade shape with so specific a ritual or magical function" (Bagley 1999: 191).

The shaft floor held a cross-shaped wooden tomb chamber, totally decayed away, the interior of which had been decorated with shell, bone and ivory inlays, pigmentation and carved patterns similar to those known from bronzes and bone. Holding the corpse and the bulk of the grave goods (looted), the chamber's floor area was 78 m² and the ceiling height 3 m (*ibid.*). The shaft was filled by the *hangtu* technique and interlayered with human and animal sacrifices. This was also the case with the fill of the ramps, which gave access to the various fill levels. The south ramp, where human sacrifice seems to have been focussed, held 59 skeletons and 42 skulls grouped into eight rows of skeletons and fourteen groups of skulls. "Except for a few infants, all the victims were teenage males with their hands tied behind them who had been lined up five or ten at a time in rows facing the shaft and beheaded. The heads were collected for later deposit in a higher level, earth was poured over the bodies and pounded hard, and the process was repeated" (Bagley 1999: 192).

The process was also repeated outside the tomb, where thirty-one pits were neatly arranged along its east perimeter. Sixty-eight humans were distributed between twenty-two pits, from one to seven corpses in a pit. Seven of the other pits contained 12 horses with decorated bridles, turquoise ornaments and small bronze bells. They were most likely chariot horses and their attendants, for near the shaft walls the excavators discovered traces of the chariot box, a shield and painted and inlaid impressions left by objects of carved wood.

While M1001 was accompanied by at least 90 victims, buried with care and accompanied by some grave goods, plus 74 without grave goods beheaded or otherwise mutilated, M1004 was the focus of no less than 1,200 sacrificial pits associated with large tombs in the eastern part of the cemetery. This group, excavated in 1934 and 1935, contained mostly human victims, laid out in east-west rows in distinct groups, apparently as sacrifices subsequent to funerals. All the pits of a group contained either complete skeletons or beheaded ones, but not both. Twenty pits contained only horses, from a single one to as many as 37 horses in a single pit. Other animal sacrifices in other pits included two elephants each in its own pit with human attendant.

In 1976 another group of 191 pits lying southeast of M1400 was found containing the remains of another 1200 victims in 22 groups corresponding it would appear, to separate sacrificial events. The smallest group comprised a single pit; the largest consisted of 47 pits with 339 victims. The average sacrifice exceeded 50 victims, some of whom were women and children, but most were young adult males. "Beheading was the normal method of sacrifice, but some victims were dismembered or cut in half and a few children seem to have been trussed up and buried alive. Skeletons were usually incomplete, heads normally buried separate from bodies" (Bagley 1999: 193).

The character *fa*, which shows an axe on a human neck, represents the most common sacrificial method mentioned in the oracle bone inscriptions (Shelach 1996: 13). In total the oracle bone texts refer to more that fourteen thousand sacrificial victims, of whom over half are referred to as Qiang, a neighbouring society to the north-west of Shang territory. Itself stratified, Qiang were preferentially hunted as victims for sacrificial murder. Indeed the Qiang were the only non-Shang victims specifically referred to in the oracle bone inscriptions (*ibid.*).

Stratigraphic relationships and oracle bone inscriptions suggest that Wu Ding and his two immediate successors were responsible for the sacrifices so far discovered. But forty pits discovered in 1978, containing mainly horses appear to be somewhat later. Later test probes around the Xibeigang cemetery suggest that a substantial part of it, covering several hectares and a considerable time-span, was a continuous sacrificial ground where human victims, sometimes by the hundred, were slaughtered for royal ancestors. With life so cheap and totally at the disposal of the ruler, no doubt human sacrifices also took place elsewhere, on other pretexts. Bagley (1999: 194) remarks that such slaughter had to have justification from religious belief; that it was necessary to secure the support of the gods and thus assure the welfare of society. But he also observes that, akin to Aztec, and other Mesoamerican sacrifices (in fact pan-American as will be seen below), such practices were instruments of terror against the population and thus were political acts, a point also made by Demarest (1984: 228) in regard to the

Mayan elite, when he says that "Classic Maya human sacrifice was both a legitimation and a sanctification of political power". Furthermore, "once human sacrifice becomes an institutionalized legitimation mechanism, rulers are forced to continue conducting wars to maintain the supply of victims necessary for the ceremonies" (Shelach 1996: 20). Indeed, "The right to perform ritual homicide, the ultimate testament of power in the arbitration of life and death, was no doubt a ceremonial spectacle divorced from all others" (Swenson 2003: 288). That is, ritual homicide manifested more power than all others, and served as the climax to a series of rites. "In fact, it seems likely that the privileged control of elite cycles of warfare, prisoner capture, and ceremonies of human sacrifice constituted the basis of Moche political relations" (Swenson 2003: 268).

What the rulers and their spin-doctors the ritual specialists said the justification was, and what the population took from such murderous displays, shows the stark realities of power. Human beings were slaughtered because they could be; when the rhetoric is removed, power is exposed and the violence is naked.[67] This would be of particular importance in formative or early state society where state apparatuses were as yet insufficiently well developed to control the population fully. Warfare too, more or less continuous, would serve to portray the warrior elite and then the state as the people's defenders, while, by imposing politico-cultural boundaries, social circumscription would help prevent people 'voting with the feet' by moving away from the demands of an incipient state.

If the rulers and their power apparatus, the state, really existed to confer the benefits of good management on society, then the conflict between the interests of rulers and ruled would not exist and the drastic devices applied by the elite would not have been required. In particular, the population would not need to have been kept cowed by the terror of becoming 'alien' like the Qiang, and sacrificed for the greater good of rulers. "Sacrificers themselves are thus empowered by the act of sacrifice. It is they who send a human being or animal from the material world into a spiritual dimension. They control 'death' as cosmological transition. Their bloody demonstration of this power enhances their own and their fellow ritual specialists' social influence" (Lewis-Williams and Pearce 2005: 126–7).

The successors to the Shang were the (Western) **Zhou**. Their texts say that Shang rulers lost the Mandate of Heaven (*tianming*) through drunkenness and indulgence, not mass murder. Likewise, texts of later periods praise the Shang for their adherence to ritual.

With nearly all tombs looted in antiquity, the only intact royal burial so far discovered is that of Fu Hao (to be read as Tzu, the name of the Shang clan) one of Wu Ding's 64 consorts. Also a shaft tomb, it is 7.5 m to the shaft floor and 5.6 m by 4 m at the opening. The *ercengtai* with its niches are above the tomb chamber, which is at the base of the shaft, and into which is cut the small *yaokeng* with its sacrificial victims.

This tomb (see Figure 6.39), number 5 at Xiaotun, Anyang, was excavated in 1976, and is still the only one whose owner is established. More than half the bronze vessels

---

[67] Discussing the "uniquely long tradition of human sacrifice" in China, Huang (1989: 80) concludes that it "can be seen a having three major causes: the long and vigorous history of interaction between ethnic Chinese and other neighbouring groups, the enduring popularity of polygamy, and the effects on Chinese social developoment of Chinese philosophical traditions, combined with the lack of an established religion" that valued human life.

*Figure 6.39: Conjectural reconstruction of the structure above Fu Hao's tomb, possibly an ancestral hall.*

(>100) and a few of the stone and jade items bear her name. Two large axe blades with her name inscribed on them may have been used to behead the sacrificial victims at her funeral. This is common at Anyang (Bagley 1999: 197). Fu Hao's wealth was extreme. Her tomb contained 1,600 kg of top quality bronzes, along with 755 jades, the largest assemblage ever encountered (Bagley 1999: 194). In addition there were 271 weapons, including 89 *ge* blades, tools and also 5 large bronze bells (*nao*)[68] and 18 smaller ones, plus four bronze mirrors and four bronze tigers or tiger heads (Chang 1980b: 42). The mirrors are imports from north-western 'China', or copies, as are the ten ring-handled knives.[69] But even this doesn't exhaust the contents, which further included: 110 objects of marble, turquoise and other minerals, plus 564 objects of carved bone of which 20 were arrowheads and 490 hairpins. Jades and the almost 7,000 cowries (currency) must have been the most valuable as they were in the inner coffin. There were even four pottery vessels and three clay whistles (*ibid.*). A display fully demonstrating that the famous consort had everything, even power.

Fu Hao's jades are particularly interesting, and not just because they were not ritual objects, but rather because they were her own personal 'jewellery' collection, some being perforated for suspension. Many were antiquities, as much as a millennium old by her time, and derived from Neolithic and Chalcolithic cultures: the Shijiahe culture of the middle Yangzi; the Liangzhu culture of the lower Yangzi; the Longshan of Shandong

---

[68] The bells, of which the largest is 14 cm high with a weight of only 600 grams, are dwarfed by Yangzi examples. One from Ninxiang in northern Hunan weighs 220 kg and is highly decorated. Its importance is manifest, while the Anyang examples seem peripheral.

[69] Knives of the northern complex have blades cast in one piece with their handles. Zhongyang blades are mounted with stems or tangs (*nei*), while northern practice in Siberia and elsewhere is to haft by means of shaft rings or tubular shaft holes (Lin Yun 1986: 254–258, with illustrations).

*Figure 6.40:* Ding *decorated with dragons, lozenges and knobs (British Museum).*

and the Hongshan of the distant north-east. Indeed the latter were well enough known and sufficiently highly regarded to inspire imitation at Anyang (Bagley 1999: 202). On the male side, the whole chariot complex seems to have been received from the north around 1200 BC, that is, in Wu Ding's time (*ibid.*: 208). A related chariot burial of this period was found at Sufutun, 400 km to the west.

The major bronzes are arranged around three sides of the shaft floor. They were probably placed in the tomb wrapped in cloth, as imprints remain on the bronze. The two largest, which are *fangding* weighing 120 kg each, are dedicated to Mu Xin, her memorial name. To the sides, at the level of the *ercengtai* ledge, can be seen niches for three of the sixteen sacrificial victims. Eight more were in the outer coffin, one was located in the *yaokeng* along with a dog, while another four were placed above the coffins (inner and outer). Sixteen is a very modest death toll for a royal tomb. However, as most human sacrifices took place during memorial rites rather than at the deceased's funeral, we do not know how many humans in total were sacrificed for Fu Hao.

As P.C. Chang (1986: 136) observes: "The Fu Hao of Wu Ding's era was a hero among women; her many capabilities included both civil and military talents. Her civil virtue sufficed to pacify the tribal allies, her military virtue served to solidify the state; within, she presided over sacrifices, while without, she led military troops to attack the four border regions". Only a member of the ruling lineage could do this.

Connections with Anyang seem to have been deadly. About 400 km to the east, at Sufutun, Yidu, in Shandong, there seems to have been either a colony or a very close ally of Anyang. There a chariot burial and four tombs were excavated in 1965–6, and

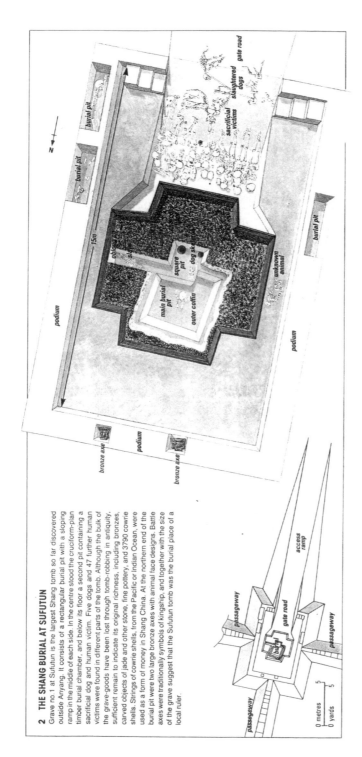

## 2  THE SHANG BURIAL AT SUFUTUN

Grave no.1 at Sufutun is the largest Shang tomb so far discovered outside Anyang. It consists of a rectangular burial pit with a sloping ramp in the middle of each side. In the centre stood the cruciform-plan timber burial chamber, and below its floor a second pit containing a sacrificial dog and human victim. Five dogs and 47 further human victims were found in different parts of the tomb. Although the bulk of the grave-goods have been lost through tomb-robbing in antiquity, sufficient remain to indicate its original richness, including bronzes, carved objects of jade and other stone, fine pottery, and 3790 cowrie shells. Strings of cowrie shells, from the Pacific or Indian Ocean, were used as a form of money in Shang China. At the northern end of the burial pit were two large bronze axes with animal face designs. Battle axes were traditionally symbols of kingship, and together with the size of the grave suggest that the Sufutun tomb was the burial place of a local ruler.

*Figure 6.41: Grave No. 1 at Sufutun (from Scarre 1988: 146).*

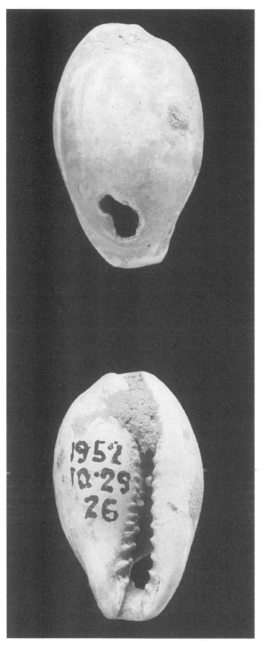

six more in 1986, dated by the excavators to Yinxu 3 or 4, which is contemporary with the later occupation of Anyang. Three of the ten tombs are said to have ramps. The largest tomb, M1, as at Anyang, had a rectangular shaft, 8 m deep with sloping walls (15 x 11 m reducing to 10 x 6 m) at the bottom of which was a cross-shaped burial chamber (Bagley 1999: 220).

See Figure 6.41: Grave No.1 at Sufutun (from Scarre 1988: 146).

The burial chamber was approached by four ramps, of which the southern, 26 m long, descended to the floor of the shaft, while the others, two of which were stepped, gave onto the *ercengtai* where seven human victims were placed. Most of the tombs had an *ercengtai*, a *yaokeng* and a coffin containing most of the grave goods. Although M1 had been stripped by looters, it still contained two large bronze axes found near the north wall of the shaft, one of the axes inscribed with the Ya Chou emblem; as also were fragments of a *jue* and an adze. M1 also contained 14 pieces of gold foil, a few jades and 3,790 cowries (*ibid.*) (see Figure 6.42). But most significantly, the tomb held no less than 48 human victims, teenagers or even younger. Two were in two separate pits in the floor of the burial chamber (one accompanied by a dog), seven as previously mentioned on the *ercengtai*, while the remaining thirty-nine, either as complete bodies or as heads alone, were buried in three layers in the south ramp, together with five dogs (*ibid.*).

## Meanwhile in the West, on the Chengdu Plain

*Figure 6.42: Cowrie money, Shang and Zhou periods (British Museum).*

The Chengdu Plain is the only large plain in Sichuan and is a physiographically independent unit in the western part of the Sichuan Basin, which is located right up against the mountain front, the eastern edge of the Qingzang (Qinghai-Tibet) Plateau

(Zhu *et al.* 2006: 248). It is more than likely that "the inhabitants of the Chengdu Plain differed in language, customs, appearance and socio-political affiliation from their contemporaries in the Shang and Zhou heartland..." though linked through a set of interaction spheres (von Falkenhausen 2006: 234). Even earlier, the strongest connections of the Neolithic Baodun Culture of the plain was with the Shijiahe Culture (*c.*2500–1900 BC) on the Middle Yangzi (von Falkenhausen 2006: 198, 212). In prehistoric and early historic periods "the plain was isolated enough to foster the development of native cultures and escape being overwhelmed by any one outside influence, but open enough to be stimulated by outside contacts" (Xu 2006a: 106) on its own terms.

The Baodun Culture is the predecessor of Sanxingdui Bronze Age Culture, that is turn is succeeded by Shi'erqiao, whose major centre is the city of Jinsha. Derivations and influences generally flowed along the Yangzi, east to west, rather than north to south (von Falkenhausen 2006: 192–212), that is, from the Huanghe to the Yangzi. Indeed the middle Yangzi might have had a more significant impact on the central plains than currently suspected according to Falkenhausen (*ibid.*: 220) who suggests that we should consider "the transmission of southern elite culture elements from Shihuaje to the Erlitou area. In a somewhat limited sense, one might conceive of Shijiahe as a fountainhead of bifurcating trajectories, one leading to central Henan [i.e. to Erlitou] the other to the Chengdu plain – two areas that remained in contact even after the demise of their common inspiration. If tenable, such a scenario might necessitate some rethinking of the privileged position conventionally granted to the Yellow River basin in accounting for the rise of the earliest Chinese states".

As mentioned above, the local Neolithic culture centred on the Chengdu Plain is the **Baodun**. As of 2003 seven walled sites are known – with Yandian the most recently discovered – distributed in an arc from south-west to north-east of Chengdu and spaced about 20–33 km apart (Xu 2001: 23). Surrounding this group of sites are other related Neolithic settlements (see Figure 6.43).

The settlements vary greatly in size, the two smallest being about 10 ha each, the next two slightly more than 30 ha and the largest 60 ha. In addition to the type site of Baodun, which is the largest prehistoric walled settlement so far discovered in south-west China (Yi 2006: 144), the others are: Yufu, Gucheng, Mangcheng, Shuanghe and Zizhu (*ibid.*). As the settlements are located on river banks, at elevations of 500–700 m in transition zones where hills meet the plain, it has been suggested that the walls (*hangtu*) are more flood than military defence, owing to some very shallow slope angles on the faces of town walls, and from sand and pebble deposits within them (*ibid.*). With the wall at Baodun 30 m at the base and 8 m in width at 4 m high (Yi 2006: 111) this is very dubious and they are most likely just defensive. However, it must be said that the weapons found so far are not plentiful and show few signs of use. Nonetheless, full circumvallation, as seen at the Mangchen site, and probably the case for all of the settlements, is rarely required for flood protection alone. At Mangchen, as at Shuanghe, there is in fact double circumvallation, the inner wall separated from the outer by 20 metres (Yi 2006: 118). Indeed Yi (*ibid.*: 131–2) remarks that those walls "are the most notable feature of the Baoduncun Culture", with pits the most ubiquitous feature. Fashioned with care to have smooth vertical sides, the pits contained large quantities of artefacts including pottery and stone implements. Yi (*ibid.*) relates this to pottery

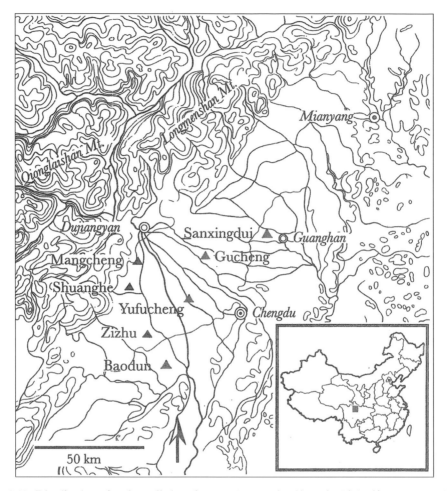

*Figure 6.43: Distribution of early walled settlement sites on the Chengdu Plain (from Wang Yi, 2006: 111).*

or stone tool production, but the construction of the pits and their contents seem to be a harbinger of the later, artefact-filled pits at Sanxingdui, the contents of which are spectacular (discussed at length below).

The most common artefacts found at the Baoduncun sites are pottery of either fine clay or coarse fabric ware, the latter grey-yellow and relatively soft, the former mostly grey-brown. The most distinctive feature of Baoduncun stone implements is their small size (Yi 2006: 139), a fact needing explanation.

> "Characteristic pottery forms include flat-bottom and ring-foot vessels, with the former outnumbering the latter. Among the vessel types are cord-marked and scalloped-rim *guan*, broad-rim *zun*, tall-neck and trumpet mouth *guan*, folded rim *guan*, ring-foot *zun* and *pan*. In addition there are a small number of stems from *dou* and cylindrical vessels. The lithic inventory consists of flaked tools, microliths and

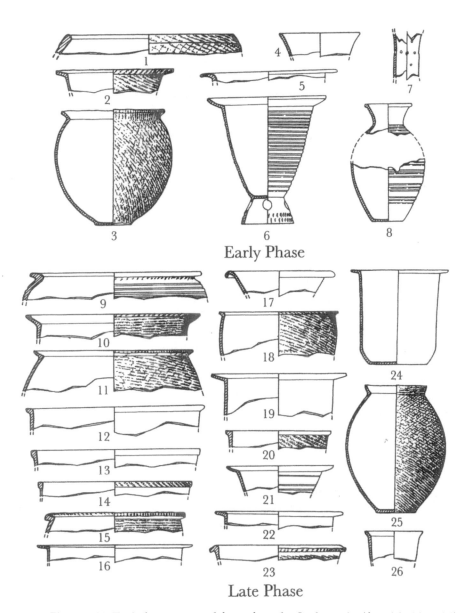

Early Phase

Late Phase

*Figure 6.44: Typical pottery vessel forms from the Gucheng site (from Yi 2006: 124).*

*Typical pottery vessel forms from the Gucheng site. (1-8 belong to the Early Phase, 9-26 to the Late Phase). 1. Constricted-mouth guan [T3(12):11]; 2,3,10,11. Cord-marked and scalloped-rim guan [T3(11): 78, H14:1, T5(13):92, H3:1]; 4. hu [H9:69]; 5,22. Flared-mouth and ring-foot zun [H22:24]; 8,17. Tall-neck and trumpet-mouth guan [H14:3, 97T9(6):9]; 9. Constricted-mouth guan [T5(13):94]; 12. Narrow-rim pen [T3(9):43]; 13,14,18,20,23. Narrow-rim guan [T2(9):49, T2(9):49, T4(11):87, T5(12):31, T5(12):13]; 15. Curved-rim guan [T5(13):129]; 16. Broad-rim and flat-bottom zun [T4(13):142, H22:35]; 25. Folded-rim and deep-belly guan [H22:34]; 26. bei [T4(13):150]. Vessels not to same scale.*

polished stone tools. Flaked stone tools include axes and knives, microliths include cores and flakes, and polished stone tools included axes, adzes and chisels. A stone axe with three perforations was exquisitely made and stylistically unique, showing no traces of wear".

This is part of Yi's (2006: 129) description of the Shuanghe site finds, but as all six sites "display a great deal of consistency in their cultural assemblages" (*ibid.*: 131), it can represent them all and one can expect spindle whorls, bone awls and whetstones, found at Zizhu, to be recovered from the other sites. Overall, "Baoduncun pottery was manufactured by coiling clay strips by hand and then finishing the vessel on a slow potter's wheel" (Yi 2006: 133). The most common vessel type was the *guan*. Course fabric wares were probably mostly used for cooking, while fine clay vessels probably served mostly as containers (*ibid.*). See Figure 6.44 for examples.

At Gucheng the foundations of a large rectangular building, F5, was found during the 1997–98 season. Measuring 50 by 11 metres, its north-west to south-east axis parallels

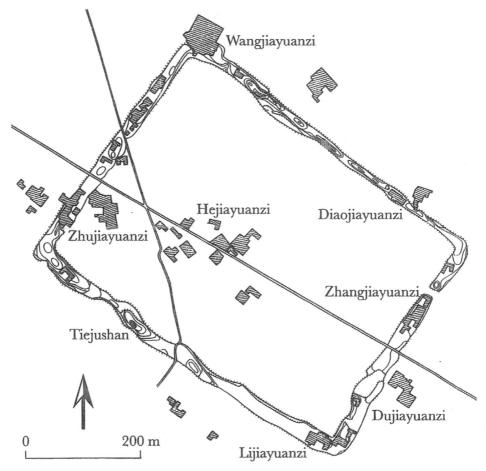

*Figure 6.45: Plan of the Gucheng walled settlement site in Pixian County (from Yi 2006: 123).*

that of the town. Construction was by wooden posts supporting bamboo matting that was then plastered on both sides with a mud-straw mixture. Yi (*ibid*.: 126) comments that "in addition to the rarity of such a large structure in Neolithic China, F5 is also unique in terms of its architectural style. It is likely to have been a site for large-scale rituals. It was built during the Early Phase of the Gucheng site and was abandoned at the end of the Late Phase".

Baoduncun Culture existed between about 5000 BP and 3700 BP, with calibrated determinations from charcoal spanning 2631 BC (highest, Baodun) to 2273 BC (Gucheng, highest); rounded: *c*.2600–*c*.2300 cal. BC (Yi 2006: 136).

The last phase, IV, of the Baodun Culture should date between Phases I and II of the Sanxingdui Culture (below) according to Yi (2006: 137), who states that this "would be equivalent to the period from the end of the Longshan Culture to the beginning of the Xia Dynasty, or approximately 4000–3700 BP". In any event, Baoduncun Culture is the direct precursor of the Sanxingdui civilization *(ibid.*: 144).

## SANXINGDUI ('The Three-Star Mounds')

This was recognised as totally new Bronze Age culture following the discovery of so-called death pits at Sanxingdui located about 10 km west of the city of Guanghan, which is 40 km northeast of Chengdu, the capital of Sichuan province (see Figure 6.43). The centre of the site is a walled enclosure of about 3.5 km², with an artefact spread covering an area of up to 17 km² along the southern bank of the Yazi river and both sides of the Mamu River (Jay Xu 2006: 150).

Here on 18 July 1986, workers at a local brick factory discovered a collection of jades and fortunately archaeologists were called immediately (Liu 2000: 23). Another pit, Pit II, was discovered on 14 August of the same year only 30 m from the first, again by the brickyard workers. Both pits were rectangular and carefully dug.[70]

Pit 1 is 4.64 x 3.48 m and 1.68 m deep; declining to 3 x 4 m at the bottom. It is approached by ramps from the south and south-east, and its corners are oriented to the cardinal directions, as are those of Pit II. This relatively shallow pit contained an astonishing array of items, 420 in total. There were 178 bronzes, 129 'jades', 70 works in stone, 39 pottery objects and four gold items (Liu *op. cit.*). Organic material included three cubic metres of charred animal bones that came from pig, sheep, goat, cow and ox, 13 elephant tusks (identified as *Elephas maximus*, which, from the presence of its teeth, seems to have been slaughtered on site; cf: Elvin 2003), 62 cowrie shells and a number of pieces of amber, quite a rare find in China.

Excavation standards in China are such that the 'jade', 'amber' and 'stone' finds were discriminated only by inspection, not even using a microscope, let alone by chemical analysis to determine, for example, true nephrite. Apparently something in the sense of 'fine hardstone' is intended by the encompassing term 'jade' (see Xu 2001 n. 32 for critical discussion). According to So (2001: 154), of the 200 or so objects from the pits classified as jade, less than six per cent are actually nephrite, most being varieties of

---

[70] Those are but a few events in the the site's excavation history; for which see Jay Xu 2006, who also provides tables of radiocarbon dates.

marble or limestone. Specifically, of the 105 'jades' in Pit 1, only four are nephrite; of 81 'jades' in Pit 2, only six are nephrite. The significance of this is that the softer materials can be worked with metal tools, while nephrite (6.5 -5 on the Mohs scale of hardness) needs to be abraded to shape (and polish) by grinding with crushed harder minerals.

First into Pit I were the 'jades', then the gold items. Next the bronze figures and vessels went in, followed by a mixed group of 'jades', bronze weapons, pottery, animal bones and the elephant tusks. Last into the pit were 'jades' of the *zhang* type (trapezoidal blades) and *ge* (daggers) along with some other pieces of pottery. All suffered from varying degrees of fire damage, including the animal bones, before being placed in the pit (*ibid.*). Indeed, "most of the objects in Pit 1 had been subject to high temperatures; some of the bronzes show traces of melting, others had melted into unrecognisable lumps. Since the walls of the pit show no sign of fire or smoke, the burning must have occurred before the objects were dumped in the pit" (Xu 2001: 30). Pit 1 contained pottery plus a large quantity of bone and ash; Pit II had none at all (*ibid.*: 31).

Apparently the site shows continuous occupation in four periods, from the 'Neolithic', equivalent to the Longshan of central China, (though Longshan is early Chalcolithic) through to the time of the Western Zhou; based upon ceramics found within dwelling areas, supported by stratigraphic analysis and radiocarbon dating (Liu 2000: 30). Period I is dated to the second half of the third millennium, Period II the first half of the second millennium, Periods III and IV lie in the second half of the second millennium. The two major pits are perhaps only separated by a generation around 1200 BC (Xu 2001: 25). A dozen small contemporary settlements have been identified in Guanghan and Shifang counties and two others have been excavated: at Xinfan Shuiguanyin and at Xindu Guilinxiang.

Pit II measures 5.3 x 2.3 m with a depth of 1.68 m and a volume of 20.48 cubic metres, nearly as large as Pit I. Though the pit is slightly smaller, the objects found here were even more remarkable, and included 735 bronzes, 61 gold pieces and 486 jades, including *zhang* blades, *ge* daggers, *fu* axes, the *zuo* chisel and the ritual *cong*. There were also turquoise items, tiger teeth and cowrie shells. According to Xu (2001b: 60) deposition of the items seems to be more methodical than in Pit I and to have taken place in three layers (*ibid.*). Small objects were placed in the bottom layer: bronze, jades, gold and stone. The bronzes of this layer comprised animal face-masks, diamond-shaped fittings (use unknown) small trees and finials. Larger bronzes were placed in the middle layer. One of those was a life-sized statue, discussed below. Another amazing piece was a large bronze tree nearly 4 m high with stylized birds on its stylized branches, which have leaves and flower buds. Falkenhausen (2006: 218) refers to those trees as 'spirit trees', while the birds that he calls 'avian-human hybrids' almost certainly represent another kind of spirit, perhaps that of shamanistic transformation. See Figure 6.46.

Apparently the largest tree was formed from over a hundred different parts cast in two-part moulds. Xu (2001b: 60) reckons that "heavy reliance on casting, and on section-mould casting in particular, is the hallmark of the bronze industry that originated at Erlitou and Erligang, and to find the same reliance at Sanxingdui is strong evidence that Sanxingdui got its bronze technology from the Zhongyuan." Or perhaps both got it from the lower/middle Yangzi, as suggested above.

*Figure 6.46 (left): Bronze spirit tree No. 27:, 396 cm high, with perching birds, possibly magical birds representing winds (feng). Figure 6.47 (right): Life-sized bronze figure, 172 cm high, with uplifted arms, and each of its hands forming a circular grip, probably for elephant tusks. From Sanxingdui Pit II.*

There are also 44 heads of varying size, bronze masks, some of which have tubular protruding eyes and some vessels containing cowrie shells and jades (*ibid.*). The top layer consists of over sixty charred elephant tusks strewn over the other layers. No other animal remains were found in this pit. But again, most of the objects had been broken and burned before being placed in the pit. Both pits were dug into virgin soil and sealed by rammed earth fill. Potsherds typical of late Period III lay above Pit I, sherds from early period IV above Pit 2 (Xu 2001: 25). Forms with pointed bottoms came into use toward the end of Period III and were popular in Period IV. Fabric too changed in Period IV (*ibid.*: 29).

Although some jades, (notably stacks of ritual jade *bi*, the complement to the *cong* ritual jade tubes), had been found at the bottom of an irrigation ditch in 1929, and a pit 2.1 x 0.9 m and 0.9 m deep excavated in 1933 by D.C. Graham, then Director of the Huaxi (now Sichuan) University Museum, the largest part of the 1929 finds had already been sold by the local landowner (So 2001: 153). Between 1964 and 1984 pits containing workshop debris, including tools and uncut stones, were encountered several times within the area enclosed by the city walls. However, none of this prepared the excavators for the quantity and the quality of the finds in 1986.[71] As Liu Yang (2000: 24) observes of Figure 6.47:

> "What most astonished the archaeologists … was the group of a hundred bronze figures, heads and masks with fantastic features, amongst them a life-size statue wearing an elaborate robe and standing on a tall square base. The figure has two long uplifted arms, and each of its hands forms a circular grip that gives the impression it originally grasped something. There are dozens of life-size heads with large slanting eyes framed by bold outlines, strongly curled nostrils and tight-lipped mouths".

Four of the heads are covered in gold leaf, and even more striking are the zoomorphic-human masks with enormous ears and 'pop-out' eyes on stalks. So striking is the impression they make, that Liu Yang (2000: 36–7) refers to them as "stylised to an almost grotesque degree of fantasy. … Undoubtedly, masked ritual played a vital role in community life of the ancient Sanxingdui inhabitants". Figure 6.48 shows one of these: A zoomorphic-human mask with enormous ears and 'pop-out eyes on stalks'. From Sanxingdui Pit II. Height 66 cm, width 138 cm.

The pits did not occur in isolation. The 'Three Mounds' were in fact part of the inner wall of a city covering some 3.5 km² situated south of the Yazi River. Surviving parts of the wall, of *hangtu* construction, are 1100 m on the east, 200 m in the south and 600 m to the west, with the river probably forming its northern perimeter, although the wall could well have been present there too (Liu Yang 2000: 29). Original dimensions are estimated to have been 1.8 km by 0.6 km in the south and 0.8 km in the west (*ibid.*: 26).

The wall was massively thick; 40 m at base, narrowing to 20 m at the top, and reaching perhaps 10 m in height. It was protected, at least to the south, by a 'moat' 2.8 m deep, probably just the ditch from which the soil was removed for wall construction. Liu Yang (*ibid.*) reports that the wall was built during the 'early Shang' period and

---

[71] In 1987 jade and stone artefacts were found in the north-eastern part of the walled area, and in 1997 and 1998 in burials outside the west wall (So 2001: 153).

*Figure 6.48: Zoomorphic-human mask with enormous ears and 'pop-out eyes on stalks'. From Sanxingdui Pit II. Height 66 cm, width 138 cm.*

was abandoned in the 'early Zhou'. Buildings inside the wall ranged from small dwellings of only 10 m², to a large hall 8.7 m x 23 m covering about 200 m². Building plans are round, square and rectangular, with an average area of 20–25 m² of the 50 or more buildings excavated so far (Xu 2001: 26). The city also had interior walls. It is not known whether this had the aim of dividing the city into districts, whether the city outgrew earlier walls, or whether they represented flood defences against the Mamu River which runs through the site. The present course of this river is, however, unlikely to be that of ancient times. The exterior walls are dated to Period II by the potsherds they contain. They have the same gently sloping sides as the Baodun walls. Cultural sequences are interrupted by blackish silt, free of artefacts, so are likely to be alluvial deposits. Commencing early in the third millennium as a Baodun Culture site (Sanxingdui Phase I), the whole site apparently was abandoned around 1000 cal. BC (Xu 2001: 25, Xu 2006: 168), possibly caused by repeated flooding.

Chengdu seems to begin as an offshoot of Sanxingdui, according to its pottery and stone tool repertoire, this especially so after the discovery of Jinsha (below), some 38 km away and only 5 km west of the centre of Chengdu (Zhu *et al.* 2006: 251–2). The type site for this successor phase was said to be **Shi'erqiao**, which lies on the western side of modern Chengdu. Its buildings are said to be contemporary with Sanxingdui III and IV, though this is difficult to establish. Xu (2001: 35) remarks that they seem more architecturally

*Figure 6.49: 'Figure with an Animal Headdress' from Sanzingdui Pit II.*

sophisticated than anything so far known at the Sanxingdui site, but this may just be a consequence of differential exposure. Shi'erqiao covers a maximum area of 3 ha, which is smaller than the Neolithic Baodun Culture sites (Xu 2006: 174). In any event the **Jinsha** site which, as already mentioned, is in the western suburbs of Chengdu itself, is a much more important site of that period. It covers in excess of 4 km² (Zhu et al. 2006: 273, editor's note) and the construction activities leading to the recognition of the site alone produced over 1300 objects of gold, bronze, jade, stone, earthenware and ivory (*ibid.*). "As of early 2002, more than 2000 important artefacts had been unearthed at Jinsha, including approximately 40 gold objects, more than 700 bronze items, over 900 jade items, nearly 300 stone items, and more than 40 ivory and bone artefacts, in addition to a large number of elephant tusks and approximately 10,000 pottery vessels and sherds" (Zhu *et al.* 2006: 261). Significantly, the pit K1 at Jinsha, which lies in the north-east corner of Lanyuan, contains eight layers of elephant tusks and in addition a large number of bronze and jade items (Zhu *et al.* 2006: 261). Feature L2 in the northern sector of Meiyuan contains a concentration of boars' tusks, deer antlers and semi-precious stones in a relatively disordered state (*ibid.*). Particularly noteworthy is a bronze figurine only 20 cm tall, but strikingly similar, particularly in the arm positions, to the life-size standing figure from Pit No.2 at Sanxingdui. Both have the 'socketed hands' designed to receive, that is, to hold, some possibly curved object, as on this 'Figure with an Animal Headdress' from Sanzingdui Pit II (Figure: 6.49), probably elephant tusks.

A different sort of figurine, so far unique, weighs 2.12 kg and is made of polished serpentine. Originally painted, it represents a kneeling man wearing pigtails, with his wrists bound behind his back, obviously a prisoner, reminiscent of Andean depictions of those soon to be sacrificed.

Also strikingly similar to the find at Sanxingdui, though on a reduced scale, is the gold-foil band from Jinsha, whose repeated 'pierced fish' design is almost identical to that on the gold sheath from Pit No.1 at Sanxingdui.

Figure 6.50 shows a masked figure, 12.4 cm high, kneeling in *guizuo* (ritual/formal) posture.

The time span of Jinsha, which probably began as a satellite of Sanxingdui, is estimated to run from the Late Shang Period to the Early Western Zhou (*ibid.*); that is, to span the last couple of centuries of the second millennium and the first century of the first millennium, and, at least for part of that period "it may well have been the capital city of an ancient state that was centred in the Chengdu Plain" (*ibid.*). The striking motif of 'spiral sun' encircled by four birds may be relevant to its role as ritual, population and power centre.

The scale of Sanxingdui city is similar to that of Shangcheng in Henan, probably the largest city of its time in China, but is larger than Zhengzhou, where the walls enclose an area of around 3 km² (Xu 2001: 27). Today Chengdu extends over 200 km². All of those ancient cities are of a particular type, namely *core and satellite*, as found at Anyang and Panlongcheng, amongst many others, indicating that this urban form is a product of deep structures in the political economy and is not a local or even a regional phenomenon. As already mentioned, in core and satellite cities the city wall encompasses only the elite centre and their immediate retainers,

*Figure 6.50: Masked figure, 12.4 cm high, kneeling in* guizuo *(ritual/formal) posture.*

while the various craftspeople (jade, bronze etc.) and essential support workers (food products, ceramics, lithics) are located in villages beyond the walls. At Jinsha, "the different parts of the site each have their own functions. These include a palace area, a ceremonial-ritual area, a residential area and a burial ground" (Zhu *et al.* 2006: 271). Further excavation is certain to reveal a number of workshop areas too.

Outside the west wall at Sanxingdui a group of 28 graves was excavated in July 1998 (*ibid.*). Small, and poorly furnished with only a few jade and stone artefacts, they were obviously burials of support workers. Five pits have been found in the northern and north-eastern parts of the site. They contained stone and jade artefacts, mostly large disks, but sometimes also rings, forked blades and other shapes (*ibid.*).

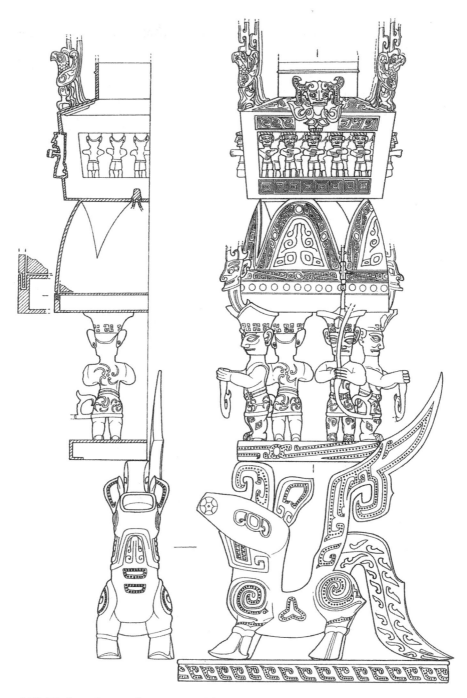

*Figure 6.51: The large bronze altar, supported by a winged-dragon, excavated from Pit II, Sanxingdui.*

They may just have been rubbish pits, for in addition to finished and half-finished objects, those pits contained raw materials, waste material and grinding stones. Similar items found in the vicinity of the pits suggest that workshops for stone and jade were located in this zone (*ibid.*: 27).

No elite burials have yet been found. If the contents of Pits I and II at Sanxingdui are not grave goods, on the Fu Hao pattern, what do they represent? The range and value of objects in the pits and the fact that they were broken and burned prior to interment, requires a fuller explanation than mere 'ritual' or 'sacrifice'. It is possible that sacrifices to royal ancestors are being made at Sanxingdui, for as Liu Yang (2000: 38) observes "in ancient Chinese art, statues portray ancestors, masks represent the spirits of dead forbears, and paintings and decorative arts employ the same motifs over and over again". And in the *Liji* (Record of Rites) and the *Zhouli* (Rites of the Zhou Dynasty), burnt sacrifices are commonly offered to heaven, the buried ones to the earth. In the pits we have both aspects. But is that all there is to it?

The standing totem figure, the large bronze altar (see Figure 6.51) and the tree are surely too exceptional and costly to be smashed up and offered in sacrifice. And surely too much is being offered up? We need to try alternative explanations even though Baodun pits might offer some kind of precedent.

Liu Yang (2000: 27–8) offers an account based on late sources, notably that of Yang Xong (53 BC–18 BC) in the (Western) Han period (206 BC–AD 9). His *Shuwang bengji* (Biography of the Shu Kings) lists five dynasties of Shu rulers: Cancong,

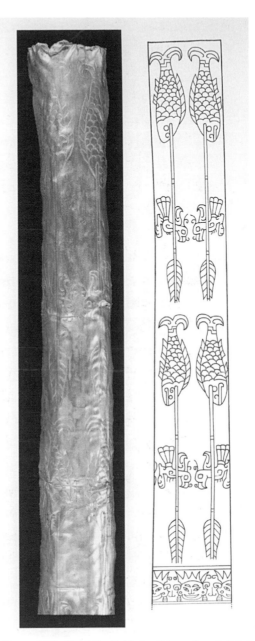

*Figure 6.52: (Right): Gold sheathing of a staff (of kingship and/or supreme priesthood?), 143 cm long, from Pit I, Sanxingdui.*

Baiguan, Yufu, Duyu and Kaiming, each spanning a century or more. The first three dynasties were based at Qushang, taken to be the Sanxingdui area. Those three dynasties apparently came from the same ethnic group. The assumption is that the

*Fig. 6.53 Bronze head with gold-leaf mask, 42.5 cm high, from Pit II. Note holes for earrings and socket-shaping of 'neck'.*

bronzes excavated from the two pits are contemporary with the period of Yufu when Sanxingdui flourished. In this scenario the late Yufu period seems to be when the destruction of Sanxingdui occurred. While a foreign invasion cannot be ruled out, dynastic change accompanied perhaps by civil war involving ethnic conflict seems more likely. "The sudden interruption of consistent settlement at Sanxingdui and the decline of this culture in the area were perhaps the consequence of a violent revolution that resulted in the triumph of Duyu and the shifting of the the ritual and political centre from Sanxingdui to Chengdu" (Liu Yang 2000: 31). In the light of recent discoveries and excavations, not exactly to Chengdu, but to Jinsha.

This is one scenario which might explain the wholesale removal of ritual objects associated with the previous regime. Flooding at Sanxingdui is another, and may also account later for the collapse of the city at Chengdu. The dynastic change scenario assumes that Sanxingdui/Chengdu is indeed the state of Shu of the (much) later texts, one of the Three Kingdoms (Shu, Wei and Wu) of a period named after them (AD 220–265/280). The Three Kingdoms were the successors to the Eastern (*i.e.* restored) Han (AD 25–221). Alternatively, destruction on such a scale could well be a consequence of a peasants' revolt and the overthrow of an oppressive regime. One of the items destroyed (burned) is a gold staff from Pit I (Figure 6.52).

The sheathing takes the form of a tube of gold, formed by hammering an ingot into a rectangular sheet, 7.2 cm by 142 cm and weighing 170.44 g (Xu 2001c: 71). The sheet had decorative designs of fish, birds and arrows raised in it, then the sheet was wrapped around a wooden rod. From Pit 2 the 172 cm commanding figure standing on its stool on a plinth, totalling 260.8 cm in height and weighing 180 kg, wears what seems to be a two-part crown formed from a headband topped by feathers. Both objects seemingly represent kingship and both were destroyed along with many other items, including the trees. Perhaps the commanding figure controlled the Tree of Life, and, when smashing him up with his symbolic tree and also the altar (Figure 6.51) possibly embodying the cosmos itself, his political grip was destroyed and with it kingship.

Peasant revolts are very well known in Chinese history, most famously perhaps those leading to the destruction of the hated Qin regime after the emperor's death in 210 BC. Popular armed support produced the victory of the commoner Liu Bang who instituted the (Western) Han dynasty (206 BC–AD 9). Extensive risings culminated in 184 AD with the famous Yellow Turbans, and remarkably, self-consciously 'levelling' risings swept the Yangzi Valley in the mid 17th century (Blunden and Elvin 1983: 134), exactly the same period as Leveller activity in the British Civil Wars.

Those are just a few of the many peasant revolts. As late as the nineteenth century the Qing lost large tracts of the country to rebellions that, like the Taiping Tianguo, could last for decades. At Sanxingdui it may even be that state or proto-state apparatuses were destroyed, and that for a time more egalitarian conditions obtained. However, once a state has arisen in an area, its experience can never be unlearned. It is likely, therefore, that from the late Bronze Age, Chengdu was always the capital of a state based in Sichuan. But those scenarios are mere speculation, which only thorough regional survey (cf: Underhill *et al.* 2002, 2008) plus sustained, rigorous and wide-ranging excavation (and publication!) can resolve. No amount of textual exegesis, artefact or contextual 'interpretation' can do so.

## The Zhou

In central plains historiography the Zhou takeover (1045 BC) of the Shang domains was an epochal event. To later, especially Confucian scholars, this was necessarily so, as it demonstrated the consequences of losing the mandate of Heaven, and Zhou served as the noble exemplar (Shaughnessy 1991: xv). However, this whole scenario is a Western Zhou construction, expediently adopted and expanded as moral history in the Eastern Zhou/Warring States period and subsequently.

> "According to Western Zhou ideas, the king was the 'counterpart' of Heaven or God. He was a 'law', a 'model' or a 'pattern' to the people and states of the earth below. He was an exemplar to whose manifest virtue they responded, and a teacher. ... He and his vassals were those who set the world in order, building walls and marking out and sharing the fields for farming. He was also 'the host to a thousand spirits', making them offerings and 'obedient to the dead princes of the clan'" (Blunden and Elvin 1983: 75).

In origin Zhou was just another bronze-using part of central plains culture, but one with particularly strong influences from and connection to the northern complex. Originally from the Wei River valley in Shaanxi province, it also received strong influences from Yangzi and western cultures. This amalgam and the resulting dynamism is what probably enabled it to takeover the Shang domains. It is probable that the Shang ruling class had become excessively ritualistic, cruel and arrogant; but in any event those failings were stressed after the Zhou conquest in 1045 BC. In neither Shang nor Western Zhou accounts is there mention of the other bronze-using cultures around or at a distance from them. Only now is archaeology beginning to show just how narrow and distorting the 'classical' written sources really are. Nonetheless, one

*Figure 6.54: A particularly important 11th-century* gui *(21.6 cm high, 42.0 cm wide, diameter 26.6 cm) with a lengthy inscription describing how King Wu's brother, Kang Hu (Duke of Kang) and Mei Situ were given territory in Wei (Henan Province) to reward them for their part in the defeat of an uprising by remnants of the Shang (British Museum).*

of the 'classic' texts, the Zuozhuan, which has contemporary inscriptional support[72], is invaluable for indicating how Zhou feudalism and the political kinship system operated:

"When king Wu had subdued Shang, king Cheng completed the establishment of the new dynasty, and chose and appointed [the princes of] intelligent virtue, to act as bulwarks and screens to Zhou. ... [The heads of] six descent groups (*zu*) of the people of Yin [i.e. Shang] – the Tiao, Xu, Xiao, Suo, Changshuo, and Weishuo lineages (*shi*) – were ordered to lead the families of their patrilineages (*zongshi*), to collect their branch lineages (*fenzu*), to conduct their distantly related dependents (*leichou*), and to repair with them to Zhou. ... To Kang Shu (the first Marquis of Wei) there were given ... seven descent groups (*zu*) of the people of Yin – the Tao, Shi, Po, Yi, Fan, Ji, and Zhongkui lineages (*shi*)..." Keightley's (1999b: 51) modified version of Legge's (1872) translation. As Shaughnessy (1996: 162) succinctly puts it: "no one in the lineage was really free, with the possible exception of the 'aristocrats'". Note that whole clans and lineages were just uprooted by command and despatched elsewhere to serve the state. This situation continued until modern times.

---

[72] E.L. Shaughnessy's *Sources of Western Zhou History* (1991) is fundamental in this regard.

In what he terms 'The age of hierarchy' existing in China from ancient to modern times, C.K. Yang (1959: 89) describes how that social hierarchy is formed structurally and psychologically: "The interlocking of these three factors, generation, age and proximity of kinship, resulted in a system of status and authority that assigned to every person in the kinship group a fixed position identified by a complex nomenclature system. The identification of status for distant relatives was facilitated by giving the same middle name to all sons born into the same generational level so that the kinship position of a person could be readily identified by the generational name whenever distant members met. An important feature of this system was that it could fit a kinship group of any size, from a small conjugal family to a vastly extended family like *a clan with ten thousand or more members*, thus giving the small family a ready organizational framework for expansion whenever economic conditions permitted. This hierarchy of status and authority imposed strong compulsion on the individual to observe his own place in the group through, amongst other factors, the operation of the mores of filial piety and veneration of age" and thus ancestors (my emphasis).

## The state formation process in China

A clan consists of a number of lineages all supposedly descended from a common ancestor, but not all the lineages are of equal standing or rank. Indeed Chang (1983a: 35) states that "the lineage (*zu*) was probably the most important social framework for coercion; *zu* rules were the society's fundamental law". Those deemed to be nearest to the founding ancestor of the clan are the most senior and politically powerful. They control the most important fecundity rituals because they are invested with potency by dint of proximity to the ancestors who are the locus of crucial power, mediating as they do between divinities and men.[73] Paul Kirchhoff (1935) called the resulting social framework *the conical clan.* In it one lineage gets promoted to the apex of a cone formed, as it were, by the branching away (by hierarchical segmentation) of related lineages.[74] It is important to realise that all native lineages have similar time-depth, and that seniority is a result of political manipulation. In this process the majority of lineages come to count for little, while one or two tend to monopolize the bulk of social

---

[73] Ritual is repeated, conventionalized symbolic behaviour, externally (publicly) and internally (psychologically) actualising aspects of the belief-system (ideology).
[74] A lineage is a descent construct whereby the living trace connections with each other through grandparents and ancestors, real or imagined. But only families actually exist at any point in time and it is their household units that can lend each other support if they have reason to do so. Lineages, by 'relating' contemporaneous family units to one another on the basis of the past and of sibling solidarity in it, provide that good reason. A lineage is, then, an organization of obligatory mutual support, since all members supposedly share the same substance. To the extent that a lineage thrives and multiplies over time, branching lines of descent constitute a clan. However, the lineage which can claim seniority, say through descent from the oldest son, can also claim to be most strongly in touch with the ancestors, and so best able to act as a channel for divine blessings, since the divinized ancestors are themselves in touch with divinity. The obverse of this is that the further away from this axial lineage others are, the more junior and subordinate they become, forming eventually just a 'mass', obliged to render services, even their lives, to the dominant lineage. In other words they become mere chattel. This is how the conical clan emerges with the 'great lineage' (*da zōng*) at its apex dominating the clan territory. Its leader is first called 'lord' (*hóu*) then with the domination over/amalgamation with other clan territories, king (*wáng*). *Wángzú* are members of the royal lineage.

surpluses and to dispose of armed power, so that the solidarity that comes from clan identity is ultimately guaranteed by armed might.

The process of state-formation thus takes place when the apical lineages (at the top of the cones) mix and marry with their clansmen no longer. Instead they marry either within their own lineage or with other elevated lineages from other clans, who likewise draw their support and revenues from, but are no longer answerable to, related but inferior lineages. Thus the conical principle, in the words of Kirchhoff ([1935] 1968: 266) "results in a group in which every single member, except brothers and sisters, has a different standing: the concept of the degree of relationship leads to different degrees of membership in the clan. In other words, some are members to a higher degree than others". The 'members of higher degree' emerge with the privileges, while the rest have the duties.

Lee and Zhu (2002: 717) argue that the earliest plausible example of lineage organization in Chinese archaeology occurs in the **Shuiquan** cemetery site in Jiaxian, which belongs to the late Peiligang Culture at the end of the 6th millennium BC. This is very early indeed; right at the beginning of the Chinese Neolithic. Gao and Lee (1993) conducted a biometric distance study of the craniofacial features of the skeletons recovered from the **Shijia** site belonging to the considerably later Yangshao Neolithic culture. The cemetery, excavated in 1976, contained 43 graves in an area of 250 m² (Li Liu 2000: 141). Of those, 40 graves contained multiple interments, from which 727 individuals were identified. The number of interments per grave ranged from four to 51, averaging 18.2 per grave, with a median of 16.5 (Gao and Lee 1993: 273).

The site has a radiocarbon date of 3785 BC (*ibid.*: 272). Lee and Zhu (2002: 718) found that "the interments of the same grave regardless of sex tend to share more phenotypic characteristics when compared to the interments of the other graves. The placement of the interments in the cemetery was obviously regulated by a biological network. The relationship among the individuals of the same graves was consanguine rather than affinal; that is, the men and women of the same graves were brothers and sisters rather than husbands and wives". This demonstrates a clear lineage relationship in a society where social differentiation was probably minimal (Li Liu 2004: 129).

Gao and Lee's (1993: 293) sophisticated statistical techniques further indicate from the skewed sex-ratio at death, 1: 1.97 F: M, that the society was patrilocal and patrilineal; some sisters are missing, presumed buried at the locus of exogamous marriage. For similar reasons, **Yuanjunmiao** burials show a sex ratio (F: M) of 1: 1.38 and **Jiangzhai** Phase II, 1: 1.70 (Li Liu 2000: 143). This indicates that females were the first to be alienated from ritual procedures for transformation into ancestors; then all of those who did not leave behind them substantial property (Li Liu 2000: 155). Thus Yangshao culture was only relatively egalitarian and the egalitarianism related to the interests of corporate kin-groups with the attendant subordination of individuals within them, something also characteristic of historical China.

## Contemporary clan contests

The importance of lineage and its ranking within the clan (and the relative power of clans) is still important today, after a century and a half of turmoil in China, brutal wars imposed by Japan, industrialisation and two revolutions, resulting in six decades of highly centralised authoritarian communist government. Mobo Gao (1999: 35–6) describing contemporary conditions in his home village and his (Gao) clan in Boyang County, Jiangxi Province, makes it abundantly plain that the number of adult males capable of fighting – 'fists' – is crucial to the relative standing of each structural unit: village, clan and lineage. Thus "everyone wants his or her own village to have more males in order to fight better with neighbouring villages. A villager from a large village feels superior, speaks louder and moves more boldly. If a brawl breaks out in a market place involving people from two villages, the villagers from the small village, knowing their place, will usually withdraw and thus loses face by avoiding a fight".

But it must not be thought that all is solidarity within villages and clans. "Even within a village, the sphere of influence and power is based on the number of fists. The proportion of power and influence of a family parallels the number of males who can fight. A family of many brothers is always respected and feared. The family with the greatest number of adult males would have the greatest say in village affairs and it could intimidate the village leader", that is, where it did not supply him. Here it must be remembered that Gao Village is a 'single-surname village' (all bear the family name Gao) signifying that all villagers have lineal kinship relations. Thus it was in prehistory, as at **Yuchisi**, a Late Dawenkou culture site in Mengcheng, north Anhui, dating to 2800–2600 BC. This moated 10 ha site (5 ha settlement within the moat) has been almost completely exposed, and of it Li Liu (2004: 99) remarks "the planned village pattern positively indicates a monolineage community. It is thus likely that the Yuchisi settlement indicates a monolineage community. However, many Yangshao settlements, such as Jiangzhai, Banpo and Beishuoling, were also well-planned, and they may have been organized monolineally as well". But Yuchisi was not one big happy family. Its sub-lineages competed for prestige and rank by means of competitive feasting. The six highest ranking burials by quantity and quality of grave goods were distributed over four separate house-clusters: II, III, VII and VIII of the nine house groups with 192 associated burials (*ibid*.).

Exactly the same considerations of potential force determine internal relationships within the clan, which can be spread over a number of villages. "In Gao Village there are five branches [of the clan]. Very often, tensions break out among different branches and sometimes conflicts break out. Again, adult male members take precedence. The branch with the greatest number of adult males will usually intimidate and bully the small branches" (*ibid*.: 36). There is nothing subtle or even ideological about it.

Solidarity is thus relative to self-interest and depends on the level of threat. Inter-clan conflicts can be of a different order of magnitude and so can expediently call-forth clan solidarity. Thus "The dispute between Gao Village and Wang Village has a long history. In 1947, both sides prepared for battle with guns and locally made cannons. Wang Village backed off before the fighting actually took place because the big Gao Village 10 km away, which is twice its size, came to the small Gao Village's help with a machine-gun, which frightened the Wang villagers" (*op. cit.* 14). I'll bet it did.

This situation of village against village and clan against clan is the historic and prehistoric pattern, and cannot be put down to the conflict prevailing in 1947 between Communists and the Guomingdang. For as recently as 1991, Gao (1999: 116), records

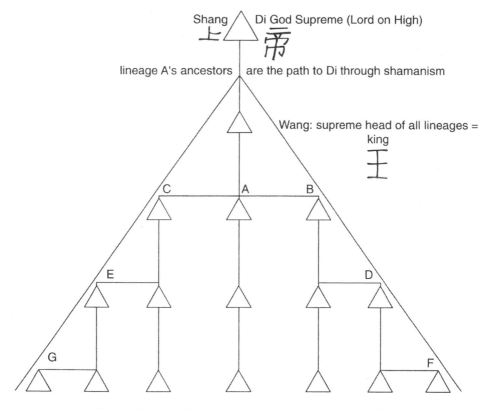

*Figure 6.55: Stratification in the Structure of the Conical Clan.*

"A telling example is a feud between Jin Village, the biggest village in Yinbaohu *xiang*[75], which has 1000 households and its neighbouring village which is much smaller. In a large scale battle involving locally made cannons and guns which took place in 1991, seventeen people from the small village were killed by Jin villagers." *Plus ça change!*

As the local security guards and county officials were overwhelmingly Jin villagers or clansmen, the 17 deaths went unpunished. Examples of such clashes are commonplace and could easily be proliferated from other accounts. The fact is that the Chinese countryside is as riddled by clan politics as is sub-Saharan Africa. What is different is that the centre of the Chinese state is not in the hands of a clan or tribe out to despoil the rest, as is often the case in Africa.

All therefore depends on who the enemy is and the extent of the danger. Are the interests of every Gao clan member across a number of villages threatened, or is it safe to advance one's own interests by intimidating related or neighbouring

---

[75] A *xiang* is a township or a district. Equivalent to that of a (former) commune, it is the lowest unit of rural administration staffed by government-appointed and paid officials. This level traditionally represents the maximal penetration of central government control into the countryside.

1. The fundamental importance of the lineage and clan, focussed by
2. Ancestor veneration (sometimes taking the form of mummification or human sacrifice), where
3. Lineages gain dominant positions by 'feasting the community', claiming proximity to ancestors and launching projects.
4. Offices, originally rotational ('cargo-like'), are 'captured' and become their permanent possession, by occupying which
5. A ruling elite forms, justified by the ideology of 'birth' and ritual practice, and which, distancing itself from the populace, is
6. Responsible only to ancestors and animistic ('higher') powers, and which therefore
7. Deploys legitimated force in protecting its position and takes life at will, paradigmatically as 'sacrifices'
8. On the basis of its power it can demand
9. Ever increasing economic resources (including corvée), the extraction of which, having reached an internal ceiling, can be
10. Augmented by raiding/subjecting neighbouring populations/expanding the territory controlled/ levying taxes or extracting tribute.

*Figure 6.56: The Dominance Escalator for clan-based societies.*

lineages? It all depends on immediate circumstances and what Evans-Pritchard called structural opposition.

Clan hierarchy in antiquity is illustrated (from Maisels 1999: 296) as shown in Figure 6.55, where the head of the 'central' or senior lineage becomes king (*wang*) because he has the most direct relationship with the ancestors and they with Shang Di (or just Di) the supreme being, the 'supreme lord' or Lord on High.

As we have seen immediately above, in getting to the top and consolidating the lineage's position there, the threat and deployment of force is essential. A lineage in a Chinese village that has no physical force to deploy cannot 'hold its head up', and a village or clan with an insufficiency of fists is of no account. But those able to combine at least two sorts of power, physical and ideological can then acquire economic power and with that combination form themselves into rulers, or similarly if the initial combination is of physical power with economic. If then they are able to develop and deploy an apparatus (agents in offices) that will do their bidding, then they have formed, if not a state, at least a complex chiefdom.

Social and thus hierarchical structures were similar in pre-Columbian Andean cultures. From a common Late Palaeolithic basis in hunting magic and shamanism, remarkably analogous ideological and political structures developed with the advent of the Neolithic.

What they have in common enables us to construct what can be called the **Dominance Escalator** for the emergence of states based upon clanship (here China and the Andes); it can be summarized as in Figure 6.56.

In his comprehensive review of Peruvian archaeology, Moseley (1993: 53) observes that "the Andean archaeological record indicates that the evolution of leadership saw the crystallization of formal offices and hierarchical posts long before such positions were co-opted by the emergence of an hereditary elite. Whereas cargo-like systems of governance seem to have great antiquity, *karaka*-like rule did not become prevalent until shortly before the Christian era."

In what he calls cargo systems of leadership, Moseley (*op. cit.* 107) claims that capable individuals rotate through a succession of formal offices. However, in the light of Andean-Indian ethnography, a more apt term would be 'big-man system', where one enjoys prestige and leadership to the extent that, and for so long as, one is able to 'feast the community.'[76] Communal feasting and drinking, especially of *chicha*, is still socially, politically and ritually important amongst indigenous Andean populations.

"*Karakas* claimed closer descent from the *ayllu's* founding ancestor than the subjects they oversaw, and local lords and those of larger polities formed a separate class of people who married among themselves..." (*ibid.*: 52). This is the consequence of the conical clan in a nutshell. Its theoretical analysis has been greatly advanced by Hage and Harary's (1991, 1996) application of graph theory, while Jenkins (2001), applying their work, has enormously clarified the structure of the *ayllu* by applying the Search Tree model to them. He finds that "the model that best characterizes the structure of a conical clan is a *depth first search tree*, which is, in effect, an algorithm for labelling a tree."[77] It is the ordering of points in the tree that gives relative rank.

And its metaphysical basis was also the same: "For commoner and *karaka* alike, ancestor veneration was a fundamental institution of Andean society. Native concepts did not maintain a sharp division between the living and the dead, and the deceased actively influenced the health and well-being of their descendants. People consulted and propitiated their progenitors on a regular basis. Forebears defined the lineage, moiety [division], and *ayllu* to which an individual belonged, and position within the hierarchy of life's relationships" (Moseley 1992: 53).

Those familiar with traditional East-Asian social organisation will immediately recognise this description. In the Andes, *ayllus*, not individual families were the units of land ownership. Even today, over 90 per cent of irrigated land in production is corporately worked in some fashion. And so,

> "Ranging from *ayllus* to the Inca state [Tiwantinsuyu], Andean social formations were held together by kin bonds based upon veneration of tangible common ancestors and mummies were the preferred symbols of founding fathers and corporate identity" (Moseley 1993: 94).

In China a key method by which a lineage could assert itself as the dominant one in a clan was by shamanism and divination. This explains the dominant role of ritual

---

[76] "By astute economic generosity and management he secures influence over his kin and neighbours, who become his debtors. People support a Big Man's political endeavours and his ambitions to build his 'name' because he contributes to their brideprice funds, bankrolls their ritual obligations and because they also, as a group, profit from investing in his increasing political renown" (Lindstrom 1996: 63).

[77] A tree is a connected acyclic graph. "To search a tree requires that it is rooted and planar (a planar graph is one that can be drawn so that no edges cross). A *rooted tree* is one in which a point is distinguished from all other points; that point is called the root, conventionally designated as the point at the top of the diagram. A *labelled tree* with *p* points has the numbers 1,2,3..., *p* assigned to its points. To search a tree means to label its points in consistent order, starting with point 1, the root, and visiting each point [using a consistent principle] until the entire tree is labelled" (Jenkins 2001: 172).

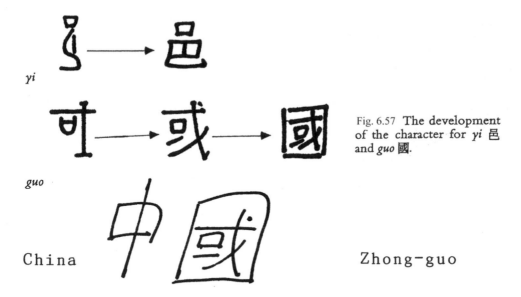

Fig. 6.57 **The development of the character for *yi* 邑 and *guo* 國.**

*Figure 6.57: The development of the character for* yi *(settlement, town) and for* guo *(state), (from Demattè 1999: 143 with additions).*

at the Chinese court right up to its overthrow by the Revolution of 1911–12.[78] It also explains how writing and calculation – which in Mesopotamia began as household and temple accounts during the fourth millennium – commenced in China as scapulimancy, a form of divination (Flad 2008: 418) examples of which have been given above. Questions to the gods and ancestors were inscribed on the shoulder blades of deer, sheep, pig, camel, dog and bear, and most commonly, cattle and turtle plastrons, the latter used from Longshan times onward. Indeed, in coastal areas and the Huai River Valley, the practice reaches back to the early Neolithic (Xingcan Chen 2008: 421–2). When exposed to fire (hence the term pyromancy) cracks formed across the inscription and were interpreted by 'experts' as answers to the king's questions. They concerned everything from harvest success through travel and hunting to warfare.

---

[78] "Ritual has been a central concern of Chinese culture for at least four thousand years. It prompted the earliest known uses of Chinese writing, as well as the making and use of virtually all the earliest examples of what we now call Chinese art. A self-defining activity of rulers and families alike, it was also a dominant issue for all the important schools of Chinese thought. While providing Chinese with a standard for distinguishing themselves from non-Chinese, and even all humans from animals, it also was viewed by no later than the third century BC as a principle of the cosmos. More terrestrially, the practice and influence of ritual stretched beyond the sphere of religious worship and even traditional rites of passage, into the quotidian world. There it gave shape to common gestures, added nuances to manners, and provided a framework for the oral and written expression of language. In fact, its impact on the organized activities of the Chinese state and court was probably far greater than in the polities and bureaucracies of other states" (McDermott 1999: 1). Confucius' emphasis on the importance of ritual to civilization, was, then, just a node in the flow of already ritualistic Chinese culture.

## Clanship Urbanism

Mobo Gao (above) has provided graphic descriptions of how clanship shaped intra-village and inter-village power relations. In antiquity clanship also defined urban formation.

Capitals dominated their territories through a network of subsidiary towns occupied by subsidiary lineages or allied clans. Indeed, Chang (1983: 362) states that:

> "the fundamental social unit throughout the Bronze Age [*c.*2200 to *c.*500 BC] was the walled town [*yi*] thousands of which dotted the loessic landscape of northern China. Physically, all these towns were similar." Founded by political fiat, most originated in a coordinated building event and "were enclosed by earthen walls on four sides. The walls were built by the ramming technique [*hangtu*]: long planks were bound together to form a trough, earth was put in and then rammed solid with stone or metal pounders, and then the planks were untied and moved to form another trough, into which earth was put to form another wall section at a higher level. The town enclosure was mostly square or rectangular, with north, south, east, and west walls. Because of the use of planks, walls were straight, and corners were right-angled. Gates opened on the walls; the south gate was the main opening and the enclosure may be said to 'face' the south with its back to the north. This orientation is not unusual for north China, with the sun, the source of all life, shining in from the south" (*ibid.*).

Accordingly, the situation at about 2,000 BC when the earliest state-level civilization was emerging, was that of a landscape dotted with walled towns, *yi*, populated by a single clan, *xing*, but actually ruled by a dominant lineage, *zu*. A state, *guo* consisted of a network of towns under a royal capital, *du*.[79]

> "Yi-settlements were built at the king's behest, recorded in the phrase *wang zuo yi*, 'the king built [i.e. had built] the settlement' and were moveable, the names travelling with the settlement. The Shang word for city-wall, variously equated to modern forms *guo* or *yong*, illustrates two roofed structures atop the walls of a square enclosure. ... A variant with four roofs is also known. The Shang graph for temple-palace, *gong*, incorporates two square elements, perhaps chambers or courtyards, below a roof" (Thorpe 1983: 31).

About 2,000 BC then, there were several thousand such 'states' (*guo*).[80] In the succeeding Shang period a couple of thousand remained, but by 770 BC that number had fallen to about 170, becoming 20 in the mid fifth century and mere seven in the late fifth century (Hui 2005: 153). By the end of third century BC there was of course only one, the 'universal empire' (Van Evera 1999: 181). It is this condition that prompts

---

[79] Despite occasional affixes, there is in general no distinction between singular and plural in Chinese ('Mandarin') nouns. Nor are there real tenses.

[80] "The ruler of a feudal *guo* was only 'first among equals'. The ruler's blood relatives all shared the right to rule by birth in accordance with the closeness of their blood ties. Higher level aristocrats had the right to hold public offices and the obligation to reprimand the ruler for his mistakes. The lowest level of the nobility or *guoren* formed the majority of the population and enjoyed substantial rights and duties. Along with the obligations to fight wars and pay taxes, *guoren* had the rights to bear arms and own land" (Hui 2005: 196–7). So the *guoren*, literally 'state people', were not the lowest class in society but rather its politico-military basis.

some writers to speak of early Chinese 'city-states'. But neither socially, economically, militarily nor in terms of settlement structure, is this a useful description. They began as small territorial states and either expanded to become or were absorbed by larger territorial states of the "village-state" type (Maisels 1987, 1990). By the middle of the first millennium BC, states were relatively few and huge in power, population, military and economic resources. For example, starting in the seventh century BC, the state of Chu spent the next four centuries gobbling up *guo* and turning them into *xian*, administrative districts. "A crucial turning point occurred when military service and land tax were extended from *guoren* to *yeren* in [the state of] Jin in 645 BC. This measure [of mobilizing the peasantry] was so effective in uplifting Jin's relative capability that it became institutionalized in Jin and gradually copied by other great powers" (Hui 2005: 197).

Whereas the Zhou regime had been essentially feudal, predicated on ranked elite lineages with the king *primus inter pares*, this broke down during the Spring and Autumn Period (770–484/475 BC) as did clanship itself (Blunden and Elvin 1983: 61). What emerged during the subsequent Warring States period (475–221 BC), between the state of Qin, the ultimate victor, and Qi, Yan, Qiao, Wei, Han and Chu, was the fully territorial state, rigorously controlled from the centre and consolidated by mass-mobilization. "As Warring States in ancient China developed the capacity to engage in near-total mobilization for war, they were literally war machines" (Hui 2005: 150).

The individual family had now become the unit of responsibility to a state which regulated and exploited the lives of its subjects ever more closely and was, if possible, even more wasteful of their lives. In 256 BC Qin extinguished the languishing Zhou court. Between 236 and 221 BC Qin devoured its enemies 'as a silkworm devours the mulberry leaf'. But this was no overnight victory resulting from one or a few decisive battles. On the contrary, as Hui (2005: 96) relates: "Qin's success involved the hard [and utterly ruthless] work of seven generations of rulers through 57 wars involving great powers (52 initiated by Qin and five initiated by other states) over the course of 135 years (356–221 BC)", in which defeated armies were brutally slaughtered, and not only soldiers but civilian adult males too (Hui 2005: 153).

The clashes during the Warring States period were momentous in scale and unparalleled in world history not only up until that time but even until the First World War, over two millennia later! The wars ended with the imperial unification of China in 221 BC under the notoriously brutal Qinshihuangdi, 'First August Emperor' (more literally 'August Celestial Deity'). Formerly King Zheng of Qin, he forced one tenth of the working population, that is 700,000 labourers who were nominally convicts, to build his 35.4 km² (22 mile²) necropolis at Lishan, and then had them buried alive to preserve its secrets! He forced an equal number, castrated, to rebuild the Qin capital, Xianyang, which included replicas of 270 palaces of the defeated states. Into those replicas Zheng forced more than 120,000 families of the defeated states. All of which are, of course, good examples of the state serving society. And the palaces, the result of all that labour and timber, did not last long: they were destroyed by the rebel general Xiang Yu in 206 BC.

Zheng's state certainly re-ordered society, family and the individual, top to bottom and inside out: "It is not an exaggeration to say that Qin developed 'the fine-grained administrative grid' characteristic of the 'high modernist state'" as a consequence of which "with onerous military service, corvée, land tax, and head tax, the subjects lived on the verge of starvation" (Hui 2005: 180, 217) and many went over the edge. But who was counting? Those familiar with Mao Zedong as emperor and his successors, will certainly recognise the continuation and development of those absolutist characteristics (Blunden and Elvin 1983: 134). No wonder Qinshihuangdi was Mao's idol.

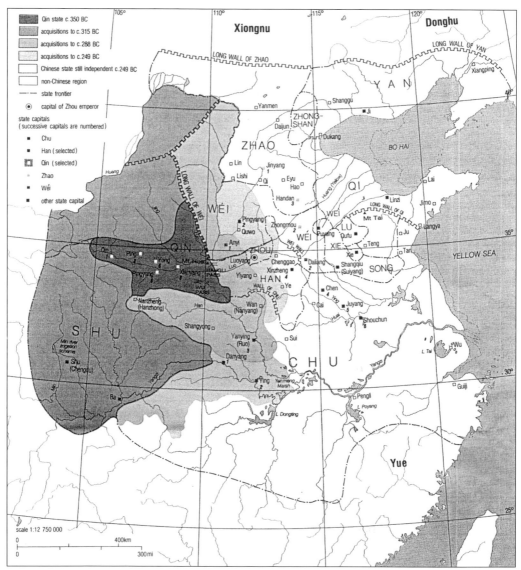

*Figure 6.58: How Qin (centre left) swallowed the other states and made China into an empire-state (from Blunden and Elvin 1983: 71).*

# CHAPTER 7

# *Andean Civilization*

In the New World the earliest complex societies emerged, not, as is generally believed, in Mesoamerica but in Peru during the third millennium. Egypt is the Nile and its delta. Ecuador, Peru, Bolivia and Chile encompass the Andes, its high plateaux and the rivers that cross the narrow coastal desert. Those countries are the product of the longest (6,500 km/4,000 miles), probably most unstable, and second highest mountain chain in the world, which, for half its length exceeds an average altitude of 3,600 m/12,000 ft. Two things are worthy of note at the outset: "the Peruvian process took place in total isolation from other societies on the continent. Indeed, the rise of civilization in Peru preceded Mesoamerica, the other centre of pristine civilization in America, by at least 1,500 years" (Ruth Shady Solis 2008: 28–9).

Coastal groups exchanged with groups exploiting the resources of Andean valleys, valleys interacted with groups on the high plateaux, with neighbours and, down the line, with groups over the mountains and into the Amazon foothills and basin. Indeed ceramics appear in Ecuador and the Amazon Rim around 3000 BC, about a millennium earlier than in Peru. The reason for Ecuador's priority is, of course environmental. The Coastal Current that flows northwards up the coast of Peru, determining the ecology of its littoral, turns westwards off Peru's Santa Valley. As this cold current is responsible for marine richness and coastal aridity, those conditions do not apply to Ecuador which is situated north of Peru. Ecuador's coastal climate is accordingly warmer and wetter, encouraging a more diverse regime of hunting, gathering and fishing with easy access to the forested interior along river valleys. It is necessary, therefore, to get to grips with the geography, though those wishing to skip this and go directly to state-formation processes can jump to Section I: The Early Horizon.

## A: The Setting

To simplify, the geography of South America can be conceptualised as comprising: an s-shaped spine of fold mountains running all down the west (Pacific) coast, in its central stretches separated from that coast by the Atacama/Peru Desert, technically a 'cold water desert'. The long narrow Pacific Coast zone is only 16 km wide in some parts of Peru, which is the third largest country in South America. The coastal zone comprises only 11 per cent of Peru, but has over 50 per cent of the modern population of 26.7 million (2002). At their northern extremity (in Colombia) the Andes fan out into three distinct cordilleras (ranges) while at the southern end, in southern Chile (south of Santiago) the mountains diminish in height and width until they break-up into thousands of

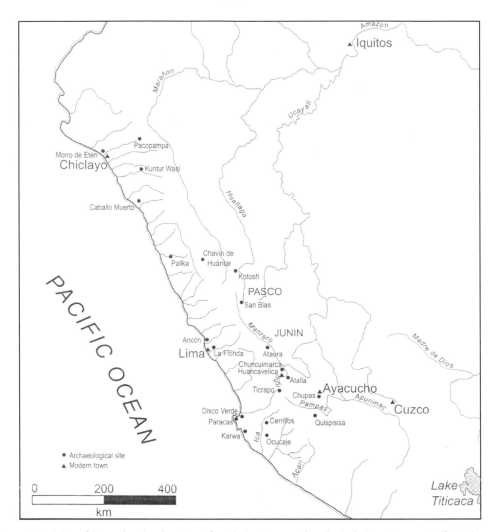

*Figure 7.1: Map of Peru showing location of Early Horizon archaeological sites, Amazon tributaries and Lake Titicaca (Drawn by George Lau, in Burger and Mendieta 2002: 154).*

islands in what is known as a 'concordant coastline' of flooded longitudinal valleys.[81] Broadly, the north and far south have plenty of rainfall; the central coast (Peru) has little, while most of the rain falls on the eastern slopes of the mountains and flows into the Amazon basin. It is important to note that as much as 90 per cent of Andean runoff descends to the Atlantic, and only 10 per cent to the Pacific. This because most of the condensate originates over the Amazon Basin and so as convectional rainfall strikes the eastern face of the mountains generating the headwaters of the Amazon.

---

[81]   North to south: Venezuela, Colombia, Ecuador, and northern Peru are tropical. Inland from the border of Peru with Chile is Bolivia, the western part of which occupies the mountains at their widest. Chile then runs down the rest of the west coast, all the way to Cape Horn.

The Callejón de Huaylas refers to the intermontane valley of the Rio Santa bounded by the Cordillera Blanca and the Cordillera Negra, respectively west and east in parallel to the coastline in the Department of Ancash, north-central Peru. "The Santa is unique in being one of the of the few coastal rivers that extend deeply into the adjacent western cordillera of the Andes" (Wilson 1987: 61). See Figure 7.2.

South of the coastal Santa Valley, where the valleys are drier and the flow more seasonal, the shoreline is rocky, good for rock-pool animals. Locally this is a 'headland and bay' ('Atlantic' type) coast, with large numbers of sea birds and sea mammals using the promontories and thus subject to human predation. North of the Rio Santa the valleys are larger with more perennial water and sandy beaches, good for launching boats (Hastorf 1999: 42), which were made of reed and/or balsa logs. Sandy beaches are, however, found all along the Peru coast (Haas 2008 pers.com.). Also north of the Santa, at 8°S, lies Trujillo, which is one of the Peruvian maritime hot-spots (*ibid.*). Farther north the upwelling currents veer far out to sea and the anchoveta (anchovies) with them (Moseley 1993: 105).

The near-shore fishery extends for a remarkable 2000 km along the coast, thanks to the cold Peru Current, when it is not disrupted by El Niño warming (which in modern times occurs around Christmas, hence the Spanish name). Cold water, with its high levels of dissolved oxygen, is the richest, and that is why polar waters are so productive in summer. The Peru Current normally has the ability to yield 100 tonnes per square kilometre of anchoveta over its length, alone able to sustain more than 6 million people. However, "near the northern end of the anchovy belt, around 8, 11, and 15 degrees South Latitude, there are fishery 'hot spots', called productivity maxima, with yields of 1,000 tonnes per square kilometre per year. It is significant that very large pre-ceramic monuments only occur along the 600 km stretch of shoreline bracketed by these hot spots. Thus, the most complex maritime societies arose where the fishery was at its richest" (Moseley 1993: 102); also "the largest littoral communities and the biggest Preceramic mounds arose in settings favourable to net fishing" (*ibid.*: 106).

In fact, just to mention the Peru (or Humboldt) Current is too simple; misleadingly so. There are two north-flowing cold ocean currents off Peru, which vary in depth. Originating in the Antarctic Circumpolar Current driven by the West Wind Drift (ocean surface currents are wind driven), they are the Humboldt Current and the Peru Coastal Current. The Humboldt is from 500–600 km wide and can be as deep as 700 m. Close to shore runs the Peru Coastal Current, which is about 100–200 km wide and rarely exceeds 200 m in depth. Flowing in the opposite direction, (south), but at a greater depth, is the Peru Undercurrent. The Peru Coastal Current/Humboldt Current flow north to within four degrees (S) of the Equator, at which latitude they turn west to become part of the South Equatorial Current that runs westward parallel to the Equator. One part of this now warmed current runs south off the east coast of Australia. The current spanning the South Pacific is called the South Pacific Gyre.[82]

---

[82]  A gyre is a roughly circular movement of water in each of the ocean basins: North Atlantic Gyre, South Atlantic Gyre, North Indian and South Indian, North Pacific and South Pacific. Warm water flows away from the Equator in the western part of basins and cold water flows back toward the Equator in the east to complete the loop. Those in the northern hemisphere rotate clockwise, in the southern hemisphere anti-clockwise, the

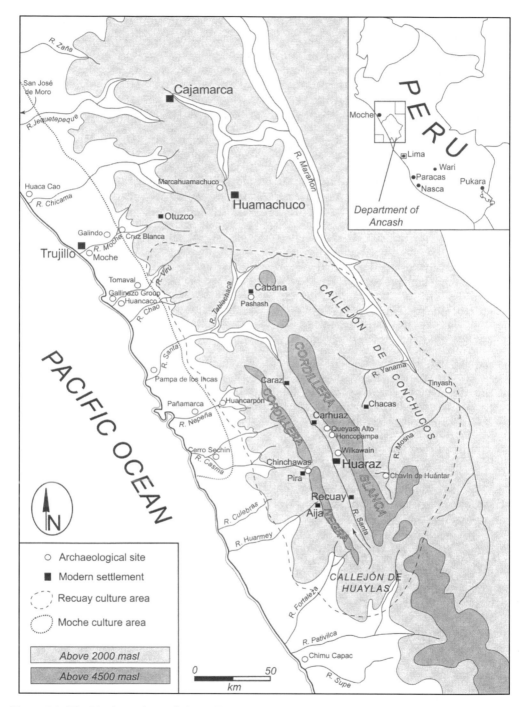

*Figure 7.2: The Rio Santa (centre) the Callejón de Huaylas and other Peruvian rivers (from Lau 2004a: 179).*

There is a deep ocean trench just offshore (the Peru-Chile Trench) where the oceanic plate is subducted (pushed down) under the continental plate, which, accordingly, is rising at the continental margin by from 5 cm to 10 cm per thousand years. This is a *subduction zone* and its proximity to the continental margin is why the coastal plain in Peru and Chile is so narrow. Subduction zones are areas of frequent and strong seismic and volcanic activity. The recurrence interval for great earthquakes in southern Peru over the past several centuries is on the order of one century (Keefer and Moseley 2004: 10878).

The Andes have a steep gradient because they are young fold mountains formed by sea floor compression and margin crumpling as the small but heavy Nasca Plate impacts the South American at a rate of around 78 mm per year (Keefer and Moseley 2004: 10878). This also means that rock strata are weak or unconsolidated, making avalanches and serious erosion highly likely during earthquakes and heavy El Niño rainfall (*ibid.*: 10879). The central Andes manifests what Shimada (1987: 130) felicitously terms 'horizontally condensed topography', a consequence of continental margin folding.

Easterly Trade Winds push the upper layers of offshore water to the west, allowing deep, cold nutrient rich water to rise to the surface. This is called 'upwelling' and it is greatly reduced during El Niño events, causing fish stocks to crash. During El Niño the strong west-blowing winds that normally confine the warmest water to the Western Pacific have weakened or changed direction, or blow in a variety of directions. Warm surface water, usually confined to the East Indies, now stretches along the Heat Equator to the Eastern Pacific, affecting coastal southern Ecuador and northern Peru most directly.

Upwelling allows nitrates and phosphates to rise into the photic zone producing a great bloom of plankton upon which fish and other animals feed. Upwellings also cause localized advection fogs, such as those characteristic of San Francisco. In South America upwellings produce *lomas*, cloud meadows, important to some prehistoric human populations in the Andes. A fog bank covers the central coast of Peru in winter and so affects Lima. This is the region where the early states formed, and it is where the valleys have water for most of the year. By contrast, the southern coastal valleys of the Department of Ica have water only for a few months per year, and states never formed there (Silverman 1996: 140).

The low temperature of the surface currents and the direction of the prevailing winds result in poor orographic (mountain triggered) rainfall in normal years (i.e. when the Walker Circulation is intact). Accordingly, altitudinal climatic zonation is extreme. Climatic and ecological differences, which in flat land would take hundreds to thousands of kilometres to be expressed, in the Andes occur in a few hundred or thousand metres of altitude. Thus a rapid descent takes one from arctic conditions through grassy plains and wooded valleys across hot desert to the cold-water currents of the Pacific.[83]

---

directions caused by the displacements of the Coriolis (Earth rotation) Effect.

[83] The West Wind Drift is the key to oceanic circulation (and, indirectly to atmospheric circulation) in the Southern hemisphere, along with the gyres. The Antarctic Circumpolar Current flows around the world in the Southern Ocean between the Antarctic Continent and the southern extremities of South America, Africa, Australia and New Zealand. The Southern is the only ocean with global extent and it balances the salt, gas,

However all valleys and coastal plains in Peru are not equal. Valleys on the central coast are relatively narrow and descend precipitously to the sea. By contrast valleys on the northern coast are wider in their lower reaches because the hills are more distant from the sea resulting in a lesser gradient. This gives rise to extensive areas of plain as one valley mouth merges into another, facilitating intervalley travel and large-scale field irrigation (Quilter 2002: 156).

This schematic transect across both Cordilleras of the Peruvian Andes (Figure 7.3), which shows the altitudinal and lateral relationships between biomes, is about 16 degrees South Latitude, cutting across the southern part of Lake Titicaca (after Waugh 1984: 27). La Paz, the world's highest capital city, is at 3,800 metres (12,400 ft), 16° 20' S, 66° 10' W. Quito, the capital of Ecuador, is the second highest, at 3000 m (9,850 ft).

The topography of South America is amazingly varied, more so, for example, than Africa, although it has over 20 per cent over the earth's land surface area compared to South America's 12 per cent (17,870,000 km²). Africa is, therefore, second only to Asia (29.6 per cent) in how much of the planet's surface area it comprises (30,097,000 km², 11,620451 miles²) but Africa has no mountain ranges to match the length and altitude of the Andes. South America does, however, have a drainage basin to match the Congo, the Amazon, with of course their associated rainforests, the world's largest remaining blocs. The Equator crosses South America in the far north (obviously in Ecuador) north even of the main Amazon drainage. By contrast the Equator cuts across the very centre of Africa, with the huge Sahara Desert to the north, extending across the widest part of the continent, from Atlantic to Indian Ocean. In South America the only desert is the long, narrow Atacama, stretching from Chile up through Peru. It exists in this form because the main rain-bearing winds are easterlies, putting the western coast in rain-shadow.[84]

Away from the Andes, the rest of the continent's biomes are either forest or grassland, the latter most continuously in the southern part of the continent (Argentina, Paraguay and Uruguay). There is a lot of grassland, both tropical and temperate. South America is ecologically a fortunate continent. It is much more temperate than Africa, which is almost symmetric about the Equator (37° N to 35° S Latitude), while South America lies farther south (extending from *c*.12° N to 55° S). In addition to the Sahara, the world's largest, Africa has deserts in the south, the Namib and Kalahari. Africa extends from the Mediterranean (Algiers 36° 42' N) through the tropics and the Equatorial regions to sub-Mediterranean South Africa (Cape Town 33° 55' S). By contrast, South America extends from the tropical Caribbean through the great Equatorial forests to temperate grasslands (*pampas*) and on to the cold, wet islands and peninsulas south of 43° S in Chile. Further, altitude in the

---

nutrient and temperature levels of the other oceans. Its circum-global flow, temperature and the fact that it generates not only the Peru Current, but also the Benguela Current off the west coast of Africa, and also the West Australia Current (plus, of course, their crucial return currents) make the West Wind Drift/Southern Ocean critical to the functioning of global climate.

[84] Wind directions are named after the direction from which they come, while ocean currents are named for the direction toward which they flow. Thus the North Atlantic Drift that warms Britain and northern Europe comprises South-westerly winds and a NE current called the Gulf Stream, which is that part of the N. Equatorial Current above the Tropic of Cancer.

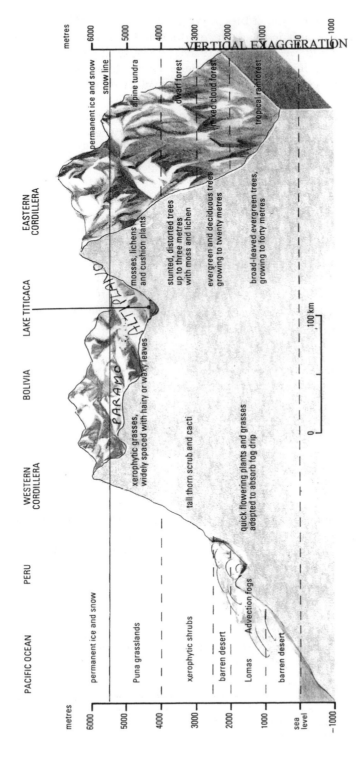

*Figure 7.3: Vegetation zones across the Andes (after Waugh 1984: 27) Yunga lies at 1,000 to 2,000 masl. Vertical exaggeration is 25.*

*cordilleras* (mountain chains) and on the high plateaux (*altiplanos*) mimics latitude to some extent.

In Peru, the *Puña* zone "is the highest area fit for human occupation, consisting of rolling grasslands spotted with flat lakeshore plains and crossed by a network of perennial streams. The altitude range of the *puña*, from about 3,900 to 5,000 m, has rather little effect on *puña* ecology, especially in central Peru. More signifiant are moisture-retention and heat-protection differences due to a variety of topographical, ground-water and bedrock exposure conditions. In general, the *puña* is best considered a fine-grained mosaic environment, which contains scattered plant resources such as berries, tubers and seeds, but with ideal grassland areas for grazing of abundant wild camelids and deer. Lakeshore areas may have been productive for waterfowl, aquatic plants and amphibians" (Rick 1988: 5). Important cultigens were developed on the lower reaches of the *puña* zone, below 4,100 m, in addition to potatoes (*Solanum* spp.), always the most important of the Andean tubers, and oca (*Oxalis tuberosa*). Cultigens include quinoa (*Chenopodium quinua*) and canihua (*Chenopodium pallidicaule*) low yielding cereal-like crops that can tolerate salinity as well as cold; also the tubers ullucu (*Ullucus tuberosus*) and mashua (*Tropaeolulum tuberosum*). Highly localised zones of high productivity are the *bofedales*, marshes, naturally occurring or created by flooding. Marshes/pools/waterholes in the *altiplano* are called *vegas*. From the *puña* to the snowline is the barren *paramo*.

East of the Andes lie the other countries of South America, the 'lands of the river basins', comprising Brazil, the largest and lushest by far; Argentina the next largest, centred on the basin of the Plata River, on the north bank of which, sandwiched between Argentina and Brazil is Uruguay with its capital Montevideo also on the Plate estuary. North of Uruguay and also sandwiched between Argentina and Brazil lies Paraguay. It is only separated from Uruguay by a finger of Argentina pointing north-west towards Surinam and the Guianas on the Atlantic. The northern shores of Colombia and Venezuela form the southern shore of the Caribbean. Colombia, at the northern end of the Andes, also has a Pacific coastline, while Ecuador and Bolivia are, respectively, north and south of Peru.

In sum, South America's regional geography comprises: the Andes; the Llanos (savannah grasslands of the Orinoco region); Amazonia (Equatorial rainforest); the Chaco (N. Argentina, forests and swamps); the Pampas (temperate grasslands of Argentina and Uruguay) and, below 40°S, Patagonia (tussock grass) split between Argentina and Chile.

## B: Outline Chronology

Grouping many Andean sites and phases,[85] the cultural periods are broadly that which can be seen in Figure 7.4. Reviewing cultural evolution and state formation in the Andes, Stanish (2001: 55) concludes that "the state originated in Moche, Wari and Tiwanaku in the first half of the first millennium". Prior to this the general view

---

[85] The state of terminology, periodization and chronology currently disturb most Andeanists (cf: Silverman 2004a; Haas and Creamer 2004, Isbell and Burkholder 2002 and Note 99 below), but a resolution is not imminent; so, cautiously, we must use what we have.

| | | | |
|---|---|---|---|
| Preceramic Period I | 11,000–9500 BC | | |
| Preceramic Period II | 9500–8000 BC | | |
| Preceramic Period III | 8000–6000 BC | ARCHAIC PERIOD | |
| Preceramic Period IV | 6000–4200 BC | | |
| Preceramic Period V | 4200–2500 BC | | |
| Preceramic Period VI | 2500–1800 BC | Cotton Preceramic | |
| Initial (Ceramic) Period | 1800–900 BC | | |
| Early Horizon** | 900–200 BC | | |
| Early Intermediate Period | 200 BC–AD 600 | | |
| Middle Horizon | AD 600–1000 | | |
| Late Intermediate Period | AD 1000–1450 | | |
| Late Horizon | AD 1450–1534 | | |

** "Horizons are periods in which a single well-defined style of material culture is found broadly distributed throughout the Andes" (Schreiber 2001: 77).

*Figure 7.4: Cultural phases and Chronology.*

is that we are dealing with chiefdoms whose integrating and compelling force was religion (Cook 2001: 139). Religion of course justifies domination, and it only needs the addition of physical force to ideological and economic controls to form a state (Stanish 2001: 57–8). And even early on the cruellest violence was perpetrated by chiefdoms on whomever they could expediently victimize, a phenomenon found in all continents (Guilaine and Zammit 2005).

We need to pick up on Cook's suggestion that it was religion that was the enabling factor in the rise of chiefdoms. I have already said that religion was also crucial in the rise of states. An extreme manifestation of this is a formation called the Sacerdotal State, which is a state run by priests, conventionally called a theocracy. A modern and historical example of a Sacerdotal State is of course the Vatican State, historically the Papal States. The Moche was a state of peculiar type (a 'coalition state' where the elites of different valleys found it expedient to rule jointly) run by warriors and priests, with the former aspect dominant. However, on present information, I think that the concept of Sacerdotal State best describes the perplexing early Nazca polity of the southern Andes and it may well describe the much earlier polity at Moxeke/Sechín Alto in the Casma Valley. Shelia. Pozorski (1987: 30) states that "In place of warfare, irrigation and religion appear to have played interacting roles in bringing about the origins of the state in Casma", where early theocratic states were established in the lower valley by about 1500 BC (*ibid.*: 15).

Nazca is introduced next because it raises questions about the adequacy of our existing ideas about chiefdoms and states (cf: Silverman 1993: 343; 2002b: 179). I then return to an account of the development of complex civilization in the Andes as a whole.

## C: Nazca: Chiefdom or State of a New (Old) Type?

The modern town of Nasca lies 400 km south of Lima in the Rio Grande de Nazca drainage which comprises nine main tributaries. Lying mostly within the Early Intermediate Period, Nazca culture (*c*.AD 1–750) is famous for the so-called 'Nazca lines' which are geoglyphs representing animals and geometric lines inscribed in the desert over some 450 km². The animal figures are early, and the straight lines later, with the culture designated 1–5, early to late. The major centre during the early to middle period was Cahuachi, a 150 hectare site; later La Muña was a, if not the, major centre. Other sites of the Nazca culture include Ventilla, Marcaya, Estudiante, Los Molinos, Puente Gentil and Los Médanos. Nazca emerged from the earlier Paracas culture (*c*. 800 BC–AD 1). See Figure 7.5 for a map of the cultural regions and sites in Peru, Chile and Bolivia (modified from Smith and Schreiber 2006: 4).

Cahuachi lies 75 km inland on the edge of the desert plateau. It contains a pyramid 30 metres high, a 'great temple', plazas and forty other structures based, like the pyramid, on the modification of natural landscape features. Built where the River Nazca emerges from its underground course, Cahuachi is obviously a highly charged ritual and pilgrimage site (Gijseghem and Vaughn 2008), but seems to have been destroyed by two natural disasters, flood and earthquake, between AD 300 and AD 350, in the later part of the Middle Nazca Period (AD 200–400). Thereafter La Muña in the Palpa Valley in the northern part of the drainage basin became the principal centre (Isla and Reindel 2008: 398). This sequence is significant and I shall return to it below.

At La Muña, Isla and Reindel have excavated tombs that "constitute the richest and most elaborate burials of Nasca Culture, of whatever period" (*op.cit.*: 393). "The tombs are located in an exclusive part of the site, separated from the surrounding area by walls of thick adobe", and accordingly "the remains can be taken as evidence for real social stratification among the Nazca in the Palpa Valleys during the Nasca 5 phase"(*ibid.*). Despite long-term and ongoing looting of Nazca tombs, Isla and Reindel (*ibid.*: 390–391) recovered at La Muña striking, and apparently professionally made ceramic vessels, including a set of pan-pipes, gold pendants in the shape of small *orcas* (killer whales) plus dozens of beads made of semi-precious stones, *Spondylus* shell, gold and copper. All of this investment in tomb construction with rich grave goods in contrast to what is normally found at the sites of other Nazca burials, according to the authors (2008: 393):

> "The La Muña tombs differ in many respects from other burials in ancient Nasca society. They consist of more than simple pits in the ground, and they have surface architecture that is reminiscent of a mausoleum. Their mortuary chambers were constructed quite deep – much deeper, for example than those of the highest status tombs described by Carmichael, which have a depth of only 4.5 m. Additionally, Carmichael's tombs contain no more than ten ceramic vessels as offerings [Carmichael 1995: table 1]".

Carmichael's contributions are not just to the excavation of Nazca sites, but also to the theory of state formation in general. Is the Nazca polity to be regarded as a chiefdom, or series of chiefdoms, a state or a series of states? He observes (1995: 162) that "a ranked society is a graded society, while a stratified society contains

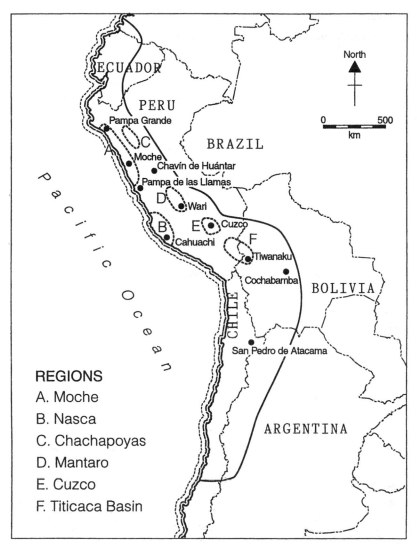

*Figure 7.5: Cultural regions and sites in Peru, Chile and Bolivia (modified from Smith and Schreiber 2006: 4).*

discontinuous social groupings", namely social classes. And while chiefdoms have ranking, dependent upon proximity especially genealogical proximity, to the chief, states possess subordinate classes. Carmichael (1995: 174) concludes from the fact that he found a gradation in the status of tombs without any separation between the various types, that "ranking was present in Nazca society, but there was a low degree of formalized social differentiation in status hierarchy". He (1995: 181) therefore regards Nasca as an 'incipient chiefdom'. Other characteristics reinforcing his view include: a) the absence of full-time specialists in a specific occupation; b) the absence of truly monumental architecture compared with that found in the known state societies of northern Peru; c) the absence of a marked hierarchy of settlements, with Cahuachi a ceremonial centre, rather than a true urban settlement.

To start with (b) and (c): Cahuachi may not have been an urban centre, that was probably at Ventilla. However, Cahuachi does contain a pyramid and many *huacas* that have to be seen as monuments, despite their description by Silverman (1993: 336) of its 25 ha of mounds as "monumentally unmonumental". In regard to (a) the quality of pottery and of metalwork does seem to indicate the presence of full-time specialists, at least during the later periods.

At Los Molinos, a predominantly Nazca 3 site, Isla and Reindel (2008: 394–5) found no evidence of food production. They argue that the high degree of uniformity manifest in textiles and pottery "shows that the whole population was well integrated throughout the territory occupied by the Nasca culture" and further that "the high quality and extreme consistency of Nasca ceramics in terms of their shape and decoration would lead us to believe that there were pottery-production centres where specialized craftsmen worked".

Despite this, Carmichael is not alone in seeing Nazca society as at most a chiefdom or series of chiefdoms. Silverman (1993: 338), herself a Nazca specialist, sees the settlement pattern as consisting of two, and at most three tiers, and she is rightly sceptical that settlement hierarchy tells us much by itself (2002b). Further, she says (1993: 339) that "status differences are visible in Nazca mortuary patterns, but true social stratification (as evidenced by exclusive and absolute differences in types of burial treatment, tomb forms, body preparation, grave goods, and spatial divisions in cemetery patterning) are not". Now just such evidence is available from La Muña. However, Silverman's further suggestion that Nazca society represents a 'sphere of religious interaction' does move us forward if taken together with the periodization of La Muña as later than Cahuachi, and as pre-eminent after the latter's decline. On this basis we could postulate Nazca during the pre-eminence of Cahuachi as a 'sacerdotal state', one run by priests in collegiate fashion, under, perhaps, a 'principal priest'. A sacerdotal state would certainly have political dimensions, but its legitimating function would be as administrator and purveyor of religious ideology, coupled with, and perhaps inseparable from, the role of administrator of the irrigation system upon which Nazca society depended (Beresford-Jones *et al.* 2009: 329).

When the ideology was seen to fail to protect Cahuachi itself, since natural disasters are not 'natural' in this worldview, then the pre-eminence of La Muña could represent the emergence of a new elite whose legitimacy, or at least power, did not reside principally in ideological matters, but in violence. Indeed, Webb (1987: 166) sees all early states as either theocratic or with a hegemonic sacerdotal role in their formation, with the next stage, that of consolidation, expansion and the reduction of members of society to subjects, taking place through militarism.

In her study of Nazca burials DeLeonardis (2000: 381) found that "by Middle Nazca disembodied heads are found in greater numbers and in a variety of settings. Caches of heads are more frequent, as is the number of heads per cache". By contrast "among whole-body burials, a shift occurs with a notable increase in grave wealth among a smaller segment of the population, signalling an emergent elite". What is clear is that this elite did not emerge and consolidate its power and privileges through a managerial imperative. Whether it was ever able to centralize its power and turn this into overall social control awaits much more extensive excavation and reporting than we have. Presently it seems that a Nazca state remained at the level of incipience, that is as a Sacerdotal State, blocked by environmental degradation and collapse (Beresford-Jones *et al.* 2009: 327).

### Environmental Risks and Possibilities

El Niño episodes possibly began around 4,000 BC. Domesticated alpaca may be present around 3500 BC at the *puña*-edge site of Telarmachay Cave. About 3000 BC post-Pleistocene sea levels become established, as elsewhere narrowing the coastal plain, now rarely exceeding 50 km, and drowning sites. Modern climatic conditions and vertical zonation become established in the Andes at about this time. However, modern levels in Lake Titicaca in southern Peru and western Bolivia are not reached until around 1600 BC (Stanish *et al.* 2002: 451–2).

Rick (1988: 40) argues that even the later Pleistocene environment was not substantially different from the present day situation. This is rather unlikely. For one thing, in Peru the shoreline at 10,000 BP was probably around 10 km farther west, according to naval charts (Chauchat 1989: 59). Temperature and humidity would also have been different. An argument could be made that vertical zonation simply gained or lost altitude, or became more or less wide; but oceanic and atmospheric circulation in the later Pleistocene was manifestly not the same as now, even excluding the effects of high altitude glaciation in the Andes.

"Except for the rich marine food chain, Andean animal life was most abundant in the high elevation *puña* grasslands of the north" (Moseley 1993: 89). So much so, that Rick (1988: 32) proposes year-round base-camp sedentism ("with occasional short-term use of hunting camps at relatively short distances from the base-camp" (Hastorf 1990: 135)) for camelid hunters on the *puña*; a treeless, windswept plateau that in places extends up to the Cordilleran peaks. Above the *puña* and extending up to the snow line, lies the *puña brava* which has no vegetation other than a few Arctic-Alpine species. The tree line, which is at 4500 metres on the Equator, decreases to 2000 m at 40° S.

## D: Preceramic Period I–II (11,000–8000 BC)

### Sedentism and the Domestication Process

The presence of game and thus settlement on the *puña* parallels coastal sedentism induced by the richness of marine animals (and seaweed). It used to be thought that the highland valley groups exploited *puña* and littoral seasonally or served as intermediaries between coastal and highland populations, but neither seems to be the case on present evidence. Rather each of the three specialized in exploiting its own environmental location, with little interaction between them. Obsidian is scarcely found at any distance from its source; shell hardly finds its way inland, and plants are not found introduced to areas distant from their zones of origin. "Fruits, vegetables and grains that cannot be grown in the *puña* would seem ideal foci for trade and interaction,

now "occurs irregularly with gaps of three or four valleys between" (*ibid*.), suggesting that individual plants were taken up by individual families for family reasons. Another aspect might be an incipient division of labour, with some specialising, say, in cotton growing, while (related families?) in adjoining valleys do not grow but manufacture cotton cloth, some of which is exchanged for staple. Alternatively, some might specialise in the growing and manufacture of hemp products, exchanged for the specialized products of other valleys, say cotton or woollen goods.

The precocity of cotton growing and its association with bottle gourds (*Lagenaria siceraria*) has a particular and important explanation. Large early river-mouth sites like Aspero arose because of the abundance of marine resources, leading Moseley (1975a) to propose a 'maritime hypothesis' for the development of complex society on the coast during the Late Archaic (Cotton Preceramic). Such sites, found in almost every valley along the coast, from Huaca Prieta in the north of Peru, to the Chinchorro sites on the north coast of Chile, also had some floodplain available to grow crops (Haas and Creamer 2004: 44). A central part of available marine resources were of course shoals of anchovies and sardines. These are small fish requiring nets for their efficient capture. Cotton fibre is ideal for net construction and the bottle gourds make excellent floats. Ample archaeological evidence exists for such usages (*ibid*.).

> "In the Cotton Preceramic VI (2500–2100 BC), domestic plants are more common at all sites and we see new, intriguing patterns. … There are now two main complexes of crops that co-occur at the sites. First, beans and peppers co-occur (with squash as well) throughout the coast, building on earlier trends. The second cluster of crops that co-occur, especially on the central coast, are gourds, cotton, achira and guava. Those plants were present in the previous phase: two industrial, one starchy food, and one fruit. Maize, avocado, potato, and manioc are present during these 4000 years, but sporadically. At this time, maize is present only every three valleys or so along the coast: in the valleys of Virú, Supe, Chancay and Chilca as well as in the Ayacucho caves" (Hastorf op. cit. 48).

Potato, domesticated in the Andes, is better nutritionally and much better adapted to mountain conditions than maize, which is susceptible to cold and frost. However, maize makes *chicha*, double-fermented beer (*akha* in Quechua), which has such cultural importance, being "worthy of special guests, the deities, and the ancestors", that it serves to facilitate social stratification. Hastorf and Johannessen (1993: 133) argue that this is achieved by means of the indebtedness created by the provision of 'free' beer at feasts and ritual occasions. To reciprocate the indebted were obliged to provide labour services. Indeed the Inca organised such prestations on an industrial scale to keep the empire provisioned through labour service. Which shows yet again that there is no such thing as free beer.

> "Locations where we find dense domesticates do seem to be where there is special architecture: La Galgada [see figure], Huaynuna [forerunner of U-shaped mound and plaza], El Aspero [and now Caral] and Huaca Prieta, thus supporting the idea that more intensive politico-religious interests included more, yet particular, foodstuffs as key elements in their cultural constructions as well the daily practice of food consumption" (Hastorf 1999: 50).

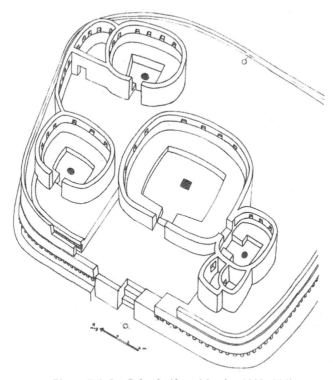

*Figure 7.6: La Galgada (from Moseley 1993: 114).*

**La Galgada** (see Figure 7.6) has two substantial mounds each supporting a Kotosh-style individual chamber. The larger mound is oval in shape, faced with fine masonry and fronted by a sunken circular court (Moseley 1993: 113). The oval sanctuaries (*huacas sanctuarias;* a huaca is any formal/public shrine) on top were stone-built set in mud mortar, clay plastered, painted pearly white and ornamented with rows of interior niches, symmetrically arranged. So that they could be sealed for rituals, a horizontal ventilation shaft passed beneath the narrow, west-facing door to supply air to the hearth in the centre (*ibid.*). A roof of clay was supported on logs. Plant remains, particularly those of chili peppers were found in fire pits. Feathers of tropical birds and deer antlers were found on some floors. Three phases of enlargement extending over a millennium saw the chambers serving as tomb vaults for men, women and children accompanied by a variety of offerings then being filled in and covered by later constructions (*ibid.*: 114). Ceramics are present during the last two episodes of platform construction at Galgada, accompanied by other technological advances, notably heddle-loom weaving. But the final phase of rebuilding, around 1200 BC, was the most dramatic, with the summit assuming a U-shaped configuration (*ibid.*: 115). Three elevated platforms now surrounded a lower central court opening to the front of the mound. The court lacked a hearth but could accommodate a much larger audience than previously.

What seems to have happened, is that the earlier lineage or clan based 'private' structures and ceremonies have been 'centralised' and made into a spectacle where the congregation are no longer participants but onlookers. An intermediate stage saw the mound tops given over to a single, much enlarged structure with an oversized fire basin, their rectangular central chambers capable of holding audiences of 50 or more *(ibid.*: 114).

## G: The Aspero Tradition and Caral

"From about 3000 to 2500 BC a striking series of stone buildings were being constructed in the area of the central coastlands. The earliest recognized are at Bandurria, Rio Seco and Aspero. The site of Los Gavilanes, north of Huarmey, is said to contain stone buildings of considerable size, which were occupied between 2850 and 2780 BC, immediately before the construction of a system of underground storage depots for housing harvests of grain" (Pineda 1988: 76).

At Bandurria there is a pyramid mound, while Rio Seco, ten miles north of Rio Chancay, has five or six (*ibid.*: 77). Occupation at Rio Seco covers 11.8 ha with a mortuary population as large as 2,500–3000 (Moseley 1993: 107). In complete contrast to Egyptian pyramids, early ones, as at Rio Seco, did not derive from *mastaba*-like underground tombs, but resulted from the successive in-filling of a room complex. Occupation zones are integrated with the pyramids suggesting a clan or *ayllu*-type basis for them and for what may or may not be the early stages of social differentiation, perhaps as clan ranking. The scale of early Andean pyramids must be realized: two at Rio Seco are only 10–15 m in diameter and a mere 3 m high; by contrast the smallest at Caral (below) is 60 m x 45 m x 10 m (Haas and Creamer 2004: 46).

**El Aspero** is a settlement at the mouth of the Supe Valley covering about 13.2 hectares (see Figure 7.7). It occupies a shallow basin in hills jutting out into the sea at the north end of a sandy delta formed at the mouth of the Supe valley (Moseley 1993: 115). The Supe is one of a group of four valleys – Huaura, Pativilca, Fortaleza and Supe – located in the Norte Chico ('Little North') region situated between what has traditionally been referred to as the Central Coast and the North Coast of Peru (Haas and Creamer 2004: 35–6). "Thus far, surveys have located 26 [now over 30]

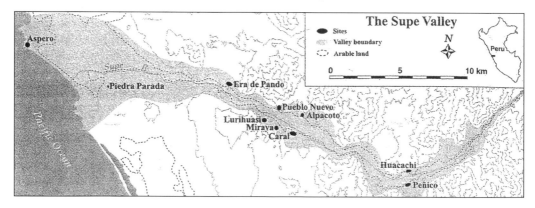

*Figure 7.7: Map of the Supe Valley (from Solis, Haas and Creamer 2001: 724).*

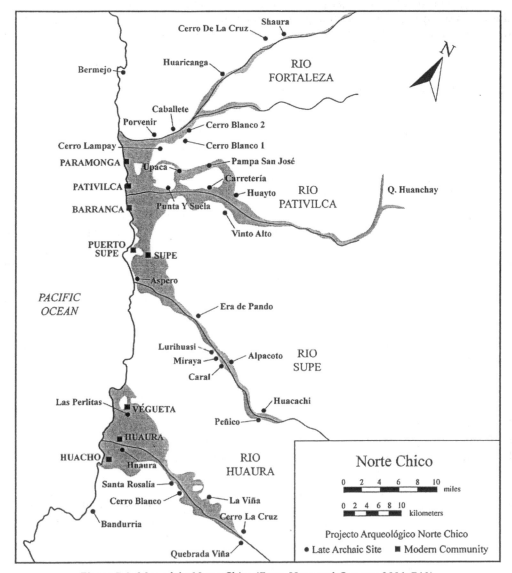

*Figure 7.8: Map of the Norte Chico (From Haas and Creamer 2006: 748).*

late Archaic sites in the Norte Chico all lacking ceramics and with monumental communal architecture. These sites range from 50 to 250 ha in area and have from one to six platform mounds ranging from 15,000 to over 300,000 m³ in volume. The Norte Chico Preceramic complex then appears to have a 'provocative' effect on other outside areas" (*ibid.*).

Haas and Creamer (2004: 48–9) following Shady (1997) state that the **Norte Chico** developments were seminal in a number of areas, particularly the standardization of

Andean religion, but more generally because "the beginnings of a distinctive Andean civilization can be traced directly to the Late Archaic occupation of the Norte Chico" (2006: 746). The Norte Chico encompasses the four river valleys already mentioned: Rios Fortaleza, Pativilca, Supe and Huaura, as shown on this Map from Haas and Creamer (2006: 748), Figure 7.8 above.

At Aspero at the mouth of the Rio Supe, the pyramid mounds resulted from the progressive in-filling of rooms. Flanking the mounds, low terraces define various patio and court areas. The terraces may also have supported housing on the northern edge of the site, and defined residential groupings. There are two kinds of underground structures perhaps serving for storage. Of 17 standing mounds, six are truncated pyramid platforms, stone-built, with heights ranging between 2 m and 10.7 m, the latter height attained when the platforms were banked up against or set upon hills. The less prominent mounds might contain housing for those in attendance on temple activities. Built of basaltic blocks rather than of rounded boulders, Huaca de la Sacrificios is a large, free standing platform. Excavation on the summit limited to the last phases of construction yielded radiocarbon dates averaging 2857 BC (Moseley 1993: 116).

Calibrated dates at El Aspero span 3055 to 2500 BC (Shady Solis 2008: 29). Dillehay *et al.* (2004: 33) state that Aspero was one of the sites of the Late Preceramic Period "when more emphasis was given to wealth goods and individual leadership". Until Period IV (last of the Preceramic periods) "social relations do not conform to the elite and non-elite dichotomy found in so many archaeological discussions of emergent social complexity in other parts of the world". Instead the people of the central Andes focussed upon building a sense of social collectivity through ritual feasting, and through the building of both large and small scale monuments manifesting identity and solidarity (*ibid.*).

Perched against a small hill, Huaca de los Idolos is one of the higher platforms at El Aspero. It takes its name "from a cache of human figurines of unbaked clay found in the summit compartment with the altar-like bench and niche, where a small alcove had a cache of objects spread over its floor before it was filled-in to support a new, higher floor" (Moseley 1993: 118). Summit structures cover an area of 20 x 30 m, reached by a wide slightly projecting ramp (Moseley 1993: 117). It gives access through a gateway to a walled but unroofed reception area, the largest structure on the summit, behind which smaller courts and rooms are irregularly disposed. On the main axis of the platform, however, was a centrally located compartment measuring about 4 x 5 m with three small rectangular niches at chest level. This compartment was subdivided by a thin wall faced with a geometric adobe frieze consisting of horizontal bands of raised plaster (*ibid.*).

About 40 km inland from the coast are some 30 sites with sunken pits. Their major concentration is in the Supe Valley, some 200 km (120 miles) north of Lima. The Supe River is presently dry for much of the year (Shady Solis 2008: 62) and it would be interesting to know whether this was so in the Late Archaic. At Chupacigarro Grande A, part of Caral (below), a pit is associated with a pyramid that possesses lateral wings. The pit at Piedra Parada "is located at the centre of a square plaza and lies at the foot of a complex of rectangular enclosures built on two parallel platforms

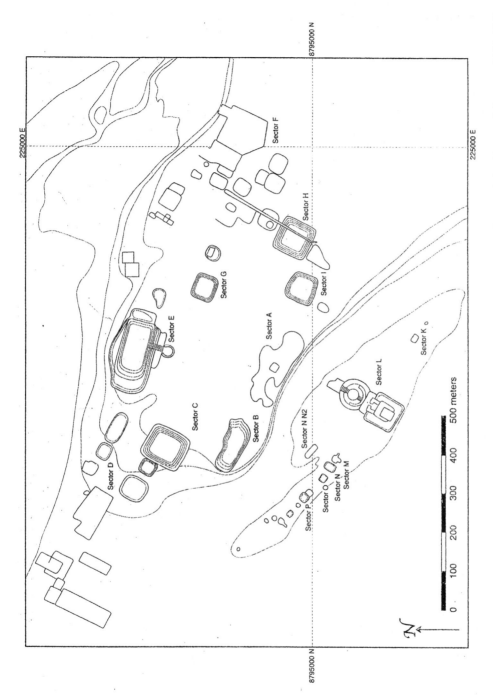

*Figure 7.9: Map of the central zone of Caral, Supe Valley, Peru (from Science Vol. 292, 27a April 2001. Solis, Haas and Creamer, 2001: 724).*

stepped into the hillside" (*ibid.*: 81). Those are considered early examples before the design was standardised. Broadly dated to the Late Preceramic, Piedra Parada, covering about 15 ha laid out in formal plan, is further along the road to urbanization than El Aspero. From mortuary data it is estimated that Rio Seco had a population of between 2,400 and 3000, with Bandurria having about the same number and El Aspero considerably more (Pineda 1988: 94), though this should be revised downward. Despite the appearance of some social differentiation in the three sites just mentioned, all of which are Preceramic, there is no evidence of maize cultivation, except at El Aspero, where it is comparatively unimportant (*ibid.*: 93). Much more important were cotton and gourds, both for industrial use. Gourds were used as fishing floats and containers. Their toughness and general utility helps explain the slow and uneven uptake of pottery.

## *Caral: First City of the Americas?*

At 66 ha Caral is the second largest of 18 Late Archaic Period archaeological sites in the Supe Valley. The largest is Era de Pando with 79.74 ha and the smallest Capilla, with only 0.16 ha (Shady Sollis 2008: 32). Of the 'top ten' largest sites of this period in the Supe Valley, Aspero is the smallest, with 18.8 ha. All are within 45 km of the coast (*ibid.*: 30), while Aspero is on the coast.

Located 23 km (14 miles) inland on a terrace 350 m above sea level on the south side of the valley, 25 m above the Supe floodplain, Caral has been known since 1905, but only recent extensive excavation and radiocarbon dating has shown its full significance to the Preceramic Period (Shady Sollis 2008: 29–30) and perhaps to the evolution of Andean culture in general. It was occupied between 2,627 and 2020 BC. Cotton (*Gossypium barbadense)* and vegetables, including squash (*Cucurbita sp.*), beans (*Phaseolus vulgaris*), lucuma (*Lucuma obovata*), great quantities of guava (*Psidium guajava*), pacay (*Inga feuillei*) and camote (*Ipomoea batatas*) were grown with the aid of irrigation canals (with a contemporary canal on the prehistoric alignment), probably commencing around 3,000 BC. Maize was present in small amounts (Shady Sollis 2008: 49). Protein was supplied by fish, mainly anchovies (*Engraulis ringens*) and sardines (*Sardinops sagax*) plus shellfish: clams (*Mesodesma donacium*) and mussels (*Chloromytilus chorus* and *Aulacomya ater*).

Caral's central zone covers 65 ha (200 acres) and contains 32 public structures, two sunken circular plazas, with another at Chupacigarro, the smaller 23 ha complex about 300 m to the south-west. The city is split into halves, upper and lower, with a residential periphery around the nuclear area (Shady Solis 2008: 34–5). Six large platform mounds are grouped around what appears to be a huge public plaza, which, "due to its size, location and its association with the circular court ... was probably the city's principal public building" (*ibid.*: 38). "Each of the six large mounds is associated with a large formally arranged residential complex. Each room complex covers an area of between 450 and 800 m², with carefully constructed and heavily plastered walls of cut stone. Domestic trash indicates that these rooms were residential in nature" (Shady Solis *et al.* 2001: 723). As this construction technique is the same as for the monumental architecture, it suggests that the residential complexes directly associated with the mounds are elite residences, perhaps of the dominant lineages. By contrast, Sector A, also a residential area and covering an area of 5500 m², consisted of small rooms constructed of flimsy and perishable materials of the wattle and daub type. This type of plebeian housing seems not to be confined to Sector A, but rather occupies the terrain between the ceremonial centre and Chuparcigarro to the south-west (Shady Solis *et al.* 2001: 723) and probably elsewhere in the vicinity. Plausibly those areas are housing for the lesser lineages and possibly incomers or temporary visitors.

The lower half of Caral is significantly different from the upper half. Buildings are generally smaller and aligned on an east-west axis, although facades face towards the upper half. The lower half contains no large-to-medium-sized pyramidal structures, only small ones (Shady Solis 2008: 42). However it does contain a feature of major significance, namely the Temple of the Amphitheatre complex. This complex comprises a circular subterranean court resembling an amphitheatre with tiered seats, platforms that ascend sequentially, a circular altar and an elite building occupying 200 m², and on the west side a group of rooms (*ibid.*). "On the upper south-west side of the court a group of 32 flutes, manufactured from condor and pelican bones, was recovered. ...Nearby, on the east side of the architectural complex, a group of 32 bugles, manufactured from camelid and deer bones, was found" (Shady Solis 2008: 45). Projecting north-east from the complex is a rectangular platform 26 m wide and 3.2 m high that has been cut on the north side by erosion (*ibid.*)

There are eight other Preceramic sites in the Supe Valley with sunken circular plazas, monumental platform mounds, and large areas of residential architecture: Piedra Parada, Era de Pando, Lurihuasi, Pueblo Nuevo, Miraya, Alpacoto, Huacachi, and Peñico, all of which exceed 30 ha, making it the largest concentration of such features in the Andes (Shady Sollis *et al.* 2001: 724). In the Norte Chico as a whole there are at least 30 large ceremonial/residential sites, 15 of those recently discovered in the Pativilca and Fortaleza Valleys (Haas and Creamer 2004: 46). However, "the sum of the volumes of mounds constructed in the valleys of Pativilca and Fortaleza (499,110.00 m³) cannot be compared with those of Supe (2,401,970.48 m³), nor have sites of equal or greater complexity been identified in other valleys of the region, or, for that matter, other regions" (Shady Solis 2006: 761).

Given their abundance in this confined area at this early date it is possible and even probable that those characteristic features originated in the Supe Valley. They do not appear elsewhere in Peru until around 1970 cal.BC (*ibid.*: 726). As already mentioned, in addition to Caral and Aspero there are 16 other substantial Preceramic sites in the Supe Valley. Eight of those (Piedra Parada, Era de Pando, Lurihuasi, Pueblo Nuevo, Miraya, Alpacoto, Huacachi, and Peñico) exceed 30 ha and possess large-scale corporate architecture (Shady Solis *et al.* 2001: 726). Clearly the Supe Valley had surplus to spare, making it a pioneer in the emergence of social hierarchy and, in Shady Solis' view, the state.

The largest of the architectural complexes at Caral is the Great Pyramid, located in the upper half of the city. "It measures 170.8 m from east to west and 149.7 m north to south; the façade which faces south is 19.3 m in height while on the north side, toward the valley, the mound reaches 29.9 m. It is comprised of a dominant circular sunken court and an imposing stepped pyramidal structure constituted by a central body, containing the bulk of the construction, and two side components (one to the east and the other to the west) of smaller size" (Shady Solis 2008: 38).

Clearly the mobilization of labour on a massive scale was now established fact, for all the six central mounds were built in only one or two phases. The method used was one that became standard for large building projects in the Andes. *Shicra* bags were woven from sedges and reeds into loose sacks or bags. It is the fibres from those bags that have been radiocarbon-dated. Deriving from annuals, the historic wood problem (Maisels 1999: 47) is avoided as also the problems in relying on dates from midden materials.[86] The labourer filled the bags with rubble at a nearby quarry and then carried the load to the site, placing it, still in the bag, in the zone allocated to his/her *ayllu*. A new bag was picked up and another load transported. The mounds were terraced, and used for administrative purposes. Not only were the side terraces used, but the tops of the 'pyramids' were also used. They contained courtyards and rooms accessed by stairs.

Caral seems to have been a true city and not merely a ceremonial centre, as many of the later centres probably were (Quilter 2002: 177). It also seems to have set the pattern for subsequent urbanism in the Andes, in both its built environment and in its social morphology. Indeed Haas and Creamer (2006: 769) are insistent on this important point: "A distinctly Andean pattern of civilization begins in the Norte Chico in the third millennium BC, and subsequent developments have historical roots in this small section of the Peruvian coast. As more work is done it will become increasingly clear that the crucible of Andean civilization is to be found at Caral and the other early sites in the Norte Chico".

As already stated, the Norte Chico contains more than 30 large sites "all with monumental architecture and all occupied in the Late Archaic" (Haas and Creamer 2006: 751). Accordingly, they cannot be encompassed by a single chiefdom nor yet do they form competing chiefdoms. Haas and Creamer (2006: 751) reject the application of the chiefdom concept here for two principal reasons: (1) "These sites range from 1 to 10 km apart, with no smaller sites in the intervening areas. The communal architecture at these sites includes multiple constructed mounds, over 50,000 m³ in volume, exceeding that of the individual and collective communal architectural remains found in ethnographically or historically known chiefdoms in Polynesia, Africa, the Caribbean and elsewhere..." (2) The other nonchiefdom-like feature of the Norte Chico is the absence of warfare. Warfare tends to be ubiquitous in chiefdom societies ... and there is no indication of conflict within or between valleys" (*ibid*.). Instead, as an alternative working hypothesis they propose (2006: 755) that "a number of commonalities bind together a broad expanse of sites along the coastal plain. Those commonalities include similar cotton textiles ... a combined maritime and domesticated plant diet, and a religious system based on a U-shaped site layout, platform mounds, and sunken circular plazas centred in the Norte Chico..." In other

---

[86]  Indeed, Stanish (2006: 764) has criticised some of Haas and Creamer's Norte Chico dates as based on midden remains that are at least half a millennium earlier than what the shicra bags indicate for the onset of monumental construction there. Haas and Creamer (2006: 767) respond by providing fibre bag calibrated dates of 2740 BC and 3040 BC at Caballete, 2740 BC and 2690 BC at Porvenir, 2740 BC at Upaca.

words, social cohesion along the coast or from the coast inland seemed to consist in a complex division of labour between the coastal fishing and the inland farming communities (assisted by some simple irrigation, especially for growing cotton, if today's practice is any guide) and within the inland settlements (growing avocado, lucuma, chili beans, pacay, squash, guava, achira, camote and maize) coupled to a shared religious and symbolic system.

Shady Solis (2008: 57) stresses that "religion functioned as the instrument of cohesion and coercion, and it was very effective. ... In this way religion was converted into the principal force of domination exercised by the state". She sees that state, based in Caral, as dominating not only the Supe Valley but perhaps also settlements in Pativilca and Fortaleza. She further argues (2008: 55–6) that "The accumulation of wealth resulting from high productivity and exchange, unequally distributed, and the formation of hierarchical social strata in a context of permanent socio-economic articulation, would have fostered the formation and centralization of an extensive state government. This would explain the formation of a system of differentiated urban centres, including the most prominent that were located in Caral's capital zone. Circular courts with public functions were constructed in nearly all urban centres, and a huge amount of labour was invested in monumental construction".

Claims made for Caral as the earliest Andean state have been firmly rejected by Mark Aldenderfer (2006: 756) on the basis that "none of the empirical data recovered from it are consistent with the existence of either an urban centre, a coercive polity, or a state level of political organization". I think that Caral must qualify as an urban centre, perhaps even 'America's first city' (Shady Solis 2008: 28), but I certainly agree with Aldendorfer and also Haas and Creamer that there is presently no evidence either for a coercive polity or a state level of political organization. Shady Solis herself (2008: 50) describes "a productive, internally complementary, agricultural-fishing economy" that was indeed "managed by the authorities of the settlements" but which, as yet perhaps, had not emerged as ruling with the ability to *command and control*. I contend that the ability to command and control is key to state *existence*, while the fusion of ideological, economic and physical power (force) is key to state *formation*. On a much larger scale, I argued in Chapter 3 that an organic division of labour and a shared religious and symbolic system are what made the Harappan civilization function without state domination (Maisels 1991, 1999). The size and urban complexity of Harappa and Mohenjo-Daro are amongst several reasons leading some scholars to assume the presence of a state governing Indus-Sarasvati society. However that is merely an assumption in the absence of the state characteristics previously specified, and that may also be the case in regarding Caral as the (non-) locus of America's first state.

Nonetheless, the catalytic *role* of the Norte Chico is suggested, *inter alia*, by the later widespread adoption of the architectural tradition of circular or rectangular sunken plazas. Indeed, Supe society "laid down the foundation of what would become the Central Andean social system" (Shady Solis 2008: 62). Also seminal was the iconic figure of the Staff God, the principal deity, crude but clear images of which were found on two gourd fragments from the Pativilca Valley, one yielding a calibrated AMS date of 2250 BC. The Staff God later played an important role in Chavín art, by which means it was disseminated throughout the Andes. Human sacrifice was also present.

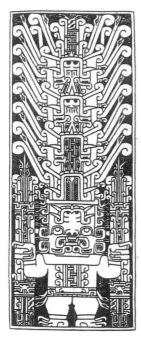

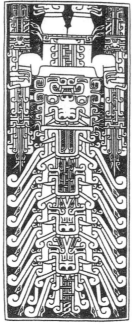

*Figure 7.10A (left): The Staff God as a Taotie.*

*Figure 7.10B (above): The Staff God on cotton cloth from Kerwa (from Moseley 1993: 156).*

That said, Isbell and Knobloch (2008: 342–3) deny that there ever was a universal ideology represented by a Staff God who "carried an encapsulated and ancient essence of Andean cosmology". Instead, they see "dynamic competition, change, reinterpretation and invention appear(ing) to have been the rule as the Rayed Head developed into Staff God worship", perhaps over half a millennium, by which time "the Staff God appears to have achieved religious supremacy by Middle Horizon 1B, that is probably synchronous with its popular appearance at both Conchopata/Huari and at Tiwanaku". In Andean cosmology we do seem to encounter shared themes and forms of representation that, despite varying emphases, syncretisms and distinctions over time and space, do form a stable and coherent set of 'cardinal tenets' (Maisels 1999: 356). Cardinal tenets are organizing principles that summarize the spontaneous folk tradition on behalf of emergent elite culture, thus encapsulating key concepts essential to the ideological structure. Cardinal tenets are elaborated and contested over time and space by ideological experts, such as theologians, but the core set of beliefs tends to remain intact with only their semantic range affected (Van Buren 2000: 77, 81). Thus the cardinal tenets of Christianity: 'divine birth/son of god/born of a virgin/redeemer who died for our sins/ resurrection' etc., survived the Reformation with the core values intact.

## El Paraiso

El Paraiso is the largest preceramic monument in the western hemisphere and was built by people who did not live at the site, only 2 km from the sea, judging by the absence of middens, so prominent at Aspero and Rio Seco. Building of the platform mounds was underway by 2000 BC and continued for a couple of centuries. In that time over

100,000 tonnes of stone were quarried to construct nine masonry complexes occupying 58 ha of the Chillón Valley. They were erected in stages by filling interconnected rectangular courts, rooms and corridors with rubble in mesh bags as previously described. Walls were of rock set in mud mortar and then plastered with adobe. This method of construction and the time taken strongly suggests the presence of *ayllus* and the absence of chiefdom or state.

> "The two largest ruins are elongated complexes that form the wings of a giant 'U'. Each wing is more than 50 m wide and more than 250 m long. They frame a spacious 7 ha plaza and the base of the U is partially closed off by several smaller ruins, while other masonry complexes are scattered around the periphery. The orientation of El Paraiso is exactly the same as later U-shaped ceremonial centres in the region, but the uneven layout suggests a piecemeal growth" (Moseley 1993: 119).

## H: Initial (Ceramic) Period (1800–900 BC)

At this time large site complexes proliferated with increasing social hierarchy. For the coastal valleys this must imply some mastery of irrigation techniques (Pineda 1988: 81–2; Pozorski and Pozorski 2002: 32), just as at Caral. U-shaped complexes have a pyramid at the centre, lateral wings and open space between, some of which was used for formal plazas. Space around the complex was probably given over to agriculture, probably for the direct or ritual support of the complex itself. Broadly three traditions of U-shaped complexes can be seen emerging between 1800 and 1500 BC, starting from such site plans as those at El Paraiso and El Olivar in the Chillón and Casma Valleys respectively. The three are: (1) the Casma Valley (Sechín Alto Complex and Las Haldas); (2) between the Huaura and Lurin rivers (La Florida, Mina Perdida and Garagay) and (3) the Moche valley (Caballo Muerto). La Florida and Mina Perdida should, according to published C[14] dates of 1800–1600 BC, constitute a first generation along with the Casma Valley sites, while the complex of Garagay (together with Chocas and Huacoy) in the Chillón Valley and Manchay Bajo at Lurin, represent a second generation (but as already mentioned, see the chronological caveats of Haas and Creamer 2004: 49–50 and the troubled issue of dating argued over in Haas and Creamer 2006).

On the central coast complexes, the circular sunken pits seem to be a later introduction from the highlands, where they had developed as independent functional units concerned, most likely, with chthonic agricultural forces, notably Pacha Mama, Mother Earth. As Moseley (1993: 112) observes: "When pits occur in front of platforms the stairways of both structures are generally aligned, indicating that ritual processions moved in a linear manner from the neutral surface of land level, to the negative plane of the sunken court, to the positive plane above it [on the platform]. One must wonder if this was not a cosmological pathway from the earth's interior to the heavens above".

### *Initial Period (1800–900 BC)*

To recapitulate, sizeable settlements originally formed around some complex stone-built ceremonial centres that began in the Late Preceramic, only a couple of millennia after

Huarango deforestation, Peru

On the south coast of Peru, at the edge of the Atacama Desert, the last surviving remnants of native dry forest are disappearing. Felled for charcoal or to make way for agriculture, their destruction is opening the way for spreading desertification.

Huarango forest has played a vital role in the lives of the people in the Nasca and Ica region for thousands of years, supplying food, timber, fodder and many other important resources. Archaeological evidence indicates that these forests were fundamental to the livelihoods of the ancient Nazca culture (responsible for the enigmatic Nazca Lines). They also house a number of increasingly rare animals, such as the slender-billed finch.

Huarango trees prevent land turning into deserts (Image: Oliver Whaley, RBG Kew)

*Figure 7.11: Death by Deforestation – Images and Text from the Royal Botanic Gardens, Kew, London (see D.G. Beresford-Jones et al., Latin American Antiquity 2009 20(2): 303–332).*

the spread of settled village farming in Peru. Cooperative subsistence efforts seem to have been reinforced by collective labour efforts creating monuments to represent the community and its place in the scheme of things.[87] Initial Period settlements on the central coast (of Peru) were of three types: large centres with public architecture (such as Garagay and Cardal); small shoreline villages (such as Ancon and Curayucu), and small inland hamlets, such as Chillaco and Palma. These three types of settlements linked-up in exchange and ceremonial networks to form small-scale internally self-sufficient subsistence systems (Burger 1995: 69).

However, the Initial Period, lasting for nearly a millennium, laid the agrarian basis for the states to come, and may even have seen early state formation at such sites as the Sechín Alto Complex (Pozorski and Pozorski 2002). It was a period of population growth based on the extensive and intensive exploitation of domesticated plants and (relatively few species of) animals, plus, of course, abundant marine resources. Given the difficult and largely inhospitable terrain, two fundamental subsistence patterns became established in the mountains and on the coast: high altitude populations became concentrated in the south, where upland basins are largest, while maritime-oasis adaptation became concentrated in the north, where desert rivers are largest (Moseley 1993: 123).

> "The Initial Period is associated with the florescence of farming economies. The average date for the appearance of ceramics on the central coast is 1800 BC. Although agricultural economies emerge at different times in different settings they generally appeared in conjunction with pottery and heddle weaving: ceramics were vital for storing, cooking and brewing agrarian comestibles; farming and herding led to increased cotton and wool supplies; and heddle weaving allowed for the mass production of cloth. South American root crops were the primary staples, complemented by beans, legumes, squash and fruits. Although present in the highlands, maize growing and llama herding remained rare or absent in coast settings. The arid mountains and rainless coast made irrigation an integral aspect of the new economic order, and irrigation influenced where and how people worked" (Moseley 1993: 125).

As already mentioned, irrigation was conducted by corporate kin groups, for "given water, almost every canal can operate independently and therefore support an independent group of people" (Moseley 1993: 126), and most rivers can sustain several canal systems. It is worth the investment, for given the high levels of light and temperatures present, irrigation permits the growing of several high yielding crops each year. Sierra basins are relatively flat and so most suitable for extensive irrigation, with the upper reaches of the Rios Zana and Santa exploited even in

---

[87] "There was not apparently, a long transition between the initiation of settled village farming and the creation of large public works in ancient Peru. On the contrary, agriculture – whether in combination with fishing and hunting – seems to have developed hand in hand with collective labour. Life revolved around cooperative efforts, both subsistence and otherwise, and public works were the conspicuous expression of this basic organizing principle" (Burger 1995: 54). Caral seems to be a particularly clear and early example of this. "Large-scale mobilization of labour was made possible by a shared community ideology and its religious and social sanctions, rather than by coercive authorities. As a consequence, the public monuments were designed to meet the spiritual and social needs of the community as a whole rather than to immortalize a particular individual or family" (*ibid.*).

preceramic times, as also in the Casma Valley, where by the Initial Period cotton, gourd, squash, avocado, lúcuma, beans, lima beans peanuts and even potatoes were grown (Pozorski and Pozorski 2002: 44). Sierra basin irrigation occurred below the zones of rainfall farming, while higher still, the steep mountain slopes could be irrigated when terraced, fed by springs and mountain streams. Irrigation thus opened up another two layers of verticality. The tendency was for corporate kinship groups to form 'vertical archipelagos'. Whether originating on the coast, mid or high altitudes, the aim was to have branches of one's own community occupy settlements in different ecological zones, so that for the purpose of basic subsistence, the kinship group would be self-reliant and adequately provided. On this secure basis, specialized craft or crop items could then be exchanged with those of other groups (Mazuda *et al.*1985 eds; Browman ed., 1987).

Near the coast, irrigation was the only way for substantial agriculture to develop in the desert conditions. This meant that farming settlements arose inland, further up the river valleys, in canyons and at valley necks where river gradients are still steep and canal construction easier. The longer canals demanded by lesser gradients nearer to the river mouths had to await the advent of state-like society (below) to mobilize the larger amounts of labour needed.

Moseley (1992: 126) argues, however, that the high levels of uncertainty produced by unpredictable river regimes, where even the flow of large rivers can fluctuate by a factor of five (between 500 and 2,500 million cubic metres within a ten year period), and where 75 per cent of the flow is concentrated between February and May (after which the smaller drainages are dry), explains the explosion of religious/ceremonial construction seen after 1800 BC, by which time agricultural dependency had reached a high level.

Accordingly, "the Initial Period is characterized by exceptional numbers of inland monuments, and those early ceremonial centres probably commemorated the rise of autonomous groups sustained by independent canal systems" (*ibid.*: 127). Bawden (1999: 175) states "leadership in this context was still largely embedded in the principles of communal ancestry and kinship that form the enduring structural fabric of Andean society".

In the Initial Period (IP) ceramics appear and agricultural production becomes both extensive and intensive with the advent of irrigation (Kembel and Rick 2004: 52–3). During the IP the old centre of La Galgada was remodelled from a Kotosh-tradition sanctuary (begun *c.*2,200 BC) into a u-shaped configuration, with three elevated platforms surrounding a lower central court opening in the front of the mound (Moseley 1993: 115). The mound-top chambers were then used as repositories for corpses. "Some mummies were accompanied by textiles and jewellery that rank among the finest of Initial Period grave goods yet recovered. The latter includes shell disks with engraved birds and a stone disc mosaic with a cat-like face that are rather similar to later Chavín artwork. The grave-goods are highly suggestive of personal wealth and status, while the gallery crypts are equally suggestive of sepulchral *huacas* of later-period nobility"(Moseley 1993: 144). But similar developments are not evident elsewhere in the Cordillera and Galgada did not trigger them. Obviously circumstances were not yet ripe for further social stratification, even at Galgada.

By the end of the Initial Period all sites sampled now have agriculture, but still not the same agriculture. Only chili peppers and beans occur everywhere (*ibid.*). The scarcity of potato and manioc is probably for good ecological (or exchange) reasons, and avocado continues only in the north. But guava is "present in two neighbouring valleys, then none for six valleys, then grown in two adjacent valleys, then none for three more valleys" (*ibid.*). Maize, a plant that does eventually become a staple and is always ritually charged, especially when transformed into *chicha*, always drunk in the context of intense social interaction (Hastorf and Johannessen 1999: 188), has a similar interrupted presence.

**The Casma Valley** is located in the Ancash Region of Peru, some 330 km (206 miles) northwest of Lima. On the coast to its south, skirted by the Panamerican Highway, lies the important 40 ha prehistoric site of Las Haldas.

In the Sechín branch of the Casma Valley, the Sechín Alto Complex has four components: Sechín Alto which spreads over 56 hectares, Taukachi-Konkan to its north, Sechín Bajo to its north-west and Cerro Sechín to its west. With no less than four square and rectangular plazas lined by smaller mounds, Sechín Alto extends in a linear, U-shaped layout for 1.2 km east of the main mound, which is 250 x 300 metres at base rising to a maximum height of 35 metres (Pozorski and Pozorski 2006: 40). Cerro Sechín[88] in the early Initial Period covered only around five hectares and consisted of a three-level stepped platform of conical adobes with a possible sunken court in front of it (Stanish 2001: 49). Nonetheless, "perhaps the most outstanding feature of Cerro Sechín", Stanish (*op.cit.*) observes, "is the numerous carvings in stone on the outer wall of the pyramid. These early Initial Period carvings depict macabre scenes of war, including decapitations, trophy heads, and body parts, plus warriors and victims in various states of subjugation". Pozorski and Pozorski (2006: 46) see those four-hundred carvings on granite slabs as a record of the suppression of a rising against the power centre of Sechín Alto, some time between 1500 and 1400 BC, after which Sechín Alto activity ceased at the site of Pampa de las Llamas Moxeke to the south. For a map of the Casma Valley area showing the location of Las Haldas, the Sechín Alto complex, and other early sites, see Figure 7.12.

From their long-term studies of the Casma Valley, Shelia Pozorski and Thomas Pozorski (2002: 44) postulate two major phases there: the Moxeke Phase (2150–1500 BC), named from the site of Pampa de las Llamas-Moxeke, which is succeeded by the Sechín Phase (1500–1400 BC) named from the site of Cerro Sechín. The greatest volume of construction at both sites, however, seems to have taken place in the Moxeke Phase, with the principal mound at Sechín Alto "the largest structure in the New World at the time it was constructed. However, this immense mound does not stand alone. It is surrounded by additional large and intermediate mounds; and a series of four plazas, two with circular courts, extend over a kilometre toward the east" (Pozorski and Pozorski 2002: 35).

From their analysis of the architecture and ceramics, "it appears that the Moxeke Phase was characterised by a cohesive polity within the Casma Valley that unified,

---

[88]  cerro = hill/mountain; quebrada = dry canyon; abra = high pass; bofedales: high altitude artificial wetlands used for grazing.

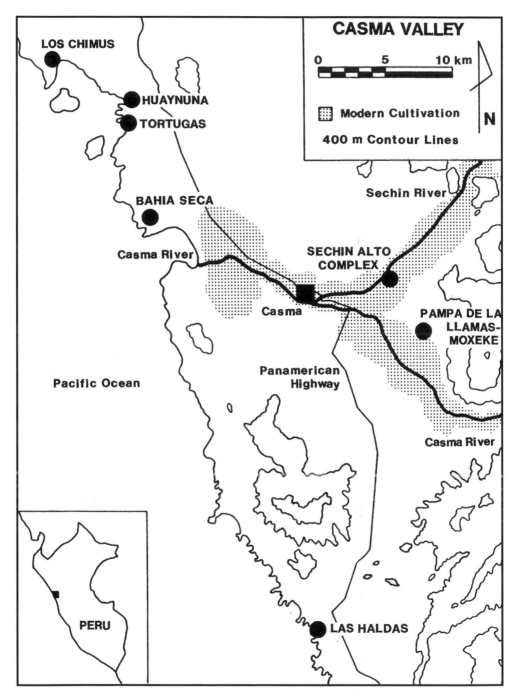

Fig. 7.12: Map of the Casma Valley area showing the location of Las Haldas, the Sechín Alto complex, and other early sites (from Pozorski and Pozorski 2006: 29)

and likely controlled, both branches of the Casma River Valley as well as a string of coastal satellites [including Huaynuná, Tortugas and Bahia Seca] north of the Casma River mouth. The square-room architectural form was symbolic of this control, and its presence at all the larger inland sites plus Bahía Seca documents both the administrative extension of the polity and the adherence of polity components to the architectural tenet that associated this architectural form with 'administration' or 'political power'. Concurrently, the site of Las Haldas existed in relative isolation as a sizeable settlement on the coast south of the river mouth" (Pozorski and Pozorski: 2002: 46).

During the Sechín Phase (1500–1400 BC) the site of Llamas-Moxeke ceased to be occupied (*ibid*.: 23) but the main site was always at the main Sechín Alto site mound, "still by far the largest construction within the valley" (*ibid*.: 46). The mound summit was remodelled removing the modular square-room unit and replacing it with rooms with common walls, such that only the corner of the room block is rounded (*ibid*.: 47). After 1400 BC Las Haldas-type ceramics appear at the inland and coastal sites formerly in the ambit of the Moxeke Culture, while Las Haldas itself becomes transformed into "what can best be described as a miniature version of the Sechín Alto site with the construction of the currently visible mound/plaza complex which represents the greatest, and perhaps the first, monumental construction at the site" (*ibid*.). But all is not as it seems. It is Las Haldas that moves inland and along the coast to take control of the Casma Valley between 1400 and 1300 BC (Pozorski and Pozorski 2006: 46). They argue (*ibid*.) that this was possible due to a double impact weakening the Sechín Alto polity between 1500 and 1400 BC. The first has already been referred to as the rising of the Moxeke population against the centralization and likely also the personalization of power at Sechín Alto. Secondly they postulate "an El Nino event about 1400 BC that would have severely affected the agricultural economy that supported and enabled the Sechín Alto polity" (Pozorski and Pozorski 2006: 46; Pozorski and Pozorski 2005).

Pozorski and Pozorski (2006: 42) posit this sequence of polities in the Casma Valley: Phase A (2150–1500 BC) formerly called the Moxeke Phase polity, and Phase B (1500–1400 BC) formerly called the Sechín Phase polity, followed by the Las Haldas takeover. They do not say what the nature of each phase might be, though they entertain the possibility that a 'palace or royal residence' exists on the principal Taukachi-Konkan mound which is the northern component of the Sechín Alto Complex (Figure 7.17). From its monumental constructions, the 38 modular square-room units that serve to compartmentalize the summit of Huaca A at Moxeke into storage units (*ibid*.: 45), the later scenes of violent suppression carved into the outer wall of the pyramid at Cerro Sechín and on the mud friezes at Moxeke, together with the limited areal extent of both polities; could it be that the earlier polity was that of a *Sacerdotal State* and the later phase at Taukachi-Konkan that of an emergent *royal state* that failed ? And if so, perhaps that failure caused the abandonment of the Pampa de las Llamas Moxeke site so opening the way around 1400 BC "for Las Haldas intruders to move across the Casma branch, into the Sechín branch, and onto the Sechín Alto mound" (Pozorski and Pozorski 2006: 49).

| City | Estimated Area sq km | Estimated Population | References |
|------|------|------|------|
| Tenochititlan | 12–15 | 160,000–200,000 | (Sanders and Webster 1988) |
| Teotihuacan | 18 | 125,000 | (Sanders and Webster 1988) |
| Cuzco | 10 | 125,000 | (Agurto 1980, Hyslop 1990:64–65) |
| Tikal | 5–10 | 60,000 | (Marcus per s. comm.) |
| Chan Chan | 6 | 50,000 | (Moseley and Mackey 1973:328) |
| Tiwanaku | 4–6 | 30,000–60,000 | (Kolata and Ponce 1992:332) |
| Wari | 5 | 10,000–70,000 | (Isbell, Brewster-Wray & Spickard 1991:24) |
| Tula | 10.75–13 | 30,000–40,000 | (Dielhl 1983:58) |
| Calakmul | 1.75 + | 50,000 | (Folan et al. 1995) |
| Huánuco Pampa | 2 | 30,000(?) | (Morris and Thompson 1985:86) |
| Copán | 2.5 | 18,000–25,000 | (Sanders and Webster 1988) |
| Sayil | 3.45 | 10,858 | (Tourtellot, Sabloff and Smyth 1990:248,261) |
| Pikillacta | 2 | ? | (McEwan 1991:100) |

*Figure 7.13: The size of Chan Chan relative to other major Prehispanic urban centres in Mesoamerica and South America (from Stanish 2002: 185).*

Pozorski (1987: 45) describe Chavín as an "amalgamator of anachronisms rather than a disseminator of ideas", and they maintain that its extent, duration and degree of influence is much less than usually thought.

> "A critical examination of the Early Horizon and Initial Period in ancient Peru has shown that the Chavín phenomenon can no longer be viewed as a 'Mother Culture' from which sprang all succeeding Andean civilizations. Instead, the foundations of Andean civilization and state development lie in the Cotton Preceramic Period when two separate networks of chiefdom level polities developed – along the coast and in the highlands."

The ideology spread by Chavín seems to have filled the gap left by the collapse of the coastal U-shaped ceremonial centres, which, by 500 BC, were largely abandoned or in disarray (Moseley 1993: 157). The Old Temple at Chavín de Huantar was itself a U-shaped ceremonial centre with a circular sunken court. Even when expanded southwards in two phases, it still retained its U-shape configuration, albeit no longer symmetrical.

The reasons for the many abandonments are not known due to limited excavation, but may have been caused by conflicts over increasing social stratification and/or environmental/climatic problems, perhaps El Niño amongst them (Burger 1988: 142–3). If this is so, the Chavín interlude (it lasted only two centuries) perhaps laid a more secure basis for future social stratification by elaborating the ideological dimension. This is manifested, for example, in the Staff God (sacrificer) that, as represented on the Raimondi Stone (a monolithic plaque) is a series of 'taoties'. Reinforcement could have come through oracles at Chavín de Huantar itself (the Lanzon Stela, a principal cult image, in the Old Temple, Figure 7.14) and many subsidiary ('wife' and 'daughter')

---

sacrificial, and contains a fundamental dichotomy or dualism between earth and sky".

*Figure 7.14: El Lanzon in the temple complex at Chavin de Huantar (Instituto Nacional de Cultura del Perú).*

oracles distributed across the Chavín sphere of influence. Indeed, in a plausible scenario, Burger (1988: 117) sees the spread of Chavín religion, not as imposed or proselytized, but as the lodging of 'approved' branch shrines of what became a fully-fledged regional cult coexisting with the intensely local shrines. Further, as Burger remarks, the implantation would be welcomed by local elites as providing a refashioned legitimacy, while the non-elites welcomed a crisis-reducing mechanism. The intensity of the new cult (recasting traditional elements) and its regional nature gave impetus to major developments in technology, notably textiles and metal-working (Burger 1988: 129).

The Chavín Period ended around 200 BC with its centres abandoned amidst widespread social dislocation. To that extent it was a failure, despite "the indelible impact it left on early Peruvian society, since it did not prevent the complete systems collapse which occurred at the end of the Early Horizon (Burger 1988: 143). Indeed, on account of its length and disruptive nature, Pozorski and Pozorski (1987: 46) think that the 'Early Horizon' should be renamed the 'Early Period'.

It was succeeded by two derivative traditions, the Salinar which represented immediate continuity and, about a century later, by the Gallinazo, which extended from the Santa Valley in the south to the present-day borders of Ecuador (Bawden 1996: 190). Salinar was the sub-stratum to Moche emergence, but the background to the rise of the Moche state was the dislocation, unrest and violence of the Early Intermediate Period. The catalyst was the rise of Serro Arena, an urban centre built along the top of a ridge jutting into the Moche Valley. It "possessed the densely clustered architecture, stratified population, corporate administrative, religious and economic facilities, and overall planning that characterise urban life" (Bawden 1996: 186). And urban life had two transformative consequences: it produced new forms of social management, and also a more intense iconography to accompany a more intense ideology. Yet, "the entire corpus of Moche art may have revolved around fewer than two dozen themes or stories. Similar to stories about the birth and resurrection of Christ or King Arthur's Camelot, Moche themes were recounted orally, depicted graphically, and acted out as pageants and rituals (Moseley 1993: 179–80)". Indeed the main foundation, charter and reproduction myths (Maisels 1990: 275) may only have been sixteen in number.[92]

## J: Early Intermediate Period (200 BC–AD 600)

*Moche: First State of the Northern Andes*

By the Middle Gallinazo Period stability had returned sufficiently for a general seaward relocation of settlements to take place, away from their former inland defensive locations. Agriculture flourished, irrigation canals were extended and population increased, indicated by the increasing number and size of settlements. Again the Moche

---

[92]  A myth is a story which purports to relate experiences or powers or events beyond the palpable or present. The purpose of myth is to 'give an account' thereby to fill a cognitive space and so an emotional need. Myth does not record facts, but tells stories as if they were true. "Myths are stories which, through symbol and metaphor, provide explanations of how human life came to be as it is." (Bawden 1996: 140). Myths can also be related in straightforward quasi-empirical terms, without either symbol or metaphor, but combinations are usual.

Valley was to the fore with the huge terraced settlement of Cerro Orejas housing several thousand inhabitants. But Moche was not alone. The Chicama Valley had Licapa, the Santa Valley held Huaca Santa covering several square kilometres, and the Virú Valley contained the extensive Gallinazo group, also a town of several thousand inhabitants (Bawden 1996: 187). There was plenty of social surplus to mobilize, so high and massive platforms were again built. Later Gallinazo platforms also employed the segmentary building technique that was to become such a marked characteristic, even into the Spanish colonial period (Moseley 1975c: 192). Thus *mit'a*-like labour organization was used to build elite houses and ceremonial structures in adobe. Commoners were, however, banned from using this material and were confined to the use of simple quarters with cane wall on stone footings. "...adobe – the substance of Pacha Mama – was reserved for quarters of the *karaka* class and for large buildings at corporate centres" (Moseley 1993: 165). Clearly social stratification was marked and of long standing and the state itself was in process of formation. A marker of its advent was the appearance of the 'Moche corporate style' in art and architecture.

> "The corporate style was extremely standardised because it served centralized political concerns. Although the style was expressed in many media, the surviving sample of Moche art is dominated by ceramics and by stirrup-spout libation vessels in particular. Most libation vessels were made in multi-piece moulds. Standardisation was apparently achieved by producing the moulds in the imperial homelands of the Moche and Chicama Valleys and shipping them to workshops in the provinces" (Moseley 1993: 179).

An alternative type of libation vessel to those three-dimensional ones made in piece moulds to represent men, animals and the usual shamanistic merger of the two, were non-moulded vessels, thereby capable of receiving naturalistic painting. These included the traditional Gallinazo negative or resist technique, but went on to use more durable pigments in clay slips in red on a white or cream base. Increasingly finer brushes were employed to produce motifs in 'fine line' depictions (in red on a buff background). Iconography was of course more extensive on murals, the largest area of which was on the Huaca de la Luna, the companion to the Huaca del Sol.

The Huaca de la Luna, was, according to Chapdelaine (2006: 30) "a multifunctional building where the governing body was also running state affairs. It might not be a typical palace, but it is certainly not a typical Moche temple either". The surface of Plaza 3A behind the main platform was covered by the skeletal remains of over seventy sacrificial victims (Bourget 2001). The cut marks found primarily on the anterior and lateral surfaces of the verterbrae, "correspond well to Moche artistic depictions of the slashing of the throat of captives to collect blood" (for drinking) according to the physical anthropologist John Verano (2001: 181). Indeed, that blood was actually drunk from goblets as shown, is confirmed by residue analysis (Bourget and Newman 1998). Limited excavations so far undertaken in adjacent Plaza 3B have revealed seven victims. The cut marks on their skeletons is indicative of defleshing, raising the possibility of cannibalism at Huaca de la Luna, according to Verano (*ibid.*: 182) or of torture, or both.

Having stated that sacrifice was a central and persistent theme in Moche ritual iconography, Bawden (1995: 262) nonetheless reproduces the emic or cultural relativist view that "sacrifice is an event that enables officiants, acting on behalf of their

*Figure 7.15: Naked captives being led to the slaughter, Moche IV fineline drawing (Sutter and Cortez 2005: 533; drawing by Donna McClelland).*

community (sic) to acquire the vitality of outside forces through ritual violence in a setting charged with supernatural power where they themselves become spiritually transcendent". Sounds noble, doesn't it! Cordy-Collins (1992: 217), relates that "from the abundant depictions of warfare and prisoner sacrifice in Moche iconography, clearly the objective of warfare was not the killing of the opponent, but rather the capture for ultimate ritual sacrifice". Prior to this act of transcendence another took place in which the blood of the bound prisoners was taken and subsequently consumed by aristocratic participants in an elaborate ceremony (Donnan 1978: 158–173).

The killers were, of course 'sacrificing' nothing: they were affirming their own power (DeLeonardis 2000: 382; De Marrais, Castillo and Earle 1996: 24; Kaplan 2000: 195–6; Dickson 2006: 129) by manipulating the base instincts of the population in which they were the dominant elite. The human head had originally been a focus for and a source of potency in life, death and fertility (George 1996). Thus, a central piece of Moche iconography (and reality!) was the figure of the Decapitator, shown with a knife in one hand and a severed head in the other (see Bawden 1999: 151). It had deep roots and enormous cultural resonance, as the concept was pan-Andean (Cordy-Collins 1992: 206). The 'Decapitator Theme' was clearly derived from earlier Chavín-related Cupisnique religion, sometimes called 'coastal Chavín' (Bawden 1996: 217). This was the ascent to high civilization.

Stressing the role of ideology in the formation of the earliest state in the Americas, namely Moche, D'Altroy (2001: 462) observes that ideology in the Andes and Mesoamerica was a "vigorous, active aspect of early complex society – perhaps morbidly so, given the frequent evidence for human sacrifice, bloodletting, and the use of hallucinogens." Further, there is now abundant material evidence "for a melding of ideological and social leadership in a set of elite individuals of both sexes, apparently linked to militarism and human sacrifice" (*ibid*.: 455). Or as Bawden (1999: 167) succinctly puts it: "By exploiting Andean shamanistic belief in the wholeness of

*Figure 7.16: Bound prisoners awaiting torture and death (Bottle sculpture, from Donnan 2001: 135).*

man and nature and the vitalizing role of blood in this relationship, they constructed an ideology of power upon which to build their dominance".

Ideology, the representation of the interests of specific groups and individuals, must necessarily justify those sectional interests by claiming that they embody universal principles and operate for the general good. As DeLeonardis (2000: 382) put it: "In Nasca art and ideology it was conveyed through images of the natural world and inextricably linked with cultural drama, ritual, combat, and power relationships. ... One could argue that head-taking had evolved from an occasional sacrifice to a more widely practiced tactic of warfare, 'ritual' or otherwise".

Discussing the significance of Huari D-shaped structures, Cook (2001: 162) states that "although the Sacrificer is a figure that predates the emergence of Middle Horizon polities, it ushers in changes from agrarian village life to a tribute-paying populace under state authority". This was facilitated because "the image of a Sacrificer is simultaneously a metaphor for rulership in which sacrifice is construed as, or made equivalent to, tribute, and a metonym of cosmology, whereby sacrificial blood is understood to be a vital fluid that recreates and generates life" (*ibid*.: 158).

All peoples of the Americas north and south, state-ordered and non-state ordered, indulged this kind of brutality[93] (Hill 2003: 289) which often involved the removal of organs or limbs from living victims. What was new, of course, was the scale and systematic nature of human 'sacrifice' amongst the likes of the Maya and Aztecs, for whose elites it was a central instrument of, and support for, state power (Schele & Miller 1986), just as the slaughter of humans and animals was in the Roman Colisseum. "Through captive sacrifice, kings provisioned gods with human flesh and blood, and in return gods rewarded kings and their supporters with agricultural abundance" (Johnston 2001: 374). Speaking of its deep roots in Archaic society in Mesoamerica, Friedel (1996: 3) remarks that "sacrifice is the key expression of the covenant between the living and the dead, human beings and gods". What kind of 'covenant' is manifested by the industrial-scale slaughter practiced by the Aztecs. One must not confuse folk roots with the political policy of states.

## What surpluses provide

The Temple of the Sun in the Moche Valley of Peru is estimated to have required more than 130 million mud bricks for its construction (Alva and Donnan 1993: 14). Much earlier, around 2150–1750 BC (uncalibrated) a large construction at La Florida in the Rimac Valley, just south of Lima, is estimated by Patterson (1991) to have a volume of 1,010,500 cubic metres. Its building would have taken 500 to 1000 labourers about two centuries. Over twice as large, however, is Sechín Alto in the Casma Valley (See Figure 7.17).

Large surpluses were therefore available from irrigation agriculture; could the rise of the Moche state be explained by the management requirements of irrigation systems?

Brian R. Billman (1996, 1999, 2002) has undertaken a thorough, quantitative and periodized study of canal building in the Moche Valley in relation to subsistence requirements, settlement patterns, monument building and the rise of the Moche state. He does not conclude that the Moche state arose out of the need to build, maintain

---

[93] Paul (2000) discussing the imagery of bodiless human heads in Paracas necropolis textile iconography from Early Horizon epoch 10 to Early Intermediate Period epoch 2 (roughly 100 BC to AD 200), during which "depictions of bodiless human heads are omnipresent" divides the representations into a Type A, where there seems to be a rope projecting from the forehead (about 25 per cent of the total), and Type B, where the head is carried by the hair. She states (*ibid*.: 76) that Type A heads "may represent trophy heads like the Paracas archaeological specimens described above", while Type B heads might be those of deceased family members or ancestors. If this is the case, then only Type A heads are 'trophy heads', that is, "the assumption that the source of the head was an enemy taken through aggressive action" (*ibid*.: 73). In any case, "the distinction made here between the two types of bodiless heads seems not to have been a critical one to the persons who produced the images" because "it is possible that these icons are not literal depictions of human heads but rather symbols of the intense concentration of power in heads" (*ibid*.: 77). If this is so then mere images would have sufficed and obtaining more heads, from whatever source, would not have been 'necessary'. But more heads confer more power on the individuals, clans or elites 'taking' the heads and there is every archaeological indication that what are portrayed are real heads. Real heads were taken throughout the Andes and Paracas was no exception. Paul's position is a clear case of denial (cf: LeBlanc 2003b).

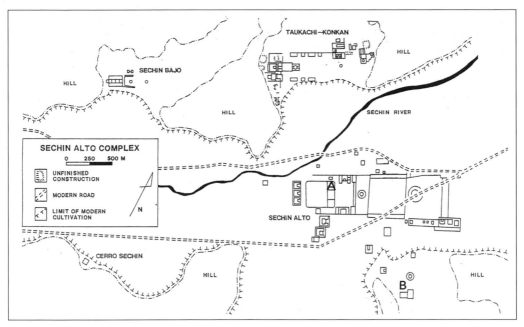

*Figure 7.17: The Sechín Alto complex (from Pozorski and Pozorski 2006: 14).*

and resolve disputes arising from canal irrigation. However once arisen the state did extend canals and build new ones, in order to extend its own power. Rather, politics are paramount, and he argues that "control of land, labour and water permitted [the elite] to create the first centralized valley-wide polity. Centralized institutions of rule were not required to construct and manage Guañape phase irrigation canals; neither warfare nor the managerial requirements of irrigation were important factors. The managerial requirements of irrigation were also probably relatively unimportant in the formation of the Southern Moche state. Warfare, highland-coastal interaction, and political control of irrigation systems created opportunities for political leaders to form a highly centralized, territorially expansive state" (2002: 395).

However, as argued further below, the Moche state may not have been centralized. The most convincing model of Moche state structure has been developed by Russell and Jackson (2001) from the work of Netherly (1977, 1984) in the Chicama Valley. Netherly's analysis was based upon reports of indigenous socio-economic organization for the near-conquest period. Russell and Jackson (2001: 161) assume that the model the reports provide "can be applied to the earlier Moche period…" a reasonable assumption. And if, as is highly likely, the Netherly/Russell/Jackson model applies to all of the Moche valleys, then for the first time we have an insight into Moche state structure, and perhaps even into other pre-Inca states.

The Huaca del Sol with the Huaca de la Luna define the central space of the urban centre, the capital of the Moche polity, that Chapdelaine (2002: 53) calls the 'Huacas of Moche'. Using one of the natural features around which it was built, others refer to the centre as Cerro Blanco and I will continue to do so since 'Huacas of Moche' is more awkward a name than Cerro Blanco (Figure 7.18). Chapdelaine (2002: 53) estimates the size of the settlement to be 60 ha during Moche IV (AD 400/450–c.700) and its population to be around 5000. This is, as he admits, very conservative. Chapdelaine (2002: 54) suggests that the situation is one of "complete occupation of the space between the two major public buildings;" that is, the population is homogeneously distributed on the plain between the Huaca del Sol (parallel to the Moche River) and the Huaca de la Luna (at the foot of Cerro Blanco). Figure 7.18 is a general map of the Huacas of Moche site from Chapdelaine (2002: 55).

Huaca del Sol was the largest solid adobe structure ever constructed in the Andes, and one of two or three largest mounds ever erected on the continent, the other being the companion Huaca de la Luna. Constructed by more than 100 kinship groups who used around 143 million adobe bricks in its construction, the Huaca del Sol once had the form of a giant cross as is clear from the Map. Reduced by over half due to Spanish 'hydraulic mining' using the 'modern canal', the Huaca del Sol presently measures 380 x 160 x 40 metres above present land surface at its highest point. As can be seen, Huaca de la Luna is a complex of courts and three interconnecting platforms extending over an area measuring 95 x 85 metres, reaching 25 metres in height. Constructed about the same time as its companion (i.e. between Moche I and IV) it was never altered. Enclosed by high adobe walls, refuse was not allowed to accumulate in the Huaca de la Luna. Its walls were covered by "the largest and most varied corpus of Moche murals yet discovered. They consist of rich polychrome depictions of anthropomorphic and zoomorphic beings, and of animated clubs, shields and other artefacts. Some share canons with the ceramic arts" (Moseley 1993: 178).

> "Sites such as Sipán and San José de Moro preserve the tombs of officials who presided over rituals involving the sacrifice of captives. The skeletal remains of their victims have now been identified at the Huaca de la Luna, and similar evidence can be expected to be buried in ceremonial compounds at other Moche sites" ( Verano 2001a: 183).

It was not, however, a simple case of a dominant centre crystallising the state and then going on to conquer its neighbours. Rather the elites of the Gallinazo tradition in some valleys saw their interests best served by a fusion to form a multi-valley state, which then expanded as much by the adherence of other elites as by the military action that also took place. The state which was thus formed was a *coalition state*, which is not the same as a segmentary state or even chiefdom, which does have a ruling centre. A coalition state has a number of ruling centres roughly equal in power although unequal in prestige.

Moche was not a particularly large state, even at its maximum extent when it stretched from the Piura Valley in the north to Huarmey is the south, a distance of 550 km (Alva and Donnan 1993: 13) (see Figure 7.19). Depth was a mere 50–80 km, so the total area was only around 35,750 km (taking a mean) most of which was desert. Accordingly, irrigation on a large scale was vital. Subsistence came from the ocean and from the land. Maize, beans, guava, avocados, squash, chili peppers and, of course, peanuts were grown (Alva and Donnan 1993: 13). Animal protein came from fish, shrimp, crabs, crayfish and molluscs (*ibid.*). Guinea pig and ducks were raised and

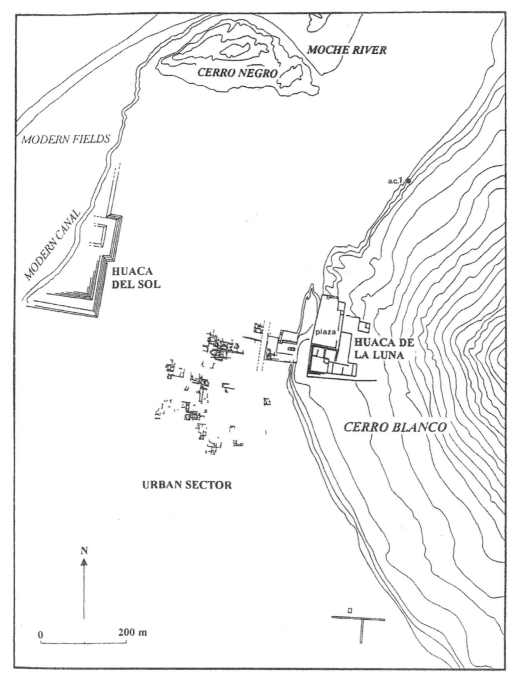

*Figure 7.18: General map of the Huacas of Moche site (Cerro Blanco).*

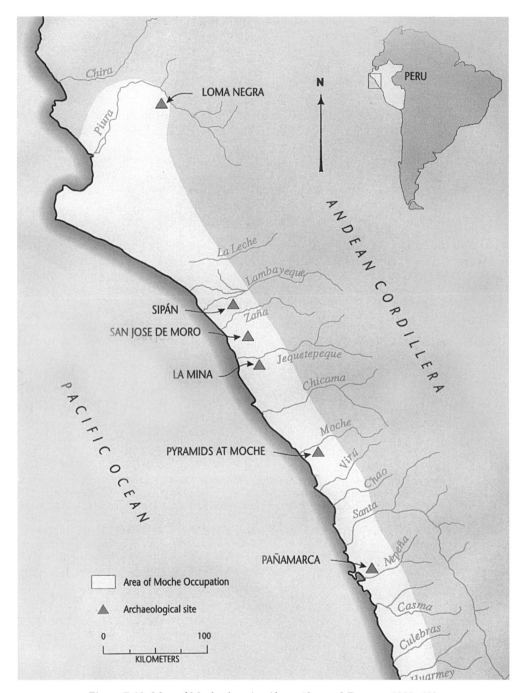

*Figure 7.19: Map of Moche domains (from Alva and Donnan 1993: 12).*

domesticated llamas were also eaten. Wild resources were hunted or gathered, and included birds, snails, other animals and plants (*ibid.*). Cerro Blanco itself, on present limited exposures, seems to have undertaken little of its own subsistence production, but to have left the fishing and arable farming to satellite villages, while the city population undertook textile production, metallurgy pottery and other crafts.

The urban population was, according to Chapdelaine's (2002: 72–3) existing exposures, grouped around a lineage core into residential compounds of those engaged in the same branch of specialised production in workshops. Further, "it seems that at Moche, storage of goods was conducted at the household level of organization, within a private context, by each leader of a compound or household" (*ibid.*: 64). Not then merely a ceremonial centre; the city manifested an urban division of labour.

Chapdelaine's (2001) excavations of compounds at Moche indicate that there were three classes (with internal sub-divisions) in and around the city: the labouring class; a middle class of skilled artisans and functionaries; and an upper class elite who constituted the ruling class. He proposes "that several individuals of the highest urban class were acting as leaders of each quarter of the city's urban nucleus, as members of a state council, heads of noble families, or leaders of large economic and/or social corporate groups. The middle class residing in the urban sector was composed of skilled craftsmen, bureaucrats, and heads of small corporate groups, all working for the governing body. A third class, residing principally outside the urban sector, was composed principally of food producers, and the labour force necessary for various operations in the city" (2001: 84), especially, one imagines, the heavy labour.

The key instrument of state formation was ideology[94] and by the end of Moche I-II, all the communities of the central valleys appear to have adopted it. By about 300 BC the elites in control of the communities of the central valleys were in the process of forming a new social order (Bawden 1996: 227).

---

[94] Ideology comes spontaneously from people's conditions of life. It is the impression the world of objects, forces and events makes upon us, producing a kaleidoscope world of flux, hearsay and some empirical knowledge. From those we construct narratives, that is, tell each other stories, in order to confer meaning on events and processes, so as to make sense of the world. Some of this is transformed into myth and made manifest in the rituals of life, fertility, death and changes of condition. Ideologues then come along (shamans, priests, scribes, politicians), who select from and elaborate upon this spontaneous material to form a coherent religious or political ideology. 'Believe what I say not what you see', is a credible refrain by ideologues, because most people's mental images of the world are piecemeal and impressionistic, especially in the key area of cause and effect, that is, the causal continuum, which comprises interactive chains of causes and effects at many levels (Maisels 1991). Further, to the naturally evolved psychodrama a conscious, artificial and political construct is added, incorporating some but not all of the elements found in spontaneous or 'folk' beliefs, which are always diffuse and malleable. This 'superstructure' has less emotional resonance, and so requires to be imposed and maintained by authority, an important part of which is manifest in monumental and public display. However folk ideology/religion/mores continue as it were 'beneath' the official ideology/religion, incorporating such new material as folk heroes, the impact of events, and also ideas and personae from the official version. But the roots of the spontaneous ideology are enduringly deep and can even impose restrictions upon the elite. Chinese emperors, for example, were bound to endless and onerous daily ritual, most of which had folk roots. In Sumer, seasonality was seen spontaneously as the death and rebirth of Dumuzi, husband of Inanna, goddess of fertility. Millennia later, in the midst of a world empire and following on from a number of sophisticated religions, the death and resurrection of Jesus appeared not as the seasonal death and rebirth of vegetation, or the sun, but as social, psychological and moral rebirth. In turn this entered folk religion, over the next millennium justifying popular revolt, as during the Peasants' Revolts in 14th Century England , 16th Century Germany and the wars of parliament against monarchy in 17th century Britain, to name but a few.

During what Bawden (1996: 222) calls the Middle Period, extending from about AD 300 to AD 600 (and thus covering the Moche III and IV stylistic phases of Larco Hoyle), Moche ideology was adopted by or imposed upon the population of the North Coast. It centred upon the much expanded settlement of Cerro Blanco with its two great power foci, the Huaca del Sol and the Huaca de la Luna. So effective was this materialization of ideology as embodied in structures, symbolic objects and public ceremonies that De Marrais, Castillo and Earle (1996: 23) declare that "through materialization, Moche elites appropriated and owned history and tradition"; which can, of course, be expediently re-manufactured when required. As Earle (1997: 151–2) justly remarks: "Ideas must be materialized to become social, to become cultural things. ... The materialization of ideologies provides the foundations for institutions of power, owned and controlled by the ruling elite. ... To the degree that ideologies are materialized, they become part of the physical world that is constructed by social labour", and manifest to all.

At this time southern valleys, Virú and its neighbours and the Santa, were home to vigorous and independent Gallinazo societies, while to their south the dominant populations of the Nepeña, Casma and Huarmey valleys appear to be part of a highland polity quite distinct from the Gallinazo. Virú was the first to be incorporated at the time of the emergence of Moche III, around AD 300 (Chapdelaine *et al.* 2001: 371). To manifest and cement this control, the new Moche rulers changed both settlement and agricultural patterns. They began the construction of platforms, the dominant and no doubt intimidating symbols of Moche power and the sites of the activities supporting it (Bawden 1996: 243).

Phases III and IV, extending from around AD 300 and ending well before AD 800 (Chapdelaine *et al.* 2001: 371), perhaps as early as AD 700, also saw Moche presence in the lower reaches of the Santa and the neighbouring Nepeña valley, with Moche hegemony now extending from the Lembayeque River in the north to the Huarmey in the south. The Santa valley must have had especial importance because a range of platforms dot the valley, ranging from the major Pampa de los Incas complex down to minor ones of local importance. As Bawden (1996: 245) observes:

> "David Wilson, who has conducted the most recent survey of the area, has described the Pampa de los Incas site as the chief locus of political control in the valley (figure 1.1; Wilson 1988: 207–12). This extensive complex of platforms, adobe walls, habitation areas, and cemeteries covered an area of over two square kilometres and was approached by the main road that entered the Santa Valley from the north. Also in the immediate environs of this site Wilson identified what was probably a pottery production workshop controlled by the polity. In this regard Wilson also noted that the pottery of this period from Santa, while displaying typical Moche characteristics, includes only a restricted number of types, a feature that Wilson ascribes to the formal dictates of a controlling central administration."

The Moche rulers concentrated population in the lower valley with the building of new canals, fields and settlements. In the process Wilson estimates that the Santa population fell from about 30,000 to around 22,000, or nearly 27 per cent, probably a consequence of military conquest and resettlement. Under Moche domination, the number of settlements in the Santa Valley fell to 84 from its previous 205 (Bawden 1996: 246). Directly to its south lies the Nepeña valley. Here 37 habitation sites were reduced to only five, and those are clustered defensively around the major centre of Panamarca in the middle of the valley adjacent to the most likely routes from the north. The settlement distribution, the fortress-like nature of Panamarca, "centred around a major terraced platform mound, which, like the Castillo de Huanaco in the Virú Valley, rises in five stages above the surrounding land surface" (Bawden 1996: 247), with famously imposing murals on the walls of the complex, indicate that this was no routine cluster, but a colony in conflict, almost certainly with people of the Recuay Culture. Recuay art reflects a preoccupation with warfare, and "disembodied heads or 'trophy heads' are common motifs, appearing as neck ornaments and clutched in bags" (DeLeonardis and Lau 2004: 86).

## K: The Netherly-Russell-Jackson Model of Moche State Structure

Firstly, Russell and Jackson (2001: 161) predicate that "extended clans and their associated lands translated into political units, which are here referred to by their colonial designation, *parcelidades*. Data from early colonial administrative records indicate how the *parcelidades* may have been hierarchically arranged", which is in a moiety system where one side was superior to the other, but both superior to those ranked beneath, as shown in the following diagram from Russell and Jackson (2001: 162) (Figure 7.20).

Secondly, Russell and Jackson (*ibid.*) state that on the ground, "the Chicama polity was divided into four subgroups, or *parcelidades*, organized into two paired moietes: the dominant moiety to the north of the Chicama River, and the lesser moiety to the south. These moieties were bounded and defined by major canal arteries whose maintenance and waters were the responsibility and entitlement of the associated landowners".

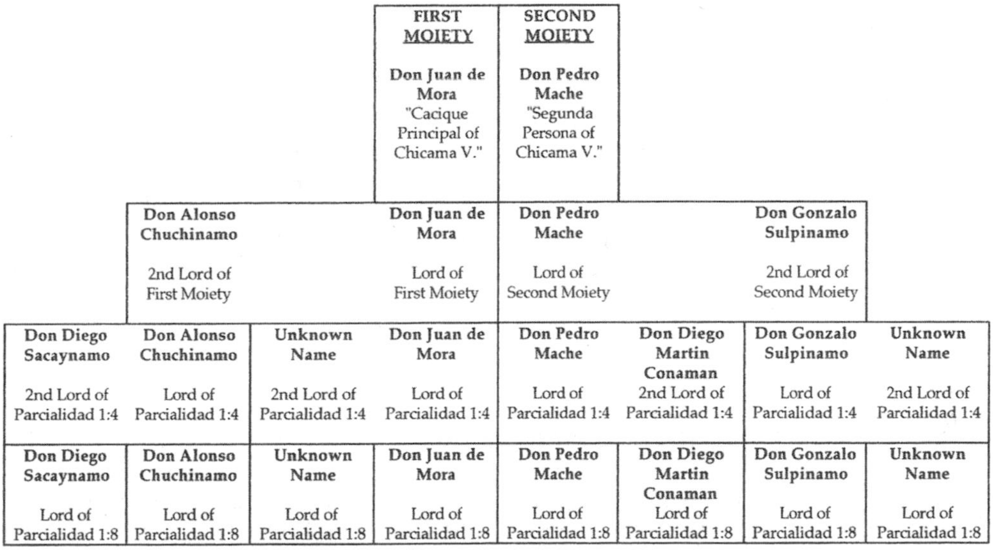

| | | | FIRST MOIETY | SECOND MOIETY | | | |
|---|---|---|---|---|---|---|---|
| | | | Don Juan de Mora "Cacique Principal of Chicama V." | Don Pedro Mache "Segunda Persona of Chicama V." | | | |
| | Don Alonso Chuchinamo 2nd Lord of First Moiety | | Don Juan de Mora Lord of First Moiety | Don Pedro Mache Lord of Second Moiety | | Don Gonzalo Sulpinamo 2nd Lord of Second Moiety | |
| Don Diego Sacaynamo 2nd Lord of Parcialidad 1:4 | Don Alonso Chuchinamo Lord of Parcialidad 1:4 | Unknown Name 2nd Lord of Parcialidad 1:4 | Don Juan de Mora Lord of Parcialidad 1:4 | Don Pedro Mache Lord of Parcialidad 1:4 | Don Diego Martin Conaman 2nd Lord of Parcialidad 1:4 | Don Gonzalo Sulpinamo Lord of Parcialidad 1:4 | Unknown Name 2nd Lord of Parcialidad 1:4 |
| Don Diego Sacaynamo Lord of Parcialidad 1:8 | Don Alonso Chuchinamo Lord of Parcialidad 1:8 | Unknown Name Lord of Parcialidad 1:8 | Don Juan de Mora Lord of Parcialidad 1:8 | Don Pedro Mache Lord of Parcialidad 1:8 | Don Diego Martin Conaman Lord of Parcialidad 1:8 | Don Gonzalo Sulpinamo Lord of Parcialidad 1:8 | Unknown Name Lord of Parcialidad 1:8 |

*Figure 7.20: The Netherly-Russell-Jackson Model of Moche state structure.*

Thirdly, "common farmers were obligated to make tribute payments to their local lord, who was called a *principal*, who in turn owed tribute to a higher level lord or *cacique*, who himself usually owed tribute to an even higher status paramount lord or *cacique principal*" (Russell and Jackson 2001: 161).

Fourthly, "Individual *caciques* retained a measure of autonomy, while ideology and ritual served as a powerful glue to hold the system together. It was a system made up of a series of reciprocal and hierarchical relationships that were codified in ritual. The reciprocal relationships operated both vertically and horizontally; between rulers and the ruled, as well as between the living and the ancestors" (*ibid.*: 172).

This is by far the most comprehensive and convincing model of (any) Andean state structure that we have, integrating as it does all known aspects of Andean social structure and culture, past and present. It seems to answer Dillehay's (2001: 277) well justified call, "that we must consider a more complex interplay between two types of ideologies in the Andes. One is the preservation of local communities and their kinship-based rituals, which is important for the development of a viable peasant substratum. The second is the aggrandisement and emulation of lords."

The model describes what is essentially a *segmentary state*. I have already referred to the Moche example as a 'coalition state'. It might not be too fanciful to imagine that two whole valleys could be paired in a super- and sub-ordinate moiety system, and that all valleys could be thus linked into a pyramid, with the Moche valley itself at the top. For some or much of the time the Moche Valley may have been hegemonic, but this does not mean that there was a 'central person' in a 'central place' in the Moche Valley who exercised rule, hence the term 'coalition state' rather than 'segmentary state'. It is likely that many Lords ruled in cooperation, competition, and sometimes, no doubt, in conflict with one another.

State formation occurred during the Middle Moche phase (from about AD 300) long after the onset of canal irrigation some two millennia previously. It was during the Middle Moche phase that "the first truly large-scale canals were constructed and when irrigation expanded into the far reaches of the north side of the valley, which is the most difficult to reclaim" (*ibid.*: 383). Again we see a state (or some members of the elite) moving from a satisficer strategy to the more precarious optimiser that maximises output. Ceremonial imperatives justify political objectives (Johnston 2001: 373) and those drive the elite (staying in power at all costs), not economic welfare. In the highly productive Santa Valley, population levels actually fell after takeover by the Moche, although new canals were built to accommodate a new, politically inspired settlement pattern, perhaps attempting to recreate the sort of political economy just described for the Chicama Valley.

Which is not to say that corporate kin society was the realm of freedom. As Moseley (*op.cit.*: 127) well observes: "access to the means of making a living was based on kinship and ancestors, and paid for by contributing to corporate undertakings. In Inca times peasant farmers did not own the land they tilled, and it is unlikely that they ever did". Long before the rise of the Inca or earlier states: "Farmers prospered and increased their numbers, but under a rather totalitarian yoke of the larger kin collectives into which they were born" (*ibid.*). Again, this condition of subordination of the individual within a corporate group (Stone-Miller 2002: 15) so conducive to hierarchy and state-formation, should be compared with East Asia, where "in Chinese culture the individual's identity has been consistently derived from particularistic relationships with others. It is always some relationship, such as position within the family or other particularistic consideration, which determines self-identity for the Chinese. Therefore they are expected to make sacrifices without hesitation for the group that provides them with their identities. ... Chinese children are generally told that their identity is totally derived from belonging to some larger group or community, and it is therefore from this 'Other' that the individual receives his or her 'greater self' or *da-wo*" (Pye 1996: 18, 21).[95] Similar considerations obtain in Japan, where the Emperor could be seen as the chief of all the clan chiefs.

## Recuay

Spanning eight centuries from *c.*AD 1–800, Recuay culture has four phases: Huaras Style (200 BC–AD 250), Recuay Style (AD 250–650); Late Recuay (AD 600–700) and Early Wari-Influenced Styles (AD 700–850). Although social stratification took place amongst Recuay populations, in none of those periods does a state seem to have formed (Lau 2004a: 180) which indicates that warfare by itself does not result in state formation, but requires the presence of other factors, as specified in Chapter 9 (cf: Figure 9.1).

Coeval cultures in addition to Moche are Salinar, Gallinazo, Cajamarca, Lima and montane forest cultures (Lau 2004a: 178). "As in other contemporary cultures, like Moche and Nasca, warfare is a recurring theme in the interpretation of Recuay groups ... with warriors, weapons, and trophy heads as common motifs in Recuay art" (*ibid.*). Indeed the whole Recuay settlement pattern can be seen as a response to ongoing conflict (Lau 2004a: 180). In addition to trophy heads, common in the Andes, Recuay warriors wore trophy hands on their headgear (Lau 2004b: 169, where illustrated).

Renowned for their distinctive cultural traditions that emerged in the early centuries AD and which persisted at least until the Wari expansion around AD 750 (Lau 2002: 282), Recuay, whose core area was that of highland Ancash, were the Early Intermediate successors of the highlanders who had earlier shared elements of Chavín ideology with the nearby coastal groups (Bawden 1996: 249). However, Recuay iconography, stressing themes of important personages and ancestor veneration, "appears to be a conscious break from the esoteric and mystifying emphases of Chavín imagery" (Lau 2004a: 178). Not only did the characteristic white-on-red iconography lack the overt and complex religious symbolism of Chavín-period pottery (Lau 2004: 189), but "at Chavín de Huántar itself. ... Huarás groups built common residential buildings and dumped refuse atop one of the most sacred places of the temple complex, the Old Temple atrium" (Lau 2004a: 191). Recuay settlements were smaller, more dispersed and egalitarian units, many in defensible hilltop positions.

Recuay Culture was centred in the Callejón de Huaylas, one of the most important intermontane valleys of northern Peru because the River Santa flows through it.

---

[95] Cf: Gao (1999: 106): "Just as before 1949, the economic and social structures in Mao's China were such that individuals were not valued in their own right. Their values were assessed as part of the household in which they lived". Cf: Shaughnessy 1996 for a review of the situation in the military activities of historical China.

Recuay itself is located in the far south of the fertile Upper Santa drainage (Figure 7.2). The Recuay site of Chinchawas, studied by Lau (2002), lies on an important route connecting Casma on the coast with the Callejón. This is not exceptional as many Recuay settlements are situated at strategic locations on trade routes. Additionally, not only did Recuay groups prosper through participating in exchanges between ecological zones, but "small communities were established to exploit high altitude agricultural lands (upper *quechua*) as well as zones for camelid pasturage or *puña*" (Lau 2004: 178).

> "Recuay sites can be characterised as small hilltop settlements, often with restrictive access, strategic positions, and fortifications. It is likely that most Recuay people lived in areas closer to their fields and pastures, but convened at those hilltop locations as refuges during periods of aggression. Large settlements often feature massive perimeter walls, baffles, parapets, and moats." (De Leonardis and Lau 2004: 83).

Conflict with the Moche seems to have been ongoing. Lau's (2004b) analysis of dress, weaponry and accoutrements shows that the combat scene which covers the body of the famous Luhrson vessel (a stirrup-spout bottle 26.5 cm high, whose rollout drawing is illustrated below in Figure 7.21), is almost certainly between Moche and Recuay warriors. This dispels the notion that combat was solely a ritual affair internal to the Moche warrior elite. At the least conflict occurred along contested frontiers, specifically in the Andean foothills and the inland valleys of North Central Peru (Lau 2004b: 180).

## L: A Coalition State

Moche III 'expansion' north of the Jequetepeque Valley raises the question of whether Moche was actually a unitary state or some kind of coalition state, with an originating centre at Cerro Blanco in the Moche Valley, linked to other essentially independent centres to the north. Indeed De Marrais, Castillo and Earle (1996: 23) conjecture that "the Moche comprised at least two independent polities ... one centred

*Figure 7.21: Rollout drawing from the Luhrson vessel (VA 666) showing combat between Moche and another less well protected and armed group (from Lau 2004b: 167).*

in the southern Moche and Chicama Valleys, the other occupying centres in the Jequetepeque and Lambayeque Valley systems [Castillo and Donnan 1994]". And while southern Moche was expansionist, the northern was not. However, even calling Moche duocentric still does not adequately capture its form. Bawden (2004: 126) speaks of a "regional network of dominant interest represented by Moche ideology support[ing] several distinct and sovereign centres of power". Indeed, polities centred around a 'lord' in each valley with the subsidiary 'lords' as mentioned above (in the Netherly-Russell-Jackson model) are the most likely (Alva 2004: 243). Chapdelaine (2006: 36) offers "the hypothesis of several states centred in different valleys and having different types of relations between them and the ruling elite at the Moche site (Bawden 1996: Castillo and Donnan 1995; Quilter 2002)".

*Figure 7.22: Sipan pyramids and Moche burial platform.*

It seems, then, that the Moche was a multi-centric or coalition polity, as indicated by the differential responses of the Moche, Lambayeque and Jequetepeque Valleys to pressure late in the sixth century AD. The Cerro Blanco polity invaded and dominated southern valleys with Gallinazo populations. But in the north, where the lowest parts of the valleys were also occupied by Gallinazo populations who were similar to Moche in ethnicity and religion and separated only by the political aspects of their shared religious beliefs (Bawden 1996: 253), coexistence seems to have been the norm. What seems to have happened is that some of the Gallinazo elites used Moche ideology and iconography to make themselves rulers, and thus, by means of "horizontal communication among the highest-status elites through exchange of the most elaborate symbolic and exotic objects" (De Marrais, Castillo and Earle 1996: 23) became part of, or at least allied to, the Moche ruling class.

The building of Sipán in the Lambayeque Valley (which is contiguous with La Leche and Zana valleys) demonstrates a local ruling class' full identification with and deployment of Moche political ideology. Indeed since the discovery of the 'royal tombs' in the small pyramid there in 1987,[96] Sipán has become archetypal for the study

---

[96] The group of three pyramids is collectively referred to as Huaca Rajada. It comprises a very large pyramid linked by a complex series of (processional?) ramps to a smaller one that appears to have about a third the volume of the largest. The smallest pyramid, containing the tombs, seems to have had at least six encapsulating building phases (Alva and Donnan 1993: 44). This small pyramid with its large platform appears to be relatively detached from the other two, connected to them only by a large plaza.

By contrast some scenes show combat between fully clothed and armoured Moche warriors and those clad only in a loincloth, with no armour and bearing different weapons and accoutrements (Verano 2001: 113; Lau 2004b: 171). What this seems to represent is attacks on surrounding populations, primarily the Recuay, to serve as sacrificial victims. Just because iconography shows combat as ritualized, this does not mean that all combat was ritual and that other, more collective ('conventional') types of warfare did not take place (Quilter 2002: 172).

The Shang predated on the Qiang peoples to their west and, as in early state China we can say with Shelach (1996: 13) that "it can be argued that the Qiang belonged to the captive-victim category, and, moreover, that to the Shang they *were* the category". As Quilter (quoted Stone-Miller 2002: 94–5) put it: "Moche was about blood in the sand under a harsh sky and the murmur of the crowd; the flash of the sacrificial knife wielded by a god impersonator", the Degollador. And as she (*ibid.*: 95) succinctly adds: "Thus, ritual sacrifice is presented as a spiritual necessity in state aesthetics"; that is, aesthetics as power-play. Commentators should not speak blandly about 'ceremonial' and an ethnographic example of such parasitism in permanence such as was most likely suffered by the remaining Gallinazo and/or highland populations, exists in regard to the headhunters of Sulawesi (Indonesia). There mountain groups preyed upon coast-dwelling trading partners amongst whom they even worked in some seasons. Kenneth George (1996: 82), their ethnographer, "points out that *pangngae* (the song and chant of a ritual headhunt) is a time for the uplanders to prey upon their coastal trading partners". Although those particular predatory uplanders are stateless, George (*op.cit.*) deals fully with the rhetoric, emotions and rituals involved.

*Figure 7.24: Moche Pitchers in the form of Prisoners.*

They offer plenty of scope for a ruthless shaman/militarist to forge a chiefdom in the right circumstances, central to which must be a fairly populous farming regime, such as the valleys of Peru provided.

Bawden (1996: 343) remarks that "great rulers like the Warrior Priest of Sipán were extreme practitioners of the shaman's art in the political sphere" (Bawden 1996: 343). The Sipán elite used precious metal to display ritual symbolism rather than fine-line pottery and portrait vessels. In fact the wealth of metal, copper, gold and silver found in the Sipán tombs is amazing, as is the quality of workmanship, applied to everything from clothing through weapons to jewellery and insignia. This is a 'local' feature that Sipán shares with Upper Piura developments, for both of them have strong connections to their north. Nonetheless, Sipán rulers' tomb chambers were surrounded by hundreds of ceramic vessels, in addition to human hands and feet "quite possibly taken from sacrificed prisoners whose bodies were dismembered, exactly as shown in Moche art" (Alva and Donnan 1993: 165). Indeed one of the striking things about Moche visual 'art' is just how literal it is in rendering the ideological power-plays of the Moche rulers.

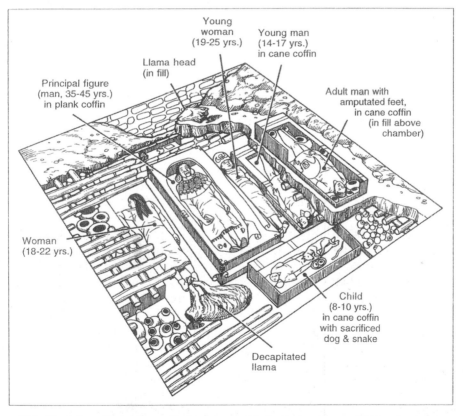

*Figure 7.25: Tomb 2 at Sipán, Peru, the burial of a Moche lord with possible family members and/or retainers. Reprinted by permission from 'Archaic States', p. 49, edited by Gary M. Feinman and Joyce Marcus. Copyright © 1998 by the School for Advanced Research, Santa Fe, New Mexico, USA.*

## Moche IV–V: The End

It was all over by AD 750. Moche V spans the period AD 600–750. Sand encroached on the entire south side of the Moche valley. This indicates abrupt environmental change including exceptional inundation events. The Cerro Blanco site was largely abandoned by the end of the Moche IV Phase (Bawden 1996: 265). Dune formation, the burial of fields and monuments "clearly indicates that the climate of the sixth century was dominated by a series of droughts, smaller ones in the first half of the century and, significantly, a 30–year event encompassing its last third. This drought has been characterised as one of the longest in history and would have caused severe problems in the already arid coastal region" (*ibid.*: 268); dependent, it must be remembered, on river-flow.

In the period under consideration major El Niños recurred in 511–12, 546, 576, 600, 610, 612, 650, 681 (based on the Quelccaya glacial corings from the Cordillera Occidental of the southern Peruvian highlands) and with similar frequency in later centuries. For late prehistoric times Satterlee *et al.* (2000: 104) report that "the ice core data indicate: (1) below average precipitation from 1000–1500; (2) drought episodes at 1250–1300 and 1450–1500; and (3) periods of ENSO activity during 1270–5, 1350–1370 and 1482–1493, with the 1350 episode being pronounced". From their research in the Osmore Drainage (the Montegua River Basin in southern Peru), Satterlee *et al.* (*op. cit.*) show that Chiribaya culture settlements and irrigation systems were wiped out by the 1350 ENSO, referred to as the Miraflores Catastrophe.

A severe drought cycle hit in the mid-to-late 6th Century, affecting highlands and lowlands. This produced the thirty year drought already referred to, stretching from 563 to 594. Good rainfall resumed in 602, lasting until 636, when another drought extended to 645. The three decades of drought had reduced precipitation by 30 per cent (Moseley 1993: 209) and ruined farmland.

Sea warming events bring drought and floods and sometimes famine. Droughts in the last part of the sixth century were followed by severe flooding episodes. There are other natural hazards to be considered, especially longer-term drying episodes not related to El Niño or La Niña. In the Andes frequent and strong earthquakes (>6.0 on the Richter Scale, which is logarithmic) have to be contended with, along with landslips and mudslides, which, separately or combined can bring disaster to irrigation channels and settlements as occurred in the Osmore Drainage. Littoral settlements can be struck by tsunamis. Geological activity in the Andes must never be underestimated; there are even geysers at 4000 metres, which is the same altitude as Tibet. The Ancash earthquake in Peru in 1970 brought down – at speeds approaching 350 km per hour – glacier ice, rock and mud 3000 m from Mount Huascaran (6768 m/22,205 ft, the highest in Peru) upon the 20,000 inhabitants of the town of Yungay, which was entirely wiped out. The port of Chimbote was also wrecked.

The 1970 earthquake that hit the Department of Ancash, through which the Santa Valley runs, was 7.8 on the Richter Scale and the estimated death toll was 66,000. Ica and Pisco were seriously hit in 2007. Such devastating earthquakes must have occurred in Precolumbian times and conferred on one valley or valley group decisive advantages over others. The violence of the mountains was (and still is) conceived of as a supernatural force by the indigenous population. Mountain deities have a variety of regional names but in the contemporary Antabamba Valley of Apurimac, Peru, the Andes are referred to as *apu* (in fact very close to the European *alp, alt* etc.). Other generally used terms are *achachila* in Quechua or Aymara, or *mallku* (Aymara) or *wamani* (Quechua). The many terms because "by far the most common landform considered sacred in the Andes is the mountain peak or prominent knoll" (Kuznar 2001: 48). As their ethnographer Gose (1986: 308) observes "the *apus* have always been slaughterers themselves", in the sense of ritual slaughterers.

Severe El Niño flooding struck Cerro Blanco in 576. Although the flood damage was to some extent repaired, the decades of drought in the late sixth century were ultimately decisive, for the city was inundated by sand, burying everything but the *huacas*. Accordingly, at the end of the Middle Period, while some use may still have been made of the Huaca de la Luna into the Late Period, settlement moved to Galindo, on the north side of the Moche Valley (Bawden 1996: 266). Located some 32 km from the sea at the junction of the coastal plain with the valley's narrow upper reaches and adjacent to the main trunk canal, the Galindo of Moche V covered 6 km² at its maximum. The density and variety of its population (probably crowded with southern refugees and those from the lower parts of its own valley) made Galindo much more genuinely urban than Cerro Blanco had ever been. In that respect it was similar to Pampa Grande in the Lambayeque Valley, 65 km from the Pacific and 165 km north of Galindo. Social control still operated through complex stratification and ideology; however the former was now clearly marked by physical compartmentalization into districts segregated by walls. Clearly ideological stabilization had ended.

Huacas no longer dominated the city by reason of their high visibility and central location, "constant reminders of elite authority and no doubt [having] the force to captivate audiences even from afar" (Swenson 2003: 284); like the cathedrals of Catholic Europe and Latin America.

On the ramps and terraces of the focal *huacas* ceremonies of awesome majesty had taken place for four and a half centuries. Up their ramps a mass of stunningly clad officiants, some dressed as divinities, had ascended, slowly and deliberately, accompanied and paced by the blaring sounds of ceramic and shell trumpets,[98] whistles and drums, to an 'inevitable' climax at the summit. Instead, the now miniscule platform was relegated to a subordinate role at the periphery of the site, and its central place was taken by the *cercadura*. This was an enclosure of small compartmentalised spaces hidden from public view by a high perimeter wall. No longer could the Moche Valley rulers use public ritual as the key tool of social control. Now secret rites took its place, supposedly confirming their 'hidden' power.

Another innovation in the Moche V transition at Galindo is the individualization of power, indicated by a ruler's palace and burial platform, both enclosed by a high wall, its interior surface adorned with a polychrome mural (Bawden 1996: 289). The wall was pierced by a single, elaborate and baffled gateway. Bawden (*ibid.*) thinks that this was the prototype for the more elaborate palace structures in the Chimú capital of Chan

---

[98] Ceramic trumpets are amongst the earliest musical instruments to be found in the Andes (Moseley 1993: 146).

Chan and indeed remarks (2001: 303) that "social identity ... at Galindo [is] difficult to characterize as 'Moche'". 'Bottom line' social control was marked by the presence of corporate storage against the scarcities of food brought on by drought, flood and sand. Accordingly, a fifth of the total occupied area was given over to small one-roomed structures filled with large wide-mouthed food storage jars (Moseley 1993: 212).

The new regime was accompanied by two related changes in funerary practices: ordinary people were interred in the stone-faced benches flanking the walls of domestic living spaces; higher status burial took place in small clusters of stone-lined chambers placed in open areas between the houses (*ibid.*: 290). Yet another innovation in belief is indicated by the position, posture and burial goods accompanying the dead; a further indicator of the cleavage between rulers and ruled. The mass of ordinary people had been removed from the sacred geography of their ancestral lands by removal to an 'artificial' city where their traditional communitarian lifestyle could not function. In Bawden's words (2001: 302) "urbanism destroyed their collective boundaries and threatened the very social identities of their members". Rejecting continuities with the socio-political past and the alienating present, the ordinary people responded "by inserting their dead into the pivotal social space of the household as sacred *huacas* and spiritual presences". In so doing, "they reconstituted the elemental relationships of their social being". As much as they could, that is. It was defiance of the new order, and that order was under threat.

Retrenchment in the Moche Valley seems to have been accomplished in haste, forced by the loss of the resources of southern valleys that had asserted their autonomy. Also, and perhaps more importantly, by the loss of the lower part of the Moche Valley to wind-blown sand. Major ideological changes necessarily accompanied such drastic political and economic ones. But this was not by itself enough to secure the position of the elite, who, embattled, tried to rule by differentiation and "coercion detached from Andean structural sanction" (Bawden 1996: 305).

## M: At Pampa Grande in the North

In the Lambayeque Valley by contrast, changes seem less severe and the ruling elite more secure, at least for a while. The city of Pampa Grande was even larger and denser than Galindo, but occupied a similar position at the neck of its valley, the Lambayeque. All the larger Moche settlements had such a location, with the exception of the coastal site of Pacatnamú (below). More of the old ways were able to continue here, marked by the presence of a dominant monumental complex at the centre of the corporate precinct of the city. It housed a series of enclosures and platforms centred upon the Huaca Grande, also called the Huaca Fortaleza. One of the largest single architectural units of the pre-Columbian period, the highest terrace of this three-tiered structure is 38 metres from ground level. The basal dimensions are 270 by 180 metres (see Figure 7.26).

The first terrace is approached by a 290 m long ascending central ramp from the northern edge of the Great Compound (Bawden 1996: 294). Yet Huaca Fortaleza is but the largest of some 30 large structures, adobe mounds and terraces, so far known at Pampa Grande (Shimada 1994: 247). Instead of painstaking construction using adobe

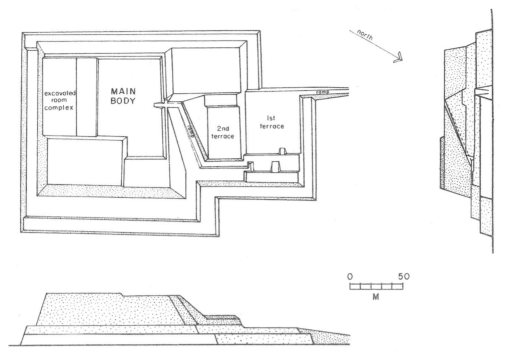

*Figure 7.26: Huaca Fortaleza, Pampa Grande in the Lambayeque Valley (Shimada, from Bawden 1996: 295).*

bricks, the Huaca Fortaleza was built using the 'chamber-and-fill method', by which a honeycomb of rectangular walled cells are filled with rubble. Re-assertion of the old ways by new methods appear to have worked, as the city of Pampa Grande was less compartmentalised and movement freer than in Galindo, even though Pampa Grande contained a large subjected Gallinazo population.

Linked with other large platforms to form a complex that includes rows of one-room storage facilities set in closely controlled walled courts, the Huaca Grande/Fortaleza dominates the city and the surrounding countryside just as earlier huacas had done. However the Pampa Grande complex was built more or less continuously, apparently up to the burning and abandonment of a least the core of the site around AD 700, perhaps by the dominated majority Galinazo population. Adobe brick platforms do however continue to exist at San José de Moro, located on a major route in the northern part of the lower Jequetepeque valley, near the Rio Chaman. The Rio Jequetepeque connects the highlands to the coastal plain. Unlike Galindo and Pampa Grande, San José was not newly established in the Moche IV period (reckoned by Chapdelaine 2002: 59 to begin around AD 400–450) but was essentially a cemetery and ceremonial centre continuously occupied for more than a thousand years (Castillo 2001: 309), beginning in the Middle Moche period. Both its modest size and its layout are traditional. Reflecting continuity and tradition, San José contains huge adobe walled and timber roofed burial chambers located in the ceremonial precinct for those of highest status. According to Bawden (1996: 297), they are amongst the most elaborate and informative ever recovered on the North Coast. Two of the occupants played key roles as priestesses in the Sacrifice Ceremony, again emphasising the importance of ritual violence as the key process that supposedly sustained society (*ibid.*: 284). In a world of 'transubstantiation' taking heads and hearts was taking another's substance in order to secure one's own wellbeing. Nonetheless, even here the rulers had to make changes, which they did by incorporating ideological symbolism derived from the central highland polity of Wari, based in the Ayacucho Valley of Peru, *c.*AD 550 –1000 (Cook 2004: 158).

As we have seen, there is as yet no evidence of Wari occupation of the North Coast. Their sphere was confined to the central and southern valleys of the Peruvian Coast, plus the associated coastal cultures: Nievería, Pachacamac and Atarco. Nonetheless this looming highland power had to have made ideological impact upon Moche consciousness, since ideology is about the representation of, and justification for, interests and power. In the Jequetepeque Valley, this even involved the adoption of a new mythic/ritual cycle, involving struggle against but eventual mastery over monstrous disorder. When representing success, ideology is power and no doubt the Moche elite needed to tap some new source in the face of hostile conditions. The alternative, of course is that a new folk synthesis was formed that could be co-opted by the elite. But this did not happen until after the Transitional Period, *c.*AD 800–950, that followed Moche collapse.

## Internal causes of Moche decline

This loss of control of natural and political circumstances most likely opened up the central fault-line in Moche society, which ran between the communitarian values of the ordinary people (which Bawden calls 'holistic') and the individuating and controlling activities of the elite. They gained their elevated position by manipulating pre-existing cosmological beliefs and social norms, which Bawden (1996: 272) characterises as shamanism, kinship, reciprocity and ancestral reverence. Rulers put themselves at the centre of, as indispensable to, social reproduction by officiating at the rituals of life, death and transformation. The latter was achieved by shamanism, the first two by the Decapitator cult, feeding the gods with blood and thereby obligating them to reward that sacrifice. When those ministrations, no doubt intensified in times of exceptional stress, proved unavailing in modifying natural forces, then social belief and consequently social cohesion must be lost. Around AD 700, Galindo was abruptly terminated amid signs of localized burning around the town. Similarly at Pampa Grande the Huaca Fortaleza had some of its adobe turned into fired brick. The elite's attempt to rule using force and foreign ideological elements was manifestly unavailing, and the population, no doubt especially the Gallinazo population, had just had enough.

The northern valleys, less affected than the Moche Valley by environmental and political circumstances, were more favourably placed, and the elite was still apparently able to draw upon traditional ideology for their rule. Nonetheless, in the Jequetepeque valley, the copying and hybridisation of pottery style with that of the Pachacamac of the Central Coast, indicates ideological defection and progressive loss of grip from the end of the Middle Period onwards. Bawden (1996: 315) highlights the reasons for this:

> "The items that made up what I have termed the language of power – those that bore the thematic iconography of the system of Moche political power – were made by specialist potters, metallurgists, and weavers under strict control of the ruling elite. These items embodied meaning that was infused with the power of myth reproduced in ritual. They manifested the mandate of the rulers in the social domain, affirming and sustaining the tenets of Moche political ideology."

Since the definition of ideology is as the representation and justification of interests, real or imagined, material and immaterial, another way to look at this process is through salesmanship. Ideology can then be seen as salesman's rhetoric used to convince the working population that they are getting in exchange for their labours on behalf of the elite, something of equivalent worth; indeed something essential to their very existence. So the price the majority are being asked to pay is a 'fair' one. The illusion of 'fair-exchange' was especially important in the Andes, given the central importance of norms of reciprocity. However, when the goods purchased fail to do as they are advertised, namely to enhance the quality of life, but instead do the opposite, then the salesmen are seen to be cheats and liars, that is, they are criminals who must be disposed of. According to Bawden (2004: 127–8) failure came first and hardest in the southernmost Moche polity, which was always the most centralised and expansionist: "Here alone, communicated though ceramic portraits, the symbolism of political ideology depicted rulers as individuals rather than solely illustrating the roles that they played in the rituals of government. It follows that it is also here that the rulers most closely linked the maintenance of a beneficent social and cosmic order to their individual prowess."

In the Jequetepeque Valley at San Jose de Moro, "the only elements that disappear [from grave goods and styles] are those most directly connected with the elite. ...This would signal an internal deterioration that might have had an element of violence, as in this era of defensive constructions, walled cities, and hilltop fortifications multiply – all indications of instability reaching violent levels and requiring action" (Castillo, 2001: 326–7). But instability in this valley permitted a new accommodation, to say the least. In this period in the Jequetepeque Valley, Swenson (2008: 126) has identified settlements, notably San Ildefonso and Catalina, both possessing tiered fortification walls with slingstones (Swenson 2008: 128). Within both, local descent/neighbourhood groups (*ayllus?*) erected low and quite small ceremonial platforms in order to engage in competitive feasting in a politico-religious context, with a highly political agenda. While this process may represent "a veritable popularization of Moche religion", as Swenson (*ibid*.: 135) puts it, it was a religion taken out of the control of the central elites and recast to serve local ideological needs, just as Catholicism has been over much of the Andes. "Therefore, the individual ceremonial sites that proliferated throughout the Jepetpeque countryside [during the Late Period] may have served as the temples of lineage divinities, who were elevated in status through identification with Moche supernaturals" (*ibid*.). This isn't new; what is new is that non-elite, non-urban groups were doing what the elite groups had previously done to render themselves elite.

Therefore "San Ildefonso might represent the union of several lineage groups who competitively maintained distinct theatres of ideological self-expression, perhaps in honouring a more inclusive or regionally revered deity" (*ibid.*). The key point is that the elite's monopoly of power was broken in the Jequetepeque.

In Pampa Grande, containing much of the population of the Lambayeque Valley, the whole elite residential, ritual and administrative centre was burned, especially the Huaca Fortaleza, while the residential areas of the rest of the population were not affected (Bawden 1996: 319). Apparently this experiment in forced urbanism was quickly repudiated as not in keeping with North Coast social structure, and a more natural, ecologically tailored, dispersed settlement pattern resumed (cf: Dillehay 2001: 273). By AD 750 then, the Moche V cities of Galindo and Pampa Grande were abandoned and a distinctive Moche symbolic complex had ceased to exist, while the abandonment of Galindo marked the total disintegration of the Moche Valley polity (Bawden 1995: 267).

## N: Middle Horizon/Late Intermediate Period (AD 600–1450)

### Sicán and other Lambayeque Culture polities

Following the collapse of the Moche polity a new one arose centred in the well-watered, densely irrigated Lambayeque Valley, employing a synthesis of Moche and Wari elements. Rooted in Lambayeque Culture whose core area lay north of the Chicama (with Chimú territory to the south), its Early Phase (AD 900–1050/1100) is termed Sicán, named after the Sicán Precinct of Batán Grande (Conlee *et al.* 2004: 212) in the Leche Valley, which was the pre-eminent centre up to the end of this phase. Later manifestations of this culture are Túcume (AD 1050–1350/1400) and Pacatnamú (AD 1100–1200/1300).

Sicán revived Moche imagery with certain of the old forms of political control, including the use of platform mounds. Sicán even re-used major Moche centres, such as Huaca El Brujo, San Jose de Moro and Pacatnamú (Bawden 1996: 330). "Reflecting the vast size of the greater Lambayeque irrigation complex, this region contains more large cities and settlements than other Andean regions" (Moseley 1996: 251). However, Sicán does not appear to have been a centralised state or empire, but a confederation of highly stratified polities as Moche had been. This makes the vast size of Batán Grande even more remarkable:

> "Covering an enormous area, this complex of domestic and monumental buildings probably contains more mounds of exceptional size than any other Andean centre of comparable antiquity. Called the Sicán Precinct, the civic core covers 4 km² and includes more than a dozen truncated pyramids. Huaca Corte is among the largest and measures 250 metres square. Many architectural features were carried over from Pampa Grande, including an emphasis on large platforms with prominent perpendicular ramps, summit colonnades, chamber and fill construction, and the use of marked adobes" (Moseley 1996: 252).

Batán Grande seems to have been fabulously wealthy judged by the quantity and quality of metal objects looted from the site and now gracing museums and private collections. "A single tomb in the central precinct yielded some 200 gold and silver

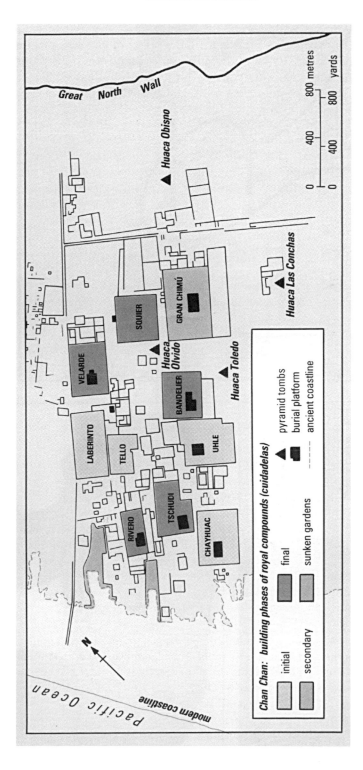

Figure 7.27: Map of Chanchan.

necklaces, mummy masks, repusse vases, *tumi* knives, and other artefacts, in addition to quantities of shell, turquoise, lapis lazuli, emerald inlays and other adornments" (Moseley 1996: 252). The city's wealth seems to have come from being both a religious centre and a commercial one. Seafaring merchants seem to have been based in Batán Grande, where a form of copper coinage called *naipes* was minted from local copper arsenical ores. These are flat I-shaped objects from 5–7 cm long and 3–5 cm wide, made from hammered and cut sheet copper. Similar objects are found in Western Mexico and coastal Ecuador, and almost certainly served as a medium of exchange. Orderly stacks of 500 were found in a tomb at Batán Grande, along with 500 kg of copper artefacts and other metal items, accompanied by 17 human sacrifices. The sheer quantity of metal indicates local extraction, smelting and production at Cerro Huaringa, evidence for which becomes clear after *c.*AD 850. The tomb also contained Spondylus shells from Ecuador, and lapis lazuli (*ibid.*: 253). Indeed, Shimada (1987: 143) "considers large-scale arsenical copper production beginning around AD 850 to have been a key variable that *promoted* (as opposed to initiated…) the evolution of the Middle Sicán state"(original emphasis).

Batán Grande's good fortune ended around AD 1100, with massive flooding. Unlike Chotuna, Batán Grande was not rebuilt. On the contrary, as the site and its elite had obviously failed their cosmological functions, the city was, with deliberation, burned and abandoned, as at Pampa Grande previously. The ensuing Late Sicán Phase was accompanied by new beliefs, with, for example, the excision of Lord Sicán or the Sicán Deity, "a standing figure of a culture hero/supernatural that can be reduced to a bust or just a head. Often with a crescent headdress and smaller attendants, he always has the eyes shaped like sideways commas that are diagnostic of this style" (Stone-Miller 2002: 158). Tomb 1 at the Huaca Loro contains a spectacular combined mask and headdress of precious metals that resembles other representations of Lord Sicán, complete with huge earspools. Huaca Loro also contained, amongst a "breathtaking array of goldwork … 2,000 square gold plaques originally sown on a ground cloth, golden feather ornaments and tall circular crowns…" (Stone-Miller 2002: 158).

It appears that the city of Purgatorio also in the Leche Valley, took over Batán Grande's metropolitan functions, while Túcume may have taken over its ritual/ceremonial functions. The 'mega-Niño' occurring at around AD 1100, seems to have forced the move from Batán Grande to Túcume, 15 km to the west. Its period of pre-eminence extended from about AD 1100–1350/1400 (Conlee *et al*. 2004: 213). Twenty-six truncated pyramids and lack of associated residential structures suggests that Túcume was primarily a ceremonial centre (*ibid.*).

Between 1350 and 1400 Chimú (below) took over the Jequetepeque Valley and the Lambayeque area north of it. But Túcume was neither destroyed nor much changed, as the Chimú rulers were content to share power with the existing rulers (*ibid.*: 217).

One hundred kilometres south of Túcume, Pacatnamú is located at the mouth of the Jequetepeque River, on high bluffs overlooking the Pacific (Conlee *et al*. 2004: 213). The site had Moche origins: in the Late Moche period it had a double defensive wall and a moat (Dillehay 2001: 271). When it flourished, from about 1100 until 1200/1300, Pacatnamú covered 1 km². In this period it seems to be a largely ceremonial centre with clusters of truncated pyramids with rooms on their summits. Huaca "complexes contain small pyramids surrounded by walls, adjacent enclosures with rooms and patios, U-shaped rooms known as *concillios*, and areas with restricted access" (Conlee *et al.* 213).

## Chimú (Chimor)

The Moche Valley itself was not stateless for long. Where the opportunity exists to exploit sedentary cultivators, some group will always want to become rulers, proffering 'protection' against hostile forces, natural and social, external and internal, in exchange for a palatial lifestyle. So again it was in the Moche Valley, where, from around AD 850 the city of Chan Chan arose as capital of the Chimor state. "At its height the empire encompassed two-thirds of all irrigated land along the desert and, by inference, two thirds of the coastal population" (Moseley 1996: 248). The second largest native state ever to exist in South America, Chimú stretched down the contiguous valleys of the Pacific coast, from Motupe in the north to the Casma Valley in the south, covering some 1300 km (800 miles). Peaking between 1400 and 1450, Chimú resisted Inca empire building until defeated and absorbed by it in 1470, not long before the Inca Empire met a similar fate at Spanish hands after 1532.

> "One of the benefits of rank in Andean society was the privilege of riding in a litter – a mark of status that was as valid for the Chimú as for the Moche – and even carrying the litter of a royal person was a mark of social standing" (Jackson 2004: 306).

At its peak Chan Chan's relatively dense central core occupied 6 km² (2.5 sq. miles), and included ten palaces of former kings. Called *ciudadelas*, 'citadels', actually compounds or palace precincts, they were enclosed by adobe walls of pressed earth (*tapia*) 12 m (40ft) high, and exhibit evidence of sectional construction (Moseley 1975b: 224; McEwan 1990: 105). Gran Chimú, the largest, measured 400 m by 600 m, or 1310 ft by 1970 ft. On his death the king was buried in a multi-tiered burial platform, made of large blocks of *tapia*, located toward the southern end of the *ciudadela*, as seen in the southeast section of the Ciudadela Rivero (Figure 7.29). The king's tomb was placed in the centre of the platform, surrounded by smaller cell-like tombs (Conlee *et al.* 204: 215). Ciudadela Tello, however, has no burial platform, but a great number of storerooms, and Klymshyn (1987: 105) argues that it was built "as a separate storage facility (which) marks the start of the allocation of more goods to general circulation through redistribution than to the royal funerary rites". She also sees Laberinto as serving the same purpose as it does not contain a burial platform "the presence of which is perhaps the most important criterion used in identifying the monumental compounds as palaces" (*ibid.*). Around the palace-compounds south of Gran Chimu, Squier and Velarde, lie 34 elite compounds (Klymshyn 1987: 100).

The core of the city, to the extent that it had one, included four huacas: (N→ S): Obispo, Las Conchas, Toledo and El Higo.

*Ciudadelas* are entered through a single gateway opening onto a vast courtyard. Beyond lies a vast complex of storerooms with U-shaped accounting and despatching rooms, accompanied by large roofed wells. J.R. Topic (2003) argues that in the U-shaped structures can be seen the transition from 'stewards to bureaucrats'; that is, between those (stewards) who closely supervise goods and people, and those (bureaucrats) who process and control information. The latter evolve to control the former as the system expands from state to empire. U-shaped structures also occur at Chimú rural sites and provincial centres.

In terms of buildings, Topic (2003: 251) associates *arcones* with stewards and *audiencias* with bureaucrats. *Arcones* have bins, *audiencias* have niches or troughs (*trocaderos*). Since *arcones* are found in the residential *barrios*, but not in the *ciudadelas*, while *audiencias* occur in the *ciudadelas* but not in the residential *barrios*, (both types occur in intermediate or elite architecture), it seems that *arcones* are receiving centres for collection from the producers, while *audiencias* are the control centres which decide final allocation. This would explain the hierarchical relationship between stewards and bureaucrats, with the stewards performing low-level clerical functions, perhaps combined with a level of enforcement, and the bureaucrats supervisory ones.

Although both Chimú and Inca empires employed large-scale storage (which has not been demonstrated for either Tiwanaku or Wari) the difference between the Chimú and Inka empires in regard to storage is threefold: (1) the Inca used portable recording devices, the *quipu* (knotted strings) and *yupana* (abacus), while Chimú used some kind of counter kept within the U-shaped structures; (2) Inca stores were dispersed across the empire while Chimú stores were concentrated at Chan Chan; (3) Inca stores mainly consisted of staples to support the army on campaign, also to provide reciprocity feasts, while the Chan Chan stores were of craft products, with the vast majority of

*Figure 7.28: Aerial photograph of part of Chan Chan.*

its population comprised of artisans. Craft items were important to Chimú political economy because, like other empires, including the Roman and the British, "the Chimú and Inca both employed a combination of señorial and bureaucratic administration, alliance-building, gift-giving and military force" (Topic 2003: 269). In other words, "a key element of the Chimú power base was the centralization and accumulation of wealth at the capital" (Conlee *et al.* 2004: 235).

The royal residential quarters lie in the northern part of the compound, the burial platforms toward the southern end. The great compounds apparently housed only the ruler's family and their immediate retainers. The ground plan of one of those palace/mortuary complexes, Rivero, is reproduced from Moore (1992:106; cf: Flannery 1998: 25). [Figure 7.29: The Rivero compound at Chanchan]. One of the smaller compounds, it covered 87,900 m², and is situated near the present coastline. It is delineated at the centre of the aerial photograph (Figure 7.28). As can be seen it comprised four distinct sectors: central, north, annex (the northernmost extension with the large wells) and the wing to the east.

The Central sector, the *raison d'etre* of the compound, contained the royal residence, with kitchens and

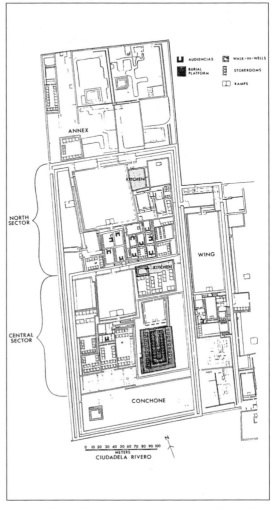

*Figure 7.29: The Rivero compound at Chan Chan (from Moore 1992: 106 after K.C. Day 1982, fig. 3.2, in Moseley and Day eds).*

storerooms, plus the burial platform with a ritual forecourt, which was the locus for despatching sacrificial victims. To the south of the residence and burial platform lay the Canchon, which probably housed, in wattle and daub structures, the population of royal retainers. Movement between and within each sector was highly restricted and there seems to have been no direct access to the Central, royal sector. Instead entry was through the North sector, which in turn was approached from the east through the wing. But this entry and the one from the west opened, in the first instance, only onto the patio, where, no doubt, all arrivals were clearly visible.

This North sector patio was even larger than the one in the central sector. It was surrounded to the south and east by storerooms and *audiencias*, through which produce was filtered. Each *audiencia* was 5–6 m², with walls a metre thick, and roofed (in contrast to most rooms). This sector also had a kitchen and, necessarily, its own walk-in well. No doubt the storeroom workers and officials lived, as well as worked, in this largely self-contained sector.

In addition the city core contained 34 'mini-palaces', with low walls, for the aristocracy. Their compounds also contained small U-shaped *audiencias* or offices, but lacked the friezes and burial mounds of the palatial compounds. Access to Chan Chan's core was highly restricted, as was access to the *ciudadelas*. The city as a whole sprawled over 20 km² (*c.*8 miles²) and had a population of about 30,000, comprising around 26,000 artisans, mostly weavers and metalworkers, wood and lapidary workers, plus about 3,000 retainers directly serving the elite and the state (Moseley 1992: 256). They lived packed closely together in irregular structures made of cane or wattle and daub. Rural as well as urban populations appear to have been highly specialised, but only artisans and retainers were allowed to live in the city – peasants and fisher folk being excluded. Figure 7.30: shows a commoner's house made of cane and mud walls (*kincha*) with rock or adobe footings, and where only the smaller rooms are roofed (from Moseley 1975b: 223).

The ratio of peasants and fishers to urban consumers would be interesting to know, especially as Chan Chan was not the only imperial settlement; Azangaro, Viracocha

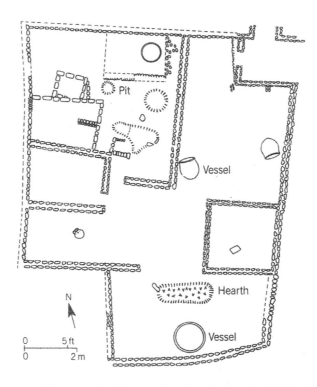

*Figure 7.30: A commoner's house made of cane and mud walls (kincha) with rock or adobe footings.*

Pampa and Pikillacta are others, with Pikillacta, probably a Wari regional capital, amongst the largest. Indeed Pikillacta, in the lower Cuzco Valley, extending over 2 km², is the largest settlement to be constructed in the southern Peruvian highlands before Inca Cuzco, with which it has a historical relationship (McEwan 1990: 104; Glowacki 2002: 267).

The El Niño floods around AD 1300 wrecked the irrigation system in the Moche Valley above Chan Chan. This system had formerly recharged the urban aquifer, tapped by use of walk-down wells. With a falling water table, a 70 km (43.5 mile) trunk canal, La Cumbre, was cut to bring water to the Moche Valley from the Rio Chicama, working from both directions. However, the surveying was deficient and it is most likely that water never flowed along its length. Accordingly, the inland growth of the city, which had required deeper wells, was halted, and "the metropolis was forced to contract toward the sea where wells could reach the depressed water table" (Moseley 1993: 260). With valley development in reverse, the Jequetepeque region was seized by Chimor and the administrative centre of Farfan built to control it (*ibid.*). It possesses a burial platform hitherto reserved for royalty at Chan Chan (Mackey 1987: 129) perhaps suggesting that a member of the royal family was sent to administer this valley.

**Manchan** is the largest known settlement south of the Virú Valley and provincial centre of the Casma Valley, where the Chimú ruled jointly with local lords (Conlee *et al.* 2004: 217). From his fieldwork around Manchan, Moore (1991: 38) has interpreted faunal, raised field construction and other lines of evidence as support for a 'mega-Niño' in the first part of the fourteenth century, perhaps around AD 1330. He observes (*ibid.*: 37) that ENSO events (El Niño /Southern Oscillation) of low but variable intensities occur every six to twenty years, with very strong events occurring once or twice a century. Regarding the impact of the early-fourteenth-century mega event on the Chimú state, Moore (1991: 42) notes "the agricultural responses included partially reconstructing irrigation systems in the Moche Valley … expansion into other coastal valleys … and, I argue, the construction of the Casma valley raised fields. … Other, currently unknown, measures may have been taken by the Chimú state, as well as by coastal farmers independent of state-directed goals". However, as argued by Thomas Pozorski (1987), the 'mega-Niño' which he dates at 1300 BC, produced one clear response. Having effectively wiped out the canal network, rebuilding was a costly failure, so the Chimú state adopted the alternative strategy of further imperial expansion, making this the 'second phase'. The consequence was that "the height of sociopolitical development on the north coast, represented by the fully extended Chimu empire, was reached some 150 years after most of these canal systems fell into disuse" (Pozorski *op.cit.* 119). A couple of decades later, in 1470, it fell to Inca expansion.

## O: Wari and Tiwanaku

Moche was outlived by Wari (Huari) in inland and upland Peru, and, at the southern pole in Bolivia by Tiwanaku around Lake Titicaca (shared between Peru and Bolivia). Tiwanaku originated about AD 200 and began its expansion as a regional power around AD 650 by incorporating the Island of the Sun in the lake (Stanish 2002: 190). It peaked between AD 800–900 and had collapsed by AD 1000 (Conlee et al. 2004:

229). The languages of Aymara and Pukina (the latter now extinct) are native to this area (ibid.). See Figure 7.31.

In the south-central Andes the states of Wari and Tiwanaku dominated the Middle Horizon (AD 600–1000). Tiwanaku was the first polity with a developed four-level settlement hierarchy in the south central Andes, and was the highest centre of an ancient empire anywhere in the world. Tiwanaku was indeed the first and only expansionist state to develop in the south-central Andes. It was not structurally similar to the Inca empire, which had almost total control over all its conquered territory (Stanish 2002: 190) even though it used a variety of political means to achieve this. By contrast Tiwanaku was a state of restricted means, which meant that outside of its core/heartland area of Lake Titicaca, its control was selective and restricted to key economic/political aims. Indeed, part of Tiwanaku's hegemony was probably derived from its role as a pilgrimage centre (Isbell and Vranich 2004: 173) and its existence was in large measure due to its integrative and ideological functions for different ethnic groups (Janusek 2004: 202) accessible owing to its position on the altiplano.

By AD 800 the city of Tiwanaku extended over 6.5 km² and contained a population of 15,000 to 30,000 (Janusek 2004: 183), though Bermann (1997: 95) estimates 30,000–40,000. The Tiwanaku state survived until about AD 1000, about the same as Wari. Janusek (2004: 203–4)[99] has a Late Tiwanaku V period, spanning 1000 to 1150. However, during that period the city was being cannibalised by a much diminished population, such that by 1150 occupation covered an area of, at most three per cent of the previous area according to Janusek's own estimation (2004: 204). Putuni, the elite residential sector had been raised to the ground, so it seems that the Tiwanaku state collapsed much earlier, around the millennium. Janusek (ibid.) mentions the systematic defacement of stone monoliths, and remarks that "defacing them effaced the power of those groups

---

[99]   There is however a major problem with Tiwanaku chronology. The conventional scheme is founded on an inadequate ceramic base, much of which was already in museum collections and inadequately provenanced. Isbell and Burkholder (2002) have subjected the conventional chronology to a devastating critique deriving from their excavations at Iwawi, a residential mound on the south shore of the Taraco Peninsula, only 23 km west of Tiwanaku city. They have two main criticisms: (1) that the chronology is unsupported by sufficient archaeology; (2) that the developmental scheme predicated on the chronology and archaeology substitutes assumptions for demonstrable evidence. Thus the nature of Tiwanaku state and society still remains to be established. They say (ibid.: 210) for example, that the assumption that Iwawi, and sites like Iwawi, were administrative centres is mistaken, and also that "Goldstein's (1993) assertion of an association between Tiwanaku government and sunken courts with megalithic stairways is in error". So far is the chronology adrift that "rectangular sunken courts, often with stairways and artificial mounds, appeared in the Bolivian and Peruvian altiplano by the end of the second millennium BC" (ibid.: 209). As for the chronological stages of Tiwanaku, Isbell and Burkholder (2002: 205) suggest that Tiwanaku II is an "essentially hypothetical [pottery] style that Ponce proposed to fill the stylistic gap between Tiwanaku I and Tiwanaku III, has never been identified and probably does not exist". Similarly, they accuse Ortloff and Kolata (1993) of moving Tiwanaku's 'collapse' back 200 years from the generally accepted AD 1200 date to AD 1000, in order to improve the temporal correlation with climatic changes documented in ice cores from Peruvian glaciers (ibid.: 206). This ice-core chronology and the prolonged twelfth-century drought that supposedly induced Tiwanaku's collapse, have received a strong critique from Calaway (2005). Meanwhile an accumulation of volcanic ash, which is clear at Iwawi and which occurred during the formative period of Tiwanaku urbanism, has been overlooked. Excavations are proceeding and a proper ceramic sequence is being established. As yet, however, no comprehensive replacement chronology has been proposed, so below I continue to use the established scheme with the caveats already mentioned.

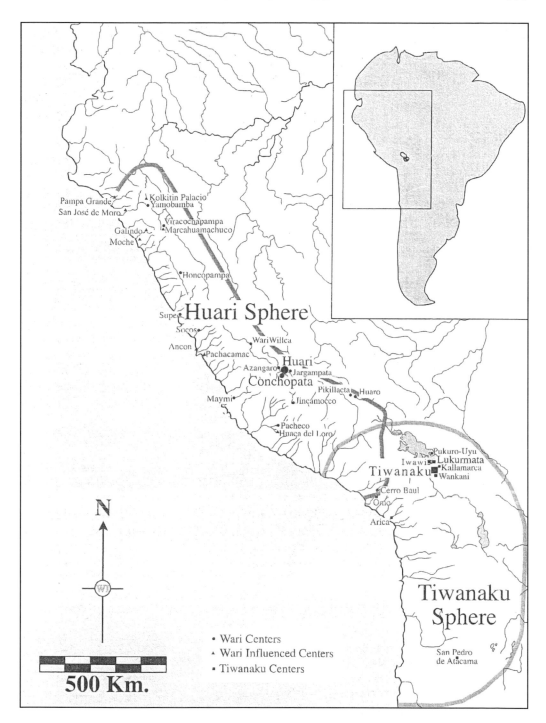

*Figure 7.31: Map of Tiwanaku and Wari domains from Isbell (2004: 5).*

and the ideological foundations of their status and identities. Ritualized hostility was directed at specific elite groups. And perhaps in a more abstract sense, at the Tiwanaku state". This is yet another example of the 'revolt of the plebs' against an Andean state, demonstrating an emic view of the state as serving elites and not society as a whole. If the state's demands kept increasing, or if its demands remained the same in a period of declining productivity, or if demographic growth took place without accompanying increases in production resulting in scarcity, then the state's demands would be seen as an intolerable imposition. This would particularly undermine the public feasting that Janusek (*ibid.*: 207) calls "massive rituals of consumption and their attendant politics". A key part of the state's rationale was that it was upholder of the natural, beneficial order of things, part of which was to be a generous host and redistributor. Now that conditions had changed for the worse, the state's claims would be seen to be empty and its legitimacy gone. Only the kin-group and the locality would then have a legitimate claim on producers.

**Wari (Huari), capital of the Wari empire**, lies at mid-elevation, between 2,700 m and 3100 m above mean sea level, in the central Andean Highlands of Peru. It is situated on the east flank of the deep and narrow Ayacucho Valley (Isbell and Vranich 2004: 175) on the undulating and irregular top of a steep sided ridge. The city of Wari is located near the headwaters of the little Ocopa River, a tributary of the main stream with which the Ocopa merges 3 km above Simpapata (Isbell 1988: 165).

Its urban core covered about 300 ha, formed upon large terraces to compensate for the topography. The Wari archaeological zone, as indicated by sherd and other refuse scatter, is reckoned to extend over an area of 15 km$^2$ (D'Altroy and Schreiber 2004: 272). At its peak in the Middle Horizon, Isbell (1988: 172) estimates that 500 ha were occupied. The city seems to have been divided up into large kinship and/or occupational compounds containing multi-storey buildings. Orthogonal in plan, the enclosures were subdivided into square or rectangular units called 'patio groups', which consisted of an open central patio "surrounded on its perimeter by long, narrow rooms called galleries. Sometimes the galleries were two or three deep, and they were two, or even three, stories tall" (Schreiber 1996: 743). Movement between patio groups was highly restricted. Indeed movement throughout the city is problematic, as Wari possessed few streets, and they were very narrow and short. Wari also lacked an obvious civic centre (Isbell and Vranich 2004: 180).

Movement could either have been along the tops of compound walls or through the compounds themselves, both types of possible movement reducing privacy (Isbell and Vranich 2004: 177–8). Indeed so restrictive was this architecture that Stone-Miller (2002: 139) speaks of "the militaristic patio group architecture that characterizes the middle years of the city". Following Isbell, she remarks (*ibid.*) that "the rise of successful generals and a militaristic aesthetic is not surprising, however, considering how widespread the Wari state became, seemingly by the use of force". Indeed, Smith and Schreiber (2006: 6) characterise Wari as an empire, in contrast to Tiwanaku, though they shared elements of iconography.

Tiwanaku was a centre for display, Wari the opposite. So much so, that Isbell and Vranich (2004: 181) call Tiwanaku "the hemisphere's first theme park, conceptualized and built as a set, within which pilgrims and residents became actors in a cosmological

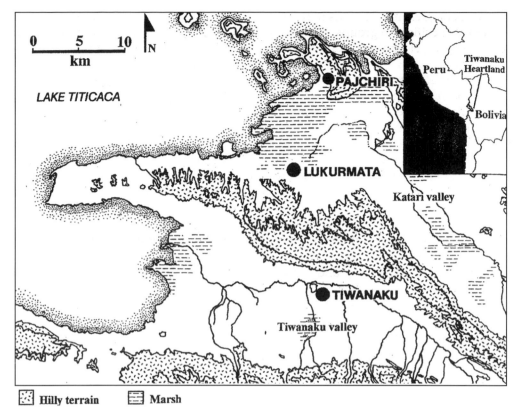

**Hilly terrain**   **Marsh**

*Figure 7.32: Map of the Tiwanaku Heartland at the southern end of Lake Titicaca (from Janusek 1999: 108).*

passion. Viewers experiencing Tiwanaku surely responded to massive pyramids set against an expansive background of residential compounds and sacred horizon markers, particularly the Illimani Mountain". By contrast, "at Wari, temples and palaces were almost indistinguishable from residential buildings. Wari's elites seem to have been content with palaces and ceremonial monuments that were little more than big versions of traditional stone-walled homes".

As in Tiwanaku, each Wari compound housed a minimal *ayllu* and each patio group a micro-*ayllu* or minimal lineage. Population density could have been about 240 persons per hectare. So if the architectural core of the city was evenly divided between public and residential space, the population density of the urban core was around 120 persons per hectare. If, at its peak, one third of Wari's 500 ha was urban core with 120 persons/ha, and two-thirds was periphery with a density of 19.5–42 persons/ha, then the population of Wari city would have ranged between 20,650 and 34,000 (*ibid.*: 173), which seems to have been about average for Andean capital cities. At its maximum extent the Wari empire was estimated by Katharina Schreiber (2001: 85) to be 320,000 km².

Architectural compounds housing kinship groupings may have been an artefact of urbanisation and state intensification, appearing, for instance, in the Tiwanaku

IV period (AD 400–800) at Tiwanaku and Lukurmata and not outliving that period (Berman 1997: 98). However, while the "shifts to larger dwellings, multiple-structure household units and increased storage space are consistent with an increase in residential group size" (*ibid*.: 98–9), this was only possible because of the pre-existing structure of the *ayllu*, which was given a more formal spatial delineation. Co-residence is contingent on economic and political factors. Berman (1997: 107) considers that "growth in household size reflects the increasing significance of the household as a unit of land transmission, typically under conditions of land scarcity". When the more usual dispersed residential pattern resumed, the conceptual structure of the *ayllu* continued. "In the Andes", Hastorf (1990: 144) observes, "people's residences are linked to political units, land, and earth deities, suggesting that as groups became more identifiable and distinct from their neighbours, their political and social structures also became more elaborate."

Wari were highland irrigation specialists, enormously successful in terracing steep sierra slopes (the *quichua* zone), which especially in times of drought and hardship, turned out to be a secure niche. Spread all over the mountains, Moseley (1993: 216) calls their spread 'adaptive dispersal', accounted for by new technology and a more flexible social structure, able to efficiently integrate different ecological zones and cultural elements. It certainly had great influence upon the contemporary Moche and interacted with Tiwanaku. Wari art incorporated coastal Nasca and highland Pucara[100] art from the Early Intermediate Period (Knobloch 2000: 387), and in its turn was very influential "as the major contributor to broad regional stylistic trends in the central highlands and coast" (Cook 2004: 155).

A near neighbour of Wari in the Ayacucho Valley was another urban centre called Conchopata, "a centre of prestige second only to the imperial capital of Wari" (Cook 2004: 155); the locus of large, state-sponsored politically charged feasts. In addition to feasting halls and the large oversized jars associated with feasting, Conchopata also contained vernacular architecture and circular or D-shaped temples (Cook 2004: 164). A site demography "skewed heavily in favour of females, inclusive of elite females" (*ibid*.) suggests the possibility that Conchopata, so close to the capital, was the locus of some kind of queen's court, charged perhaps with key ritual roles, complementary to the presumably male imperial centre at Wari.

Huaro appears to have been the principal Wari settlement in the Cuzco Valley, such that its multi-component role, including administration, persisted into the second

---

[100] "The Pucara culture (250 BC – AD 380) was centred at the eponymous type-site near the village of Pucara, located in the Ayaviri-Pucara valley of the Peruvian altiplano at an elevation of 3950 m asl. The Pucara site's monumental pyramidal platforms indicate an advanced degree of planning and labour organization, and with an area of 6 sq.km, Pukara can also be described as one of the altiplano's first urban sites" (Goldstein 2000: 338). According to Isbell and Knobloch (2008: 319–10) "The Pucara style is best understood as a late and exuberant version of the Yaya-Mama Tradition, that developed and spread through the northern altiplano between approximately 200 BC and AD 200. The first monumental altiplano capital was constructed at Pucara, a site 60 km north of Lake Titicaca. ... Pucara ceremonial architecture in the capital included at least three sunken courts crowning a monumental platform complex, suggesting some kind of confederacy. Each court was surrounded by a D-shaped complex of rooms that may have facilitated large ritual activities by providing storage facilities for costumes, food and other essentials. ...The extent of Pucara political domination is unknown, but it was probably a sizeable polity".

epoch, despite the existence of Pikillacta (Glowacki 2002: 279). The agricultural centre of the Huaro complex was Hatun Cotuyoc, where oblong saucer-shaped basalt stones, averaging 20 x 16 x 6 cm, were found. Similar stones have been found on Inca sites and they are taken to be 'counting stones' (Glowacki 2002: 281). Wari developed an extensive road network linking provincial centres, later taken over and extended by the Incas (D'Altroy and Schreiber 2004: 255) and perhaps those 'counting stones' were employed to compensate for the fact that Andean people never developed a writing system (McEwan *et al.* 2002: 288).

Recent radiocarbon dates from Middle Horizon contexts at Chokepukio in the bend of the Rio Huatanay at the north-eastern end of the Cuzco Valley, and those from the site of Pikillacta across the river, suggest that the Wari occupied Cuzco for perhaps as long as four hundred years from around AD 600 to about AD 1000 (McEwan *et al.* 2002: 292). Their occupation of the Lucre basin at the eastern end of the Valley of Cuzco seems to have been particularly intense and included the large complex at Batan Urqo, only 17 km east of Pikillacta (*ibid.*). Following the decline or collapse of the Wari Empire, it would appear that a state-level polity of some sort survived in the Lucre basin. At the other, western, end of the Cuzco valley there is a different ceramic with different motifs. This is K'illke style, which owes nothing to Wari, but derives from a local Middle Horizon style called Qotakalli. "In very general terms it can be said that Inca ceramics consist of K'illke influenced motifs painted on pottery influenced by Lucre ceramic technology (McEwan *et al.* 2002: 295). In 1997 Arminda Gibaja discovered a number of ritually buried *huacas* (shrines) at Chokepukio. McEwan *et al.* (2002: 297) remark on the possibility that "the act of sealing those *huacas* and including a joint offering of the two styles represents the merging of those two groups" namely the Wari and the K'illke, and from that fusion the Inca polity arose sometime after AD 1200.

## P: Late Horizon (AD 1450–1534)

### Chimú and Inca empires

The Inca absorbed Chimú (Chimor) around 1470 and moved its artisans and its ruler to Cuzco, deliberately causing the death of the city of Chan Chan. And as Moseley (1993: 261) sums the trajectories:

> "From the perspective of multi-linear evolution, the long trajectory of maritime-oasis lowland development culminated in Chan Chan and Chimor; while the Inca carries mountain and highland evolution to fruition. From a geopolitical perspective, the rise of these competitive nations pitted the two great demographic centres of the Andes against one another in a protracted struggle for suzerainty over the Cordillera. Ultimately the greater forces of the southern highlands prevailed over those of the southern lowlands. This brought about the final political synthesis of the Andes that was known as Tahuantinsuyu and the Late Horizon of unity was the last".

The Inca Empire was the latest and largest indigenous empire. With a population estimated at anywhere between 6 and 30 million, the empire of Tawantinsuyu (Tahuantinsuyu as above) incorporated over 100 societies spread over one million km²/386,000 miles² (D'Altroy 1996: 340). Within a century of its foundation, the empire, with an average depth of 320 km, reached from the Ancasmayo River to the Maule River near Santiago, Chile, a distance of 4000 km/2,485 miles. It was held together by 30,000 km/18,640 miles of road with 2000 way stations, constructed and maintained by mit'a (corvée) labour.

The Inca Empire had a command economy. As Charles Stanish (1996: 343) states in his review of Inca economic organisation: "Darrell La Leone has demonstrated that there was no market economy in the Inca state. La Leone notes the lack of true money, the absence of marketplaces, and the lack of merchants. Even in the huge Inca imperial system, the basic exchange structure was organized around 'asymmetrical reciprocity', or complex redistributive relationships woven into a vast and extremely hierarchic political economy". Asymmetrical reciprocity of course means that more was extracted than was returned.

All of this control direct and indirect, military, economic and ideological (especially the cult of the Inca as son of the sun) needed a large administrative apparatus backed up by armed force, all the more necessary when new lands were being conquered and whole populations moved around the empire for the purposes of pacification and economic productivity. Inca storehouses, such as the ones at Huanuco Pampa could hold as much as 36 million litres of grain; to be expected when one considers that the state demanded about two-thirds of all agricultural and manufactured output.

Justificatory myth even said that the Inca lineage, nobles and commoners had separate chthonic origins. Beset by civil war and smallpox, the Inca state was destroyed by the Spaniards after November 1532. In one of the bitter ironies with which History abounds, by imposing their own state institutions upon the Indians and rendering them even more oppressed, the Spaniards forced on them a pseudo-egalitarianism based on exclusion from power, marginality, the struggle for physical and cultural survival, and thus competition for distinction in the community through religious ceremonial and cult functions.

## Q: The Peasant Household

The basis of pre-Inca, Inca and Spanish colonial society, indeed of every agrarian society, was the peasant household. Hagstrum (1999: 271) in her ethnoarchaeology of villagers in the Upper Mantaro, illustrates striking continuities in prehistoric and contemporary pottery and maintains (*ibid.*: 269) that "the household group has continued to be the fundamental unit of agricultural and ceramic production in this region of the Andes" for at least seven centuries. She speaks of "the semi-autonomous household as an ecological adaptation [that] actually represents the basic building block of this Andean phenomenon ... [where] autonomy and self-sufficiency appear to be guiding principles".

Such direct ethnographic continuities make it worthwhile to attempt to model the Political Ecology of the Andean Peasant Household, which I have based largely on the work of Hagstrum (1999) informed by the contributors to Kuznar (2001). See Figure 7.33 above. The left-hand side shows the contribution to family production by its members; the right-hand side shows what happens to the output and what proportions are redistrbuted to the contributors.

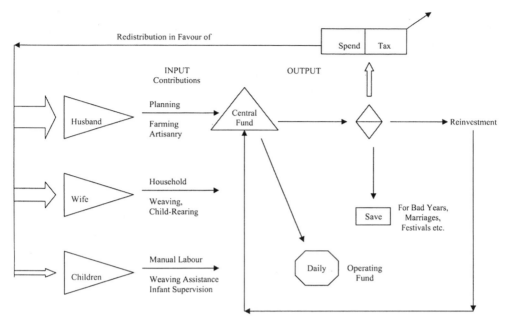

*Figure 7.33: Domestic Economy of the Peasant Household (of Farmer-Potters) in the Peruvian Andes.*

Hagstrum states (*ibid.*: 280) that "the Mantaro farming household is typically a nuclear family" and that "for agriculturalists who are also artisans, a self-sufficient household labour force for farming and artisanry affords flexibility in scheduling and undertaking those two economic activities. To guarantee themselves a team of workers to accomplish their agricultural and ceramic tasks without drawing on outside labour, farmer-potters have bigger families" (*ibid.*: 273); numbering 7.86 at Quicha Grande (farmer-potters), 5.83 at Llacuari Pueblo (farmers). When outside help is required, it is not actually 'outside' help that is called upon. In order not to incur any reciprocal debt so as to retain maximum household autonomy, members of an extended family are called upon. Members help one another without expecting any specific repayment (*ayuda*).

So notions that the Andean state arose to facilitate vertical integration between coasts, valleys and high plains or between adjoining valleys are just dissolved by the evidence. Such exchanges went on perfectly well for lengthy periods prior to the advent of the state and after the collapse of states, for example in the post-Tiwanaku or Late Intermediate Period. Does this mean that prior to the emergence of the state Andean societies were peacefully egalitarian? It does not; hierarchy and armed conflict existed. What did not exist was an institution predicated on negative reciprocity: a perpetual extraction machine. The best that might be said for the existence of such states is that the political conditions they established permitted economic output to rise sufficiently to compensate for the demands in produce and labour it made upon the population, such that families were no worse off. But such a claim, and it is not exactly a proud one, would have to be demonstrated with strong quantitative evidence given the known negatives. It would also have to deal with the repeated uprisings against the various states mentioned, an indigenous response that provides a rather decisive evaluation of their worth.

# CHAPTER 8

## Politics, Culture and Social Structure

**Politics** is the traffic between economic power, physical force and ideology. Politics inheres within and shapes all social activities: domestic, workplace, social gatherings, all organizations (for instance, universities) and of course the state. It also structures Culture, which is diachronic, and Culture both produces and responds to ideologies. I have previously (eg: 1990: 41, 1999: 2) defined *Culture as the cumulative intergenerational transmission of techniques (technology) beliefs and institutions that together result in shared conceptions and perceptions of reality with the standards and expectations that flow therefrom.* This of course is not to deny that ideologies contradict one another, but it does claim that without a preponderance of shared assumptions no Culture is possible. From an *action* or better, *agent's* perspective, Ward Goodenough's (1957: 167) operational definition of culture has never been bettered. He states that "a society's culture consists of whatever it is one has to know or believe in order to operate in a manner acceptable to its members, and to do so in any role that they accept for one of themselves".

So a way to restate what Culture comprises is as follows: **Culture** *is the combination of ways of doing things (institutions and technology) with patterns of belief and also expectations arising from the combination.* As the various social classes and statuses, including gender statuses, have different engagements with institutions, production, consumption and belief, cultures are rarely uniform or smoothly integrated. Rather, they are contradictory and unstable, especially when faced with external pressures, natural, technological or political (Maisels 1991). Cumulation in culture is, then, not simply additive but vectoral. If individual human behaviour is represented as a series of wiggly lines causing 'interference' amplitudes around various norms, then the resulting variation in the disturbances shifts aspects of the culture in a certain direction. An example from British culture in the last few generations is the present acceptability of cohabiting non-married couples, their production of children and also the acceptability of single-parent families. In this case an initial ideological opening in the 1960's licensed cohabitation in subsequent decades. Those practices latterly received administrative and legal endorsement.

**Ideology** has three aspects: (1) that of the spinners of ideology, the mythmakers, transmitters such as writers, artists, lawyers, preachers etc.; (2) its adoption by followers and other advocates; and (3) its acceptance by some of the population at large, which is its *raison d'etre*. But 'acceptance' itself has to be unpacked, resulting in fives modes: (a) where it is, or appears to represent the material interests of the acceptor (AK) (b) where it is, or appears to be in AK's non-material interests [e.g. for status] (c) where

AK's family and peers believe it, so social harmony requires belief (d) where it is expedient to believe for occupational/career reasons (e) where it is imposed by the state. Thus (c), (d) and (e) often go together.

Ideology is the representation of the real interests of those for whom the ideology is spun (e.g. nationalist politicians, fundamentalist sects, business lobbyists). However, the point is to make the public believe it and to induce the decision-makers to act upon it. This is achieved by two means: (1) universalisation, where the aims of the interest group are made out to be the interests of society as a whole; (2) naturalization, essentially an earlier version of universalisation, whereby a particular social arrangement (such as divine kingship) is made out to be indispensable for the successful reproduction of society in Nature.

So a summary definition of Ideology would be: *the representation of individual and sectional interests as general or collective interests.* This is accomplished by rhetorically and ritually stepping out of the practical realities of life; 'going up a level' to the intangible or metaphysical where the supposed fundamental forces or spiritual powers reside; making some changes or accommodation there, then stepping down to the earthly or mundane level having changed social conditions for the better through that higher level intervention.

Such devices are possible because most people's heads are full of a confusing mixture of impressions about daily and current events, hearsay, disconnected fact-fragments, received, religious or folk wisdom, bits of half-remembered school learning etc. What is in everyone's head is a bit different, because even within the same family, no two biographies and thus no two sets of experiences are identical. Differences are of course all the more marked between the sexes, generations and occupations and most marked when social stratification exists. Therefore, when what seems like a coherent scheme is advanced that seems to 'make sense' of the world for a part of the population, it will be accepted by that part. How does this work psychologically?

*The ideologists tell you what to believe and you find your own reasons for believing it, based on your own background and present situation,* as indicated by modes (a) to (e) above. The internalization/justification process is most compelling, of course, when the ideology has been established for generations and each generation is socialized to it. It is implanted during the most impressionable and formative younger years, and as an adult, even were one to perceive contradictions in it, no other coherent explanatory scheme may be available to you. Even where it is, early imprinting establishes patterns of thought, that, being deeply imbedded or structuring, one can be unable to get free of, for at an unconscious level it conditions all thought processes (cf: Boyer 2001). Conditioned from one's earliest days, it may be almost impossible to 'think out of the box', because a singular frame of reference has formed a mind-set that refuses the acceptance of any other frames of reference. This will apply especially when one's *biographic capital* (time, effort, sacrifices, emotions and life-goals) have been invested in it. Only trauma changes minds thus fixed.

**Ideologues** are salesmen. They figure out what they want you to believe, then find culturally acceptable themes with which to sell their product just as those in the advertising industry do. For instance, lawyers have developed **legalist ideology,** a notion with which English-speaking cultures have been indoctrinated, namely that lawyers should regulate everything and everyone, and that there can be 'rights' independent of obligations. To spin this very successful ideology they have deployed the rhetorical themes of 'fairness', 'justice' (by which they mean the legal *process* itself, not *outcomes* that are just), 'due process' and 'civilized behaviour' (cf: Fuller 1969: 106–118). The omnipresence of lawyers and litigation is of course inimical to those professed 'principles' as proven by the ever-rising crime rates in Britain and the U.S. This is unsurprising as lawyers and judges never define justice as such; a signal absence that is not accidental but symptomatic: *mauvaise confiance, mauvaise conscience* (bad faith, bad conscience). But not L.L. Fuller (1969: 176), who, with his characteristic perceptiveness and honesty, states that "As lawyers we have a natural inclination to 'judicialize' every function of government. Adjudication is a process with which we are familiar and which enables us to show to advantage our special talents".

## Leadership and the ideology of fame or celebrity

All leaders at all times need to be celebrities to hold power (e.g. Napoleon) or win elections (Churchill as a very old man in the 1950s). The extreme example of this is Soviet-style 'cult of personality', which all dictatorships promote. Of course not all celebrities aspire to political leadership. However, Al Gore, though he was Vice President, failed to make himself a celebrity and so failed to become U.S. President, while Clinton the celebrity could survive several own-goals plus all his enemies could throw at him.

One doesn't need charisma to become a celebrity. A celebrity is just someone who gets noticed and has been able to institutionalize attention. In our times, with its all-embracing entertainment culture, it so happens that most celebrities come from and are manufactured by the various fields of entertainment: film, television, sport and the arts. Only a few minor celebrities derive from the world of science. Einstein is the exception, but then he brought about a scientific revolution in the age of mass media.

Anyone can be some kind of celebrity. We all know of those who are famous for being famous, that is, for being in tabloid newspapers and pulp magazines. All it needs is continuous self-promotion through the media. Of course, you have to be driven to want this, and that is a matter of early character formation. If you connect yourself with a political movement they will foster your self-promotion. Do this well enough and obsessively enough and you can end up leading the movement. This will get you society-wide attention, which can be traded in for other celebrity roles even if you do not achieve supreme power.

Chiefdoms cannot become states until the elite have generated a suitably wide and deep universalistic scheme, central to which is the sacralized position of the ruler as a vehicle for bestowing divine benefits on society. We see this happening in Egypt toward the end of the fourth millennium, when a state-church is formed with the king as the pivot of state and church, the one serving the other in a process of mutual reinforcement. This is what made such a large territorial state possible (along with the Nile as a highway) securing and secured by military and economic power. Wilkinson (2000: 23) sums this up most succinctly when discussing the interlocking changes in ideology, art and burial practices in the time of Narmer, who presided over the crucial transition in the concept of the ruler. "The spectacular achievements of pharaonic Egypt would have been impossible, even unimaginable", he writes, "without the driving force of ideology; and that ideology centred on the role of the king. The creation and promulgation of the institution of kingship [was] a concept so powerful that it survived for three thousand years [and] must rank as the supreme accomplishment of Egypt's early rulers".

It is clear that ideology is no epiphenomenon, but a history-forming force. People may be driven by military and economic power, but they are led by ideology. Religion or cult is a mental representation of forces or powers. Those powers can be translated into political power via the political triangle, the arena of contest-exchange framed at the vertices by ideology, economics or physical force (Maisels 1984, 1990). The area enclosed is the political terrain where struggles for dominance are fought out by those able to deploy one or several of those resources. The state is dominant in the political arena because it possesses more of each of the three key resources and has built interlocking and mutually sustaining institutions on that basis.

The failed states of Europe, Latin America, Africa and Asia, and there are many, have failed in precisely this regard. And they have failed because sectional interests control more of the three key resources than does the state, which itself is violently and destructively fought over and dominated by those sectional interests: class, ethnic, religious etc. Control of the state is then used for personal enrichment, sectional aggrandisement and the destruction of opposition, so no stable 'public interest' and public commitment can emerge. *But only a constant commitment to the public good justifies the existence of a state.*

Every single area of social life is a political arena and at every level the three resource groups mentioned are the ones being exchanged in contest, in order that individuals obtain their own best advantage (which includes that of their offspring). If that can be instituted permanently and society-wide by a group, then social classes have come into being. As stated in Chapter 3, *social classes consist of those with a shared position in the relations of production.* Those comprise the Forms of Productive Cooperation (how work is organized) and the Forms of Ownership and Control, which together animate the Forces of Production: the instruments (tools, machines), the labour power and the objects worked upon, as also stated there.

To enter the political game as a player and not an object, once must come to it with one's own resources. Those however are various: not just economic resources but bodily strength, beauty or charisma, intelligence, 'noble birth', knowledge or cunning, ideological and rhetorical skills, the loyalty of a following, kinship or locality based, daring or ruthlessness; most likely some combination of those. The point is that one brings what one has to get what one wants. And there is no free-run or free lunch. Always there are rival bidders and blockers (even, or especially, within a royal family) for everyone is out to maximize benefits to themselves.

The political field has of course many levels extending from the inter-state level to that of individual psychology. It inheres in all interpersonal relationships: sexual, intra-familial, intra-peer group and so on, wherever people interact, that is, in all and every aspect of social life. Indeed R.D. Laing has pointed out (*pers. comm.*) that contest-exchange is ultimately a struggle going on within each individual, between wants and needs, means and ends, hopes and fears, available resources and wished-for goals, instrumental actions versus existential satisfactions. So one can say that, once ideological cloaks are stripped away, political problems are psychological problems (emotional plus cognitive).[101]

Social exchanges will be as unequal and forced as possible and forcing-in-permanence is what the state does. The triangle of figure 1.1 thus helps to explain the Indus anomaly: ultimate control of the means of production, of protection and destruction, is what characterizes the state. However, each of the states we looked at had different methods for, and extent of, control over those crucial resource areas. This is of course a consequence of different ecologies and technologies and thus different trajectories into state formation from the Neolithic village. If however, different sections of the population, particularly a geographically widespread population with different ethnic origins, has enough in common to form a single society united through the division of labour (organic solidarity or complementariness) – then there will be no structural cleavage into rulers and ruled, into producers and unproductive consumers, but rather an *oikumene* or commonwealth will exist. There will be no overarching vertical stratification, but horizontal specialization. Those are a lot of 'ifs', and that is why the Indus experience is unique. It is also why many scholars are sceptical of Indus statelessness, even though they cannot point to the usual attributes of state presence.

Some commentators have found the terms *oikumene* or *commonwealth* insufficiently explanatory, so in Chapter 3 I attempted to make the reference more transparent by calling Harappan society 'a heterarchy', stating that:

> "In some instances a *heterarchy* may emerge to integrate a society through a series of overlapping and interacting competencies in different activities in adjacent geographical areas. In contrast to vertical integration by *hierarchy* (top down), a heterarchy is a mode of horizontal integration between different but complementary places and organisations. Hierarchies can exist within a heterarchy, each in its own sphere, but no hierarchy there is so dominant as to be able to subject the whole society. The outstanding instance is Indus civilization, where there is no dominant centre or class of rulers. This does not mean that there are no differences of wealth or standing. There surely were a whole set of gradations in wealth and standing, but not the usual dichotomy between a 'mass' of producers and a dominant elite who ran society in their own interests as consumers of the social surplus."

This is a consequence of the three fundamental sources of social power – economic, physical force and ideology – being held by and within separate social groups and their elites, who did not fuse to form, nor did they become subordinated to, a ruling centre and apparatus.

---

[101] Emotions can be primary or secondary. Primary ones are instinctive, secondary emotions are those generated by self-consciousness and include: shame, pride, regret and guilt.

# Chapter 9

## How do states form?

Despite all the talk and identification of elites and stratification, it should not be thought that the process of state formation is automatic; *agents* cause states to form when the conditions are right. How do they do it?

---

- Agricultural communities form
- They enjoy a period of equality
- They begin to differentiate internally as
- Some households/lineages are more successful than others for contingent reasons. They 'feast' the community, launch projects and build support, including amongst neighbouring communities
- They seize the opportunity to promote themselves by emphasizing/capturing key aspects of the common religion which they manipulate and modify
- They use their religious eminence/privileges to gain economic privileges as 'rights', entitling themselves to the labours of others
- Stratification has arrived
- The household/lineage/clan gains adherents enabling it to deploy force ('fists') to reinforce its position internally and to extend hegemony externally by raids
- It secures tribute some of which is shared with followers
- Success breeds success and more adherents are gained
- Ideological elaboration accompanies this and with it further social elevation
- An elite has formed exchanging wives only with other elites
- A charismatic arises who can catalyse the religious/ideological dimensions with the economic and violence, making him supreme within the elite and utterly dominant over the rest of the population
- Dynastic succession and functional elaboration mean that
- The state has formed.

---

*Figure 9.1: The State Formation Process.*

Weber (1947: 328–9) identified three forms of political authority: traditional, legal-rational and charismatic. He saw charisma as the personal magnetism of aspiring leaders, especially populist ones, such as Napoleon, Gandhi, Nasser and Hitler, giving them the means to build personal power bases by developing a personal following of devotees. "In the case of charismatic authority, it is the charismatically qualified leader as such who is obeyed by virtue of personal trust in him and his revelation, his heroism or his exemplary qualities…" Traditional authority is held by those we now refer to as having 'ascribed' status, such as kings in dynastic succession. For legal-bureaucratic authority Weber (*ibid*.: 330) has in mind positions such as presidents and prime ministers elected or appointed according to law, as well as those in positions of some power in the bureaucracy, always a more important feature of German societies than Anglo-American. Accordingly I use the term 'organizational' authority for Weber's legal-bureaucratic, since it makes clear the sort of authority possessed by the CEO of a corporation as well as in the ranks of the military, where recruits are told that it is the rank in the organization that is being saluted and not the person holding it. Weber (*ibid*.: 328) does say rational-legal authority belongs to the office, while traditional authority belongs to the person sanctioned by tradition. Thus, he says, "the modern army is essentially a bureaucratic organization administered by that peculiar type of military functionary, the 'officer' (*ibid*.: 335).

Crucially, Weber sees an evolutionary development from charismatic through the 'routinization of charisma' in traditional authority to the legal-bureaucratic ('organizational') that he thought characterised nineteenth- and twentieth-century Europe and North America. He thought this was a logical sequence, but I think we can see it also in the archaeological data contained in this volume, with the exception of Sumer, where the early city-states had organizational leadership from the temple. Kingship came later, under northern impact. Thus Gilgamesh, 'great king' of Uruk in the Early Dynastic period was obviously a charismatic of legendary status. His burning ambition was to throw off the overlordship of Kish, and his "heroism or exemplary character" (Weber) was strong enough to mobilise those of fighting age to do so. However, as with other charismatic leaders, exemplary here does not mean 'moral' in our ethical sense, as the Gilgamesh narratives make plain.

It has been stressed that states form differently and have differing characters. Thus in the formation of city-states the element of force is least, and here the notion of mutual advantage and social contract has some substance (Postgate 2003: 23; Small 1997: 110–111). Indeed, Berent (1998: 333) has gone so far as to argue that the Greek *polis* should be described as a 'stateless society'. But this is a step too far; for one thing there were slaves in *polis* societies. By contrast, states that arise through the domination of clans and the consolidation of chiefdoms rely on a high level of force, even terror (Walter 1969). City-states justified themselves as representing a community of economic interest and in terms of organizing security; or better, as managing both in a broadly consensual way (Charlton and Nichols 1997a: 10). By contrast, territorial states justified themselves as interceding between the human realm and the cosmic and human forces that jeopardised life. As Kolata (1997: 253) so succinctly put it: "Moral, political and military authority in the Andean capital flowed from the ruling lineages and their coterie of kin, fictive kin, retainers and camp followers. The capitals, perhaps to a greater degree than urban centres in other parts of the preindustrial world, were autocratic, built for and dominated by a native aristocracy. In this sense, Andean capitals were truly patrician cities – places for symbolically concentrating the political and religious authority of the elites".

Once in power, elites do what they have to do to stay there. If this involves 'buffering' or infrastructure development, then they might do this if they are aware of where their long-term interests lie. But fundamentally the state did not arise for such functional purposes, and that is why ancient states had such a poor rate of technological and for that matter, cultural, development. As I have previously shown (Maisels 1990: 36–9; 302–309) ancient states upon formation quickly reached a technological and cultural plateau, where they remained until their collapse. Developments come mostly in spurts at formation and upon dissolution, because once the relations of production are established, it is rarely in the interests of the power-holders that they be substantially modified, as is usually required to incorporate significantly new technology. Further, as technical advances generally derive from those actually doing the work, if, by their subordination they are deprived of initiative and rewards deriving from innovation, they will not produce many. Also, producers who exist on the cusp of adequacy or scarcity/famine will be highly risk-averse and will stick to what they know works.

As Egypt was basically stable during its first three thousand years, it is not surprising that "it is a striking feature of native Egyptian culture at all periods that it is not technically innovative" (Baines and Malek 1980: 140). This despite the fact that connections between Nile and Levant were already well established in the Badarian period (Wilkinson 1999: 161). But it is not just about stability; as already mentioned, dependency is also a key factor. Mesopotamia contained the most innovative early complex society. But even in the largest institutions, namely palaces and temples with their continuously high demand for foodstuffs, craft products and trade goods, the grinding of flour was always done by hand in the Neolithic manner. Textile weaving, which produced the key export commodity, was also done by hand, again in a manner that had scarcely improved since the Neolithic. This despite the fact that in the late third millennium, in excess of 13,000 weavers worked in the city of Ur alone! The huge numbers were required because cloth and garment production was excruciatingly slow, indicating very low productivity. Neither water nor wind power was employed, and thus the mill, the 'mother of machines' was absent.[102] This was because both grinding and weaving (but not fulling) was undertaken by women, who could be made to overcome technical deficiencies with long hard labour. By contrast irrigation works and ploughing/sowing techniques reached standards in the third millennium BC not again achieved until late in the second millennium AD, as grain was the pillar of Mesopotamian society.

Thus the state did not arise for functional reasons; rulers' ministrations were less tangible and effective than that. For example, in no ancient (and few modern!) societies could the state guarantee the population something as basic as clean drinking water (hence the importance of beer in ancient Mesopotamia, Egypt and England). Instead, state elites justified themselves by advertising their roles as bridges between heaven and earth, between ancestors and the living, or as protectors of the people against outside attack and the upholders of law and order. Only notionally did they lighten the burdens of the vast majority. In good times taxation was a burden upon the peasantry, often removing their buffers against privation and starvation (Gilman 1995: 238). In bad times dynastic struggles and self-aggrandizement through warfare and monument-building impaired and destroyed countless lives, while adding further to producers' burdens

---

[102]   By contrast in the area of England covered by the Domesday Book of 1086 AD, basically the Midlands, East Anglia and the Southern Counties (34 counties in all), an astonishing 5,624 water mills were recorded (Gimpel 1988: 12). As soon as paper reached Europe in the 13th century, it was being produced in mills (*ibid.*). Almost as important as the application of inanimate power to production was the model of, and skills involved in the building of mills, with their gears, cams etc.

and inhibiting infrastructural and cultural development. As Wilkinson (1999: 114) says of ancient Egypt:

> "In a way, economic management was simply a means to an end. The end was the ability to mount impressive projects to glorify the king and maintain the status of those around him".

Thus all functional arguments are fundamentally misconceived. States arise when power is concentrated by, and in the interests of, a small group, not 'society as a whole' or the majority's 'systemic requirements'. And if the old power-holders lose their grip, new groups come along who impose their will by force and rule in their own selfish interests. Indeed in evolutionary terms, the *state is an institution favouring power-holders' reproductive success.*

Generations of anthropologists and archaeologists have been seeking functional, that is, adaptive explanations for the advent of the state. Cohen's suggestion (1981: 114) is "that a major common feature of centralized governments and the role for which they were primarily 'selected' is that of buffering human populations against ecological disasters – replacing natural buffers lost when saturation of usable space necessitated sedentism". In a recent major work already cited, Yoffee (2005: 16) argues that "in complex societies a central authority develops in order to bring relatively autonomous subsystems within the contours of a larger institutional system". I contend, however, that the explanation for the advent of the state resides not in a collective social response to the natural environment or to advancing social complexity, but is to be found in human nature itself. Human response is never truly collective, but comes down to groups and individuals taking initiatives, with the rest being entrained (Joyce 1997; Brothwell 2005: 955).

Accordingly, where two conditions are met: (1) the existence of a dense and extensive agricultural population, and (2) the ability of an elite to extend its ideological control to include physical and economic force; then the state will certainly arise.[103] That is why, to employ Henry Wright's phraseology (2006: 305), political experiments in state formation have been made from prehistory to the present, independently and derivatively in all parts of the world. This is a consequence of the human desire to get something for nothing, which can only be achieved by exploiting others. In Durkheimian terms this is negative reciprocity, and in Darwinian terms it is genotypic/phenotypic advantage. However it is termed, it is institutionalized by class stratification and state domination.

## Summation: human nature as primate behaviour

States did not emerge because they were 'adaptive', in the sense of answering the needs of society as a whole as it became more complex. States became part of the problem, not the solution. The permissive conditions of their rise were the subsistence surpluses generated in the wake of the Neolithic Revolution; surpluses that were storable and disposable. That has long been agreed by all scholars. What is only now becoming clear and is not yet agreed by all scholars (or perhaps even a majority) is that the advent of

---

[103] My own contrary example, namely Indus Civilization where no state emerged, indicates that the second criterion was not met: elites were not able to extend their ideological power to incorporate physical and economic force.

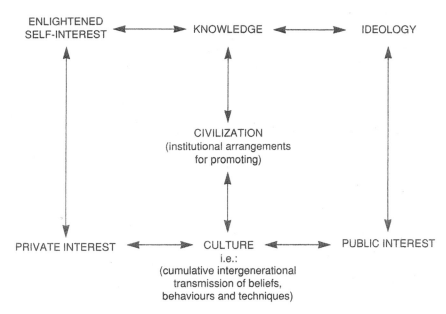

*Figure 9.2: Civilization in Popular Understanding (from Maisels 1993: 205).*

the state is due to the selfish human desire to privilege oneself (Trigger 2003a: 41), the motivation for this springing from our genetic programme which functions to promote the success of the phenotype (the individual carrying the genome) in order to succeed in displacing other genotypes (gene packages).

We are all selfish phenotypes, our genes make us so. It is the basic survival, reproduction and evolutionary mechanism that cannot be denied.[104] Recognising this, the good society is one which obliges us to pursue *enlightened* self-interest (Trigger 2003a: 42). This involves self-discipline, delayed gratification, regard for others and treating them as you would wish to be treated. A state which does not promote those norms is illegitimate. A legitimate state promotes a sense of honour in its citizens. This is the self-worth that comes from taking responsibility for one's actions and for one's obligations to others. Excuses are demeaning and denial is dangerous, personally, socially and historically. Most people know this, and expect a 'civilized' state to function by promoting the public good and restricting self-interest, especially of the rulers and the rest of the elite, which in advanced economies includes the top managers of all businesses (see Figure 9.2 (from Maisels 1993: 205)).

The proof is in the practice. There is never a shortage of contestants for the top jobs, despite the alleged 'pressures and burdens of office'; the material and psychological rewards are much too great. People will do anything to get power and to keep it; the

---

[104] Some will try to deny this fact on the basis that some people will undertake self-sacrifice because of 'principle' or 'conscience'. Where the sacrifice is genuine, the maintenance of personal integrity and the satisfaction to be gained from 'doing the right thing' – one with the implicit or explicit approbation of others – produces a 'self-reward' that boosts self-worth and self-esteem, and so is a major benefit to the sacrificer, potentially outweighing the cost.

problem lies in wresting power from them. States were and are part of the feedback processes that constitute social evolution, bought, of course, at enormous cost to people and the environment (Elvin 1993, 1998, 2002; Shapiro 2001). Brothwell (2005: 955) rightly observes that the twentieth century saw the deaths of 100 million people from warfare alone, and this was undertaken by states. Currently, failed states are generating huge amounts of suffering, disease and death, so states have been and remain one of mankind's greatest problems. They cannot be un-invented but they must be made to serve the common good and only truly democratic states can do that. Democracy is not without its problems, but in democratic states the good outweighs the bad and humanistic principles are fostered, while in tyrannies characterised by one-party-states and absolutist ideologies, the bad massively outweighs any good they can do.

> "Finally, we have to remember that democracy, in itself, is government by discussion. It is government 'by the word'; and all things are thrown for settlement into an arena in which 'one shrewd thought devours another'" (Barker 1960: 4).

By contrast, Samuel Dill (1958: 281) in his unsurpassed work on the last centuries of the Roman Empire, most eloquently summarized what human nature can do even in those rare cases when a potentate has the best of intentions:

> "The system of bureaucratic despotism, elaborated finally by Diocletian (AD 284–305) and Constantine (AD 306–337), produced a tragedy in the truest sense, such as history has seldom exhibited; in which, by an inexorable fate, the claims of fancied omnipotence ended in a humiliating paralysis of administration; in which determined effort to remedy social evils only aggravated them until they became unendurable; in which the best intentions of the central power were, generation after generation, mocked and defeated alike by irresistible laws of human nature, and by hopeless perfidy and corruption in the servants of government".

This work has posed four key questions of social analysis:

1) What component of human behaviour is organic, that is, is a function of biology
2) Since that component is not zero, what proportion is a result of social factors
3) In dealing with social factors, what part does geography play and what part the historical trajectory (= Culture/Civilization)
4) To what extent are societies unique, each possessed of a singular set of characteristics.

And the conclusion reached: If societies are indeed comparable in regard to their evolved structures and institutions, then it must be a consequence of underlying behavioural characteristics generated by human nature itself. It is human nature to privilege oneself at the expense of others. This leads to hierarchy and, if the sequence given in Figure 9.1 is followed to finality, the state.

# Appendix A

## *The Socio-Political Contract and the Lessons of History*

While regimes can be changed, the state cannot be abolished and so must be made to serve a population's needs. However, most states in the world are still only serving the needs of the rulers. The chronic incapacity of Third World states' response to major natural disasters tragically demonstrates the fact. The unwillingness of the Burmese military rulers to respond to the vast destruction wrought by Cyclone Nargis (2008), the second most powerful in history, was just obscene.

All too often power-holders' power is self-serving to the extent that they like dealing with other elites and other governments and their agencies but hate dealing with their own populations and their needs, whom they regard as chattel to be exploited. This of course is disguised by nationalist, populist, anti-imperialist and other collectivist rhetoric. Favoured justifications for failure are that the country's poverty and poor infrastructure are responsible for the lack of basic disaster preparation and response. From states that cannot even provide clean water for their populations, this is scarcely surprising. Their priorities are elsewhere and this is where the money goes.

This is not accidental. Only the citizens of a democracy can enter into a political contract in which they expect and require some worthwhile response to their own interests. "Democracy itself is a process, and its success requires long-standing habits and traditions of civic engagement, not merely the miraculous appearance of good constitutions or enlightened legal codes" (Wrangham and Peterson 1996: 245). Or, for that matter, an unceasing supply of 'Aid'.

The alternative is some mode of authoritarian imposition of policies which may or may not be 'in the best interests' of society as a whole. Usually people are the best judges of their own best interests. Usually they wish to express those and get some persons to carry them forward, allowing the rest of the population to get on with their lives in the expectation of an improvement in its quality. From this certain propositions follow:

1. Modern democratic government is a contract between rulers and ruled. Professional politicians undertake the efficient management of economy and society in exchange for certain perquisites: a career, good income, foreign travel, a lot of free 'hospitality' and, when out of office or out of active politics, good pensions with the chance to earn large sums in business, media or education.
2. What holds politicians to this bargain are elections. However balloting by itself is no guarantee of public sovereignty. A dictatorship can get itself 'elected' and 're-elected'. Hitler was elected and more recently Mugabe, when he failed to get

re-elected despite using his usual combination of violence, racism and bribery, just stayed in power with the support of the army and police.

3.  In continental Europe, notably in France and Italy, an elite and fairly closed political class simply play musical chairs through elections, with party leaders running through a series of top jobs such as Mayor, Prime Minister, then President, eventually ending up as European Commissioner or lodged somewhere else in the state or para-state apparatus or on the Boards of companies, especially those which are state-owned.

4.  Elections are but part of the process of being able to sanction those in power, the key sanction being the ability to turn them out of power, and also to apply the criminal law to them. In Italy until recently this was impossible: the ballot, using proportional representation, simply legitimized the holding of executive power by one part of the political class who shared their prerogatives with the rest of the political class. This effectively made Italy a one-party-state, despite that fact that the politicians were grouped into a range of parties from Communist to Fascist, through all shades of social democracy, liberalism and conservatism. Also, the criminal law scarcely applies in Italy, and in courts defendants and witnesses are allowed to lie (they do not have to swear to tell the truth).

5.  Free media are essential, along with freedom of speech, assembly, movement and political party formation. But they are by no means sufficient. There are additional requirements for the functioning of a genuine democracy, which, to reiterate, is one where popular sovereignty sanctions the political class thereby holding them to account:

    a)  The administrative and legal apparatus of the state must be detached from the political struggle and political instruction. Courts must be autonomous and continuous in their functioning, which of course does not mean that judges and prosecutors should not be elected; rather the reverse. The state apparatus in general must not be the instrument of any political party or ethnic group. Its members must therefore be recruited by merit from the whole of society, reflecting society's diversity. Recruitment must be by open competitive examination to ensure both competence and detachment. 'Appointments', 'recommendations' and quotas allow political parties and ethnic groupings to stuff the lower echelons with their people and to 'seed' the higher. This produces intolerable partisanship and brings the apparatus into contempt; which it then deserves. Patronage – the appointment of individuals to para- or quasi-governmental bodies because of their political acceptability – is likewise unacceptable.

    b)  Strong civilian control of military and police forces regarding aims, ethos, methods and finances, is vital to a democracy. On the other hand open/merit recruitment to the military and to the police prevents those services being staffed by a single class or stuffed with political appointees. It also reduces the tendency for the police and military to isolate themselves from the rest of society, looking only to their own sectional interests and ignoring the wishes and needs of the society which they supposedly serve.

    c)  The role of the armed forces in a democracy is to prevent subjugation of one people by another. This threat can also be an internal one, obtaining where certain politicians wish to rig things such that they will remain permanently in power by abusing elections to abolish them, or where they wish to seize key areas of social activity for themselves and those they represent. This breaches the 'democratic contract' and so justifies the President and/or armed forces taking control until a more normal political regime returns.

d) A normal political regime is one in which different interests are represented and negotiated, not suppressed. The central forum for representation and negotiation is of course parliament, and it is accordingly crucial that the government is collectively and individually answerable to parliament as a body.

e) A parliament that can be prorogued for lengthy periods and convened to 'approve' executive measures is not a parliament. *A real democratic parliament is the ultimate locus of legitimate power.* It has sovereignty and will not cede any of it. Supreme power to make and unmake all laws and treaties has to reside in it, and not with a monarch, president, commission, armed forces or the legal or religious establishment, or some combination of those.

f) Universal suffrage in the modern sense began with the Prussian Reichstag in 1867. However, the government was appointed by the king and so was not answerable to parliament. Long before the establishment of the Reichstag, Prussia and the other German states were *Rechtsstaats*; states governed by laws and constitutions. Indeed, modern jurisprudence (legal theory) originates in nineteenth century Germany with so many lawyers in high office. However the cult of legality (*legalism*) neither promoted democracy nor secured it against anti-democratic forces.[105] Hitler's indulgent treatment by the legal apparatus after his failed *putsch* in 1923 is signal. Legalist ideology also restrained Socialists and Jews from assassinating Hitler, although his aims and intentions were clear from 1923, the time of the Munich *putsch*. While 'imprisoned' after its failure he wrote, or rather dictated *Mein Kampf*, which was published in 1925. After this no one could say they didn't know. However Jews and liberals were convinced that the *Rechtsstaat* – laws, courts, police and the *Beamtenstaat*, the all-enveloping civil service – would protect them (Hilberg 1985). Of such illusions are tragedies made. It was only a matter of months after 30 January 1933, when Hitler became Chancellor, that the *Rechtsstaat* became a *Machtstaat*.

g) An avoidable tragedy was the genocide perpetrated at Srebrenice in Bosnia in July 1995, which was supposedly a United Nations safe haven guarded by Dutch 'peacekeepers', a role in which they prided themselves. Like the Belgians in Rwanda the previous year, when asked why they had stood aside, allowing the massacre to take place over several days, they pathetically claimed that 'they did not want to exceed their 'legal' mandate'! Of course this is just an excuse for cowardice, but it demonstrates one of the uses of legalism as ideology. Legalism is at root the ideology of lawyers, justifying their control of all aspects of society. They do this by deliberately conflating *political rights* – notably to vote and to have this vote determine the rise and fall of governments – with *processual or juridical rights*, which are not rights at all, but procedures (cf: Fuller 1969: 96–7) designed to protect the status and prerogatives of the legal profession. Under those procedural 'rights', an accused need not answer for himself to his peers (the jury) and a judge can dismiss evidence *not* because it is

---

[105] In a blast against wilful naivety, Hui (2005: 181) writes: "Scholars often presume that a body of impersonal law provides a bulwark against arbitrary rule. However, in the absence of constitutional democracy, feudal customs were in fact better than positive laws at checking against domination in both early modern Europe and ancient China. Feudal customs carried the weight of tradition and could not be arbitrarily changed by kings and princes. Positive laws, by contrast, were based on the will of the sovereign. When the king could re-write the law according to his wishes, there could only be rule *by* law (with ruler above the law), not the rule *of* law (with rulers subject to the law)."

weak or false but because of the way it was obtained, and can even collapse a case on those, or other, bases at his or her own discretion. In England judges can even direct juries as to their findings!

h) Legalism is not about, and does not promote but rather undermines, law and order in a community. Legalism is a secular replacement for the Pre-Reformation church's claim of its 'right' to control all aspects of life and thought (Moynahan 2002). A decent society is not a product of the proliferation of law and lawyers, but is the product of social cohesion, self-discipline, moral pressure and a sense of honour amongst the citizens.

i) A fateful meeting of Nazi party and state officials took place in a grand villa on the shore of Berlin's Lake Wannsee, on 20 January, 1942. It decided on the 'final solution' (by transportation and gassing) of the so-called 'Jewish problem'. A large proportion of those present were lawyers (Roseman 2002: 96). In effect, the Wannsee meeting was a meeting of lawyers and SS to ensure that genocide was legal as well as efficient! Legality is no guarantee of morality, indeed, it is often the opposite, and neither is the *Bildung* (education) or *Kultur* (culture) in which the German middle-classes placed so much faith. Even after the War such legalism persisted, as Fuller (1969: 40) explains: "Some of the later decisions [of German courts] rested the nullity of judgements rendered by the courts under Hitler not on the ground that the statutes applied were void, but on the ground that the Nazi judges misinterpreted the statutes of their own government". To such monstrous absurdities does legalism reduce itself! Instead, courts had merely to declare that all Nazi laws and court decisions were void on account of the Nazi Party constituting a criminal conspiracy and the regime a criminal association, so making all their acts illegal.

In sum: to be legitimate, modern states must ensure security from external attack and internal crime. But they must also justify their costs by using taxes (and Aid where present), actively to improve the living conditions of society. This means that the money and management at their disposal must be deployed to produce a multiplier effect of social benefits. Well-directed government spending on the hard and soft infrastructures (Figure 1.3) produces a chain-reaction of improvements in the quality of life of the population. This is not optional. Failure to do so makes a state a failed state with all the ensuing consequences.

Finally: if *History is philosophy from examples*, as Dionysius of Halicarnassus said, what lessons can be drawn from this survey?

The First Lesson of History is that people are inherently selfish.

The Second is that, as we are obliged to live socially, good governance is everything.

The Third is that only the full panoply of democracy can secure good governance, and

The Fourth lesson is that 'legalism' is no guarantee of good governance, but on the contrary undermines it.

In the absence of good governance nothing flourishes, no progress is made and the sum of human happiness is not increased. People are forced to live in society, and so if its dominant agencies are in effect working against it, then the quality of life will at best stagnate and at worst degenerate, as presently in the Congo, Zimbabwe and Sudan where things are as dire as when Joseph Conrad wrote *Heart of Darkness* over a century ago. Blaming outsiders individually or collectively is an ugly but essential part of undemocratic rulers' self-justifying rhetoric.

But governance is a consequence of a society's derived cultural configuration, making the rectification of governance inherently difficult. This is a historically produced culturo-structural problem, and not a result of 'national indebtedness', or 'the structure of international trade', the 'colonial legacy' or any other of the all-too-many excuses for misgovernance. Like peasant indebtedness to local landowners and urban usurers, those countries' problems are a consequence of elites possessing the power to despoil the population and to plunder the country's resources. Nigeria is a prime example: because its oil riches have been wasted and stolen by a series of Lagos ('national') governments of northern warlords, Nigeria remains underdeveloped in terms of economy, infrastructure and society.

Though rare in practice, good governance is in fact straightforward. It requires that taxes be levied on the basis of ability to pay without exception or favouritism, and that the revenue raised be spent for the betterment of the population as a whole, with minimal deductions for the expenses of running the state apparatus and the lifestyles of its incumbents.

How can we tell whether misgovernance is happening? It is usually very obvious. If the police and armed forces are brutal, incompetent or corrupt, or are political and just don't do civil policing (recovering stolen property, bearing down on anti-social behaviour, investigating and prosecuting rape, solving murders), then the condition is obvious. Just listen to what those affected say. And if you need an 'objective' index, observe the levels of corruption. Is it widespread or institutionalised? Then so is misgovernance, for widespread corruption rots the social fabric, and it is within the powers, and it is certainly the duty of a government to tackle this. But of course all too often that is just not expedient and in all too many cases the motivation for being in power is to enrich oneself by any means.

Culture is the key. Britain was a free society (in that its members enjoyed liberty) long before it was a democracy, in the sense of being ruled by a government elected by the population as a whole (not until 1918, when women gained the franchise). Thus cultural expectation preceded and drove forward political democracy in Britain, identifiably from the 13th century onwards (Magna Carta 1215; Simon de Montfort).

Politics in democracies consists in the trading of interests such that a sufficiently broad consensus is formed – that there's 'something in it for everuone', even if that is merely the prospect of future gains – enabling a state to exist semi-detached from politics, enjoying popular support and tasked with ensuring that adequate provision is made for security (internal and external), the health  and progress of the economy (thus jobs and wealth) plus the hard and soft infrastructures (Figure 1.3) that facilitate everything. In other words the state is obliged to do by collective action what individuals and private organizations cannot do

# Appendix B

## Science v. Ideology

Ideology is the representation of interests, real or imagined, material or non-material. Ideology represents the real interests of its originators and propagators, but only the imagined interests of those who receive it. (Self-) interest is what distinguishes ideological from scientific explanations, even failed scientific explanation. Ptolemy of Alexandria (*c*. AD 90–168) was a polymathic scientist, as befits the superintendent of the Museum established to do scientific research, the only one in antiquity. An astronomer, geographer and mathematician, Ptolemy's works became the standard for the next millennium and a half. Unfortunately his astronomy was Geocentric and thus wrong. It is therefore failed science, but science nevertheless, for science resides in the exact explication of mechanism. However, once adopted by the Catholic Church as doctrine, Ptolemaic/Aristotelian cosmology became mere ideology, where facts are fitted to interests. Indeed, it was for championing Copernicus' new astronomy against the Aristotelian, for saying that the Earth moved around the sun and not vice versa, that Gordiano Bruno (1548–1600) was burned at the stake.

Lavoisier, the great eighteenth-century chemist, rejected the then emerging thermodynamic explanation of heat, and instead maintained that heating was due to the absorption of an 'element' called caloric. This was retrogressive and utterly wrong as the Anglo-American polymath Count Rumford (1753–1814) proved by measuring the conversion of motion into heat. Nonetheless, Lavoisier was practicing science and not ideology. His conjecture was testable, it was found wanting and it was replaced. By contrast, Lysenko's claims for, and the state's imposition of, a 'red science of biology', meant that soviet biology was not science and its failure contributed to the permanent food shortages that lasted as long as the Soviet Union.

Archaeology is a science (Kuznar 1996), but if undertaken for, or captured by nationalism, ethnicism or religion (and those frequently go together), becomes mere ideology, where the facts are fitted to interests. Categorization is one, necessary, thing; but categories are verbal models and models are simplifications of aspects of reality to facilitate cognition and action. Within ideology, however, categories serve either as substitutes for reality or as a template to which reality has to conform, with all the costs that ensue from this. Isbell and Knobloch (2008: 312–3) expose some of those abuses in Andean archaeology, and show how such ideology (in this all too common instance, for 'priority earliness') still confuses Andean chronology. Kaulicke (2008: 105) commenting on what Burger has called the "artificial buffer-zone of ignorance" in relation to research conditions along the Peru/Ecuador border, notes how "comprehension is also hindered by nationalistic or 'separatistic' trends in both nations' archaeologies', different chronological schemes, and therefore the absence of serious comparative approaches". Li Liu and Hong Xu (2007: 899–900) have exposed the official 'Xia-Shang-Zhou Chronology Project' as "a kind of political propaganda" for the historicity of culturally important texts.

Lynn Meskell (1998: 60–2) refers to an 'archaeology of desire' in relation to what Çatalhöyük represents for some people, namely "the search for a utopian model"; but the concept of an 'archaeology of desire', or wish-fantasy, has wider application in all continents and periods. In the last two decades of the 20th century some claimed that 'grand narrative ideology' was dead. We now see that this was grossly mistaken, the outcome of a temporary conjuncture in the West. Some earlier grand narrative ideologies died of bankruptcy, but the desire for the product is always there, and where there's demand...

As we have seen, ideology is the form in which interests – real and imagined, material and immaterial – are represented to a wider public. Because ideology is not seamless and well-integrated but inherently contradictory, over the longer term change does come to ideology through its internal conflicts. As ideologies depend upon denying facts not recognising them, their failure to agree with reality has to be defended by excuses or special pleading. This is called 'secondary elaboration' (of the primary propositions) but it cannot rest there. The need for excuses has to be explained away by other excuses and so on in an extending line of excuses that are mere falsehoods. People cannot be argued out of ideologies to which they have committed themselves (or been committed by their parents) by pointing to facts; they will be declared 'non-facts' or 'not relevant facts'.

"The ideologist mistakes the prodding of neurosis for the law of history, the ordinance of class or race. But ideology envelops him in intellectual [and emotional] ramparts which make him immune to criticism. He has a complete world-system with prefabricated answers to every question, and he is *impervious to disconfirming evidence.* Above all, ideology, by dividing people into two classes, one elected, the other rejected, sets the stage for untrammelled violence and warfare. No one is so ruthless as those who believe themselves denominated by history as the children of light" (Feuer 1975: 193, emphasis added).

**Why is ideology attractive? People like stories and ideologies are political stories.** Children like to be told a story at bedtime. Parents are recommended to do this as storytelling assists their children's imaginative development and helps them sleep soundly.

Satisfactory stories have a beginning, scene-setting stage, a middle where most of the action takes place and a resolution at the end. This is an analogue for a satisfactory life, for when an account is given retrospectively, it is a narrative, a story, a connected set of meaningful activities and events, of causes and consequences. When this is done socially or collectively, it is an historical account.

Right back at the origins of writing in late fourth millennium Sumer there are lists and bookkeeping accounts. The earliest piece of literature in the world, from third millennium Sumer, is a story or rather a set of tales that are attached to Gilgamesh, culture-hero and tyrant-king of the city-state of Uruk (Unug). It is a story of hubris and nemesis, of surpassing strength and weakness, the search for immortality and its futility. It is in fact a story of human ambition, trials, failings and finally, of having to come to terms with human transitoriness. 'Gilgamesh' is a superb set of tales whose poetry still has the power to move, and it indicates that not much progress has been made in literature over five thousand years.[106] Most of the themes are the same, which is not surprising as in one way or another, all stories deal with the human condition. Indeed, the Gilgamesh stories circulated verbally before writing and, in unified narrative, form a 'quest', involving the hero in a series of tests, some of which he fails. In the collation and translation by Andrew George (1999), some opening stanzas (ll.9–12, 41–44) relate how: -

> "He came a far road, was weary, found peace,
> and set all his labours on a tablet of stone.
> He built the rampart of Uruk-the-Sheepfold
> of holy Eanna, the sacred storehouse.

> "…who scoured the world ever searching for life,
> and reached through sheer force Uta-napishti {Noah} the Distant;
> who restored the cult-centres destroyed by the Deluge,
> and set in place for the people the rites of the cosmos".

Adults like to be told stories of different but overlapping types. Gilgamesh encompasses them all:

1. myths that relate people to the great scheme of things; ontological or religious stories;
2. stories that deal with human encounters with one another;
3. stories about life challenges; overcoming tests and difficulties of all kinds: illnesses, tragedies, natural events, as they affect ordinary people;
4. stories about heroes, extraordinary or semi-divine people.

As social animals we have evolved to take account of the feeling and motives of others and to internally model, the better to manipulate, the dynamics of interpersonal relationships (Byrne and Whiten 1988). We also have to model our relationships with the natural environment (Mithen 1996).

> "We know that human minds are narrative or literary minds. That is, minds strive to represent events in their environment, however trivial, in terms of causal *stories,* sequences where each event is the result of some other event and paves the way for what is to follow. People everywhere make up stories, avidly listen to them, are good judges of whether they make sense. But the narrative drive goes deeper. It is embedded in our mental representation of whatever happens around us" (Boyer 2001: 233, original emphasis).

Narrative is, indeed, a function of the maturing of the brain's pre-frontal cortex and that is recent in evolutionary terms, 40,000–30,000 years ago.

Stories are, then, models worked out in chains of causes and effects through the interplay of ideas, circumstances and personalities. Stories as seen in everyday gossip – which are stories about acquaintances – have had an important evolutionary role in network-building within one's group (Dunbar 1993, Boyer 2001).

---

[106] Or, for that matter, in visual art over the last 30,000 years, judging from the wall-paintings at Lascaux, Chauvet or Altamira.

Soap opera works on the same human propensities (Mithen 1996: 118): the writers spin a yarn and the viewer finds characters and plot lines with which to identify. The same obtains with regard to the novel and drama, of which television 'soap' is but the lowest common denominator form. By instinct we are programmed to seek pleasure and avoid pain. Cognitively and emotionally we seek meaning for our existence and a value for it in the greater scheme of things: 'society', 'cosmos' or 'history'. Traditionally, surviving to be an 'ancestor' was a central way of achieving meaning and value, and even a sort of immortality. In developed countries where children are not an economic asset but a liability, this is still the major motive for people to have children. People imagine trajectories for themselves with their children, and much more vaguely of their children after the death of the parents. This is a story or narrative told internally and never articulated in full or at all. But it is the implicit story underlying and parallel to the stories we are told about other people. The key thing is narrative as trajectory and vice versa. People tell themselves stories and weave them into the received stories about the history of their societies, the meaning of life and so on (Trevarthen 2006: 238). Ideologies are political stories.

The story form is crucial because it is relational: people to each other, past, present and future – family, lovers, friends, strangers, enemies – and their relationships with the natural environment. Central to the narrative form is *sequence*; this, then that, then the next, with explication and elucidation in the form of motives and responses (Boyer 2001).

Meanings are present because stories deal in outcomes. Stories are meaningful because they conform to, and sometimes help illuminate, the pattern of life. Language, causalities and the stages of life are sequential and thus susceptible to narrative, which is accordingly the preferred mode of human exposition and explanation. Narrative forms thus seem 'natural' whereas mathematics and physical science do not (Wolpert 1992). Mathematics and physical science deal with puzzle-solving, systemic analysis and relational transformations. Accordingly, if you don't know the mechanism you haven't done the science. Such mindsets feel alien to most people, whereas narrative-based accounts seem 'natural', like natural language, which has a history spanning 250,000 years. And that is one major reason why ideology flourishes much more readily than scientific accounts and scientific scepticism, even where science plays a huge role in society (Shermer 1997).

"What is distinctive in ideology is the drama it sets forth as the 'meaning' of the historical process, together with its assignment of the roles of leadership elite, chosen class, and historical culmination. There is no dualism of fact and value in ideology but only because both are transfigured (and *aufgehoben*) in myth" (Feuer 1975: 4). We adopt positions on an emotional-ideological basis; then, using argumentation, attempt to justify those positions to ourselves and to others. This process constitutes rationalization, not reason.

## Appendix C[107]

## Leadership Attributes

### I: How to make a chiefdom/state/empire in twelve simple steps:

1) Get born as a charismatic alpha male of elite parentage, but outside the main line of succession, so that you have to struggle for it. This sharpens the mind. Julius and Octavius Caesar are your models.
2) Get a reputation, or develop it through being famous or notorious for something, preferably as a warrior (as above).
3) Get a core following of psychological dependents (as above).
4) Get a cause, e.g. restoring legitimacy. This gets you more followers and the justification that you are not just antisocially ambitious (as above).
5) Get aggressive. Destroy the local opposition/rivals/early supporters and make yourself internally dominant (as above).
6) Get some early, even if minor, victories over neighbours that make you the 'glorious leader' (as above).
7) Get the ideologues going on your personal qualities and on 'destiny' (Octavian much better than Julius here; he tried to do his own 'spin').
8) Bolster this by setting in train infrastructural works that develop the economy. Autobahns are good.
9) Get consolidated. Delegate various functions to loyal followers, especially the raising of levies and taxes. When things go wrong, they get the chop, not you.
10) Use the income to: (a) build yourself a huge palace; 'because you can' (shows potency) and 'because you are worth it'; (b) build up the armed formations; (c) build up the secret police; (d) get more ideologists (priests, lawyers, artists etc) pay them well and build more ideological monuments (temples, law-courts, art-galleries, sports stadia etc.) for the glorification of the regime. Get a smooth well-educated foreign minister who understands foreigners, lies convincingly and can see trouble coming. Zhou Enlai is your model here.

---

[107] Since writing this I have discovered an excellent ten-point checklist of 'How to be an agent of state formation' in Flannery (1999: 14–15). He is always in the vanguard of archaeological thought and those of us who practise anthropological archaeology are greatly in his debt. I particularly like his statement (p. 18) that "most processes are just long-term patterns of behaviour by multiple agents", producing and responding to unintended as well as intended consequences. See the volume of essays in honour of Kent V. Flannery: 'Cultural Evolution, Contemporary Viewpoints', edited by Gary Feinman and Linda Manzanilla (2000) Kluwer Academic/Plenum Publishers, New York.

11) Under cover of your ideologists, launch wars of expansion, or at least mobilise the population 'for defence of the country'. China and North Korea are the models for this.

12) Repeat from 6, remembering to consolidate at home by (a) developing a welfare system, and (b) promoting the cult of popular stupefaction by means of total entertainment. Bread and circuses are a time-proven winning combination that now must include all international spectator sports and reality TV shows. So stage the Olympic Games and any other of the global sportsfests that you can lay your hands on.

## II: The suitable candidate:

1. Will have a personality disorder
2. Will be totally amoral, self-serving and ruthless
3. Will possess (or be possessed by) anger, jealousy and ambition in equal measure
4. Will need to compensate for what is felt to be deprivation or abuse as a child and lack of recognition/dignitas as a youth. Now you'll show them, especially your father and the girls who spurned you.
5. Will know that you have special gifts and so have been called to provide deliverance by God, Destiny, History or the Nation; preferably by all of those.
6. Will be convinced *and can convince others* that you do not do this for yourself but for 'your people', for 'justice', 'liberation' or 'civilization'.
7. Will be prepared to 'sacrifice yourself ' for the cause, although many others have to be sacrificed first. This is noble and purifying.
8. Will be absolutely convinced that Right and History are on your side. Whatever happens, you will never waver and admit that you were wrong, only that unforeseeable circumstances and/or conspiracies were against you. After all, you are the chosen one.

If you fit the personality profile, then the last section shows you how to: -

## III: Become a dictator ('saviour/liberator') in the modern world:

1) Be born in the lower middle class.
2) Do not go to university: go to some low-level college and nurse a sense of grievance.
3) Do not get a proper profession; use your unemployment to do some 'self-education' and/or become an army officer.
4) Do plunge into a political party. If none are suitable join an underground conspiracy and turn it into a political party while retaining its conspiratorial attributes.
5) Get to be its boss as quickly as possible by trickery, bribery, intimidation and elimination. There is no time to lose.

6) Do a state coup and call it a 'people's revolution'. Before, during and after, you will need extra security apparatus.
7) Eliminate other parties and also your own party rivals. Get control of the media, but leave a few newspapers and a TV channel independent (but under threat and so self-censoring) for window-dressing.
8) Change the constitution if you have not already done so. Merge the party with the state to form the party-state. All government posts must be held by party members answerable to you.
9) Under the rhetorical smokescreen of national revival, mission or salvation, control everything and everyone.
10) When this results in economic disaster blame foreign agents, foreign companies and foreign governments working with native saboteurs. Victimise some minority to divert attention and provide an emotional outlet. When attacked for those policies, declare with outrage that those matters are 'purely internal, nobody else's business, in the national interest', and bluster that 'international law demands non-interference' and that only imperialists/racists would dare to say otherwise.

Always remember the Golden Rule: whatever it is, it is always someone else's fault!

# BIBLIOGRAPHY

Abu Al-Soof, B. (1969) 'Excavations at Tell Qalinj Agha (Erbil)', *Sumer* 25: 3–42.

Abu Al-Soof, B. (1985) *Uruk Pottery*. Baghdad State Organisation of Antiquities and Heritage.

Abusch, T. (2002) ed., *Riches Hidden in Secret Places: Ancient Near Eastern Studies in Memory of Thorkild Jacobsen*. Eisenbrauns, Winona Lake.

Abusch, T. and van der Toorn, K (2000) eds, *Studies in Ancient Magic and Divination 1*. Groningen, Styx.

A'dami, K. (1968) 'Excavations at Tell es-Sawwan (second season)'. *Sumer* 24: 57–94.

Adams, B. (1995) 'Ancient Nekhen: Garstang in the City of Hierakonpolis.' *Egyptian Studies Association Publication* No. 3, New Malden.

Adams, B. (1996) *Elite tombs at Hierakonpolis*. In Spencer ed., pp. 1–15.

Adams, B. (1998/1999) 'Discovery of a predynastic elephant burial at Hierakonpolis'. *Archaeology International*, 46–50.

Adams, B. (2002) 'Seeking the roots of Ancient Egypt. A unique cemetery reveals monuments and rituals from before the Pharaohs'. *Archéo-Nil 12*: 11–28.

Adams, B. and Ciałowicz, C. (1997) *Protodynastic Egypt. Princes Risborough*, Shire Publications.

Adams, Douglas (1979) *The Hitch-Hikers Guide to the Galaxy*. London, Pan Books.

Adams, R.L. (2005) 'Ethnoarchaeology in Indonesia illuminating the ancient past at Çatalhöyük?' *American Antiquity* 70(1): 181–188.

Adams, R. McC. (1981) *The Heartland of Cities: Surveys of Ancient Settlement and Land Use on the Central Floodplain of the Euphrates*. Chicago and London, University of Chicago Press.

Adams, R. McC. (1992) *Ideologies: unity and diversity*. In Demarest and Conrad, pp. 205–21.

Adams, R. McC. (2000) 'Scale and complexity in archaic states: Review of Archaic States', edited by G.M. Feinman and Joyce Marcus. *Latin American Antiquity* 11(2): 187–193.

Adcock, F.E. (1959) *Roman Political Ideas and Practice*. Ann Arbor, University of Michigan Press.

Adler, M. and Wlshusen, R. (1990) 'Large-scale integrative facilities in tribal societies: cross-cultural and Southwestern U.S. Examples'. *World Archaeology* 22(2): 133–146.

Agrawal, D.P. and Sood, R.K. (1982) 'Ecological factors and the Harappan Civilization'. In Possehl ed., pp.223-231.

Agrawal, D.P. (1984) *Palaeoenvironmental and prehistoric studies in the Kashmir Valley*. In Kennedy and Possehl eds, pp. 33–40.

Agrawal, D.P. and Chakrabarti, D.K. (1979) eds, *Essays in Indian Protohistory*. Delhi, B.R. Publishing Corporation.

Aiello, L.C. and Dunbar, R.I.M. (1993) 'Neocortex size, group size and the evolution of language'. *Current Anthropology* Vol. 34: 184–193.

Akkermans, P.M.M.G. (1989a) 'The Neolithic of the Balikh Valley, Northern Syria: a first assessment'. *Paléorient* 15/1: 122–134.

Akkermans, P.M.M.G. (1989b) *Halaf mortuary practices: a survey*. In Haex, Curvers and Akkermans eds, pp. 75–98.

Akkermans, P.M.M.G. (1989) ed., 'Excavations at Tell Sabi Abyad: Prehistoric Investigations in the Balikh Valley, Northern Syria'. *BAR* 468, Oxford.

Akkermans, P.M.M.G. (1990) *Villages in the Steppe: Later Neolithic Settlement and Subsistence in the Balikh Valley, Northern Syria*. Leiden, Rijks Museum van Oudheden.

Akkermans, P.M.M.G. (1991) 'New radiocarbon dates for the Later Neolithic of Northern Syria'. *Paléorient* 17/1: 121–125.

Akkermans, P.M.M.G. (1996) ed., *Tell Sabi Abyad: The Late Neolithic Settlement*, Vol. 2. Istanbul, Nederlands Historisch-Archaeologisch Instituut.

Akkermans, P.M.M.G. (2001) Abstract of paper '*Neolithic communities in Syria: equality or chiefly power?*' given at the conference on '*The Fifth Millennium BC in the Near East*', University of Liverpool, 15–18 November; and pers. comm.

Akkermans, P.M.M.G. (2004) *Hunter-gatherer continuity: The transition from the Epipalaeolithic to the Neolithic in Syria*. In Aurenche, Le Miere and Sanlaville eds, pp. 281–293.

Akkermans, P.M.M.G., Cappers, R., Cavallo, C., Nieuwenhuyse, O., Nilhamn, B. and Otte, I.N. (2006) 'Investigating the Early Pottery Neolithic of northern Syria: New evidence from Tell Sabi Abyad'. *American Journal of Archaeology* 110: 123–56.

Akkermans, P.M.M.G. and Duistermaat, K. (1997) 'Of storage and nomads: The sealings from Late Neolithic Sabi Abyad, Syria'. *Paléorient* 22(2): 17–44.

Akkermans.P.M.M.G. and Duistermaat, K. (2004) More seals and sealings from Neolithic Tell Sabi Abyad, Syria'. *Levant* 36: 1–11.

Akkermans, P.M.M.G. & Le Miere, M. (1992) 'The 1988 excavations at Tell Sabi Abyad, a Later Neolithic village in Northern Syria'. *American Journal of Archaeology* 96: 1–22.

Akkermans, P.M.M.G. and Schwartz, G.M. (2003) *The Archaeology of Syria: From Complex Hunter-Gatherers to Early Urban Societies (ca. 16,000–300 BC)*. Cambridge, CUP.

Akkermans, P.M.M.G. and Verhoeven, M. (1995) 'An image of complexity: the Burnt Village at Late Neolithic Sabi Abyad, Syria'. *American Journal of Archaeology* 99: 5–32.

Albarracin-Jordan, J. (1996) 'The Tiwanaku settlement system: the integration of nested hierarchies in the Lower Tiwanaku Valley'. *Latin American Antiquity* 7(3): 183–210.

Alcock, S.A., D'Altroy, T.N., Morrison, K.D. and Sinopoli, C.M. (2001) eds, *Empires: Perspectives from Archaeology and History*. Cambridge, CUP.

Alcock, S.E. (2000) *Classical order, alternative orders, and the uses of nostalgia*. In Richards and Van Buren eds, pp. 110–119.

Aldenderfer, M.S. (1993) 'Ritual, hierarchy, and change in foraging societies'. *JAA* 12: 1–40.

Aldenderfer, M.S. (1993) ed., *Domestic Architecture, Ethnicity and Complementarity in the South-Central Andes*. Iowa City, University of Iowa Press.

Aldenderfer, M.S. (1998) *Maritime Foragers: Asana and the South-Central Andean Archaic*. Iowa City, University of Iowa Press.

Aldenderfer, M.S. (2006) 'Comment on Haas and Creamer'. *CA* 47(5)756–7.

Algaze, G. (1993) *The Uruk World System: The Dynamics of Expansion of Early Mesopotamian Civilization*. Chicago, The University of Chicago Press.

Algaze, G. (2001a) *The prehistory of imperialism: The case of Uruk Period Mesopotamia*. In Rothman ed., pp. 27–83.

Algaze, G. (2001b) 'Initial social complexity in Southwestern Asia: the Mesopotamian advantage'. *Current Anthropology* 42: 199–233.

Algaze, G. (2001c) 'Reply to Frangipane 2001b'. *Current Anthropology* 43 (3): 416–7.

Algaze, G. (2004) 'Trade and the origins of Mesopotamian civilization'. *Bibliotheca Orientalis* 61(1–2): 6–20.

Algaze, G. (2007) *The Sumerian takeoff*. In Stone ed., pp. 343–368.

Allan, S. (2007) 'Erlitou and the formation of Chinese civilization: Toward a new paradigm'. *Journal of Asian Studies* 66: 461–96.

Allan, S. (2008) 'Comment on Flad'. *CA* 49.3: 420.

Allard, F. (2002) 'Mortuary ceramics and social organization in the Dawenkou and Majiayao Cultures'. *JEAA* 3(3–4): 1–21.

Allchin, B. (1984) ed., *South Asian Archaeology 1981*. Cambridge, CUP.

Allchin, B. (1994) ed., *Living Traditions: Studies in the Ethnoarchaeology of South Asia*. Oxford and New Delhi, Oxford, IBH Publishing.

Allchin, B. and Allchin, F.R. (1997) *Origins of a Civilization: the Prehistory and Early Archaeology of South Asia*. New Delhi, Viking.

Allchin, R. and Allchin, B. with Elston, G. and Straza-Majewski, O. (1997) eds, *South Asian Archaeology 1995: Proceedings of the 13th Conference of the European Association of South Asian Archaeologists*. New Delhi and Calcutta, Oxford and IBH Publishing and Science Publishers Inc., USA.

Allen, E.S. (2002) *Palaeoethnobotany: Preliminary results*. In Garfinkel and Miller eds, pp. 236–246.

Alon, D. and Levy, T.E. (1989) 'The archaeology of cult and the Chalcolithic sanctuary at Gilat'. *Journal of Mediterranean Archaeology* 2: 163–221.

Al-Soof, B.A. (1969) 'Excavations at Tell Qalinj Agha (Erbil); Summer 1968'. *Sumer* 25:3-42.

Aufrecht, W.E. Mirau, N.A. and Gauley, S.W. (1997) eds, 'Urbanism in Antiquity: from Mesopotamia to Crete'. *JSOT Supplement Series* 244. Sheffield. Sheffield Academic Press.

Alva, W. (1988) 'Discovering the world's richest unlooted tomb'. *National Geographic* 174(4): 510–549.

Alva, W. (1990) 'New royal tomb unearthed'. *National Geographic* 176(6): 2–16.

Alva, W. (2001) *The royal tombs of Sipán: art and power in Moche society*. In Pillsbury ed., pp. 223–245.

Alva, W. and Donnan, C.B. (1993) *Royal tombs of Sipán*. Los Angeles, Fowler Museum of Cultural History, University of California.

Anderson, E.N. (1988) *Food of China*. New Haven, Yale University Press.

Anderson, P.C. (1997) *History of harvesting and threshing techniques for cereals in the prehistoric Near East*. In Harlan Symposium, pp. 145–159.

Anderson, P.C. (1999) ed., *Prehistory of Agriculture: New Experimental and Ethnographic Studies*. Los Angeles, The Institute of Archaeology, University of California, Monograph 40.

Anderson, W. (1992) 'Badarian burials: evidence for social inequality in Middle Egypt during the Early Predynastic era'. *Journal of the American Research Centre in Egypt (JARCE)* 29: 51–66.

Antonova, E. (1992) 'Images on seals and the ideology of the state formation process'. *Mesopotamia* XXVII: 77–87.

Anyang Excavation Team (1977) *Anyang Yinxu nuli jisikeng de fajue (The excavation of the slave sacrificial pits at the Yin Site of Anyang)*. Kaogu 1: 20–36.

Ardeleanu-Jansen, A. (1989) *A short note on a steatite sculpture from Mohenjo-Daro*. In Frifelt and Sorensen eds, pp. 196–210.

Ardeleanu-Jansen, A. (1991) *The sculptural art of the Harappa Culture*. In Jansen *et al.* eds, pp. 167–178.

Arkush, E. and Stanish, C. (2005) 'Interpreting conflict in the ancient Andes: implications for the archaeology of warfare'. *Current Anthropology* 46(1): 3–28.

Arnold, J.E. (1993) 'Labour and the rise of complex hunter-gatherers'. *Journal of Anthropological Archaeology* 12: 75–119.

Arriaza, B.T. (1995) *Beyond Death: The Chinchorro Mummies of Ancient Chile*. Washington DC, Smithsonian Institution Press.

Arsebuk, G., Mellink, M.J. and Schirmer, W. (1998) eds, *Light on Top of the Black Hill; Studies Presented to Halet Çambel*. Istanbul, Ege Yayinlari.

Asthana, S. (1979) *Indus-Mesopotamian trade: Nature of trade and structural analysis of operative system*. In Agrawal and Chakrabarti eds, pp. 31–47.

Atre, S. (1989) 'Toward an economico-religious model for Harappan urbanism'. *South Asian Studies* Vol: 5 pp. 49–58.

Aufrecht, W.E., Mirau, N.A. and Gauley, S.W. (1997) eds, *Urbanism in Antiquity: From Mesopotamia to Crete*. Sheffield, Sheffield Academic Press.

Aurenche, O. (1996) *Famille, fortune, pouvoir et architecture domestique dans les villages du Proche Orient*. In Veenhof ed., pp. 1–16.

Aurenche, O., Evin, J. and Hours, F. (1987) eds, 'Chronologies in the Near East: Relative Chronologies and Absolute Chronology, 16,000–4,000 BP. C.N.R.S. International Symposium, Lyon, 24–28 Nov. 1986'. Oxford, *BAR 379(i,ii)*.

Aurenche, O., Galet, P., Regagnon-Caroline, E. and Evin, J. (2001) 'Proto-Neolithic and Neolithic cultures in the Middle East – the birth of agriculture, livestock raising and ceramics: a calibrated $C^{14}$ chronology 12,500–5,500 cal BC'. *Radiocarbon* 43(3): 1191–1202.

Aurenche, O., Le Miere, M. and Sanlaville, P. (2004) eds, 'From the River to the Sea: The Palaeolithic and the Neolithic on the Euphrates and the Northern Levant. Studies in Honour of Lorraine Copeland'. Oxford, *BAR International Series 1263*.

Austin, M.M. and Vidal-Naquet, P. (1977) *Economic and Social History of Ancient Greece: An Introduction*. London, Batsford.

Ayala, F.J. (2006) *Biological evolution and Human Nature*. In Jeeves ed., pp. 46–64.

Badawi, F.A. (2003) 'A preliminary report on 1984–86 excavations at Maadi-West'. *MDAIK* 59: 1–10.

Badler, V.R. (2002) *A chronology of Uruk artefacts from Godin Tepe in central Western Iran and implications for the interrelationships between the local and foreign cultures*. In Postgate ed., pp. 79–110.

Bagley, R.W. (1977) 'P'an-lung-ch'eng: A Shang City in Hupei'. *Artibus Asiae* 39: 165–219.

Bagley, R.W. (1987) *Shang Ritual Bronzes in the Arthur M. Sackler Collection*. Cambridge Mass., Harvard University Press.

Bagley, R.W. (1988) 'Sacrificial Pits of the Shang Period at Sanxingdui in Guanghan County, Sichuan Province'. *Arts Asiatiques* 43: 76–86.

Bagley, R.W. (1990) *A Shang city in Sichuan Province. Orientations*, November, pp. 52–67.

Bagley, R.W. (1999) *Shang Archaeology*. In Loewe and Shaughnessy, pp. 124– 231.

Bagley, R.W. (2001) ed., *Ancient Sichuan: Treasures from a Lost Civilization*. Seattle Art Museum, University of Princeton Press.

Baines, J. and Lacovara, P. (2002) 'Burial and the dead in ancient Egyptian society: Respect, formalism, neglect'. *Journal of Social Archaeology*, Vol. 2(1): 5–36.

Baines, J. and Malek, J. (1980) 'Atlas of Ancient Egypt'. *Facts on File*. Oxford.

Baines, J. and Yoffee, N. (1998) *Order, legitimacy and wealth in Ancient Egypt and Mesopotamia*. In Feinman and Marcus eds, pp. 200–260.

Baines, J. and Yoffee, N. (2000) *Order, legitimacy and wealth: setting the terms*. In Richards and Van Buren eds, pp. 13–17.

Baird, D. (2005) 'Pinarbasi'. *Anatolian Archaeology* 11: 12–13.

Baird, D., Campbell, S. and Watkins, T. (1996) 'Excavations at Kharabeh Shattani, Vol. II'. *Occasional Papers* No: 18, Edinburgh University Dept. of Archaeology.

Ball, J.W. and Tascheck, J.T. (2007) 'Sometimes a 'stove' *is* just a stove: a context based reconsideration of three-prong 'incense burners' from the Western Belize Valley'. *Latin American Antiquity* 18(4): 451–470.

Bamforth, D.B. (2002) 'Evidence and metaphor in Evolutionary Archaeology'. *American Antiquity*, 67(3) 435–452.

Bandy, M.S. (2004) 'Fissioning, scalar stress, and social evolution in early village societies'. *American Anthropologist* 106(2): 322–333.

Bandy, M.S. (2005) 'Energetic efficiency and political expediency in Titicaca Basin raised field agriculture'. *Journal of Anthropological Archaeology* 24: 271–296.

Bandy, M.S. (2008) *Early village society in the Formative Period in the southern Lake Titicaca Basin*. In Isbell and Silverman eds, pp. 210–236.

Banning, E.B. (1997) *Spatial perspectives on early urban development in Mesopotamia*. In Aufrecht *et al.* eds, pp. 17–34.

Banning, E.B. (2000) *The Archaeologist's Laboratory: The Analysis of Archaeological Data. Interdisciplinary Contributions to Archaeology*. New York, Kluwer Academic/Plenum Publishers.

Banning, E.B. (2001) 'Making up for lost time: Chronological problems in the Late Neolithic'. Paper read at the Conference on the Fifth Millennium in the Near East, University of Liverpool, 15–18 November, 2001.

Banning, E.B. and Byrd, B.F. (1987) 'Houses and changing residential unit: Domestic architecture at PPNB "Ain Ghazal". *Proceedings of the Prehistoric Society* 53: 309–325.

Bar-Matthews, M., Ayalon, A., Kaufman, A. and Wasserburg, G.J. (1999) 'The Eastern Mediterranean palaeoclimate as reflection of regional events: Soreq Cave'. *Israel Earth and Planetary Science Letters* 166: 85–95.

Bar-Yosef, O. (1991) *The archaeology of the Natufian Layer at Hayonim Cave*. In Bar-Yosef and Valla eds, pp. 81–92.

Bar-Yosef, O. (1995) *Earliest food producers – Pre Pottery Neolithic (8000–5500)*. In Levy ed., pp. 190–201.

Bar-Yosef, O. (1998) 'The Natufian Culture in the Levant, threshold to the origins of agriculture'. *Evolutionary Anthropology* Vol. 6, Issue 5, pp. 159–177.

Bar-Yosef, O. and Gopher, A. (1997) eds, 'An Early Neolithic Village in the Jordan Valley Part 1: The Archaeology of Netiv Hagdud'. Cambridge, Mass. *School of Prehistoric Research Bulletin* 43.

Bar-Yosef, O. and Kra, R.S. (1994) *Late Quaternary Chronology and Palaeoclimates of the Eastern Mediterranean*. Tucson, Radiocarbon, Univ. of Arizona.

Bar-Yosef, O. and Valla, F. (1991) eds, 'The Natufian Culture in the Levant'. *International Monographs in Prehistory* 1. Ann Arbor, Mich..

Bard, K.A. (1997) *Urbanism and the rise of complex society and the early state in Egypt*. In Manzanilla, ed., pp. 59–86.

Bard, K.A. (2000) *The emergence of the Egyptian state (c.3200–2686 BC)*. In Shaw ed., pp. 61–88.

Barker, E. (1960) *Greek Political Theory*. London, Methuen.

Barkow, J.H., Cosmides, L. and Tooby, J. (1993) eds, *The Adapted Mind: Evolutionary Psychology and the Generation of Culture*. New York, OUP.

Barnard, N. (1973) 'Records of discoveries of bronze vessels in Chinese literary sources – and some pertinent remarks on aspects of Chinese historiography'. *Journal of the Institute of Chinese Studies of the Chinese University of Kong Kong* 6(1) 455–544.

Barnard, N. (1986) *A new approach to the study of clan-sign inscriptions of Shang*. In Chang ed., pp. 141–206.

Barnard, A. and Spencer, J. (1996) eds, *Encyclopaedia of Social and Cultural Anthropology*. London and New York. Routledge.

Bartel, B. (1979) 'A discriminant analysis of Harappan Civilization human population'. *Journal of Archaeological Science* 6: 49–61.

Barth, F. (1965) *Political Leadership among Swat Pathans*. Oxford, OUP.

Baruch, U. and Goring-Morris, A.N. (1997) 'The arborial vegetation of the central Negev Highlands at the end of the Pleistocene: evidence from archaeological charcoal wood remains'. *Archaeobotany and Vegetation History* 6/4: 249–259.

Bastien, J. (1978) 'Mountain of the Condor: Metaphor and Ritual in an Andean Ayllu. Washington D.C.', *American Ethnological Society Monograph* 64.

Bauer, J., Englund, R.K. and Krebernik, M. (1999) 'Mesopotamien, Späturuk-Zeit und Früdynastische-Zeit, Annäherungen 1', in P. Attinger, M. Wäfler (eds) *Orbis Biblicus et Orientalis Band* 160/1, Universitätsverlag, Freiburg.

Bavay, L., De Putter, T., Adams, B., Navez, J. and Andre, L. (2000) 'The origin of obsidian in Predynastic and Early Dynastic Upper Egypt'. *MDAIK* 56: 5–20.

Bawden, G. (1982) 'Community organization reflected by the household: A study of pre-Columbian social dynamics'. *Journal of Field Archaeology* 9: 165–181.

Bawden, G. (1995) 'The structural paradox: Moche Culture as political ideology'. *Latin American Antiquity* 6(3): 255–273.

Bawden, G. (1996) *The Moche*. Oxford UK., Blackwell Publishers.

Bawden, G. (2001) *The symbols of Late Moche social transformation*. In Pillsbury ed., pp. 285–305.

Bawden, G. (2004) *The art of Moche politics*. In Silverman ed., pp. 116–129.

Bayly, S. (1999) *Caste, Society and Politics in India from the Eighteenth Century to the Modern Age*. Cambridge, CUP.

Bazelmans, J. (1999) *By Weapons Made Worthy: Lords, Retainers and their Relationship in Beowulf*. Amsterdam, Amsterdam University Press.

Beck, R.A. (2004) 'Architecture and polity in the formative Lake Titicaca Basin, Bolivia'. *Latin American Antiquity* 15(3): 323–343.

Becker, C. (1998) 'The role of hunting in Pre-Pottery Neolithic pastoralism and its ecological implications'. *Anthropozoologica* 27: 67–78.

Beckman, G. (2005) *How religion was done*. In Snell ed., pp. 366–376.

Bedigan, D. (1997) *Early history of sesame cultivation in the Near East and beyond*. In Harlan Symposium, pp. 93–107.

Behrens, H., Loding, D. and Roth M.T. (1989) *Studies in Honor of A.W. Sjoberg*. Philadelphia, The University Press.

Begley, V. and De Puma, R.D. (1991) eds, *Rome and India: The Ancient Sea Trade*. Madison, University of Wisconsin Press.

Beijing University (1983) *Yuanjunmiao*. Beijing, Wenwu Press.

Belfer-Cohen, A. (1988) 'The Natufian graveyard in Hayonim Cave'. *Paléorient* 14(2): 297–308.

Belfer-Cohen, A. (1991) 'The Natufian in the Levant'. *Annual Review of Anthropology* 20: 167–186.

Belfer-Cohen, A. and Bar-Yosef, O. (2000) *Early sedentism in the Near East: a bumpy ride to village life*. In Kuijt ed., pp. 63–98.

Belfer-Cohen, A. and Goring-Morris, N. (2002) 'Recent developments in Near Eastern research'. *Paléorient* 28(2): 143–48.

Belfer-Cohen, A. and Goring-Morris, N. (2005) *Which way to look? Conceptual frameworks for understanding Neolithic processes*. In Gebel and Rollefson eds, pp. 22–24.

Bellamy, J.A. (1989) *The Arabic alphabet*. In Senner ed., pp. 91–102.

Bellwood, P. (2005) *First Farmers: the Origins of Agricultural Societies*. Malden (MA) Blackwell.

Benco, N.L. (1992) 'Manufacture and use of clay sickles from the Uruk Mound, Abu Salabikh, Iraq'. *Paléorient* 18(1): 119–133.

Benson, E.P. (2001) *Why sacrifice?* In Benson and Cook eds, pp. 1–20.

Benson, E.P. and Cook, A.G. (2001) *Ritual Sacrifice in Ancient Peru: New Discoveries and Interpretations*. Austin, University of Texas Press.

Benz, M. (2004) 'The emic view: social questions of the Neolithisation of the Near East'. *Neo-Lithics* 1/04: 27–8.

Berelov, I. (2006) 'Signs of sedentism and mobility in an agro-pastoral community during the Levantine Middle Bronze Age'. *Journal of Anthropological Archaeology* 25: 117–143.

Bermann, M. (1997) 'Domestic life and vertical integration in the Tiwanaku heartland'. *Latin American Antiquity*, 8(2): 93–112.

Bernbeck, R., Coursey, C., & Pollock, S. (1996) 'Excavations of Halaf Levels at Kazane, SE Turkey'. *Neo-Lithics* 2/96: 4

Bernbeck, R., Pollock, S. and Coursey, C. (1999). 'The Halaf settlement at Kazane Hoyuk: Preliminary Report on the 1996 and 1997 Seasons'. *Anatolica* XXV: 109–147.

Berent, M. (1998) 'Stasis, or the Greek invention of politics'. *History of Political Thought* XIX(3).

Beresford-Jones, D.G., Torres, S.A., Whaley, O.Q. and Chepstow-Lusty, A.J. (2009) 'The role of *Prosopis* in ecological and landscape change in the Samanca Basin, Lower Ica Valley, South Coast of Peru from the Early Horizon to the Late Intermediate Period'. *LAA* 20(2): 303–332.

Berreman, G.D. (1979) 'Caste and Other Inequities'. *Ved Prakash Vatuk*, Folklore Institute, Meerut.

Berreman, G.D. (1993) *Sanskritization as female oppression in India*. In Miller ed., 366–392.

Bettinger, R. (1991) *Hunter-Gatherers: Archaeological and Evolutionary Theory*. New York, Plenum.

Bhan, K.K., Sonawane, V.H., Ajithprasad, P. and Pratapchandran, S. (2005) 'A Harappan trading and craft production centre at Gola Dhoro (Bagasra)'. *Antiquity* No. 304, Project Gallery.

Bienert, H.D. (1991) 'Skull cult in the prehistoric Near East'. *Journal of Prehistoric Religion* 5: 9–23.

Bienert, H.D. (1995) *The human image in the Natufian and Aceramic Neolithic of the Middle East*. In Waldren *et al.* eds, pp. 75–103.

Bigelow, L. (2000) 'Zooarchaeological investigations of economic organization and ethnicity at Late Chalcolithic Hacinebi: A preliminary report'. *Paléorient* 25(1): 83–89.

Billman, B.R. (1996) *The Evolution of Prehistoric Political Organizations in the Moche valley, Peru*. Unpublished Ph.D. dissertation, Dept. of Anthropology, University of California, Santa Barbara.

Billman, B.R. (1999) *Reconstructing prehistoric political economies and cycles of power in the Moche valley, Peru*. In Billman and Feinman eds, pp. 131–159.

Billman, B.R. (2002) 'Irrigation and the origins of the southern Moche state on the North Coast of Peru'. *Latin American Antiquity* 13(4): 371–400.

Billman, B.R. and Feinman, G.M. eds (1999) *Settlement Pattern Studies in the Americas: Fifty Years Since Virú*. Washington DC, Smithsonian Institution Press.

Bindra, S.C. (2002–3) 'Lothal: a Harappan port town revisited'. *Puratattva* 33: 1–22.

Binford, L.R. (1987) 'Data, relativism and archaeological science'. *MAN* Vol. 22(3): 391–404.

Binford, M.W., Kolata, A.L., Brenner, M., Janusek, J.W., Seddon, M.T., Abbott, M. and Curtis, J.H. (1997) 'Climate variation and the rise and fall of an Andean Civilization'. *Quaternary Research* 47: 235–248.

Bisht, R.S. (1991) 'Dholavira: A new horizon of the Indus Civilization'. *Puratattva* 20: 71–82.

Bisht, R.S. (1998–9) 'Dholavira and Banawali: Two different paradigms of the Harappan *urbis forma'*. *Puratattva* 29: 15–37.

Bisht, R.S. & Asthana, S. (1979) *Banawali and some other recently excavated Harappan sites in India*. In Taddei ed., pp. 221–239.

Blackham, M. (2002) 'Modelling Time and Transition in Prehistory: the Jordan Valley Chalcolithic (5500–3500 BC)'. Oxford, BAR *S1027*.

Blackman, M.J. (2000). 'Chemical characterization of local Anatolian and Uruk style sealing clays from Hacinebi'. *Paléorient* 25(1): 51–56.

Blake, M. (1999) ed., *Pacific Latin America in Prehistory: The Evolution of Archaic and Formative Cultures*. Pullman, Washington State University Press.

Blakeley, B.B. (1988) 'In search of Danyang, I: Historical geography and archaeological sites'. *Early China* 13: 116–152.

Blanton, R.E. (1994) *Houses and Households: A Comparative Study*. Plenum Press, New York.

Blanton, R.E. (1995) *The cultural foundations of inequality in households*. In Price and Feinman eds, pp. 105–127.

Blanton, R.E. (1998) *Beyond centralization: Steps toward a theory of behaviour in archaic states*. In Feinman and Marcus eds, pp. 135–172.

Blanton, R.E., Feinman, G.M., Kowalewski, S.A. and Peregrine, P.N. (1996) 'A dual processional theory for the evolution of Mesoamerican Civilization [Agency, ideology and power in archaeological theory, 1]'. *Current Anthropology* 37(1): 1–14.

Bloch, M. (1992) *Prey into Hunter: The Politics of Religious Experience*. Cambridge, CUP.

Blum, J. (1961) *Lord and Peasant in Russia from the Ninth to the Nineteenth Century*. New Jersey, Princeton University Press.

Blunden, C. and Elvin, M. (1983) *Cultural Atlas of China*. Oxford, Equinox.

Bocquet-Appel, J.-P. and Naji, S. (2006) 'Testing the hypothesis of a worldwide Neolithic demographic transition'. *Current Anthropology* 47(2): 341–365.

Boese, J. (1986–7) 'Excavations at Tell Sheikh Hassan: Preliminary report on the Year 1987 campaign in the Euphrates Valley'. *Annales Archéolgiques Arabes Syriennes* 36–37: 67–100.

Bohannan, P. (1967) ed., *Law and Warfare: Studies in the Anthropology of Conflict*. Austin and London, University of Texas Press.

Boivin, N. (2000) 'Rythms and floor sequences: excavating time in rural Rajastan and Neolithic Çatalhöyük'. *World Archaeology* 31(3): 367–88.

Boivin, N. (2005) 'Orientalism, ideology and identity: examining caste in South Asian archaeology'. *Journal of Social Archaeology* 5(2): 225–252.

Bonavia, D. and Grobman, A. (1989) *Andean maize: its origins and domestication*. In Harris and Hillman eds, pp. 456–470.

Bonogofsky, M. (2004) 'Including women and children: Neolithic modelled skulls from Jordan, Israel, Syria and Turkey'. *Near Eastern Archaeology* 67(2): 118–9.

Boone, E.H. (1984) ed., *Ritual Human Sacrifice in Mesoamerica*. Washington DC, Dumbarton Oaks Research Library and Collection.

Bourdieu, P. (1977) *Outline of a Theory of Practice*. Cambridge, Cambridge University Press.

Bourget, S. (2001a) *Children and ancestors: ritual practices at the Moche site of Huaca de la Luna, North Coast of Peru*. In Benson and Cook eds, pp. 93–118.

Bourget, S. (2001b) *Rituals of sacrifice: its practice at Huaca de la Luna and its representation in Moche iconography*. In Pillsbury ed., pp. 89–109.

Bourget, S. and Newman, M.E. (1998) 'A toast to the ancestors: ritual warfare and sacrificial blood in Moche culture'. *Baessler-Archiv* 46(1): 85–106.

Bourke, S.J. (2002) 'The origins of social complexity in the Southern Levant: new evidence from Teleilat Ghassul, Jordan'. *Palestine Excavation Quarterly*, 134(1) 2–27.

Boxer, C.R. (1957) 'Sakoku, or the Closed Country (1640–1854)'. *History Today*, Vol. 7(2): 80–88.

Boyer, P. (2001), *Religion Explained: The Human Instincts that Fashion Gods, Spirits and Ancestors*. London, Heinemann.

Braun, E. (2000) *Area G of Afridar, Palmahim Quarry 3 and the earliest pottery of Early Bronze Age I: part of the 'missing link'*. In Philip and Baird eds, pp. 113–128.

Carneiro, R.L. (1970) 'A theory of the origin of the state'. *Science* 169: 733–38.

Carneiro, R. L. (1981) *The chiefdom: precursor of the state*. In Jones and Kautz eds, pp. 37–79.

Carneiro, R.L. (1992) *Point counterpoint: ecology and ideology in the development of New World civilization*. In Demarest and Conrad, pp. 175–203.

Carr, C. and Neitzel, J.E. (1995) eds, *Style, Society and Person. Archaeological and Ethnological Perspectives*. New York, Plenum.

Carrasco, D. (1999) *City of Sacrifice: The Aztec Empire and the Role of Violence in Civilization*. Boston M.A., Beacon Press.

Carter, E., Campbell, S. and Gauld, S. (2003) 'Elusive complexity: new data from Late Halaf Domuztepe in South Central Turkey'. *Paléorient* 29(2): 117–134.

Carter, R. and Philip, G. (2006) *The Ubaid and beyond: exploring the transmission of culture in the developed prehistoric societies of the Middle East. Outline of key themes emerging from the Durham Ubaid Conference, April 2006*, circulated to participants.

Carus-Wilson, E.M. (1967) *Medieval Merchant Venturers: Collected Studies*. London, Methuen & Co.

Casal, J.-M. (1964a) 'Fresh digging at Amri'. *Pakistan Archaeology* I: 57–65.

Casal, J.-M. (1964b) *Fouilles d'Amri. 2 Vols*. Publications de la Commission des Fouilles Archéologiques, Fouilles du Pakistan. Paris.

Case, H. and Payne, J.C. (1962) 'Tomb 100: the decorated tomb at Hierakonpolis'. *Journal of Egyptian Archaeology* 48: 5–18.

Casson, L. (2001) *Libraries in the Ancient World*. New Haven and London, Yale University Press.

Castillo, L.J. (2001) *The last of the Mochicas: a view from the Jequetepeque Valley*. In Pillsbury ed., pp. 307–331.

Castillo, L.J. and Donnan, C.B (1994) 'La ocupación Moche de San José de Moro, Jequetepeque'. In Uceda and Mujica (eds.), pp. 93-146.

Cauvin, Jacques (1994) *Naissance des divinités, naissance de l'agriculture: La revolution des symboles au Néolithique*. Paris, CNRS.

Cauvin, Jacques, (2000a) *The Birth of the Gods and the Origins of Agriculture*. Cambridge, CUP.

Cauvin, Jacques, (2000b) *The symbolic foundations of the Neolithic Revolution in the Near East*. In Kuijt ed., 235–251.

Cauvin, Jacques (2001) 'Ideology before economy'. *Cambridge Archaeological Journal* 11(1): 106–7.

Cauvin, J. and Cauvin, M.-C. (1993) 'La séquence néolithique PPNB au Levant nord'. *Paléorient* 19: 23–27.

Chagnon, N.A. (1968) *Yanomamö: The Fierce People*. New York, Holt, Rinehart and Winston.

Chagnon, N.A. (1988) 'Life histories, blood revenge, and warfare in a tribal population'. *Science* 239: 985–992.

Chakrabarti, D.K. (1979) *Size of the Harappan settlements*. In Agrawal and Chakrabarti eds, pp. 205–215.

Chakrabarti, D.K. (1995) *The Archaeology of Ancient Indian Cities*. Oxford, OUP.

Chakrabarti, D.K. (1999) *India: An Archaeological History*. New Delhi, Oxford University Press.

Chang, K.C. (1974) 'Urbanism and the king in Ancient China'. *World Archaeology* 6(1): 1–14.

Chang, K.C. (1977a) ed., *Food in Chinese Culture: Anthropological and Historical Perspectives*. New Haven, Yale University Press.

Chang, K.C. (1977b) *Food in ancient China*. In Chang ed., pp. 23–52.

Chang, K.C. (1977c) *The Archaeology of Ancient China, 3rd edition*. New Haven, Yale University Press.

Chang, K.C. (1980a) *Shang Civilization*. New Haven, Yale University Press.

Chang, K.C. (1980b) *The Chinese Bronze Age: a modern synthesis*. In Fong ed., pp. 35–50.

Chang, K.C. (1983a) *Art, Myth and Ritual: the Path to Political Authority in Ancient China*. New Haven, Yale U.P.

Chang, K.C. (1983b) *Settlement patterns in Chinese archaeology: A case study from the Bronze Age*. In Vogt and Leventhal eds, pp. 361–374.

Chang, K.C. (1986a) *The Archaeology of Ancient China (4th ed.)*. New Haven, Yale University Press.

Chang, K.C. (1986b) ed., *Studies of Shang Archaeology: Selected Papers from the International Conference on Shang Civilization*. New Haven and London, Yale U.P.

Chang, K.C. (1986c) *Yin-hsu tomb number five and the question of the P'an Keng/Hsiao Hsin/Hsio Yi Period in Yin-hsu Archaeology.* In K.C. Chang ed., pp. 65–80.

Chang, P.C. (1986) *A brief description of the Fu Hao Oracle Bone Inscriptions.* In K.C. Chang ed., pp. 121–140.

Chang, T.T. (1989) *Domestication and the spread of cultivated rices.* In Harris and Hillman eds, pp. 408–417.

Chapdelaine, C. (2001) *The growing power of a Moche urban class.* In Pillsbury ed., pp. 69–87.

Chapdelaine, C. (2002) *Out in the streets of Moche: urbanism and sociopolitical organization at a Moche IV urban centre.* In Isbell and Silverman eds, pp. 53–88.

Chapdelaine, C. (2006) *Looking for Moche palaces in the elite residences of the Huacas of Moche site.* In Christie and Sarro eds, pp. 23–43,

Chapdelaine, C., Pimentel, V. and Bernier, H. (2001) 'A glimpse at Moche Phase III occupation at the Huacas of Moche site, Northern Peru'. *Antiquity* 75: 361–72.

Charlton, T.H. and Nichols, D.L. (1997a) *The City-State concept: Development and applications.* In Nichols and Charlton eds, pp. 1–14.

Charlton, T.H. and Nichols, D.L. (1997b) *Diachronic studies of City-States: permutations on a theme – Central Mexico from 1700 BC to AD 1600.* In Nichols and Charlton eds, pp. 169–207.

Chase-Dunn C. and Hall, T.D. (1997) *Rise and Demise: Comparing World Systems.* Westview Press, Boulder.

Chauchat, C., Wing, E.S., Lacombe, J.-P., Demars, P.-Y., Santiago, E., Uceda, C. and Deza, C. (1992) *Préhistoire de la cote nord du Pérou: Le Paijanien de Cupinisque. Cahiers du Quaternaire*, 18. Paris: Centre Régional de Publications de Bordeaux, Éditions CNRS.

Chen, Xingcan (2008) 'Comment on Flad'. *CA* 49(3): 421–2.

Chen, Lie (1996) *The ancestor cult in ancient China.* In Rawson ed., pp. 269–272.

Cheng Chen-Hsiang (1986) *Bronzes with the 'Ssu T'u Mu' inscriptions excavated from the Fu Hao tomb.* In Chang ed., pp. 81–102.

Chippendale, C. (1993) *Ambition, deference, discrepancy, consumption: The intellectual background to a post- processual archaeology.* In Yoffee and Sherratt eds, pp. 27–36.

Childs-Johnson, E. (1988) ed., *Ritual and Power: Jades of Ancient China.* New York, China Institute of America.

Childs-Johnson, E. (1991) 'Jades of the Hongshan culture: the dragon and fertility cult worship'. *Ars Asiatique* 46: 82–95.

Christie, J.J. and Sarro, P.J. (2006) eds, *Palaces and Power in the Americas: From Peru to the Northwest Coast.* Austin (TX), University of Austin Press.

Chłodniki, M. and Ciałowicz, K.M. (2002) 'Tell el-Farka seasons 1998–1999: preliminary report'. *MDAIK*58: 89–117.

Ciałowicz, K.M. (1992) *La composition, le sens et la symbolique des scènes zoomorphes prédynastiques en relief.* In Friedman and Adams eds, pp. 247–258.

Ciałowicz, K.M. (2000) 'Review of Wilkinson, Toby A.H. [1999] Early Dynastic Egypt'. *Bibliotheca Orientalis* LVII (5–6): 575–577.

Claessen, H.J.M. & Skalnik, P. (1978) *Limits: the beginning and end of the Early State.* In Claessen and Skalnik eds, pp. 619–635.

Claessen, H.J.M. & Skalnik, P. (1978b) eds, *The Early State.* The Hague, Mouton.

Claessen, H.J.M. & Skalnik, P. (1981) eds, *The Study of the State.* The Hague, Mouton.

Clark, J. and Pye, M. (2000) *Olmec Art and Archaeology in Mesoamerica.* New Haven, Yale University Press.

Clarke, M.V. (1926) *The Medieval City State.* London, Methuen and Co.

Close, A.E. (2002) 'Sinai, Sahara, Sahel: The introduction of domestic caprines to Africa'. *Jennerstrasse* 8 (eds) pp. 459–469.

Coe, M.D. (1981) *Religion and the rise of Mesoamerican state.* In Jones and Kautz eds, pp. 157–171.

Cohen, M.N. (1981) *The ecological basis of New World state formation: General and local model building.* In Jones and Kautz eds, pp. 105–122.

Cohen, R. and Service, E.R. (1978) eds, *Origins of the State: The Anthropology of Political Evolution.* Philadelphia, ISHI.

Cole, S. (1994) 'Marsh formation in the Borsippa region and the course of the Lower Euphrates'. *JNES* 53: 81–109.

Colledge, S., Conolly, J. and Shennan, S. (2004) 'Archaeobotanical evidence for the spread of farming in the Eastern Mediterranean'. *Current Anthropology* 45(S): 35–58.

Collins, P. (2000) 'The Uruk Phenomenon: The Role of Ideology in the Expansion of the Uruk. Culture during the 4th Millennium BC'. Oxford, Archaeopress, *BAR* 900.

Collins, P. (2006) 'Trees and gender in Assyrian art'. *Iraq* LXVIII: 99–107.

Collon, D. and Reade, J. (1983) 'Archaic Nineveh'. *Baghdader Mitteilungen* 14: 33–41.

Conkey, M. and Hastorf, C. (1990) eds, *The Uses of Style in Archaeology*. Cambridge, CUP.

Conlee, C.A. (2003) 'Local Elites and the reformation of Late Intermediate Period sociopolitical and economic organization in Nasca, Peru'. *Latin American Antiquity*, 14(1): 47–65.

Conlee, C.A., Dulanto, J., Mackey, C.J. and Stanish, C. (2004) *Late Prehispanic sociopolitical complexity*. In Silverman ed., pp. 209–236.

Conrad, G.W. and Demarest, A.A. (1984) *Religion and Empire: The Dynamics of Aztec and Inca Expansionism*. New York, CUP.

Constantini, L. (1984) *The beginning of agriculture in the Kachi plain: the evidence of Mehrgarh*. In B. Allchin ed., pp. 29–33.

Constantini, L. (1990) *Harappan agriculture in Pakistan: The evidence of Nausharo. South Asian Archaeology 1987, Part* 1, pp. 321-332.

Constantini, L. and Lentini, A. (2000) *Studies in the vegetation history of Central Baluchistan, Pakistan: Palynological investigations of a Neolithic sequence at Mehrgarh*. In Taddei and De Marco, pp. 133–159.

Cook, A.G. (1992) 'The stone ancestors: idioms of imperial attire and rank among Huari figurines'. *Latin American Antiquity* 3: 341–364.

Cook, A.G. (2001) *Huari D-shaped structures, sacrificial offerings and divine rulership*. In Benson and Cook eds pp. 137–163.

Cook, A.G. (2004) *Wari art and society*. In Silverman ed., pp. 146–166.

Cooke, G.A. (1987) 'Reconstruction of the Holocene coastline of Mesopotamia'. *Geoarchaeology* 2: 15–28.

Cooper, J.S. (1983) *The Curse of Agade*. Baltimore, Johns Hopkins University Press..

Cooper, J.S. (1986) *Sumerian and Akkadian Royal Inscriptions, I. Presargonic Inscriptions*, New Haven, American Oriental Society.

Cooper, J.S. (2000) *Sumerian and Semitic writing in most ancient Syro-Mesopotamia*. In Van Lerberghe and Vogt eds, pp. 61–77.

Cope, C. (1991) 'Gazelle hunting strategies in the Southern Levant'. In Bar-Yosef and Valla (eds), pp. 311-358.

Copeland, L. and Hours, F. (1987) *The Halafians, their predecessors and their contemporaries in Northern Syria and the Levant, relative and absolute dating*. In Aurenche *et al.* eds, pp. 401–425.

Cordy-Collins, A. (1992) 'Archaism or tradition? The decapitation theme in Cupisnique and Moche iconography'. *Latin American Antiquity* 3(3): 206–220.

Cordy-Collins, A. (2001a) *Blood and the Moon Priestesses: Spondylus shells in Moche ceremony*. In Benson and Cook eds, pp. 35–53.

Cordy-Collins, A. (2001b) *Labretted ladies: foreign women in Northern Moche and Lambayeque art*. In Pillsbury ed., pp. 247–257.

Cork, E. (2005) 'Peaceful Harappans? Reviewing the evidence for the absence of warfare in the Indus Civilization of north-west India and Pakistan (c. 2500–1900 BC)'. *Antiquity* 79: 411– 423

Cotterell, A. (1980) ed., *The Encyclopaedia of Ancient Civilizations*. New York, Mayflower Books.

Covey, R.A. (2000) 'Inka Administration of the far south coast of Peru'. *Latin American Antiquity*, 11(2): 119–138.

Crawford, H. (1998) *Dilmun and its Gulf Neighbours*. Cambridge, CUP.

Crawford, G.W. and Chen Shen (1998) 'The origins of rice agriculture: recent progress in East Asia'. *Antiquity* 72: 858–866.

Crawford, G.W., Underhill, A., Zhao, Z., Lee, G-A., Feinman, G., Nicholas, L., Luan, F., Yu, H., Fang, H. and Cai, F. (2005) 'Late Neolithic plant remains from Northern China: preliminary results from Liangchengzhen, Shandong'. *Current Anthropology* 46(2): 309–317.

Cross, F.M. (1989) *The invention and development of the alphabet*. In Senner ed., pp. 77–90.

Cruells, W. and Nieuwenhuyse, O. (2004) 'The Proto-Halaf period in Syria. New sites, new data'. *Paléorient* 30/1: 47–68.

Crumley, C.L. (1976) 'Toward a locational definition of state systems of settlement'. *American Anthropologist* 78(1): 59–73.

Culbert, T.P. (1988) *The Collapse of Classic Maya civilization*. In Yoffee and Cowgill eds, pp. 69–101.

Cupere, B. de and Duru, R. (2003) 'Faunal remains from Neolithic Höyücek (SW Turkey) and the presence of early domestic cattle in Anatolia'. *Paléorient* 29(1): 107–120.

Curtis, J. (1981) *Arpachiya*. In Curtis ed., pp. 30–36.

Curtis, J. (1981) ed., *Fifty Years of Mesopotamian Discovery*. London, British School of Archaeology in Iraq.

Curvers, H.H. and Schwartz, G.M. (1990) 'Excavations at Tell al-Raqa'i: a small rural site of early urban Mesopotamia'. *AJA* 94: 3–23.

Daggett, R. (1987) *Toward the development of the state on the north central coast of Peru*. In Haas, Pozorski and Pozorski, eds, pp. 70–82.

Damania, A.B. (1997) 'Diversity of major cultivated plants domesticated in the Near East'. *Harlan Symposium*, pp. 51–64.

Damania, A.B., Valkoun, J., Willcox, G. and Qualset, C.O. (1997) eds, *The Origins of Agriculture and Crop Domestication. Proceedings of the Harlan Symposium, 10-14 May 1997, Aleppo, Syria*. Aleppo, ICARDA, IPGRI, FAO, and UC/GRCP.

Damerow, P. and Englund, R.K. (1989) 'The Proto-Elamite Texts from Tepe Yahya'. *American School of Prehistoric Research, Bulletin* 39. Peabody Museum of Archaeology and Ethnology, Harvard University.

Davidson, T.E. and McKerrell, H. (1980) 'The neutron activation analysis of Halaf and 'Ubaid pottery from Tell Arpachiyah and Tepe Gawra'. *Iraq* 42: 155–67.

Davis, N. (1984) *Human sacrifice in the Old World and the New: Some similarities and differences*. In Boone ed., pp. 211–226.

Davis, S. (1984) 'Climatic change and the advent of domestication: The succession of ruminant artiodactyls in the Late Pleistocene-Holocene in the Israel region'. *Paléorient* 8: 5–15.

Davis, W. (1989) *The Canonical Tradition in Egyptian Art*. Cambridge, CUP.

D'Altroy, T. N. (1996) *Inca Civilization: Introduction*. In Fagan ed., pp. 340–1.

D'Altroy, T.N. (2001a) *A view of the plains from the mountains: Comments on Uruk by an Andeanist*. In Rothman ed., pp. 445– 475.

D'Altroy, T.N. (2001b) *Politics, resources and blood in the Inka empire*. In Alcock *et al.* eds, pp. 201–226.

D'Altroy, T.N. and Schreiber, K. (2004) *Andean empires*. In Silverman ed., pp. 255–279.

De Bary, W.T. and Bloom, I. (1999) compilers: *Sources of Chinese Tradition: from Earliest Times to 1600*. New York, Columbia University Press.

Debono, F. and Mortensen, B. (1990) 'El Omari: A Neolithic Settlement and Other Sites in the Vicinity of Wadi Hof, Helwan'. *Archäologische Veröffentlichungen* 82. Mainz, Philipp von Zabern.

Deckers, K. and Riehl, S. (2004) 'The development of economy and environment from the Bronze Age to the Early Iron Age in Northern Syria and the Levant. A case-study from the Upper Khabur region'. *Antiquity* Vol. 78, No. 302, Project Gallery.

De Cupere, B. and Duru, R. (2003) 'Faunal remains from Neolithic Höyücek (SW Turkey) and the presence of early domestic cattle in Anatolia'. *Paléorient* 29(1): 107–120.

De Leonardis, L. (2000) 'The body context: Interpreting Early Nasca decapitated burials'. *Latin American Antiquity* 11(4): 363–386.

De Leonardis, L. and Lau, G.F. (2004) *Life, death and ancestors*. In Silverman ed., pp. 77–115.

Del Olmo Lete, G. and Montero Fenellos, J.-L., eds (1999) *Archaeology of the Upper Syrian Euphrates: The Tishrin Dam Area*. Barcelona, Editorial AUSA.

Delougaz, P. and Kantor, H.J. (1996) 'Choga Mish, Volume 1: The First Five Seasons of Excavations 1961–1971. Part 1 Text, Part 2 Plates.' Chicago, *Oriental Institute Publications Volume* 101.

Demarest, A.A. (1984) *Overview: Mesoamerican human sacrifice in evolutionary perspective*. In Boone ed., pp. 227–247.

Demarest, A.A. (2006) *Sacred and profane mountains of the pasión: Contrasting architectural paths to power*. In Christie and Sarro eds, pp. 1176–140.

Demarest, A.A. and Conrad, G.W. (1992) eds, *Ideology in Pre-Columbian Civilizations*. Santa Fe (NM), School of American Research Press.

Demattè, P. (1999) 'Longshan-era urbanism: the role of cities in Predynastic China'. *Asian Perspectives* 38(2): 119–53.

De Marrais, E. (2004) 'Tiwanaku, urbanization, and the 'practice' of statecraft in the Andes. Review article'. *Cambridge Archaeological Journal*, 12(2): 289–91.

De Marrais, E., Castillo, L.J. and Earle, T. (1996) 'Ideology, materialization, and power strategies [Agency, Ideology, and Power in Archaeological Theory 2]'. *Current Anthropology* Vol. 37 (1): 15–31.

De Polignac (1995 [1984]) *Cults, Territory and the Origins of the Greek City-State*. Chicago, University of Chicago Press.

Dhavalikar, M.K. (1993) Harappans in Saurashtra: The mercantile enterprise as seen from recent excavation of Kuntasi. In Possehl ed., pp. 555–568.

Dhavalikar, M.K. and Possehl, G.L. (1992) 'The Pre-Harappan Period at Prabhas Patan and the Pre-Harappan Phase in Gujarat'. *Man and Environment* XVII(1): 71–78.

Diakonoff, I.M. (1974) 'Structure of Ancient Society and State in Early Dynastic Sumer'. *Monographs of the Ancient Near East 1(3)*. Undena, Malibu.

Diakonoff, I.M. (1983) 'The structure of Near Eastern society before the middle of the second millennium BC' *Oikumene* 3: 7–100.

Diakonoff, I.M. (1996) *Extended family households in Mesopotamia (III-II Millennia BC)*. In Veenhof ed., pp. 55–59.

Diaz, H.F. and Markgraf, V. (1992) eds *El Niño: Historical and Palaeoclimatic Aspects of the Southern Oscillation*. Cambridge CUP.

Di Cosmo, N. (2002) *Ancient China and its Enemies: The Rise of Nomadic Power in East Asian History*. Cambridge, CUP.

Dickson, D.B. (2006) 'Public transcripts expressed in theatres of cruelty: the Royal Graves at Ur in Mesopotamia'. *Cambridge Archaeological Journal* 16(2): 123–44.

Diehl, R.A. (2004) *Olmecs: America's First Civilization*. London, Thames and Hudson.

Diehl, R.A. and Coe, M.D. (1996) *Olmec archaeology*. In Rosenbaum ed., pp. 11–25.

Dill, S. (1958 [1898]) *Roman Society in the Last Century of the Western Empire*. New York, Meridian Books.

Dillehay, T.D. (1995) ed., *Tombs for the Living: Andean Mortuary Practices*. Washington DC, Dumbarton Oaks Research Library and Collection.

Dillehay, T.D. (2001) *Town and country in Late Moche times: A view from two northern valleys*. In Pillsbury ed., pp. 259–283.

Dillehay, T.D., Bonavia, D. and Kaulicke, P. (2004) *The first settlers*. In Silverman ed., pp. 16–34.

Divale, W.T. and Harris, M. (1976) 'Population, warfare and the male supremacist complex'. *American Anthropologist* 78(3): 521–538.

Dixon, P. (1992) *'The cities are not populated as once they were'*. In Rich ed., pp. 145–160.

Dolce, R. (1998) 'The palatial Ebla Culture in the context of North Mesopotamian and North Syrian main powers'. *Subartu* 4/2: 67–81.

Donnan, C.B. (1978) *Moche Art of Peru: Pre-Columbian Symbolic Communication*. Los Angeles, Fowler Museum of Culture History, University of Los Angeles.

Donnan, C.B. (1991) ed., *Early Ceremonial Architecture in the Andes*. Dumbarton Oaks, Washington D.C.

Donnan, C.B. (1992) *Ceramics of Ancient Peru*. Fowler Museum of Cultural History, UCLA.

Donnan, C.B. (2001) *Moche ceramic portraits*. In Pillsbury ed., pp. 127–139.

Donnan, C.B. (2004) *Moche Portraits from Ancient Peru*. Austin, University of Texas Press.

Donnan, C.B. and Castillo, L.J. (1992) 'Finding the tomb of a Moche priestess'. *Archaeology* 45(6): 38–42.

Donnan, C.B. and McClelland, D. (1999) *Moche Fineline Painting: Its Evolution and its Artists*. Los Angeles, University of California, Fowler Museum of Cultural History.

Dorado, M.R. (1997) *Clues to the system of power in the city of Oxkintok*. In Manzanilla ed., pp. 169–180.

Dransart, P. (2000) *Clothed metal and the iconography of human form among the Incas*. In McEwan ed., pp. 76–91.

Dreyer, G. (1993) 'A hundred years at Abydos'. *Egyptian Archaeology* 3: 10–12.

Dreyer, G. (2000) 'Egypt's earliest historical event'. *Egyptian Archaeology* 16: 6–7.

Driver, T. and Chapman, G (1996) eds, *Time-scales and Environmental Change*. London, Routledge.

Druc, I.C. (2004) 'Ceramic diversity in Chavín de Huantar, Peru'. *Latin American Antiquity* 15(3): 344–363.

Duistermaat, K. (1996) *The seals and sealings*. In Akkermans pp. 339–401.

Dunbar, R.I.M. (1988) *Primate Social Systems*. London, Chapman and Hall; Ithaca, Cornell University Press.

Dunbar, R.I.M. (1993) 'Coevolution of neocortex size, group size and language in humans'. *Behavioural and Brain Sciences* 16(40): 681–735.

Dunn, A. (2004) *The Peasants' Revolt*. Oxford, Tempus.

Düring, B.S. (2005) 'Building continuity in the Central Anatolian Neolithic: exploring the meaning of buildings at Aşikli Höyük and Çatalhöyük'. *Journal of Mediterranean Archaeology* 18.1(3–29).

Durrani, F.A., Ali, I. and Erdosy, G. (1991) 'Further excavations at Rehman Dheri'. *Ancient Pakistan* 7: 61–146.

Earle, T.K. (1987) 'Chiefdoms in archaeological and ethnohistorical context'. *Annual Review of Archaeology* 16: 279–308.

Earle, T.K. (1995) *Chiefdoms: Power, Economy, and Ideology*. Cambridge, Cambridge University Press.

Earle, T.K., D'Altroy, T.N., Hastorf, C.A., Scott, C.J., Costin, C.L., Russell, G.S. and Sandefur, E.C. (1987) *Archaeological Field Research in the Upper Mantaro, Peru 1982–1983: Investigations of Inka Expansion and Exchange*. Los Angeles, University of California, Institute of Archaeology, Monograph 28.

Echallier, J.C. (1981) 'La production des céramiques protohistoriques de Shortugai (Afghanistan). Études pétrographiques'. *Paléorient* 7(2): 115–19.

Edens, C. (2000) 'The chipped-stone industry at Hacinebi: Technological styles and social identity'. *Paléorient* 25(1): 23–33.

Edens, C. and Wilkinson, T.J. (1998) 'Southwest Arabia during the Holocene: Recent archaeological developments'. *Journal of World Prehistory* 12: 55–119.

Edmonds, R.L. (1998) ed., *Managing the Chinese Environment: SOAS Studies on Contemporary China*. Oxford, OUP.

Edwards, P.C., Meadows, J., Sayej, G. and Westway, M. (2004) 'From the PPNA to the PPNB: New views from the Southern Levant after excavations at Zahrat adh-Dhra'2 in Jordan'. *Paléorient* 20(2): 21–60.

Edzard, D. (1997) *Gudea and his Dynasty*. Toronto, University of Toronto Press.

Eidem, J. and Warburton, D. (1996) 'In the land of Nagar: a survey around Tell Brak'. *Iraq* 58: 51–64.

El-Baghdadi, S.G. (2003) 'Proto- and Early Dynastic necropolis at Minshat Ezzat, Dakahlia Province, Northeast Delta'. *Archéo-Nil* 13: 143–152.

El-Wailly, F. and Abu el-Soof, B. 'Excavations at Tell es-Sawwan', *Sumer* 21: 17–32.

Eliade, M. (1972 [1951]) 'Shamanism: Archaic Techniques of Ecstacy'. *Bollingen Series* LXXVI. New Jersey, Princeton University Press.

Eliade, M. (1957) *The Sacred and the Profane: The Nature of Religion*. New York, Harcourt Brace Jovanovich.

Ellis, M. de J. (1977) ed., *Essays on the Ancient Near East in Memory of J.J. Finkelstein. Hampden, Memoirs of the Connecticut Academy of Arts and Sciences*, Vol. XIX.

Elvin, Mark (1984) 'Why China failed to develop an endogenous industrial capitalism: a critique of Max Weber's explanation'. *Theory and Society* 3(3): 379–391.

Elvin, Mark (1993) 'Three thousand years of unsustainable growth: China's environment from archaic times to the present'. *East Asian History* 6:

Elvin, Mark (1998) *The environmental legacy of Imperial China*. In Edmonds ed., pp. 9–32.

Elvin, Mark, (2002) 'The unavoidable environment: reflections on premodern economic growth in China. Papers from the Third International Conference on Sinology, History Section'. Taipei, Institute of History and Philology, *Academia Sinica*, 2002, pp. 1–86.

Elvin, Mark (2004) 'Some reflections on the use of 'styles of scientific thinking' to disaggregate and sharpen comparisons between China and Europe from Sòng to mid-Ching times (960–1850 CE)'. *History of Technology* 25: 53–103.

Forest, J.-D. (2005) *The state: The process of state formation as seen from Mesopotamia.* In Pollock and Bernbeck eds, pp. 184–206.

Forest, J.-D. (2006) *Abstract of paper given to the Ubaid Conference, Durham University, April 2006.*

Forest-Foucault, C. (1980) 'Rapport sur le fouilles de Kheit Khasim III'. *Paléorient* 6: 221–4.

Fortes, M. (1953) 'The structure of unilineal descent groups'. *American Anthropologist* 55: 17–41.

Fortes, M. (1959) 'Descent, filiation and affinity'. *Man* 59: 193–197 and 206–212.

Foster, B.R. (1977a) *Ea and Saltu.* In M.de J. Ellis ed., pp. 79–84.

Foster, B.R. (1977b) 'Commercial activity in Sargonic Mesopotamia'. *Iraq* 39: 31–44.

Foster, B.R. (1981) 'A new look at the Sumerian temple state'. *JESHO* 24: 225–241.

Foster, B.R. (1982) 'Archives and record keeping in Sargonic Mesopotamia'. *Zeitschrift für Assyriologie* 72(1): 1–27.

Foster, B.R. (2005) *Transmission of knowledge.* In Snell ed., pp 261–268.

Frame, M. (2001) *Blood, fertility and transformation: interwoven themes in the Paracas necropolis embroideries.* In Benson and Cook eds, pp. 55–92.

Francfort, H.P. (1981) 'About the Shortugai sequence from Mature Harappan to Late Bactrian: Bronze Age in Eastern Bactria (N.E. Afghanistan)'. *Puratattva* 10: 91–4.

Francfort, H.P. (1984) *The early periods of Shortugai (Harappan) and the Western Bactrian culture of Dashly.* In Allchin ed., pp. 170–75.

Franco, R., Gálvez, C., Vasquez, S. and Murga, A. (1999) 'Reposición de un muro Mochica con relieves policromos, Huaca Cao Viejo, complejo El Brujo'. *Arkinka* 4(43): 82–91.

Frangipane, M. (1993) *Local components in the development of centralized societies in Syro-Anatolian regions.* In Frangipane *et al.* eds, pp. 133–161.

Frangipane, M. (1997a) *Arslantepe-Malatya: external factors and local components in the development of early state society.* In Manzanilla ed., pp. 43–58.

Frangipane, M. (1997b) 'A 4th Millennium temple/palace complex at Arslantepe-Malatya. North-South relations and the formation of early state societies in the Northern Regions of Greater Mesopotamia'. *Paléorient* 23/1: 45–73.

Frangipane, M. (2001a) *Centralization processes in Greater Mesopotamia: Uruk 'expansion' as the climax of systemic interactions among areas of the Greater Mesopotamian region.* In Rothman ed., pp. 307–347.

Frangipane, M. (2001b) 'On models and data in Mesopotamia'. *Current Anthropology* 43(3): 415–416.

Frangipane, M. (2002) *'Non-Uruk' developments and Uruk related features on the northern borders of Greater Mesopotamia.* In Postgate ed., pp. 123–148.

Frangipane, M., Hauptmann, H., Liverani, M., Matthiae, P. and Mellink, M. (1993) eds, *Between the Rivers and Over the Mountains: Archaeologica Anatolica et Mesopotamica Alba Palmieri Dedicata.* Rome. Dipartimento di Scienze Archeologiche e Antropologiche dell'Antichita Universita di Roma 'La Sapienza'.

Frank, R.H. (1988) *Passions within Reason: The Strategic Role of the Emotions.* New York, Norton.

Frayne, D.R. (1993) 'Sargonic and Gutian Period (2334–2113 BC). The Royal Inscriptions of Mesopotamia'. *Early Periods*, Vol. 2. Toronto, Buffalo, New York, University of Toronto Press.

Freidel, D.A. (1981) *Civilization as a state of mind: the cultural evolution of the Lowland Maya.* In Jones and Kautz eds, pp. 188–227.

French, D.H. (1988) 'Canhasan Sites 1. Canhasan I: Stratigraphy and Structures'. *British Institute of Archaeology at Ankara Monograph* No. 23. Ankara, British Institute of Archaeology.

Friberg, J. (1984) 'Numbers and measures in the earliest written records'. *Scientific American* 250: 110–118.

Friberg, J. (1999) 'Counting and accounting in the proto-literate Middle East: Examples from two new volumes of proto-cuneiform texts'. *Journal of Cuneiform Studies* 51: 107–138.

Fried, M.H. (1957) 'The classification of corporate unilineal descent groups'. *Journal of the Royal Anthropological Institute* 87: 1–29.

Friedman, E. (2000) *Post-Deng China's right populist authoritarian foreign policy.* In Lau and Shen eds, pp. 1 ff.

Friedman, R.F. (1996) *The ceremonial centre at Hierakonpolis: Locality HK29A.* In Spencer ed., 16–35.

Friedman, R.F. and Adams, B. (1992) eds, *The Followers of Horus: Studies Dedicated to Michael Allen Hoffman (1944–1990).* Oxford, Oxbow Books

Friedman, R.F., Watrall, E., Jones, J., Fahmy, A.G., Van Neer, W. and Linseele, V. (2002) *Excavations at Hierakonpolis*. *Archéo-Nil* 12: 55–68.

Frifelt, K. and Sorensen, P. (1989) eds: *South Asian Archaeology, 1985*. London, Curzon Press.

Fuller, C.J. (1997) ed., *Caste Today*. New Delhi, Oxford University Press.

Fuller, D.Q., Harvey, E. and Qin, L. (2007) 'Presumed domestication? Evidence for wild rice cultivation and domestication in the fifth millennium BC of the Lower Yangzi region'. *Antiquity* 81: 316–331.

Fuller, D.Q., Qin, L. and Harvey, E. (2007) 'Rice archaeobotany revisited: comments on Liu et al'. *Antiquity* 82(315):

Fuller, L.L. (1969) *The Morality of Law* [revised edition]. New Haven and London, Yale University Press.

Fung, Pineda R. (1988) *The Late Preceramic and Initial Period*. In Keatinge ed., pp. 67–96.

Fung, C. (2000) 'The drinks are on us: ritual, social status, and practice in Dawenkou burials, North China'. *JEAA* 2(1–): 67–91.

Furst, P.T. (1996) *Shamanism, transformation and Olmec art*. In Rosenbaum ed., pp. 69–81.

Galili, E., Gopher, A., Rosen, B. and Horwitz, L. (2004) *The emergence of the Mediterranean fishing village in the Levant and the Neolithic anomaly of Cyprus*. In Peltenburg and Wasse eds, pp. 91–101.

Galili, E., Gopher, A., Eshed, V. and Hershkovitz, I. (2005) 'Burial practices at the submerged Pre-Pottery Neolithic C site of Atlit-Yam, northern coast of Israel'. *BASOR* 339: 1–19.

Gálvez, C. and Briceño, J. (2001) *The Moche in the Chicama Valley*. In Pillsbury ed., pp. 141–157.

Gansell, A.R. (2007) 'Identity and adornment in the third-millennium BC Mesopotamian "Royal Cemetery" at Ur'. *CAJ* 17(1): 29–46.

Gao, Mobo C.F. (1999) *Gao Village: A Portrait of Rural Life in Modern China*. London, Hurst & Company.

Gao, Q. and Lee, Y.K. (1993) 'A biological perspective on Yangshao kinship'. *Journal of Anthropological Archaeology* 12(3): 266–98.

Garazhian, O. (2009) 'Darestan: a group of Pre-Pottery Neolithic (PPN) sites in south-eastern Iran'. *Antiquity* Vol.83, issue 319: Project gallery.

Gardiner, A.H. (1961) *Egypt of the Pharaohs*. Oxford, OUP.

Gardner, J.F. (1974) *Leadership and the Cult of Personality*. London and Toronto, Dent/Hakkert.

Garge, T. (2001–2) 'Is every circular fire-pit in Harappan levels a "tandoor"?' *Purattatva* 32: 25–32.

Garfinkel, S.J. (2000) *Private Enterprise in Babylonia at the End of the Third Millennium BC* PhD. Diss., Columbia University.

Garfinkel, S.J. (2002) 'Turam-Ili and the community of merchants in the Ur III Period'. *Journal of Cuneiform Studies* 54: 29–48.

Garfinkel, S.J. (2005) *Public versus private in the ancient Near East*. In Snell ed., pp. 406–418.

Garfinkel, Y. (1994) 'Ritual burial of cultic objects: the earliest evidence'. *Cambridge Archaeological Journal* 4(2): 159–88.

Garfinkel, Y. (2001) 'Dancing or fighting? A recently discovered predynastic scene from Abydos, Egypt'. *Cambridge Archaeological Journal* 11: 241–54.

Garfinkel, Y. and Ben-Shlomo, D. (2002) *Sha'ar Hagolan architecture in its Near Eastern context*. In Garfinkel and Miller eds, pp. 71–84.

Garfinkel, Y., Korn, N. and Miller, M.A. (2002) *Art from Sha'ar Hagolan: Visions of a Neolithic village in the Levant*. In Garfinkel and Miller, pp. 188–208.

Garfinkel, Y. and Miller, M.A. (2002) eds, *Sha'ar Hagolan 1: Neolithic Art in Context*. Oxford, Oxbow Books.

Garfinkel,Y. (2003) *Dancing at the Dawn of Agriculture*. Austin, University of Texas Press.

Garfinkel, Y., Ben-Shlomo, D., Freikman, M., and Vered, A. (2007) 'Tel Tsaf: The 2004–2006 excavation seasons'. *Israel Excavation Journal* 57(1): 1–33.

Garfinkel, Y., Vered, A. and Bar-Yosef, O. (2006) 'The domestication of water: The Neolithic well at at Sha'ar Hagolan, Jordan Valley, Israel'. *Antiquity* 80: 686–696.

Garrard, A. (1999) 'Charting the emergence of cereal and pulse domestication in south-west Asia'. *Environmental Archaeology* 4: 67–86.

Gat, Azar (1999) 'The pattern of fighting in simple, small-scale, pre-state societies'. *Journal of Anthropological Research*, Vol. 55: 563–583.

Gebauer, A.B. and Price, T.D. (1992) eds, *Transitions to Agriculture in Prehistory*, Madison, Wisconsin, Prehistory Press.

Gebauer, A.B. and Price, T. D. (1995) eds, *Last Hunters, First Farmers: New Perspectives on the Prehistoric Transition to Agriculture*. Santa Fe, SAR.

Gebel, H.G.K. and Koslowski, S.K. (1994) eds, *Neolithic Chipped Stone Industries of the Fertile Crescent*. Berlin, Ex Oriente.

Gebel, H.G.K. (2005) *On PPN ritual centralities*. In Gebel and Rollefson eds, pp. 27–29.

Gebel, H.G. K., Hermansen, B.D. and Jensen, C.H. (2002) eds, *Magic Practices and Ritual in Early Near Eastern Production, Subsistence and Environment*. Berlin, Ex Oriente.

Gebel, H.G. and Rollefson, G.O. (2005) eds, 'Dialogue: The Early Neolithic Origin of Ritual Centres'. *Neo-Lithics* 2/05 (Special Issue).

Gelb, I.J. (1979) *Household and family in Ancient Mesopotamia*. In Lipinsky ed., I: 1–98

Gelb I.J. (1992) *Mari and the Kish Civilization*. In Young ed., pp. 121– 202.

Gelb, I.J., Steinkeller, P. and Whiting, R.M. (1991) 'Earliest Land Tenure Systems in the Near East: Ancient Kudurrus, 2 vols'. *Oriental Institute Publications 104*. Chicago, The University of Chicago.

Geller, J.R. (1992) *From prehistory to history: Beer in Egypt*. In Friedman and Adams, pp. 19–26.

George, A. (1999) *The Epic of Gilgamesh*. London, Penguin Books.

George, K.M. (1996) *Showing Signs of Violence: The Cultural Politics of a Twentieth-Century Headhunting Ritual*. Berkeley, University of California Press.

Ghezzi, I. (2008) *Religious warfare at Chankillo*. In Isbell and Silverman eds, pp. 67–84.

Ghiselin, M.T. (1974) *The Economy of Nature and the Evolution of Sex*. Berkeley, University of California Press.

Ghosh, A., Kar, A. and Hussain, Z. (1979) 'The lost courses of the Saraswati River in the Great Indian desert: New evidence from Landsat imagery', *The Geographical Journal* 145(3): 446–451.

Gibson, McG. (1972) *The City and Area of Kish*. Coconut Grove, Florida, Field Research Projects.

Gibson, McG. (1975) *Excavations at Nippur, Eleventh Season – with appendices by Civil, M., Johnson, J. and Kaufman, S.* University of Chicago, Oriental Institute Communications No. 22.

Gibson, McG. and Biggs, R.D. (1977) eds, *Seals and Sealing in the Ancient Near East*. Malibu, Calif., Undena Publications.

Gibson, McG. and Biggs, R.D. (1987) eds, 'The Organization of Power: Aspects of Bureaucracy in the Ancient Near East'. *SAOC* 46. University of Chicago, The Oriental Institute.

Gibson, McG., Franke, J.M.., Civil, J., Bates, M., Boessneck, J. and Butzer, K. (1992) 'Excavations at Nippur', *Oriental Institute Communications* No. 23. Twelfth Season. University of Chicago.

Gijseghem, H.V. (2001) 'Household and family at Moche, Peru: An analysis of building and residence patterns in a prehispanic urban centre'. *LAA* 12(3): 257–273.

Gijseghem, H.V. and Vaughn, K.J. (2008) 'Regional integration and the built environment in middle-range societies: Paracas and early Nasca houses and communities'. *JAA* Vol. 27(1): 111–130.

Gilbert, G.P. (2004) 'Weapons, Warriors and Warfare in Early Egypt'. Oxford, *BAR International Series* 1208.

Gilead, I. (2001) *'Smiths and shamans come from the same nest': magic and craftsmanship in 5th millennium Palestine. Abstract of paper given at the conference on 'The 5th Millennium BC in the Near East', University of Liverpool, November 2001*.

Gilman, A. (1995) *Prehistoric European chiefdoms: rethinking 'Germanic' societies*. In Price and Feinman eds, pp. 235–251.

Gimpel, J. (1988) *The Medieval Machine: The Industrial Revolution of the Middle Ages*. London, Pimlico.

Ginter, B. and Kozlowski, K. (1994) 'Predynastic Settlement near Armant. Heidelberg, Heidelberger Orientverlag'. *Studien zur Archäologie und Geschichte Altägyptens* 6.

Glowacki, M. (2002) *The Huaro archaeological site complex: Rethinking the Huari occupation of Cuzco*. In Isbell and Silverman eds, pp. 267–285.

Glowacki, M. and Malpass, M. (2003) 'Water, *huacas*, and ancestor worship: Traces of a sacred Wari landscape'. *Latin American Antiquity* 14: 431–48.

Godelier, M. (1977) *Perspectives in Marxist Anthropology*. Cambridge Studies in Social Anthropology, CUP.

Godelier, M. (1986) *The Mental and the Material*. London and New York, Verso.

Goelet, O. (1999) *Town and 'country' in ancient Egypt*. In Hudson and Levine eds, pp. 65–116.

Goepper, R. (1996) *Precursors and early stages of the Chinese script*. In Rawson ed., pp. 273–281.

Goldstein, P. S. (1993) 'Tiwanaku temples and state expansion: a Tiwanaku sunken-court temple in Moquegua, Peru'. *Latin American Antiquity* 4(1): 22–47.

Goldstein, P. S. (2000) 'Exotic goods and everyday chiefs: Long-distance exchange and indigenous sociopolitical development in the South Central Andes'. *Latin American Antiquity* 11(4): 335–361.

Goodenough, W. H. (1956) 'Residence rules'. *Southwestern Journal of Anthropology* 12: 22–37.

Goodenough, W.H. (1957) 'Cultural Anthropology and Linguistics'. In P.L. Garvin (ed.) *Report of the 7th Annual Round Table on Linguistics and Language Study*. Washington D.C., Georgetown University Press.

Goodenough, W.H. (1970) *Description and Comparison in Cultural Anthropology: The Lewis Henry Morgan Lectures*. Cambridge, CUP.

Goodison, L. and Morris, C. (1998) eds, *Ancient Goddesses*. Madison, University of Wisconsin Press.

Goody, J. (1971) *Technology, Tradition and the State in Africa*. London, Hutchinson University Library for Africa.

Gopher, A. and Gophna, R. (1993) 'Cultures of the 8th and 7th millennia BP in the southern Levant: A review for the 1990's'. *Journal of World Prehistory* 7(3): 297–353.

Gopher, A. and Goren, Y. (1995) *The beginning of pottery*. In T.E. Levy ed., pp. 224–5.

Gophna, R, (1992) *The contacts between 'En Besor Oasis, Southern Canaan, and Egypt during the Late Dynastic and the threshold of the First Dynasty. A further assessment*. In van den Brink, pp. 385–394.

Gophna, R. (1996) *The earliest phase of relations between Egypt and Canaan*. In Krzyzaniak *et al.* eds, pp. 311–314.

Gophna, R. (2002) *Elusive anchorage points along the Israel littoral during the Early Bronze Age* I. In Van den Brink and Levy eds, pp. 418–421.

Gopnik, H. and Rothman, M.S. (2009) eds, *On the High Road: The History of Godin Tepe, Iran*. Toronto, Royal Ontario Museum/Mazda Press.

Goren, Y., Segal, I. and Bar-Yosef, O. (1993) 'Plaster artefacts and the interpretation of the Nahal Hemar Cave'. *Journal of the Israel Prehistoric Society* 25: 120–131.

Goring-Morris, N. (1993) 'From foraging to herding in the Negev and Sinai: the Early to Late Neolithic Transition'. *Paléorient* 19/1: 65–89.

Goring-Morris, N. (2000) *The quick and the dead: The social context of aceramic Neolithic mortuary practices as seen from Kfar Hahoresh*. In Kuijt ed., pp. 103–136.

Goring-Morris, N. and Belfer-Cohen, A. (1998) 'The articulation of cultural processes and Late Quaternary environmental changes in Cisjordan'. *Paléorient* 23: 107–19.

Goring-Morris, N. and Belfer-Cohen, A. (2002) *Symbolic behaviour from the Epipalaeolithic and early Neolithic of the Near East: Preliminary observations on continuity and change*. In Gebel *et al.* eds, pp. 67–79.

Goring-Morris, N. and Horwitz, L.K. (2007) 'Funerals and feasts during the Pre-Pottery Neolithic B of the Near East'. *Antiquity* 81: 902–919.

Gorsdorf, J., Dreyer, G., and Hartung U. (1998) 'C$^{14}$ Dating results of the archaic royal necropolis Umm el-Qaab at Abydos'. *MDAIK* 54: 169–175.

Gosden, C. and Hather, J. (1999) eds 'The Prehistory of Food: Appetites for Change'. *One World Archaeology* 32, London, Routledge.

Gose, P. (1986) 'Sacrifice and the commodity form in the Andes'. *MAN* 21(2): 296–310.

Gose, P. (1996) 'Oracles, divine kingship, and political representation in the Inka state'. *Ethnohistory* 43(1): 1–32.

Gourdin, W.H. and Kingery, W.D. (1975) 'The beginnings of pyrotechnology: Neolithic and Egyptian lime plaster'. *Journal of Field Archaeology* 2: 133–150.

Graf, D.A. (2000) *Dou Jiande's dilemma: Logistics, strategy and state formation in seventh-century China*. In Van de Ven ed., pp. 77–105.

Graffam, G.C. (1992) 'Beyond state collapse: Rural history, raised fields and pastoralism in the South Andes'. *American Anthropologist* 94: 882–904.

Green, M.W. (1989) *Early cuneiform*. In Senner ed., pp. 43–57.

Green, S.W. and Perlman, S.M. (1985) eds, *The Archaeology of Frontiers and Boundaries*. New York, Academic Press.

Greenhill, B. (1975) *Archaeology of the Boat: A New Introductory Study*. London, A. & C. Black.

Gregory, R.L. (1987) ed., *The Oxford Companion to the Mind*. Oxford and New York, OUP.

Grigson, C. (2001) *Culture, environment and pigs – a case study in the northern Negev. Abstract of papers given at the conference on 'The fifth millennium BC in the Near East', University of Liverpool, November 2001*.

Gropp, G. (1992) *A 'Great Bath' in Elam. In* C. Jarrige ed., pp. 113–118.

Grosman, L. (2003) 'Preserving cultural traditions in a period of instability: the Late Natufian of the hilly Mediterranean zone'. *Current Anthropology* 44(4): 571–580.

Guilaine, J. and Zammit, J. (2005) *The Origins of War: Violence in Prehistory*. Oxford, Blackwell.

Guinan, A. (1996) *Social constructions and private designs: The house omens of Šumma Alu*. In Veenhof ed., pp. 61–68.

Guo Dashun (1995) *Lower Xiajiadian culture*. In Nelson ed., pp. 147–181.

Gupta, S.P. (1996) *The Indus-Saraswati Civilization: Origins, Problems and Issues*. Delhi, Pratibha Prakashan.

Gupta, S.P. (2000–2001) 'River Saraswati in History, Archaeology and Geology'. *Puratattva* 31: 30–38.

Gut, R.V. (2002) *The siginificance of the Uruk sequence at Nineveh*. In Postgate ed., pp. 17–48

Haaland, R. (1999) *The puzzles of the late emergence of domesticated sorghum in the Nile Valley*. In Gosden and Hather eds, pp. 397–418.

Haas, J. (1981) *Class conflict and state in the New World*. In Jones and Kautz eds, pp. 80–104.

Haas, J. (1982) *The Evolution of the Prehistoric State*. New York, Columbia University Press.

Haas, J. (1987) *The exercise of power in early Andean state development*. In Haas, Pozorski and Pozorski eds, pp. 31–35.

Haas, J. (1999) *The origins of war and ethnic violence*. In Carman and Harding eds pp. 11–24.

Haas, J. (2001a) *Warfare and the evolution of culture*. In Price and Feinman eds, pp. 329–350.

Haas, J. (2001b) *Nonlinear paths of political centralization*. In Haas ed., pp. 235–243.

Haas, J. (1990) ed., *The Anthropology of War*. Cambridge, CUP.

Haas, J. (2001) ed., *From Leaders to Rulers*. New York, Kluwer Academic/Plenum Publishers.

Haas, J. and Creamer, W. (2004) *Cultural transformations in the Central Andean Late Archaic*. In Silverman ed., pp. 35–50.

Haas, J. and Creamer, W. (2006) 'Crucible of Andean civilization: The Peruvian coast from 3000 to 1800 BC'. *Current Anthropology* 47(5): 745–775.

Haas, J., Pozorski, S. and Pozorski, T. (1987) eds, *The Origins and Development of the Andean State*. Cambridge, CUP.

Haex, O.M.C., Curvers, H.H. and Akkermans, P.M.M.G. eds (1989) *To the Euphrates and Beyond: Archaeological Studies in Honour of Maurits van Loon*. Rotterdam/Brookfield, A.A. Balkema.

Hage, P. and Harari, F. (1991) *Exchange in Oceania: A Graph Theoretic Analysis*. New York, Clarendon Press.

Hage, P. and Harari, F. (1996) *Island Networks: Communication, Kinship and Classification Structures in Oceania*. Cambridge, CUP.

Hagstrum, M.B. (1999) 'The goal of domestic autonomy among Highland Peruvian farmer-potters: Home economics of rural craft specialists'. *Research in Economic Anthropology* 20: 265–298.

Hall, N. (1992) *Introduction*. In Hall, pp. 7–21.

Hall, N. (1992) ed., *The New Scientist Guide to Chaos*. Harmondsworth, Penguin Books.

Hammade, H.Y. and Yamazaki, Y. (1993) 'Some remarks on the Uruk levels at Tell al'Abr on the Euphrates'. *Akkadica* 84–5: 53–62.

Hansen, M.H. (2000a) *The impact of City-State cultures on world history. Conclusion to Hansen 2000b*.

Hansen, M.H. (2000b) ed., *A Comparative Study of Thirty City-State Cultures: An Investigation Published by the Copenhagen Polis Centre*. Copenhagen, C.A. Reitzels.

'Harlan Symposium' (1997) *The Origins of Agriculture and Crop Domestication: Proceedings of the Harlan Symposium, 10–17th May 1997, Aleppo, Syria*. Published jointly by ICARDA, IPGRI, FAO and University of California/GRCP.

Harris, D.R. (1994) ed., *The Archaeology of V. Gordon Childe: Contemporary Perspectives.* London, UCL Press.

Harris, D.R. (1996) ed., *The Origins and Spread of Agriculture and Pastoralism in Eurasia.* London, UCL Press.

Harris, D.R. (1997) 'The spread of Neolithic agriculture from the Levant to Western Central Asia.' In *Harlan Symposium*, pp. 65–82.

Harris, D.R. (1998) 'The origins of agriculture in southwest Asia'. *The Review of Archaeology* 19: 5–11.

Harris, D.R. and Hillman, G.C. (1989) eds, *Foraging and Farming: The Evolution of Plant Exploitation.* London, Unwin and Hyman.

Harris, M. and Ross, E.B. (1987) *Death, Sex and Fertility: Population Regulation in Preindustrial and Developing Societies.* New York, Columbia University Press.

Harrison, R., Gillespie, M., and Peuranki-Brown, M. (2002) eds, *Eureka: The Archaeology of Innovation and Science.* Calgary, University of Calgary Press, Chacmool Society.

Hart, H.L.A. (1961) *The Concept of Law.* Oxford, Oxford University Press, Clarendon Law Series.

Hartung, U. (2002) 'Abydos, Umm el-Qaab: le cemetière prédynastique U'. *Archéo-Nil* 12: 87–93.

Hartung, U. (2003a) 'Predynastic subterranean dwellers in Maadi, Cairo'. *Egyptian Archaeology* 22: 7–9.

Hartung, U. (2003b) 'Maadi, fouille de sauvetage aux confins du Caire'. *Archéo-Nil* 13: 29–36.

Hartung, U. (2003c) 'Bouto, fouille d'habitat dans le Delta du Nil'. *Archéo-Nil* 13: 73–76.

Hartung, U. (2004) *Rescue excavations in the Predynastic settlement of Maadi.* In Hendrickx *et al.* eds, pp. 337–356.

Hassan, F.A. (1988) 'The Predynastic of Egypt'. *Journal of World Prehistory*, 2(2): 135–185.

Hassan, F.A., Tassie, G.J. and Rowland, J.M. (2003) 'Social dynamics at the Late Predynastic to Early Dynastic site of Kafr Hassan Dawood'. *Archéo-Nil* 13: 37–45.

Hastings, C.M. (1987) *Implications of Andean verticality in the evolution of political complexity; a view from the margins.* In Haas, Pozorski and Pozorski eds, pp. 145–157.

Hastorf, C.A. (1990a) *The ecosystem model and long-term Prehistoric change: An example from the Andes.* In Moran, ed., pp. 131–157.

Hastorf, C.A. (1990b) *One path to the heights: negotiating political inequality in the Sausa of Peru.* In Upham ed., pp. 146–176.

Hastorf, C.A. (1999) *Cultural implications of crop introductions in Andean Prehistory.* In Gosden and Hather eds, pp. 35–58.

Hastorf, C.A. (2003) 'Community with the ancestors: ceremonies and social memory in the Middle Formative at Chiripa, Bolivia'. *Journal of Anthropological Archaeology* 22: 305–332.

Hastorf, C.A. (2005) 'Comment on Arkush and Stanish'. *CA* 46(1): 17.

Hastorf, C. A. and Johannessen, S. (1993) 'Pre-Hispanic political change and the role of Maize in the Central Andes of Peru'. *American Anthropologist* 95(1): 115–138.

Hauptmann, H. (1993) *Ein Kultgebaüde in Nevali Çori.* In Frangipane *et al.* eds, pp. 37–69

Hawass, Z.A., Hassan, F.A. and Gautier, A. (1987) 'Chronology, sediments and subsistence at Merimda Beni Salama'. *Journal of Egyptian Archaeology* 74: 31–38.

Hawkes, J.G. (1989) *The domestication of roots and tubers in the American Tropics.* In Harris and Hillman eds, pp. 481–503.

Hayashi, M. (1993) 'Concerning the inscription "May sons and grandsons eternally use this [vessel]"'. *Artibus Asiae* 53(1/2): 51–58.

Hayden, B. (1990) Nimrods, piscators, pluckers and planters: The emergence of food production. *JAA* 9: 31–69.

Hayden, B. (1995) *Pathways to power: Principles for creating socioeconomic inequalities.* In Price and Feinman eds, pp. 15–86.

Heesterman, J.C. (1985) *The Inner Conflict of Tradition.* Chicago, University of Chicago Press.

Heiser, C.B. (1989) *Domestication of Cucurbita: Cucurbita and Lagenaria.* In Harris and Hillman eds, pp. 471–503.

Helwing, B. (1999) 'Cultural interaction at Hassek Höyük, Turkey. New evidence from pottery analysis'. *Paléorient* 25(1): 91–99.

Jiang, Leping and Liu, Li (2005) 'The discovery of an 8000–year-old dugout canoe at Kuahuqiao in the Lower Yangzi River, China'. *Antiquity* Vol. 79 No. 305, Project Gallery.

Jimenez-Serrano, A. (2002) 'Royal Festivals in the Late Predynastic Period and the First Dynasty'. Oxford, *BAR*.

Jimenez-Serrano, A. (2003) 'Chronology and local traditions: the representation of power and the royal name in the late predynastic period [of Egypt]'. *Archéo-Nil* 13: 93–142.

Jing, Yuan and Flad, R.K. (2002) 'Pig domestication in ancient China'. *Antiquity* 76: 724–32.

Jing,Yuan and Flad, R.K. (2005) 'New zooarchaeological evidence for changes in Shang Dynasty animal sacrifice'. *Journal of Anthropological Archaeology* 24: 252–270.

Jing, Z. and Rapp, G. (1995) 'Holocene landscape evolution and its impact on the Neolithic and Bronze Age sites in the Shangqiu area, northern China'. *Geoarchaeology* 10: 481–513.

Jing, Z., Rapp, G. and Gao, T. (1997) 'Geoarchaeological aids in the investigation of early Shang civilization on the floodplain of the Lower Yellow River, China'. *World Archaeology* 29(1): 36–50.

Joffe, A.H. (2000) 'Egypt and Syro-Mesopotamia in the 4th millennium: Implications of the new chronology'. *Current Anthropology* 41: 113–123.

Johns, T. (1989) *A chemical-ecological model of root and tuber domestication in the Andes.* In Harris and Hillman eds, pp. 504–519.

Johnson, G.A. (1980) 'Rank-size convexity and system integration: A view from archaeology'. *Economic Geography* 56(3): 234–247.

Johnson, G.A. (1982) *Organizational structure and scalar stress.* In Renfrew, Rowlands and Segraves eds pp. 389–421.

Johannessen, S. and Hastorf, C.A. (1989) 'Corn and culture in central Andean prehistory'. *Science* 244: 690–692.

Johnston, K.J. (2001) 'Broken fingers: Classic Maya scribe capture and polity consolidation'. *Antiquity* 75: 373–381.

Jones, D. (1995) *Boats (Egyptian Bookshelf).* London, British Museum Press.

Jones, G.D. and Kautz, R.R. (1981) I*ssues in the study of New World state formation.* In Jones and Kautz eds, pp. 1–34.

Jones, G.D. and Kautz, R.R. (eds) (1981) *The Transition to Statehood in the New World. New Directions in Archaeology,* Cambridge, CUP.

Jones, J. (2001) *Innovation and resplendence: metalwork for Moche lords.* In Pillsbury ed., pp. 207–221.

Jones, S. (1997) *The Archaeology of Ethnicity. Constructing Identities in the Past and Present.* London, Routledge.

Jones, T.B. (1976) *Sumerian administrative documents: An essay.* In Lieberman ed., pp. 41–61.

Jonker, G. (1995) *The Topography of Remembrance: The Dead, Tradition and Collective Memory in Mesopotamia.* Leiden, E.J.Brill.

Joyce, A.A. and Winter, M. (1996) 'Ideology, power, and urban society in pre-Hispanic Oaxaca [Agency, Ideology, and Power in Archaeological Theory 3]'. *Current Anthropology,* Vol. 37(1): 33–86.

Joyce, A.A. (1997) *Ideology, power, and state formation in the Valley of Oaxaca.* In Manzanilla ed., pp. 133–168

Joyce, R.A. (2000) *High culture, Mesoamerican civilization, and the classic Maya tradition.* In Richards and Van Buren eds, pp. 64–76.

Jurmain, R.D. (2001) 'Palaeoepidemiological patterns of trauma in a prehistoric population from Central California'. *American Journal of Physical Anthropology* 115: 15–23.

Kafafi, Z., & Rollefson, G.O. (1995) 'The 1994 Excavations at Ayn Ghazal: Preliminary Report'. *Annual of the Department of Antiquities of Jordan* 39: 13–29.

Kafafi, Z. (2005) *Stones, walls and rituals.* In Gebel and Rollefson eds, pp. 32–34

Kahl, J. (2001) 'Hieroglyphic writing during the fourth millennium BC: An analysis of systems'. *Archéo-Nil,* 11: 103–25.

Kalgren, B. (1963) 'Loan characters in Pre-Han texts, I'. *Bulletin of the Museum of Far Eastern Antiquities* 35: 1–128.

Kane, V.C. (1974–5) 'The independent bronze industries in the south of China contemporary with the Shang and Western Chou Dynasties'. *Archives of Asian Art* 28: 77–107.

Kane, V.C. (1982–3) 'Aspects of Western Chou appointment inscriptions: The charge, the gifts and the response'. *Early China* 8: 14–28.

Kaplan, J. (2000) 'Monument 65: A great emblematic depiction of throned rule and royal sacrifice at Late Preclassic Kaminaljuyu'. *Ancient Mesoamerica* Vol. 11(2): 185–198.

Katz, D. (2003) 'Review of Flückiger-Hawker [1999]'. *Bibliotheca Orientalis* LX(3–4): 394–399.

Kaulicke, P. (2008) T*he Vicús-Mochica relationship.* In Isbell and Silverman eds, pp. 85–111.

Kay, C.E. (1994) 'Aboriginal overkill: the role of native Americans in structuring western ecosystems'. *Human Nature* 5: 359–98.

Keatinge, R.W. (1981) *The nature and role of religious diffusion in the early stages of state formation: An example from Peruvian prehistory.* In Jones and Kautz eds, pp. 172–187.

Keatinge, R.W. (1988b) *Preface.* In Keatinge ed., pp. xiii–xxvii.

Keatinge, R.W. (1988a) ed., *Peruvian Prehistory.* Cambridge, CUP.

Keatinge, R.W. and Conrad, G. (1983) 'Imperialist expansion in Peruvian prehistory: Chimú administration of a conquered territory'. *Journal of Field Archaeology* 10: 255–283.

Keay, J. (1991) *The Honourable Company: A History of the English East India Company,* London, Harper Collins.

Keeley, L.H. (1995) *Proto-agricultural practices among hunter-gatherers: A cross-cultural study.* In Price and Grebauer eds, pp. 243–272.

Keeley, L. H. (1996) *War Before Civilization: The Myth of the Peaceful Savage.* New York, OUP.

Keefer, D.K. and Moseley, M.E. (2004) 'Southern Peru desert shattered by the great 2001 earthquake: Implications for paleoseismic and paleo-El Nino-Southern Oscillation records'. *Proceedings of the National Academy of Sciences (U.S.)* Vol. 101(30): 10878–10883.

Keightley, D.N. (1978) *Sources of Shang History: The Oracle-Bone Inscriptions of Bronze Age China.* Berkeley, University of California Press.

Keightley, D.N. (1979) 'The Shang State as seen in the Oracle Bone Inscriptions'. *Early China* 5: 25–34

Keightley, D.N. (1989) *The origins of writing in China. Scripts and cultural contexts.* In Senner ed., pp. 171–202.

Keightley, D.N. (1999a) *The Oracle Bone Inscriptions of the Late Shang Dynasty.* In De Bary and Bloom eds, pp. 3–23.

Keightley. D.N. (1999b) 'At the beginning: The status of women in Neolithic and Shang China'. *NAN NÜ: Men, women and gender in early and imperial China.* Vol. 1(1): 1–63, Brill.

Keightley, D.N. (1999c) 'Theology and the writing of history: truth and the ancestors in the Wu Ding divination records'. *JEAA* 1: 207–230.

Keightley, D.N. (2008) 'Comment on Flad'. *CA* 49(3) : 425–6.

Kelly, R.C. (2000) *Warless Societies and the Origin of War.* Ann Arbor, University of Michigan Press.

Kelly, R. and Rappaport, R. (1975) 'Function, generality and explanatory power: A commentary and response to Bergmann's arguments'. *Michigan Discussions in Anthropology* 1: 24–44.

Kembel, S.R. and Rick, J.W. (2004) *Building authority at Chavín de Huantar.* In Silverman ed., pp. 51–76.

Kemp, B.J. (1968) 'Merimda and the theory of house burial in Prehistoric Egypt'. *Chronique d'Egypte* 43: 22–33.

Kemp, B.J. (1989) *Ancient Egypt: Anatomy of a Civilization.* London, Routledge.

Kemp, B.J. (1995a) 'How religious were the ancient Egyptians?' *Cambridge Archaeological Journal* 5: 25–54.

Kemp, B.J. (1995b) *Unification and urbanization of ancient Egypt.* In Sasson ed., Vol. II, pp. 679–690.

Kemp, B.J. (2000) 'The colossi from the early shrine at Coptos in Egypt'. *Cambridge Archaeological Journal* 10(2): 211–242.

Kemp. B.J. (2001) 'Just like us? (Review article)'. *Cambridge Archaeological Journal* 11(1): 123–129.

Kennedy, K.A.R. (1982). *Palaeodemographic perspectives of social structural change in Harappan society.* In Pastner and Flam eds, pp. 211–218.

Kennedy, K.A.R. and Possehl, G. (1984) eds, *Studies in the Archaeology and Palaeoanthropology of South Asia.* New Delhi, Oxford and IBH.

Kenoyer, J.M. (1989a) *Socio-economic structures of the Indus Civilization as reflected in specialized crafts and the question of ritual segregation.* In Kenoyer ed., pp. 183–192.

Kenoyer, J.M. (1991a) 'The Indus Valley tradition of Pakistan and Western India'. *Journal of World Prehistory* 5(4): 331–385.

Kenoyer, J.M. (1991b) *Urban process in the Indus Tradition: A preliminary model from Harappa.* In Meadow ed., pp. 29–60.

Kenoyer, J.M. (1994) *The Harappan State, was it or wasn't it ?* In Kenoyer ed., pp. 71–80.

Kenoyer, J.M (1998) *Early city-states in South Asia: Comparing the Harappan Phase and Early Historic Period.* In Nichols and Charlton eds, pp. 51–70.

Kenoyer, J.M. (2000) *Wealth and socioeconomic hierarchies of the Indus Valley Civilization.* In Richards and Van Buren eds, pp. 88–109.

Kenoyer, J.M. (1989b) ed., 'Old Problems and New Perspectives in the Archaeology of South Asia'. *WAR* 2. Madison, Wisconsin, University of Wisconsin, Dept. of Anthropology.

Kenoyer, J.M. and Meadow, R.H. (2000) *The Ravi Phase: A new cultural manifestation at Harappa.* In Taddei and De Marco eds, pp. 55–76.

Kesarwani, A. (1984) *Harappan gateways. A functional reassessment.* In Lal *et al.* eds, pp. 63–73.

Khatri. J.S. and Acharya, M. (1995) 'Kunal: A new Indus-Sarasvati site'. *Puratattva* 25: 84–86.

Khadkikar, A.S., Rajshekhar, C. and Kumaran, K.P.N. (2004) 'Palaeogeography around the Harappan port of Lothal, Gujarat, western India'. *Antiquity* 78: 896–903.

Khan, F. (1984) *The potential of Ethnoarchaeology, with special reference to recent archaeological work in Bannu District, Pakistan.* In B. Allchin ed., pp. 83–99.

Kirchhoff, P. (1935) 'The principles of clanship in human society'. In M. Fried ed., *Readings in Anthropology,* II: 260–270. New York, Thomas Y. Crowell [1968].

Kislev, M.E. (1997) *Early agriculture and paleoecology of Netiv Hagdud.* In Bar-Yosef and Gopher eds, pp. 209–236.

Klengel, H. and Renger, J. (1999) eds, 'Landwirtschaft im Alten Orient'. *Berlin Beiträge zum Vorderen Orient Band* 18. Berlin, Dietrich Reimer Verlag.

Klymshyn, A.M.A. (1987) *The development of Chimu administration in Chan Chan.* In Haas, Pozorski and Pozorski eds, pp. 97–110.

Knapp, R.A.. (2000a) *China's Walled Cities. Images of Asia,* OUP (China) Ltd.

Knapp, R.A. (2000b) *China's Old Dwellings.* Honolulu, University of Hawaii Press.

Knobloch, P.J. (2000) 'Wari ritual power at Chonchopata: An interpretation of *Anadenanthera columbrina* iconography'. *Latin American Antiquity* 11(4): 387–402.

Kobayashi, T. (1992) 'On Ninazu, as seen in the economic texts of the Early Dynastic Lagas'. *Orient* Vol. XXVIII: 75–95.

Kobusiewicz, M., Kabacinski, J., Schild, R., Irish, J.D. and Wendorf, F. (2004) 'Discovery of the first Neolithic cemetery in Egypt's western desert'. *Antiquity* 78: 566–578.

Kohl, P.L. and Fawcett, C. (1995) eds, *Nationalism, Politics and the Practice of Archaeology.* Cambridge, CUP.

Köhler, E.C. (2003) 'The new excavations in the Early Dynastic necropolis at Helwan'. *Archéo-Nil* 13: 17–27.

Kohlmeyer, K. (1996) *Houses in Habuba Kabira South: Spatial organization and planning of Late Uruk residential architecture.* In Veenhof ed., pp. 89–103.

Kohlmeyer, K. (1997) *Habuba Kabira. In The Oxford Encyclopaedia of Archaeology in the Near East,* E. Meyers ed., pp. 446–48. New York, OUP.

Kolata, A.L. (1986) 'The agricultural foundations of the Tiwanaku State: a view from the heartland'. *American Antiquity* 51(4): 748– 762.

Kolata, A.L. (1989) ed., *Arqueología de Lukurmata,* Vol. 2. Instituto Nacional de Arqueología and Ediciones Puma Punku, La Paz.

Kolata, A.L. (1991) 'The technology and organization of agricultural production in the Tiwanaku State'. *Latin American Antiquity,* 2(2): 99–125.

Kolata, A.L. (1992) *Economy, ideology and imperialism in the South-Central Andes.* In Demarest and Conrad eds, pp. 65–85.

Kolata, A.L. (1997) *Of kings and capitals: Principles of authority and the nature of cities in the native Andean state.* In Nichols and Charlton eds, pp. 245–254.

Kolata, A.L. (1996) ed., 'Tiwanaku and its Hinterland: Archaeology and Palaeoecology of an Andean Civilization, Vol. 1'. *Smithsonian Series in Archaeological Enquiry,* Washington DC, Smithsonian Institution Press.

Kolata, A.L. (2003) ed., 'Tiwanaku and its Hinterland: Archaeological and Palaeoecological Investigations of an Andean Civilization, Vol. II'. *Smithsonian Series in Archaeological Enquiry*, Washington DC, Smithsonian Institution Press.

Kolata, A.L., Binford, M.W., Brenner, M., Janusek, J.W. & Ortloff, C. (2000) 'Environmental thresholds and the empirical reality of state collapse: a response to Erickson [1999]'. *Antiquity* 74: 424–6.

Kolata, A.L. and Ortloff, C. R.(1989) 'Thermal analysis of Tiwanaku raised field systems in the Lake Titicaca Basin of Bolivia'. *Journal of Archaeological Science*, 16: 233–263.

Kolata, A.L. and Ortloff, C.R. (1996) *Tiwanaku raised-field agriculture in the Lake Titicaca Basin of Bolivia*. In Kolata ed., pp. 109–152.

Kolata, A.L., Rivera, O., Ramirez, J.C. and Gemio, E. (1996) *The natural and human setting*. In Kolata ed., pp. 203–230.

Kolb, R.T. (1990–91) 'Anmerkungen zu *Sanctioned Violence in Ancient China* von Mark Edward Lewis'. *Monumenta Serica* 39: 356.

Kornbacher, K.D. (1999) 'Cultural elaboration in prehistoric coastal Peru: An example of evolution in a temporally variable environment'. *JAA* 18: 282–318.

Kottak, C.P. (1972) 'Ecological variables in the origin and evolution of African states: the Buganda example'. *Comparative Studies in Society and History*, 14: 351–380.

Kouchoukas, N. and Wilkinson T. (2007) *Landscape archaeology in Mesopotamia: Past, present and future*. In Stone ed., pp. 1–18.

Kozlowski, S.K. and Aurenche, O. (2005) 'Territories, Boundaries and Cultures in the Neolithic Near East'. Oxford, *BAR S3162*.

Kramer, C. and Douglas, J.E. (1992) 'Ceramics, caste and kin: Spatial relations in Rajasthan, India'. *Journal of Anthropological Archaeology* 11: 187–201.

Kramer, K.L. and Boone, J.L. (2002) 'Why intensive agriculturalists have higher fertility: A household energy budget approach'. *Current Anthropology* 43(3): 511–517.

Kramer, S.N. (1983) 'The Sumerian Deluge Myth: reviewed and revised'. *Anatolian Studies* 33: 115–121, *Journal of the British Institute of Archaeology at Ankara*.

Krapf-Askari, E. (1972) *Women, spears and the scarce good: A comparison of the sociological function of warfare in two Central African societies*. In Singer and Street eds, pp. 19–40.

Krispijn, Th.J.H. (2001) *The Sumerian lexeme *urum, a lexico-etymological study*. In van Soldt *et al.* eds, pp. 251–261.

Kroeper, K. (1996) *Minshat Abu Omar – Burials with Palettes*. In Spencer ed., pp. 70–92.

Kroeper, K. (2004) *Minshat Abu Omar: Aspects of the analysis of a cemetery*. In Hendrickx *et al.* eds, pp. 859–880.

Kromer, B. and Schmidt, K. (1998) 'Two Radiocarbon dates from Göbekli Tepe (South-eastern Turkey)', *Neo-Lithics* 3.

Krzyzaniak, L. and Kobusiewicz, M. (1989) eds, 'Late Prehistory of the Nile basin and the Sahara'. *Studies in African Archaeology* 2, Poznan, Poznan Archaeological Museum.

Krzyzaniak, L., Kroeper, K. and Kobusiewicz, M. (1996) eds, 'Interregional Contacts in the Later Prehistory of Northeastern Africa'. *Studies in African Archaeology*, Vol. 5. Poznan, Poznan Archaeological Museum.

Kuijt, I. (2000a) ed., *Life in Neolithic Farming Communities: Social Organization, Identity, and Differentiation*. New York, Plenum Press.

Kuijt, I. (2000b) *Life in Neolithic farming communities: An Introduction*. In Kuijt ed., pp. 3–13.

Kuijt, I. (2000c) *Keeping the peace: Ritual, skull caching, and community integration in the Levantine Neolithic*. In Kuijt ed., pp. 137–164.

Kuijt, I. (2000d) 'People and space in early agricultural villages: Exploring daily lives, community size, and architecture in the Late Pre-Pottery Neolithic'. *JAA* 19: 75–102.

Kuijt, I. (2004) 'Pre-Pottery Neolithic A and Late Natufian at 'Iraq ed-Dubb, Jordan'. *Journal of Field Archaeology* 29 [2002–2004] pp. 291–308.

Kuijt, I. and Chesson, M.S. (2005) *Lumps of clay and pieces of stone: Ambiguity, bodies, and identity as portrayed in Neolithic figurines*. In Pollock and Bernbeck eds, pp. 152–183.

Kuijt, I. and Goring-Morris, N. (2002) 'Foraging, farming and social complexity in the Pre-Pottery Neolithic world of the Southern Levant: A review and synthesis'. *Journal of World Prehistory* 16(4): 361–440.

Kuit, I. and Mahasneh, H. (1998) 'Dhra: an early Neolithic village in the Southern Jordan Valley'. *Journal of Field Archaeology* 25: 153–161.

Kuznar, L.A. (1990) 'Pastoralism temprano en la sierra alta del Departamento de Montegua, Peru'. *Chungara* 24/25: 53–68.

Kuznar, L.A. (1996) *Reclaiming a Scientific Anthropology*. Lanham, MD, Altamira.

Kuznar, L.A. (2001a) ed., *Ethnoarchaeology of Andean South America: Contributions to Archaeological Method and Theory*. An Arbor, Michigan, International Monographs in Prehistory, Ethnoarchaeological Series 4.

Kuznar, L.A. (2001b) *An introduction to Andean religious ethnoarchaeology: Preliminary results and future directions*. In Kuznar ed., pp. 38–66.

La Rocca, C. (1992) *Public buildings and urban change in northern Italy in the early mediaeval period*. In Rich ed., pp. 161–180.

Laban, S. (2004) *A Second Domesday? The Hundred Rolls of 1279–80*. Oxford, OUP.

Lahiri, N. (1999) *The Archaeology of Indian Trade Routes up to c.200 BC: Resource Use, Resource Access and Lines of Communication*. New Delhi, OUP.

Lal, B.B. (1979) *Kalibangan and Indus Civilization*. In Agrawal and Chakrabarti eds, pp. 65–97.

Lal, B.B. (1984) *Some reflections on the structural remains at Kalibangan*. In Lal, Gupta and Asthana eds, pp. 55–62.

Lal, B.B. (1994) *Chronological horizon of the Mature Indus Civilization*. In Kenoyer ed., pp. 15–25.

Lal, B.B., Gupta, S.P., & Asthana, S. (1984) eds: *Frontiers of the Indus Civilization: Sir Mortimer Wheeler Commemoration Volume*. New Delhi, Books and Books.

Lamberg-Karlovsky, C.C. (1999) *Households, land tenure and communication systems in the 6th–4th millennia of Greater Mesopotamia*. In Hudson and Levine eds, pp. 167–201.

Lambert, P.M. (1994) *War and Peace on the Western Front: a Study of Violent Conflict and its Correlates in Prehistoric Hunter-gatherers of Coastal Southern California*. Unpublished PhD Dissertation, Dept. of Anthropology, University of California, Santa Barbara.

Lambert, P.M. (1997) *Patterns of violence in prehistoric hunter-gatherer societies of coastal southern California*. In Martin and Frayer eds, pp. 77–109.

Lambert, P.M. (2002) 'The archaeology of war: a North American perspective'. *Journal of Archaeological Research* 10(3): 207–241.

Lambert, W.G. (1987) 'Goddesses in the pantheon: a reflection of women in society?'. In *RAI* 33 pp. 125–130.

Landels, J.G. (1978) *Engineering in the Ancient World*. London, Constable.

Langdon, J. (2004) *Mills in the Mediaeval Economy: England 1300–1540*. Oxford, OUP.

Langdon, S. (1924) *Excavations at Kish Vol. I, Excavations 1923–24*. Paris, Paul Geuthner.

Lansing, J.S. and Miller, J.H. (2005) 'Cooperation, games and ecological feedback: Some insights from Bali'. *Current Anthropology* 46(2): 328–334.

Lau, G.F. (2002) 'Feasting and ancestor veneration at Chinchawas, North Highlands of Ancash, Peru'. *Latin American Antiquity* 13(3): 279–304.

Lau, G.F. (2004a) 'The Recuay culture of Peru's north-central highlands: A reappraisal of chronology and its implications'. *Journal of Field Archaeology* 29 [2002–2004] pp. 177–202.

Lau, G.F. (2004b) 'Object of contention: An examination of Recuay-Moche combat imagery'. *Cambridge Archeological Journal* 14(2): 163–184.

Lau, G.F. (2006) 'Ancient Andean space and architecture: New syntheses and debates'. *Review Article. Antiquity* 80 (309): 720–724.

Lau, G.F. (2007) 'Tiwanaku and beyond: Recent research in the South Central Andes'. *Antiquity* 81(311): 214–216.

Lau Chung-ming and Jianfa Shen (2000) eds, *China Review 2000*. Hong Kong, The Chinese University Press.

Leach, H.M. (1999) *Food processing technology: Its role in inhibiting or promoting change in staple foods*. In Gosden and Hather eds, pp. 129–138.

Leach, H.M. (2003) 'Human domestication reconsidered'. *Current Anthropology* 44(3): 349–368.

LeBlanc, S.A. (2003a) *Constant Battles: The Myth of the Peaceful Noble Savage*. New York, St. Martins Press.

LeBlanc, S.A. (2003b) 'Prehistory of warfare'. *Archaeology* 56(3): 18–25.

LeBlanc, S.A. and Watson, P.J. (1973) 'A comparative statistical analysis of painted pottery from seven Halafian sites'. *Paléorient* 1: 117–133.

Ledderhose, L. (2000) 'Ten Thousand Things: Module and Mass Production in Chinese Art. The A.W. Mellon Lectures in the Fine Arts, 1998'. *Bollingen Series* XXXV.46. New Jersey, Princeton University Press.

Lee, G-A., Crawford, G.W., Liu, L. and Chan, X. (2007) 'Plants and people from the early Neolithic to Shang periods in North China'. *PNAS* 104(3): 1087–92.

Lee, R.B. and DeVore, I. (1968) eds, *Man the Hunter*. Chicago, Aldine.

Lee, Y.K. (2002) 'Building the chronology of early Chinese history'. *Asian Perspectives* 41(1): 15–42.

Lee, Y.K. (2004) 'Control strategies and polity competition in the lower Yi-Luo Valley, North China'. *Journal of Anthropological Archaeology* 23: 172–195.

Lee, Y.K. and Zhu, N. (2002) 'Social integration of religion and ritual in prehistoric China'. *Antiquity* 76: 715–23.

Legge, James (1872) *The Chinese Classics, Vol. 5: The Ch'un Ts'ew, with the Tso Chuen*. Reprint, Hong Kong 1960.

Leick, G. (2001) *Mesopotamia: The Invention of the City*. London, Penguin Books.

Lekson, S. H. (2002) 'War in the Southwest, war in the world'. *American Antiquity* 67(4): 607–624.

Lete, G. del Olmo and Fenollos, J.-L. Montero (1999) eds, 'Archaeology of the Upper Syrian Euphrates – The Tishrin Dam Area'. *Proceedings of the International Symposium Held at Barcelona, 28–30 January 1998*. Barcelona, Editorial Ausa.

Levine, L. D. and Young, T.C. (1977) *Mountains and Lowlands*. Malibu, Undina Press.

Levi-Strauss, C. (1982) *The Way of the Masks*. Seattle, University of Washington Press.

Levy, T.E. (1986) 'The Chalcolithic period'. *Biblican Archaeologist* 49: 82–108.

Levy, T.E. (1995) ed., *The Archaeology of Society in the Holy Land*. London and Washington, Leicester University Press.

Levy, T.E., Van den Brink, E.C.M. and Alon, D. (1995) 'New light on King Narmer and the Protodynastic Egyptian presence in Canaan'. *Biblical Archaeologist* 58: 26–36.

Lewis, M.E. (1999a) *The 'feng' and 'shan' sacrifices of Emperor Wu of the Han*. In McDermott ed., pp. 50–80.

Lewis, M.E. (1999b) *Warring States political history*. In Loewe and Shaughnessy eds, pp. 587–650.

Lewis, M.E. (2000) *The Han abolition of universal military service*. In Van de Ven ed., pp. 33–76.

Lewis-Williams. D. and Pearce, D. (2005) *Inside the Neolithic Mind*. London, Thames and Hudson.

Li Boqian (1999) 'The sumptuary system governing Western Zhou rulers'cemeteries viewed from a Jin ruler's cemetery'. *Journal of East Asian Archaeology* 1: 251–276.

Lieberman, S.J. (1976) ed., 'Sumerological Studies in Honor of Thorkild Jacobsen on his Seventieth Birthday'. *Assyriological Studies* No. 20. Chicago and London, University of Chicago Press.

Li, Xueqin, Harbottle, G., Zhang, Juzhong and Wang, Changsui (2003) 'The earliest writing? Sign use in the seventh millennium BC at Jiahu, Henan Province, China'. *Antiquity* 77: 31–44.

Lindstrom, L. (1996) *'Big Man'*. In Barnard and Spencer eds, pp. 55–6.

Lipinsky, E. (1979) ed., 'State and Temple Economy in the Ancient Near East. 2 vols'. Leuven, *Orientalia Lovaniensa Analecta* 6.

Lipinsky, E. (2002) 'Some thoughts on ancient Mesopotamian magic and religion [review of Abusch and van der Toorn 2000]'. *Bibliotheca Orientalis* LIX (5–6): 468–486.

Lipo, C.P., Madsen, M.E., Dunnell, R.C. and Hunt, T. (1997) 'Population structure, cultural transmission and frequency seriation'. *JAA* 16: 310–333.

Lipschitz, N., Gophna, R., Harman, M. and Biger, G. (1991) 'The beginning of olive (*Olea europaea*) cultivation in the Old World: a reassessment'. *Journal of Archaeological Science* 18: 441–453.

Littauer, M.A. and Crouwel, J.H. (1979) *Wheeled Vehicles and Ridden Animals in the Ancient Near East*. Leiden, Brill.

Littauer, M.A. and Crouwel, J.H. (1990) 'Ceremonial threshing in the ancient Near East'. *Iraq* 52: 15–19.

Liu, Li (1996a) 'Mortuary ritual and social hierarchy in the Longshan culture'. *Early China* 21: 1–46.

Liu, Li (1996b) 'Settlement patterns, chiefdom variability, and the development of early states in North China'. *Journal of Anthropological Archaeology* 15(3): 237–88.

Liu, Li (1999) 'Who were the ancestors? The origins of Chinese ancestral cult and racial myths'. *Antiquity* 73: 602–613.

Liu, Li (2000) 'Ancestor worship: an archaeological investigation of ritual activities in Neolithic North China'. *Journal of East Asian Archaeology* 2(1–2): 129–64.

Liu, Li (2003) ''The products of minds as well as of hands': Production of prestige goods in the Neolithic and early state periods of China'. *Asian Perspectives*: 42(1): 1–40.

Liu, Li (2004) *The Chinese Neolithic: Trajectories to Early States*. Cambridge, CUP.

Liu, Li and Chen Xingcan (2003) *State Formation in Early China*. London, Duckworth.

Liu, L., Chen, X., Lee, Y.K., Wright, H.T. and Miller-Rosen, A. (2004) 'Settlement patterns and development of social complexity in the Yi-Luo region, North China'. *Journal of Field Archaeology* 29: 1–26.

Liu, L. and Xu, H. (2007) 'Rethinking Erlitou: legend, history and Chinese archaeology'. *Antiquity* 81: 886–901.

Liu, X., Hunt, H.V. and Jones, M.K. (2009) 'River valleys and foothills: changing archaeological perceptions of North China's earliest farms'. *Antiquity* 83: 82–95.

Liu, Yang (2000) *Behind the masks: Sanxingdui bronzes and the culture of the ancient Shu*. In Liu and Capon eds, pp. 23–44.

Liu, Yang and Capon, Edmund (2000) eds, *Masks of Mystery: Ancient Chinese Bronzes from Sanxingdui*. Sydney, Art Gallery of New South Wales.

Liverani, M. (1993) ed., 'Akkad, The First World Empire: Structure, Ideology, Traditions'. *History of the Ancient Near East, Studies (HANE /S)* Vol. 5, Padua.

Liverani, M. (1996) 'Reconstructing the rural landscape of the Ancient Near East'. *Journal of the Economic and Social History of the Orient (JESHO)* 39(1): 1–41.

Liverani, M. (2001) *The fall of the Assyrian empire: Ancient and modern interpretations*. In Alcock *et al.* eds, pp. 374–391.

Loewe, M. (1999) *The imperial way of death in Han China*. In McDermott ed., pp. 81–111.

Loewe, M. and Shaughnessy, E.L. (1999) eds, *The Cambridge History of Ancient China: From the Origins of Civilization to 221 BC*. Cambridge, CUP.

Lu Liancheng (1993) 'Chariot and horse burials in Ancient China'. *Antiquity* 67: 824–838.

Lu, Tracey L.-D. (1998) 'Some botanical characteristics of green foxtail (*Setaria viridis*) and harvesting experiments on the grass'. *Antiquity* 72: 902–7.

Lu, Tracey L.-D. (1999) 'The Transition from Foraging to Farming and the Origin of Agriculture in China'. *BAR International Series* 774, Tempus Reparatum, Oxford.

Lu, Tracey L.-D. (2006) 'The occurrence of cereal cultivation in China'. *Asian Perspectives* 45(2): 129–158.

Lupton, A. (1999) 'Stability and Change. Socio-political Development in North Mesopotamia and Southeast Anatolia, 4000–2700 BC'. Oxford, *BAR Int. Series* 627.

Lynton, N. (1984) *The use of Ethnoarchaeology in interpreting South Asian prehistory*. In Kennedy and Possehl eds, pp. 63–71.

Lyonnet, B. (1981) 'Établissements chalcolithiques dans le Nord-Est de l'Afghanistan: leur rapports avec les civilizations du bassin de Indus'. *Paléorient* 7(2): 57–74.

McAnany, P.A. (2000) *Living with the ancestors: kinship and kingship in Ancient Maya society*. In Smith and Masson eds, pp. 483–487.

McAndrews, T., Albarracin-Jordan, J. and Bermann, B. (1997) 'Regional settlement patterns in the Tiwanaku Valley of Bolivia'. *Journal of Field Archaeology* 24: 67–83.

Macauley, M. (1999) *Social Power and Legal Culture: Litigation Masters in Late Imperial China*. Stanford, Stanford University Press.

McCorriston, J. (1992) 'The Halaf environment and human activities in the Khabur Drainage, Syria'. *Journal of Field Archaeology*, 19(3): 315–333.

McCorriston, J. (1994) 'Acorn eating and agricultural origins: Californian ethnographies as analogues for the ancient Near East'. *Antiquity* 68: 97–107.

McCorriston, J. (1997) 'The fibre revolution: Textile extensification, alienation and social stratification in Ancient Mesopotamia'. *Current Anthropology* 38(4): 517– 49.

McDermott, J.P. (1999a) editor, *State and Court Ritual in China*. Cambridge, CUP.

McDermott, J.P. (1999b) *Introduction.* In McDermott 1999a, pp. 1–19.

McDermott, B. (2004) *Warfare in Ancient Egypt.* Stroud, Glos., Sutton Publishing.

McDowell, A.G. (1999) *Village Life in Ancient Egypt: Laundry Lists and Love Songs*, Oxford, OUP.

McEwan, C. (2000) ed., *Precolumbian Gold: Technology, Style and Iconography.* London, British Museum Press.

McEwan, C. and Haeberli, J. (2000) *Ancestors past but present: Gold diadems from the far south coast of Peru.* In McEwan ed., pp. 16–27.

McEwan, G.F. (1990) 'Some formal correspondences between the imperial architecture of the Wari and Chimú Cultures of ancient Peru'. *Latin American Antiquity* 1(2); 97–116.

McEwan, G.F. (1996) 'Archaeological investigations at Pikillacta: A Wari site in Peru'. *Journal of Field Archaeology* 23: 169–86.

McEwan G.F., Chatfield, M. and Arminda, G. (2002) *The archaeology of Inca origins: Excavations at Chokepukio, Cuzco, Peru.* In Isbell and Silverman eds, pp. 287–301.

McGrew, W.C. (2004) *The Cultured Chimpanzee: Reflections on Cultural Primatology.* Cambridge, CUP.

McGuire, R.H. (1983) *Breaking down cultural complexity: Inequality and heterogeneity. Advances in Archaeological Method and Theory*, Vol.6: 91–141. Academic Press.

McIntosh, R. (1999) 'Clustered cities and alternative courses to authority in prehistory'. *Journal of East Asian Archaeology* 1: 63–86 [Festschrift in honour of K.C. Chang].

Mackay, E.J.H. (1935) *The Indus Civilization.* London, Lovat Dickinson and Thompson.

Mackay, E.J.H. (1938) *Further Excavations at Mohenjo-daro*, I–II. Delhi, Government of India Press.

Mackay, E.J.H. (1943) 'Chanhu-daro Excavations, 1935–36'. *American Oriental Series*, 20. New Haven, Connecticut.

Mackey, C.J. (1987) *Chimú administration in the provinces.* In Haas, Pozorski and Pozorski eds, pp. 121–129.

McNeish, R.S. (1981) *The transition to statehood as seen from the mouth of a cave.* In Jones and Kautz eds, pp. 123–156.

MacNeish, R.S. and Libby, J.G. (1995) eds, *Origins of Rice Agriculture.* El Paso, University of Texas Press.

Maeda. T. (2005) 'Royal inscriptions of Lugalzagesi and Sargon'. *Orient* XL: 3–30.

Maekawa, K. (1987) 'The management of domain land in UrIII Umma: a study of BM 110116'. *Zinbun* 22: 25–82.

Maekawa, K. (1996) *The governor's family and the 'temple households' in UrIII Girsu.* In Veenhof ed., pp. 171–179.

Makowski, K. (2002) *Power and social ranking at the end of the Formative Period: The Lower Lurin Valley cemeteries.* In Isbell and Silverman eds, pp. 89–129.

Maisels, C.K. (1978) *Ratagan: A Forestry Village in the West Highlands of Scotland.* Dissertation, University of Edinburgh, Dept. of Social Anthropology.

Maisels, C.K. (1984) *The Origins of Settlement, Agriculture and the City-State in Mesopotamia.* Doctoral Thesis, University of Edinburgh, Dept. of Social Anthropology,

Maisels, C.K. (1987) 'Models of Social Evolution: Trajectories from the Neolithic to the State'. *MAN*, Vol. 22 (2): 331–359.

Maisels, C.K. (1990) *The Emergence of Civilization: from Hunting and Gathering to Agriculture, Cities and the State in the Near East.* London, Routledge.

Maisels, C.K. (1991) *Trajectory versus typology in Social Evolution. Cultural Dynamics*, Vol. IV(3): 251–269.

Maisels, C. K. (1993a) *The Emergence of Civilization: from Hunting and Gathering to Agriculture, Cities and the State in the Near East.* Revised paperback edition. London, Routledge.

Maisels, C. K. (1993b) *The Near East: Archaeology in the 'Cradle of Civilization'.* London, Routledge.

Maisels, C.K. (1999) *Early Civilizations of the Old World: the Formative Histories of Egypt, the Levant, Mesopotamia, India and China.* London, Routledge.

Malek, J. (1983) *Gîza.* In Smith and Hall eds, pp. 25–36.

Malek, J. (2000) *The Old Kingdom.* In Shaw ed., pp. 89–117.

Malone, C. (1998) ed., 'Special Section on Rice Domestication'. *Antiquity* 72: 857–907.

Malpass, M.A. and Stothert, K.E. (1992) 'Evidence for preceramic houses and household organization in Western South America'. *Andean Past* 3: 137–163.

Mani, B.R. (2004–5) 'Pre-Harappan village settlements and early farming communities in northern South Asia (c. 9th–4th millennia BC)'. *Puratattva* 35: 7–20.

Manuel, J. (2004–5) 'Harappan environment as one variable in the preponderance of Rhinoceros and paucity of Horse'. *Puratattva* 35: 21–26.

Manzanilla, L. (1992) *Akapana: Una pirámide en el centro del mundo.* Instituto de Investigaciones Antropológicas. Universidadal Autónoma de México, México, D.F.

Manzanilla, L. (1996) 'Corporate groups and domestic activities at Teotihuacan'. *Latin American Antiquity* 7: 228–246.

Manzanilla, L. (1997) ed., *Emergence and Change in Early Urban Societies.* New York and London, Plenum.

Manzanilla, L. (1997a) *Early urban societies: Challenges and perspectives.* In Manzanilla ed., pp. 3–42.

Manzanilla, L. (1997b) *Teotihuacan: Urban archetype, cosmic model.* In Manzanilla ed., pp. 109–132.

Manzanilla, L (1997c) *Recapitulation and concluding remarks.* In Manzanilla ed., pp. 275–286.

Manzanilla, L. and Woodward, E. (1990) 'Restos humanos asociados a la pirámide de Akapana (Tiwanaku, Bolivia)'. *Latin American Antiquity* 1: 133–149.

Margueron, J.-Cl. (1996) *La maison orientale.* In Veenhof ed., pp. 17–38.

Marcus, J. (1998) *The peaks and valleys of ancient states: An extension of the Dynamic Model.* In Feinman and Marcus eds, pp. 59–94.

Marshall, J. (1931) *Mohenjo Daro and the Indus Civilization,* 3 Vols., London, Arthur Probsthain.

Martin, D.L. and Freyer, D.W. (1997) eds, 'Troubled Times: Violence and Warfare in the Past'. *War and Society* Vol. 6. Amsterdam, Gordon and Breach Publishers.

Martin, G.T. (1983) *Saqqâra.* In Smith and Hall eds, pp. 37–44.

Martin, L.A. (2000) 'Mammalian remains from the Eastern Jordanian Neolithic and the nature of caprine herding in the steppe'. *Palaeorient* 25(2): 87–104.

Maschner, H.D.G and Reedy-Maschner, K.L. (1998) 'Raid, defend (repeat): the archaeology and ethnohistory of warfare on the North Pacific Rim'. *JAA* 17: 19–51.

Maskarinec, G.G. (1995) *The Rulings of the Night: An Ethnography of Nepalese Shaman Oral Texts.* Madison and London, The University of Wisconsin Press.

Mathews, J.E. (1997) *Population and agriculture in the emergence of complex society in the Bolivian Altiplano: The case of Tiwanaku.* In Manzanilla ed., pp. 245–274.

Matthews, R.J. and Fazeli, H. (2004) 'Copper and complexity: Iran and Mesopotamia in the fourth millennium BC'. *Iran* 42: 61–75.

Matsuzawa, T. (1978) 'The Formative site of Las Haldas, Peru: Architecture, chronology and economy. Translated by Izumi Shimada'. *American Antiquity* 43: 652–73.

Matthiae, P. (1993) *On this side of the Euphrates: a Note on the urban origins in Inner Syria.* In Frangipane *et al.* eds, pp. 523–530.

Matthiae, P., Enea, A., Peyronel, L. and Pinnock, F. (2000) eds, *Proceedings of the First International Congress on the Archaeology of the Ancient Near East.* Roma, Dipartimento di Scienze Storiche, Archeologiche e Entropologiche Dell'Antichita', Universita La Sapienza.

Matthews, R.J. (1992) 'Jemdet Nasr: The site and the period'. *Biblical Archaeologist,* Dec. 1992: 196–202.

Matthews, R.J. (1993) 'Cities, Seals and Writing: Archaic Seal Impression from Jemdet Nasr and Ur'. *Materialen zu den Frühen Schriftzeugnissen des Vorderen Orients,* Vol. 2. Berlin, Gebr. Mann Verlag.

Matthews, R.J. (2000a) ed., *Ancient Anatolia: Fifty Years Work by the British Institute of Archaeology at Ankara.* London, British Institute of Archaeology at Ankara.

Matthews, R. J. (2000b) *Sampling an urban centre: Tell Brak excavations 1994–1996.* In Matthiae *et al.,* pp. 1005–1010.

Matthews, R.J. (2002) 'Zebu: harbingers of doom in Bronze Age Western Asia?' *Antiquity* 76: 438–46.

Matthews, R.J., Matthews, W. and McDonald, H. (1994) 'Excavations at Tell Brak, 1994'. *Iraq* 56: 177–194.

Mayer, A.C. (1956) 'Some hierarchical aspects of caste'. *Southwestern Journal of Anthropology,* Vol. 12(2): 117–144.

Mayr, R.H. (2002) 'The seals of the Turam-Ili archive'. *Journal of Cuneiform Studies* 54: 49–65.

Mazuda, S., Shimada, I. and Morris, C. (1985) *Andean Ecology and Civilization: An Interdisciplinary*

*Perspective on Andean Ecological Complementarity.* Tokyo, University of Tokyo Press.

Mazzoni, S. (1999) 'Tell Afis and its region in the Late Chalcolithic Period'. *Annales Archéologiques Arabes Syriennes* 43: 97–117.

Meadow, R.H. (1991) ed. 'Harappa Excavations 1986–1990: A Multidisciplinary Approach to Third Millennium Urbanism'. *Monographs in World Archaeology* No. 3. Madison, Wisconsin, Prehistory Press.

Meadow, R.H. & Kenoyer, J.M. (1994). *Harappa excavations 1993: the city wall and inscribed materials.* In Parpola and Koskikallio eds, II: 451–470.

Meadow, R.H. & Kenoyer, J.M. (2003) *Recent discoveries and highlights from excavations at Harappa: 1998–2000.* Downloaded 30.8.08.

Meggers, B. J. (1987) *Comment.* In Haas, Pozorski and Pozorski eds, pp. 158–160.

Mehra, K.L. (1999) *Subsistence changes in India and Pakistan; the Neolithic and Chalcolithic from the point of view of plant use today.* In Gosden and Hather eds, pp. 139–147.

Melbye, J. and Fairgrieve, S.I. (1994) 'A massacre and possible cannibalism in the Canadian Arctic: New evidence from the Saunaktuk site (NgTn-1)'. *Arctic Anthropology* 31: 57–77.

Mellaart, J. (1967) *Catal Huyuk: a Neolithic Town in Anatolia.* London, Thames and Hudson.

Melleuish, G. (2002) 'The state in world history: Perspectives and problems'. *Australian Journal of Politics and History* 48(3): 322–335.

Merpert, N. Ya. and Munchaev, R.M. (1984) 'Soviet Expedition's Research at Yarim Tepe III Settlement in Northwestern Iraq, 1978–79'. *Sumer* 43 (1–2): 54–68.

Merpert, N. Ya. and Munchaev, R.M. (1987) 'The Earliest Levels at Yarim Tepe I and Yarim Tepe II in Northern Iraq'. *Iraq* 49: 1–36.

Merpert, N. Ya. and Munchaev, R.M. (1993) *Yarim Tepe I.* In Yoffee and Clark eds, pp. 75–114.

Méry, S. and Blackman, J. (2000) 'Harappa et Mohenjo-Daro: deux zones de production de jarres à engobe noir au Pakistan à la Période Indus'. *Paléorient* 25(2): 167–177.

Meskell, L. (1998) *Twin peaks: The archaeologies of Çatalhöyük.* In Goodison and Morris eds, pp. 46–62.

Meskell, L. (1999) *Archaeologies of Social Life: Age, Sex, Class in Ancient Egypt.* Oxford Blackwell.

Michalowski, P. (1993) 'Letters from Early Mesopotamia (Writings from the Ancient World)'. Atlanta, *Society of Biblical Literature* 3.

Midant-Reynes, B., Buchez, N., Crubezy, E. and Janin, T. (1996) *The predynastic site of Adaima: settlement and cemetery.* In Spencer ed., pp. 93–97.

Midant-Reynes, B. (2000) *The Naqada Period (c.4000–3200 BC).* In Shaw ed. pp. 44–60.

Millaire, J.-F. (2004) 'The manipulation of human remains in Moche society: delayed burials, grave reopening, and secondary offerings of human bones on the Peruvian north coast'. *Latin American Antiquity*, 15(4): 371–388.

Miller, B.D. (1993) ed., *Sex and Gender Hierarchies*, Cambridge, Cambridge University Press.

Miller, D. (1985) 'Ideology and the Harappan Civilization'. *Journal of Anthropological Archaeology*, 4: 31–71.

Millett, N.B. (1990) 'The Narmer Macehead and related objects'. *JARCE* 27: 53–59.

Millon, R. (1988) *The last years of Teotihuacan dominance.* In Yoffee and Cowgill eds, pp. 102–164.

Mills, B.J. (2004) 'The establishment and defeat of hierarchy: inalienable possessions and the history of collective prestige structures in the Pueblo Southwest'. *American Anthropologist* 106(2): 238–251.

Milner, G.R., Anderson, E. and Smith, V.G. (1991) 'Warfare in late prehistoric west-central Illinois'. *American Antiquity* 65: 581–603.

Milner-Gulland, R. (1999) *The Russians.* Oxford, Blackwell.

Milton, G. (2000) *Big Chief Elizabeth: How England's Adventurers Gambled and Won the New World.* London, Hodder and Stoughton.

Misra, V.N. (1996) 'Review of Gupta (1996)'. *Puratattva* 26: 138–9.

Mithen, S., Finlayson, W., Pirie, A., Carruthers, D. and Kennedy, A. (2000) 'New evidence for economic and technological diversity in the Pre-Pottery Neolithic A: wadi Faynan 16'. *Current Anthropology* 41(4) 655–663.

Molleson, T. and Hodgson, D. (2003) 'The human remains from Woolley's excavations at Ur'. *Iraq* LXV: 91–129.

Moore, A.M.T. (2002) 'Pottery kiln sites at Al'Ubaid and Eridu'. *Iraq* LXIV: 69–77.

Moore, A.M.T., Hillman, G.C. and Legge, A.J. (2000) eds, *Village on the Euphrates: from Foraging to Farming at Abu Hureyra*. New York, OUP.

Moore, D.M. (1981) *Pride of India: genus 'Melia'.* In Hora ed., pp. 241–2.

Moore, J.D. (1991) 'Cultural responses to environmental catastrophes: Post El-Niño subsistence on the prehistoric North Coast of Peru'. *Latin American Antiquity* 2(1): 27–47.

Moore, J.D. (1992) 'Pattern and meaning in prehistoric Peruvian architecture: The architecture of social control in the Chimú state'. *Latin American Antiquity* 3(2): 95–113.

Moore, J.D. (1996) *Architecture and Power in the Ancient Andes: The Archaeology of Public Buildings.* Cambridge, CUP.

Moorey, P.R.S. (1984) 'Where did they bury the kings of the IIIrd Dynasty of Ur?'. *Iraq* 46: 11–18.

Moorey, P.R.S. (1986) 'The emergence of the light horse-drawn chariot in the Near East c.2000–1500 BC'. *World Archaeology* 18: 203–4.

Moorey, P.R.S. (1990) 'From the Gulf to the Delta in the fourth millennium BC: the Syrian connection'. *Eretz Israel* 21: 62–9.

Moorey, P.R.S. (1994) *Ancient Mesopotamian Materials and Industries: The Archaeological Evidence.* Oxford, OUP.

Morales, V.B. (1990) 'Figurines and other clay objects from Sarab and Çayönü'. *Chicago, Oriental Institute Communications,* No. 25.

Moran, E.F. (1990) ed., *The Ecosystem Approach in Anthropology: From Concept to Practice.* Ann Arbor, University of Michigan Press.

Morris, C. (1998) *Inka strategies of incorporation and governance.* In Feinman and Marcus eds, pp. 293–309.

Morris, I. (1987) *Burial and Ancient Society: The Rise of the Greek City-State.* Cambridge, CUP.

Morris, I. (1991) *The early polis as city and state.* In Rich and A. Wallace-Hadrill eds, pp. 24–57.

Morris, I. (1997) *The archaeology of equalities? The Greek city-states.* In Nichols and Charlton eds, pp. 91–105.

Moseley, M.E. (1975a) *The Maritime Foundations of Andean Civilization.* Menlo Park, CA, Cummings.

Moseley, M.E. (1975b) 'Chan Chan: Andean alternative to the preindustrial city'. *Science* Vol. 187 (4173): 219–225.

Moseley, M.E. (1975c) 'Prehistoric principles of labor organization in the Moche Valley'. *American Antiquity* 40: 191–196.

Moseley, M.E. (1978) 'The evolution of Andean civilizations'. In *Ancient Native Americans,* ed. J.D. Jennings, pp. 491–541. San Francisco, Freeman.

Moseley, M.E. (1992) 'Maritime foundations and multilinear evolution: retrospect and prospect'. *Andean Past* 3: 5–42.

Moseley, M.E. (1993) *The Incas and Their Ancestors: The Archaeology of Peru.* London, Thames and Hudson.

Moseley, M.E. and Cordy-Collins, A. (1990) eds, *The Northern Dynasties: Kingship and Statecraft in Chimor.* Dumbarton Oaks Research Library and Collection, Washington DC.

Moseley, M.E. and Day, K.C. (1982) eds, *Chan Chan: Andean Desert City.* Albuquerque, University of New Mexico Press.

Moynahan, B. (2002) *William Tyndale: If God Spare My Life.* London, Little, Brown.

Mughal, M.R. (1974) 'New evidence of the Early Harappan culture from Jalilpur, Pakistan'. *Archaeology* (Cambridge, Mass.) Vol. 27: 106–113.

Mughal, M.R. (1982) *Recent archaeological research in the Cholistan Desert.* In Possehl ed. pp. 85–95.

Mughal, M.R. (1990) 'The Harappan settlement patterns in the Greater Indus Valley'. *Pakistan Archaeology* No. 25: 1–72.

Mughal, M.R. (1994) *The Harappan nomads of Cholistan.* In B. Allchin ed., 1994, pp. 53–68.

Mughal, M.R. (1997) 'A preliminary review of archaeological surveys in Punjab and Sindh: 1993–95'. *South Asian Studies* 13: 241–249.

Muller, B. (1996) *Les maquettes architecturales: Reflet de l'habitat domestique?* In Veenhof ed., pp. 39–60.

Müller-Neuhof, B. (2006) 'An EPPNB human sculpture from Tell Sheikh Hassan'. *Neo-Lithics* 2006: 32–38.

Munchaev, R.M., Merpert, N.Ya., and Bader N.O. (1984) 'Archaeological Studies in the Sinjar Valley, 1980'. *Sumer* 43 (1–2): 32–53..

Munchaev, R.M. and Merpert, N.Ya. (1998) *Tell Hazna I: The most ancient cult centre in north-east Syria*. In Arsebük, Mellink and Schirmer eds, pp. 499–514.

Munro, N.D. (2004) 'Zooarchaeological measures of hunting pressure and occupation intensity in the Natufian: implications for agricultural origins'. *Current Anthropology* 45(S): 5–33.

Nadel, D. and Werker, E. (1999) 'The oldest ever brush hut plant remains from Ohalo II, Jordan Valley, Israel (19,000 BP)'. *Antiquity* 73: 755–64.

Naqin, S. (2000) *Peking: Temples and City-Life, 1400–1900*. Berkeley, University of California Press.

Nath, A. (1999) 'Further excavations at Rakhigarhi'. *Puratattva* 29: 46–49.

Nath, A. (2000–2001) 'Rakhigarhi: 1999–2000'. *Puratattva* 31: 43–45.

Naveh, D. (2003) 'PPNA Jericho: a socio-political perspective'. *CAJ* 13(1): 83–96.

Nelson, S.M. (1995) ed., *The Archaeology of Northeast China: Beyond the Great Wall*. London, Routledge.

Nelson, S. M. (1995) 'Ritualized pigs and the origins of complex society: Hypotheses regarding the Hongshan Culture'. *Early China* 20: 1–16.

Nemet-Nejat, K.R. (1998) *Daily Life in Ancient Mesopotamia*. Peabody, Mass., Hendrickson Publishers.

Nesbitt, M. (2002) *When and where did domesticated cereals first occur in southwest Asia?* In Cappers and Bottema eds, pp. 113–132.

Nesbitt, M. (2004) 'Can we identify a centre, region, or a super-region for Near Eastern plant domestication'. *Neo-Lithics* 1/04: 38–40.

Netherly, P. (1977) *Local Level Lords on the North Coast of Peru*. Ph.D Diss., Dept. of Anthropology, Cornell University, Ithaca.

Netherly, P. (1984) 'The management of Late Andean irrigation systems on the North Coast of Peru'. *American Antiquity*, 49: 227–254.

Nezafati, N., Pernicka, E. and Momenzadeh, M. (2006) 'Ancient tin: Old question and a new answer'. *Antiquity* No. 308, Project gallery.

Nichols, D.L. and Charlton, T.H. (1997) eds, *The Archaeology of City-States: Cross-Cultural Approaches*. Washington and London, Smithsonian Institution Press.

Nielsen, A.E. (2001) *Ethnoarchaeological perspectives on caravan trade in the South-Central Andes*. In Kutznar ed., pp. 163–201.

Nielsen, A.E. (2005) 'Comment on Arkush and Stanish'. *CA* 46(1): 17–18.

Nieuwenhuyse O. (1997) 'Following the Earliest Halaf: Some later Halaf Pottery from Tell Sabi Abyad, Syria', *Anatolica* XXIII: 227–241.

Nigam, J.S. (1996) 'Sothi pottery at Kalibangan: A reappraisal'. *Puratattva* 7 14.

Nigro, L. (1996) 'Visual role and ideological meaning of the Enemies in the Royal Akkadian Relief. 43e'. *RAI*, Prague 1996:283-297.

Nigro, L. (1998) 'The two steles of Sargon: Iconography and visual propaganda at the beginning of the Royal Akkadian Relief.' *Iraq* Vol 60: 85-102.

Nishiaki, Y and Matsutani, T. (2001) *Tell Kosak Shamali, Vol. 1. The Archaeological Investigations on the Upper Euphrates, Syria: Chalcolithic Architecture and the Earlier Prehistoric Remains*. Oxford, Oxbow and The University Museum, University of Tokyo.

Nissen, H.J. (1988) *The Early History of the Ancient Near East: 9000–2000 BC*. Chicago and London, University of Chicago Press.

Nissen, H. J. (2001) *Cultural and political networks in the Ancient Near East during the fourth and third millennia BC*. In Rothman ed., pp. 149–179.

Nissen, H.J. (2002) *Uruk: key site of the period and key site of the problem*. In Postgate ed., pp. 1–16.

Nissen, H.J. (2007) *Archaeological surveys and Mesopotamian history*. In Stone ed., pp. 19–28.

Nissen, H.J., Damerow, P. and Englund, R.K. (1993) *Archaic Bookkeeping: Early Writing and Techniques of Economic Administration in the Ancient Near East (trans. Paul Larsen)*. Chicago, University of Chicago Press.

Nivison, D.S. (1983) 'The dates of Western Chou'. *Harvard Journal of Asiatic Studies* 43(2): 481–580.

Oates, J. (1978) 'Religion and ritual in sixth-millennium BC Mesopotamia'. *World Archaeology* 10:

117–24.

Oates, J. (1993) *An Akkadian administrative device from Brak*. In Frangipane *et al.* eds, pp. 289–305.

Oates, J. (2002) *Tell Brak: the fourth millennium sequence and its implications*. In Postgate ed., pp. 111–122.

Oates, J. and Oates, D. (1997) 'An open gate: Cities of the fourth millennium BC (Tell Brak 1997)'. *Cambridge Archaeological Journal* 7: 287–96.

Oates, D., Oates, J. and MacDonald, H. (2001) *Excavations Tell Brak, II: Nagar in the Third Millennium BC*. Cambridge, McDonald Institute for Archaeological Research.

O'Brien, A.A. (1996) 'The Serekh as an aspect of the iconography of early kingship'. *JARCE* 33: 123–138.

O'Connor, D. (1989) 'New funerary enclosures (Talbezirke) of the Early Dynastic Period at Abydos'. *Journal of the American Research Center in Egypt* 25: 51–86.

O'Connor, D. (2000) *Society and individual in early Egypt*. In Richards and Van Buren eds, pp. 21–35.

O'Connor, D. and Silverman, D.P. (1995) eds, *Ancient Egyptian Kingship*. Leiden and New York, E.J. Brill.

O'Day, K. (2000) *The goldwork of Chimor: The technology and iconography of wealth accumulation*. In McEwan ed., pp. 62–75.

Odell, G. (1996) ed., *Stone Tools: Theoretical Insights in Human Prehistory*, New York, Plenum.

Ökse, A. T. (2006) 'Gre Virike (Period I) – Early Bronze Age ritual facilities on the Middle Euphrates River'. *Anatolica* XXXII: 1–27.

Ortloff, C. R., Feldman, R.A. and Moseley, M.E. (1985) 'Hydraulic engineering and historical aspects of the Pre-Columbian intra-valley canal systems of the Moche Valley, Peru'. *Journal of Field Archaeology* 12(1): 77–98.

Ortloff, C. and Kolata, A. (1993) 'Climate and collapse: agro-ecological perspectives on the decline of the Tiwanaku State'. *Journal of Archaeological Science* 20: 195–221.

Özbal, H., Adriaens, A. and Earl, B. (2000) 'Hacinebi metal production and exchange'. *Paléorient* 25(1): 57–65.

Ozdogan, M. (1998) 'Anatolia from the last glacial maximum to the Holocene climatic optimum: cultural formations and the impact of environmental setting'. *Paléorient* 23/2: 25–38.

Ozdogan, M. and Ozdogan, A. (1993) *Pre-Halafian pottery of southern Anatolia*. In Frangipane *et al.* eds, pp. 87–103.

Ozdogan, M. and Ozdogan, A. (1998) *Buildings of cult and the cult of buildings*. In Arsebuck *et al.* eds, pp. 581–601.

Pal, Y., Sahai, B., Sood, R.K. and Agrawal, O.P. (1980) 'Remote sensing of the 'lost' Sarasvati River'. *Proceedings of the Indian Academy of Sciences (Earth Plant Science)* pp. 317–331.

Panjwani, P. (2004–5) 'Early Chalcolithic traditions of Gujarat'. *Puratattva* 35: 38–43.

Pankenier, D.W. (1981–2) 'Astronomical dates in Shang and Western Zhou'. *Early China* 7: 2–37.

Park, T.K. (1992) 'Early trends toward class stratification. Chaos, common property, and flood recession agriculture'. *American Anthropologist* 94: 90–107.

Parpola, A. (1984) *New correspondences between Harappan and Near Eastern glyptic art*. In Allchin ed., pp. 176–195.

Parpola. A. (1986) 'The Indus Script: a challenging puzzle'. *World Archaeology* 17: 399–419.

Parpola. A. (1993) 'The Assyrian Tree of Life: Tracing the origins of Jewish monotheism and Greek philosophy'. *Journal of Near Eastern Studies* 52(3): 161–208.

Parpola, A. & Koskikallio, P. (1994) eds, *South Asian Archaeology 1993: proceedings of the twelfth international conference of the European Association of South Asian Archaeologists held in Helsinki University 5–9 July 1993; 2 vols.* Helsinki, Suomalainen Tiedeakatemia.

Pärsinnen, M. (1992) 'Tawantinsuyu: The Inca State and its political administration'. Helsinki, *Societas Historica Finlandiae, Studia Historica* 43.

Pastner, S. and Flam, L. (1982) 'Anthropology in Pakistan: Recent Socio-Cultural and Archaeological Perspectives'. *South Asia Occasional Papers and Theses* No. 8, South Asia Program, Cornell University.

Patel, A. (1997) *The pastoral economy of Dholavira: a first look at animals and urban life in third millennium Kutch*. In Allchin and Allchin eds, pp. 101–113

Patterson, T.C. (1991) *The Huaca La Florida, Rimac Valley, Peru*. In Donnan ed., pp. 59–70.

Paul, A. (2000) 'Bodiless human heads in Paracas necropolis textile iconography'. *Andean Past* 6: 69–94.

Paul, A. and Turpin, S.A. (1986) 'The ecstatic shaman theme of Paracas textiles'. *Archaeology* 39(5): 20–27.

Payne, J.C. (1993) 'Tomb 100: the decorated tomb at Hierakonpolis confirmed'. *Journal of Egyptian Archaeology* 59: 31–5.

Payne, J.C. (1993) *Catalogue of the Predynastic Egyptian Collection in the Ashmolean Museum*. Oxford, Clarendon Press.

Paynter, R. (1989) 'The archaeology of equality and inequality'. *Annual Review of Anthropology* 18: 369–399.

Pearce, J. (2000) 'Investigating ethnicity at Hacinebi: Ceramic perspectives on style and behaviour in 4th millennium Mesopotamian-Anatolian interaction'. *Paléorient* 25(1): 35–42.

Pearsall, D.M. (1999) *The impact of Maize on subsistence systems in South America: an example from the Jama River Valley, coastal Ecuador*. In Gosden and Hather eds, pp. 419–437.

Pearson, C.E. (1980) 'Rank-size distributions and the analysis of prehistoric settlement systems'. *Journal of Anthropological Research* 36(4): 453–462.

Pearson, J.L. (2002) *Shamanism and the Ancient Mind: A Cognitive Approach to Archaeology*. Walnut Creek, Altamira.

Pearson, M.P. (2003) 'Food, Culture and Identity in the Neolithic and Early Bronze Age'. Oxford, *BAR* S1117.

Pearson, M.P. and Thorpe, I.J.N. (2005) 'Warfare, Violence and Slavery in Prehistory'. Oxford, Archaeopress, *BAR* S1374.

Pearson, R. (1998) *The Chuzan Kingdom of Okinawa as a City-State*. In Nichols and Charlton eds, pp. 119–134.

Pearson, R. (2005) 'The social context of early pottery in the Lingnan region of south China'. *Antiquity* 79: 819–828.

Pei, Anping (1998) 'Notes on new advancements and revelations in the agricultural archaeology of early rice domestication in the Dongting Lake region'. *Antiquity* 72: 878–85.

Peltenburg, E. (2007) ed. *Euphrates River Valley Settlement: The Carchemish Sector in the Third Millennium BC*. Levant Supplementary Series Volume 5. Oxford, Oxbow Books

Peltenburg, E. and Wasse, A. (2004) eds, *Neolithic Revolution: New Perspectives on Southwest Asia in the Light of Recent Discoveries on Cyprus*. Levant Supplementary Series Volume 1. Oxford, Oxbow Books.

Peters, J., Helmer, D., von den Driesch, A. and Sana Segui, M. (1999) 'Early animal husbandry in the Northern Levant'. *Paléorient* 25(2): 27–47.

Peterson, C.E. and Drennan, R.D. (2005) 'Communities, settlements, sites, and surveys: regional-scale analysis of prehistoric human interaction'. *American Antiquity* 70(1): 5–30.

Peterson, J. (2002) *Sexual Revolutions: Gender and Labor at the Dawn of Agriculture*. Walnut Creek (CA), Altamira.

Petrie, W.F. (1902) *Abydos*, Part 1. London, Egyptian Exploration Society.

Petrie, W.F. and Quibell, J.E. (1896) *Naqada and Ballas*. London, Quaritch.

Pettinato, G. (1991) *Ebla: A New Look at History*. Baltimore, Johns Hopkins University Press.

Philip, G. (2002) *Contacts between the 'Uruk' world and the Levant during the fourth millennium BC: evidence and interpretation*. In Postgate ed., pp. 207–236.

Philip, G. and Baird, D. (2000) eds, *Ceramics and Change in the Early Bronze Age of the Southern Levant*. Sheffield, Sheffield Academic Press.

Pickersgill, B. (1989) *Cytological and genetic evidence on the domestication and diffusion of crops within the Americas*. In Harris and Hillman eds, pp. 426–439.

Pickersgill, B. and Heiser, C.B. (1977) *Origins and distribution of plants domesticated in the New World Tropics*. In Reed ed., pp. 803–835.

Piggott, S. (1983) *The Earliest Wheeled Transport*. Ithaca, N.Y., Cornell University Press

Piggott, S. (1992) *Wagon, Chariot and Carriage*. London, Thames and Hudson.

Pillsbury, J. (2001) ed., 'Moche Art and Archaeology in Ancient Peru'. Washington D.C., *National Gallery of Art: Studies in the History of Art* 63.

Pineda, R.S. (1988) *The Late Preceramic and Initial Period*. In Keatinge ed., pp. 67–96.

Pingree, D. (1996) *Astronomy in India*, In Walker ed., pp. 123–142.

Pinker, S. (1994) *The Language Instinct: The New Science of Language and Mind.* Harmondsworth, Penguin.

Pinker, S. (2002) *The Blank Slate: The Modern Denial of Human Nature.* London, Allen Lane.

Pinnock, F. (1985) 'About the trade of Early Syrian Ebla'. *M.A.R.I.* 4: 85–92.

Pinnock, F. (2001) 'The urban landscape of Old Syrian Ebla'. *JCS* 53: 13–34.

Pinnock, F. (2006) 'Ebla and Ur: Relations, exchanges and contacts between two great capitals of the ancient Near East'. *Iraq* LXVIII: 85–97.

Pittman, H. (1993) *Pictures of an administration: the Late Uruk scribe at work.* In Frangipane *et al.* eds, pp. 221–245.

Pittman, H. (1994) 'The Glazed Steatite Glyptic Style: the Structure and Function of an Image System in the Administration of Protoliterate Mesopotamia'. Berlin, *Berliner Beiträge zum Vorderen Orient* 16.

Pittman, H. (2000) 'Administrative evidence from Hacinebi tepe: An essay on the local and the colonial'. *Paléorient* 25(1): 43–50.

Pittman, H. (2001) *Mesopotamian interregional relations reflected through glyptic evidence in the Late Chalcolithic 1–5 Periods.* In Rothman ed., pp. 403–443.

Plog, F. (2003) 'Social conflict, social structure and processes of culture change: book review essay'. *American Antiquity* 68(1)182–88.

Podzorsky, P.V. (1988) 'Predynastic Egyptian seals of known provenience in the R.H. Lowie Museum of Anthropology'. *JNES* 47: 259–68.

Pollock, S. (1999) *Ancient Mesopotamia.* Cambridge, CUP.

Pollock, S. (2001) *The Uruk Period in southern Mesopotamia.* In Rothman ed., pp. 181–231.

Pollock, S. and Bernbeck R. (2005) eds, *Archaeologies of the Middle East: Critical Perspectives.* Oxford, Blackwell.

Porat, N. and Adams, B. (1996) *Imported pottery with potmarks from Abydos.* In Spencer ed., pp. 98–107.

Porter, A. (2002) 'The dynamics of death: ancestors, pastoralism and the origins of a third millennium city in Syria'. *BASOR* 325: 1–36.

Possehl, G.L. (1979) *Pastoral nomadism in the Indus Civilization: an hypothesis.* In Taddei ed., pp. 533–551.

Possehl, G.L. (1982) ed., *Harappan Civilization: a Contemporary Perspective.* Warminster, Aris and Phillips.

Possehl, G.L. (1984) *A note on Harappan settlement patterns in the Punjab.* In Kennedy and Possehl eds, pp. 83–87.

Possehl, G.L. (1986) *Kulli: An exploration of ancient civilization in South Asia.* Durham, Carolina Academic Press.

Possehl, G.L. (1990) 'Revolution in the urban revolution: the emergence of Indus Civilization'. *Annual Review of Anthropology* 19: 261–282.

Possehl, G.L. (1992) ed., *South Asian Archaeological Studies: Essays in Honour of Walter A. Fairservice.* Publisher not named.

Possehl, G.L. (1995) *Seafaring merchants of Meluhha.* In Allchin & Allchin eds, pp. 87–100.

Possehl, G.L. (1997) 'The transformation of the Indus Civilization'. *Journal of World Prehistory,* Vol. 11(4): 425–472.

Possehl, G.L. (1998) *Sociocultural complexity without the State: the Indus Civilization.* In Feinman and Marcus eds, pp. 261–291.

Possehl, G.L. (2002) *The Indus Civilization: A Contemporary Perspective.* New York and Oxford, Altamira Press.

Possehl, G.L. (2003) ed., *Harappan Civilization: A Recent Perspective.* New Dehli , American Institute of Indian Studies and Oxford and IBH Publishing Co.

Possehl, G.L. (2007) *The Harappan settlement of Gujarat.* In Stone ed., pp. 213–234.

Postgate, J.N. (1992) *Early Mesopotamia: Society and Economy at the Dawn of History.* London, Routledge.

Postgate, J.N. (1994) 'How many Sumerians per hectare ? – Probing the anatomy of an early city'. *Cambridge Archaeological Journal* 4(1): 47–65.

Postgate, J.N. (2003) 'Learning the lessons of the future: trade in prehistory through a historian's lens'. *Bibliotheca Orientalis*. 60(1–2): 6–26.

Postgate, J.N. (2002) ed., 'Artefacts of Complexity: Tracking the Uruk in the Near East. London', *Iraq Archaeological Reports*, 5; British School of Archaeology in Iraq.

Postgate, J.N., Wang, T. & Wilkinson, T. (1995) 'The evidence for early writing: utilitarian or ceremonial'. *Antiquity* 69: 459–80.

Potts, D.T. (1997) *Mesopotamian Civilization: the Material Foundations*. London, Athlone Press.

Potts, D.T. (1999) *The Archaeology of Elam: Formation and Transformation of an Ancient Iranian State*. Cambridge, CUP.

Potts, T.F. (1994) *Mesopotamia and the East*. Oxford, Oxford University Committee for Archaeology, Monograph 37

Pournelle, J.R. (2007) *KLM to CORONA: A bird's-eye view of cultural ecology and early Mesopotamian urbanization*. In Stone ed., pp. 29–62.

Powell, M.A. (1987) ed., 'Labor in the Ancient Near East'. New Haven, *American Oriental Society*.

Powell, M.A. (1996) 'Money in Mesopotamia'. *JESHO* 39(3): 224–242.

Pozorski, S. (1987) *Theocracy vs. militarism: The significance of the Casma Valley in understanding early state formation*. In Haas *et al.* eds, pp. 15–30.

Pozorski, S. and Pozorski. T. (1986) 'Recent excavations at Pampa de las Llamas-Moxeke, a complex Initial Period site in Peru'. *Journal of Field Archaeology* 13: 381–401.

Pozorski, S. and Pozorski. T. (1987) *Chronology*. In Haas, Pozorski and Pozorski, pp. 5–8.

Pozorski, S. and Pozorski. T. (1990) 'Re-examining the critical preceramic/ceramic period transition: New data from coastal Peru'. *American Anthropologist* 92: 481–91.

Pozorski, S. and Pozorski. T. (1992) 'Early civilization in the Casma Valley, Peru'. *Antiquity* 66: 845–70.

Pozorski, S. and Pozorski. T. (1994) 'Early Andean Cities'. *Scientific American* 270(6): 66–72.

Pozorski, S. and Pozorski T. (2002) *The Sechín Alto Complex and its place within Casma Valley Initial Period development*. In Isbell and Silverman eds, pp. 21–51.

Pozorski, S. and Pozorski T. (2006) 'Las Haldas: An expanding Initial Period polity of coastal Peru'. *Journal of Anthropological Research*, 62: 27–52.

Pozorski, T. (1987) *Changing priorities within the Chimu state: the role of irrigation agriculture*. In Haas, Pozorski and Pozorski eds, pp. 111–120.

Pozorski, T. and Pozorski, S (1987) *Chavín, the early Horizon and the Initial Period*. In Haas, Pozorski and Pozorski, pp. 36–46.

Pozorski, T. and Pozorski, S. (2005) 'Architecture and chronology at the the site of Sechín Alto, Casma Valley, Peru'. *Journal of Field Archaeology* 30: 1–19.

Price, B.J. (1977) 'Shifts in production and organization: a cluster-interaction model'. *Current Anthropology* 18(2): 209–33.

Price, T.D. and Brown, J.A. (1985) eds, *Prehistoric Hunter-Gatherers: Emergence of Cultural Complexity*. New York, Academic Press.

Price, T.D. and Feinman, G.M. (1995) eds, *Foundations of Social Inequality*. New York, Plenum.

Price, T.D. and Feinman, G.M. (2000) eds, *Archaeology at the Millennium: A Sourcebook*. New York, Kluwer Academic/Plenum.

Price, T.D. and Gebauer, A.B. (1995) eds, *Last Hunters, First Farmers: New Perspectives on the Prehistoric Transition to Agriculture*. Santa Fe, School of American Research.

Proulx, D.A. (1971) 'Headhunting in Ancient Peru'. *Archaeology* 24: 16–21.

Proulx, D.A. (2001) *Ritual uses of trophy heads in Ancient Nasca society*. In Benson and Cook eds, pp. 119–136.

Puri, V.M.K and Siddiqui, M.A. (1996) 'Glacial Deformation and Strain Rate Tensor Analysis of Gangotri Glacier, Uttarkashi Distt., U.P. Proc. Symp'. *North-West Himalaya and Foredeep, Geological Survey of India, Special Publication* 21(2): 307–310.

Puri, V.M.K. and Verma, B.C. (1998). 'Geological and glaciological source of Vedic Saraswati in the Himalayas'. *Itihas Darpan*, Vol. IV No. 2, pp. 7–21.

Pye, L.W. (1996) *The state and the individual: an overview interpretation*. In Hook ed., pp. 16–42.

Quigley, D. (1993) *The Interpretation of Caste*. Oxford, Clarendon Press.

Quilter, J. (1985) 'Architecture and chronology at El Paraiso, Peru'. *Journal of Field Archaeology* 12: 279–297.

Quilter, J. (1990) 'The Moche revolt of the objects'. *Latin American Antiquity* 1: 42–65.

Quilter, J. (1991) 'Late Preceramic Peru'. *Journal of World Prehistory* 5: 387–438.

Quilter, J. (1997) 'The narrative approach to Moche iconography'. *Latin American Antiquity* 8(2): 113–83.

Quilter, J. (2001) *Moche mimesis: continuity and change in public art in Early Peru*. In Pillsbury ed., pp. 21–45.

Quilter, J. (2002) 'Moche politics, religion and warfare'. *Journal of World Prehistory* 16: 145–95.

Quintero, L.A. & Wilke, P.J. (1995) 'Evolution and economic significance of naviform core-and-blade technology in the Southern Levant'. *Paléorient* 21/1: 17–33.

Quirke, S. (1992) *Ancient Egyptian Religion*. London, British Museum Press.

Quivron, G. (1997) *Incised and painted marks on the pottery of Mehrgarh and Nausharo-Baluchistan*. In Allchin and Allchin *et al.* eds, pp. 45–62.

*RAI (1987)* = Rencontre Assyriologique Internationale 33. 'La Femme dans le Proche-Orient Antique. Compte rendu'. Paris, Éditions Recherche sur les Civilisations.

Raaflaub, K. and Rosenstein, N. (1999) eds, *War and Society in the Ancient and Mediaeval Worlds: Asia, the Mediterranean, Europe and Mesoamerica*. Cambridge, MA, Centre for Hellenic Studies, Harvard University.

Rackham, O. (1986) *The History of the Countryside*. London, J.M. Dent.

Radhakrishna, B.P. and Merh, S.S. (1999) eds, 'Vedic Saraswati'. *Memoir* 42, Geological Society of India, Bangalore.

Raglan, Baron (Fitzroy Richard Somerset IV) 1979 [1936] *The Hero: A Study in Tradition, Myth, and Drama*. New York and London, Meridian.

Rainville, L. (2005) 'Investigating Upper Mesopotamian Households using Micro-Archaeological Techniques'. Oxford, *BAR* S1368.

Ramirez, S.E. (2005) 'Comment on Sutter and Cortez', *Current Anthropology* 46(4): 539–40.

Rao, L.S., Sahu, N.B., Sahu, P., Shastri, U.A. and Diwan, S. (2004) 'Unearthing Harappan settlement in Bhirrana (2003–4)'. *Puratattva* 34: 20–4.

Rao, S.R. (1973) *Lothal and the Indus Civilization*. New York, Asia Publishing House.

Rao, S.R. (1985) 'Lothal, A Harappan Port Town, 1955–62'. New Delhi, *Memoirs of the Archaeological Survey of India*, No. 78, Vol. 2.

Rappaport, R.A. (1968) *Pigs for the Ancestors: Ritual in the Ecology of a New Guinea People*. New Haven, Yale University Press.

Ratnagar, S. (1991) *Enquiries into the Political Organization of Harappan Society*. Ravish Publishers, Pune.

Ratnagar, S. (2001) 'The Bronze Age: unique instance of a pre-industrial world system?'. *Current Anthropology* 42(3): 351– 379.

Rawson, J. (1980) *Ancient China: Art and Archaeology*. London, British Museum Publications.

Rawson, J. (1989) 'Statesmen or barbarians? The Western Zhou as seen through their bronzes'. *Proceedings of the British Academy* 75: 81–4.

Rawson, J. (1990) *Western Zhou Ritual Bronzes from the Arthur M. Sackler Collections*. Cambridge Mass., Harvard University Press.

Rawson, J. (1993) 'Ancient Chinese Ritual Bronzes: The evidence from tombs and hoards of the Shang and Western Zhou Periods'. *Antiquity* 67: 805–23.

Rawson, J. (1995) *Chinese Jade from the Neolithic to the Qing*. London, British Museum Press.

Rawson, J. (1996) ed., *Mysteries of Ancient China: New Discoveries from the Early Dynasties*. London, British Museum Press.

Rawson, J. (1999) *Ancient Chinese ritual as seen in the material record*. In McDermott, pp. 20–49.

Reddy, S.N. (1997) 'If the threshing floor could talk: integration of agriculture and pastoralism during the Late Harappan in Gujarat, India'. *Journal of Anthropological Archaeology* 16: 162–187.

Redfield, R. (1968) [1953] *The Primitive World and its Transformations*. Harmondsworth, Penguin Books.

Redford, D.B. *The Ancient Egyptian 'city': figment or reality*. In Aufrecht *et al.* eds, pp. 210–220.

Redmond, E.M. (1998) ed., *Chiefdoms and Chieftaincy in the Americas*. Gainsville, University of Florida.

Reed, C.A. (1977) *Origins of Agriculture*. The Hague and Paris, Mouton World Anthropology.

Reilly, F.K. (1996) *Art, ritual and rulership in the Olmec world*. In Rosenbaum ed., pp. 27–45.

Reitz, A.J. and Wing, E.S. (2008) *Zooarchaeology*. Cambridge, CUP.

Renfrew, C., Rowlands, M. and Segraves, B.A. (1982) eds, *Theory and Explanation in Archaeology*. Academic Press , New York.

Renger, J. (1994) 'On economic structures in Ancient Mesopotamia'. *Orientalia* 18: 157–206.

Reyna, S.P. and Downs, R.E. (1994) eds, *Studying War: Anthropological Perspectives*. Amsterdam, Gordon and Breach.

Rhodes, P.J. (1986) *The Greek City-States: A Source Book*. London and Sydney, Croom Helm.

Rice, P. (1999) 'On the origins of pottery'. *Journal of Anthropological Method and Theory* 6: 1–54.

Rich, J. (1992) ed., *The City in Late Antiquity*. London, Routledge.

Rich, J. and Wallace-Hadrill, A. (1991) eds, *City and Country in the Ancient World*. London, Routledge.

Richards, J. (2000) *Modified order, responsive legitimacy, redistributed wealth: Egypt, 2260–1650 BC*. In Richards and Van Buren, pp. 36–45.

Richards, J. and Van Buren, M. (2000) eds, *Order, Legitimacy and Wealth in Ancient States*. Cambridge, CUP, New Directions in Archaeology.

Richerson, P.J., Boyd, R. and Bettinger, R.L. (2001) 'Was agriculture impossible during the Pleistocene but mandatory during the Holocene? A climate change hypothesis'. *American Antiquity* 66(3): 387–411.

Rick, J.W. (1980) *Prehistoric Hunters of the High Andes*. New York, Academic Press.

Rick, J.W. (1988) *The character and context of highland preceramic society*. In Keatinge ed., pp. 3–40.

Ridley, M. (1993) *The Red Queen: Sex and the Evolution of Human Nature*. London, Viking.

Ridley, M. (1996) *The Origins of Virtue*. London, Viking.

Rissman, P. (1988) 'Public displays and private values: a guide to buried wealth in Harappan archaeology'. *World Archaeology* 20(2): 209–28.

Rivera, M.A. (1991) 'The prehistory of Northern Chile: a synthesis'. *Journal of World Prehistory*, 5: 1–47.

Rizkana, I. and Seeher, J. (1984) 'New light on the relation of Maadi to the Upper Egyptian cultural sequence'. *MDAIK* 40: 237–252.

Rizkana, I. and Seeher, J. (1985) 'The chipped stones at Maadi: Preliminary reassessment of a Predynastic industry and its long-distance relations'. *MDAIK* 41: 235–255.

Rizkana, I. and Seeher, J. (1987) *Maadi I: The Pottery of the Predynastic Settlement*. Mainz am Rhein, Philip von Zabern.

Rizkana, I. and Seeher, J. (1988) *Maadi II: The Lithic Industries of the Predynastic Settlement*. Mainz am Rhein, Philip von Zabern.

Rizkana, I. and Seeher, J. (1989) *Maadi III: The Non-Lithic Small finds and the Structural Remains of the Predynastic Settlement*. Mainz am Rhein, Philip von Zabern.

Rizkana, I. and Seeher, J. (1990) *Maadi IV: The Predynastic Cemeteries of Maadi and Wadi Digla.*. Mainz am Rhein, Philip von Zabern.

Roaf, M. (2000) *Survivals and revivals in the art of Ancient Mesopotamia*. In Matthiae at al. eds, pp. 1447–1459.

Roaf, M. and Galbraith, J. (1994) 'Pottery and p-values: "Seafaring merchants of Ur?" re-examined'. *Antiquity* 68: 770–783.

Roaf, M. and Galbraith, J. (2001) *Does the Neutron Activation Analysis of Halaf pottery provide evidence of trade? A re-examination of Davidson and Mckerrell's investigation of Halaf pottery from the Khabur in eastern Syria*. London, LSE Dept. of Statistics, Research Report, Nov. 2001.

Roberts, N. (2002) 'Did prehistoric landscape management retard the Post-Glacial spread of woodland in Southwest Asia?' *Antiquity* 76: 1002–10.

Robson, E. (1999) *Mesopotamian Mathematics, 2100–1600 BC: Technical Constraints in Bureaucracy and Education*. Oxford, Clarendon Press.

Rodewald, C. (1975) *Democracy: Ideas and Realities*. London and Toronto, Dent/Hakkert.

Rodman, A.O. (1992) 'Textiles and ethnicity: Tiwanaku in San Pedro de Atacama, North Chile'. *Latin American Antiquity* 3: 316–340.

Rollefson, G.O. (1996) *The Neolithic devolution: Ecological impact and cultural compensation at 'Ain Ghazal, Jordan.* In Seger ed., pp. 219–229.

Rollefson, G.O. (1998a) ''Ain Ghazal (Jordan): ritual and ceremony III'. *Paléorient* 24(1): 43–58.

Rollefson, G.O. (1998b) *The Aceramic Neolithic of Jordan.* In Henry ed., pp. 102–126.

Rollefson, G. O. (2000) *Ritual and Social Structure at Neolithic 'Ain Ghazal.* In Kuijt ed., pp. 165–190.

Rollefson, G.O. (2005) *Early Neolithic ritual centres in the Southern Levant.* In Gebel and Rollefson eds, pp. 3–13.

Rollefson, G.O. and Kohler-Rollefson, I. (1989) *The collapse of Early Neolithic settlement in the Southern Levant.* In Hershkovitz, pp. 73–89.

Rollefson, G.O. and Kohler-Rollefson, I., (1993) 'PPNC adaptations in the first half of the sixth millennium BC'. *Paléorient* 19(1): 3–42.

Rollefson, G.O., Simmons, A.H. and Kafafi, Z. (1992) 'Neolithic cultures at 'Ain Ghazal, Jordan'. *Journal of Field Archaeology* 19: 443–471.

Ronan, C. (1996) *Astronomy in China, Korea and Japan.* In Walker ed., pp. 245–268.

Roscoe, P.B. (1993) 'Practice and political centralization: A new approach to political evolution'. *Current Anthropology* Vol. 34(2): 111–140.

Roseman, M. (2002) *The Wannsee Conference and the Final Solution.* New York, Henry Holt and Co.

Rosen, S.A. (1996) *The decline and fall of flint.* In Odell ed., pp. 129–158.

Rosen, S.A. (1997a) *Craft specialization and the rise of secondary urbanism: A view from the Southern Levant.* In Aufrecht *et al.* eds, pp. 82–91.

Rosen, S.A. (1997b) 'Geoarcheology of Holocene environments and land-use at Kazan Höyük, Southeast Turkey'. *Geoarcheology* 12: 395–416.

Rosen, S.A. (2002a) *Invention as the Mother of Necessity: An archaeological examination of the origins and development of pottery and metallurgy in the Levant.* In Harrrison *et al.* eds, pp. 11–21.

Rosen, S.A. (2002b) *The evolution of pastoral nomadic systems in the Southern Levantine Periphery.* In Van den Brink and Yannai eds, pp. 23–44.

Rosen, S.A., Savinetsky, A.B., Plakht, Y., Kisseleva, N.K., Khassanov, B.F., Pereladov, A.M. and Haiman, M. (2005) 'Dung in the desert: preliminary results of the Negev Holocene ecology project'. *Current Anthropology* 46(2): 317–327.

Rosenberg, M. and Davis, M. (1992) 'Hallan Çemi Tepesi, an Early Aceramic Neolithic site in Eastern Anatolia: Some preliminary observations concerning material culture'. *Anatolica* 18: 1–18.

Rosenberg, M. (1994) 'Hallan Çemi Tepesi: some further observations concerning stratigraphy and material culture'. *Anatolica* 20: 121–40.

Rosenberg, M., Nesbitt, R.M., Redding, R.W. and Strasser T.F. (1995) 'Hallan Çemi Tepesi: some preliminary observations concerning Early Neolithic subsistence behaviours in Eastern Anatolia'. *Anatolica* 21: 1–12.

Rosenberg, M., Nesbitt, R.M., Redding, R.W. and Peasnall, B.L. (1998) 'Hallan Çemi pig husbandry and post-Pleistocence adaptations along the Taurus-Zagros arc (Turkey)'. *Paléorient* 24: 25–41.

Rosenberg, M. and Redding, R.W. (2000) *Hallan Çemi and early village organization in Eastern Anatolia.* In Kuijt ed., pp. 39–61.

Rosenbaum A. (1996) ed., *The Olmec World: Ritual and Rulership.* The Art Museum, Princeton University, in association with Harry N. Abrams Inc.

Roth, A.M. (1993) 'Social change in the Fourth Dynasty: The spatial organization of pyramids, tombs and cemeteries'. *JARCE* 30: 33-55.

Rothman, M.S. (1987) 'Graph Theory and the interpretation of regional survey data'. *Paléorient* 13(2): 73–91.

Rothman, M.S. (1993) *Another look at the 'Uruk Expansion' from the Tigris Piedmont.* In Frangipane *et al.* eds, pp. 163–176.

Rothman, M.S. (2001a) *The local and the regional: An introduction.* In Rothman ed., pp. 3–26.

Rothman, M.S. (2001b) *The Tigris Piedmont, Eastern Jazira, and Highland Western Iran in the fourth millennium BC.* In Rothman ed., pp. 349–401.

Rothman, M.S. (2001c) ed., *Uruk Mesopotamia and its Neighbours: Cross Cultural Interactions in the Era of State Formation*. Santa Fe, School of American Research Press.

Rothman, M.S. (2002) *Tepe Gawra: chronology and socio-economic change in the foothills of Northern Iraq in the era of state formation*. In Postgate ed., pp. 49–78.

Rothman, M.S. (2004) 'Studying the development of complex society: Mesopotamia in the late fifth and fourth millennia BC.' *Journal of Anthropological Research*, Vol. 12(1): 75–118.

Rothman, M.S. (2007) *The archaeology of early administrative systems in Mesopotamia*. In Stone ed., pp. 235–254.

Rothman, M.S. and Peasnall, B. (2000) 'Societal evolution of small pre-state centres and polities: the example of Tepe Gawra in northern Mesopotamia'. *Paléorient* 25(1): 101–114.

Routledge, B. (1997a) *Learning to love the King: urbanism and the state in Iron Age Moab*. In Aufrecht *et al.* eds, pp. 130–144.

Routledge, C. (1997) *Temple as the centre in ancient Egyptian urbanism*. In Aufrecht *et al.* eds, pp. 221–235.

Rowton, M.B. (1973) 'Urban autonomy in a nomadic environment'. *Journal of Near Eastern Studies* 32: 201–215.

Rowton, M.B. (1974) 'Enclosed nomadism'. *Journal of the Economic and Social History of the Orient*. 17(1): 1–30.

Rubio, G. (2005) *The languages of the Ancient Near East*. In Snell ed., pp. 79–109.

Russell, G.S. and Jackson, M.A. (2001) *Political economy and patronage at Cerro Mayal, Peru*. In Pillsbury ed., pp. 159–177.

Safar, F. Mustafa, M.A. and Lloyd, S. (1981) *Eridu*. Baghdad, Ministry of Culture and Information: State Organization of Antiquities and Heritage.

Sage, S.F. (1992) *Ancient Sichuan and the Unification of China*. Albany, State University of New York Press.

Sahlins, M. (1983) 'Other times, other customs: the anthropology of history'. *American Anthropologist* 85: 517– 44.

Samzun, Λ. (1992) *Observations on the characteristics of the Pre-Harappan remains, pottery and artefacts at Nausharo, Pakistan (2700–2500 BC)*. In C. Jarrige ed., pp. 345–352.

Sandweiss, D.H., Maasch, K.A., Burger, R.L., Richardson III, J.B., Rollins, H.B. and Clement, A. (2001) 'Variations in Holocene El Niño frequencies: climate records and cultural consequences in ancient Peru'. *Geology* 29(7): 603–606.

Sandweiss, D.H., Richardson III, J.B., Reitz, E.J., Rollins, H.B. and Maasch, K.A. (1996) 'Geoarchaeological evidence from Peru for a 5000 BP onset of El Niño'. *Science* 273: 1531–1533.

Sanlaville, P. (1989) 'Considérations sur le évolution de la basse Mésopotamie au cours des derniers millénaires'. *Paléorient* 15/2: 5–27.

Sanlaville, P. (1996) 'Changements climatiques dans la région Levantine à la fin du Pléistocène Supérieur et au début de l'Holocène'. *Paléorient* 22/1: 7–30.

Santoni, M. (1984) *Sibri and the south cemetery of Mehrgarh: third millennium connections between the northern Kachi Plain (Pakistan) and Central Asia*. In Allchin ed., pp. 52–60.

Sasson, J.M. (1995) ed., *Civilizations of the Ancient Near East, Vol. II*. New York, Charles Scribner's Sons.

Satterlee, D.R., Moseley, M.E., Keefer, D.K. and Tapia, J.E. (2000). 'The Miraflores El Niño disaster: Convergent catastrophes and Prehistoric agrarian change in Southern Peru'. *LAA* 6: 95–116.

Savage, S.H. (1997) 'Descent group competition and economic strategies in Predynastic Egypt'. *Journal of Anthropological Archaeology* 16: 226–268.

Savage, S.H. (2001) 'Some recent trends in the archaeology of Predynastic Egypt'. *Journal of Archaeological Research*, 9(2): 101–155.

Savard, M., Nesbitt, M. and Gale, R. (2003) 'Archaeobotanical evidence for early Neolithic diet and subsistence at M'lefaat (Iraq)'. *Paléorient* 29/1: 93–106.

Saxena, A. (2004–5) 'A study of Early Harappan pottery motifs'. *Puratattva* 35: 27–37.

Scarborough, V.L., Schoenfelder, J.W. and Lansing, J.S. (1999) 'Early statecraft on Bali: The water temple complex and the decentralization of the political economy'. *Research in Economic Anthropology* 20: 299–330.

Scarre C. (1988) ed., *Past Worlds: The Times Atlas of Archaeology*. London, Harper-Collins.

Scheffler, H.W. (1973) *Kinship, descent and alliance*. In Honigmann ed., pp. 747–793.

Schele, L. (1984) *Human sacrifice among the Classic Maya*. In Boone ed., pp. 7–48.

Schele, L. (1996) *The Olmec Mountain and Tree of Creation in Mesoamerican Cosmology*. In Rosenbaum ed., pp. 105–117.

Schele, L. and Miller, M.E. (1986) *The Blood of Kings: Dynasty and Ritual in Maya Art*. George Braziller, New York; in association with the Kimbell Art Museum, Fort Worth.

Schiffer, M.B. (1976) 'Archaeological context and systemic context'. *American Antiquity* 37(2): 157–165.

Schiffer, M.B. (1987) *Formation Processes of the Archaeological Record*. Albuquerque, University of New Mexico Press.

Schloen, J.D. (2001) *The House of the Father as Fact and Symbol: Patrimonialism in Ugarit and the Ancient Near East*. Winona Lake, Eisenbrauns.

Schmandt-Besserat, D. (1989) *Two precursors of writing: plain and complex tokens*. In Seener ed., pp. 27–41.

Schmandt-Besserat, D. (1998) ''Ain Ghazal 'monumental' figures'. *BASOR* 310: 1–17.

Schmandt-Besserat, D. (2003) *Stone Age death masks*. Odyssey, March/April 19–27.

Schmidt, K. (1995) 'Investigations in the Upper Mesopotamian Early Neolithic: Göbekli Tepe and Gürcütepe'. *Neo-Lithics* 2/95: 9–10.

Schmidt, K. (1998a) 'A new LPPNB figurine type: the Tell Assouad Type'. *Neo-Lithics* 1/98: 7–8.

Schmidt, K. (1998b) 'Beyond daily bread; evidence of early Neolithic ritual from Göbekli Tepe'. *Neo-Lithics* 2/98: 1–5.

Schmidt, K. (1999) 'Boars, ducks and foxes – the Urfa-project'. *Neo-Lithics* 3/99: 12–15.

Schmidt, K. (2000a) 'Göbekli Tepe and the rock art of the Near East – Göbekli Tepe ve On Asya Kaya Resim Sanati'. *TUBA-AR* 3: 1–14.

Schmidt, K. (2000b) 'Zuerst kam der Tempel, dann die Stadt' ['First came the temple, then the state']. Vorläufiger Bericht zu den Grabungen am Göbekli Tepe und am Gürcütepe 1995–1999'. *Istanbuler Mitteilungen des Deutchen Archaeologischen Instituts* 50: 5–41.

Schmidt, K. (2001a) 'Göbekli Tepe, southeastern Turkey. A preliminary report on the 1995–1999 excavations'. *Paléorient* 26(1): 45–54.

Schmidt, K. (2001b) 'Göbekli Tepe and the Early Neolithic sites of the Urfa region: a synopsis of new results and current views'. *Neo-Lithics* 1/01: 9–11.

Schmidt, K. (2002a) 'Göbekli Tepe – Southeastern Turkey. The seventh campaign, 2001'. *Neo-Lithics* 1/02: 23–25.

Schmidt, K. (2002b) 'The 2002 excavations at Göbekli Tepe (Southeastern Turkey) – Impressions from an enigmatic site'. *Neo-Lithics* 2/02: 8–12.

Schmidt, K. (2005) *'Ritual centres' and the Neolithisation of Upper Mesopotamia*. In Gebel and Rollefson eds, pp. 13–21.

Schmidt, K. (2006) 'Animals and a headless man at Göbekli Tepe'. *Neo-Lithics* 2/06: 38–40.

Schortman, E., Urban, P. and Ausec, M. (1996) 'Comment on Blanton *et al.*: Agency, Ideology and Power'. *Current Anthropology* Vol. 37(1): 61–3.

Schreiber, K. J. (1987) *From state to empire: the expansion of Wari outside the Ayacucho Basin*. In Haas *et al.* eds, pp. 91–96.

Schreiber, K.J. (1992) 'Wari Imperialism in Middle Horizon Peru'. *Anthropological Papers* 87, Museum of Anthropology, University of Michigan, Ann Arbor.

Schreiber, K. J. (1996) *The Wari Empire*. In Fagan ed., pp. 743–4.

Schreiber K. J. (2001) *The Wari empire of Middle Horizon Peru*. In Alcock *et al.* eds, pp. 70–92.

Schuldenrein, J., Wright, R. and Khan, M.A. (2007) *Harappan geoarchaeology reconsidered: Holocene landscapes and environments of the Greater Indus Plain*. In Stone ed., pp. 83–116.

Schwartz, G.M. (2001) *Syria and the Uruk Expansion*. In Rothman ed., pp. 233–263.

Schwartz, G.M., Hollander, D., and Stein, G. (2000) 'Reconstructing Mesopotamian exchange networks in the 4th Millennium BC: Geochemical and archaeological analyses of bitumen artefacts from Hacinebi Tepe, Turkey'. *Paléorient* 25(1): 67–8.

Schwartz, G.M., Curvers, H.H., Dunham, S. and Stuart, B. (2003) 'A third-millennium BC elite tomb and other new evidence from Tell Umm el-Marra, Syria'. *American Journal of Archaeology* 107: 325–61.

Seaman, G. and Day, J.S. (1994) eds, *Ancient Traditions: Shamanism in Central Asia and the Americas*. Niwot, CO: University Press of Colorado.

Seger, J.S. (1996) ed., *Retrieving the Past: Essays on Archaeological Research and Methodology in Honor of Gus. W. Van Beek*. Winona Lake Indiana, Eisenbrauns.

Seidlmeyer, S.J. (1996) *Town and state in the early Old Kingdom: A view from Elephantine*. In Spencer ed., pp. 108–127.

Seidlmeyer, S.J. (2000) *The First Intermediate Period*. In Shaw ed., pp. 118–147.

Sellen, D.W. and Mace, R. (1997) 'Fertility and mode of subsistence: a phylogenetic analysis'. *Current Anthropology* 38: 878–89.

Senner, W.M. (1989) ed. *The Origins of Writing*. Lincoln and London, University of Nebraska Press.

Serpico, M. and White, R. (1996) *A report on the analysis of the contents of a cache of jars from the tomb of Djer*. In Spencer ed., pp. 128–139.

Service, E. (1960) 'Kinship terminology and evolution'. *American Anthropologist* 62: 747–63.

Service, E. (1962) *Primitive Social Organization: an Evolutionary Perspective*. New York, Random House.

Service, E. (1975) *Origins of the State and Civilization: The Process of Cultural Evolution*. New York, W.W. Norton and Co.

Shady, R. (1997) *La cuidad sagrada de Caral-Supe en los albores de la civilización en el Peru*. Lima, Universidad Nacional Mayor de San Marcos.

Shady, R., Haas, J. and Creamer, W. (2001) *Dating Caral, a Preceramic site in the Supe Valley on the Central Coast of Peru*. Science Vol. 292, pp. 723–726.

Shady Solis, R. (2008) *America's first city? The case of Late Archaic Caral*. In Isbell and Silverman eds, pp. 28–66.

Shafer, B.E. (1991) ed., *Religion in Ancient Egypt: Gods, Myths and Personal Practice*. Ithaca, Cornell University Press.

Shaffer, J.G. (1982a) *Harappan Culture: A reconsideration*. In Possehl ed., pp. 41–50.

Shaffer, J.G. (1982b) *Harappan commerce: An alternative perspective*. In Pastner and Flam eds, pp. 166–210.

Shaffer, J,G. (1984) *Bronze Age iron from Afghanistan: Its implications for South Asian Protohistory*. In Kennedy and Possehl eds, pp. 41–62.

Shaffer, J.G. (1987) *Cultural developments in the Eastern Punjab*. In Jacobson (1987b) ed., pp. 137–173.

Shaffer, J.G. and Lichtenstein, D.A. (1989) *Ethnicity and change in the Indus Valley Cultural Tradition*. In Kenoyer ed., pp. 117–126.

Shao, Wangping (2000) 'The Longshan Period and incipient civilization'. *Journal of East Asian Archaeology* 2(1–2): 195–226. [Festschrift in honour of K.C. Chang]

Shapiro, J. (2001) *Mao's War Against Nature: Politics and the Environment in Revolutionary China*. Cambridge, CUP.

Sharer, R.J. and Grove, D.C. (1989) eds, *Regional Perspectives on the Olmec*, Cambridge, CUP.

Sharma, V.C. (1991) 'Defence system in ancient India, based on literary and archaeological evidence'. *Puratattva* 21:19-69.

Sharvit, J., Galili, E., Rosen, B. and Van den Brink, E.C.M. (2002) *Predynastic maritime traffic along the Carmel coast of Israel; a submerged find from North Atlit Bay*. In Van den Brink and Yannai eds, pp. 159–166.

Shaughnessy, E.L. (1988) 'Historical perspectives on the introduction of the chariot into China'. *HJAS* 48: 189–237.

Shaughnessy, E.L. (1989) 'Historical Geography and the extent of the earliest Chinese kingdoms'. *Asia Major* 11(2): 1–22.

Shaughnessy, E.L. (1990) 'The role of Grand Protector Shi in the consolidation of the Zhou conquest'. *Ars Orientalis* 19: 51–77.

Shaughnessy, E.L. (1991) *Sources of Western Zhou History: Inscribed Bronze Vessels*. Berkeley and Los Angeles, University of California Press.

Shaughnessy, E.L. (1996) 'Military histories of early China: A review article'. *Early China* 21: 159–182.

Shaughnessy, E.L. (1999) *Western Zhou history*. In Lowe and Shaughnessy eds, pp. 292–351.

Shaw, I. (2000a) ed.: *The Oxford History of Ancient Egypt*. Oxford, OUP.

Shaw, I. (2000b) *Introduction: Chronologies and cultural change in Egypt*. In Shaw ed., pp. 1–16.

Shaw, I. (2000c) *Egypt and the outside world*. In Shaw ed., pp. 314–329.

Shaw, I. (2000d) ed., *Ancient Egyptian Materials and Technology*. Cambridge, Cambridge University Press.

Shaw, I. and Nicholson, P. (1995) *The British Museum Dictionary of Ancient Egypt*. London, British Museum Press.

Shaw, T., Sinclair, P., Andah, B. and Okpoko, A. (1993) eds, *The Archaeology of Africa: Food, Metals and Towns*. London, Routledge.

Shelach, G. (1994) 'Social complexity in north China during the Early Bronze Age: a comparative study of the Erlitou and Lower Xiajiadian cultures'. *Asian Perspectives* 33(2): 261–291.

Shelach, G. (1996) 'The Qiang and the question of human sacrifice in the Late Shang period'. *Asian Perspectives* 35(1): 1–26.

Shelach, G. (1998) 'A settlement pattern study in northeast China: Results and potential contributions of western theory and methods to Chinese archaeology'. *Antiquity* 72: 114–27.

Shelach, G. (2000) 'The earliest Neolithic cultures of Northeast China: recent discoveries and new perspectives on the beginning of agriculture'. *Journal of World Prehistory*, Vol. 14(4): 363–413.

Shelach, G. (2002) 'Apples and oranges: a cross-cultural comparison of burial data from Northeast China'. *JEAA* 3 (3–4):

Shelach, G. (2006) 'Economic adaptation, community structure, and sharing strategies of households at early sedentary communities in northeast China'. *Journal of Anthropological Archaeology* 25: 318–345.

Shendge, M.J. (1985) 'The inscribed calculi and the invention of writing: the Indus view'. *JESHO* 28(1): 50–80.

Sheridan, M.J. (2002) 'An irrigation intake is like a uterus: culture and agriculture in precolonial North Pare, Tanzania'. *American Anthropologist* 104(1): 79–92.

Shermer, M. (1997) *Why People Believe Weird Things: Pseudoscience, Superstition and Other Confusions of Our Time*. New York, W.H. Freeman & Co.

Sherratt, A. (1995) 'Reviving the grand narrative: archaeology and long-term change'. *Journal of European Archaeology* 3: 1–32.

Sherratt, A. (1997) 'Climatic cycles and behavioural revolutions: the emergence of Modern Humans and the beginning of farming'. *Antiquity* 71: 271–87.

Sherratt, A. (1999) *Cash-crops before cash: Organic consumables and trade*. In Gosden and Hather eds, pp. 13–54.

Shimada, I. (1987) *Horizontal and vertical dimensions of prehistoric states in north Peru*. In Haas, Pozorski and Pozorski eds, pp. 130–144.

Shimada, I. (1994) *Pampa Grande and the Mochica Culture*. Austin, University of Texas Press.

Shimada, I. (1998) ed., *Andean Ceramics: Technology, Organization and Approaches*. Philadelphia, Museum Applied Science Centre for Archaeology, University of Pennsylvania Museum of Archaeology and Anthropology.

Shimada, I. (2001) *Late Moche urban craft production: a first approximation*. In Pillsbury eds, pp. 177–205.

Shimada, I., Griffin, J.A. and Gordus, A. (2000) *The technology, iconography and social significance of metals: a multi-dimensional analysis of Middle Sicán Objects*. In McEwan ed., pp. 28–41.

Shimada, I., Schaaf, C.B., Thompson, L.G. and Moseley-Thompson, E. (1991) 'Cultural impacts of severe drought in the Prehistoric Andes: Application of a 1,500 year ice core precipitation record.' *World Archaeology* 22(3): 247–270.

Shinde, V. (1992) 'Padri and the Indus Civilization'. *South Asian Studies* 8: 55–66.

Shirai, N. (2005) 'Walking with herdsmen: in search of the material evidence for the diffusion of agriculture from the Levant to Egypt'. *Neo-Lithics* 1/05: 12–17.

Silverman, H. (1993) *Cahuachi in the Ancient Nazca World*. Iowa City, University of Iowa Press.

Silverman, H. (1996) 'The Formative Period on the south coast of Peru: A critical review'. *Journal of World Prehistory* 10(2): 95–146.

Silverman, H. (2002) *Nasca settlement and society on the Hundredth Anniversary of Uhle's discovery of the*

*Nasca Style*. In Isbell and Silverman eds, pp. 121–158.

Silverman, H. (2002b) *Ancient Nazca Settlement and Society*. Iowa City, University of Iowa Press.

Silverman, H. (2004a) *Editor's Preface to Silverman 2004c*.

Silverman, H. (2004b) *Introduction: Space and time in the Central Andes*. In Silverman ed., 1–15.

Silverman, H. (2004c) ed., *Andean Archaeology*. Oxford, Blackwell, Blackwell Studies in Global Archaeology.

Silverman, H. and Proulx, D.A. (2002) *The Nasca*. Oxford, Blackwell.

Simoons, F.J. (1968) *A Ceremonial Ox of India: The Mithan in Nature, Culture and History*. Madison WI, University of Wisconsin Press.

Singer, A. and Street, B.V. (1972) eds, *Zande Themes: Essays Presented to Sir Edward Evans-Pritchard*. Oxford, Blackwell.

Sjoberg, A.W. (1977) *A blessing of King Urninurta*. In Ellis ed., pp. 189–195.

Small, D. (1997) *City-State dynamics through a Greek lens*. In Nichols and Charlton ed., pp. 107–118.

Smith, A.B. (1996) *The Near Eastern Connection II: cultural contacts with the Nile Delta and the Sahara*. In Krzyzaniak *et al.* eds, pp. 29–35.

Smith, H.S. and Hall, R. (1983) eds, *Ancient Centres of Egyptian Civilization*. London, The Egyptian Education Bureau.

Smith, M.E. and Masson, M.A. (2000) eds, *The Ancient Civilizations of Mesoamerica: A Reader*. Oxford, Blackwell.

Smith, M.E. and Schreiber, K.J. (2005) 'New World states and empires: Economic and social organization'. *Journal of Archaeological Research* 13: 189–229.

Smith, M.E. and Schreiber, K.J. (2006) 'New World states and empires: Politics, religion and urbanism'. *Journal of Archaeological Research* 14(1): 1–52.

Snell, D.C. (1982) *Ledgers and Prices: Early Mesopotamian Balanced Accounts*. New Haven, Yale University Press.

Snell, D.C. (1997) *Life in the Ancient Near East*. New Haven and London, Yale UP.

Snell, D.C. (2005) ed., *A Companion to the Ancient Near East*. Oxford, Blackwell Publishing.

Snodgrass, A.M. (1991) *Archaeology and the study of the Greek city*. In Rich and Wallace-Hadrill eds, pp. 1– 23.

So, Jenny F. (2001) *Jade and stone at Sanxingdui*. In Bagley ed., pp. 153–175.

Sonawane, V.H. (1992) 'Fresh light on the specialized crafts of the Harappans in Gujarat'. *Eastern Anthropologist* 45(1–2): 155–72.

Sonawane, V.H. (2000) 'Early farming communities of Gujarat, India'. *Indo-Pacific Prehistory Bulletin* 19: 137–146. (Melaka Papers, Volume 3).

Soper, D.L. (2000) *Harappan Period hearths: New insights from ethnoarchaeological data*. In Taddei and De Marco, pp. 101–114.

Spalinger, A.J. (2005) *Warfare in Ancient Egypt*. In Snell ed., pp. 245–257.

Spencer, A.J. (1993) *The Rise of Civilization in the Nile Valley*. London, British Museum Press.

Spencer, A.J. (1996) ed., *Aspects of Early Egypt*. London, British Museum Press.

Spencer, C.S. (1993) 'Human agency, biased transmission, and the cultural evolution of chiefly authority'. *Journal of Anthropological Archaeology* 12: 41–74.

Spencer, C.S. (1998) 'A mathematical model of primary state formation'. *Cultural Dynamics* 10: 5–20.

Spielman, K.A. (2002) 'Feasting, craft specialization, and the Ritual Mode of Production in small-scale societies'. *American Anthropologist* 104(1): 195–207.

Srinivas, M.N. (1962) *Caste in Modern India and Other Essays*. London, Asia Publishing House.

Stanish, C. (1989) *Tamaño y complejidad los asentamientos nucleares de Tiwanaku*. In Kolata ed., pp. 41–57.

Stanish, C. (1992) *Ancient Andean Political Economy*. Austin, University of Texas Press.

Stanish, C. (1994) 'The Hydraulic Hypothesis revisited: Lake Titicaca Basin raised fields in theoretical perspective'. *Latin American Antiquity* 5(4): 312–332.

Stanish, C. (1996) *Inca economic organization*. In Fagan ed. p. 343.

Stanish, C. (2001) 'The origin of state societies in South America'. *Annual Review of Anthropology*, 30: 41–64.

Stanish, C. (2002) *Tiwanaku political economy*. In Isbell and Silverman eds, pp. 169–198.

Stanish, C. (2003) *Ancient Titicaca: The Evolution of Complex Society in Southern Peru and Northern Bolivia*.

Berkeley, University of California Press.

Stanish, C. (2006) 'Comment on Haas and Creamer'. *CA* 47(5): 763–64.

Stanish, C., Burger, R.L., Cipolla, L.M., Glascock, M.D. and Quelima, E. (2002) 'Evidence for early long-distance obsidian exchange and watercraft use from the southern Lake Titicaca Basin of Bolivia and Peru'. *Latin American Antiquity* 13(4): 444–454.

Stanley, D. and Zhongyuan Chen (1996) 'Neolithic settlement distributions as a function of sea level controlled topography in the Yangtze Delta, China'. *Geology* 24(12): 1083–86.

Starr, C.G. (1982) *The Roman Empire, 27 BC–AD 476: A Study in Survival.* New York, OUP.

Staubwasser, M., and Weiss, H. (2006) *Holocene climate and cultural evolution in late prehistoric-early historic West Asia.* Quaternary Research.

Steadman, S.R. (2000) 'Spatial patterning and social complexity on prehistoric Anatolian tell sites'. *JAA* 19: 164–199.

Steele, J. and Shennan, S. (1995) eds, *The Archaeology of Human Ancestry.* London, Routledge.

Stein, G.J. (1994a) *Economy, Ritual, and Power in 'Ubaid' Mesopotamia.* In Stein and Rothman eds, pp. 11–22.

Stein, G.J. (1994b) *The organizational dynamics of complexity in Greater Mesopotamia.* In Stein and Rothman eds, pp. 35–46.

Stein, G.J. (1996) *Producers, patrons, and prestige: craft specialists and emergent elites in Mesopotamia from 5500–3100 BC.* In Wailes ed., pp. 25–38.

Stein, G.J. (1998) 'Heterogeneity, power and political economy: Some current research issues in the archaeology of Old World complex societies'. *Journal of Archaeological Research* 6(1): 1–44.

Stein, G.J. (2000) 'Material culture and social identity: The evidence for a 4th millennium BC Mesopotamian Uruk colony at Hacinebi, Turkey'. *Paléorient* 25(1): 11–22.

Stein, G.J. (2001) *Indigenous social complexity at Hacinebi (Turkey) and the organization of Uruk colonial contact.* In Rothman ed., pp. 265–305.

Stein G.J. (2002) *The Uruk expansion in Anatolia: a Mesopotamian colony and its indigenous host community at Hacinebi, Turkey.* In Postgate ed., pp. 149–172.

Stein, G.J. and Edens, C. (2000) 'Hacinebi and the Uruk expansion: Additional comments'. *Paléorient* 25(1): 167–171.

Stein, G.J. and Özbal, R. (2007) *A tale of two Oikumenai: Variation in the expansionary dynamics of 'Ubaid and Uruk Mesopotamia.* In Stone ed., pp. 329–342.

Stein, G.J. and Rothman, M.S. (1994) eds, *Chiefdoms and Early States in the Near East: The Organizational Dynamics of Complexity.* Madison Wisconsin, Prehistory Press.

Steinkeller, P. (1989) *Sale Documents of the Ur III Period. Freiburger Altorientalische Studien.* Stuttgart, Franz Steiner Verlag.

Steinkeller, P. (1992) *Third-millennium Legal and Administrative Texts in the Iraq Museum, Baghdad. Mesopotamian Civilizations* Vol. 4. Winona Lake, Eisenbrauns.

Steinkeller, P. (1993) *Early political development in Mesopotamia and the origins of the Sargonic Empire.* In Liverani ed., pp. 107–129.

Steinkeller, P. (1999) *Archaic city seals and the question of Early Babylonian unity.* In Abusch ed., pp. 1–12.

Steinkeller, P. (2001) 'New light on the hydrology and topography of Southern Babylonia'. *ZA* 91: 60–65.

Steinkeller, P. (2007) *City and countryside in third-millennium southern Babylonia.* In Stone ed., pp. 185–212.

Stephen, M.K. and Peltenberg, E. (2002) *Scientific analyses of Uruk ceramics from Jerablus Tahtani and other Middle-Upper Euphrates sites.* In Postgate ed., pp. 173–190.

Sterling, S. (1999) 'Mortality profiles as indicators of slowed reproductive rates: Evidence from Ancient Egypt'. *JAA* 18: 319–343.

Stevenson, I.N. (1974) *Andean Village Technology.* Oxford, Pitt Rivers Museum.

Stone, E.C. (1997) *City-States and their centres: The Mesopotamian example.* In Nichols and Charlton eds, pp. 15–26.

Stone, E.C. (1999) *The constraints on state and urban form in Ancient Mesopotamia.* In Hudson and Levine eds, pp. 203–219.

Stone, E.C. (2002) 'The Ur III-Old Babylonian transition: An archaeological perspective'. *Iraq* LXIV:

79–84.

Stone, E.C. (2005) *Mesopotamian cities and countryside*. In Snell ed., pp. 157–170.

Stone, E.C. (2007a) ed., *Settlement and Society: Essays Dedicated to Robert McCormick Adams*. Los Angeles, Cotsen.

Stone, E.C. (2007b) *The Mesopotamian urban experience*. In Stone ed., pp. 213–234.

Stone, E.C. and Zimansky, P. (1995) 'The tapestry of power in a Mesopotamian city'. *Scientific American*. April, pp. 117–123.

Stone-Miller, R. (2002) *Art of the Andes*. London, Thames and Hudson.

Stordeur, D. (1998) 'Jerf el Ahmar et l'horizon PPNA en Haute Mesopotamie: Xe-IXe millenaire avant J.C'. *Subartu* 4: 13–29.

Stordeur, D. (2000) 'New discoveries in architecture and symbolism at Jerf el Ahmar (Syria), 1997–1999'. *Neo-Lithics* 1/00: 1–4.

Stordeur, D. (2003a) 'Tell Aswad: résultats préliminaires des campagnes 2001 et 2002'. *Neo-Lithics* 1/03: 7–15.

Stordeur, D. (2003b) 'Des crânes surmodelés à Tell Aswad de Damascène (PPNB-Syrie)'. *Paléorient* 29/2: 109–115.

Stordeur, D. (2004) 'New insights and concepts: two themes of the Neolithic in Syria and South-East Anatolia'. *Neo-Lithics* 1/04: 49–51.

Stordeur, D. and Jammous, B. (1995) 'Pierre à rainure à decor animal trouvée dans l'horizon PPNA de Jerf el Ahmar (Syrie)'. *Paléorient* 21/1: 129–131.

Surenhagen, D. (1986) *The dry-farming belt: The Uruk Period and subsequent developments*. In Weiss ed., pp. 7–43.

Surenhagen, D. (2002) *Death in Mesopotamia: The 'Royal Tombs' of Ur revisited*. In Al-Gailani Werr *et al.* eds, pp. 324–338.

Suter, C.E. (2000) *Gudea's Temple Building: The Representation of an Early Mesopotamian Ruler in Text and Image*. New York and Leiden, Brill.

Sutter, R.C. and Cortez, R.J. (2005) 'The nature of Moche human sacrifice: A bio-archaeological perspective'. *Current Anthropology* 46(4): 521–549.

Swenson, E.R. (2003) 'Cities of violence: Sacrifice, power and urbanization in the Andes'. *Journal of Social Archaeology*, Vol. 3(2) 256–296.

Swenson, E.R. (2008) *Competitive feasting, religious pluralism and decentralised power*. In Isbell and Silverman eds, pp. 112–142.

Taddei, M. (1979) ed., *South Asian Archaeology 1977*: 2 Vols. Naples, Instituto Universitario Orientale, Seminario Di Studi Asiatici.

Taddei, M. and De Marco, G. (2000) eds, *South Asian Archaeology 1997*. Rome, Instituto Italiano per l'Africa e l'Oriente.

Tang, S., Min, S. and Sato, Y.I. (1993) 'Investigating the origin of *keng* rice (*Japonica*) in China'. *Journal of Chinese Rice Science* 7: 129–136.

Taylor, J.H. (2001) *Death and the Afterlife in Ancient Egypt*. London, British Museum Press.

Tekin, Halil (2005) 'Hakemi Use: a new discovery regarding the northern distribution of Hassunan/ Samarran pottery in the Near East'. *Antiquity* Vol. 79 http: //antiquity.ac.uk/ProjGall/tekin/

Temple, R.K.G. (1986) *China: Land of Discovery and Invention*. Wellingborough, Patrick Stephens Ltd.

Teng Shu-P'ing (=Deng Shuping) (2000) 'The original significance of *bi* disks: insights based on Liangzhu jade *bi* with incised symbolic motifs'. *JEAA* 3 (1–2): 165–193.

Testart, A. (1982) *Les chasseurs-cueilleurs ou l'origine des inegalites*. Paris, Societie d'Ethnographie.

Testart, A. (1987) 'Game sharing systems and kinship systems among hunter-gatherers'. *MAN* 22(2): 287–304.

Thomas, K. (1999) *Getting a life: stability and change in the social and subsistence systems on the North-West Frontier, Pakistan, in later prehistory*. In Gosden and Hather eds, pp. 306–321.

Thompson, L.G., Mosley-Thompson, E., Bolzan, J.F. and Koci, B.R. (1985) 'A 1500 year record of tropical precipitation in ice cores from the Quelccaya ice cap, Peru.' *Science* 229: 971–973.

Thompson, L.G., Mosley-Thompson, E., Dansgaard, E. and Grootes, P.M. (1986) 'The Little Ice Age as recorded in the stratigraphy of the Quelccaya ice cap'. *Science* 234: 361–364.

Thompson, L.G., Mosley-Thompson, E., Davis, M.E., Lin, p.-N., Henderson, K.A., Cole-Dai, J., Bolzan,

J.F. and Liu, K.-b. (1995) 'Late Glacial Stage and Holocene tropical ice core records from Huarascan, Peru'. *Science* 269: 46–50.

Thompson, L.G., Mosley-Thompson, E. and Thompson, P.A. (1992) *Reconstructing interannual climate variability from tropical and subtropical ice-core records*. In Diaz and Markgraf eds, pp. 295–322.

Thorp, R.L. (1983) 'Origins of Chinese architectural style: The earliest plans and building types'. *Archives of Asian Art* 36: 22–39.

Thorp, R.L. (1999) *Sacrifical pits at Sanxingdui, Guanghan, Sichuan Province*. In Yang Xiaoneng ed., pp. 206–227.

Thorpe, I.J.N. (2003) 'Anthropology, archaeology, and the origin of warfare'. *World Archaeology* 35(1): 145–165.

Tobler, A. (1950) *Excavations at Tepe Gawra*, Vol. 2. Levels IXX–XX. Philadelphia: University of Pennsylvania Press.

Tomka, S.A. (2001) *'Up and down we move…': Factors conditioning agro-pastoral settlement organization in mountainous settings*. In Kutznar ed., pp. 138–162.

Tooby, J. and Cosmides, L. (1992) *The psychological foundations of culture*. In Barkow *et al.* eds, pp. 19–136.

Toorn, K. van der (1996) *Domestic religion in ancient Mesopotamia*. In Veenhof ed., pp. 69–78

Topic, J.R. (2003) 'From stewards to bureaucrats: Architecture and information flow at Chan Chan, Peru'. *Latin American Antiquity* 14(3): 243–274.

Topic, J.R. and Topic T.L. (1987) *The archaeological investigation of Andean militarism: some cautionary observations*. In Haas, Pozorski and Pozorski eds, pp. 47–55.

Topic, J.R., Topic, T.L. and Cava, A.M. (2002) *Catequil: The archaeology, ethnohistory, and ethnography of a major provincial huaca*. In Isbell and Silverman eds, pp. 303–336.

Tracer, D.P. (2003) 'Selfishness and fairness in economic and evolutionary perspective: an experimental economic study in Papua New Guinea'. *Current Anthropology* 44(3): 432–438.

Trentin, M.G. (1993) *The early reserved slip wares horizon of the Upper Euphrates Basin and Western Syria*. In Frangipane *et al.* eds, pp. 177–199.

Trevarthen, C. (1987) *Brain development*. In Gregory ed., pp. 101–110.

Trevarthen, C. (2006) *Human nature before words*. In Jeeves ed., pp. 223–245.

Trigger, B.G. (1974) 'The archaeology of government'. *World Archaeology* 6(1): 95–106.

Trigger, B.G. (1990) 'Monumental architecture: A thermodynamic explanation of symbolic behaviour'. *World Archaeology* 22(2): 119–32.

Trigger, B.G. (1995) *Early Civilizations: Ancient Egypt in Context*. New York, Columbia UP.

Trigger, B.G. (1998) *Sociocultural Evolution: Calculation and Contingency*. Oxford, Blackwell Press.

Trigger, B.G. (1999) 'Shang political organization: a comparative approach'. *Journal of East Asian Archaeology* 1: 43–62 [Festschrift in Honour of K.C. Chang].

Trigger, B.G. (2003a) 'All people are [not] good'. *Anthropologica* 45: 39–44.

Trigger, B.G. (2003b) *Understanding Early Civilizations: A Comparative Study*. Cambridge, CUP.

Trigger, B.G. (2006) *A History of Archaeological Thought (Second Edition)*. Cambridge, CUP.

Trivers, R.L. (1971) The evolution of reciprocal altruism'. *Quarterly Review of Biology* 46: 35–57.

Tubb, K.W. and Grissom, C.A. (1995) ''Ayn Ghazal: A comparative study of the 1983 and 1985 statuary caches'. *Studies in the History and Archaeology of Jordan* 5: 437–447.

Turner, V. (1974) *Dramas, Fields and Metaphors*. Ithaca, Cornell University Press.

Uceda, S. (2001) *Investigations at Huaca de la Luna, Moche valley: an example of Moche religious architecture*. In Pillsbury ed., pp. 47–67.

Uceda, S and Mujica, E. (eds) (1994), *Moche: Propuestas y Perspectivas*. Trujillo, Universidad Nacional de la Libertad.

Uceda, S., Mujica, E. and Morales, R. (1997) *Investigaciones en la Huaca de la Luna 1995*. Trujillo, Universidad Nacional de la Libertad.

Uerpmann, M. and Uerpmann, H.-P. (1996) 'Ubaid pottery in the Eastern Gulf – new evidence from Umm al-Qaiwan (U.A.E.)'. *Arabian Archaeology and Epigraphy* 7: 125–139.

Ugent, D., Pozorski, S. and Pozorski, T. (1982) 'Archaeological potato tuber remains from the Casma Valley of Peru'. *Economic Botany* 36: 82–192.

Uglow, J. (2002). *The Lunar Men: The Friends Who Made the Future*. London, Faber and Faber.

Underhill, A.P. (1991) 'Pottery production in Chiefdoms: the Longshan Period in Northern China'.

*World Archaeology* 23(1): 12–27.

Underhill, A.P. (1994) 'Variation in settlements during the Longshan Period of Northern China'. *Asian Perspectives*, Vol. 33(2): 197–228.

Underhill, A.P. (1997) 'Current issues in Chinese Neolithic archaeology'. *Journal of World Prehistory*, 11(2) 103–160.

Underhill, A.P. (1999) 'Analysis of mortuary ritual at the Dawenkou site, Shandong, China'. *JEAA* 2(1–2): 93–127.

Underhill, A.P. (2002) *Craft production and social change in northern China*. New York (NY), Kluwer Academic/Plenum.

Underhill, A.P., Feinman, G.M., Nicholas, L.M., Bennett, G., Fang, H., Luan, F., Yu, H. and Cai, F. (2002) 'Regional survey and the development of complex societies in southeastern Shandong, China'. *Antiquity* 76: 745–55.

Underhill, A.P., Feinman, G.M., Nicholas, L.M., Fang, H., Luan, F., Yu, H. and Cai, F. (2008). 'Changes in regional settlement patterns and the development of complex societies in southeastern Shandong, China'. *JAA* 27(1): 1–29.

Upham, S. (1990) ed., *The Evolution of Political Systems*. Cambridge, CUP/SAR.

Usai, D. and Salvatori, S. (2007) 'The oldest representation of a Nile boat'. *Antiquity* Vol. 81 (314), Project Gallery.

Ussiskin, D. (1980) 'The Ghassulian shrine in En-Gedi'. *Tel Aviv* 7: 1–44.

Valdez, L.M. (1994) 'Cahuachi: New evidence for an Early Nasca ceremonial role'. *Current Anthropology* 35(5):675–679.

Valdez, L.M. (2006) 'Maize beer production in Middle Horizon Peru'. *Journal of Anthropological Research*, 62: 53–80.

Valdez, L.M., Bettcher, K.J. and Valdez, J.E. (2002) 'New Wari mortuary structures in the Ayacucho Valley, Peru'. *Journal of Anthropological Research* 58: 389–407.

Valla, F.R. (1995) *The first settled societies – Natufian (12,500–10,200 BP)*. In Levy ed., pp. 169–185.

Valla, F.R., Le Mort, F. and Plisson, H. (1991) *Le fouilles en cours sur la Terrase d'Hayonim*. In Bar Yosef and Valla eds, pp. 93–110.

Vallat, F. (1986) 'The most ancient scripts of Iran: the current situation'. *World Archaeology* Vol. 17(3)335–347.

Van Buren, M. (2000) *Political fragmentation and ideological continuity in the Andean highlands*. In Richards and Van Buren eds, pp. 77–87.

Van Buren, M. (2001) 'The archaeology of El Niño events and other "natural disasters"'. *Journal of Archaeological Method and Theory* 8(2): 129–49.

Van Buren, M. and Richards, J. (2000) *Introduction: ideology, wealth, and the comparative study of 'civilizations'*. In Richards and Van Buren, pp. 3–12.

Van de Mieroop, M. (1986) 'Turam-Ili: An Ur III merchant'. *Journal of Cuneiform Studies* 38: 1–80.

Van de Ven, H. (2000) ed., *Warfare in Chinese History*. Leiden, Brill.

Van den Brink. E.C.M. (1992) ed., *The Nile Delta in Transition: 4th-3rd Millennia BC*. Tel Aviv, E.C.M. Van den Brink.

Van den Brink, E.C.M. (1996) *The incised serekh-signs of Dynasties 0–1, Part I: complete vessels*. In Spencer ed., pp. 159–174.

Van den Brink, E.C.M. and Braun, E. (2003) 'Egyptian elements and influence on the Early Bronze Age I of the Southern Levant'. *Archéo-Nil* 13: 77–91.

Van den Brink, E.C.M. and Levy, T.E. (2002) eds, *Egypt and the Levant. Interrelations from the 4th through the early 3rd Millennium BCE*. London, Leicester University Press.

Van den Brink, E.C.M. and Yannai, E. (2002) eds, *In Quest of Ancient Settlements and Landscapes: Archaeological Studies in Honour of Ram Gophna*. Tel Aviv, Tel Aviv University, Ramot Publishing.

Van der Toorn, K. (1996) *Family Religion in Babylonia, Syria and Israel: Continuity and Change in the Forms of Religious Life*. Leiden, Brill.

Van Driel, G. (1983) 'Seals and sealings from Jebel Aruda 1977–1978'. *Akkadica* 3: 34–62.

Van Driel, G. (1999–2000) 'The size of institutional Umma'. *Archiv für Orientforschung*, pp. 80–91.

Van Driel, G. (2000) 'Closer to Mesopotamia's Proto-History [Review of Bauer et al.1999]'. *Bibliotheca Orientalis* LVII (5–6): 493–509.

Van Driel, G. (2001) *On villages*. In van Soldt et al. eds, pp. 104–118.

Van Driel, G. (2002) *Jebel Aruda: variations of a Late Uruk domestic theme*. In Postgate ed., pp. 191–206.

Van Evera, S. (1999) *Causes of War: Power and the Roots of Conflict*. Ithaca, New York, Cornell University Press.

Van Gijseghem, H. (2001) 'Household and family at Moche, Peru: an analysis of building and residence patterns in a Prehispanic urban centre'. *Latin American Antiquity* 12(3): 257–273.

Vanhaeren, M. and d'Errico, F. (2005). 'Grave goods from the Saint-Germain-la-Rivière burial: Evidence for social inequality in the Upper Palaeolithic'. *Journal of Anthropological Archaeology* 24: 117–134.

Van Haarlem, W.M. (2000) 'Tell Ibrahim Awad'. *Egyptian Archaeology* 18: 33–5.

Van Koppen, F. (2002) 'Review of D.T. Potts [1997]'. *Bibliotheca Orientalis* LIX (3–4): 333–341.

Van Leberghe, K. and Vogt, G. (1991) 'Sippar-Amnānum: The Ur-Utu Archive'. *Mesopotamian History and Environment Series* III, Texts 1. Ghent, University of Ghent.

Van Leberghe, K. and Vogt, G. (2000) eds, 'Languages and Cultures in Contact: At the Crossroads of Civilizations in the Syro-Mesopotamian Realm'. *Proceedings of the 42nd RAI. Leuven, Orientalia Lovaniensa Analecta* 96.

Van Soldt, W.H. (2001) editor in charge: *Veenhof Anniversary Volume: Studies Presented to Klaas R. Veenhof on the Occasion of his 65th Birthday*. Leiden, Nederlands Instituut voor her Nabije Oosten.

Van Zeist, W. (1999) *Evidence for agricultural change in the Balikh Basin, Northern Syria*. In Gosden and Hather eds, pp. 350–373.

Vaughn, K.J. (2004) 'Households, crafts, and feasting in the ancient Andes: the village context of early Nasca craft consumption'. *Latin American Antiquity* 15(1): 61–88.

Vecihi Özkaya & Aytaç Coşkun (2009) 'Körtik Tepe, a new Pre-Pottery Neolithic A site in south-eastern Anatolia'. *Antiquity* Vol. 83 issue 320 June 2009, Project Gallery.

Veenhof, K.R. (1996) ed., *Houses and Households in Ancient Mesopotamia: Papers read at the 40th Rencontre Assyriologique Internationale, Leiden 1993*. Leiden/Istanbul, Nederlands Historisch-Archaeologisch Instituut Te Istanbul.

Verano, J.W. (1997) 'Human skeletal remains from Tomb 1, Sipán (Lambayeque River Valley, Peru); and their social implications'. *Antiquity* 71(273): 670–682.

Verano, J.W. (2001a) *The physical evidence of Human Sacrifice in Ancient Peru*. In Benson and Cook eds, pp. 165–184.

Verano, J.W. (2001b) *War and death in the Moche world: osteological evidence and visual discourse*. In Pillsbury ed., pp. 111–125.

Verano, J.W., Uceda, S., Chapdelaine, C., Tello, R., Paredes, M.I., and Pimentel, V. (1999). 'Modified human skulls from the urban sector of the Pyramids of Moche, Northern Peru'. *Latin American Antiquity* 10(1): 59–70.

Verhoeven, M. (1999) *An Archaeological Ethnography of a Neolithic Community: Space, Place and Social relations in the Burnt Village at Tell Sabi Abyad, Syria. (PIHANS LXXXIII)*. Leiden, Nederlands Inst. V.h. Nabije Oosten.

Verhoeven, M. (2001a) *Transformations of society: The changing role of ritual practice and symbolism in the Pre-Pottery Neolithic B and Pottery Neolithic periods in the Levant, Syria and south-east Anatolia. Abstract of paper given at the Conference on 'The 5th Millennium BC in the Near East'*, University of Liverpool, November 2001. (2002b) : PALEORIENT 28/1: 5-14.

Verhoeven, M. (2001b) 'Person or penis? Interpreting a 'new' PPNB anthropomorphic statue from the Taurus foothills'. *Neo-Lithics* 1/01: 8–9.

Verhoeven, M. (2002a) 'Ritual and ideology in the Pre-Pottery Neolithic B of the Levant and Southeast Anatolia'. *Cambridge Archaeological Journal* 12 (2): 233–58.

Verhoeven, M. (2004) 'Tell Sabi Abyad II – a Late Pre-Pottery Neolithic B village in northern Syria: report on architecture and related finds of the 2001 campaign'. *Anatolica* XXX: 179–200.

Verhoeven, M. (2005) *Ethnoarchaeology, analogy and ancient society*. In Pollock and Bernbeck eds, pp. 251–270.

Verhoeven, M. and Akkermans, P.M.M.G. (2000) eds, *Tell Sabi Abyad II. The Pre-Pottery Neolithic B Settlement. Report on the Excavations of the National Museum of Antiquities Leiden in the Balikh Valley, Syria*. Istanbul, Nederlands Historisch-Archaeologisch Instituut.

Vernus, P. (1993) 'La naissance de l'écriture dans l'Egypt Ancienne'. *Archéo-Nil* 3: 75–108.

Vidale, M. (1989) *Specialized producers and urban elites: on the role of craft industries in Mature Harappan urban contexts*. In Kenoyer ed., pp. 171–181.

Vidale, M. and Miller, H.M.-L. (2000) *On the development of Indus technical virtuosity and its relation to social structure*. In Taddei and De Marco, pp. 115–132.

Vining, D. (1986) 'Social versus reproductive success: The central theoretical problem of human sociobiology'. *Behavioural and Brain Sciences* 9: 167–187.

Vogt, E.Z. and Leventhal, R.M. (1983) eds, *Prehistoric Settlement Patterns: Essays in Honour of Gordon R. Willey*. University of New Mexico Press and Peabody Museum of Archaeology and Technology, Harvard University.

Voigt, M.M. (2000) *Çatal Höyük in context: ritual in Early Neolithic sites in central and eastern Turkey*. In Kuijt ed., pp. 253–293.

Wagner, D.B. (1993) *Iron and Steel in Ancient China*. Leiden, E.J. Brill.

Wailes, B. (1996) ed., *Craft Specialization and Social Evolution: In Memory of V. Gordon Childe*. Philadelphia, The University of Pennsylvania Museum.

Waldren, W.H., Ensenyat, J.A. and Kennard, R.C. (1995) eds, 'Ritual, Rites and Religion in Prehistory: 3rd Deya International Conference of Prehistory'. Oxford, *BAR Int. Series* 611(i,ii).

Walker, C. (1983) 'The myth of Girra and Elamatum'. *Anatolian Studies* 33: 145–151. *Journal of the British Institute of Archeology at Ankara*.

Walker, C. (1996) ed., *Astronomy Before the Telescope*. London, British Museum Press.

Walker, P.L. (2001) 'A bioarchaeological perspective on the history of violence'. *Annual Review of Anthropology* 30: 573–96.

Wallace-Hadrill, J.M. (1971) *Early Germanic Kingship in England and on the Continent*. Oxford, The Clarendon Press.

Walter, E.V. (1969) *Terror and Resistance: A Study of Political Violence*. New York, OUP.

Wang, Aihe (2000) *Cosmology and Political Culture in Early China*. Cambridge, CUP.

Wang, Ming-Ke (1999) 'Western Zhou remembering and forgetting'. *JEAA* 1: 231–250

Wang, Ninsheng (1985–6) 'Yangshao burial customs and social organization: a comment on the excavation of Hengzhen site, Huayin, Shaanxi'. *Kaoguxue Jikan* 4: 1–39. Beijing, Chinese Social Science Press.

Wang, X., Jiang, Q.H. and MacNeish, R.S. (1995) *Palynology and palaeoenvironment in the Dayuan Basin*. In Macneish and Libby eds, pp. 59–68.

Wang Yi (2006) 'Prehistoric walled settlements in the Chengdu Plain'. *JEAA* 5 (1–4): 109–148.

Washburn, S.L. and Lancaster, C.S. (1968) *The evolution of hunting*. In Lee and DeVore eds, pp. 293–303.

Wasse, A. (2002) 'Final results of an analysis of the sheep and goat bones from Ain Ghazal, Jordan'. *Levant* 34: 59–82.

Wason, P.K. (1994) *The Archaeology of Rank*. Cambridge, CUP.

Watkins, T. and Campbell, S. (1987) *The chronology of the Halaf Culture*. In Aurenche *et al.* eds, pp. 427–460.

Watrin L. (2000) *Pottery as an economical parameter between Palestine and Egypt during the 4th millennium BC: From the Palestinian presence in the Nile Delta (c.3900–3300 BC) to the Egyptian rule of Southern Palestine (c.3300–3000 BC)*. In Matthiae *et al.* eds Vol. 2, pp. 1751–1776.

Waugh, D. (1984) *North and South America*. Edinburgh, Thomas Nelson and Sons.

Webb, M.C. (1987) *Broader perspectives on Andean state origins*. In Haas, Pozorski and Pozorski eds, pp. 161–67.

Weber, Max (1947) *The Theory of Social and Economic Organization*. New York, OUP.

Webster, D. (1996) *Copán*. In Fagan ed., pp. 151–2.

Webster, D. (1998) *Warfare and status rivalry. Lowland Maya and Polynesian comparisons*. In Feinman and Marcus eds, pp. 311–351.

Weisgerber, G. (1984) *Makan and Melluha – third millennium copper production in Oman and the evidence of contact with the Indus Valley*. In Allchin ed., pp. 196–200.

Weisheu, W. (1997) *China's first cities: the walled site of Wangchengang in the Central Plain region of North China*. In Manzanilla ed., pp. 109–132.

Weiss, H. (1986) ed. *The Origins of Cities in Dry-Farming Syria and Mesopotamia in the Third Millennium BC*. Four Quarters Publishing, Guilford, Connecticut.

Weiss, H. (1986b) *The origins of Tell Leilan and the conquest of space in third millennium North Mesopotamia.* In Weiss ed., pp. 71–108.

Weiss, H., Courty, M.-A., Wetterstrom, W., Guichard, F., Senior, L., Meadow, R. and Curnow, A. (1993) 'The genesis and collapse of third millennium North Mesopotamian Civilization'. *Science* 261: 995–1004.

Weiss, H., Kislev, M.E., Hartmann, A. (2006) 'Autonomous cultivation before domestication'. *Science* 312: 1608–10.

Weissleder, W. (1978) *Aristotle's concept of political structure.* In Cohen and Service eds, pp. 187–203.

Wells, R.A. (1996) *Astronomy in Egypt.* In Walker ed., pp. 28–41.

Wells, L. and Noller, J.S. (1997) 'Determining the early history of El Niño'. *Science* 276: 966.

Wengrow, D. (2006) *The Archaeology of Early Egypt: Social Transformations in North-East Africa, 10,000 to 2650 BC.* Cambridge, Cambridge University Press.

Wenke, R. J. (1997) *City-states, nation-states, and territorial states: the problem of Egypt.* In Nichols and Charlton ed., pp. 27–49.

Wenke R.J., Long, J.E. and Buck, P.E. (1988) 'Epipalaeolithic and Neolithic subsistence and settlement in the Fayum Oasis of Egypt'. *Journal of Field Archaeology* 15:29-51.

Al-Gailani Werr, L., Curtis, J., Martin, H., McMahon, A., Oates, J. and Reade, J. (2002) eds, *Of Pots and Plans: Papers on the Archaeology and History of Mesopotamia and Syria Presented to David Oates in Honour of His 75th Birthday.* London, NABU.

Westenholz, J.G. (1998) *Goddesses of the Ancient Near East: 3000–1000 BC.* In Goodison and Morris eds, pp. 63–82.

Wetterstrom, W. (1993) *Foraging and farming in Egypt: The transition from hunting and gathering to horticulture in the Nile Valley.* In Shaw *et al.* eds, pp. 165–226.

Wheeler, R.E.M. (1968) *The Indus Civilization (3rd edition).* Cambridge, CUP.

White, L (1962) *Medieval Technology and Social Change.* New York, OUP.

Whitehead, W.T. (2008) *Redefining plant use at the Formative site of Chiripa in the southern Titicaca Basin.* In Isbell and Silverman eds, pp. 258–278.

Whitmore, T.C. (1981) *Trees of Tropical America.* In Hora ed., pp. 265–269.

Whittow, J. (1984) *The Penguin Dictionary of Physical Geography.* Harmondsworth, Penguin Books.

Wiggermann, F.A.M. (1992) 'Mesopotamian Protective Spirits: The Ritual Texts'. *Cuneiform Monographs* 1. Groningen, Styx.

Wilcke, C. (1989) *Genealogical and geographical thought in the Sumerian King List.* In Behrens *et al.* eds, pp. 557–71.

Wilk, R.R. (1990) *Household Ecology: decision making and resource flows.* In Moran ed., pp. 323–356.

Wilkes, G. (1989) *Maize: domestication, racial evolution, and spread.* In Harris and Hillman eds, pp. 440–455.

Wilkinson, R.H. (1985) 'The Horus name and the form and significance of the serekh in the Royal Egyptian titulary'. *Journal of the Society for the Study of Egyptian Antiquities (JSSEA)* 15: 98–104.

Wilkinson, Toby, A.H. (1996a) *State Formation in Egypt: Chronology and Society.* Oxford, Tempus Reparatum, BAR 651.

Wilkinson, Toby, A.H. (1996b) 'A Re-examination of the Early Dynastic necropolis at Helwan'. *MDAIK* 52: 337–354.

Wilkinson, Toby, A.H. (1999) *Early Dynastic Egypt.* London, Routledge.

Wilkinson, Toby, A.H. (2000a) 'What a king is this: Narmer and the concept of the ruler'. *Journal of Egyptian Archaeology* 86: 23–32.

Wilkinson, Toby, A.H. (2000b) 'Political unification: towards a reconstruction'. *MDAIK* 56: 377–395.

Wilkinson, Toby, A.H. (2002) *Uruk into Egypt: imports and imitations.* In Postgate ed., pp. 237–248.

Wilkinson, Toby, A.H. (2005) *The Thames and Hudson Dictionary of Ancient Egypt.* London, Thames and Hudson.

Wilkinson, T.J. (1994) 'The structure and dynamics of dry farming states in Upper Mesopotamia'. *Current Anthropology* 35: 483–520.

Wilkinson, T.J. (2003) *Archaeological Landscapes of the Near East.* Tucson, University of Arizona Press.

Willcox, G. (1997) 'Archaeobotanical evidence for the beginnings of agriculture in Southwest Asia'. In *Harlan Symposium*, pp. 25–38.

Willcox, G. (1999) *Agrarian change and the beginning of cultivation in the Near East: evidence from wild progenitors, experimental cultivation and archaeobotanical data.* In Gosden and Willcox eds, pp. 478–500.

Willcox, G. (2004) 'Last gatherers/first cultivators in the Near East: regional and supra-regional developments'. *Neo-Lithics* 1/04: 51–2.

Williams, P.R. (2001) 'Cerro Baúl: a Wari administrative centre on the Tiwanaku frontier'. *Latin American Antiquity,* 12(1): 67–83.

Williams, P.R. (2002) 'Rethinking disaster-induced collapse in the demise of the Andean Highland States: Wari and Tiwanaku'. *World Archaeology* 33(3): 361–374.

Williams, P.R. and Nash, D.J. (2002) *Imperial interaction in the Andes: Huari and Tiwanaku at Cerro Baúl.* In Isbell and Silverman eds, pp. 243–265.

Winter, I.J. (2007) *Representing abundance: the visual dimension of the agrarian state.* In Stone ed., pp. 117–138.

Wilson, D.J. (1987) *Reconstructing patterns of early warfare in the Lower Santa Valley: new data on the role of conflict in the origins of complex north coast society.* In Haas, Pozorski and Pozorski eds, pp. 56–69.

Wilson, D.J. (1988) *Prehispanic Settlement Patterns in the Lower Santa Valley Peru: A Regional Perspective on the Origins and Development of Complex North Coast Society.* Washington D.C., Smithsonian Institution Press.

Wilson, D.J. (1997) *Early state formation in the North Coast of Peru: A critique of the City-State Model.* In Nichols and Charlton eds, pp. 229–244.

Wilson, P. (2003) 'The prehistoric period at Saïs (Sa el-Hagar)'. *Archéo-Nil* 13: 65–72.

Wilson, P. and Gilbert, G. (2002) 'Pigs, pots and postholes: prehistoric Saïs'. *Egyptian Archaeology* 21: 12–13.

Wing, E.S. (1977) *Animal domestication in the Andes.* In Reed ed., pp. 837–859.

Winkelman, M. (2002) 'Shamanism and cognitive evolution'. *Cambridge Archaeological Journal* 12.1: 71–101.

Winkelmann, S. (2000) *Some new ideas about the possible origin of the anthropomorphic and semi-human creature depictions on Harappan seals.* In Taddei and de Marco eds, pp. 341–361.

Winter, I.J. (2007) *Representing abundance: The visual dimension of the agrarian state.* In Stone ed., pp. 117–148.

Winterhalder, B. (1986) 'Diet choice, risk and food-sharing in a stochastic environment'. *JAA* 5: 369–92.

Wittfogel, K (1957) new ed. 1981. *Oriental Despotism: A Comparative Study of Total Power.* New York, Vintage Books.

Wolpert, L. (1992) *The Unnatural Nature of Science: Why Science Does Not Make (Common) Sense.* Faber and Faber, London.

Wood, J.W. (1998) 'A theory of preindustrial population dynamics'. *Current Anthropology* 19(1): 99– 135.

Wrangham, R.W. and Peterson, D. (1996) *Demonic Males: Apes and the Origins of Human Violence.* London, Bloomsbury.

Wrangham, R. W., Holland Jones, J., Laden, G., Pilbeam, D., & Conklin-Britain, N. (1999) 'The raw and the stolen'. *Current Anthropology* 40: 567–594.

Wright, H.E. (1998) *Origin of the climate and vegetation in the Mediterranean area.* In Arsebuk, Mellink and Schirmer eds, pp. 765–774.

Wright, H.T. (1977) 'Recent research on the origins of the state'. *Annual Review of Anthropology* 6: 379–397.

Wright, H.T. (1998) *Uruk states in Southwestern Iran.* In Feinman and Marcus eds, pp. 173–197.

Wright, H.T. (2001) *Cultural action in the Uruk world.* In Rothman ed., pp. 123–147.

Wright, H.T. (2006) 'Early State dynamics as political experiment'. *Journal of Anthropological Research* 62(3): 305–319.

Wright, H.T. (2007) *Ancient agency: Using models of intentionality to understand the dawn of despotism.* In Stone ed., pp. 175–184.

Wright, H.T. and Johnson, G.A. (1975) 'Population, exchange and early state formation in southwestern Iran', *American Anthropologist* 77: 267–89.

Wright, H.T. and Rupley, E.S.A. (2001) *Calibrated radiocarbon age determinations of Uruk-related assemblages.* In Rothman ed., pp. 85–121.

Wu Hung (1997) '"All about the eyes": two groups of sculptures from the Sanxingdui Culture'. *Orientations* 28.8: 58–66.

Xu, Jay (2001a) *Bronze at Sanxingdui*. In Bagley ed., pp. 59–151.

Xu, Jay (2001b) 'Reconstructing Sanxingdui imagery: some speculations'. *Orientations* 32.5: 32–44.

Xu, Jay (2001c) *Sichuan before the Warring States period*. In Bagley ed., pp. 21–37.

Xu, Jay (2006a) 'Guest editor's Preface to: The Art and Archaeology of the Sichuan Basin'. *Special Section of the Journal of East Asian Archaeology* 5, 1–4.

Xu, Jay (2006b) 'Defining the archaeological cultures at the Sanxingdui site'. *JEAA* 5 (1–4): 149–190.

Yakar, R. and Hershkovitz, I. (1990) 'Nahal Hemar Cave: the modelled skulls.' *Atiqot* 18: 59–63.

Yan, Wenming (1986) 'An analysis of the Hengzhen cemetery'. *Wenwu yu Kaogu Lunji* 6: 66–77. Beijing, Wenwu.

Yan, Wenming (1999) 'Neolithic settlements in China: latest finds and research'. *Journal of East Asian Archaeology* 1(1–4): 130–47 [Festschrift in Honour of K.C. Chang].

Yang, C.K. (1959) *Chinese Communist Society: The Family and the Village*. Cambridge Mass., MIT Press [1965].

Yang, Hongxun (1987) *Jianzhu kaogu xue lunwen ji*. Beijing.

Yang, Xiaoneng (1999) ed., *The Golden Age of Chinese Archaeology: Celebrated Discoveries from the People's Republic of China*. New Haven and London, Yale University Press.

Yang, Xiaoneng (2004) *Chinese Archaeology: New Perspectives on China's Past in the 20th Century*. New Haven, Yale University Press.

Yasin, W. (1970) 'Excavations at Tell es-Sawwan 1969. Report of the sixth season's excavations'. *Sumer* 26: 3–35.

Yates, R.D.S. (1997) *The city-states in ancient China*. In Nichols and Charlton eds, pp. 71–90.

Yates, R.D.S. (2001) *Cosmos, central authority, and communities in the early Chinese empire*. In Alcock *et al*. eds, pp. 351–368..

Yekutieli, Y. (2000) *Divine royal power*. In Van den Brink and Yannai eds, pp. 243–254.

Yener, K.A. (2007) *Transformative impulses in Late Bronze Age technology: A case study from the Amuq Valley, Southern Turkey*. In Stone ed., pp. 369–386.

Yoffee, N. (2000) *Law courts and the mediation of conflict in ancient Mesopotamia*. In Richards and Van Buren eds, pp. 46–63.

Yoffee, N. (2005) *Myths of the Archaic State: Evolution of the Earliest Cities, States and Civilizations*. Cambridge, CUP.

Yoffee, N. and Cowgill, G.L. (1988) eds, *The Collapse of Ancient States and Civilizations*. Tucson, University of Arizona Press.

Yoffee, N. and Sherratt, A. (1993) eds, *Archaeological Theory: Who Sets the Agenda*. Cambridge, CUP, New Directions in Archaeology.

Youkana, D.G. (1997) *Tell es-Sawwan. The Architecture of the Sixth Millennium BC*. London, Nabu Books, Edubba 5.

Yuan, J. (1996) 'Yuchanyan Huo Shuidao Qiyuan Zhingyao Xinwuzheng [Important evidence for the origin of rice cultivation discovered in the Yuchan cave]'. *Zhongguo Wenwubao [Chinese Antiquity News]* 3rd March, front page.

Young, G.D. (1992) ed., *Mari in Retrospect: Fifty Years of Mari and Mari Studies*. Winona Lake, Eisenbrauns.

Zeder, M.A. (1991) *Feeding Cities: Specialized Animal Economy in the Ancient Near East*. Washington D.C., Smithsonian Institution Press.

Zeder, M.A. and Hesse, B. (2000) 'The initial domestication of goats (*Capra hircus*) in the Zagros Mountains 10,000 years ago'. *Science* 287: 2254–2257.

Zeidler, J.A. (1991) 'Maritime exchange in the early formative period of coastal Ecuador: geopolitical origins of uneven development'. *Research in Economic Anthropology* 13: 247–268.

Zhang Juzhong & Wang Xiangkun (1998) 'Notes on the recent discovery of ancient cultivated rice at Jiahu, Henan Province: a new theory concerning the origin of *Oryza japonica* in China'. *Antiquity* 72: 897–901.

Zhang, C. (1997) 'The rise of urbanism in the Yangzi Valley'. *Indo-Pacific Prehistory Association Bulletin* 16: 63–67. *Chiang Mai Papers*, Volume 3.

Zhang, C. (2002) 'The discovery of early pottery in China'. *Documenta Praehistorica* XXIX: 29–35.

Zhang, F. (2000) 'The Mesolithic in South China'. *Documenta Praehistorica* XXVII: 225–31.

Zhang, W. and Pei, A. (1997) 'Lixian Mengxi Bashidang Chutu Daogu de Yanjiu [A study on the ancient rice found at Bashidang, Mengxi in Lixian county]'. *Wenwu [Relics]* 1: 36–41.

Zhang, W. and Yuan, J. (1998) 'A preliminary study of ancient excavated rice from Yuchanyan site, Dao County, Hunan Province, PRC'. *Acta Agronomica Sinica* 24(4): 416–20.

Zhang, Zhongpei (1985) 'The social structure reflected in the Yuanjumiao cemetery'. *JAA* 4: 19–33.

Zhao, C. and Wu, X. (2000) 'The dating of Chinese early pottery and a discussion of some related problems'. *Documenta Praehistorica*, XXVII: 233–9.

Zhao, Z., Pearsall, D.M. and Jiang, Q.H. (1995) *Analysis of phytoliths from Xianrendong and Wangdong.* In McNeish and Libby, pp. 47–52.

Zhao, Zhijun (1998) 'The Middle Yangtze region in China is one place where rice was domesticated: phytolith evidence from the Diaotonghuan Cave, Northern Jiangxi'. *Antiquity* 72: 885–97.

Zhu Zhangyi, Zhang Qing and Wang Fang (2006) 'The Jinsha site: an introduction'. *JEAA* 5: 247–276.

Zohary, D., Tchernov, E. and Horwitz, L.K. (1998) 'The role of unconscious selection in the domestication of sheep and goats'. *Journal of Zoology (London)* 245: 129–135.

Zou Heng (1999) 'The Yanshi Shang City: a secondary capital of the early Shang'. *JEAA* 1: 195–206.

# INDEX